Mobility and Migration in
Ancient Mesoamerican Cities

Mobility and Migration in Ancient Mesoamerican Cities

edited by
M. Charlotte Arnauld,
Christopher Beekman,
and Grégory Pereira

UNIVERSITY PRESS OF COLORADO
Louisville

© 2021 by University Press of Colorado

Published by University Press of Colorado
1580 North Logan Street, Suite 660
PMB 39883
Denver, Colorado 80203-1942

 The University Press of Colorado is a proud member of
the Association of University Presses.

The University Press of Colorado is a cooperative publishing enterprise supported, in part, by Adams State University, Colorado State University, Fort Lewis College, Metropolitan State University of Denver, Regis University, University of Colorado, University of Northern Colorado, University of Wyoming, Utah State University, and Western Colorado University.

ISBN: 978-1-64642-072-8 (hardcover)
ISBN: 978-1-64642-659-1 (paperback)
ISBN: 978-1-64642-073-5 (ebook)
https://doi.org/10.5876/9781646420735

Library of Congress Cataloging-in-Publication Data

Names: Arnauld, Marie-Charlotte, editor. | Beekman, Christopher, editor. | Pereira, Grégory, editor.
Title: Mobility and migration in ancient Mesoamerican cities / edited by M. Charlotte Arnauld, Christopher Beekman, and Grégory Pereira.
Description: Louisville, CO : University Press of Colorado, 2020. | Includes bibliographical references and index.
Identifiers: LCCN 2020032146 (print) | LCCN 2020032147 (ebook) | ISBN 9781646420728 (hardcover) | ISBN 97816464659I (paperback) | ISBN 9781646420735 (ebook)
Subjects: LCSH: Indians of Mexico—Migrations. | Indians of Central America—Migrations. | Migration, Internal—Mexico. | Migration, Internal—Central America. | Indians of Mexico—Urban residence. | Indians of Central America—Urban residence. | Indians of Mexico—Antiquities. | Indians of Central America—Antiquities.
Classification: LCC F1219.3.M54 M63 2020 (print) | LCC F1219.3.M54 (ebook) | DDC 972.8/01—dc23
LC record available at https://lccn.loc.gov/2020032146
LC ebook record available at https://lccn.loc.gov/2020032147

Cover illustrations © Sylvie Eliès

Contents

Part IV: Discussion

Figures

Tables

Mobility and Migration in
Ancient Mesoamerican Cities

Mobility and Migration in Ancient Mesoamerican Cities

An Introduction

M. CHARLOTTE ARNAULD,
CHRISTOPHER S. BEEKMAN,
AND GRÉGORY PEREIRA

This volume addresses human mobility and migration in ancient Mesoamerica, a complex preindustrial and agrarian society. The studies presented herein focus upon the periods and regions in which Mesoamerica was becoming increasingly urbanized. Large villages, towns, and cities dotted the landscape, and the movement of people within and between them made social interaction more dynamic than has been appreciated (figure 0.1). In this volume, we examine population movement in relation to urbanization and de-urbanization among ancient Mesoamerican societies and polities during the first fifteen hundred years AD.

In support of this project, both theoretical and methodological advances open new avenues for research. We aim to disrupt the conceptual dichotomy of sedentism versus mobility to highlight the physical dynamism embedded in Mesoamerican subsistence structures, economic activities, and political strategies. We consider *mobility* to encompass the broad range of habitual physical movements that facilitate (or complicate) social and cultural practices. *Migration* is then a form of movement that takes place under unusual circumstances ("a transgressive social act" [Cabana and Clark 2011b, 8–9]). From this perspective,

DOI: 10.5876/9781646420735.c000

FIGURE 0.1. *Map of Mesoamerica, showing major centers and locations mentioned in the chapters.*

sedentism has been overly idealized as a default and absolute state (Morrissey 2015), from which embedded residential and logistical mobility (Binford 1980) takes place. In reality, changing patterns of mobility are constantly transforming society and preventing anything approaching a steady state. When we speak of *urbanism*, we refer to those settlements whose size and complexity make them the loci for multiple social institutions, but whose specific organizational and scalar thresholds will vary locally. Prior researchers have noted the idealized nature of the sedentism-mobility dichotomy (e.g., Kent 1992), though most commonly as part of research into nomadic hunters and gatherers (e.g., Sapignoli 2014). We argue that mobility is also an underappreciated aspect of town- and city-based societies in the ancient world, and that this population throughput is important for subjects as wide ranging as exchange, social organization, and political dominance.

PAST PERSPECTIVES

Archaeological research relies on the imposition of structure to our data— typologies of societies, settlements, and people. While categories can provide something tangible to analyze, they have outlived their usefulness when they begin to stand in the way of our understanding. One of the primary examples in archaeology is the continuum from mobility to sedentism to urbanism, the latter associated with complex political systems. But urban centers are formed and maintained by rural to urban movement, and polities possess porous boundaries through which people regularly pass and return in the pursuit of the goods, power, and social interaction that constitute complex society.

In the renewal of migration studies following the influential paper by Anthony (1990), much has been written about how migration became discredited during the height of processual archaeology (see Cabana 2011; Cabana and Clark 2011a, 2011b). Migration was sidelined as a subject for theoretical research, because it was seen as an exogenous and unpredictable event that disturbed what were considered self-contained systems. But over the years Mesoamericanists continued to document population movements at the foundation and collapse of cities, particularly at rupture points in urban sequences when population displacement was accompanied by changes in material culture (e.g., several in Demarest et al. 2004; Fowler 1989; LeBlanc 2015).

Archaeologists have slowly recognized that not all Mesoamerican peasants stayed in one location and that large villages and cities maintained their high demographic profiles through constant in-migration (Storey 1992). Without returning to migration as an explanatory crutch, Post-processual archaeologists (in the broadest sense) acknowledged that sedentism can take various forms that still encompass mobility (e.g., "short-term sedentism" in Bernardini 2011, 34; Nelson and LeBlanc 1986; "village drift" in Darling et al. 2004; "serial migrations" in Fowles 2011, 48; "urbanized nomads" in Fox 1967). Some scholars began to analyze migration as "conscious, strategic responses to certain kinds of problems" (Beekman and Christensen 2003, 113–114). Population movement has become a topic of interest with the goal of analytical inquiry, most notably in the US Southwest, with its environmental and social dynamism (Alexiades 2009; Hard and Merrill 1992; Kent 1992; Kohler 1992; Nelson and Strawhacker 2011; Ortman and Cameron 2011; Schachner 2012; Stone 2005). Moreover, increased attention to the demographic trajectories of urban settlements revitalized the topic of population movements. "Internal" population growth had been used as a prime mover by archaeologists for decades, yet George Cowgill stressed two basic issues—that population growth (or decline) is not just the output of specific ratios between mortality and fertility, but also of population movements; and that the spatial scale of the unit under study determines whether growth and movement are external or internal:

> The mathematics of population growth also have implications about the role of
> migration as a demographic process. Clearly we should be always explicit about
> the boundaries of the regions we are investigating, and we should remember that,
> depending on how we define the region, the same movement of people may be
> seen either as an internal rearrangement in population density patterns, or as
> another process besides birth and death that actually adds to, or subtracts from
> the population total. Moreover, when the unit of analysis is a single settlement . . .

in- or out-migration may play a major role or even totally swamp effects due to internal birth and death rates (Cowgill 1975, 509)

Ancient urban settlements did not therefore grow or decline solely due to the fertility/mortality balance, but primarily through population movements in and out (see also M. Cohen 2008; Davis 1973; Joyce and Winter 1996; M. E. Smith 2014, 528). Blanton and colleagues (1996) operationalized Cowgill's points in what can now be seen as a pioneering evaluation of migration in the sequence of urbanization and de-urbanization in the central valleys of Oaxaca. They emphasized the dynamics implied in the formation and construction of a central capital at Monte Alban and elsewhere in its polity. Their general argument was based on the quantification of local and regional settlement demography phase by phase (500 BC–AD 1520), and they noted the ethnohistoric evidence for poor, mobile, landless tenants (*terrazgueros*) in colonial Oaxaca. They explicitly sought convergence between preindustrial movements in Mesoamerican agrarian society, and present-day migrations triggered by changing conditions of wage labor (see C. Smith 1982; M. E. Smith 2014). Twenty years on, we can see that this research was significant for illustrating Cowgill's point as to the importance of population movement. Their work also stressed the rural/urban dimension, as well as the directly political importance of prehispanic migration processes through time and space. As they state, "The human condition in prehispanic Oaxaca was not 'naturally sedentary'" (Blanton et al. 1996, 36; see Morrissey 2015).

THEORETICAL CONSIDERATIONS: CONTRASTING MOBILITY AND MIGRATION

We accept Anthony's general position that population movement is a patterned human behavior (1990, 895). As Tilly (1978) and Osborne (1991) have shown, movement can take many forms linked to the specificities and idiosyncrasies of culture, as well as historical circumstances. Access to this diversity is, however, markedly constrained by the methodologies of detection available to archaeologists. Broad categories of movement can be defined in relation to documented social structures, economic systems, and cultural practices, as well as events with profound consequences for human communities. To begin with a simple dichotomy, mobility is an element of *habitus*—it is embedded within those structures, systems, and practices—whereas migration generally follows more disruptive events or processes. Our definition of migration largely follows that used by Tsuda et al. (2015), who focused on this disruptive aspect, but we define mobility more narrowly than Quirk and Vigneswaran (2015), who are interested in the political manipulation of all kinds of movement.

Two contributions to mobility research provide inspiration and theoretical underpinning for this volume. One is Takeshi Inomata's (2004) consideration of the mobility of nonelites among the Classic-period Maya, the second being

Michael Smith's (2014) synthesis of local migration in the context of urbanization. These studies ask us to consider the degree to which everyday practices of mobility may have shaped not only social relations but also political authority and urbanism in ancient Mesoamerica. Mobility has of course been most frequently considered in studies of nomadic hunters and gatherers (Barnard and Wendrich 2008; Binford 1982; Kelly 1995; Sellet et al. 2006; and innumerable others), or among farmers who shifted residence with the seasons (e.g., Nelson and Strawhacker 2011; Snead et al. 2011). The assumption that populations practicing intensive agriculture were stable and remained *in situ* over long periods of time has been taken for granted, leaving a significant gap in our understanding of the role of mobility in complex social formations such as urban centers. Encompassing not only intraurban but also rural/rural and rural/urban movements, mobility was (and is) "built in" to Mesoamerican societies. Multiresidence households, customary exogamic marriage, long-distance trade, ceremonial circuits, and pilgrimages—all could be associated with routine socioeconomic and religious activities in urban contexts. Mobility is used in an analogous sense in Southwestern archaeology even though urbanization had never been as intense as in Mesoamerica (see Clark 2001; Kahn 2013, 251). Anthony (1990, 901) described these modes of mobility as "short-distance movements within a local area" (see also Cameron 2013, 219). How "short" and "local" such moves may have been in the past depends on a number of parameters, among them local and regional topography, as well as physical distance between centers. This is frequently more than a two-day walk in open topography, but social embeddedness in local/regional circuits and networks defines mobility better than does distance.

Whether landless or affiliated with social groups having access to land, peasants did not necessarily become fully sedentary wherever and whenever. In tropical and temperate environments alike, traditional crop agriculture has been recognized as a risky endeavor that did not necessarily warrant or even allow residential stability (e.g., Baden 1987; Beekman and Baden 2011; Campbell and Overton 1991; Inomata et al. 2015; Killion 2013; Pohl and Pohl 1994). Complex residential arrangements linked to *milpa* agriculture—an extensive, swidden-crop system—have been analyzed in detail in ancient and modern agrarian societies (Atran 1993; S. Brown 2002; Hanks 1990; Liffman 2000; Lucero 2002; Wilk 1991). People moved from one niche to another for many reasons, including soil exhaustion (Baden 1987, 2005), tending multiple fields, and reducing the costs of transporting the harvest (Hard and Merrill 1992). People also periodically supplemented farming with part-time craft activities (Hirth 2009), and with trading expeditions that linked settlements, markets, and resources. People maintained urban residences for one or two generations and then left for the hinterlands, or split from their households to dwell for some period in the family field hut

(Arnauld 2014). Religious practices, fairs, pilgrimages, and public ceremonies drew people into centers or conversely out into the countryside (Kubler 1984; Palka 2014; Wells and Nelson 2007) and placed short-term demands for housing upon their hosts. Monthly ceremonies drew people into the centers, while markets periodically rotated between communities. Exogamous alliances, marital residence rules, and political allegiances structured these movements. Social ties as well as topographic pathways thus channeled mobility along well-worn paths within and between centers.

Mobility would then be defined as the use of temporary residences structured by an urbanized settlement system, involving circular, irregular, or regular movement that follows a seasonal, annual, or multiannual tempo. Defined in this way, ancient Mesoamerican mobility had traits in common with modern urban and rural/urban mobility. However, ancient contexts rarely encompassed modern conceptions, values, and norms of state territory (e.g., linear boundaries that defined fiscal status and citizenship). Instead, Mesoamerican mobility originated in the incomplete overlap between groups of affiliation and groups of coresidence. People attended specific socioeconomic, ritual, and/or political activities while still pertaining to a group with a shared residential locus, most explicitly laid out in the "House" model (Gillespie 2000; Lévi-Strauss 1979), but present to some extent with most corporate groups. Thus, it follows that mobility was not—and in socially appropriate contexts, still is not—chaotic and aimless wandering. Mobile individuals or groups maintained a fixed, primary residence, generally the house of older kin, as a point of return and a place to invest resources and plan future activities (Arnauld 2014). This can be observed in contemporary Mesoamerican short- and long-distance wage migration, increasingly articulated with circular mobility owing to modern transport technologies, in which individuals and groups accumulate wealth elsewhere in a conscious mobility "project" so as to invest it in a primary residence or new land at their original locale (Piedrasanta et al. 2010; Quesnel 2009). In the past, "durable houses" (Beck 2007b) were often built to be occupied, modified, and rebuilt at the same place over centuries. Beginning in the Late Formative or Early Classic periods, the stone used for public architecture was extended to private residences. In Classic to Postclassic Maya urban centers, domestic buildings came to outstrip public architecture. Elaborate and prestigious housing satisfied the increased need for creating roots, or what can be called an "anchoring process," for mobile populations (Arnauld et al. 2017b). It follows that embedded patterns of mobility should not be confused with general "interaction." Mobility was not just about exchanging economic and cultural values, but it encompassed the multiple strategies of people moving to resolve the contradictions embedded in, for instance, their simultaneous experience of rural landscapes and urban communities.

In contrast, some forms of movement occurred in response to a surge of problems deriving from environmental change, volcanic eruption, economic downturn, or military conquest. Cabana and Clark (2011b, 5) define *migration* as a "one-way residential relocation to a different 'environment' by at least one individual" (see also Tsuda et al. 2015), alternately phrased by Bernardini (2011, 31) as "a singular, disruptive event." When faced with transgressive displacement that disrupts individual *habitus*, migrants cross political, environmental, or social boundaries, whereas mobility does not cross boundaries any more dramatic than those between the urban and the rural, or between neighborhoods or cities. Although frequent in mobility, cycles of displacement are rare in migration as it results in a new pattern of movements. In response to drastic events or circumstances, migration uproots migrants with a shift in "anchoring." The whole system of mobility must then be rebuilt, centered on the new anchor point, or what Binford called the "residential hub" (1982, 4, 14), but it could equally be thought of as a new basis for *habitus* and the establishment of new bodily practices.

Defining migration as outside the usual range of mobility means that it is motivated by relatively disruptive phenomena. These may be rapid, catastrophic events, or more long-term processes, like extended climatic shifts that encourage movement north or south, or what Ben Nelson and colleagues (2014) call "transformative relocation" of villages and cities, by which entire social groups abandoned a place to found and build a new place. Ancient Mesoamerica is not unique in having cities whose formation, growth, and dissolution were largely politically driven. Even in relatively medium-sized towns, urbanization was simultaneously polity formation, in which previously distant groups came together. De-urbanization could similarly take place along the cleavage planes between factions (Stone 2005). More than units of consumption, distributional markets, or simple crossroads with congregated populations, Mesoamerican cities were communities and polities in and of themselves (see Houston et al. 2003). City institutions were political institutions, and urban demography was a political stake. Political leaders would have sought to attract migrants and to control both mobility and migrations (Beekman 2015, 81–87; Joyce and Winter 1996; Quirk and Vigneswaran 2015):

> Mesoamerican polities, like many polities elsewhere, would have derived their power and authority from the populations that they could draw into their orbit. Governments were dependent on people for foodstuffs, construction labor, soldiers, and the products of skilled labor, such as textiles or lapidary work. Although rarely singled out as something requiring theoretical explanation, the rise and fall of many Mesoamerican centers as far back as circa 1400 BC essentially involved the attraction and eventual loss of population. (Beekman 2015, 82; see also Beekman and Christensen 2011, 160–161)

Mesoamerican migration must be seen within this framework of complex, urbanized societies in which many medium- or large-sized settlements had primarily political functions (with economic functions subsumed). They formed, fluctuated, and finally broke up or dissolved through displacements of population. Most large urban settlements in Mesoamerica were segmented into neighborhoods and districts (Arnauld et al. 2012; Daneels and Gutiérrez 2012; Hirth 2003; Manzanilla and Chapdelaine 2009; M. E. Smith 2010b). Those modular groupings came into existence not only through urban interaction (M. L. Smith 2003), but also through mobility and immigration, and as factions they facilitated migration into and out of the city (Brumfiel and Fox 1994; see Cameron 2013, 222–223; Stone 2015 in the Southwest). Even relatively short-distance migratory movements induced a strong "ethnic" identity due to the political orientation of constituent groups, each with an agenda that concealed or exacerbated such identity. This is well exemplified in indigenous tales of migration (Beekman and Christensen 2011, 148–149; Graulich 1981, 1984). Forced resettlement also contributed to the emergence of large cities, and consolidated territories that needed protection, especially during the Epiclassic, Postclassic, and even Colonial periods (see Beekman 2015; Cowgill 2013; Manzanilla 2005a; Pereira et al. 2005; Rivera Villanueva and Berumen Félix 2011). While migrations are unusual and likely to be preserved as historical content in tales, myths, or ceremonies (indeed, migration tales may be reshaped to give them additional symbolic significance—Boone 1991; M. E. Smith 1984; 2011, 478–480; Vapnarsky 2009), mobility due to its very banality may go unrecorded and be accessible primarily through archaeology.

The contrast or continuum that we draw between mobility and migration is a heuristically useful abstraction, but in many real cases there may be some overlap between them, making the dichotomy between *mobile* and *migrant* peoples somewhat difficult to apply (even without mentioning the term *refugees*). For example, a noble marriage that sanctions the integration of migrants into the local city may combine elements of each. Another example that shows the overlap between these categories is that of "ethnic" enclaves identified in the great Mesoamerican cities. The iconic case of Teotihuacan, where Zapotec, Veracruzano, and Michoacano barrios have been identified (Gómez Chávez 1998; Price et al. 2000; Rattray 1987; Spence 1992), demonstrates the permanent presence of foreign populations that maintained links with their homeland through what Spence (2005) calls "diaspora networks." These imply a continuous flow of wealth, persons, and ideas between the enclaves and their place of origin, combining cyclical and continuous mobility as new members migrate in while existing members tend to assimilate (Manzanilla 2017). Peter van Dommelen (2014, 479) recently called for "exploring the multiple and interlocking scales of mobility and migration," a topic with much potential. Mobility may for example "pave the way" for migration in more than one sense (Nelson and Crider 2005; Quesnel 2009). Through normal patterns of mobility, groups accumulate knowledge about potential destinations (Anthony 1990, 899–900). Mobility prepares individuals and social groups for migratory movements as it anticipates and establishes an organizational framework for one-way relocations (Inomata's [2004] "mobility as a capacity"), making movement available as a solution to crisis. Similarly, deeply etched pathways of mobility can "bound" a system (Anthony 1990; Cabana 2011, 20; Cameron 1995). But the "thick" boundary (Monod Becquelin 2012) created by habitual mobility can become a secondary system through which people may build new modes of movement. Today this is what leads to the *coyotes* in Mexico and the *passeurs* in Turkey and Greece—they frequently moved across these boundaries and ended up creating new pathways.

Migration and mobility interrelate along scalar and temporal lines as well. By defining mobility as the habitual and the recurrent, it could be seen as internal to a "system" while migration is external to it. Yet it is not true that mobility occurs on the local scale alone, as transport facilities and social embeddedness in local/regional networks frame mobility better than mere distance. Mobility and migration relate temporally as well. Migrations that appear singular and disruptive may be seen to recur when viewed at the scale of the *longue durée*, as people move in concert with millennial- (Paulsen 1976) or century-scale (Black et al. 2011) climatic changes. The scale effect is also an issue of temporal resolution in the sense that repeated mobility over the centuries could be conceptualized by the archaeologist as a single large migration. However, "the long-term directionality and near irreversibility of the transition" (Leppard 2014, 486) would still need to be explained (see one case of reversibility in Carot 2001). But these are only potentials—the intensification of mobility does not necessarily lead a population to become displaced, and conversely not all migrations originate in habitual mobility. For the archaeologist, it is a real challenge to identify the best spatial and temporal scales for analysis. It requires a deep knowledge of the cultural and historical contexts in which movements have been detected. For instance, the migration of a lineage or other corporate group into a host community requires a different detection method than the establishment of an entire settlement of migrants. The former could easily be missed by inadequate sampling procedures, and by methods designed for aggregate populations rather than individuals.

METHODS FOR ADDRESSING THE PROBLEM

If population movements are not simply demographic displacement from one point to another, but also patterned behavior involving many social and cultural aspects (Anthony 1990; Cabana and Clark 2011, 6), then there must be many approaches for the detection of those movements, with variation to be observed in human physical remains and material culture, but also in changes to settlement patterns or urban layouts. For example, the rapid emergence of a large urbanized settlement in one region is better explained by rural/urban mobility, or a single migration, than *in situ* population growth. The answer should be in the structure of the settlement itself and the demographic trajectory of each of its neighborhood components (Arnauld et al. 2012; Arnauld et al. 2017b; M. L. Smith 2003). Recurring episodes of abandonment and return in a given settlement may differentiate internal mobility from outmigration, requiring the occupational history of each residential unit to be reconstructed (M. E. Smith 2014). Epigraphy and iconography at some Classic Maya cities declare or portray rulers as foreign, requiring that new methodologies in bioarchaeology be applied to their physical remains in order to validate their presumed origins (e.g., Cucina 2015a, 2015b; Price et al. 2008, 2010; Wright et al. 2010). So far, there is no general methodology that universally distinguishes mobility from migration. Each has its own peculiarities, and the distinction between them emerges from the available evidence, inducing the archaeologist to develop specific strategies for her/his data. Hopefully the case studies will accumulate and build up reference inventories of patterned movements to be related to past Mesoamerican contexts. We are just starting to develop a cumulative record now, and face certain difficulties.

As suggested above, five broad classes of methods useful for studies of mobility and migration can be delineated:

1. those based on biogeochemical analysis of human remains, with the limitations inherent to the environmental influence on body chemistry,
2. genetic and morphological biodistance studies of human remains, though the data for human genetic variation (DNA) are particularly vulnerable to taphonomic factors,
3. those focusing on variations in material culture and behaviors, including forms of housing, burial, and other ritual practices, although they may have causes independent from mobility and/or migration,
4. those more demographic- and urban-based methods that concentrate on temporal and spatial variation in settlement size, composition, layout, and location, and
5. those more economic and geographic proxies that index changing relations between urban settlements and their hinterlands.

Fortunately, in many cases at least two of these methodological categories can be applied to the evidence. Moreover, in Mesoamerica linguistics and ethnohistory provide relevant, abundant documentation of population movement, and tap into aspects of migration that cannot be approached effectively through archaeology (Peregrine et al. 2009). It is important to note that in each case, not all the parameters of the movement under analysis—origin, destination, size, tempo, demographic structure, motivations—can be determined. In addition, not all such parameters have the same priority or relevance to every research project.

To begin with biogeochemical approaches, isotopic analyses that reliably track immigrants in any given population depend on the spatial distribution of distinct geologic formations (Hodell et al. 2004). In geologically homogeneous regions like the western or central Maya lowlands, long-distance migrants are more easily detected, whereas short-range mobility remains obscured. But the latter can be evaluated in the much more heterogeneous eastern lowlands of Belize. Both short- and long-range movements are generally thought to be underestimated (e.g., Scherer 2007; Scherer and Wright 2015, 115). When they work, isotopic methods can tell us something about demographic structure, origins, and destination locales of mobile/migrant groups, and we can correlate them with independently documented socioeconomic and political systems to differentiate mobility from migration. The capacity of isotopic analysis to develop spatial life histories for individuals makes them particularly ideal for discerning patterns of mobility (Manzanilla 2015, 2017; Price et al. 2000). But this method is unable to identify the succeeding generation of locally born descendants, a topic that can only be addressed through morphometric, nonmetric, and genetic studies. Some biological anthropologists have shown how migrant traces may potentially disappear into their host communities after just a few generations (Frankenberg and Konigsberg 2011). Mesoamerican archaeologists are scarcely capable of documenting population age structures, due to the lack of large numbers of well-preserved human remains. However, when the opportunity arises, those structures can be impacted by migrations, for example by producing an abnormal proportion of young men or women (e.g., Cameron 2011). Finally, setting aside properly biological markers, we cannot forget that biocultural practices were common in Mesoamerica and constitute a good indicator of foreign origin. Various authors have shown how these irreversible modifications to physical appearance, whether instituted in the first years of life (head shaping) or in adolescence (dental modifications), can signify a person's foreign origin (Pereira 1999, 165–168; 2018; Serrano et al. 1993; Tiesler 2014, 2015).

Most archaeological studies of population movements hope to identify them through formal variations in material culture, but this has well-known weaknesses (e.g., Tourtellot and González 2004). Archaeologists have long passed the point where we accept that material culture simply reflects identity, as people may choose to stand out or blend in with their new neighbors based on many factors (Beekman and Christensen 2011; Hegmon et al. 2016; Stone and Lipe 2011). Thus, portable material culture, house forms, and ritual behaviors may or may not vary between those who have moved and their new neighbors. But mobility should be inherently more difficult to identify in this manner. While we define migration as non-systemic and into areas with which the migrants may have only had narrowly structured prior contact, mobility involves repeated, cyclical movements among people who are already familiar with one another, and the transplants may feel little need to express difference from others through material culture (Beekman 2015, 77–78; Beekman and Christensen 2011, 160–161; Bernardini 2011, 32). We may be able to address this difficulty through the recognition of a "focal residence" (Anthony 1990, 904), around which regular mobility revolves. But in any case, it is important that we break with the older expectation that movement should be directly reflected by formal changes in artifacts.

As a more idiosyncratic movement that breaks with normal mobility, migration is expected to be more dramatic and to result in more visible variation in material culture. Even so, migrants can be absorbed into communities when the advantages of rapid and complete integration at the destination locale are seen as important, or when local efforts to enforce homogenization and assimilation are strong (Beekman and Christensen 2011; Clayton 2013; Cowgill 2013; Hegmon et al. 2016; Stone 2003). It is probable that migrants will still be visible through demographic variation in settlement composition, private behaviors such as food preparation, or unconscious practices embedded in technological style (Clark 2001). Furthermore, material culture signatures exist not only at the destination, but also at the origin locale where the decision to migrate may have been accompanied by specific behaviors such as rituals of abandonment, which may take the form of patterned destruction including the extraction of buried ancestral remains (Barrientos et al. 2014; Lamoureux-St-Hilaire 2015). This last example illustrates well how migration provokes a disruption in residential life by forcing the migrants to decouple from one location and reestablish themselves in a new place, and that migrants may be distinguished by evidence subtler than artifact styles.

Demographic assessments of urban settlements should incorporate settlement size, composition, and density using a multiscalar approach that considers residential units, neighborhoods, large districts, and the whole community. In spite of the diversity and abundance of Classic/Postclassic Mesoamerican urban forms, studies of this type have been developed mainly at Teotihuacan (Cowgill 2015a; Manzanilla 2015; Manzanilla and Chapdelaine 2009), Monte Albán (Blanton 1978; Blanton et al 1996), Copan (Webster et al. 2000), and to a certain extent Tikal (see Chase et al. 1990). "Population surges" indicative of pronounced immigration events are sometimes discussed (Arnauld et al. 2017b; Blanton et al. 1996; Webster 2014), but methods of evaluating population density and variation through time and space are still the subject of many disagreements. This is, however, one of the most promising avenues of research when combined with demography, urban studies, and the politico-ideological process of "place-making" (Fash and López Luján 2009). Place-making creates archaeological signatures through ideologically designed city layouts and selective placement on the landscape. Fundamental changes to city layouts may be the results of concepts imposed by migrants, while accretionary changes may be accommodations to the demands of mobility. The concept of "transformative relocation" similarly confers upon migration a primary role in polity formation and dynamics: "As in the Mimbres, Hohokam, and Classic Maya cases, in the La Quemada example people stopped living in large settlements in what had been their main area of occupation, and many families must have relocated to form new social configurations" (Nelson et al. 2014, 177). This must be seen as particularly prevalent in the Mesoamerican Epiclassic and Postclassic periods, and as such studied in detail (Manzanilla 2005b). It underlines the often-subtle aspects of human migration, even though coercion and forced resettlements in wartime may also have been part of many Mesoamerican stories.

Finally, mobility (more than migration) can be detected by reviewing the relationships between cities and their hinterlands, and can be documented through pedestrian or remote-sensing surveys, geographical assessments of landscape diversity, and through paleoenvironmental proxies documenting local human land-use. As demonstrated by Southwestern archaeologists, mobility patterns are dependent upon this type of knowledge, linking archaeological and environmental evidence to various residential systems along with specific mixes of crop agriculture or other subsistence modes. Dual residences (anchor houses, field huts) involving a high degree of mobility may have the same archaeological signature as stable social groups with strongly marked hierarchy (e.g., such as the use of slave labor at the site of agricultural production). The longevity of a household in a single locale may show frequent gaps in occupation resulting from regular mobility, but mobility that only involves a part of the social group may be undetectable.

Other disciplines may have a role to play (Beekman and Christensen 2003), but only with careful attention paid to their relative strengths and weaknesses. Different temporal and spatial scales often make it difficult to synchronize different datasets. Linguistic reconstruction is most applicable at the regional scale (e.g., Hill 2015), unless specific inscriptions are available. Ethnohistoric accounts can provide quite specific details and insights into perceived motivations for movement, but may also assign symbolic significance to migrations by working them into archetypal myths. Whether this is a plus or a minus depends on one's research question.

HOW OUR CONTRIBUTORS ADDRESSED THE PROBLEM

Even though all the chapters in this volume combine several of the approaches that we briefly delineated above, the four of them that form the volume's first part illustrate primarily bioanthropological methodologies. The four chapters that then follow combine more archaeological and geographical approaches to mobility in the Classic (AD 250–950) Maya lowlands. The last part assembles four archaeological studies of migration over Mesoamerica, mostly in post-Teotihuacan times (AD 550–1520), with attention given to ethnohistorical sources. Finally, Dominique Michelet presents a useful, factual, and realistic discussion in the last chapter.

Chapter 1 by Carolyn Freiwald uses isotopic analyses applied to a broad corpus of data with further attention to burial patterns, while in chapter 2 Julie Hoggarth, Carolyn Freiwald, and Jaime Awe supplement these proxies with distinct bioanthropological markers, burial patterns, and variation in material culture (cuisine ceramics and lithics). Each chapter documents primarily regional-scale mobility in the eastern Maya lowlands, along with some possible late immigrations during the Postclassic period (after AD 900). They both show a clear concern for the issue of "visibility" of mobile people versus stable people in terms of material culture, suggesting that mobility may have actually engaged a high proportion of the studied population at any given moment.

Another two chapters by Andrea Cucina et al. and Meggan Bullock, respectively, combine isotopic sourcing with osteological analyses. Andrea Cucina and colleagues (chapter 3) take a much broader perspective on composite movements across the Yucatán peninsula, as they use the proxies of dental nonmetrics and isotopic assessments from a large series of skeletal remains obtained at the seaport of Xcambo in northern Yucatán. They assess temporal variation from the Early Classic (AD 200–600) to the Terminal Classic (AD 800–1000) periods. The authors consider variation in settlement layout, composition, and proximity to salt production sites. They conclude that the population was composed of diverse but relatively local groups.

Meggan Bullock (chapter 4), after reviewing ethnohistorical and archaeological information about the role of Cholula in Classic/Postclassic Central Mexico to assess the relevance of migration and mobility at the site, applies isotopic, paleodemographic, and paleopathological analyses to skeletal remains obtained from a low-status cemetery located in the epicenter of the great city. Bullock summons large sets of ethnohistoric data bearing on group migrations into Postclassic Cholula, while also discussing mobility induced by marriage moves, urban "enclaves," neighborhoods and their "homelands," along with pilgrimage and market "visits." She concludes that there were numerous individual and family migrations into the city, stressing that the corresponding burial practices do not stand out from those of the local population.

The following chapters dedicated to the Maya switch their focus to the relationship between city and hinterland, primarily addressing mobility. Elizabeth Graham and Linda Howie (chapter 5) present a synthetic approach to the issue of Terminal Classic/Postclassic trade and mobility in northern Belize. They find contrasting datasets, namely a marked heterogeneity in visible material culture and burial patterns with limited isotopic evidence for nonlocal populations, against a backdrop of sociopolitical continuity at Lamanai and less so at the associated seaport of Marco Gonzalez. Short-range mobility seems widespread, and the authors argue for some degree of cosmopolitanism among the new local elites relative to traditional elites, and little migration that might have destabilized the exchange system. The situation seems to have been volatile, which would have been the case well into the Postclassic and even Colonial periods.

In chapter 6, Nancy Gonlin and Kristin Landau review the demographic trajectory of the Maya city of Copan, concluding that migration played a role in the urbanizing process, something that several independent isotopic analyses tend to confirm. But they go further in calling on a variety of archaeological evidence to suggest that ongoing mobility between the city and its hinterlands (subsumed under Tilly's categories of migrations) may have also contributed to local urban dynamics. Although mostly punctuated and dispersed, specific data identify field huts, and show a degree of heterogeneity in construction modes, rituals, and ceramics that suggest both regional mobility and some migration from lower Central America.

Chapter 7 by Nicholas Dunning, Michael Smyth, Eric Weaver, and David Ortegón Zapata starts from a geographical and sociocultural analysis of Puuc settlement patterns in the northern Maya lowlands. They evaluate mobility as a plausible peasant strategy during the Late Preclassic (200 BC–AD 150) and Classic (AD 200–800) periods. They use material culture, residential morphology, and water-storage technology (chultuns, or reservoirs) to suggest a degree of control by local social hierarchies. Demographic evidence, like the burst of population at the large city of Uxmal in the ninth century, also suggests another avenue for research on regional mobility. Their cautious, integrated approach finds only limited regional-scale mobility in the Puuc region due to the constraints associated with water distribution, but also due to stabilizing factors like the formation of noble estates and agricultural intensification.

Charlotte Arnauld, Eva Lemonnier, Dominique Michelet, and Mélanie Forné (chapter 8) infer from the long-term demographic trajectories of a few selected lowland Maya cities—where they have developed research projects—that mobility and migration must have frequently shaped and dissolved urban settlements. In a multiscalar approach centered on (mainly Classic period) intra-settlement evidence, the stratigraphy of minimal household units, episodes of monumental construction, and developments in residential architecture, they characterize mobility within, into, and away from urban settlement. Mobility should help further in characterizing the final abandonment of inner lowland cities by AD 800–1000.

The last four chapters on several Mesoamerican regions, including the Maya, revert to the more conventional theme of migration. In chapter 9, Sarah Clayton takes as her starting point the demise of Teotihuacan at the onset of the Epiclassic (AD 600–900). She evaluates possible migration from Teotihuacan to a peripheral settlement in the southeastern Basin of Mexico by looking for changes in community size and composition. After discussing the migration issue at the end of Teotihuacan, Clayton attempts to integrate the demographic trajectory of Chicoloapan Viejo with material culture variation on the household scale, in order to conclude that the settlement expansion would have followed immigration of families from Teotihuacan and elsewhere in the Basin, with subsequent settlement reorganization.

Chapter 10, by Grégory Pereira, Marion Forest, Elsa Jadot, and Véronique Darras, reviews the narrative from the *Relación de Michoacán* of Postclassic migrations into and off the Zacapu lava flows in the Michoacán highlands, where several large cities appear to quickly come and go from AD 1200 to 1520. They use such archaeological proxies as demographic trajectory, neighborhood composition and expansion, ceramic-waste accumulations, and quantities of burials compared to demographic population estimates. They find that these centers rapidly formed and dispersed along a north–south trajectory over time. This study does focus on the singular urban tradition of Mesoamerica with its sweeping migratory movements. The stake is to attain chronologies of sufficiently high resolution and precision to assess the relocations of short-time settlements.

Prudence Rice (chapter 11) starts from the ethnohistorically rich documentation of migrations across the Maya lowlands during the Terminal Classic (AD 800–1000), Postclassic (1000–1520), and Colonial (1520–1697) periods, and interrogates their veracity using a wide array of archaeological evidence from the Petén Lakes region and elsewhere. She ranges from the elite, strongly ethnicized sphere (public architecture and associated funerary rituals, settlement layout, and location), to the inner, intimate sphere of households (ceramic technological styles and decoration, forms associated with specific foodways). Even though some mobility may be involved, the movements documented are largely migratory. The author also discusses related issues of sociopolitical fission and fusion.

Chapter 12 by Chris Beekman takes place in the heterogeneous ethnic landscape between the Tarascan and Aztec Empires of the Late Postclassic period (AD 1450–1520). He considers historically documented and politically driven migrations into the Tarascan Empire that formed enclaves, and why some of them retained their ethnolinguistic identity over time. He notes parallels in how these migrations were organized and carried out when compared to the more "mythical" migration narratives from the Early to Middle Postclassic. He compares the lessons learned from these documented enclaves to earlier archaeological case studies in the central Mexican highlands. Archaeological evidence for the existence of earlier enclaves with strong, persisting identity is then discussed (at Teotihuacan, Chingu, and Ucareo settlements). Beekman argues that the fate of migrant communities depends greatly on their "institutional completeness," and whether they maintained their independence or relied upon the host economy to meet social needs.

FINAL WORDS

The position taken in the present volume is that urban mobility and migration must be studied as modalities that partially overlapped and articulated, thereby opening the way to more differentiated perspectives on the Classic, Epiclassic, and Postclassic periods in distinct urbanized areas of Mesoamerica. The balance between systemic mobility and idiosyncratic migration was dynamic, and changed across time and space. The array of methodologies that can be combined now allows us to envision various lines of research, and we stress that there must be a shift away from simply documenting population movements to developing our understanding of the role that mobility and migration played in an ancient complex agrarian society.

We support a wider dialogue that includes modern population migrations (Baker and Tsuda 2015), which have accelerated rapidly alongside many political and economic events and processes. Movement will continue to increase as climatic and environmental hazards upset current cycles of mobility and dislodge anchored farmers (Black et al. 2011). The scale of movement will not be captured by narrow definitions of individual versus household migration, as larger groups will send members as scouts to develop opportunities, and new diaspora networks will form (Faist 2013, 1638). Whereas disruptive events and circumstances today often force people to take to the road with no greater goal than survival, in many cases the role of underlying patterns of mobility in supporting the more widely discussed migrations remains to be clarified. By focusing on ancient urbanization and deemphasizing the modern focus on borders, we hope to shift attention to the urban "poverty traps" to which so many migrants are drawn in search of solutions to insurmountable problems.

Bioanthropological Approaches

1

Urban and Rural Population Movement Patterns during the Late and Terminal Classic in the Belize River Valley, Belize

CAROLYN FREIWALD

Migration in ancient cultures used to be described as understudied, neglected, or poorly understood, but new methods and innovative theoretical frameworks now allow archaeologists to ask who moved, where the migrants came from, and even when or why they chose—or were forced—to move. Direct radiocarbon dating of burials allows for more precise ceramic and settlement chronologies (Ebert et al. 2016; Hoggarth et al. 2014), and data from historic accounts and epigraphic texts may reveal the reasons people moved (Bullock, chapter 4, this volume; McAnany et al. 2016). Studies of modern migration behaviors offer a theoretical framework to predict broader population movement patterns (Ezzo et al. 1997; Freiwald 2011a), and biodistance studies of similarities and differences in human tooth and bone metrics and morphology offer a means to test them (Aubry 2009; Miller 2015; Scherer 2004, 2007; Scherer and Wright 2015; Willermet et al. 2013; Wrobel 2004).

Biogeochemical methods have proved particularly informative in reconstructing population movement and how it relates to key anthropological questions, from the range of early hominins (Copeland et al. 2011; Richards et al. 2008), to

DOI: 10.5876/9781646420735.c001

migration patterns at the onset of the European Neolithic (Bentley et al. 2003; Grupe et al. 1997; Price et al. 2004) and mobility within states and empires (Buzon et al. 2007; Killgrove and Montgomery 2016; Knudson 2008; Prowse et al. 2007; Turner et al. 2009). In the Maya region, research has focused on key questions that include the growth of large cities such as Copan and Tikal (Price et al. 2014; Wright 2012) and the origins of important historic figures and their relation to foreign powers during critical moments of Classic-period (AD 250–900) culture change (Buikstra et al. 2004; Wright 2005a; Wright et al. 2010). More important, population movement has been identified at nearly every center studied using biogeochemical methods, including both large and small settlements in the Maya region (Awe et al. 2017; Chinchilla Mazariegos et al. 2015; Cucina et al. 2011, 2015; das Neves 2012; Davies 2012; Donis 2013; Freiwald 2011a, 2011b, 2019; Freiwald et al. 2014; Freiwald and Pugh 2018; Green 2016; Hoggarth et al., chapter 2, this volume; Krueger 1985; Micklin 2015; Miller 2015; Miller Wolf and Freiwald 2018; Mitchell 2006; Novotny 2015, Novotny et al. 2018; Patterson and Freiwald 2016; Price et al. 2008, 2010, 2014, 2015, 2018; Rand et al. 2015; Sierra Sosa et al. 2014; Somerville et al. 2016; Spotts 2013; Sutinen 2014; Trask 2018; Trask et al. 2012; White et al. 2001; Wright 2005a, 2005b, 2007, 2012; Wright and Bachand 2009; Wright et al. 2010; Wrobel et al. 2014, 2017), as well as elsewhere in Mesoamerica (e.g., Bullock Kreger 2010; Manzanilla 2017; Price et al. 2000; Wells et al. 2014; White et al. 2002, 2004a).

More recently, the focus has shifted from identifying population movement, which now is acknowledged as an ordinary occurrence (M.E. Smith 2014), to understanding its structure and the information that different methods can (and cannot) provide. For example, biogeochemical methods are not useful for identifying ongoing mobility related to trade, warfare, pilgrimages, or visits. Strontium, oxygen, and more recently sulfur and lead, provide better indicators of migration, defined as a change in residence that is long-term or permanent and breaks with previous habits (*sensu* Arnauld et al., chapter 8, this volume; Cabana and Clark 2011a). The term *migration* also describes movement across a political border, regardless of distance (Finnegan 1976; Hoerder 2004). Ancient political and social boundaries in the Maya region are not well understood and were likely different than the geologic and geographic boundaries that form the basis for isotopic variation.

Migration in this chapter is interpreted as a change in residence between locations with distinct strontium isotope values, which may include movement within and across political boundaries as well as social ones in parts of the Maya lowlands. More specifically, it is a difference in isotope values in early-forming tooth enamel that represents the place of birth, and the place of burial, which serves as a proxy for the residence at the end of life. The term *nonlocal* refers to individuals whose isotope values are statistical outliers from the sample population, and *local* describes individuals with isotope values found nearby, with the understanding that similar values may exist elsewhere in the Maya region.

This study uses a rural community in the eastern Maya lowlands to explore migration patterns among the Maya during the Late and Terminal Classic period (AD 700–900). Barton Ramie was a hinterland settlement located on the floodplain of the Belize River in a region where isotopic studies suggest substantial population movement. Strontium isotope values for individuals buried at 20 surface sites and caves suggest that nearly a quarter of the Belize Valley population relocated at least once between birth and burial (Freiwald 2011a; also see Freiwald 2011b; Green 2016; Krueger 1985; Micklin 2015; Mitchell 2006; Novotny 2015; Spotts 2013; Wrobel et al. 2014, 2017). At Barton Ramie, 14 percent of individuals sampled ($n = 28$) had origins elsewhere in the Belize Valley or neighboring regions (Freiwald 2011a). Movement into rural communities shows that migration was not limited to Maya cities, which has important implications for settlement, biodistance, and demographic studies.

I begin by describing population movement in the Belize River Valley and the baseline data used to interpret isotope studies in the Maya region, and then focus on individuals buried in six residential groups in the Barton Ramie settlement. Strontium isotope values suggest that both men and women moved and were interred in the same burial locations as those who were locally born. Certain aspects of funerary treatment are linked to origin, but the burials of some migrants were indistinguishable from the rest of the burial population. Carbon and nitrogen isotope values show that individuals with nonlocal origins also shared the same diet, even though they came from different places. I also present a possible association between nonlocal origins in the Belize Valley and dental modification, including inlays and filing of incisors and canine teeth. The main finding is that Maya social and political organization appears to have accommodated population movement in rural as well as urban areas, and that migration was an important demographic process during the Late / Terminal Classic periods.

BARTON RAMIE AND THE BELIZE RIVER VALLEY

Barton Ramie is located in the Belize River Valley (figure 1.1) and is best known for Willey and colleagues' pioneering 1954–1956 excavations, which still serve as a reference for household archaeology and Belize Valley burial practices (Freiwald 2011a; Schwake 2008; Welsh 1988; Willey et al. 1965; Yaeger 2003). The site consists of small clusters of house mounds and residential groups, with occupation beginning during the Middle Preclassic (~1000 BC) and possibly extending into the Postclassic period after AD 900. This study focuses on the Spanish Lookout phase, which marks the Late / Terminal Classic periods (AD 700–900). Individuals buried at the site also were used in one of the first studies of population movement using strontium isotope assays (Krueger 1985), have figured prominently

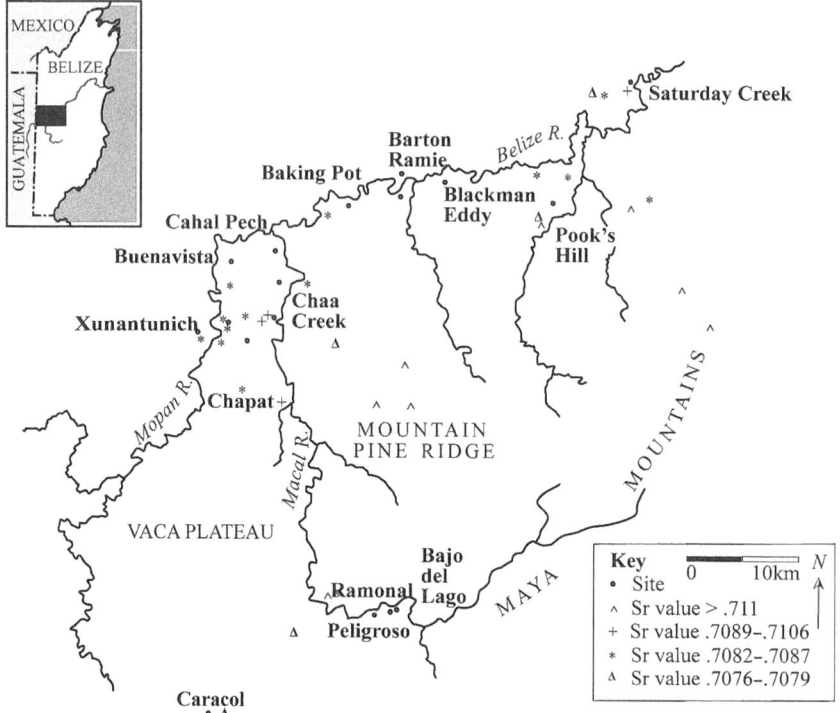

FIGURE 1.1. *Barton Ramie and Belize Valley sites, with strontium isotope values from flora and fauna in the region. (Freiwald 2011a, 412–414.)*

in dietary analyses using carbon, nitrogen, and oxygen isotope values (Freiwald 2011a; Gerry 1993; Gerry and Krueger 1997) as well as body modification practices (Tiesler 2014), and form one of a small number of osteological collections to be restudied by multiple researchers.

The site consists of eight loosely defined clusters of house mounds and plazuela groups that are located near Baking Pot, Blackman Eddy, and Lower Dover (figure 1.1), but lack clear social or political ties to these large centers (Aimers et al. 2000; Audet and Awe 2005; Driver and Garber 2004; Guerra and Collins 2015; Helmke and Awe 2012; LeCount and Yaeger 2010b; Leventhal 2010). Many of the 122 burials identified in the 1950s excavations were only partially uncovered or left *in situ*, with observations on age, sex, and burial treatment made under these conditions in the field (Willey et al. 1965). Twenty of the individuals in this study come from large trenches or horizontal excavations in mounds BR-1, BR-123, and BR-144, and test units, generally in the center of the mounds, in BR-75, BR-130, and BR155 (figure 1.2). Krueger (1985) sampled eight additional individuals, but the precise burial numbers and locations were not provided.

FIGURE 1.2. *Map of Barton Ramie and mounds used in this study. (Willey et al. 1965, 288: figure 171, modified from Yaeger 2003.)*

ISOTOPE METHODS FOR MEASURING MIGRATION

The element strontium serves as a good marker of migration because the proportion of two of its isotopes, $^{87}Sr/^{86}Sr$, varies according to the age and type of bedrock (Bentley 2006; Ericson 1985). Populations living in places with different bedrock may have distinct isotope ratios if they consume mainly local resources (Price et al. 2002), which the Maya likely did (but see Wright 2005a). Hundreds of isotope values in plants, water, and rocks (Gilli et al. 2009; Hodell et al. 2004; also see Laffoon et al. 2012) and in animal and human populations (Freiwald 2011a; Price et al. 2008, 2010; Thornton 2011; Wright 2005b) show average isotope ranges across much of Mesoamerica that allow us to identify long-distance population movement (figure 1.3). In the Maya region, $^{87}Sr/^{86}Sr$ values decrease gradually from the limestone bedrock of the northern Yucatán ($\sim$0.709) to the southern lowlands ($\sim$0.707), with intermediate values along the coast and in the central lowlands ($\sim$0.708). Higher strontium isotope values are identified mainly in the Maya Mountains and their foothills (>0.7092), and low values are found along the Pacific Coast (0.704–0.705) and in the metamorphic geology in southern Guatemala and western Honduras (0.706).

Some sites located only a few kilometers apart in both the eastern and western lowlands have distinct $^{87}Sr/^{86}Sr$ values, showing that aerial and fluvial inputs

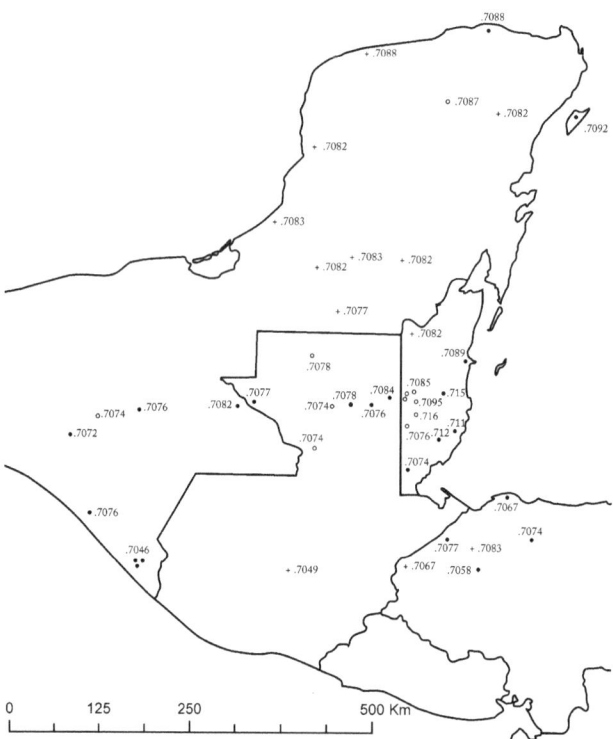

FIGURE 1.3. *Strontium isotope values in the Maya region. Black dots represent nonhuman values processed by the author, and with colleagues Miller Wolf and Freiwald (2018; Price et al. 2008). Open circles are average human values by author, and with colleagues (Patterson and Freiwald 2016). Crosses mark published values (das Neves 2012; Krueger 1985; Price et al. 2010, 2018; Wells et al. 2014; Wright et al. 2010).*

can affect isotopic signatures and that in some places, local and regional movement can be documented (Freiwald 2011a; Price and Gestsdóttir 2006; Price et al. 2008). For example, values change over short distances in and around the Belize Valley, increasing from the Vaca Plateau, to the Belize Valley and Yucatán coast, and to the foothills of the Maya Mountains and the Mountain Pine Ridge (table 1.1). Human populations in each of these regions reflect these baseline values (Freiwald 2011a), but tend to have slightly higher average $^{87}Sr/^{86}Sr$ values, which may stem from use of imported foods such as sea salt or salted marine fish (McKillop and Aoyama 2018; Wright 2012; also see Fenner and Wright 2014).

Although these values are grouped by UTM coordinates (table 1.2), isotopic landscapes (e.g., Hodell et al. 2004) are not necessarily predictable in the Maya

TABLE 1.1. Average strontium isotope values in central Belize

Location	No. of samples	Mean $^{87}Sr/^{86}Sr$
Belize River floodplain	17	0.708503
Lower Macal River floodplain	3	0.709989
West of Maya Mountains	5	0.711742
North of Maya Mountains	4	0.714268
East of Maya Mountains	2	0.711585
Mountain Pine Ridge	3	0.722228
Vaca Plateau	4	0.707743

region. For example, average human values at Chaa Creek (0.07095 $^{87}Sr/^{86}Sr$) are distinct from those at Cahal Pech (0.7084 $^{87}Sr/^{86}Sr$) less than 5 km away (Freiwald 2011a, 129, table 5.2). Belize Valley values in the 0.708 range may extend into the Petén in Guatemala (Davies 2012; Freiwald, Mixter, and Billstrand 2014; Freiwald, Yaeger, Awe, and Piehl 2014), where lower values are predicted, and similar short-range variability may exist in the western lowlands as well (Freiwald 2011; Price et al. 2008). Portions of the Maya region form a mosaic of strontium isotope values that change over short distances due to geologic variation and soil formation processes, while other areas share similar values over hundreds of kilometers.

THE BARTON RAMIE SAMPLE

Isotopic ratios in other elements such as oxygen, carbon, sulfur, and lead, and differences in trace elements, may be used to track migration, but the focus of this study is on 28 strontium isotope values in tooth enamel of individuals, including 10 men, five women, two adults of unknown age and sex, three juveniles who died before the age of 18, and Krueger's (1985) samples (table 1.3; also see Freiwald 2011a, 418–421). I attempted to include a proportional number of males and females from households with a large number of excavated and well-documented burials, but also chose individuals that Gerry (1993) included in his dietary analysis in order to compare the record of adult diet (bone isotope ratios) with childhood diet (tooth enamel values). I preferentially selected the first molar because, along with deciduous teeth, it captures the earliest residence since the enamel begins to form *in utero*. However, I substituted later-forming teeth when first molars were not available due to antemortem loss, poor preservation, or other factors.

Each tooth was measured and photographed with a high-resolution macro lens and then mechanically cleaned using a variable-speed dental drill equipped with a diamond burr to remove surface contamination (Freiwald 2011, 106–108). Five milligrams of clean tooth enamel were processed at the University of North

TABLE 1.2. Strontium isotope values from flora and fauna in the Maya lowlands and some neighboring regions*

Location (UTM coordinates, zones 15 and 16)	$^{87}Sr/^{86}Sr$	Sample	Lab No.
Blue Creek, Belize (town) (281698, 1792066)	0.707444	Riverine *jute* snail, shell (*Pachychilus indiorum*)	F4524
Saturday Creek, Belize (site) (308073, 1913386)	0.707572	Terrestrial snail, shell	F4939
Caracol, Belize (site) (273753, 1854383)	0.707630	Terrestrial snail, shell (*Neocyclotus* sp.)	F4521
Caracol Road, Belize (280732, 1862863)	0.707712	Iguana, bone (Iguanidae)	F1755
Roaring Creek, Belize (303043, 1894443)	0.707768	Riverine *jute* snail, shell (*Pachychilus indiorum*)	F3384
San Antonio, Belize (town) (284791, 1889275)	0.707863	Opossum, bone (Didelphidae)	F1754
Western Highway, Belize (276023, 1892227)	0.708208	Terrestrial snail, shell	F5276
Western Highway, Belize (305063, 1905607)	0.708219	Toad, bone (Bufonidae)	F5278
San Pedro Siris, Belize (site) (288402, 1920784)	0.708252	Terrestrial snail, shell (*Neocyclotus* sp.)	F4525
Buenavista, Belize (site) (1895200, 273250)	0.708285	Cow, tooth enamel (*Bos taurus*)	F4526
Cristo Rey, Belize (town) (282102, 1895200)	0.708320	Opossum, bone (Didelphidae)	F4527
Arenal, Belize (site) (276836, 1882948)	0.708342	Basilisk lizard, bone (*Basiliscus vittatus*)	F4941
Caves Branch, Belize (site/resort) (321643, 1900085)	0.708366	Terrestrial snail, shell (*Neocyclotus* sp.)	F4520
Western Highway, Belize (298473, 1905421)	0.708380	Tiger rat snake, bone (*Spilotes pullatus*)	F5274
Caracol Farms, Belize (modern) (286372, 1902758)	0.708397	Opossum, bone (Didelphidae)	F1751
Succotz, Belize (town) (272103, 1890417)	0.708477	Iguana, bone (Iguanidae)	F1753
Western Highway, Belize (284804, 1900796)	0.708527	Toad, bone (Bufonidae)	F5277
Spanish Creek (waterway), Belize (327614, 1939737)	0.708615	Frog, bone (Anura)	F4938
San Lorenzo, Belize (site) (273316, 1891806)	0.708629	Terrestrial snail, shell (*Neocyclotus* sp.)	F5275
Succotz, Belize (town) (272103, 1890417)	0.708719	Armadillo, bone (*Dasypus novemcinctus*)	F1752
Saturday Creek, Belize (site) (0308073, 1913386)	0.708820	Rabbit, bone (*Sylvilagus* sp.)	F4940

continued on next page

TABLE 1.2—*continued*

Location (UTM coordinates, zones 15 and 16)	$^{87}Sr/^{86}Sr$	Sample	Lab No.
Ladyville, Belize (town) (362966, 1941958)	0.708912	Iguana, bone (Iguanidae)	F1750
Chaa Creek, Belize (site) (277612, 1892312)	0.708942	Terrestrial snail, shell (*Neocyclotus* sp.)	F5272
Saturday Creek, Belize (site) (310807, 1914565)	0.709077	Opossum, bone (Didelphidae)	F5273
Chaa Creek, Belize (site) (277949, 1892212)	0.710373	Terrestrial snail, shell (*Neocyclotus* sp.)	F5271
Martz Farm, Belize (281103, 1881143)	0.710653	Terrestrial snail, shell (*Neocyclotus* sp.)	F4943
Blue Hole, Belize (320884, 1899551)	0.711136	Terrestrial snail, shell (*Neocyclotus* sp.)	F4942
Guacamayo Bridge, Belize (282759, 1865966)	0.711414	Riverine *jute* snail, shell (*Pachychilus indiorum*)	F4523
Guacamayo Bridge, Belize (282759, 1865966)	0.711755	Riverine *jute* snail, shell (*Pachychilus indiorum*)	F3385
Roaring Creek, Belize (303043, 1894443)	0.713917	Riverine *jute* snail, shell (*Pachychilus indiorum*)	F4522
Hummingbird Community, Belize (town) (331818, 1886422)	0.715170	Tree, seed pod (species not identified)	F4933
Mango Creek, Belize (346367, 1831352) + A48	0.710636	Pine, wood (species not identified)	F7707
Bladen River, Belize (333383, 1821711)	0.713789	Pine, wood (species not identified)	F7708
Swasey River, Belize (333425, 1827119)	0.710215	Pine, wood (species not identified)	F7709
Deep River, Belize (313825, 1818962)	0.711840	Pine, wood (species not identified)	F7710
Payne Creek, Belize (308020, 1809861)	0.712231	Pine, wood (species not identified)	F7711
Mountain Pine Ridge, Belize (292650, 1886003)	0.716212	Toad, bone (Bufonidae)	F4934
St. Margaret, Belize (town) (327536, 1890212)	0.716847	Opossum, bone (Didelphidae)	F4932
Mountain Pine Ridge, Belize (290381, 1879762)	0.724951	Toad, bone (Bufonidae)	F4935
Mountain Pine Ridge, Belize (293619, 1879712)	0.725520	Pine cone (species not identified)	F4936
Chiapas, Mexico, San San Cristóbal de las Casas (town) (538773, 1848614)	0.707394	Terrestrial snail, shell	F2964
Chiapas, Mexico, San San Cristóbal de las Casas (town) (538773, 1848614)	0.707651	Terrestrial snail, shell	F2966

continued on next page

TABLE 1.2—*continued*

Location (UTM coordinates, zones 15 and 16)	$^{87}Sr/^{86}Sr$	Sample	Lab No.
Chiapas, Mexico, San San Cristóbal de las Casas (town) (538773, 1848614)	0.707747	Terrestrial snail, shell	F2965
Chiapas, Mexico, Chiapa de Corzo (town) (498951, 1847289)	0.706584	Riverine *jute* snail, shell (*Pachychilus indiorum*)	F2971
Chiapas, Mexico, Chiapa de Corzo (town) (498951, 1847289)	0.707363	Riverine *jute* snail, shell (*Pachychilus indiorum*)	F2970
Chiapas, Mexico, Chiapa de Corzo (town) (498951, 1847289)	0.707392	Riverine *jute* snail, shell (*Pachychilus indiorum*)	F2972
Chiapas, Mexico, Chiapa de Corzo (town) (498951, 1847289)	0.707481	Riverine *jute* snail, shell (*Pachychilus indiorum*)	F2976
Chiapas, Mexico, Mirador (site) (461224, 1824404)	0.707177	Riverine *jute* snail, shell (*Pachychilus indiorum*)	F3360
Chiapas, Mexico, Mirador (site) (461224, 1824404)	0.707201	Riverine *jute* snail, shell (*Pachychilus indiorum*)	F3361
Western lowlands, Mexico, Yaxchilan, Mexico (site) (715498, 1871905)	0.708188	Terrestrial snail, shell (*Neocyclotus* sp.)	F3288
Western lowlands, Mexico, Yaxchilan, Mexico (site) (715498, 1871905)	0.708222	Terrestrial snail, shell (*Neocyclotus* sp.)	F3287
Western lowlands, Mexico, Bonampak (site) (676454, 1862225)	0.707701	Riverine *jute* snail, shell (*Pachychilus indiorum*)	F3290
Western lowlands, Mexico, Bonampak (site) (676454, 1862225)	0.707727	Riverine *jute* snail, shell (*Pachychilus indiorum*)	F3289
Pacific Coast, Mexico, Ojo de Agua (site) (565331, 1647413)	0.704628	Cow, tooth enamel (*Bos taurus*)	F2980
Pacific Coast, Mexico, Izapa (site) (589693, 1647549)	0.704663	Sheep/goat, tooth enamel (Caprinae)	F2979
Pacific Coast, Mexico, Paso de la Amada (site), Buenos Aires (town) (555949, 1646180)	0.704771	Cow, rib (*Bos taurus*)	F2978
Pacific Coast, Mexico, Chilo (site) (555492, 1649375)	0.705100	Terrestrial snail, shell	F2977
Pacific Coast, Mexico, Pijijiapan (town) (477416, 1735555)	0.707213	Dog, tooth enamel (*Canis lupus familiaris*)	F2975
Pacific Coast, Mexico, Pijijiapan (town) (477416, 1735555)	0.707680	Dog, bone (*Canis lupus familiaris*)	F2974
Pacific Coast, Mexico, Pijijiapan (town) (477416, 1735555)	0.707759	Dog, bone (*Canis lupus familiaris*)	F2973

* Also see Freiwald (2011a, 412–414).

Carolina at Chapel Hill Geochronology and Geochemistry Laboratory using a VG Sector 54 thermal ionization mass spectrometer (TIMS). Strontium was isolated using Sr-Spec ion exchange resin manufactured by Eichrom Industries in micro columns (~35 µL resin bed volume). Samples were loaded in single rhenium filaments in phosphoric acid and tantalum chloride solution and analyzed in triple dynamic multicollector mode with $^{88}Sr = 0.1194$, which assumes exponential fractionation behavior. Analytic uncertainty is estimated using the NBS-987 strontium standard ($^{87}Sr/^{86}Sr = 0.710268 \pm 0.000020$, 2σ; $n = 134$), with standard error for analyses generally exceeds 0.000011, 2σ.

RESULTS

Four of the 28 Barton Ramie samples (14.3%) have strontium isotope ratios that indicate a different origin (see table 1.3, shaded rows). The dataset is small, and a larger sample size with more isotopic variability or that extends over a broader geographic area could make it more difficult to differentiate the local from the nonlocal populations. I use both mean- and median-based statistics and a faunal baseline for the site and region to interpret three of the 20 values (excluding Kruger's 1985 data) as statistical outliers. $^{87}Sr/^{86}Sr$ values of three baseline samples collected within 2–8 km of the site (average 0.708435, range 0.70838–0.70853) are similar to those along the Belize River floodplain (average 0.708503, range 0.70821–0.70908). $^{87}Sr/^{86}Sr$ values for the human sample population range from 0.707650 to 0.709584. Mean-based statistics exclude two individuals, BR-144 B2 and BR-123 B9, because they do not fall within two standard deviations of the average for the sample. These values are extreme outliers from the interquartile range, based on the median value, which also excludes BR-123 B18 as an outlier from the dataset. Each of these three outlier values also falls outside of the range of the Belize Valley baseline fauna (figure 1.4). Excluding outlier values, the mean strontium isotope value of the Barton Ramie sample burial population is 0.70862 ± 0.0002.

Two individuals have values that are higher than those found in along the Belize River floodplain, including a female >45 years old at the time of death (0.709584 $^{87}Sr/^{86}Sr$) and a probable adult male in mound BR-123 (0.70916 $^{87}Sr/^{86}Sr$). One of Krueger's (1985) samples (0.70918 $^{87}Sr/^{86}Sr$), for whom no information is reported, is also an outlier value (not shown in figure 1.4). These values most likely represent short- or medium-distance population movement. $^{87}Sr/^{86}Sr$ values in excess of 0.7092 in human populations have only been identified in proximity to the Maya Mountains (Freiwald 2011a; Wrobel et al. 2017), although isolated nonhuman samples with high values are reported in Guatemala's Motagua Valley and in western Honduras (Hodell et al. 2004; Miller Wolf and Freiwald 2018). An adult male buried in mound BR-144 has a low value (0.707650 $^{87}Sr/^{86}Sr$) that suggests a birthplace or childhood home in the southern lowlands.

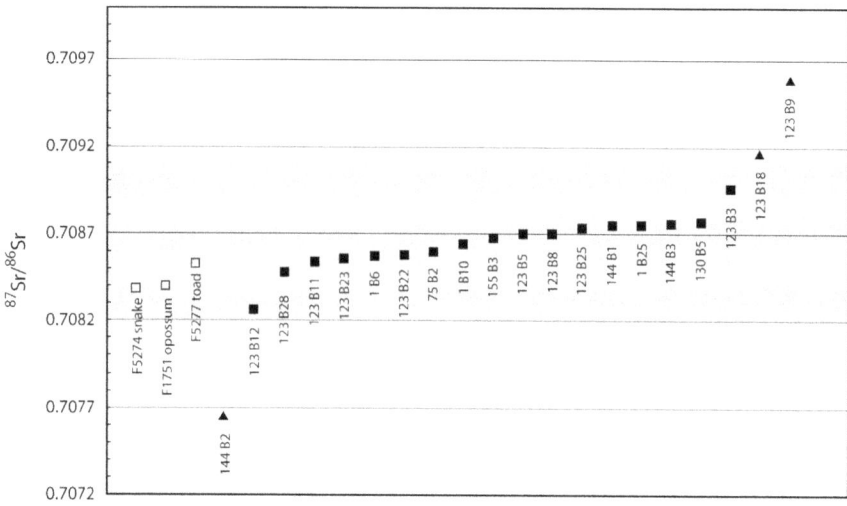

FIGURE 1.4. *Barton Ramie strontium isotope values. Human values in black and fauna sampled near the site in white. Squares represent local values and triangles show nonlocal values. Shaded area shows faunal baseline values along the Belize River.*

Similar values exist in the Vaca Plateau, as well as from the Petén Lakes region in Guatemala to Chiapas, Mexico (see table 1.2). The range of the 17 remaining values (0.708262–0.708958 ^{87}Sr/^{86}Sr) matches that of baseline values along the Belize River floodplain (0.70821–0.70908 ^{87}Sr/^{86}Sr) (see figure 1.1). This suggests a local origin for each of these individuals, but does not rule out movement among sites within the Belize Valley, from another part of the Maya region, or even from elsewhere in Mesoamerica where similar values exist (Davies 2012, 296; Freiwald 2011a, 308; Miller Wolf and Freiwald 2018; Price et al. 2015). Understanding the meaning of the values, however, requires a close examination of burial treatment in a broader regional context.

DISCUSSION

The small sample of Barton Ramie burials mirrors trends identified in the larger Belize Valley sample, including four findings presented here. First, both males and females had nonlocal origins; migration was not limited to a single demographic. There also is a linkage between burial orientation and isotopic origin, even as people who relocated to Barton Ramie shared the same general diet as those born in the region. A final point is a possible relationship between dental modification and migration that merits further exploration.

Two of the nonlocal isotope values were found in mound BR-123, where Willey and colleagues (1965, 90) recovered 35 burials, 11 of which are included

TABLE 1.3. Barton Ramie $^{87}Sr/^{86}Sr$ isotope values

Burial Information	$^{87}Sr/^{86}Sr$ value	Sex and age-at-death	Body position and orientation	Date
MOUND BR-123				
BR-123 B3	0.708958	female	Extended, prone position, with the head to the south	Late–Terminal Classic period
N8857.90	URM3?	adult		
F5877				
BR-123 B5	0.708697	female?	unknown	Late–Terminal Classic period
N8857.25	ULM1?	adult		
F5869				
BR-123 B8	0.708699	male	Extended, prone position, with the head to the south	Late–Terminal Classic period
N8857.32	LLM2	adult		
F5873				
BR-123 B9	0.709584	female	Extended, prone position, with the head to the south and the lower legs flexed (ventrally placed, legs flexed)	Late–Terminal Classic period
N8857.33	LLM1	>45 years		
F5871				
BR-123 B11	0.708535	5–6 years	Probably extended, with the head to the south	Late–Terminal Classic period
N8857.83	URP3			
F5875				
BR-123 B12	0.708262	female?	Extended, prone position, with the head to the south	Late–Terminal Classic period
N8857.84	URM1	adult		
F5876				
BR-123 B18	0.70916	male?	Extended, prone position, with the head to the south	Late–Terminal Classic period
N8857-7	LLM2	adult		
F5864				
BR-123 B22	0.708578	4–5 years	Extended, prone position, with the head to the south	Late–Terminal Classic period
N8857-8	ldm2			
F5863				

continued on next page

TABLE 1.3—*continued*

Burial Information	$^{87}Sr/^{86}Sr$ value	Sex and age-at-death	Body position and orientation	Date
BR-123 B23	0.708560	male?	Extended, prone position, with the head to the south and lower legs flexed	Late–Terminal Classic period?
N8857.42	LRM1	12–18 years		
F5870				
BR-123 B25	0.708733	male	Extended, prone position, with the head to the south	Late–Terminal Classic period
N8857.55	URP3	adult		
F5874				
BR-123 B28	0.708481	20–35 years	Extended, prone position, head to the south, facing west	Late–Terminal Classic period?
N8857.134	LLM1			
F5879				
MOUND BR-1				
BR-1 B6	0.708575	adult?	Seated position, facing west	Late–Terminal Classic period
N8857.36	LLM1			
F5872				
BR-1 B10	0.708641	male	Extended, prone position, head to the south, facing east	Late–Terminal Classic period
N8857.141	URC	40–60 years		
F5881				
BR-1 B25	0.708746	14–18 years	Extended, supine position, head to the south, facing east	Late–Terminal Classic period
N8857.142	LRM1			
F5882				
MOUND BR-144				
BR-144 B1	0.708745	female?	Probably extended, head to the south and facing west	Late–Terminal Classic period or later
N8857.21	LRM1	adult		
F5866				
BR-144 B2	0.70765	male?	Extended, prone position, head to the south, facing down	Late–Terminal Classic period or later

continued on next page

TABLE 1.3—*continued*

Burial Information	$^{87}Sr/^{86}Sr$ value	Sex and age-at-death	Body position and orientation	Date
N8857.22	LRM1?	adult		
F5867				
BR-144 B3	0.708753	male	Extended, prone position, head to the south, facing down	Late–Terminal Classic period or later
N8857.23	LLM1	adult		
F5868				
MOUND BR-75				
BR-75 B2	0.708601	male?	Extended, prone position, with the head to south.	Late–Terminal Classic period
N8857.127	URM1	adult		
F5878				
MOUND BR-130				
BR-130 B5	0.708771	male?	Seated (?)	Late–Terminal Classic period
N8857.17				
F5865	LRM1	adult		
MOUND BR-155				
BR-155 B3	0.708675	male	Extended, prone position, with the head to the south	Late–Terminal Classic period or earlier?
N8857.137	LLM1	40–50 years		
F5880				
UNKNOWN BURIAL LOCATION (KRUEGER'S 1985 STUDY)				
BR-12	0.70871	No information available (Krueger 1985)		
BR-14	0.70851	No information available (Krueger 1985)		
BR-15	0.70853	No information available (Krueger 1985)		
BR-2	0.70884	No information available (Krueger 1985)		
BR-24	0.70858	No information available (Krueger 1985)		
BR-38	0.70844	No information available (Krueger 1985)		
BR-39	0.70867	No information available (Krueger 1985)		
BR-40	0.70918	No information available (Krueger 1985)		

Sources: Burial number from Willey et al. (1965), with accession numbers from the Peabody Museum at Harvard University and University of Wisconsin–Madison lab numbers. Information on sex, age, and burial context derive from Willey et al. (1965), with modifications to age and sex assignments from Tiesler (personal communication 2009) and observations by Freiwald (2011a, 418–421).

in this sample. Nine of these individuals have strontium isotope values consistent with a Belize Valley origin. One probable male (Burial 18, 0.709160 ^{87}Sr/^{86}Sr) shows funerary treatment typical of the Belize Valley, with a prone, extended body placement and a southern orientation. He was buried with a slightly higher number of grave goods ($n = 6$) than most burials in this mound (no items, $n = 16$; 1–5 items, $n=16$; 5–10 items, $n = 2$), but not to the extent of the 46 items buried with Burial 30, who was not sampled (Willey et al. 1965, 550). Grave goods are not indicative of origin at Barton Ramie, where two-thirds of the burials had no offerings (Willey et al. 1965) and no goods linked individuals to nonlocal places of birth.

The isotope ratio in Burial 9 (0.709584 ^{87}Sr/^{86}Sr) suggests a nonlocal origin even though the burial was oriented to the south and interred in a prone position (Willey et al. 1965, 114). The lower legs, however, were fully flexed in a very atypical position for the Maya region. The VPLF, or ventrally placed, legs flexed body position, begins to appear at coastal sites such as Marco Gonzalez at the end of the Classic period and spreads inland over time to Chau Hiix and Lamanai, as well as several Belize Valley locations (Graham and Howie, chapter 5, this volume; Graham et al. 2013; also see Donis 2013; Wrobel and Graham 2015). Two locations north of the Maya Mountains, Chaa Creek and the Uayazba Kab rockshelter, have similar average human strontium isotope values, but ^{87}Sr/^{86}Sr baseline values east of the Maya Mountains show that a coastal origin also is possible (see table 1.2; also see Hodell et al. 2004).

In contrast, the low nonlocal ^{87}Sr/^{86}Sr value for BR-144 Burial 2 (0.707650) is not associated with an anomalous burial position. The burial was located near six others in a test unit excavated in the medium-sized mound. Two other burials (Burials 1 and 3) have strontium isotope values consistent with a local origin. Although these were only partially excavated, Willey and colleagues (1965, 553–554) described prone body positions and southern orientations for each of the three individuals in this sample.

These findings reflect broader trends in the Belize Valley. Descriptions of body position and orientation were available for two-thirds (67.5%) of the 148 individuals in my regional Belize Valley study: 89 percent of the individuals with strontium isotope values in the local range were buried with a southern orientation, with the bodies most commonly in a prone, extended position (Freiwald 2011a, 317). However, variability in burial position is present at most Maya sites. For example, Barton Ramie individuals with local isotope values were buried in seated body positions, which are widely reported but represent fewer than 1.5 percent of Classic-period burials in the Maya region (Freiwald 2019). Three of 24 burials in mound BR-1 had strontium isotope values typical of the Belize River floodplain. BR-1 Burial 6 was unique not only for the large quantity of grave goods, including 20 vessels and 16 other stone, bone, and shell objects, but because the individual was placed in a seated position, facing west (Willey et al. 1965, 545–546). A second probable seated burial was found in a test unit in the BR-130 mound; Burial 5 was likely placed in a seated position and has a local strontium isotope value, as do Late / Terminal Classic seated burials individuals at Actuncan (Freiwald 2019) and Saturday Creek (Freiwald 2011a; Lucero 2006). In fact, nearly all seated burials have strontium isotope values considered local to their burial locations (Freiwald 2019).

The supine position of the individual in Barton Ramie Burial 25, which had a local strontium isotope value, also is relatively uncommon in this region but represents the norm elsewhere in the Maya lowlands (Schwake 2008; Welsh 1988). Micklin (2015) also identified a Late Classic burial at Actuncan (Burial 13) with an individual whose supine body position was anomalous, but whose local isotope value and southern orientation were similar to the other six prone interments located in the same area. Orientation seems to be more consistent than position as a marker for origin; other variation in burial practice may relate to one or more variables such as time period, age, status, occupation, or even idiosyncratic adaptations to accepted funerary traditions.

Long-term dietary differences, however, were not indicated by a small sample of carbon ($^{13}C/^{12}C$) and nitrogen ($^{15}N/^{14}N$) isotope assays. $\delta^{13}C$ isotope values in the Maya region generally determine the extent to which maize was consumed (versus other plants). They are used in conjunction with $\delta^{15}N$ values to determine the types of plant, terrestrial, or marine proteins in the diet (e.g., Gerry 1993; J. Metcalfe et al. 2009; Piehl 2006; Somerville et al. 2013; Tykot 2002; White et al. 2001; Whittington and Reed 1997; Wright 2006). I built on John Gerry's (1993) carbon and nitrogen dietary analysis to assess the extent to which a person's origin might explain some Maya lowland dietary differences (table 1.4). Bone collagen samples were processed at the University of Illinois at Urbana-Champaign under the direction of Dr. Stan Ambrose following procedures modified from Balasse et al. (2002). See Freiwald (2011a, 260) and Gerry (1993) for descriptions of sample preparation.

Average Barton Ramie isotope values in this sample are similar to those identified at some sites in Belize, including Caledonia and Minanha (e.g., Gerry 1993; Rand et al. 2015; Williams et al. 2017). Isotope values indicate different dietary inputs at Lamanai and Pacbitun, but average values at most sites fall within −9‰ to −11‰ $\delta^{13}C$ and 8‰ to 10‰ $\delta^{15}N$ average values (also see Mansell et al. 2006, 183; Somerville et al. 2013; White et al. 1993; Wright 2006). Variability has been attributed to sex, age, status, and location, but this sample suggests that at Barton Ramie, migrants did not maintain dietary differences, at least in ways that isotope values might detect in this small sample size.

A final discussion point relates to dental modification. Three of the individuals in the Barton Ramie sample had modified teeth, including BR-1 B6 (Type

TABLE 1.4. Bone collagen values for Barton Ramie burials*

Burial	$^{87}Sr/^{86}Sr$	$\delta^{13}C_{co}$	$\delta^{15}N$	C:N ratio
BR-144 B2	0.707650	−10.79[†]	9.31[†]	3.33, 3.29
BR-1 B10	0.708641	−10.13	8.84	3.26
BR-1 B6	0.708575	−13.00	8.10	3.40
BR-75 B2	0.708601	−10.00	8.80	3.25
BR-123 B3	0.708958	−11.10	8.70	—
BR-123 B8	0.708699	−13.30	8.90	3.42
BR-123 B9	**0.709584**	−13.30	8.80	3.35
BR-123 B12	0.708262	−12.80	8.20	—
BR-123 B18	**0.709160**	−11.40	9.50	3.40
BR-123 B23	0.708560	−10.60	9.20	3.37
BR-123 B25	0.707833	−11.10	8.90	3.31
BR-123 B28	0.708481	−12.30	8.60	3.22
BR-144 B3	0.708753	−11.80	8.90	3.34
BR-155 B3	0.708675	−12.00	9.40	—
Average value of samples		−11.80	8.80	

* Individuals with nonlocal strontium isotope values are **bold**; Gerry's (1993, 207–210) data are *italic*.
[†] Average of two values (Freiwald 2011a, 432–433).

A1), BR-1 B25 (Type B-4), and BR-155 B3 (Type F9), which differed from others at the site (Willey et al. 1965, 540). Each of these individuals had local origins; however, a disproportionate number of individuals with modified teeth in the Belize Valley had strontium isotope values that differed from those found near their burial locations. Fifty-three individuals buried at seven Belize Valley sites include 15 examples of dental modification, 10 of whom had nonlocal strontium isotope values (Freiwald 2011a, 335). This is not surprising: head shapes signaled regional identities in many parts of Mesoamerica (Sierra Sosa et al. 2014; Tiesler 2014), and these data pose an intriguing starting point for further investigation. A larger sample in the region and detailed analysis of the type of filing or inlays and the extent of modification on the entire dental arcade is needed before any convincing conclusions can be drawn.

CONCLUSIONS

In sum, 14.2 percent of the burial population sampled at Barton Ramie has nonlocal strontium isotope values, similar to other sites in the Belize Valley (Freiwald 2011a). In fact, nearly every study in the Maya region shows that between 10 and 40 percent of the individuals sampled moved at least once between birth and burial. This is a staggering finding when the shortcomings of isotopic studies of migration are considered. Isotopic methods only identify first-generation migrants and a single relocation, not the multiple moves an individual might have made as a child, adolescent, or adult. Isotope assays also will miss return migration and population movement within and between regions with similar isotope values. Moreover, isotope values do not vary on a fine-enough scale to identity residential mobility, or movement within a settlement or city, which is the most common type of movement found in modern migration studies. However, the concepts of return migration and migration streams (Cadwallader 1992) suggest that the places people came from might also be where they moved, providing theoretical support for interpreting broader patterns of movement from isotopic studies.

Barton Ramie results also illustrate other aspects of population movement within the Belize Valley. First, migration included individuals in hinterland settlements and residential groups interpreted as commoner residences. Population movement was not limited to elite individuals or to those residing at major centers. Second, migration was not limited to exogamy, as both men and women moved. Marriage likely was one of many reasons for population movement, which clearly was occurring throughout the Maya region. Finally, all presumed migrants were buried in close proximity to individuals interpreted as local to the Barton Ramie settlement. The intimate nature of a residential burial, in which the dead are incorporated into the lives of the living generation after generation, tells a story of assimilation in which the place of birth played a less important role than other factors in an individual's identity.

In the case of the Belize Valley, movement was mainly within an area with shared ceramic, dietary, and burial patterns. It is not surprising, then, that "migrants," who may have relocated over only a short distance, followed many of the same practices in both their new and old residences. However, shared genetic traits among many Maya centers indicate that not all movement was necessarily among neighboring regions (Scherer 2004), suggesting that Maya social organization must have accommodated population movement on a wider scale. This does not mean that migrants could assimilate seamlessly into a new community; in fact, some nonlocal individuals received "local" burial treatment, while others are marked by distinctive funerary treatments (Freiwald, Yaeger, Awe and Piehl 2014). The frequency and direction of population movement we identify using isotopic assays could have implications for understanding social and political boundaries and the extent to which rulers could control or influence peoples' movements. Settlement-pattern studies and population-density estimates also are impacted by migration patterns, and the ability to measure multiple isotope ratios over decades of an individual's life suggest that the next decade of research will contribute significantly to our understanding of Maya culture.

ACKNOWLEDGMENTS

The Peabody Museum of Archaeology and Ethnology at Harvard University and the Belize Institute of Archaeology provided permission to include samples from Barton Ramie. Funding came from the Ruth Dickie GWIS–Beta Chapter, the University of Wisconsin–Madison Anthropology Department, a NSF Award 0413047 Human Migration in Mesoamerica to T. Douglas Price and colleagues, and a Heinz Foundation for Latin American Studies grant to Dr. Jason Yaeger. Thank you to James H. Burton and T. Douglas Price of the University of Wisconsin–Madison Laboratory for Archaeological Chemistry, to Paul Fullagar of the University of North Carolina at Chapel Hill, Stanley Ambrose of the University at Illinois Urbana–Champaign, and to Vera Tiesler, Gabriel Wrobel, Mark Robinson, and the three reviewers who contributed to this study.

2

Classic and Postclassic Population Movement and Cultural Change in the Belize Valley, Belize

JULIE A. HOGGARTH,
CAROLYN FREIWALD,
AND JAIME J. AWE

Research on migration and mobility has become more prevalent in the archaeological literature on the ancient Maya in recent years (see Freiwald, chapter 1, this volume; Cucina 2015b; Price et al. 2015; Scherer et al. 2014; Wright 2012). These studies are important, especially for understanding population aggregations and/or dispersals that may be linked to cycles of political development and disintegration of regional centers across the Maya lowlands. In their DNA study on contemporary Maya populations, Ibarra-Rivera and colleagues (2008) identified little genetic variability, suggesting that mobility and migration were frequent occurrences. Using dental metrics, Scherer (2007) also identified little variation among Classic-period Maya groups, supporting the presence of population movement rather than isolation. Isotopic analyses offer new possibilities for identifying both regional and long-distance population movement that complement ethnohistoric descriptions of high levels of mobility and migration during the Postclassic and Colonial periods (Farriss 1984; Jones 1998, 8–13; Restall 1997; Rice et al. 1998; Robinson 1981). Understanding patterns of mobility in the prehistoric past is especially important, as large-scale population movements

DOI: 10.5876/9781646420735.c002

have been described for both the northern and southern lowlands during the Postclassic period (Jones 1998; Pugh 2003, 2004; Rice, chapter 11, this volume).

We present an archaeological case study from the Belize Valley that presents new data from Baking Pot that makes a strong case for migration into a depopulated area, rather than continuity in occupation after the Classic period (Hoggarth et al. 2014). We offer new ideas about the geographic origin of the Postclassic occupants of the site and the nature of migration and mobility during this time. Classic-period populations were mobile, but more large-scale movement is indicated by settlement patterns, material culture, burial patterns, and the biogeochemistry of human remains, which suggest that a new population moved to Baking Pot during the Postclassic period.

BELIZE VALLEY

Baking Pot is located in western Belize (figure 2.1) on the southern bank of the Belize River (figure 2.2). Navigable for more than 200 miles, the Belize River served as a major transportation route between the Caribbean coast and the interior, making the Belize Valley an important trade route for more than two millennia. Baking Pot was initially occupied during the Middle Preclassic period (~cal 700 BC), reaching its apogee at the end of the Late Classic period (cal AD 600–800) (Audet 2006; Helmke 2008; Hoggarth et al. 2014). Despite the sociopolitical collapse of the site around cal AD 750–900, there is evidence for Postclassic occupation in the site's peripheral areas (Audet and Awe 2004; Ehret and Conlon 2000; Hoggarth 2012; Hoggarth et al. 2014). Postclassic ceramics from Baking Pot and the site of Barton Ramie nearby have previously been interpreted as evidence for continuous Classic to Postclassic occupation (Aimers 2004; Willey et al. 1965). However, recent radiocarbon dating of burials with Postclassic ceramics from Baking Pot's settlement has placed all three directly dated individuals within the Late Postclassic period (cal AD 1280–1420) (Hoggarth et al. 2014). In this chapter, we examine the existing bioarchaeological, biogeochemical, and archaeological data to identify evidence for population movement into the region and how it changed from the Classic to Postclassic periods. Changes in settlement patterns, material culture, burial traditions, and the isotopic origins of Baking Pot inhabitants indicate reoccupation during the Late Postclassic period rather than demographic continuity.

BIOARCHAEOLOGICAL AND BIOGEOCHEMICAL APPROACHES: ISOTOPIC EVIDENCE

Isotope values in bones and teeth provide a direct line of evidence to investigate the origin and mobility of Classic and Postclassic populations in the Belize Valley. Strontium ($^{87}Sr/^{86}Sr$) isotope values are most commonly used to differentiate local and nonlocal individuals in Mesoamerican archaeological

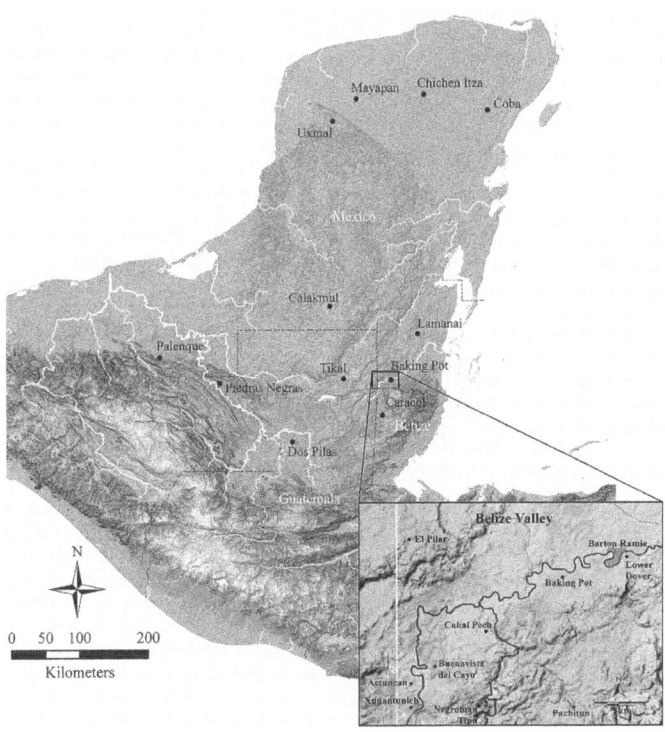

FIGURE 2.1. *Location of Baking Pot and the Belize Valley in the central Maya lowlands.*

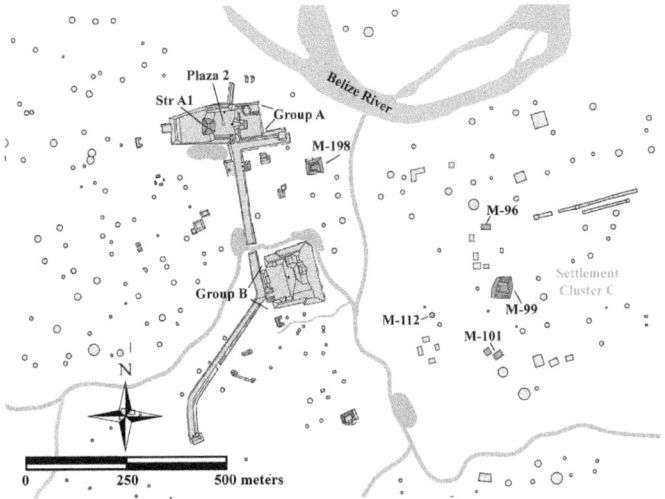

FIGURE 2.2. *Map of Baking Pot site core and settlement, showing the locations of structures with dated and sampled burials.*

populations (Freiwald 2011a, 2011b; Price et al. 2010, 2015; Sierra Sosa et al. 2014; Thornton 2011; Wright 2005a, 2012; Wright et al. 2010; Wrobel et al. 2014), and oxygen isotope values ($\delta^{18}O$) provide complementary information on both diet and residence (Price et al. 2010; White et al. 2000, 2004a, 2004b, 2007). Both elements are incorporated into tooth enamel, which forms during infancy and childhood, and bone, which remodels continually throughout life. Enamel is less subject to diagenetic contamination than other body tissues, and teeth are mechanically and chemically cleaned to remove potential surface contamination (see Freiwald, chapter 1, this volume).

Both isotopes vary in predictable ways in Mesoamerica. Bedrock geology, soil formation processes, and diet form the basis for strontium isotope variability (Bentley 2006). $^{87}Sr/^{86}Sr$ ratios decrease gradually from the north to the south in the Maya region due to geologic differences between the Cretaceous limestone bedrock of the Yucatán Peninsula, the igneous rocks of the Maya Mountains, and the volcanic-derived sediments of the Guatemalan highlands and Pacific coast results in high values (see Freiwald, chapter 1, this volume; Hodell et al. 2004; Price et al. 2008). Most Maya-lowland populations have a similar range of oxygen isotope ratios, but enriched values are found in the central lowlands and depleted ones along the Pacific coast and in the Guatemalan highlands (Freiwald 2011a; Lachniet and Patterson 2009; Marfia et al. 2004; Price et al. 2010; Scherer et al. 2014).

Hundreds of published strontium and oxygen isotope values recorded for the Maya lowlands show population movement into nearly every Maya center investigated, including Tikal, Copan, and Caracol (Freiwald 2011a; Miller 2015; Price et al. 2015; Wright 2012). Most research focuses on the Classic period (but see Wright 2007), and there has been limited discussion of change in migration patterns over time (but see Spotts 2013; Wright 2012). The Belize Valley is one of the most intensively sampled parts of the Maya region; strontium isotope values are available for more than 200 individuals buried in the Belize Valley and neighboring regions. Nearly one-fourth of the population moved at least once between birth and burial (Freiwald 2011a; Mitchell 2006; Spotts 2013), including 28 Classic-period individuals from Baking Pot and 28 from Barton Ramie (Freiwald 2011a, 2011b, and chapter 1, this volume).

At Baking Pot, 31 individuals were sampled for isotopic measurement, with 28 dating to the Classic period and three dating to the Postclassic period. Most individuals have $^{87}Sr/^{86}Sr$ values that we interpret as isotopically local; that is, values that are found near Baking Pot and the Belize River. Mean-based statistics for 16 modern faunal samples, ranging from 0.70821 to 0.70908 $^{87}Sr/^{86}Sr$, provide an expectation for the isotope values of people living on the Belize River floodplain. Six Classic-period individuals have values that are statistical outliers, or more than two standard deviations from the mean of the baseline fauna (0.70850

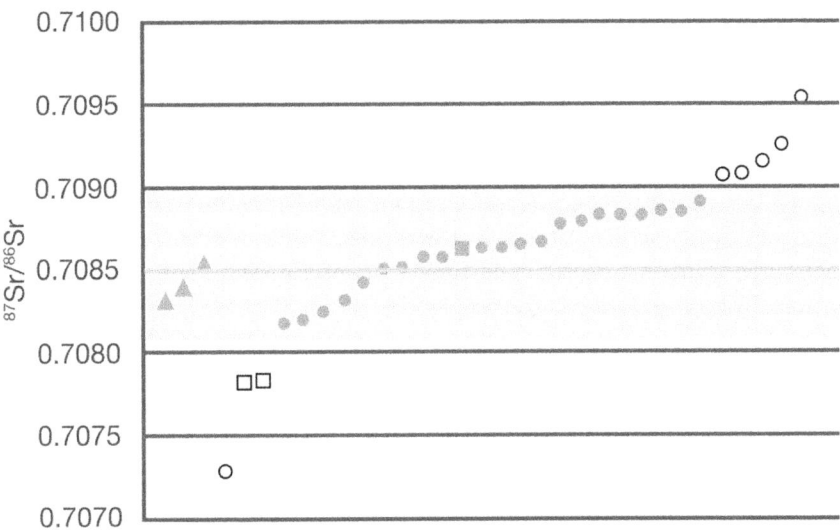

FIGURE 2.3. *Strontium isotope values for Classic-period samples (circles) and the three Postclassic individuals (squares) compared to fauna collected near the site (triangles) and the range of Belize valley fauna (shaded area). White markers represent values interpreted as nonlocal.*

$\pm$ 0.00026 $^{87}Sr/^{86}Sr$ in Freiwald 2011a, 85). Comparing the population to a faunal baseline results in a high proportion of samples classified as isotopically nonlocal, providing a conservative estimate of the local population. Using a baseline of human values in the Belize Valley ($n = 115$) provides a conservative estimate of movers, resulting in four outlier values that fall within two standard deviations from the human mean of 0.7086 (0.708146 to 0.709142 $^{87}Sr/^{86}Sr$ in Freiwald 2011a, 128). There are multiple ways to interpret isotope values, and the addition of new values may shift the statistical boundaries (Freiwald 2011a, 2011b). Therefore, we consider a range of values, from 14–21 percent of the burial sample, as isotopically nonlocal to Baking Pot (figure 2.3).

Five high $^{87}Sr/^{86}Sr$ values (0.70955, 0.70926, 0.70916, 0.70908, 0.70909) and one low one (0.70729) may reflect Classic-period population movement patterns in the Belize Valley. First, movement into Baking Pot came from different places. Values higher than 0.709 $^{87}Sr/^{86}Sr$ are found in a limited number of locations in the Maya region, but in human populations have been identified only in and around the Maya Mountains to the south. One site, Chaa Creek, is located less than 5 km from Baking Pot (Freiwald 2020; Hodell et al. 2004; Wrobel et al. 2017). Values in the 0.707 $^{87}Sr/^{86}Sr$ range are found in the southern lowlands, and the outlier value in this case represents long-distance movement into the Belize

Valley (Freiwald 2011a; Hodell et al. 2004). The only Classic-period oxygen isotope value was sampled from this individual (−4.27 $^{18}O/^{16}O$). It is not a statistical outlier from Belize Valley sites (−2.9 ± 0.99 $^{18}O/^{16}O$) but it also fits values identified to the south (Price et al. 2010).

A second Classic-period trend is that burials of isotopically nonlocal individuals followed Belize Valley norms, which included a southern orientation and prone body position. Unfortunately, contextual information on the individual with the lowest outlier value is not available. Third, individuals with nonlocal isotope values are buried in different residences during the Early, Late, and Terminal Classic periods, suggesting movement into Baking Pot from different locations. In sum, relocation into Classic-period Baking Pot households did not result in pronounced changes to burial patterns or material culture, perhaps because most movement was from places with similar practices and traditions.

Isotope values of the small Postclassic sample of three individuals show a different pattern. Two individuals (Burials 101-1 and 99E-1) have strontium isotope values that also are statistical outliers from the Baking Pot population and the rest of the Belize Valley. Burials 101-1 (0.707824 $^{87}Sr/^{86}Sr$) and 99E-1 (0.707815 $^{87}Sr/^{86}Sr$) have values that match those found in the central lowlands. Potential places of origin span a large area that includes the Vaca Plateau near Caracol, the central Petén near Lake Petén Itzá, or as far west as San Cristóbal in Chiapas, Mexico. Oxygen isotope values also support a nonlocal origin for Burial 101-1 (1.07‰) and are similar to enriched values reported in the Petén region (Lachniet and Patterson 2009; Price et al. 2010). In contrast, the $\delta^{18}O$ for Burial 99E-1 (−3.10‰) is similar to those reported for the Belize Valley with mean values of −2.99 and −3.20‰ at different sites in the region (n = 32; Freiwald 2011a, 268). Burial 198-2, a Late Postclassic infant burial, has a strontium isotope ratio that is consistent with the local range of values. In fact, the value is nearly the same as a burial dated to the Middle Preclassic in the same structure, suggesting that these individuals, who lived and died centuries apart, consumed resources with the same local signatures.

Values found at Petén Lakes sites provide the closest match for the two Baking Pot Postclassic individuals with nonlocal values. Strontium isotope values from fauna at the Postclassic sites Zacpeten (0.7076 $^{87}Sr/^{86}Sr$) and Topoxte (0.7077 $^{87}Sr/^{86}Sr$) are similar to findings at other sites in the region (Freiwald and Pugh 2018, 89; Hodell et al. 2004; Thornton 2011). If populations were moving into Baking Pot from the north, we would expect values similar to those found in central Belize. Wright (2007) reports values ranging from 0.7086 to 0.7089 $^{87}Sr/^{86}Sr$ at Mayapan (also see Gilli et al. 2009), and work by Price and colleagues (2010) shows similar values along the coastal Yucatán Peninsula, including near Lamanai (but see Thornton 2011). To the south, values identified near Tipu should exceed 0.711 $^{87}Sr/^{86}Sr$, though the isotopic analyses of wild game show that the catchment used by site residents extended into areas with both lower and higher values (Freiwald 2011a; Thornton 2011; Yaeger and Freiwald 2009). Drawing conclusions from a small sample of only three individuals poses more questions than answers, but it is clear that Postclassic population movement and burial patterns represent an important change in the Belize Valley.

ARCHAEOLOGICAL APPROACHES

Biogeochemical and archaeological data offer strong support for the presence of new populations moving into the Belize Valley during the Postclassic period who brought with them distinct traditions. The isotope data offer some support for links with the nearby Petén Lakes region, but the data set is small and similar strontium and oxygen isotope values exist in many other places. However, archaeological evidence shows cultural similarities that we can compare to the biological data. Distinct changes in burial traditions, settlement patterns, and material culture at Baking Pot during the Postclassic period show a distinctive break from Classic-period traditions. The introduction of new types of technology, materials, settlement choices, and ideology also supports our interpretation of migration into the area during this time.

Burial Patterns

Exploring burial patterns in conjunction with the isotopic evidence offers an additional line of evidence through which to explore mobility. Distinctive burial practices can be identified in the Belize Valley, forming an important aspect of social identity for the residents of the area that distinguished its population from those in nearby regions. Our research has recorded important changes in burial practices at Baking Pot during the Postclassic period, including body position, orientation, and burial location.

Burials in the Belize Valley during the Late and Terminal Classic periods typically included a single individual oriented to the south, with the body placed in a prone, extended position (Freiwald 2012; Schwake 2008; Welsh 1988; Willey et al. 1965; Yaeger 2003) (figure 2.4a). For example, of the 29 Classic-period samples in this chapter, five (17%) were interred in a prone body position with a southern orientation, and eleven (38%) in an extended, prone body position with the head oriented to the south (Freiwald 2011a, 190–191).

However, like most of the Maya lowlands, there is considerable variability in burials at Baking Pot and within the region. Seated, supine, and flexed body positions are described at Belize Valley sites and at Baking Pot, but always make up a small portion of the burial positions during the Classic period (e.g., Freiwald, Mixter, and Billstrand 2014; Helmke 2000; Hoggarth 2012; Iannone 1996; Lucero 2006; Novotny 2012). However, orientation and origin are closely linked: 89 percent of Belize Valley individuals ($n = 100$) with "local" strontium isotope values were buried with a southern orientation, and often in a prone, extended body position. Fewer than 20 percent of those with values not found in Belize Valley human populations were buried in this manner (Freiwald 2011a, 317). This pattern is identified for the Baking Pot burial population during the Classic period as well. Twenty-seven individuals with known burial information had strontium and/or oxygen isotope values local to the Belize Valley or the adjacent foothills of the Maya Mountains: 90 percent were oriented to the south ($n = 19/21$), 88 percent were placed in an extended body position ($n =15/17$), and 82 percent were interred in a prone position ($n= 18/22$) (Freiwald 2011a, 189–201).

Postclassic Baking Pot burial patterns are strikingly different. Individuals are buried in flexed and semiflexed body positions oriented to the north and northwest in off-platform locations. This is a notable break in centuries-old regional burial patterns (Schwake 2008; Willey et al. 1965; Yaeger 2003). It may signify an influx of individuals who had not recently lived in the Belize Valley, supporting other data for large-scale depopulation at the site and reoccupation by a new population (Hoggarth et al. 2014). Hoggarth's (2012, 187–189) multidimensional scaling of burial locations, orientations, goods, and mortuary architecture showed a distinct form of organization for the two adult Postclassic burials in comparison with Classic burials. The attributes that show the dissimilarity with earlier burials include the off-platform burial locations, low burial investment (stone-lined pits adjacent to or built into the outside walls of platforms), and atypical orientations and positions identified for Burial 99E-1 and Burial 101-1 (Hoggarth 2012, 189). The Baking Pot Late Postclassic burials likely reflect broader temporal changes that include a focus on flexed body positions, as the patterns represent a significant change from previous Belize Valley traditions.

Burial 99E-1 (figure 2.4b) is a male individual interred beside the platform wall in a cist, and a greenstone celt (Hoggarth 2012). The body was placed in a fully flexed position with the left arm extended. It is likely that the body slumped to the right early in the postburial decomposition process because the bones remained articulated, with the exception of the head, which rotated out of anatomical position at a 90-degree angle. The cranium was found on its left side adjacent to the left shoulder with the face to the south, although it might have originally faced west or been placed in a prone position (see figure 2.4b). In addition, if the body originally was aligned with the legs, the individual was oriented to the northwest and not to the north.

Burial 101-1 includes one male individual who was buried adjacent to the wall of the Structure M-101 platform in a simple lined cist with an obsidian blade and an Augustine Red vessel foot fragment (Hoggarth 2012; Zweig 2011). The individual was interred in a supine position with the right arm fully flexed and the left in a semiflexed position on the chest so that the two lower arms lay in parallel on the right side of the body. The legs were flexed and in an upright position, with the right leg lying on the left. The individual's skull was oriented approximately

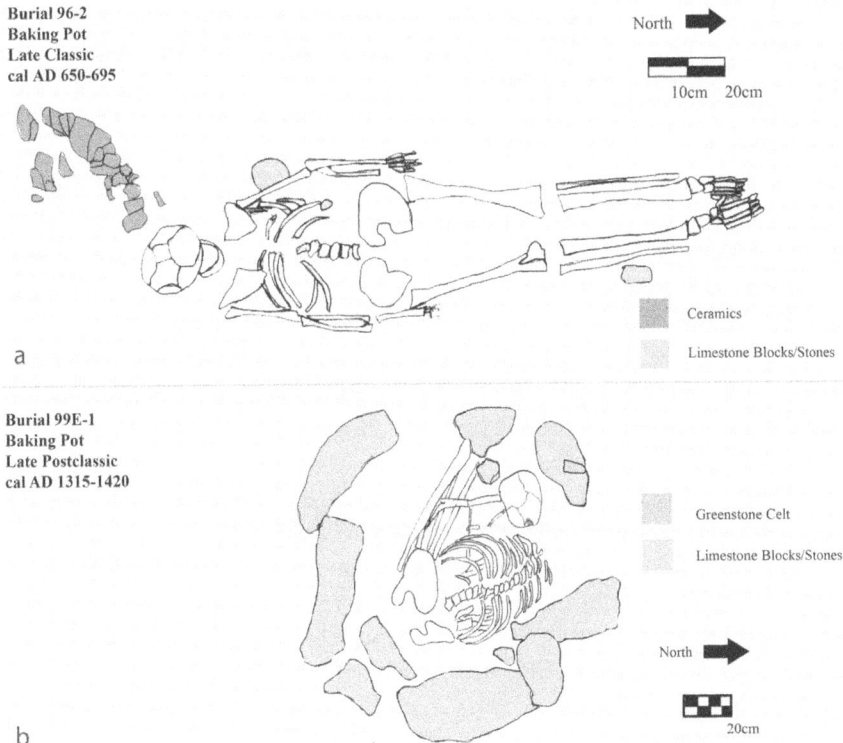

Burial 96-2
Baking Pot
Late Classic
cal AD 650-695

North

10cm   20cm

Ceramics

Limestone Blocks/Stones

a

Burial 99E-1
Baking Pot
Late Postclassic
cal AD 1315-1420

Greenstone Celt

Limestone Blocks/Stones

North

20cm

b

FIGURE 2.4. *Baking Pot: (a) Burial 96-2, showing the Classic extended burial position; (b) Burial 99E-1, showing a flexed Postclassic burial position.*

to the north, and although a tree root may have partially moved the position of the cranium, it appears that the individual may have faced east.

A third Late Postclassic burial, Burial 198-2, includes one infant buried in a mixed Classic/Postclassic deposit in the Yaxtun Group (M-198) excavated by Carolyn Audet (2002) during the 2000 and 2001 field seasons. No distinctive burial pattern was described for this individual.

As in the Classic period, burial patterns were diverse during the Early and Late Postclassic periods, and burial locations, body positions, and grave goods varied regionally and temporally (A. Chase 1983; D. Chase 1982; D. Chase and Chase 1988; Graham et al. 2013). Some burial practices show continuity from the Classic period, such as a preference for the use of eastern structures. Other practices, such as the seated burial position or cremation, are identified more frequently after AD 900 (D. Chase 1997; Weiss-Krejci 2003). Baking Pot's Postclassic funerary traditions are new to the region but show no direct link to any specific Postclassic site.

Body position and orientation represent the most basic and perhaps the most fundamental change. Postclassic burials show a preference for flexed positions that may emphasize bundling bodies, which signaled not only a change in body preparation but in beliefs about death and the afterlife (D. Chase and Chase 1988; Graham et al. 2013). For example, Masson (1997, 300) reports that Late Postclassic/Colonial burials were interred in flexed positions at Caye Coco and Laguna de On. At Lamanai, individuals were interred in a prone position with the lower legs fully flexed behind the body in the VPLF (ventrally placed, legs flexed) burial positions (Graham and Howie, chapter 5, this volume; Graham 2004, 235; Wrobel and Graham 2015, 87). The VPLF burial position also is identified at Marco Gonzalez during the Terminal Classic period and during the Early Postclassic at San Pedro on Ambergris Caye (Graham et al. 2013), suggesting that the new style of interring the dead spread across parts of northern Belize. This pattern has not been identified at Baking Pot.

Another form of flexed body position, the upright seated burial, also became more widespread. At Santa Rita Corozal, Diane Chase (1997) noted a pattern of upright flexed burials. She also reported seated burials at Nohmul, though flexed or partially flexed positions were most common ($n = 10$) compared to other positions (seated $n = 3$ and extended $n = 4$). Maya-style burials have been noted on the fringes of the Colonial church and at nearby houses at Tipu in flexed or seated positions as well (Graham et al. 1989). Arlen Chase (1983, 1285–1288) reported an even distribution of extended and flexed positions in 12 burials at Tayasal, which shows continuity from Late Classic–period burial practices, where 11 of the 20 burials were extended and seven were flexed. However, Pugh and Shiratori's more recent work in the Petén Lakes region suggests that seated burials represent a regional variation of the flexed body position (Pugh et al. 2012; Pugh et al. 2016; Shiratori 2014). A single seated burial (Burial 96-4) was noted in Hoggarth's excavations at Baking Pot. However, this burial appears to be Late/Terminal Classic (based on stratigraphy and ceramics) and has not yet been directly dated.

Variation in grave goods also suggests that new regional styles had developed by this time. Oland and Masson (2005, 226–227) reports burials interred with deer bone, along with many other types of objects. Smashed vessels marked some seated burials at Tayasal (Shiratori 2014); interments with vessel feet may be a local variation of a Petén Lakes Itza tradition. However, there is currently very limited information on Postclassic occupation, especially burials, in the Belize Valley. Willey et al. (1965) list several burials from Barton Ramie that possibly postdate the Late Classic, but it is not known whether these burials date to the Late/Terminal Classic Spanish Lookout complex or are associated with the Postclassic New Town complex. Overall, these burials appear to follow Classic-period traditions (Willey et al. 1965) and likely are earlier than the small Baking Pot Postclassic burial sample.

Baking Pot Postclassic burials represent a change from a strong Classic-period regional mortuary tradition. Continuities were indicated by a preference for the eastern side of architectural groups, and by uncommon flexed positions (Freiwald and Billstrand 2014; Freiwald et al. 2014a). However, the body positions, their northern orientation, the type of grave goods (vessel feet), and the location of the graves are completely different. Each was located on the exterior of a structure, whereas not a single Classic-period burial was discovered in a similar location in the site's settlement. Other burial locations reported for Postclassic sites include burials in front of mounds at Caye Coco, both inside and outside of structures at Mayapan, and in middens at Lamanai (Oland and Masson 2005, 226–227; Pendergast 1981). Diane Chase (1982) notes burial locations behind structures at Santa Rita Corozal, but no other Postclassic site shows exactly the same burial practices. It is possible that participation in and influence from the nearby Itza and/or Kowoj sociopolitical and economic spheres may have been transformed to form a new regional pattern at Baking Pot.

Settlement Patterns

Archaeological research in the Maya lowlands has identified differences in the organization, construction, and quality of architecture at sites between the Classic and Postclassic periods. For example, Postclassic construction is described as smaller in scale than Classic-period architecture, often utilizing recycled materials (Masson 1997; Pugh et al. 2012). Specific architectural traits, such as colonnaded structures, circular shrines, and C-shaped benches, are noted beginning in the Terminal Classic and continuing into the Postclassic period in the northern lowlands. Awe (2015) also recently argued that other cultural traits introduced during the Classic/Postclassic transitional period in the Belize Valley include balustrades on stairways, an increase in the frequency of Tlaloc imagery, slateware ceramics, Jaina-style figurines, and vertical hoops on ballcourts (e.g., at Naranjo and Xunantunich). Thompson (1970) suggested that the presence of similar architectural features, associated with Terminal Classic architecture in the Yucatán, provided evidence for the eastward movement of Chontal Maya from the Gulf Coast (also see Kowalski and Kristan-Graham 2011). Whether or not these traits represent the movement of people or ideas is debatable, but there is no question that they do serve as markers of cultural transformations occurring across the Maya region.

Temporal changes in architecture at Baking Pot include changes in construction activity, the architectural configuration of house groups, and the quality of building materials. Construction of all eight house groups that Hoggarth (2012) excavated for her doctoral research reached its maximum at the end of the Late Classic period (~AD 600–800). Construction declined during the Terminal Classic period, with only the noble house group (M-99) maintaining the same rate of construction. Radiocarbon evidence suggests the site experienced a collapse of political systems and large-scale abandonment by the end of the Terminal Classic period (~cal AD 800–900), with a reoccupation during the Late Postclassic period (cal AD 1280–1420) (Hoggarth et al. 2014). Very little to no new construction has been noted for the Postclassic period, with limited evidence recovered in the settlement areas at the M-99 and M-184 domestic groups. C-shaped bench structures have not been identified at Baking Pot, unlike architecture identified in the Sibun Valley (Harrison-Buck and McAnany 2006) and at sites around the Petén Lakes (Schwarz 2009). However, L-shaped structures have been identified for Late / Terminal Classic domestic groups. In addition, the "ticketbooth" structure along the central causeway of the site core is circular in form (Audet 2006), which may suggest influence from the north at the end of the Classic period.

Postclassic settlement is concentrated in the central and eastern sections of Baking Pot. This area includes some of the most fertile alluvial soils along the river and suggests a preference for settlement in the areas that were agriculturally more productive. Despite the widespread nature of Postclassic activity in the site's periphery, the absence of new ceremonial or monumental construction may be more indicative of a shorter-term reoccupation or a lack of access to labor and / or construction materials. Directly dated burials in the eastern settlement at Baking Pot all cluster between cal AD 1280 and 1420 (Hoggarth et al. 2014). No substantial ceremonial construction or nonlocal architectural styles have been identified during this period. These data—along with the absence of radiocarbon dates in the Early Postclassic period (AD 900–1250)—offer evidence for the depopulation of the site around cal AD 850–900, with around 400 years that appear to be either a hiatus in occupation or low-scale population. This was followed by a reoccupation of the settlement areas at Baking Pot by the beginning of the Late Postclassic period (AD 1250).

Material Culture

Evidence for cultural disjunction has been identified in the material culture at Baking Pot. Ceramic forms and decoration from Settlement Cluster C at Baking Pot provide indications of changing strategies of household and community organization through time. Polychrome decoration on ceramics declined in the Terminal Classic and Postclassic periods, a pattern identified across other regions of the Maya lowlands (Hoggarth 2012, 150). The proportion of serving vessels and faunal remains in high-status households increased during these same periods. This evidence indicates the development of new forms of interhousehold relationships beginning in the Terminal Classic period in the form of large-scale community feasting (Hoggarth 2012, 143–162). These activities may have increased in intensity during the Late Postclassic period. Other ceramic

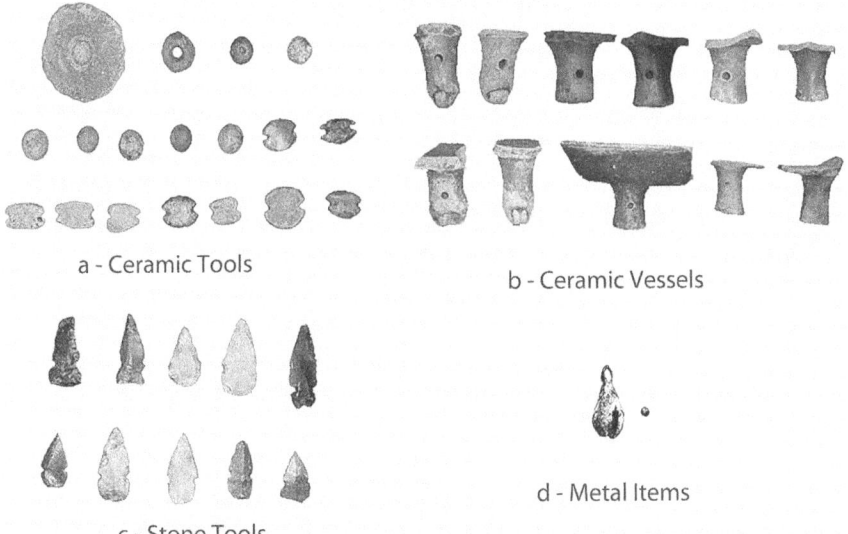

a - Ceramic Tools

b - Ceramic Vessels

c - Stone Tools

d - Metal Items

FIGURE 2.5. *Postclassic material culture from Baking Pot. (a) Ceramic tools recovered in Postclassic contexts include net sinkers and spindle whorls. (b) Ceramic vessel types were predominated by Augustine Red, Paxcaman Red, and Topoxte Red types. (c) New types of stone tools introduced during the Postclassic period include small notched points used in bow and arrow hunting. (d) Metal objects introduced during the Postclassic included copper bells that are commonly associated with ornamentation.*

artifacts appear in higher frequencies in Terminal Classic and Postclassic contexts, including modeled ceramic net sinkers and balls (figure 2.5). Aimers (2004) has previously described disjunctions in the material culture, including the introduction of new vessel types such as the *comal*, which may indicate the introduction of new types of cuisine. In the excavations at the Yaxtun group, Carolyn Audet (2002) identified a ceramic mask in a Postclassic midden and suggested that it might depict the Postclassic merchant god. If accurate, this may suggest integration into broader Postclassic ideological systems. Together, this evidence points to distinct shifts in ceramic artifacts that may suggest the introduction of ideas or people into the area.

New types of materials and technology, such as copper bells and notched arrow points, were identified in Postclassic contexts at Baking Pot (Hoggarth 2012). A small number of copper bells were recovered from several of the largest residential groups. While some were plain, several excavated by Audet (2002) included faces worked into the body of the bells. Copper bells dominate the assemblage of copper items at Mayapan (85%) (Paris 2008). Evidence for the production and consumption of copper items has also been noted at Lamanai in northern Belize (Simmons 2005). Simmons and Shugar (2013) have noted that over 42 percent of copper items at Lamanai are bells. Simmons and colleagues (2009) suggest that copper bells, as well as copper rings, may have been produced on a small scale from imported material and items. They also argue that copper rings are common during the Early Postclassic, while bells are more prevalent during the Late Postclassic period. This pattern aligns well with the Late Postclassic radiocarbon dates from Baking Pot Postclassic burials. However, no evidence for the production or re-smelting of copper materials has been identified at Baking Pot. The current sample of copper bells ($n = 3$) recovered at Baking Pot is low, which limits substantive comparisons with other Postclassic sites.

The presence of notched points in Postclassic contexts provides evidence for the spread of bow and arrow technology into the area during this time. Notched points at Baking Pot appear to be distinct from points at other Postclassic sites in Belize and in the adjacent Petén Lakes region (Meissner 2014). The majority of tools were made from local chalcedony (67%, 10/15), although smaller numbers of obsidian notched points have also been identified (Meissner 2014). Chalcedony was also noted in higher quantities in the Quexil Islands in the Petén Itzá ethnopolity (Meissner 2014, 549), which could suggest economic interaction or population exchange from this area. These patterns complement other cultural changes noted by Schwarz (2009) and suggest cultural similarities in the material culture between the Belize Valley and Petén Lakes region.

In sum, the changes in material culture during the Postclassic period at Baking Pot suggest interaction with Petén polities, but do not clearly demonstrate movement of people during this time. Settlement patterns may indicate smaller-scale occupation than during Classic times, and materials may show the exchange of ideas between regions. However, new burial and isotopic patterns that suggest in-migration did occur, along with the exchange of new ideas and the transformation of social and ritual practices.

CONCLUSIONS

This research represents the initial stages of investigations at Baking Pot that focus on understanding population movement during the Classic and Postclassic periods. Using an approach that examines population mobility from multiple lines of evidence, including biogeochemical and archaeological approaches, we have identified patterns that may represent local developments in the Belize Valley prior to the political collapse and demographic decline of the region at the end of the Classic period that left much of the Belize Valley sparsely populated. Postclassic patterns offer evidence for subsequent in-migration and reoccupation of the region.

Biogeochemical data indicate that the majority of the Classic-period individuals that we sampled exhibit local strontium isotopic values, with population movement coming from multiple locations but mainly from the south. Burial patterns support these data, with most individuals buried in the typical Belize Valley orientation and body position. Material culture at Baking Pot during the Classic period largely included locally made ceramics and other materials, with most obsidian from the El Chayal source. Few examples of architecture influenced by nonlocal stylistic traditions have been identified at Baking Pot, including a circular shrine adjacent to the central causeway, which dates to the Terminal Classic period. No examples of C-shaped benches in domestic groups have been identified, unlike sites in the Petén Lakes dating to the Terminal Classic period.

Radiocarbon data indicate that Baking Pot was depopulated by ~cal AD 900. Burials in Baking Pot's settlement area show that the area was reoccupied between cal AD 1280–1420, although no Postclassic-period monumental construction has been identified (Hoggarth et al. 2014). Three burials from Baking Pot's settlement area date to the Postclassic. The two adult burials have nonlocal strontium isotope values and burial patterns that differ from Classic-period traditions, offering evidence that a different population reoccupied the site. Flexed burials located adjacent to domestic platforms also have been identified in northern Belize and the Petén Lakes regions. The third burial is an infant located in a midden that has a local strontium isotope signature.

Major disjunctions in the material culture are noted for the Postclassic period. New ceramic forms, similar to those from the Petén Lakes, suggests that these migrants moved from this adjacent region. Bow and arrow technology was introduced during the Postclassic period, as well as metal ornamental items such as copper bells. Obsidian from Postclassic contexts has higher proportions from the Ixtepeque source in the Guatemala highlands. Very little construction is noted for Postclassic times, with only minor floor construction episodes in domestic groups.

Congruencies between the material culture at Postclassic Baking Pot and in the Petén Lakes may indicate exchange of not only ideas and materials, but perhaps of people from sites in and around this region. However, this hypothesis will be tested in future research, along with more extensive comparisons of the material culture with other Postclassic centers, to provide a more detailed view on mobility and migration at Baking Pot and in the Belize River Valley.

ACKNOWLEDGMENTS

Funding for this study was provided by the Belize Valley Archaeological Reconnaissance (BVAR) project, the National Science Foundation (BCS-1460369, Hoggarth), a Sigma Delta Epsilon/Graduate Women in Science Eloise Gerry Fellowship (Freiwald), and the Social Sciences Research Council of Canada (Awe). We want to thank Doug Kennett and Brendan Culleton for their ongoing contributions to the Baking Pot radiocarbon project, Paul Fullagar and the

Department of Geological Sciences at the University of North Carolina at Chapel Hill, David Dettman and the University of Arizona Department of Geosciences, and T. Douglas Price and James Burton of the University of Wisconsin–Madison for work with the isotope data. Permission for sampling came from the Belize Institute of Archaeology and the Peabody Museum at Harvard University. Claire Ebert assisted with the figures, and students and staff of the BVAR project contributed to the fieldwork.

3

The Bioarchaeology of Maya Population Mobility, Trade, and Settlement Growth during the Classic Maya Period

A View from the Yucatecan Coastal Port of Xcambo, Mexico

ANDREA CUCINA,
THELMA N. SIERRA SOSA,
AND VERA TIESLER

During the Classic period (~AD 250–900), the ancient Maya economic organization was based on a "city-state" structure in which small polities gravitated around their main capitals. Urban city governments watched over a regional system that was tied internally by cultural bonds and extensive political and economic interactions (M. E. Smith 2004). In this scenario, small local producers sold their products in regional markets with the help of local small-scale traders, while professional merchants transported commodities long distances towards ports of trade or larger regional markets (Masson 2002a). Coastal polities produced and traded salt and marine resources in exchange for other essential or luxury goods. The presence of inland corridor sites (Dunning and Andrews 1994) along the Yucatecan coastline promoted the distribution of goods from a coastal maritime trade network to inland sites through so-called gateways (Dahlin and Ardren 2002; Jackson and McKillop 1989; Masson and Freidel 2002). In turn, short- and long-distance inland trade networks distributed or redistributed goods among the inland communities not easily reached by the coastal trade (González de la Mata and Andrews 1998).

DOI: 10.5876/9781646420735.c003

Doubtlessly, short- and long-distance movements of both luxury goods and basic produce were commonplace across the Maya area, regulated either by the elite from ruling centers or as part of a local, small-scale distribution of goods. In ancient Maya society, trading did not rule the day as in today's capitalistic view, but most probably was handled within much larger political, social, and cosmological frames. Such relationships were complex, multifaceted, and not solely driven by the forces of supply and demand (McAnany 2010, 3).

Also, population movement, through individual change in residence or more collective migrations, defined the ancient Maya. Population movement could be associated either with trade activities or with subjective, individual, family, or kin-related needs (see also Bullock, chapter 4, in this volume). Bioarchaeological research has been generating significant databases that demonstrate that short- and long-distance biological interaction was much more common and far ranging than formerly suspected. In fact, as also Graham and Howie (chapter 5, this volume) note in the case of coastal Belize, some degree of mobility was the norm, not the exception. The evidence of $^{87}Sr/^{86}Sr$ and $\delta^{18}O$ ratios in dental enamel has brought to light the ample presence of nonlocally born individuals within a growing number of archaeologically retrieved skeletal collections (see for example Price et al., 2008, 2014; Scherer and Wright 2015; Tiesler et al. 2017; Wright 2005a, 2005b, 2012; Wright et al. 2010). A complementary perspective on mobility is provided by dental morphology and morphometry. This line of research examines the biological diversity and change through a (micro)evolutionary lens by assessing the extent of morphological affinities among ancient human groups (Cucina 2015b; Cucina and Ortega 2014; Cucina et al. 2018; Scherer 2007; Tiesler and Cucina 2012; Wrobel 2004).

Unfortunately for scholarship, the causes that led to individual or broader population movements can rarely be inferred from the archaeological human collections themselves. Neither can modern migration theories (most of which were developed during the second half of the last century, based on market economy) be used as proxies to explain migratory patterns in ancient, noncapitalistic societies (Arango 2000; Cameron 2013). Champion and Hugo (2004) critically discuss the stereotypical and preconceived dichotomy between urban and rural contexts in modern societies, demonstrating that the borders between the two are more and more often blurred nowadays.

Yet, undeniably, economy and commerce have always played important (albeit never unique) roles in the development and destiny of hamlets, towns, or societies as a whole. In such a perspective, it follows that the socioeconomic and political evolution of a town, its urbanization or de-urbanization, must have direct consequences also on the structure of Maya settlement populations. Here, too, from a biological point of view, internal population dynamics and structures range by definition between the two opposite poles of "urbanized" versus "rural" contexts.

On the high end of the population conglomerates, Webster and Sanders (2001) address the concept of Maya "cities" and stress how these must have differed from pivotal Mesoamerican population aggregates like Teotihuacan with its large, multiethnic population, densely packed living quarters, and its extensive urban planning and sociopolitical hierarchy (Manzanilla and Chapdelaine 2009). Nonetheless, whatever name the centers of administrative and residential compounds are given in the Maya area, the high number and density of inhabitants, inner heterogeneity (in terms of wealth, political power, and economic functions) and group identity are the essential variables for the development of preindustrial urban ecologies in this area of Mesoamerica (Webster and Sanders 2001, 47–48).

The present chapter revolves around the other pole of population conglomerates; namely, those hamlets or villages that were small *per se* (sites ranked as type IV in the Archaeological Atlas of Mexico; Velásquez Morlet et al. 1988) but do not fall into the categories of *"hinterland"* or "satellite communities" serving larger capitals. Also, small-sized settlements could function as centers of far-reaching and active networks, especially on the coastline, where a large part of long-distance trading was accomplished by boat. Such a settlement is showcased by the Classic-period Maya settlement of Xcambo (AD 250–700/750) (figure 3.1), which we explore in the following. This port was nested on the edges of the coastal marshland inside the northern shores of the Yucatán peninsula. Different lines of evidence suggest that this compact and densely populated site experienced affluence and growth at the onset of the Late Classic period (~AD 550), when local salt beds triggered an ever more active and relatively autonomous trade involvement in far-reaching trading networks (Sierra Sosa 2004).

Based on a critical view of sociocultural migration theories, and resting on the background of evolutionary theory, this chapter explores, from the very lens of bioarchaeology (i.e., those very actors who played on the stage of ancient Maya society), the effects that economic changes had on population structure and human mobility in this archaeological context. Contrary to material culture, it discusses how the skeletal remains provide a unique and direct source of information that allows us to reconstruct population dynamics that mirror processes of urbanization in ancient societies.

This contribution relies on previously published bioarchaeological datasets, as well as on novel information on this community's internal population dynamics through time. In particular, we focus on biological variability, demographic patterns, and individual migration as consequences of the site's socioeconomic evolution from the Early to the Late Classic phases of occupation.

THEORIZING HUMAN MOBILITY AND CONGLOMERATION

Human migration and mobility have been extensively studied under the multiple lenses of sociology and economics (Cameron 2013; Champion and Hugo

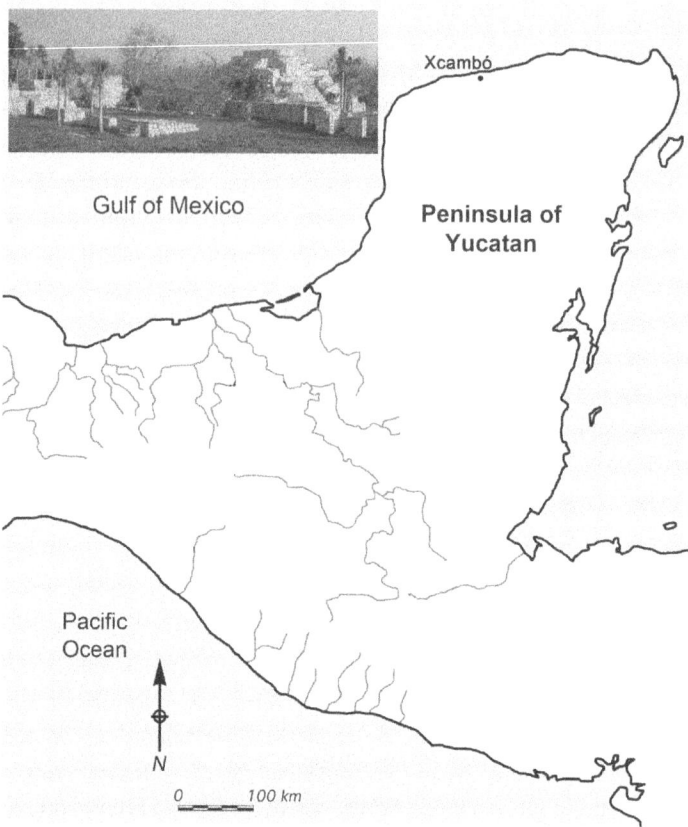

FIGURE 3.1. *Geographical location of the site of Xcambo along the northern coast of the Yucatán peninsula. The inset photo shows the main plaza's southern structure. (Map and photo by A. Cucina.)*

2004). Although a thorough discussion of the different theories of migration and human mobility is beyond the scope of this chapter, a brief overview of the basic concepts allows us to place into context the empirical evidence accrued and combined after a multidisciplinary study of archeological and bioarchaeological datasets. As Greene (1986; see also M. E. Smith 2004) suggested, archaeology plays a major role in the analysis of ancient states' economy, because it can provide a set of parameters that are of paramount importance for reconstructing the economic models of ancient societies. Far beyond exploration of the historical record alone, archaeological evidence of increased agricultural production, population growth, rise of craft production and regional exchange, and intensified long-distance commerce among different loci of domestic consumption—all provide invaluable clues in regard to ancient economies (M. E. Smith 2004, 74).

The neoclassical approach to human migration developed as a consequence of twentieth-century economic growth. Similar to functionalist theory, it addresses human migration as the product of positive forces that attract individuals to the place of destination (pull), and at the same time retain local folk in the area. Conversely, negative forces (push) tend to impel the migrants from their place of origin and prevent new immigration (Arango 2000; Cameron 2013). The push-pull theory interprets population movement as the result of economic factors, and the decision to move is entirely dependent on the individual's or group's rational decision. In line with this neoclassic economic view is the close identification of economic disparity (between origin and destination) as a migration motor (Arango 2000). Note that forced migration (due to political reasons or warfare) is often not considered a true "migration" because the individuals ("refugees") are not free to choose whether to move or not (Cameron 2013).

Other, more conflict-oriented theories do not separate migration causes from their consequences. In this scheme, human mobility is not seen just as the product of unequal development or natural causes, but as contributing to and reinvigorating inequality and unequal development. This circular thinking is considered particularly suitable to understanding the population dynamics in modern capitalistic societies and their relationships with less-developed or underdeveloped ones.

World system theory (WST) assumes that the components that make up this "system" eventually influence the cultural ones. They are structured around core countries as well as semiperipheral and peripheral areas. According to this perspective, movements of people (on an individual basis or as a group) respond to a wide array of biological, cultural, economic, and social (political or administrative) conditions. However, like conflict theory, WST brings capitalism into play as a motor to increase inequality between peripheral areas and core countries. Initially supported by colonial regimes, WST is nowadays sustained by multinational corporations and is only applicable on a global level (Papademetriou and Martin 1991).

Migration theories tend to simplify complex migration dynamics by seeing them as the consequence of only economic factors while neglecting the specific human and cultural dimensions of all population movements (Arango 2000). Migration networks usually consist of all those interpersonal relationships (family and friends) that link a potential migrant to other folk who have already migrated. Although economic reasons may always stand behind the personal decision to move, the migration network may not be strictly tied to the movement of a labor force. Interestingly, network systems represent some sort of intermediary step between purely individual choices (micro) and their collective structural determinants (macro) (Arango 2000).

It is worthwhile to stress that all theoretical approaches tend to leave aside the complexity of migratory processes themselves; their heterogeneous and multifaceted, polymorphic dynamics, forms, types, actors, motivations, and socioeconomic contexts. As Arango points out (2000, 295), most of these can hardly be considered at the level of real "theory," as they are not generalizable.

Last, all migration "theories" developed as a consequence of economic expansion at a global level, in particular during the second half of the twentieth century. Instead of being created *ante quam* as guidelines for empirical research with the goal of developing generalizable research hypotheses that could be confronted with verifiable facts, they were built on the basis of heuristic, commonsense, empirical observations, turning the latter into theories or conceptual frameworks. Although some of them can find a substrate on which to work at the national level (such as, for example, the rural/urban relationship), the majority of them find fertile terrain at the international level.

Finally, evolutionary scientists draw a completely different perspective on the causes and (more so) on the consequences of migration. Physical anthropologists and human biologists conceive that migration is embedded in human genes, and therefore consider that social and cultural factors are profoundly interwoven with human biology (Campbell and Crawford 2012). Independent of the fact that social actors may be actively or passively involved in migratory phenomena, and regardless of the theoretical (sociological, economic, geographical) frames that may best explain specific processes, migrants are also human, biological actors. In their recent edited volume, the contributors to the volume by Campbell and Crawford (2012) therefore stress the biological consequences that migrations have on human health, genetic population structure and demography (see also Gage et al. 2012).

SETTLING THE MAYA PORT OF XCAMBO, YUCATÁN

The archaeological Classic Maya site of Xcambo is located in the middle of the marshlands on the fringes of the northern coast of Yucatán. The settlement was laid out on a small, natural but artificially expanded mound that measures 700 m × 150 m (Sierra Sosa 2004). Initially recognized by Andrews in 1976, it was thoroughly and extensively excavated between 1996 and 2000 by one of the authors of this chapter (T.S.S.). The archaeological explorations permitted us to draw the site's architectural plan and to trace its administrative areas, as well as most of its residential compounds. The combined analyses of a wide array of conventional archaeological datasets, together with the examination of burial patterns, mortuary contexts, and of the more than 600 human skeletons themselves, have granted a fairly detailed reconstruction of the site's occupational history (Sierra Sosa 2004).

Although Xcambo shows uninterrupted human presence since the Middle Preclassic, it flourished only during the Classic period. The complex ceramic sequence differentiates two major occupation phases (Ceballos 2003; Jimenez

2002). The first dates to the Early Classic period (AD 250–550) and the second to the two centuries that followed (AD 550–700/750). The archaeological record indicates that no true political elite governed the site and no royal burials have ever been discovered; rather, the kind and variety of objects recovered from the mortuary record suggest that, during the Late Classic, the site was characterized by a relatively homogeneous wealthy middle class of merchants and administrators (Sierra Sosa 2004).

After AD 700, the site seems to have been entirely abandoned within a few generations (Sierra Sosa 2004). The abandonment was likely a consequence of the shift in the political sphere of influence in the region at the dawn of the regional hegemony by Chichen Itza (Sierra Sosa et al. 2014). Postclassic occupation is limited to four structures erected in the main plaza: two small, stone-roofed temples were placed in the plaza's northeastern corner, while two altar-platforms were constructed close to the southeastern corner. Stylistically, they bear close similarities to the style found along the eastern coast of the peninsula and they may have been used seasonally. The site is nowadays the object of pilgrimages to a small *capilla* (chapel) built in late Colonial times.

The shifting architectonic layout informs us that during the Early Classic period, Xcambo was still a small settlement composed of an administrative and ceremonial center surrounded by small residential patio platforms. On top of the round-cornered, stucco-covered platforms stood wooden huts. Around the site, conical stone foundations were likely used as storage facilities (Sierra Sosa 2004). At the onset of the Late Classic, the site experienced sudden prosperity; structures grew in number and complexity, many built on top of the earlier ones. Residential compounds expanded throughout the mound and two public plazas replaced the early period's ceremonial and administrative structures and storage facilities. The central plaza was surrounded in its entirety by 11 structures, which represent the largest and better-built edifices, embellished with carved stones, and whose arrangement is conspicuous in comparison with the rest of the site (Sierra Sosa 1999a, 1999b). The plaza likely hosted civic, religious, and administrative functions. A pier built on the northern side of the mound facing the marshland and the *ria* (the fringe zone where fresh and salt water mix), where salt mines were located (and still are nowadays), witnessed the site's port activities (Sierra Sosa 2004). In this later and last phase of occupation, a second, U-shaped plaza surrounded by three structures was built some 250 m east from the main plaza. A 100-m-long *sak be'* (white path or white road) connected this secondary plaza to a small residential compound located at the easternmost side of the settlement. Similarly, two more unpaved roads from this plaza led to the inland agricultural settlements of Misnay and Cemul (see figure 3.1).

Given the limited extension of the site, which is surrounded by marshlands, space was intensely exploited. The majority of the residential areas were built around the plazas, and working facilities like storage rooms, workshops, and areas of domestic activities were erected in close proximity to one another. Note that the compounds' distribution and organization differ between the main plaza's western and eastern sides. The western structures seem to be the earliest ones, built during the Early Classic and remodeled in the later phase of occupation. Stone-walled structures covered with straw roofs were erected on raised platforms and located around small, inner patios, or laid out to form quadrangles, resulting all together in a densely built compound without interruption (Sierra Sosa 2004). In contrast, the plaza's eastern limits show (continuous) occupation only during the Late Classic period. They were constructed with wooden walls and perishable roofs on stone-walled rectangular foundations raised on top of low, wide mounds. The eastern compounds were not as densely built nor as numerous as the edifices on the western side. Large open-air spaces were probably used for outdoor production and recreational activities.

BIOLOGICAL VARIABILITY AT XCAMBO

Biological variability is the result of microevolutionary phenomena that characterize a population. Based on evolutionary theory, evolutionary forces work to increase or decrease variability within a population. Gene flow increases intrasite variability as a result of migratory processes that bring in new people from other contexts; out-migration, genetic drift, or endogamic processes have the opposite effect and reduce a population's intrasite variability (O'Rourke and Enk 2012).

Dental Morphology and Diversity

At Xcambo, the population's biological (morphological) structure has been explored from the perspective of dental morphology. Dental morphological traits have been used extensively in biodistance studies to assess morphological/biological affinities among archaeological human groups (Scott and Turner 1997). The majority of dental traits present a range of degrees of expression, from absent to highly expressed, and the number of degrees depends on every individual trait. In order to handle them statistically, traits are dichotomized into present versus absent categories. A trait is considered *present* in an individual when its degree of expression is equal to, or higher than, a previously fixed threshold; otherwise, it is considered to be *absent* (Scott and Turner 1997).

In the Maya region, previous studies based on dental morphological traits show that Xcambo presents affinities with other coastal sites during the Classic and Postclassic periods, suggesting the existence of a biological corridor around the peninsula that followed the economic coastal trade network (Cucina 2015b; Cucina and Ortega 2014). Despite this communication route, it seems that Xcambo did not establish profound biological relationships with inland sites in

TABLE 3.1. Xcambo, 24 scored dental morphological traits*

Upper I1 Shoveling	Lower M1 Anterior Fovea
Upper I1 Double Shoveling	Lower P4 Cusp Number
I2 Interruption Groove	M2 Groove Pattern
Upper I1 Tuberculum Dentale	Lower M1 Cusp Number
Upper P3 Cusp Number	Lower M2 Cusp Number
Upper M3 Metacone	Lower M1 Deflecting Wrinkle
Upper M2 Hypocone	Lower M1 Middle Trigonid Crest
Upper M1 Cusp 5	Lower M1 Protostylid
Upper M1 Carabelli's Cusp	Lower M2 Cusp 5
Upper M2 Root Number	Lower M1 Cusp 6
Upper M2 Enamel Extension	Lower M1 Cusp 7
Lower C Distal Accessory Ridge	Lower M2 Root Number

* Following the ASUDAS system.

the northern Maya lowlands and towards the Chenes region (Cucina et al. 2015; Tiesler et al. 2017).

Contrary to the common use of dichotomized dental morphological traits for biodistance analyses, in this study we have analyzed individual data by sex and period, taking into consideration the degree of expression of every trait. Twenty-four traits were selected out of 79 scored following the ASUDAS system (Scott and Turner 2007) (table 3.1). In order to accentuate individual differences within the site, selection of traits was based on the trait's higher degree of intra-site variability.

For statistical elaborations, we selected from the site's database on dental morphology six male and six female individuals from the Early Classic period, and 22 females and 29 males belonging to the Late Classic period. This reduced sample size results from the selection of all those individuals presenting the fewest number of empty cells in the raw-data matrix used to perform multidimensional scalings (MDS). MDS was executed using statistical package STATISTICA 7.1 (StatSoft®), substituting empty cells with the trait's mean. Figure 3.2 shows the individual distribution by sex for the Early Classic and Late Classic periods.

For the early phase of occupation, figure 3.2a shows that males and females overlap in the center of the bidimensional distribution (lighter shadow highlights the distribution of females, darker shadow encompasses males, and the darkest shadow indicates overlapping distributions). Half of the males on the positive side of the first (horizontal) dimension distance themselves from the female range of variability. The same occurs for two female individuals along the negative side of the plot. In turn, the distribution by sex in the Late Classic (figure 3.2b) shows a marked overlap between male and female morphologies.

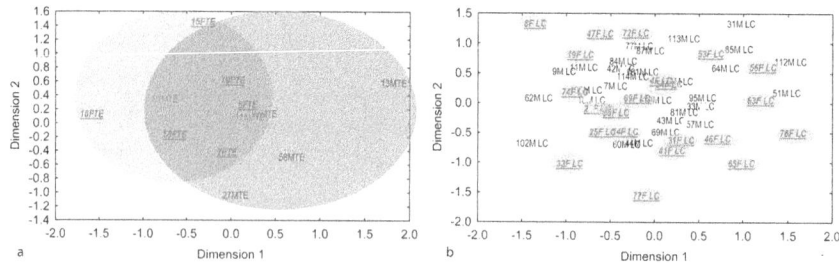

FIGURE 3.2. *MDS distribution of male and female individuals for the (a) Early Classic (TE) and (b) Late Classic (LC) periods. Shaded areas in a show the respective ranges of variability for males (darker shade) and females (lighter shade). In b, female labels are underlined, in italics, and are also individually shaded.*

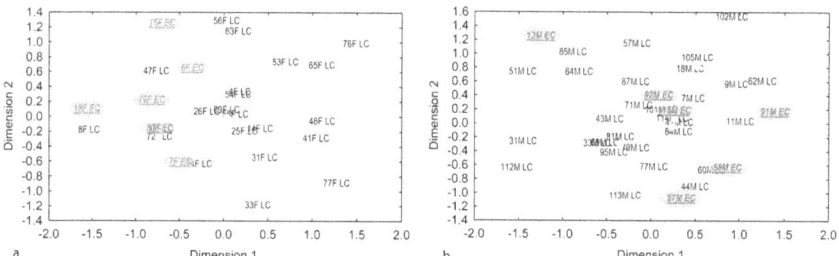

FIGURE 3.3. *MDS distribution of (a) female and (b) male individuals, regardless of period: EC, Early Classic (in shadowed circles); LC, Late Classic.*

Figure 3.3 shows the same MDSs for females (3.3a) and males (3.3b), regardless of the chronological period. As we can appreciate, female individuals belonging to the Early Classic period tend to be set on the negative side of the first, horizontal dimension. Their distribution only slightly overlaps with the range that encompasses the Late Classic females. Conversely, male individuals tend to overlap more evenly than females between periods, even though the majority of the male individuals from the Early Classic are set on one side of the overall distribution of males. Resting on the scale of *x*- and *y*-axes of figures 3.3a and 3.3b, we can appreciate a marked overlap of Late Classic individuals, coupled with a more even distribution of Early Classic males, while contemporary females are spread on the edges of the overall distribution. Although we cannot rule out that the Early Classic reduced sample size may affect the individuals' distribution in the MDS plots, the Late Classic sample shows a noticeably higher level of morphological variability, in particular when compared to the series of Early Classic females, substantiating a real trend in population dynamics.

POPULATION STRUCTURE AND MOBILITY

Paleodemography

The internal paleodemography of a given population (composition by age and sex) is an important parameter to assess life expectancy, mortality and, more importantly, the extent of fertility of ancient people (Sattenspiel and Harpending 1983). Population structures are therefore essential for reconstructing and under-standing the population's evolutionary history. Not all the skeletal collections are, however, suitable for paleodemographic analyses. First, skeletal series repre-sent the ages at death and not those of the living. Second, not all the collections are representative of the once-living population. As Weiss has already under-lined (1973), any demographic reconstruction from a nonrepresentative sample is not likely to be productive. Third, the estimation of age at death tends to mimic the age structure of the reference samples (Hoppa and Vaupel 2002). Last, and this is particularly true for the Maya area, poor skeletal preservation severely hampers demography by limiting the applicability of multiple techniques to determine sex and to estimate age at death. In this perspective, the specific con-ditions of Xcambo's marshland substrate represent a welcome exception. The archaeological excavations unearthed some 600 skeletons in a heterogeneous though relatively good state of preservation. The individuals span the entire period of occupation (AD 250–700/750): the majority (351 individuals) belong to the Late Classic (AD 550–700/750), 81 individuals have been assigned to the Early Classic (AD 250–550), and the remainders could not be assigned specifically to any of the two periods. Because of sample size and representativeness, Tiesler and colleagues (2005) only discussed the demographic structure of the site during the Late Classic phase of occupation. The small size of the Early Classic sample, together with the limited information obtained for age at death and sex of this chronological segment of the population, prevented a thorough comparison between the two periods. Notwithstanding this and within the limits of such analyses, a small-scale comparison between early and late phases of occupation will permit us to highlight some of the differences in population structure and the site's evolutionary history.

In the first place, the striking difference in sample size between the two peri-ods is worth mentioning, as only 81 individuals compose the Early Classic sample in comparison with 351 confidently assigned to the Late Classic. This 1:4.3 ratio between the two periods cannot be justified by poor preservation alone, or by differential excavation, since the site was excavated in its entirety. A more likely scenario is an actual increase in population density itself. From the archaeo-logical perspective, Sierra Sosa (2004) delineated a less-dense settlement pattern during the early period, in which residential structures were limited mostly to the westernmost side of the mound. The reduced number of skeletal remains

TABLE 3.2. Life table of the Late Classic period calculated for growth rate $r = 0$.

Age	$d''(x)$	$l(x)$	$q(x)$	$L(x)$	$e(x)$	$C(x)$	$FB(x)$
0	37	100.00	0.107	0.947	25.85	0.037	0.000
1	30	89.34	0.098	0.850	27.87	0.033	0.000
2	13	80.58	0.046	0.787	29.85	0.030	0.000
3	13	76.84	0.048	0.750	30.28	0.029	0.000
4	11	73.12	0.044	0.715	30.79	0.028	0.000
5	18	69.90	0.074	3.367	31.19	0.130	0.000
10	17	64.76	0.077	3.114	28.46	0.120	0.000
15	20	59.79	0.097	2.844	25.62	0.110	0.041
20	15	53.96	0.082	2.588	23.12	0.100	0.112
25	18	49.56	0.108	2.344	19.95	0.091	0.112
30	24	44.20	0.158	2.035	17.07	0.079	0.091
35	25	37.19	0.194	1.679	14.81	0.065	0.063
40	21	29.96	0.203	1.346	12.79	0.052	0.026
45	22	23.87	0.271	1.032	10.41	0.040	0.005
50	22	17.41	0.365	0.712	8.350	0.028	0.000
55	17	11.06	0.439	0.432	6.700	0.017	0.000
60	10	6.20	0.500	0.233	5.000	0.009	0.000
65	10	3.10	1.000	0.078	2.500	0.003	0.000
Total	351						

clearly indicates that population concentration was low, with fewer families living at the site. In turn, the Late Classic reorganization of structures—which led to more densely built residential compounds all around the settlement, together with the building of the small plaza at the site's eastern side—is indicative of increased population size and density, as mirrored by the larger skeletal sample. Based on the archaeological structures' density, Ortega-Muñoz et al. (2018) estimated a population between 860 and 1,073 people during the Early Classic, in contrast with a population ranging between 1,103 and 1,728 during the Late Classic. Such population growth can be highlighted also when the demographic profile is investigated. The mortality table for the Late Classic sample (table 3.2, redrawn from Tiesler et al. 2005), calculated for a growth rate of $r = 0$ (a stable and stationary population), shows that 19.8 percent of the population is represented by infants who died before one year of age, while 39.6 percent died before age 10. Such mortality distribution can also be appreciated in figure 3.4.

Based on Weiss's (1973) function, such mortality distribution would be characterized by a gross reproductive rate (daughters per woman) of 2.25, a mean number of offspring of 3.35, translating into a total fertility rate (TFR) of 4.5

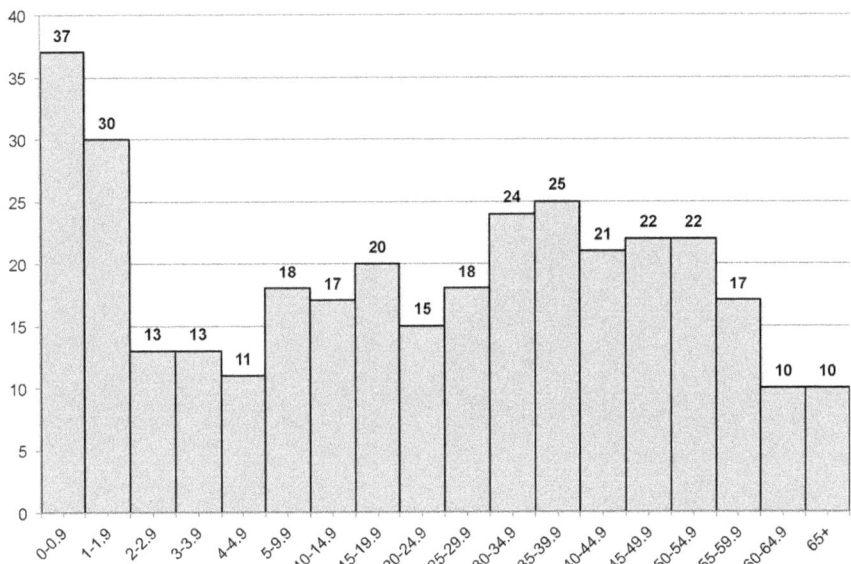

FIGURE 3.4. *Histogram showing the distribution of mortality by age classes for the Late Classic sample. Data are from table 3.2.*

children per woman and a birth and death rate of 0.0387 (given $r = 0$). Cook and Borah (1974, 29) suggest that, in Mexico, an average of five to six persons per family can be safely assumed. This would imply a figure similar to, or higher than, 3.35 of offspring, moving the TFR value above 4.5. Based on this, the demographic solution curve hypothetically estimated for this population structure (figure 3.5) indicates a TFR of five children, for a growth rate above 1 percent ($r = 0.01$), and a TFR of 5.5 for 2 percent growth ($r = 0.02$). Although the skeletal remains do not provide direct information on the number of pregnancies per woman, and the ethnohistorical evidence (Cook and Borah 1974) may not be fully applicable to prehispanic eras, the combined evidence confirms that the population of Xcambo was experiencing a period of demographic growth during the Late Classic period.

Regarding the Early Classic, of the 81 individuals composing the sample, three were newborns/neonates, 16 died in their first infancy (between birth and age 3 years), eight before age 10 years, and 12 were subadults between age 10 and 20 years. The remaining individuals were adults, of whom 11 died between 20 and 30 years of age. Due to preservation, in many cases age at death could only be estimated as a range, which limits a detailed comparison with the Late Classic period. Moreover, the small sample size does not permit us to make demographic inferences, because it is not representative of the whole

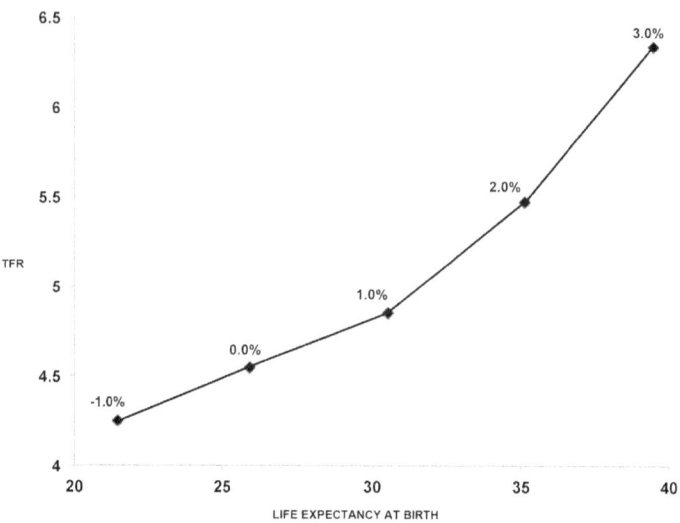

FIGURE 3.5. *Demographic solution curve for the Late Classic sample.*

population—which is why Tiesler and colleagues (2005) could not perform demographic analyses on the early sample. Notwithstanding this, the frequency of individuals dying before age three is slightly lower in the early sample than in the later one (23.5% versus 26.5%) and also slightly fewer infants died before age 10 (33.3% compared to 39.6%). Although taking these results with much caution (due to the small Early Classic sample size and the inherent difficulties in getting more precise age estimations for many individuals), the results seem to suggest that the population growth rate might have been higher during the Late Classic period, indicating a faster population expansion in comparison to the previous period. Similar conclusions were also drawn by Ortega-Muñoz and colleagues (2018), based on an archaeodemographic analysis of the site.

Individual Provenience and Mobility

In archaeologically retrieved remains, the ratio of $^{87}Sr/^{86}Sr$ isotopes can express local versus nonlocal geographic provenience. This rests on the assumption that the isotopic ratio between ^{87}Sr and ^{86}Sr in any individual reflects the local bioavailable geological ratio of the place in which each individual is born (Montgomery 2010; Price et al. 2002; Slovak and Paytan 2011; for an in-depth explanation of the principles of strontium isotope analysis and methodology, see Price et al. 2002). As opposed to bony tissue, which is subject to a process of turnover that replaces all the organic and inorganic phases every 10 to 15 years, dental enamel does not undergo any remodeling once it is laid down. Therefore, the enamel of teeth that form during the early years of life will incorporate the $^{87}Sr/^{86}Sr$ ratio of the place in which that individual is born, like the permanent first molar whose crown usually forms during the first three years of infant life (Hillson 2014).

A site's bioavailable strontium ratio can be measured following two complementing procedures. The most direct and commonly used method is represented by the analysis of archeological or modern faunal remains of species that spend their lives within a short radius (such as, for example, small mammals or terrestrial snails) and that shared the habitat of the ancient human settlers; the $^{87}Sr/^{86}Sr$ ratio is indicative of the "biologically available" strontium that is expected to be found in individuals who were born at the site (Price et al. 2008: Wright 2005a, 2005b, 2012). The second approach, which was followed by Wright (2012, 339), assumes that in any site the majority of the population would have been born locally, so that the "local" individuals' isotopic ratios should approximate a normal distribution and are expected to form a plateau. Any individuals deviating from this pattern are likely to be nonlocals. When the individual migrates to a different place, he/she will be exposed to a different $^{87}Sr/^{86}Sr$ ratio, the same that will be assimilated into the individual's bony tissue but not into the dental enamel that has already formed (Price et al. 2002). Therefore, once the bioavailable $^{87}Sr/^{86}Sr$ ratio of any archaeological site is known, the analysis of the isotopic ratio in bones and teeth of the skeletal individuals will permit us to reconstruct long- and short-term migratory history (Katzenberg and Krause 1999).

At the settlement of Xcambo itself, the ratio of $^{87}Sr/^{86}Sr$ isotopes has been successfully applied by our colleagues T. Douglas Price and James H. Burton of the University of Wisconsin in Madison to detect the presence of foreign individuals (Sierra Sosa et al. 2014). Here, the analysis of $^{87}Sr/^{86}Sr$ ratio in a series of terrestrial animal remains provided a "local" range between 0.7089 and 0.7091 (Sierra Sosa et al. 2014). Because of the close vicinity to the coast, and given that seawater has a ratio of 0.7092, the authors established the local ratio at Xcambo to range between 0.7089 and 0.7092 (Sierra Sosa et al. 2014, 232). All the localities along the western and northern coasts of Yucatán present this range in common with Xcambo.

Overall, 131 individuals from the site were analyzed for their isotopic ratio in teeth (Sierra Sosa et al. 2014). Strontium analysis was performed on permanent first molars (either maxillary or mandibular), whose crown forms during the first three years of life. In the few cases where the permanent first molar was not available, a permanent anterior tooth was selected, because teeth forming during the same period of time are supposed to show the same strontium ratio (see also Freiwald, chapter 1, this volume, who describes a similar methodological approach).

According to the authors, 20 individuals (15.3%) presented a strontium ratio below the minimum threshold of 0.7089, and have been considered as nonlocals. Of these, only one individual is reported from the early phase of occupation, while 19 have been assigned to the Late Classic period.

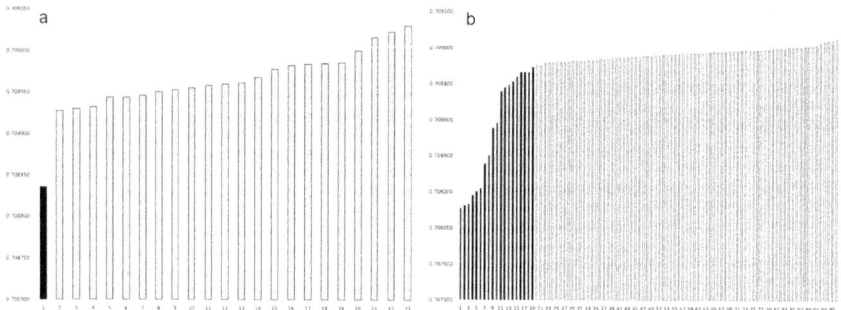

FIGURE 3.6. $^{87}Sr/^{86}Sr$ *ratios of the (a) Early Classic and (b) Late Classic samples. Bold black bars indicate nonlocal individuals, while gray bars show the locals for both periods.*

A more detailed analysis of the database, not presented by Sierra Sosa et al. (2014), shows that 12 individuals could not be assigned to any specific phase, though all of them present $^{87}Sr/^{86}Sr$ ratios above 0.7089 and are therefore considered locals. Of the remainder, 23 clearly belong to the Early Classic, and 96 to the Late Classic. From this, the presence of foreigners in the two continuous periods of occupation corresponds to 4.3 percent (1/23) in the earlier period, and 19.8 percent (19/96) in the later period. Figure 3.6 presents the distribution of locals (gray-shaded bars) and nonlocals (solid black bars) respectively for the Early Classic and Late Classic. If we proportionally assign the 12 individuals of unknown period to the Early and the Late Classic groups, about three would be allocated into the Early Classic and nine into the Late Classic. This would drop the frequency of non-locals to 3.8% in the Early Classic (1/26) and to 18.1% in the Late Classic (19/105).

The only nonlocal individual dated to the earlier period shows an $^{87}Sr/^{86}Sr$ ratio of 0.708836, slightly below the minimum value that characterizes the local people. Such a value is very common in inland areas adjoining the peninsula's northern coasts (Sierra Sosa et al. 2014), indicating that this foreign person, a male young adult, was likely not born at Xcambo but may have arrived there from a relatively close, inland area.

The inhabitants of the site tell a compellingly different story during the Late Classic period. During this phase, as above mentioned, almost one out of five individuals was of nonlocal origin. As figure 3.6b shows, the nonlocals' $^{87}Sr/^{86}Sr$ ratios present a much wider variability, ranging from 0.708109 to 0.708893. Considering the plateau in figure 3.6b, and the variability expressed by locals, it cannot be ruled out that one, or a few, of those considered as nonlocals might have been born at the site. Nonetheless, the difference between the two periods, although not statistically significant, due to the small sample size of the early period (Fisher exact test $p > 0.10$), is still remarkable and indicative of the site's cultural changes. Moreover, contrary to the Early Classic period, foreigners in the Late Classic originated from disparate regions. While some of them can be of close geographical origin to the peninsula's inland northern territories, 10 individuals ranging from 0.708109 to 0.708583 seem to come from places as far south as the Petén or the Usumacinta region (Sierra Sosa et al. 2014). Interestingly, of the 15 nonlocal adult folk for whom sex could be determined, about half (7/15) are females; this, as discussed below, opens a window on gender-related issues related to migration.

DISCUSSION

According to Champion and Hugo (2004, 8), population conglomerates such as towns and cities have been described based on a set of stereotyped features that include, among others: population density, demographic patterns and fertility, presence or absence of a marked socially stratified society, occupational structure, educational level, ethnicity, and migration. However, the authors' critique against this set of parameters is that it is mainly directed to modern societies and to the increasingly subtle and blurred borders between modern rural and urban contexts. Pumain (2004) stresses the historical difficulties in clearly defining an urban context and she notes how the various social sciences use different parameters to define it.

Xcambo can hardly be considered a city, as it did not possess the specific, required features to be defined as such. Apart from its small settlement area, no highly stratified social sectors spread among its quarters, nor is it the locus of multiple social institutions (Arnauld et al., chapter 8, this volume). It shows no centralized power: no aristocracy ruled the place, either considered as the core settlement or the networks radiating from it. Xcambo lacks evidence for intellectual specialization (like writing) or religious infrastructure, such as ballgames (Laporte 2001). Nonetheless, given the other sets of variables that could be assessed, the evolution of Xcambo's internal socioeconomic structure obliges us to consider that an *in situ* process of conglomeration occurred at the site with the shift from the Early Classic small settlement to the Late Classic administrative center for salt production and exchange. The *in situ* concept concerns the transformation (or reclassification) of a settlement without much geographical relocation of the residents (Zhu 2004, 207). Indeed, although increases in population density and architectural clustering have been documented at Xcambo, unlike normal dynamics of "urbanization," Xcambo did not (nor could it) expand outside the small mound in the northern coastal marshland.

From the perspective of those migration and population models that are applicable to Xcambo (Arango 2000; Cameron 2013), the archaeological and bioarchaeological evidence suggests that the neoclassical push-pull model might fit, at least to some extent. More to the point, we may argue that the available evidence allows us to detect the "pull" component of the model (i.e., those forces that attracted people to the site), a component that could be identified with the site's economic position within the region's goods production and trade network. In fact, paleodemography indicates an expanding population, while dental morphology reveals an increased level of intrinsic biological variability, which suggests exogamy and gene flow from external groups.

Cucina (2015b) noted that Xcambo's level of intrasite variability, based on the frequency of presence and absence of dental morphological traits, is the second highest among 18 dental collections from the Maya realm, and similar to that calculated for large cities (like Calakmul) or important trade centers (like Cozumel). Migrants, in fact, are more than the simple vehicle of ideas or "culture," as social theory claims, or of specialized labor skills and economic goods, as in liberal economy theories; migrants are also biological individuals who carry their own genetic setup to new places (Campbell and Crawford 2012). Strontium isotopes, which show that about one out of five individuals is nonlocal, confirm this idea, as does the increase in diversity of artificial cranial shapes as a visible sign of heterogeneous group identity and most probably origin (Tiesler 2014). However, the same analysis of intrasite variability applied separately to the Early and Late Classic samples does not reveal relevant differences between the two periods, which indicates a relatively variable population in both periods.

Apart from the trend itself, little or nothing can be said about the precise motivations that might have pushed people to move to Xcambo, since we would need to have full knowledge of the places from which the immigrants came. The $^{87}Sr/^{86}Sr$ ratios do, indeed, provide only general evidence, as none of the nonlocal values permits us to spot one specific location in the Maya realm at first sight. We have speculated cautiously, therefore, that family and coastal population networks grew over time in space and went along with mobility. These should have left their mark in the genetic setup of Xcambo's folk.

In this dynamic, and given the absence of political dependence, we can hardly conceive that coercing forces operated at the base of population movement to the site and its expansion. As already mentioned, no political elite lived at Xcambo, and the mortuary record suggests the inhabitants of this site belonged to a relatively homogeneous wealthy class of merchants and administrators, as seen from the Classic-period graves (Medrano 2005; Sierra Sosa et al. 2014). If working forces dedicated to salt mine activities arrived at the site, they are not likely to be represented in the skeletal record of Xcambo. On the contrary, the skeletal evidence indicates a marked reduction in male individuals' skeletal robusticity during the Late Classic period (Maggiano et al. 2008; Wanner et al. 2007), while females maintained a similar level of skeletal robusticity through time. In this biomechanics' scheme, Late Classic males switched to a more sedentary lifestyle when the site became an autonomous port of trade, and they (likely) dedicated their efforts to the site's administrative tasks. Such a change in activity patterns and daily lifestyle is common in the shift from rural to more urban-like contexts (Champion and Hugo 2004).

The demographic information on sex and age at death, combined with the stable isotopic analysis, provides additional insights on the nature of individuals' movement to the site. Gage and colleagues (2012, 373) indicated that marital migration, one of the most common causes of individuals' movement in past and present societies, by definition must be sex biased in strongly matrilocal or patrilocal societies. In other words, in those societies structured around a patrilineal social organization, those integrating with a preexisting group should be mainly females, while the opposite should occur in matrilineal societies. However, marital movement does not seem to have been the driving factor for nonlocal people to settle at the site. Among the 19 individuals considered non-locals from strontium ratios, eight are males and seven are females (four are of undetermined sex). This evidence by itself makes it difficult to infer, at least in principle, whether Xcambo's society was matri- or patrilocal. It is likely, however, that reasons behind individuals' decisions to move to the site might not have been related strictly to matrimonial affairs. Interestingly, among those who migrated to the site, three individuals are subadults. More specifically, one was an infant (younger than 10), another was between six and 10 years of age, and the last was a juvenile. The $^{87}Sr/^{86}Sr$ shows that all three of those subadults likely originated in regions close to the peninsula's northern coast. In this regard, the presence of nonlocal older infants suggests a more complex scenario at the site, in which whole families might have migrated to the settlement, apart from relatively fewer adult couples or single adults.

Last, despite the high rates of infant mortality at Xcambo, which was the rule in pre-antibiotic societies, the high life expectancy indicates increased longevity of those who survived infancy (Gage et al. 2012). Márquez et al. (2002) reported a life expectancy of 26.9 years at birth and 14.88 years at age 20 at Palenque, and consider the site's overall mortality to be the lowest when compared to other large urban settlements like Monte Alban, Cholula, and Tenochtitlan. Although the authors estimated a growth rate of 1.5 percent ($r = 0.015$) and added 30 percent infants to balance the underestimation of individuals in this age range, which limits the comparability with the $r = 0$ at Xcambo, life expectancy at birth at Xcambo is very similar (25.9 years), while it is much higher at age 20 (23.12 years). Moreover, Márquez and colleagues (2002) reported only two individuals above age 50, while at Xcambo, the life table shows that about 17 percent of the population died after age 50, which supports the hypothesis of a long-living population at the site.

Life expectancy at Xcambo would be among the highest reported by Gage and colleagues (2012, 707) for prehistoric populations. Specifically for the Maya area, Gage and colleagues report life expectancy at birth in Copan at 25.5 years, and at age 15 at 21.15 years. Although Xcambo cannot be considered a "town," its demographic values mirror (or exceed) those found in large urbanized centers in Mesoamerica. Similar to the problems faced by the Palenque population (Márquez et al. 2002), the population at Xcambo was not exempt from the spread of infectious diseases, due to its small settlement size and the increased population density. However, it is very likely that Xcambo's transition toward a more "urban-like" demographic pattern can be explained by the site's socio-economic level during the Late Classic period, characterized by an increasing number of people devoted to less-strenuous physical activities (Sierra Sosa et al. 2014), and with an occupational structure more oriented to administration and service activities in contrast to agriculture and related occupations (Champion and Hugo 2004).

CONCLUSION

In conclusion, the archaeological and bioarchaeological evidence from the Classic-period Maya port of Xcambo indicates that the shift from a small settlement to an autonomous center for salt production and trade during the Late Classic period determined a consistent change in population structure, lifestyle, and living conditions. In-site migration increased considerably, likely related to the center's new economic position within the sphere of trade and salt production. Although the site cannot be considered a proper "city" or even a "town" because of the geographic constraints on settlement expansion and the lack of other peculiar features, the process that it experienced in the Late Classic does mirror some of those that characterize larger centers, as echoed by the settlement population's in- and out-migration according to its shifting role in the administration and production of sea salt, and consequently in the coastal trade networks. We consider, therefore, that, against the backdrop of increasing regional trade, the growth and changing composition of Xcambo's population serve as important proxies for understanding the population dynamics that led to the rise of Terminal Classic trading networks controlled by Chichen Itza.

ACKNOWLEDGMENTS

The research was funded by CONACyT grants CB-2010-01 n. 154750, CB-2017-2018 n. A1-S-10037, and I0010-2014-02 n. 232831 to A.C. and was carried out under the auspices of the UC MEXUS program at the University of California–Riverside.

Immigrant Lives

Mobility and Migration in Postclassic Cholula, Mexico

MEGGAN BULLOCK

Mobility and migration undoubtedly helped shape the population dynamics of Postclassic Cholula, one of the larger urban centers in central Mexico, as well as a major market and pilgrimage site. Cholula is known to have attracted temporary visitors such as merchants and religious pilgrims (Durán 1971, 128–136; Motolinía 1971, 339–344; Rojas 1985, 130–132), and indigenous narratives assert that migrations played a significant role in the urban center's history (Berlin and Rendon 1947; Kirchhoff 1947). A recent strontium and oxygen isotope study of skeletons from a low-status Postclassic habitational zone near the Great Pyramid indicates that slightly more than 40 percent of individuals included in the sample have nonlocal isotope signatures, suggesting a significant movement of individuals and families into this residential area over an extended period of time (Bullock et al. in preparation). As part of a paleodemographic and paleopathological study of 309 skeletons from this residential area, data on age, sex, and health were collected from individuals with both local and nonlocal isotope signatures. While archaeological data and ethnohistoric texts provide contextual information on mobility and migration to prehispanic Cholula and the surrounding

DOI: 10.5876/9781646420735.c004

region, bioarchaeological analyses of nonlocal individuals offer complementary insights into their identity, their possible reasons for relocating to this community, and the reality they experienced upon arriving to the urban center.

MOBILITY AND MIGRATION IN PREHISPANIC MESOAMERICA

As Arnauld, Beekman, and Pereira discuss in the introductory chapter to this volume, the movement of individuals and groups has often been treated as an anomaly in archaeological investigations as opposed to an integral part of ancient social and economic organization. Advances in isotopic and genetic techniques over the last decades have led to renewed archaeological interest in migration by providing a means to clearly identify the movement of people, as opposed to the spread of material goods or cultural practices (Anthony 1990; Van Dommelen 2014, 479). Van Dommelen (2014, 477) has, in fact, asserted that migration can be considered "a fundamental part of being human" and should, therefore, be assumed to have been a common feature in the demography of ancient populations.

There is clearly no disciplinary consensus in the use of the terms *mobility* and *migration*, as illustrated by the fact that no fewer than four definitions (albeit with some degree of conceptual overlap) have been proposed by various chapter authors in this volume alone (see Arnauld, Beekman, and Pereira's introduction; Freiwald, chapter 1; Gonlin and Landau, chapter 6; and Graham et al., chapter 5). Distance is often considered to be one of the most important characteristics in theoretical treatments of mobility and migration (Anthony 1990). Tilly (1978), for example, defines *mobility* as short-distance relocations in which previous social relationships remain largely intact, while *migration* refers to longer-distance moves that involve a degree of dissolution of the individual's social support network. In sociological and anthropological studies of mobility and migration, distance is an easy-to-apply criterion that serves as a proxy for the much more difficult-to-measure factors that investigators are ultimately attempting to evaluate: the cultural and/or personal impact of the relocation. The further the individual moves, the more likely he or she is to encounter changes in political authority, cultural traditions, social networks, linguistic environments, religious practices, and so on that imply a need for the individual to modify his or her own behavior to adapt to new circumstances. The host community may also undergo cultural changes with significant movement to the area as novel ideas and practices are introduced.

However, as has been noted by various authors, including Tilly (1978) himself, the dividing line between what constitutes a short-distance move and what constitutes a long-distance move is difficult to pinpoint (Anthony 1990; M. E. Smith 2014). Notably, Arnauld, Beekman, and Pereira do not specify distance in their definitions of mobility and migration. Rather, they draw an important distinction between movement that is normalized by socioeconomic organization and movement that occurs outside of these cultural norms. *Mobility* in their definition is, therefore, "the broad range of habitual physical movements that facilitate (or complicate) social and cultural practices" while *migration* is "a form of movement that takes place under unusual circumstances" and that results from "disruptive events or processes" (Arnauld, Beekman, and Pereira, Introduction, this volume).

The editors require us to reorient studies of mobility and migration in prehispanic Mesoamerica. Archaeological investigations and isotopic studies have been indispensable in advancing our understanding of population movements; however, such research has typically been focused on establishing that movement has, in fact, occurred and from where. While obviously an important starting point, an understanding of mobility and migration in ancient societies requires us to move beyond details of the movement itself, such as distance, and consider the cultural attitudes and practices that either permit or restrict such movement. The editors' definitions of mobility and migration shift our focus to the cultural context and perceptions of the move. Such a reorientation encourages us to adopt a more culturally centered approach that includes such issues as the identity and motivations of migrants, the socioeconomic and political environments in both the original and host communities, and cultural attitudes towards movement.

Furthermore, by deemphasizing distance and instead focusing on the social and cultural aspects of movement, they open the doors to a new understanding of mobility in prehispanic Mesoamerica by specifically rejecting the idea that mobility involves only "local" movements (Arnauld, Beekman, and Pereira, Introduction, this volume). Instead, they suggest that social and economic structures in prehispanic Mesoamerica promoted regional interconnectivity that allowed regular movements over somewhat longer distances (relatively speaking) to occur within a framework that was still culturally defined and regulated. Their definitions, therefore, force us to consider population movements within an appropriate cultural context rather than imposing outside conceptions of mobility and migration.

POSTCLASSIC CHOLULA

Although Cholula suffered a decline sometime around the Late Classic period following the eruption of the nearby Popocatépetl volcano (Plunket and Uruñuela 2005, 2006, 2008; Uruñuela and Plunket 2005), in the Postclassic period (AD 900–1521) the urban center enjoyed a resurgence as an economically and religiously influential city (Durán 1971, 128–136; Motolinía 1971, 339–344; Müller 1973; Rojas 1985). Given that extensive trade networks, a common iconography and symbol set, and a religious focus on the god Quetzalcoatl characterized

Postclassic Mesoamerican cultures (M. E. Smith and Berdan 2003), Cholula's role as both a major market center and a pilgrimage site for Quetzalcoatl must have made it a prominent player within the region. Participation in these inter-regional networks surely influenced mobility and migration to the urban center.

THE SKELETAL ASSEMBLAGE

During the Postclassic period, religious activity at Cholula shifted to a cere-monial center dedicated to Quetzalcoatl, and the area surrounding the Great Pyramid was repurposed as a habitational zone (López et al. 1976; McCafferty 2000, 356). The 1967–1970 field seasons of the Proyecto Cholula, which focused on excavation of areas surrounding the Great Pyramid, resulted in the recovery of a total of 346 Postclassic burials (López et al. 1976).[1] While some of these interments, particularly those located near the Central Altar, were identified as ceremonial or sacrificial burials, skeletons associated with domestic architecture appear to represent families who resided in the zone (López et al. 1976).

Archaeological information regarding daily life within the residential area is essential to reconstructing mobility and migration within this urban commu-nity; however, the habitational zone and its domestic contexts have not been extensively studied (Hernández 1970; López el al. 1976; Messmacher 1967; Noyola 1992). Residents of this zone are assumed to have been commoners, based upon the style of residential construction, the type of associated domestic artifacts, and observed funerary practices (López el al. 1976). For the purposes of the cur-rent investigation, ceremonial and sacrificial burials as identified by López et al. (1976) were not included in any of the paleodemographic, paleopathological, or isotopic studies, as many of these individuals may not have been residents of Cholula. Consequently, a total of 309 individuals from residential areas were considered for the present analysis.

Osteological Methods

AGE AND SEX

As part of a paleodemographic analysis of the Cholula assemblage, data on age and sex were collected from skeletons in the collection. Adult sex deter-mination was based on a morphological evaluation of the skull, pelvis, and general robusticity of the skeleton (Buikstra and Ubelaker 1994). Subadult age estimation prioritized dental development and the union of epiphyses, and ages were assigned according to the criteria established by Ubelaker (1989). In cases in which these methods could not be applied,[2] age was assigned based on metric analysis of available skeletal elements following Fazekas and Kosa (1978) or Ubelaker (1989), as appropriate. Adult ages were estimated using tran-sition analysis, and maximum likelihood estimates of age based on a uniform prior probability were generated using the ADBOU Age Estimation Software

TABLE 4.1. Summary of paleodemographic data, Cholula*

Age	All Number	%	Isotope Sample Number	%	Local Number	%	Nonlocal Number	%
INFANTS (0–1)	32	10.40	0	0.00	0	0.00	0	0.00
CHILDREN (1–14)	95	30.70	7	14.00	5	17.20	2	10.00
ADULTS								
Male	84	27.20	23	46.00	13	44.80	10	50.00
Female	83	26.90	18	36.00	10	34.50	7	35.00
Undetermined	15	4.90	2	4.00	1	3.40	1	5.00
Total	309		50		29		20	

* The data for the entire assemblage (309 individuals) is listed as ALL. Also shown are sex and age data for those individuals included in the isotope sample (ISOTOPE SAMPLE) as well as the individuals from the isotope sample identified as having local signatures (LOCAL) and those identified as having nonlocal signatures (NONLOCAL) (Bullock et al. 2013; Bullock et al. in preparation; Bullock Kreger 2010). The category "Adults" refers to individuals age 15+.

(Boldsen et al. 2002). Age and sex data for the 309 skeletons in the collection (ALL) are listed in table 4.1. The age-at-death distribution for the entire assemblage (ALL) is shown in figure 4.1.

SKELETAL PATHOLOGIES

Skeletons were also evaluated for pathological skeletal lesions reflecting general stress, nutritional deficiencies, and infectious disease. For all bones of the skeleton, preservation was scored following Buikstra and Ubelaker (1994). Only bones with good preservation (75–100% complete) were included in the paleopathological analyses unless otherwise noted. Observed skeletal pathologies are described below.

Enamel hypoplasias are grooves on the teeth that occur when periods of nutritional stress and/or disease temporarily interrupt enamel formation (Goodman and Armelagos 1985; Goodman et al. 1984; Goodman and Rose 1990; Skinner and Goodman 1992). Central maxillary incisors, mandibular canines, and first, second, and third mandibular molars were scored for the presence and number of hypoplasias on each tooth. For each individual, the left tooth was scored, unless it was absent or unobservable, in which case the corresponding right tooth was substituted. Only permanent teeth were included in the present analysis. Teeth with extreme wear were classified as unobservable.

Cribra orbitalia refers to a pathological condition in which porosities and expansion of the diploë are observed in the orbital roof. Porotic hyperostosis is a related pathology that causes similar lesions in the bones of the cranial vault.

Age-at-Death Distributions for Postclassic Cholula

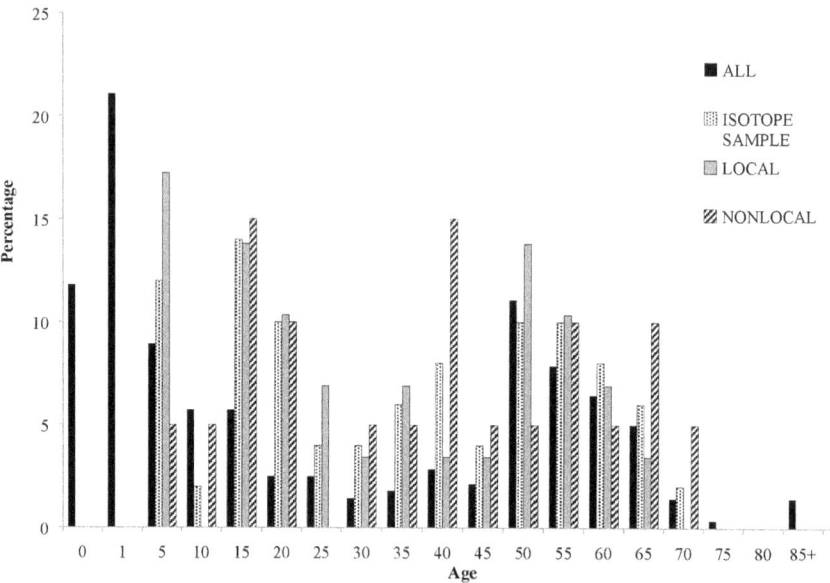

FIGURE 4.1. *Age-at-death distribution for the Cholula skeletal assemblage (ALL). Also shown are the age-at-death distribution of individuals included in the isotope sample (ISOTOPE SAMPLE) and the age-at-death distributions of those from the isotope sample identified as local (LOCAL) and nonlocal (NONLOCAL) (Bullock 2013; Bullock et al. 2013; Bullock et al. in preparation; Bullock Kreger 2010).*

In New World populations, cribra orbitalia and porotic hyperostosis are thought to be most commonly linked to megaloblastic (Walker et al. 2009) and/or iron-deficiency anemia (El-Najjar et al. 1976; Holland and O'Brien 1997; McIlvaine 2015; Mensforth et al. 1978; Oxenham and Cavill 2010; Palkovich 1987, 528–529; Stuart-Macadam 1985, 1987, 1991; Wright and Chew 1998, 925), although scurvy may also cause similar porosities (Ortner 2003; Ortner et al. 1999; Walker et al. 2009). The orbits, the frontal squama, the parietals, and the occipital were scored for the presence or absence of porosities and expansion of the diploë. As cribra orbitalia and porotic hyperostosis are bilateral conditions, good preservation (75–100%) of at least one orbit or one parietal was sufficient for inclusion in the study.

Scurvy is caused by a deficiency in Vitamin C. It is reflected in the skeleton by porous lesions and bone proliferation on the orbital roof, the bones of the cranial vault, the sphenoid, parts of the maxilla, parts of the mandible, the scapula, and the tibia (Ortner 2003; Ortner et al. 1999; Walker et al. 2009). The presence or absence of lesions on the greater wing of the sphenoid were assessed to evaluate scurvy in the collection, as sphenoidal lesions are likely pathognomonic for this deficiency (Ortner 2003; Ortner et al. 1999). Good preservation (75–100% complete) of either the left or right greater wing of the sphenoid was sufficient for inclusion in the study.

The presence or absence of proliferative skeletal lesions were recorded on each bone to identify nonspecific infections (periostitis and osteomyelitis) (Ortner 2003; Ortner and Putschar 1981). The long bones were more frequently affected than other skeletal elements; therefore, analysis focused on the humerus, radius, ulna, femur, tibia, and fibula. Good preservation (75–100% complete) of the diaphysis of the long bone was sufficient for inclusion in the study.

ISOTOPE STUDY

In order to identify nonlocal individuals in the assemblage, 50 enamel samples from permanent teeth were selected from 50 individuals for strontium and oxygen isotope analysis.[3] Characteristics of individuals included in the isotope sample are summarized in table 4.1 and figure 4.1.[4] The isotope data were analyzed and interpreted by Dr. T. Douglas Price and Dr. James Burton from the Laboratory for Archaeological Chemistry at the University of Wisconsin–Madison. A total of 20 nonlocal individuals were identified in the sample based on both within-sample variation and comparison to local archaeological faunal values, suggesting that approximately 40 percent of individuals included in the sample spent at least part of their childhoods outside of Cholula (Bullock et al. in preparation).

MOBILITY AND MIGRATION IN CHOLULA AND THE SURROUNDING REGION

While the isotopic data from this low-status residential zone in Postclassic Cholula clearly establish the settlement of nonlocal[5] individuals in this community, interpretation of the bioarchaeological data requires a contextual framework that takes into account social and cultural practices with respect to population movements in Cholula and the surrounding region. Ethnohistoric documents detailing population movements, in conjunction with archaeological data and information gleaned from anthropological demography, can provide some insights into cultural perceptions and attitudes towards movement. The bioarchaeological data can then be analyzed in terms of this established cultural context to draw some limited conclusions regarding mobility and migration in prehispanic Cholula.

Evidence of Group Migrations

From a cross-cultural demographic perspective, mobility and migration occur more frequently among individuals and families (Castro and Rogers 1983, 1984; Rogers and Castro 1981, 1984; Rogers et al. 1978); however, group migrations are a recurring theme in Mesoamerican codices and ethnohistoric documents referencing Cholula and the Puebla-Tlaxcala region. Long-distance migrations, which feature prominently in the origin stories of a number of Mesoamerican ethnic groups, are typically presented as defining moments in the groups' histories (Beekman and Christensen 2003; Berlin and Rendon 1947; Kirchhoff 1947; Reyes García 1988a, 1988b; M. E. Smith 1984). As Arnauld, Beekman, and Pereira (introduction to this volume) point out, these movements were recorded precisely because they were culturally anomalous and resulted from political, social, or economic upheavals. In this sense, these narratives describe population movements that clearly correspond to the definition of migration offered by the editors. While elements of these stories are mythologized, native histories of migrations speak to indigenous perceptions of population movements and the incorporation of immigrant groups into a new homeland (Beekman and Christensen 2003; M. E. Smith 1984).

A number of ethnohistoric accounts describe group migrations involving Cholula and the surrounding region. The dominant ethnic group in Cholula at the time of the Conquest, the Tolteca-Chichimeca, had their own narrative explaining how they had come to rule the urban center. The *Historia Tolteca-Chichimeca* (Berlin and Rendon 1947; Kirchhoff 1947) provides a detailed account of the journey of the Tolteca-Chichimeca, from their origins in Chicomoztoc, where they lived along with a number of other Chichimec tribes, to their eventual conquest of Cholula. Early on in their migration they settled at a site they named Tollan, where they began referring to themselves as Toltecas. When political unrest gripped the urban center many years later, the group left and began a migration that would last decades, with the emigrants temporarily residing in a number of different sites. When they finally arrived in Cholula sometime in the twelfth century, they were forced into servitude by the ruling ethnic group, the Olmeca-Xicalanca. The Tolteca-Chichimeca, discontent with their lowly status, attempted to take control of Cholula. While they were initially triumphant, tribes allied to the Olmeca-Xicalanca soon began a war against the new rulers of the urban center. The Tolteca-Chichimeca asked the Chichimec tribes with whom they had lived in Chicomoztoc to migrate to Cholula in order to help them defeat their enemies. The Tolteca-Chichimeca ultimately prevailed and, consequently, rewarded their allies with nearby lands, where the Chichimec tribes established themselves in various polities, among them Cuauhtinchan (Berlin and Rendon 1947; Kirchhoff 1947; Reyes García 1988a).

The *Historia Tolteca-Chichimeca* (Berlin and Rendon 1947, paragraphs 322–327, cited in Reyes García 1988a, 56–59) mentions the migration of another ethnic group, the Mixteca-Popolloca, who also settled in the Puebla-Tlaxcala region. The Mixteca-Popolloca arrived in Çacauilotlan, a polity in the region, shortly after the founding of Cuauhtinchan. According to the narrative, the Chimalpaneca-Xalcomolca, an ethnic group from Cuauhtinchan, graciously welcomed them to the area and arranged for intermarriages between the two groups. The Mixteca-Popolloca resided in Çacauilotlan for several decades before eventually migrating on to other polities (Reyes García 1988a, 56–59).

Both the *Historia Tolteca-Chichimeca* (Berlin and Rendon 1947, Paragraphs 337–338; Reyes García 1988a, 62–66) and the *Manuscript of 1553* (Reyes García 1988b, 85–86, 98) describe a migration of *calpulli* from Cholula to Cuauhtinchan. According to these texts, 25 Tolteca-Chichimeca *calpulli* (Reyes García 1988a, 65) left Cholula in the middle of the thirteenth century following an attack on the urban center. As a result of the famine that ensued, the *calpulli* decided to abandon Cholula and seek their fortunes in nearby Cuauhtinchan. The ruling lineage of Cuauhtinchan was one the Chichimec groups that had aided the Tolteca-Chichimeca in their conquest of Cholula, and in compensation for their military service, Tolteca-Chichimeca women had married into their group. Consequently, the Cholula *calpulli* were welcomed into Cuauhtinchan and provided with lands free of the usual tribute obligations as well as women to marry. The *calpulli* remained in Cuauhtinchan for more than two centuries before eventually emigrating elsewhere (Berlin and Rendon 1947, paragraphs 337–338; Reyes García 1988a, 62–66; Reyes García 1988b, 85–86, 98). This narrative is particularly interesting in that is demonstrates just how fine the line between mobility and migration can be. Although unusual factors provoked their initial movement, preexisting marriage alliances embedded in common social practices allowed these *calpulli* to be readily incorporate into their new community.

Archaeological evidence from the Puebla-Tlaxcala region as well as the Basin of Mexico suggests that mass migrations could have been linked to natural disasters. At the end of the Formative period, the volcano Popocatépetl erupted and inhabitants of nearby settlements were forced to flee. Many of those displaced by this natural disaster may have relocated to Cholula and Teotihuacan, thus accounting for some of the demographic growth these urban centers experienced around the same time (Plunket and Uruñuela 2005, 2006, 2008; Uruñuela and Plunket 2005).

From the ethnohistoric accounts as well as archaeological data, it would appear that large-scale group migrations were precipitated by political discord and war (Berlin and Rendon 1947; Calnek 1976, 289–290; Kirchhoff 1947), famine (Quiñones Keber 1995; Reyes García 1988a, 62–66), or natural disasters (Plunket and Uruñuela 2005, 2006, 2008; Uruñuela and Plunket 2005). These migrations clearly represented movement born out of exceptional events that required migrating groups to establish themselves in a new community, often far from the homeland.

The process of assimilation of these groups into a new community involves several recurring themes. Political leaders clearly capitalized on the arrival of immigrant groups in various ways (Arnauld, Beekman, and Pereira, introduction to this volume). In some cases, such as the arrival of the Tolteca-Chichimeca in Cholula, immigrants were forced into service. However, it would appear that diplomacy won out in many accounts, and political leaders found alternative means to benefit from the migration. Lands on which to settle were often gifted to groups (Berlin and Rendon 1947; Kirchhoff 1947; Reyes García 1988a, 62–66; Reyes García 1988b, 85–86, 98; M. E. Smith 1984), and intermarriage to members of migrating groups was a common means of establishing and maintaining both political and social alliances (Reyes García 1988a, 56–59, 62–66; Reyes García 1988b, 85–86, 98). By and large, ethnohistoric accounts suggest at least tolerance, if not outright acceptance, of these group migrations and a willingness to integrate migrants into the host communities.

Evidence of Mobility and Migration among Individuals and Families

The relocation of individuals and small family groups may occur as culturally sanctioned and regulated movements within the socioeconomic structures of a society, or it may be sparked by "disruptive" phenomena such as political discord or famine (Calnek 1976, 289–290). Unfortunately, these types of small-scale movements seldom appeared in ethnohistoric documents unless they involved high-ranking members of the elite precisely because they were not perceived as noteworthy (Arnauld, Beekman, and Pereira, introduction to this volume).

Marriage and economic opportunities are among the most common reasons for movement in populations throughout the world (Castro and Rogers 1983, 1984; Rogers and Castro 1981, 1984; Rogers et al. 1978; Storey 1992, 162). As seen in the ethnohistoric accounts, intermarriage served as important means of alliance-building in prehispanic Mesoamerica (Berlin and Rendon 1947; Kirchhoff 1947; Molloy and Rathje 1974; Reyes García 1988a, 62–66; Reyes García 1988b, 85–86, 98; Stone et al. 1985). However, mobility and migration in the commoner population linked to marriage was not well documented. One study of sixteenth-century marriage registers from the *cabecera* of Tecali, located in the Puebla-Tlaxcala region, found that in slightly more than 4 percent of commoner marriages, at least one of the spouses had relocated (Olivera 1978, 127, 136–137). Females appear to have been somewhat more mobile than males with respect to marriage, likely due to a preference for patrilocality, and almost all moves involved only short-distance relocations within the Puebla-Tlaxcala region itself (Olivera 1978, 137–138). The fact that nonlocal spouses were typically of ethnicities already represented in Tecali and that most were from towns or cities politically allied with the *cabecera* suggests that they would have been readily integrated into their new community (Olivera 1978, 137–138). Olivera (1978, 138) speculates that marriages involving the relocation of at least one of the spouses would have been more common in prehispanic times, as the political and organizational system imposed by the Spanish interfered with traditional political and social alliances between indigenous groups and reduced the mobility of the population, both of which contributed to increased numbers of local marriages.

By and large, ethnohistoric documents indicate that immigrant spouses in Mesoamerica would have been accepted into the host community, as many seem to have come from allied political or social groups (Berlin and Rendon 1947; Kirchhoff 1947; Reyes García 1988a; Reyes García 1988b). Immigrants from ethnic groups that held a position of political or economic power within their new community might have even found their foreign origins to be of benefit. Archaeological investigations of immigration in Teotihuacan have demonstrated that some individuals identified as nonlocal were able to obtain a degree of social status within their communities (White, Storey, Longstaffe, and Spence 2004; White et al. 2010). On the other hand, hostile relationships between ethnic groups could undoubtedly prove problematic for immigrants. The *Historia Tolteca-Chichimeca* (Berlin and Rendon 1947, paragraphs 392–395) describes a case in which a previously friendly relationship between ethnic groups in Cuauhtinchan suddenly soured, resulting in fatal attacks on spouses and children from the now-rival group.

In demographic studies of both modern and historic societies, economic considerations often weigh heavily into decisions to move to urban areas (Castro and Rogers 1983, 1984; Clark and Souden 1988; Luu 2005; Rogers and Castro 1981, 1984; Rogers et al. 1978; Whyte 2000). For prehispanic central Mexico, we still have relatively little information on individuals emigrating to urban areas specifically to pursue economic opportunities, but as Michael E. Smith (2014, 524) points out, mass rural-to-urban movements have been identified through archaeological research (Plunket and Uruñuela 2005, 2006, 2008; Sanders et al. 1979; Uruñuela and Plunket 2005), and various archaeological studies have demonstrated significant mobility in prehispanic Mesoamerican rural populations (M.E. Smith 2014; see also in this volume Freiwald, chapter 1; Arnauld, Lemonnier, Michelet, and Forné, chapter 8; Gonlin and Landau, chapter 6; Graham and Howie, chapter 5; and Cucina et al., chapter 3). In early modern Europe, many individuals migrated from rural to urban areas in order to pursue apprenticeships in the city (Clark and Souden 1988; Luu 2005; Whyte 2000). There is virtually no evidence that similar means of learning crafts existed in prehispanic Mesoamerica (see Calnek 1976, 297, for one exception). Instead, learning a craft specialization seems to have been a skill typically passed down within family units or corporate groups. In Tenochtitlan-Tlatelolco, for example, the existence of ethnic barrios of craft specialists suggests that particular family or *calpulli* groups specialized in the production of certain products (Sahagún 1950–1969, book 9; Calnek 1976, 289).

It is, therefore, unclear if knowledge of craft production would have been imparted to unrelated immigrants arriving to Mesoamerican cities, but marriage would have been a possible means of integrating new workers into the community Preferred postmarital residence patterns could have even been ignored in some cases in favor of economic considerations (White, Storey, Longstaffe, and

Spence 2004). An oxygen isotope study of the Tlajinga 33 apartment compound in Teotihuacan, which housed a corporate group of low-status craft producers, identified a number of nonlocal individuals residing within the compound, suggesting that immigrants might have been incorporated into this familial group of economic specialists, possibly through marriage, to work in the craft industry (Storey 1992; White, Storey, Longstaffe, and Spence 2004).

Access to land could have been another economic incentive for mobility and migration (M. E. Smith 2014). While *calpulli* members held hereditary usufruct rights to land, *mayeque* had no such hereditary claims and were, instead, beholden to the lord of a noble house for land, which was granted in exchange for fulfilling service and tribute obligations (Hicks 1982, 1991, 202–203; Lockhart 1992, 96–99). Available land was inadequate in some cases, obligating individuals to move in search of alternatives. In the Puebla-Tlaxcala region during the Postclassic period, *mayeque* seem to have been more numerous than *calpulli* members, perhaps as a result of landless individuals moving in search of economic opportunities (Hirth 2003, 75; Lockhart 1992, 98–99; Reyes García 1988a).

Ethnic Barrios

Ethnohistoric and archaeological accounts of ethnic neighborhoods provide indirect information about the movement of people in prehispanic Mesoamerica. Of course, these neighborhoods could have been established through both mobility and migration (Arnauld, Beekman, and Pereira, introduction to this volume), and both individual and group movements could have played a part in their formation. Much of the archaeological and ethnohistoric information we have concerning ethnic barrios comes from urban centers in the Basin of Mexico rather than the Puebla-Tlaxcala region. Tenochtitlan-Tlatelolco appears to have had a number of ethnic barrios, some of which were associated with groups of craft producers, as mentioned previously (Calnek 1976, 288–290).

In Teotihuacan, ethnic barrios have been identified through archaeological investigations of their ceramic industries, architectural features, and burial styles (Rattray 1987, 1990; Spence 1992, 1996), and isotopic studies of these communities have confirmed the presence of nonlocal individuals (Price et al. 2000; White et al. 1998; White, Spence, Longstaffe, and Law 2004). Oxygen isotope data from the Oaxaca Barrio offer interesting insights into mobility and migration within this ethnic enclave. Residents of this neighborhood were evidently highly mobile, moving between their Oaxaca homeland, Teotihuacan, and even other Zapotec enclaves (White, Spence, Longstaffe, and Law 2004).

Ethnohistoric accounts also provide limited evidence for ethnic communities in Cholula. The Colomochco were said to have migrated to the urban center after residing briefly in Cuauhtinchan (Berlin and Rendon 1947, paragraph 334; Reyes García 1988a, 60–62). Evidence of their migration is limited to postcontact

Spanish documents referencing a *cabecera* that appears to be named for this migrant group (Carrasco 1971, 366; Reyes García 1988a, 60–62), suggesting that they were granted lands within the urban center on which they settled.

Evidence of Mobility: Temporary Visitors to the City

As a market and pilgrimage site, Cholula would have attracted a number of foreign visitors to the urban center to worship at the temple of Quetzalcoatl or to exchange goods in the markets. Arnauld, Beekman, and Pereira (introduction to this volume) discuss these movements in the context of mobility, as they are "associated with routine socio-economic and religious activities in urban contexts." Religious pilgrims came to the temple of Quetzalcoatl from distant regions simply to demonstrate their devotion or to seek relief from illnesses associated with the god (Durán 1971, 128–136; Motolinía 1971, 339–344; Rojas 1985, 131–132). The investiture ceremonies of new rulers, even those of other polities, were also said to have taken place in Cholula at the temple of Quetzalcoatl (Rojas 1985, 130–131). How long these individuals would have remained in Cholula and how the urban center provided accommodations for them is unclear. Motolinía refers to temporary housing in Cholula maintained by different polities where pilgrims could stay while visiting the city: "each province had its rooms and houses within Cholula, where [pilgrims] were lodged" (Motolinía 1971, 70–71, author's translation).[6] Whether these houses were used exclusively by nobles or whether such accommodations were also available to commoners is not specified. Ethnohistoric sources make reference to hostels in Tenochtitlan-Tlatelolco (Calnek 1976, 291), and similar arrangements may have been available in Cholula as well.

Cholula had one of the largest markets in the region, likely attracting thousands of visitors daily (Cortés 1985, 104; see also Hicks 1986, 50–53 for a discussion of central Mexican markets). Not only would merchants and traders have frequented the urban center peddling their wares, but individuals from surrounding areas would have also traveled to Cholula in order to sell products or to purchase needed items. This constant flow of foreigners into and out of the urban center may have profoundly influenced mobility and migration to Cholula, as information about the urban center would have circulated widely, and such knowledge often contributes to decisions regarding movement (Lee 1966).

MOBILITY AND MIGRATION TO CHOLULA: THE BIOARCHAEOLOGICAL DATA

The strontium and oxygen isotope study of skeletons from this residential zone in Cholula indicates a significant amount of movement by the commoner population during the Postclassic period. Funerary contexts, demographic profiles, and evidence of morbidity in nonlocal individuals, when considered in conjunction with the ethnohistoric and archaeological data on migration presented above, offer insights into their motivations for relocating to this community and the processes of acclimatization and acculturation (table 4.2). Taken as a whole, these data suggest that movement into this community was likely facilitated by social and economic links that extended beyond the urban center.

Throughout the following discussion, some of the limitations of isotopic studies should be kept in mind. First, as Freiwald (chapter 1, this volume) points out, rural-to-urban movements may not be captured by isotope analysis, nor will local movement within the urban center. Only mobility and migrations from regions with distinct isotopic signatures will be visible. Consequently, the presence of individuals with nonlocal isotope values necessarily implies movement over a certain distance, as they must have come from areas outside of Cholula and its immediate hinterlands. Second, samples for the strontium and oxygen isotope studies were taken from the permanent dentition, which largely forms from birth to late childhood (Ubelaker 1989). Nonlocal isotope signatures simply indicate that the individual spent at least part of his or her childhood outside of Cholula. However, given Arnauld, Beekman, and Pereira's discussion (introduction to this volume) of the cyclical nature of mobility, in which movement may take place while maintaining a "home base," we cannot entirely rule out that some individuals with nonlocal signatures could have had familial connections within this habitational zone.

Individual or Family Movements into the Habitational Zone
Movement into this residential zone in Cholula is probably largely attributable to individual or family movements as opposed to group migrations (Bullock et al. in preparation). The isotopic data indicate that one nonlocal individual likely spent his childhood in the Gulf Coast and several nonlocal individuals might possibly have come from the Basin of Mexico (Bullock et al. in preparation). The nonlocal isotope signatures of most individuals could not be definitively identified as to region, but the fact that nonlocal individuals spent their childhoods in various regions and that movement into the community occurred over time argues against a group migration (Bullock et al. in preparation). In addition, archaeological features of the habitational zone, including architectural styles, artifacts, and burial practices, were identified as local by the archaeologists and physical anthropologists who participated in the excavations, meaning that the residential zone is also unlikely to have been an ethnic enclave (Lagunas 1994; López et al. 1976).

Motivations for Relocating
The demographic profiles of nonlocal individuals give some indications as to what may have brought them to this community. Sorting out whether such

TABLE 4.2. Summary of data for individuals identified as nonlocal, Cholula

Skeleton	Age	Sex	Offerings*	Burial Type†	Pathologies
127	21	M	Absent	Primary	Enamel hypoplasias
151	20	F	Absent	Primary	Healed proliferative lesions, enamel hypoplasias
178	48	F	Absent	Primary	Enamel hypoplasias
186	41	F	Absent	Primary	Healed proliferative lesions, enamel hypoplasias
206	68	M	Absent	Primary	Enamel hypoplasia
208	41	M	Present (cajete)	Primary	Healed proliferative lesions
213	7	?	Absent	Primary	Lesions associated with scurvy
245	42	F	Absent	Primary	Active and healed proliferative lesions, enamel hypoplasias
291	63	F	Absent	Undetermined ("salvage")	Healed proliferative lesions, porotic hyperostosis, enamel hypoplasia
292	57	M	Absent	Undetermined ("salvage")	Enamel hypoplasias
294	57	F	Absent	Primary	Healed proliferative lesions
295	15	?	Absent	Primary	Active and healed proliferative lesions, enamel hypoplasias
299	23	M?	Absent	Primary	None
301	36	M	Absent	Secondary	Healed proliferative lesions, enamel hypoplasias
302	32	M	Absent	Primary	Enamel hypoplasias
328	18	F	Absent	Primary	Healed proliferative lesions, cribra orbitalia and porotic hyperostosis, enamel hypoplasia
400–3	10	?	Absent	Primary	Enamel hypoplasias
420	69	M?	Absent	Primary	Healed proliferative lesions
424	51	M	Present (shell pieces)	Primary	Healed proliferative lesions, enamel hypoplasias
428	71	M?	Present (awl, spindle whorl, 2 needles)	Primary	Enamel hypoplasia

Source: Bullock Kreger 2010; Bullock et al. in preparation; López et al. 1976.
* Lopez et al. (1976, 46–48, 107–118).
† Information taken from Lopez et al. (1976, 41–43, 95–106).

movements are more accurately described as mobility or migration is challeng-ing, and (frankly) likely unproductive, as there may have been significant overlap between the two processes. Of the 18 adults identified as nonlocal, 10 are male, seven are female, and one is an adolescent whose sex could not be determined. Two subadults, aged seven and 10 at the time of death, were also among nonlocal individuals (Bullock et al. in preparation). The presence of these two juveniles strongly suggests that family groups relocated to Cholula.

Demographic studies have demonstrated that population movements are conditioned on age—a pattern that has been shown to apply across cultures (Castro and Rogers 1983, 1984; Rogers and Castro 1981, 1984; Rogers et al. 1978). Migrants are most frequently young adults, as marriage and the pursuit of economic opportunities typically motivate decisions to relocate. Some of these young adults are the parents of young children, who may accompany them (Castro and Rogers 1983, 1984; Rogers and Castro 1981, 1984; Rogers et al. 1978; Storey 1992). Thus, the identification of family movements into this residential area is consistent with what we know from anthropological demography. Interpreting the bioarchaeological data in light of these demographic studies (Castro and Rogers 1983, 1984; Rogers and Castro 1981, 1984; Rogers et al. 1978), adults who were identified as having spent part of their childhood outside Cholula in a distinct isotopic region could have moved to the urban center as children[7] along with their parents or other family members, or they could have moved to Cholula in young adulthood. Interestingly, the nonlocal individual thought to be from the Gulf Coast most likely migrated as a young adult, as his third molar, which forms during late childhood and early adolescence, was tested (Bullock et al. in preparation).

These studies of migration (Castro and Rogers 1983, 1984; Rogers and Castro 1981, 1984; Rogers et al. 1978) also suggest that the movement of these nonlocal individuals into this community was, in some way, linked to marriage or economic pursuits (Bullock et al. in preparation; Storey 1992; White et al. 2004). The ethnohistoric documents detailing group migrations discussed above clearly indicate the importance of marriage in establishing and maintaining social relationships in prehispanic Mesoamerica, and they indirectly imply that patrilocality was considered to be the cultural norm, as the women "gifted" to other ethnic groups relocated to live with their husbands (Reyes García 1988a, 63–64). Historic documents also suggest that women more frequently moved upon marriage (Carrasco 1971; Olivera 1978). We, therefore, cannot discard the possibility that some of the nonlocal females, and perhaps some males as well, were integrated into the community after marrying a resident. Furthermore, the fact that several nonlocal individuals may have come from the same region, the Basin of Mexico, could indicate an alliance or connection with a group or groups in that area (Bullock et al. in preparation).

The movement of family groups into this residential zone indicates that economic opportunities, whether real or perceived, influenced the relocation of some nonlocal individuals (Bullock et al. in preparation). The archaeological data do not point to a specific craft specialization or occupation for the residents of this habitational zone. Lithic workshops and ovens were identified in habi-tational areas, suggesting that some craft production may have occurred in the community (Hernández 1970). Unfortunately, it is not entirely clear if these fea-tures were contemporaneous with the Postclassic burials analyzed here, and the material evidence indicates only a limited number of participants in any case (Hernández 1970). However, as has been suggested for Tlajinga 33, marriage could have facilitated the integration of non-related individuals into the eco-nomic activities of the community (White, Storey, Longstaffe, and Spence 2004).

One possible answer to the question of how immigrants could have been incorporated into Mesoamerican urban communities could very well lie, at least in part, with preexisting mobility networks (Arnauld, Beekman, and Pereira, introduction to this volume). To illustrate some hypothetical—and clearly simplified—ways in which movements into this residential zone could have occurred, I offer three examples of how mobility could have fostered migration and vice versa. This is not to imply in any way that these three scenarios are the only possibilities or that they are necessarily mutually exclusive. To help clarify my examples, I discuss movement between a hypothetical community in the Basin of Mexico and this residential zone in Cholula.

1. TRADE-ORIENTED MOBILITY. Individuals from other regions undoubtedly visited Cholula to sell or purchase goods in the urban center, movements that Arnauld, Beekman, and Pereira (introduction to this volume) argue can best be classified as mobility. These trips into the urban zone by the inhabitants of our hypothetical community in the Basin of Mexico, though only temporary in nature, could have put them into contact with residents of this habitational zone in Cholula. Establishing such social and/or economic connections could have led to migration (by a trader or his or her social contacts within the home com-munity, for example) and longer-term settlement in this community in Cholula to explore economic opportunities. Once this link was established, it would have opened the doors to additional migration and possibly even cultural shifts that eventually resulted in mobility.

2. MARRIAGE ALLIANCES. Social or economic relationships established through market trade and exchange could have also resulted in marriage alli-ances between social or ethnic groups. Intermarriages between residents of this habitational zone in Cholula and our community in the Basin of Mexico could have paved the way for the migration of individuals or families from the allied group looking to pursue economic opportunities in the urban center, and it would have eased their social and economic incorporation into this habita-tional zone.

3. DOUBLED HOME BASES. Yet another possibility is that marriages between residents of this habitational zone in Cholula and members of our community in the Basin of Mexico resulted in the establishment of two "home bases" (Arnauld,

Beekman, and Pereira, introduction to this volume) for these couples—that of the husband and that of the wife. The family, young children in tow, might have then decided to move between these communities depending on available economic opportunities. In such a scenario, children would have social and familial ties to both communities, allowing for movements between the two. Potentially, an individual could spend part of his or her childhood in the Basin of Mexico before moving to Cholula, either with his or her parents or later on as an adult to pursue marriage or economic opportunities in the urban center. It is not difficult to imagine how, over time, movements like the ones described above could have become socially normalized and regulated.

The (In)Visibility of Nonlocal Individuals

Perhaps tellingly, these nonlocal individuals are practically invisible in the material culture of the zone. Ethnicity is typically identified in archaeological contexts from architectural styles, the material remains of domestic activities, evidence of ritual practices (including funerary customs), symbols and iconography, and corporal modifications and personal adornments, all of which express cultural identity (Emberling 1997; Stone 2003). It is, thus, notable that archaeological indicators of migration are largely absent within this community (López et al. 1976). While funerary practices often reflect ethnicity (Stone 2003, 43–44), the burials of nonlocal individuals are very similar to those of individuals with local isotope signatures (Lagunas 1994; López et al. 1976, 2002). Seventeen of the 20 nonlocal individuals were primary direct burials in either seated or flexed positions, almost all of whom were facing north or northeast, an orientation that reflects that the deceased was destined for the afterworld of Mictlán (Lagunas 1994, 91–92; López et al. 1976, 2002). Both the burial positions and the orientation of the skeletons are typical of this residential zone (López et al. 1976), and no statistically significant differences in the type of interment were observed between local and nonlocal individuals (table 4.3). Furthermore, burials excavated from the UA-1 domestic compound, another Postclassic residence in Cholula, were interred with similar positions and orientation, providing additional evidence that these practices are typical of Cholula (McCafferty 2007).

Many of the burials found in domestic contexts contained no grave goods at all, and most others had only modest offerings of lithics, ceramics, shell, or animal remains, such as dogs (López et al. 1976). Only three of the nonlocal individuals were buried with offerings: Skeleton 208 was interred with a *cajete*; Skeleton 424 was buried with shell; and Skeleton 428 was found with a spindle whorl, an awl, and two needles (López et al. 1976, 46–48, 107–118). None of these offerings is unusual within burials from this habitational zone, nor are they items that signal that the deceased originated in a different region. Artifacts thought to be from the Gulf Coast and Oaxaca were found in a few burials, although they were not

TABLE 4.3. Burial types, Cholula*

Burial Types	All (%)	Local (%)	Nonlocal (%)
Primary	76	66	85
Secondary	21	31	5
Undetermined	3	3	10

* Results are not statistically significant. Funerary data reported in López et al. (1976, 41–43, 95–106).

associated directly with any of the individuals identified as nonlocal (Lagunas 1994, 94; López et al. 2002, 99). While the presence or absence of grave goods does not mark any individual burial as being that of an immigrant, when considered collectively, nonlocal individuals were buried with fewer grave goods than local individuals. When considering the entire assemblage from this habitational zone, 40 percent of burials were accompanied by grave goods. However, when considering the isotope sample, 66 percent of those individuals identified as having local isotope values were buried with grave goods while only 15 percent of nonlocal individuals were accompanied by funerary offerings (López et al. 1976, 46–48, 107–118). These differences are statistically significant and suggest that the funerary treatment of nonlocal individuals may have differed somewhat from local individuals, perhaps as a result of having fewer familial or social ties within the community.

Intentional cultural modifications of the skeletons of nonlocal individuals do not signal an ethnic identity distinct from that of individuals with local isotope values. Romano (1973) classified cranial deformation in the burials excavated during the Proyecto Cholula and found the tabular erect modifications were, by far, the most common form of cranial modification in the Postclassic population of the site (Romano 1973). In the current study, good preservation of the bones of the cranial vault was required to assess the presence or absence of cranial modification. Of the 11 nonlocal individuals who could be evaluated, two present without modification and nine (81.8%) present with tabular erect modifications, the most common form of cranial modification observed in the population. Cranial modifications are present in 90.1 percent of the assemblage as a whole and in 93.3 percent of individuals identified as local (table 4.4). There are no statistically significant differences in the presence of cranial modification in local and nonlocal individuals.

The absence of clear evidence of mobility and migration from the archaeological data, funerary contexts, and corporal modifications suggests that nonlocal individuals would not have been identified as such without isotopic studies, meaning a significant amount of movement to Cholula would have gone unrecorded. This raises the question of whether much of the mobility and migration that occurred in prehispanic Mesoamerica is, in fact, invisible

TABLE 4.4. Individuals with cranial modification, Cholula*

Cranial Modification	All	Local	Nonlocal
Present	128	14	9
Absent	14	1	2
Unobservable	167	14	9
% affected	90.1	93.3	81.8

* Results are not statistically significant.

in the archaeological record. The lack of clear archaeological signals of population movements, particularly in regards to funerary practices, could be explained by nonlocal individuals holding religious or cultural beliefs similar to those of local residents of the urban center. With respect to the nonlocal individuals potentially from the Basin of Mexico, if they were, indeed, Nahuatl speakers, they would have shared many ideologies with residents of Cholula. The fact that similar forms of corporal modifications are present in both local and nonlocal individuals may be indicative of some shared cultural practices, as these modifications typically occur in early childhood, potentially prior to the movement of some of these individuals to Cholula. However, it should be mentioned that tabular erect cranial modifications were common in many Postclassic populations from central Mexico (Romano 1973, 1974). Finally, we cannot rule out the possibility that some of these nonlocal individuals could have had at least one parent who was originally from Cholula and who continued his or her own cultural practices despite living with his or her child in a different region for a time.

Alternatively, local residents of the habitational area may have chosen to inter nonlocal individuals according to local burial traditions without regard to ethnic differences in funerary rituals. While we often think of burials as straightforward representations of the identity of the deceased, more often they are complicated reflections of the social relationships between the living and the dead (Gillespie 2001, 76–78). The construction of a burial may be heavily influenced by the beliefs, customs, feelings, and interests of the living who participate in the funerary ritual. Any apparent disregard for the beliefs of the deceased need not be intentional nor even disrespectful. If the living do not share an ethnic identity with the deceased, they may be unfamiliar with the funerary rituals of the deceased's culture of origin.

Another possible explanation for the lack of clear signs of ethnic affiliation among nonlocal individuals is that they chose to suppress their ethnic identity so as to more readily assimilate into the community. Given the absence of markers of foreign ethnic identity in domestic architecture and household objects within this habitational zone, it seems likely that any nonlocal individuals with distinct ethnic affiliation were choosing to limit expressions of their cultural origins during life. Emberling (1997) and Stone (2003) point out that the choice to express or, conversely, repress ethnicity is based upon whether individuals perceive it to be to their advantage to do so within a given social context. In an analysis of ethnic identity and migration in three archaeological populations in Arizona, Stone (2003) found that the ethnic identity of immigrants was minimally expressed in material culture when they were incorporated into existing communities gradually over time. However, an ethnic enclave established by a larger group migration left definitive material indicators of the ethnic identity of the inhabitants of the community (Stone 2003).

Immigrants that have significant contact with other members of their ethnic group may find value in actively expressing their ethnic identity as a means of maintaining ties and establishing support networks with people who share a common origin (Emberling 1997; Stone 2003). Individual immigrants whose primary interactions include lifelong residents or immigrants from other areas may instead find it beneficial to minimize their perceived differences so as to be more readily assimilated (Emberling 1997; Stone 2003). In the case of Cholula, nonlocal residents entered the community as individuals or families, and they come from different homelands (Bullock et al. in preparation). Consequently, downplaying their ethnic identities may have allowed them to incorporate more readily into the existing social structure.[8] Many nonlocal individuals may have had familial or conjugal ties with local residents of Cholula, which would have further aided in their assimilation into the community (Bullock et al. in preparation).

The burial context of nonlocal individuals does indicate something about how they were treated upon their arrival to Cholula. The fact that these skeletons were buried in and around habitational units that housed local residents of the urban center suggests that they were incorporated into existing socioeconomic and/or familial structures. Furthermore, the sheer number of nonlocal individuals that were present in this habitational zone is evidence that they were easily integrated into this society. Given that Cholula was an urban center with extensive contacts with other Mesoamerican cultures, it is perhaps not surprising that immigrants would have been readily assimilated. That their burials are indistinguishable from those of local individuals indicates that in death they were treated similarly to lifelong residents of the community. While most nonlocal individuals were not interred with offerings, many local individuals lacked offerings as well (López et al. 1976, 2002).

Morbidity and Mortality
Studies of both historic and modern migrant populations in urban areas have demonstrated higher morbidity and mortality in migrants when compared to individuals who lived their entire lives in the urban environment (Dufour and

Piperata 2004; Galley 1998, 105–106; Landers 1993, 152–156). Movement into an urban center from a non-urban area may be associated with a significant change in the immigrant's epidemiological environment (Galley 1998; Landers 1993; Storey 1992). Furthermore, studies of modern migration have indicated that in addition to dealing with economic problems, immigrants may have little social support and considerable stress levels related to the process of acculturation (Ben-Sira 1997; Thomas 1995). Chronic stress has, in turn, been linked to increased morbidity and mortality (Cohen and Williamson 1991; Cohen et al. 1991; Peterson et al. 1991).

Nonlocal individuals in Cholula could very well have faced some of the same challenges. The residential area under study is clearly low status, meaning all the residents likely suffered some degree of economic hardship. Moreover, although these nonlocal individuals appear to have been assimilated into the community, they may have had a more limited social network than local individuals, as demonstrated by their lack of grave goods. Furthermore, assimilation into the community does not indicate that nonlocal individuals escaped the stress of adapting to a different cultural environment.

An analysis of pathological lesions in the skeletons of nonlocal individuals and comparison to those observed in local individuals allows us to reflect on the childhood living conditions of these nonlocal individuals as well as their experience upon arriving to the urban environment. Methodological challenges with respect to the interpretation of skeletal pathologies (Wood et al. 1992) and small sample sizes make it difficult to draw definitive conclusions regarding the comparative health of local and nonlocal individuals, but some general inferences can be made.

Pathological lesions that form during childhood are present in a number of the individuals identified as nonlocal, indicating that almost all of them experienced impoverished backgrounds in which economic stresses were frequent and the disease burden was likely high (see table 4.2). It is possible that some of these individuals, or their families, could have been spurred to move by poor conditions in their place of origin (Clark and Souden 1988; Luu 2005; Whyte 2000). Of the 17 individuals who could be assessed for enamel hypoplasias, 15 have at least one hypoplasia and 10 have hypoplasias on multiple teeth (tables 4.2, 4.5). Many of these individuals experienced multiple episodes of physiological stress during childhood. Furthermore, nine individuals, eight of whom died before the age of 50, have enamel hypoplasias on their permanent second and/or third molar, indicating significant stress episodes occurring in later childhood. Enamel hypoplasias on these teeth have, in turn, been linked to higher mortality in this population (Bullock 2013; Bullock Kreger 2010). In addition to this general indicator of stress, two adults have signs of healed porotic hyperostosis, indicating that they suffered nutritional deficiencies during childhood (tables 4.2, 4.6).

TABLE 4.5. Presence of one or more enamel hypoplasias*

Presence/Absence of Enamel Hypoplasias	All	Local	Nonlocal
INCISOR			
Present	61	7	9
Absent	49	6	3
Unobservable	199	16	8
% affected	55.5	53.8	75.0
CANINE			
Present	111	16	11
Absent	14	1	1
Unobservable	184	12	8
% affected	88.8	94.1	91.7
FIRST MOLAR			
Present	48	11	6
Absent	87	9	5
Unobservable	174	9	9
% affected	35.6	55.0	54.5
SECOND MOLAR			
Present	44	9	8
Absent	79	8	6
Unobservable	186	12	6
% affected	35.8	52.9	57.0
THIRD MOLAR			
Present	26	4	3
Absent	51	8	3
Unobservable	232	17	14
% affected	33.8	33.0	50.0

* Results are not statistically significant.

Other pathological lesions observed in nonlocal individuals are equivocal with respect to whether they reflect living conditions in the community of origin or the new community in Cholula. Eleven of the 20 nonlocal individuals had healed proliferative lesions indicative of systemic infections (tables 4.2, 4.7). As these lesions are healed, it is not possible to determine when they occurred in relation to relocation, but they are consistent with generally poor health in the years preceding their deaths. One nonlocal child had active lesions associated with scurvy (table 4.8), and one adolescent female had both healed and active proliferative lesions at the time of death. As these individuals are at ages in which migration

TABLE 4.6. Individuals affected by cribra orbitalia and porotic hyperostosis*

Cribra Orbitalia and Porotic Hyperostosis	All	Local	Nonlocal
ORBITS			
Present	12	0	1
Absent	114	13	6
Unobservable	183	16	13
% affected	9.5	0.0	14.3
FRONTAL SQUAMA			
Present	3	0	0
Absent	161	16	14
Unobservable	145	13	6
% affected	1.8	0.0	0.0
PARIETAL			
Present	18	1	2
Absent	170	19	11
Unobservable	121	9	7
% affected	9.6	5.0	15.4
OCCIPITAL			
Present	12	1	1
Absent	146	14	10
Unobservable	151	14	9
% affected	7.6	6.7	9.1

* Results are not statistically significant.

might have occurred shortly before their deaths, it is unclear if the disease processes responsible for the pathologies occurred before or after moving. However, the active proliferative lesions observed in one middle-aged nonlocal individual are more likely to be associated with conditions in this residential area of Cholula.

While it would appear that some nonlocal individuals may have experienced poor health while living in Cholula, they were not necessarily any worse off than local individuals. Observed frequencies of pathological lesions are similar in the assemblage as a whole and in local and nonlocal individuals identified in the isotope sample. No statistically significant differences were noted among the groups (see tables 4.5–4.8). Almost all local individuals also had at least one enamel hypoplasia and approximately half had multiple hypoplasias. Although a higher percentage of nonlocal individuals presented with at least one hypoplasia of the first maxillary incisor and the third mandibular molar, these differences did not reach the level of statistical significance.

TABLE 4.7. Individuals with proliferative lesions of the long bones*

Proliferative Lesions	All	Local	Nonlocal
HUMERUS			
Present	7	0	1
Absent	154	18	11
Unobservable	148	11	8
% affected	4.3	0.0	8.3
RADIUS			
Present	7	0	1
Absent	135	16	11
Unobservable	167	13	8
% affected	4.9	0.0	8.3
ULNA			
Present	23	1	2
Absent	129	13	9
Unobservable	157	15	9
% affected	15.1	7.1	18.2
FEMUR			
Present	30	1	3
Absent	126	13	9
Unobservable	153	15	8
% affected	19.2	7.1	25.0
TIBIA			
Present	78	7	11
Absent	99	6	5
Unobservable	132	16	4
% affected	44.0	53.8	68.8
FIBULA			
Present	51	6	4
Absent	110	11	10
Unobservable	148	12	6
% affected	31.7	35.3	28.6

* $p = 0.057$, statistically significant value at $p < 0.1$.

Only one local individual out of the 23 who could be assessed had signs of porotic hyperostosis or cribra orbitalia. While a slightly greater percentage of nonlocal individuals showed evidence of cribra orbitalia and porotic hyperostosis,

TABLE 4.8. Individuals with lesions of the sphenoid*

Lesions of the Sphenoid	All	Local	Nonlocal
Present	3	0	1
Absent	87	7	7
Unobservable	219	22	12
% affected	3.3	0.0	12.5

* Results are not statistically significant.

these differences were again not statistically significant. Evidence of scurvy was noted in only three individuals in the entire assemblage, one of whom was the nonlocal individual mentioned above, but, again, this is not a statistically significant finding.

Approximately half of the local individuals who could be assessed also had evidence of infectious disease, but comparing the frequency of proliferative lesions observed in the long bones, no statistically significant differences were observed in local and nonlocal individuals at $p < 0.05$. Nonlocal individuals did present with a statistically significant greater percentage of tibial lesions at $p < 0.1$; however, given the limitations of the data mentioned above and the inability to determine when these disease processes were active in relation to the timing of migration, it is difficult to draw any meaningful conclusions regarding this finding.

The paleopathological analyses of local individuals in this habitational zone are largely useful in that they demonstrate that they, too, suffered from nutritional stress and infectious disease, thus confirming the economic deprivation of all residents of this community. Nonlocal individuals did not necessarily suffer greater morbidity than local individuals, either in their home communities or in Cholula. The presence of pathologies in nonlocal individuals does not necessarily reflect less access to resources or poorer living conditions than local individuals of Cholula. Rather, conditions within the habitational zone were less than optimal for all residents. If perceived economic opportunities motivated movement into this community, such expectations may not have been fulfilled.

CONCLUSIONS

Given the prominent role Cholula played in Postclassic Mesoamerica, it is, perhaps, not surprising that the urban center saw such a heavy influx of immigrants during this time period. The interregional connections fostered by temporary forays into the urban zone, as well as social structures that placed importance on establishing alliances through intermarriage, would have favored cultural attitudes allowing for considerable mobility in the population. The bioarchaeological and isotopic data, when contextualized by ethnohistoric accounts, archaeological information, and cross-cultural demographic studies of migration, suggest that mobility in prehispanic Cholula did extend beyond local movements due to these regional interactions (Arnauld, Beekman, and Pereira, introduction to this volume). Whether these nonlocal individuals chose to move to the urban center to marry a resident of Cholula or to pursue economic opportunities for themselves or their families, socioeconomic structures were such that they were readily assimilated into a local community.

ACKNOWLEDGMENTS

I am especially appreciative to T. Douglas Price and James Burton from the Laboratory for Archaeological Chemistry at the University of Wisconsin–Madison, as well as Paul Fullagar and David Dettman, for their roles in analyzing the strontium and oxygen isotope samples from Cholula and interpreting the results. Special thanks also go to the Dirección de Antropología Física (DAF) and the Consejo de Arqueología of the Instituto Nacional de Antropología e Historia (INAH) for permitting access to the Cholula skeletal material. José Concepción Jiménez, David Volcanes, and Irma Martínez greatly facilitated the collection of data from the Cholula skeletons. Ken Hirth provided helpful insights into prehispanic economic organization. This chapter has been significantly improved by suggestions from the editors as well as anonymous reviewers, although any shortcomings are my own. Funding for the paleodemographic study of the Cholula skeletons was provided by the Foundation for the Advancement of Mesoamerican Studies, Inc., and a Hill Fellowship, a Sanders Award, and a Research and Graduate Studies Award from the Pennsylvania State University. The isotopic study of Cholula was funded by a grant from the Wenner-Gren Foundation.

NOTES

1. Some of these burials include multiple individuals. The archaeologists and physical anthropologists who worked on the Proyecto Cholula identified 68 of these burials as Cholulteca II and 278 as Cholulteca III, based, at least in part, on Müller's ceramic chronology (López et al. 1976; Müller 1970, 1978). However, considerable disagreement exists regarding the ceramics chronology and phase designations of the urban center (Lind 1994; McCafferty 1994, 1996, 2001; Müller 1970, 1978; Noguera 1954; Plunket and Uruñuela 2005; Uruñuela and Plunket 2005). Since these phase designations have been questioned, the burials will be more generally dated to the Postclassic period, as they clearly postdate the abandonment of the Great Pyramid and yet predate European contact (Bullock et al. in preparation; López et al. 1976; McCafferty 2000). Burials dated to Cholulteca IV were also recovered, but they were not included in any of the present studies.

2. All subadult individuals included in the isotope sample were aged through dental remains.

3. To be included in the isotope sample, skeletons had to have associated permanent teeth that could be clearly identified as belonging to that individual. Skeletal elements necessary for age and preferably sex (in the case of adults) determination also had to be present. Qualifying skeletons were then divided into age groups, and individuals were randomly selected from within each age group. Due to the original research objectives of the isotope project, young adults were oversampled. Children (<15) were undersampled because of the qualifying criteria and concerns about preserving the integrity of the collection for future research (see table 4.1 and figure 4.1).

4. One sample did not yield results. Consequently, only 49 of the 50 individuals were identified as having local or nonlocal origins (Bullock et al. in preparation).

5. The terms *local* and *nonlocal* are used here as shorthand to refer to residents of this community with known isotope signatures. *Local* indicates individuals with local isotope signatures and *nonlocal* refers to individuals with nonlocal isotope signatures. These terms are being used to acknowledge certain limitations that exist with respect to the isotopic data, which are addressed later in the chapter. Many of the individuals with nonlocal isotope values may have spent a significant portion of their lives in Cholula, and the use of the term *nonlocal* should not be taken as a commentary on their degree of social integration into this community.

6. "cada provincia tenía sus salas y casas dentro de Chololla, donde se aposentaban."

7. Obviously, this move would have had to occur at some point after the tooth that was tested in the isotope study formed. Childhood migration is most common in infancy and declines from there to reach a low at approximately age 10 (Castro and Rogers 1983, 1984; Rogers and Castro 1981, 1984; Rogers et al. 1978).

8. It should also be noted that the expression of ethnic identity through material culture may require access to goods or products from the home community. The existence of large numbers of individuals from the home culture, such as in an ethnic enclave, or significant ongoing contact with the home community makes it more likely that these material objects are available. Individuals incorporated into communities consisting almost entirely of local individuals may have limited access to goods that reflect their culture of origin, meaning the lack of expression of their ethnic identity through material culture may not always be a true choice.

PART II

Classic Lowland Maya Mobility

5

Mobility as Resilience

A Perspective on Coastal to Inland Migration in the Eastern Maya Lowlands

ELIZABETH GRAHAM AND LINDA HOWIE

In the introduction to this volume, Arnauld, Beekman, and Pereira highlight a feature that is critical to our understanding of mobility and migration of the cultures of Mesoamerica, which is "the physical dynamism embedded in Mesoamerican subsistence structures, economic activities, and political strategies." As they emphasize, urban centers were formed and maintained by movement, both to and from cities. Such an adaptation to the movement of people, even in conditions of urbanism, must have deep roots. Adjusting to mobility might in part be a historical consequence of the swidden system. Among the Belize Maya who cultivated swidden in the 1970s, 1980s, and 1990s, as communities grew, new ones were established as spinoffs of the original founding community but social relationships were maintained even with distance (Graham 1994, 325). Movement in precolumbian times must have been necessary when individuals were required to fulfil a work tax, or scribes were required to reside in courts of rulers. Longer-distance movements of households were also enabled by Maya cultural and social practices. The occurrence today of a suite of Maya surnames (e.g., Pech, Cohuoj, Chi, Cunil, Cocom, Itza, Uck

DOI: 10.5876/9781646420735.c005

[Graham 2011, xvii]) in Yucatán and Guatemala as well as in Belize suggests that patronym groups (*chibalob*) facilitated regional movements and connections (Restall 1997, 17–18). The sort of mobility, in which families, as parts of larger social groups, moved about the peninsula, is prominent in the Chilam Balam accounts of Tizimin and Chumayel (Edmonson 1982, 1986). From a coastal perspective, the movements of traders and merchants loom large. Merchants and merchant families who plied the circumpeninsular waters almost certainly established interregional and long-distance bonds, because they would have relied on each other to build networks and to make commercial transactions effective (Lacadena 2010). Bonds among coastal families surely involved marriage. An individual from Ambergris Caye was perhaps as likely to marry someone from Cozumel or coastal Campeche or the islands off Honduras as to choose someone from Caracol or Cahal Pech. The coastal ties created over time would have facilitated movement of both individuals and goods.

MOVEMENT AND MIGRATION

The movements and changes of place so far described are characterized differently by different researchers. To Tilly (1978), what we sketched out above would be examples of his local, circular, chain, and career "migrations." Arnauld, Beekman, and Pereira (introduction to this volume) advise using *migration* more cautiously and critically (see also Leloup 1996); if mobility can be an element of *habitus*, as they attest, then a degree of mobility is essential to all the movement we have so far described. They suggest further that migration follows more disruptive events or processes. We are in accord with their analysis of terms, but we would like to add three cautionary points.

The first point is a product of the limitations of the English vocabulary. An individual defines herself as an "immigrant" to Britain because *immigrant* is the only noun that exists in English to describe this sort of change of residence. No word derived from *mobility* exists that can apply to someone who decides to move from one sedentary location to another. Therefore, despite the fact that the individual has neither moved as part of a larger social group nor as the result of a disruptive event or process, she has nonetheless "migrated." In fact, her move is very much a feature of the mobility inherent in modern urbanized settlement systems, but a word that might reflect sensitivity to this nuance, "mobilitant," does not exist.

A second caution relates to level of analysis. The terms *mobility* and *migration* operate at different levels of analysis, and from different perspectives. Often when the term *migrated* is used, the context is one in which a larger-scale shift has already been recognized historically so that the movement of individuals is seen in retrospect as part of a larger-scale phenomenon. The many individuals who moved to the United States from Italy in the late nineteenth and early twentieth century are said to have been part of a migration. Yet if one questions individuals, each has a different story about why he or she decided to change location. Stimuli seem to have been varied: economic, political, social, or just a plain sense of adventure. It is the passage of time that has allowed us to generalize so that individuals or families who decided to move—for whatever reasons, and not even necessarily permanently—have become part of a "migration." This is not to say that the term is not apt as a descriptor of what we now view as having happened in history, but only that the term *migration* may not be useful as the first step in analyses undertaken to examine the details of the stimulus for movement.

The third caution is about the baggage that comes with the term. *Migration* is paired generally with a collective noun (such as *population* or *Aztec*). An individual can be a migrant, although this usage reflects, as we noted above, either the limited choice of the English language or a context in which a larger-scale shift or movement of people is already known or believed in retrospect to have taken place. In the case of the larger-scale shift, the implications of "migration" can take on a mythic dimension. The late nineteenth- and early twentieth-century movement of individuals from Naples or Puglia referred to above is attributed in the United States to the desire for both freedom (apparently unattainable in either of these places) and/or a better life in a nation that sees itself as welcoming people with open arms to fill its empty spaces. With time, and from a macro-perspective, individuals and families became "populations" and the places of origin became a single locus: "Italy." Most families considered themselves Napolitano or Pugliese or Calabrese. They *became* both "Italian" and a united "other" in the American historical narrative. Ethnic or cultural differences recognized at the time and other potentially important factors in the decision to move become blurred by the construction of a narrative and an agenda. When narratives such as the books of Chilam Balam (e.g., Edmonson 1982) attribute movement of groups across swaths of land or sea, we have to ask—in addition to who moved, when, and where—what stimulated the telling and what the agenda might be.

Another narrative that has reached almost mythic status is the claim that populations migrated from Petén to Yucatán as a result of the Classic collapse (see the chapters in Demarest et al. 2004). We know that investment in masonry architecture diminished or ceased entirely, but there are few initiatives that have been aimed at discovering whether Postclassic communities, with their wooden structures, farms, orchards, and fields, were absent entirely from what had once been an urban landscape. Coe's Tikal Time Spans 1 and 2, for example, which cover the postcollapse years from about AD 900 through the nineteenth century, provide a fascinating glimpse of a range of activities in the former urban center itself (Coe 1990, 866–874). Considering the fertility of the land and the diversity of vegetation that are associated with abandonment, especially once city architecture began to collapse (Graham 1998, 2006a; Graham et al. 2017; Lambert and Arnason 1982; Rico-Gray and García-Franco 1991), it is highly unlikely that Petén remained uninhabited, and that people—either originally Tikal-based or from surrounding regions—would not have taken advantage of rich farm land, a diversity of plants and fruit trees, local springs, building material, and even the potential to plunder tombs (Coe 1990, 871). Populations may not have been as high or as concentrated as in the Classic period, and dynastic collapse almost assuredly initiated some measure of instability, but the scale and nature of movement have yet to be ascertained. A mass migration to Yucatán should not be so widely accepted based on present evidence, which arises from an excavation focus on masonry buildings of the Classic period (Graham 1985). If we wish to hypothesize about causes of, or stimuli to, the movement of people, the terminology we use in the first instance should perhaps exclude both *population* and *migration*. We might start by thinking about what would stimulate an individual or family to move. *Migration* in particular should not be part of the question at the first level of analysis because in a sense it is already an answer.

APPROACHING MOBILITY AND MIGRATION

Given the continuity of occupation at the sites of Lamanai, on the New River Lagoon in northern Belize (Graham 2004; Pendergast 1982, 1986), and Marco Gonzalez, on Ambergris Caye (Graham 1989; Graham and Pendergast 1989; Graham et al. 2017; Simmons and Graham 2017) (table 5.1) during the time of the Maya collapse, evidence from these sites has something to tell us about mobility and migration during a critical period of transition. Following on from Arnauld, Beekman and Pereira's introduction (this volume), we structure our discussion to address three broad questions: Did conditions exist that facilitated mobility and if so, what were they? What was the scale of movement? Who moved, and in what direction? The framework of our argument is presented below as Points A, B, and C, followed by detailed discussion of each and then by implications and suggestions for further study.

POINT A. The sites taken together tell us that many types of goods and materials were transported via marine and riverine routes to and from inland locations from Preclassic to Postclassic times. The movement of goods reflects not only the economic demands of trade and exchange but also concomitant social networks of travel and communication. Merchants, markets, resources, and exchange generated conditions foundational to the ease with which people could have moved, if they chose to do so. Our working assumption for both Lamanai and Marco Gonzalez—given their intensive involvement in commerce and trade—is that a degree of mobility was the norm, not the exception.

POINT B. At Lamanai, from at least Late Classic to Early Postclassic times (ca. AD 600 to 1250) (the period on which ceramic studies were focused), there existed

TABLE 5.1. Provisional chronologies for Lamanai and Marco Gonzalez*

Period	Lamanai	Ambergis Caye (Marco Gonzalez, San Pedro)
Independence	1981 to present	
Self-governing Crown Colony	1964 to 1981	
British colonial period	1700 to 1964 (Activity beginning in 1630s)	
Spanish colonial period	1492/1500 to 1700	
Late Postclassic	1350 to 1492/1500	
Middle to Late Postclassic	1200/1250 to 1350	
Early Postclassic	950/1000 to 1200/1250	
Terminal Classic	750/800 to 950/1000	
Late Classic (late facet)	660/700 to 750/800	550/600 to 750/800
Late Classic (early facet)	590/600 to 660/700	
Early Classic	250/300 to 590/600	
Terminal Preclassic (late facet)	150 to 250/300	100 BC to AD 250/300
Terminal Preclassic (early facet)	100 BC to AD 150	
Late Preclassic	400 100 BC	
Middle Preclassic (late facet)	600 to 400 BC	*No data*
Middle Preclassic (early facet)	900 to 600 BC	*No data*
Early Preclassic	1600 to 900 BC	*No data*

* The sequence is based on relative stratigraphy, ceramic typology, and epigraphic and historical records. Radiocarbon dates exist for Lamanai's Late Classic through Early Postclassic periods, and for the Early Preclassic (Hanna et al. 2016; S. Metcalfe et al. 2009; Rushton et al. 2013).

a high degree of stability in the support of a "nonelite" population (Howie 2012, 150–155, 213–214). At the same time, both ceramic-production studies and isotopic analyses indicate that some migration at the level of intraregional movement took place in the Terminal Classic period (Howie 2012; Howie et al. 2010) with intraregional mobility at the level of individuals suggested by isotopic analyses of the Postclassic population (Donis 2013). At Marco Gonzalez in the Terminal Classic period (ca. AD 750/800 to 950/1000), there is burial evidence that could be used to generate hypotheses about the arrival of a new group of people, although local adoption of new beliefs and burial patterns is also an option. Indeed, such local adoption, if it was the case, would not have taken place without some level of movement of individuals or the sharing of ideas.

POINT C. In terms of the dynamics of change—that is, who moved, in what direction, and why—we think we can argue for movement of both commoner families and those, not necessarily noble, who were pursuing control of resources and expansion of wealth as new heads of communities. Owing to conflation of time periods in the studies that have been carried out—the entire Postclassic in the case of Donis's study (Donis 2013), and the combining of the Terminal Classic and Early Postclassic in the study by Howie and colleagues (Howie et al. 2010)—we cannot at this time provide more detail. Given the chronological definition that we have at both Lamanai and Marco Gonzalez, however, future work holds the promise of filling in the gaps.

Conditions Facilitating Mobility

Data from a range of coastal sites and from inland communities on rivers near the sea support the idea that mobility was a norm among the Maya rather than an exception (Guderjan and Garber 1995; MacKinnon and Kepecs 1989; McKillop 2002, 2009; Mock 1997; Murata 2011). Figure 5.1 is modified from a previous work (Graham 1989, 144, 146), in which an attempt was made to visualize coastal-inland and intracoastal relationships in Belize. Local movement of groups of people from inland riverine communities to the coastal lagoons and near-shore cayes probably accounts for the small size of the sites on the lagoons and near-shore cayes, and the lack of evidence, such as burials (at least at the two Colson Point sites [Graham 1994]), of year-round settlement. To an individual, both locations—the village on the coast and the inland town—may well have been considered "home" or *cah* (Restall 1997, 20–40), a notion that accords well with mobility as an element of *habitus* (Arnauld, Beekman, Pereira, introduction to this volume).

The case is slightly different with regard to the barrier reef coral islands or cayes. The evidence from Ambergris Caye (Guderjan and Garber 1995; Simmons and Graham 2017) suggests that the island supported communities independent of mainland administration or civic authority; people from these communities are most likely to have been those who seasonally or periodically inhabited and exploited the atolls (Graham 1998; MacKie 1963). At some times, the caye communities interacted predominantly with the mainland directly to the west; at others, the direction of trade and interaction was more intensely circumpen-insular (McKillop 1996; Simmons and Graham 2017). The "stability through change" that is said to have characterized Lamanai (Pendergast 1986) can also apply to Ambergris Caye. Changes in orientation of trade and exchange were part and parcel of a life based in commerce, and hence change can be said to have been a persistent and "stable" feature. The abundant remains of Early Classic polychromes (especially from AD 250 to about 500 but continuing to a lesser extent in the sixth century) at Marco Gonzalez and the Colson Point sites (along the coast in south-central Belize) indicate that inhabitants of caye and coastal sites moved large quantities of goods along the coast and then to inland sites (Graham 1986, 1994, 197–234, figures 5.27–32, 5.35; Graham et al. 2017). Salt was produced at Marco Gonzalez in the Late Classic on a scale large enough to

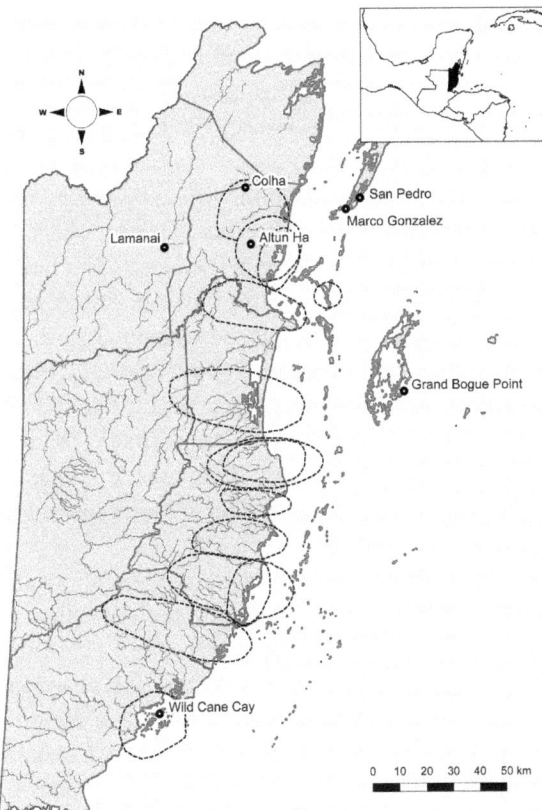

FIGURE 5.1. *Locations of Lamanai, Marco Gonzalez, and sites discussed in the text as well as proposed coastal-inland spheres. (Map by Panos Kratimenos, adapted from Graham 1989, 147, figure 10.6.)*

imply major inland consumption (Graham et al. 2017). A number of sites produced salt along Belize's coast and cayes in the Late Classic (Andrews and Mock 2002; MacKinnon and Kepecs 1989; McKillop 2002, 2016; Mock 1998; Murata 2011), and the direction of movement seems to have been east–west, from the cayes to inland communities in Belize, although coastal transport to key distribution nodes was likely. A much-diminished (compared to Early Classic times) trade in pottery, mainly polychrome vases and bowls, is also in evidence, although petrographic studies of vessels' geographic origins are still required to establish movement from specific sites or areas. In the Terminal Classic (ninth and early tenth centuries), during the heyday of Chichen Itza, salt declined dramatically as an export item in Belize and the town at Marco Gonzalez seems to have been heavily engaged in the importation—or perhaps the transshipment—of a wide range of goods: chert (present as nodules as well as artifacts), granite metates, obsidian, pottery, and shell, worked and unworked, are all present. One export item may have been worked shell (Simmons and Graham 2017). Overall, the dynamics of trade and the travel it entailed at the end of the Late Classic (end of the eighth century) through the Terminal Classic at Marco Gonzalez were decidedly circumpeninsular, and although exchange continued with the mainland, material culture shared affinities with Chichen Itza and its sphere.

Lamanai, on the other hand, seems to have lain outside the Chichen sphere in the Terminal Classic. Based on the ceramics from caches and burials in major structures in Late and Terminal Classic times, continuity is indicated in the nature of polychrome decoration. There are some changes—for example, the red ground of the seventh century changed to orange in the eighth, but black and red lines continued to mark the rim interiors of large bowls or dishes, and the vessel interiors were marked in their centers by line-drawn animals such as felines or deer, or sometimes by an abstract flower motif (Graham 2004, 2006b; Howie 2012). Through the Terminal Classic, the decoration became simplified and sketchier, and glossy surface finishes disappeared. The dramatic change to decorated exteriors came with the Early Postclassic Buk phase at Lamanai, when polychromy disappeared and incised and gouged decoration replaced it (Pendergast 1982).

In the Early Postclassic period (AD 950/1000 to ca. 1250/1300), Lamanai stepped in to fill the vacuum left by Chichen Itza's decline in the eleventh century, possibly by AD 1000 (Andrews et al. 2003; Hoggarth et al. 2016). There are no indications at Lamanai or on the caye of the drastic decline and abandonment that characterized the major centers of the Pasión-Usumacinta regions (Demarest et al. 2004, 550–551). Central Petén during the Terminal Classic seems to have experienced demographic flux rather than abandonment, although construction of monumental architecture at sites such as Tikal ceased (Demarest et al. 2004, 554–555; Valdés and Fahsen 2004). At Lamanai, monumental architectural construction persisted into the Postclassic to some degree (Pendergast 1981), although it did not match the investment in masonry construction of the Classic period. Evidence for occupation continuity is robust, however (Graham 2004; Pendergast 1981, 1982, 1986). Pottery manufacture was marked by continuity in complex knowledge of local resources (Howie 2012), an important indicator of stability of the local nonelite population. Additionally, there was continuity from the Terminal Classic in aspects of vessel form (Graham 1987), which suggests that there was no disruption in cultural memory at one level, and hence that the local population remained stable. The overall repertoire changed dramatically in appearance, however, and was almost certainly a response to new demands and possibly new cultural values. Those making the demands were not connected politically to the old Classic dynasties, and ideologically they reinforced their positions in new ways. The extent to which mobility or migration was involved in these changes is discussed in the next section.

The nature of the trade networks in the Early Postclassic remains unclear. The ceramic inventory at both Lamanai and Marco Gonzalez is dominated by the Zakpah ceramic group (e.g., Zakpah Orange-red and Zalal Gouged-incised [Walker 1990]), which indicates strengthening of connections between the caye and communities in northern Belize (Ting 2013) and hence sheds light on intraregional network dynamics. At the same time, on the caye both green obsidian and turquoise were imported, reflecting continuity in long-distance (circumpeninsular?) trade networks. We emphasize that at no time were networks exclusively one or the other—that is, circumpeninsular at the expense of coastal-mainland or vice versa—but commercial dynamics especially seem to have fluctuated between the lucrative and broad Mesoamerican or peninsular connections (Preclassic, Early Classic, Terminal Classic, Late Postclassic) and the pull of more localized or regional market networks based on the proximal mainland (Late Classic, Early Postclassic). In Middle/Late Postclassic times (ca. AD 1250 to 1492), the scene changed again. We have less information from this period, but the abundant remains of ancient San Pedro—where the modern town lies, about 7 km north of Marco Gonzalez (figure 5.1)—reflect intensive activity (Pendergast and Graham 1991). San Pedro was positioned, as was Marco Gonzalez before mangrove encroachment (Dunn and Mazzullo 1993), to take advantage of both windward and leeward canoe traffic, which suggests the existence of a bustling port keyed into circumpeninsular and mainland movements of people and goods.

In the Late Postclassic, as in all periods, sites on the cayes and coast were not on or very near good agricultural land, and a range of foods had to be imported, probably from sites such as Lamanai. Mobility is therefore what characterized the caye and coastal zones: people shifting from their inland communities to coastal way stations to fish and to access trade goods; people traveling to the reef and beyond to fish and collect shells; people traveling westward to the mainland to carry salt and smoked fish and to bring back supplies; and people circum-navigating the peninsula, transporting an array of goods to exchange, and establishing long-term social ties in the process. Although it has been traditional in Maya archaeology to promote the Postclassic as the time when sea trade became important, there is consensus among archaeologists who have worked in coastal areas that marine networks of trade and exchange have deep roots in Mesoamerican history (Andrews and Mock 2002; Graham 1989, Graham 1994, Graham 2011, 116; Masson 2000, Masson 2002b; McKillop 2002, 2016). Merchants and traders may well have developed a consciousness as a class or group (Graham 2006b), and by the Late Classic, they may have shared a common "international" language (Tokovinine and Beliaev 2013: 194). Bilingual coastal communities are documented for coastal Yucatán at the time of the Conquest (see Graham 2011, 121). The critical implication is that networks established under these conditions for both travel and communication would have been a major means by which mobility—and the attendant sociocultural dynamics and expectations engendered by mobility—would have been facilitated since Middle Preclassic times. To reinforce the observations of Arnauld, Beekman and Pereira (introduction to this volume), regular circulation over territories partly determined larger population movements.

The Scale of Movement

Detecting any kind of movement of people archaeologically is a challenging task. Stable isotope analysis via bone-tooth comparisons can tell us if an individual spent his or her early years in a locale different from the final place of death. In limestone-dominated northern Belize and Yucatán, however, detailed knowledge of local geological distinctiveness within the larger pattern is necessary to permit differentiation among sites as concerns the geographic origins (i.e., provenance) of material goods. Aside from the work that has been done at Lamanai (Howie 2012), connecting sites to resource zones is not the norm. New types of pottery reflect change, but details of paste composition and production must be known if we are to be able to determine whether the change is the result of actual transport or import of vessels by immigrants to the community, or of adoption of new styles by local potters. To date, stable isotope analysis geared specifically to exploration of the movement of people has been carried out only on a sample of Lamanai skeletal material (Donis 2013) and not on skeletal material from Marco Gonzalez. Petrographic study, too, has a longer history at Lamanai and has encompassed a wide sector of the ceramic collection (Howie 2012), but a significant start has been made on Early Postclassic material at Marco Gonzalez (Ting 2013).

LAMANAI: A CASE FROM CERAMIC PETROGRAPHY
FOR IMMIGRATION ON THE GROUP LEVEL

At Lamanai, knowledge of the details of ceramic production from the Late Classic through the Postclassic periods has produced evidence of potential immigration. Even if the detailed knowledge of ceramic production cannot always be linked directly to immigration, however, cognizance of the variety of approaches used in a community to make pots is essential for assessing the context in which changes take place and hence for hypothesizing about the possible sources of change. The Lamanai study (Howie 2012) tells us three important things. The first is that different potters working in the vicinity of Lamanai made pottery using distinct sets of local raw material ingredients and different forming, finishing, and firing methods, and the distinct paste technologies apparent in the Late Classic period can be traced back to at least Late Preclassic times (Howie et al. 2016). The second is that local potters, informed by longstanding local traditions of technical and environmental knowledge, were the primary producers of ceramics for both ceremonial and utilitarian purposes. The third is

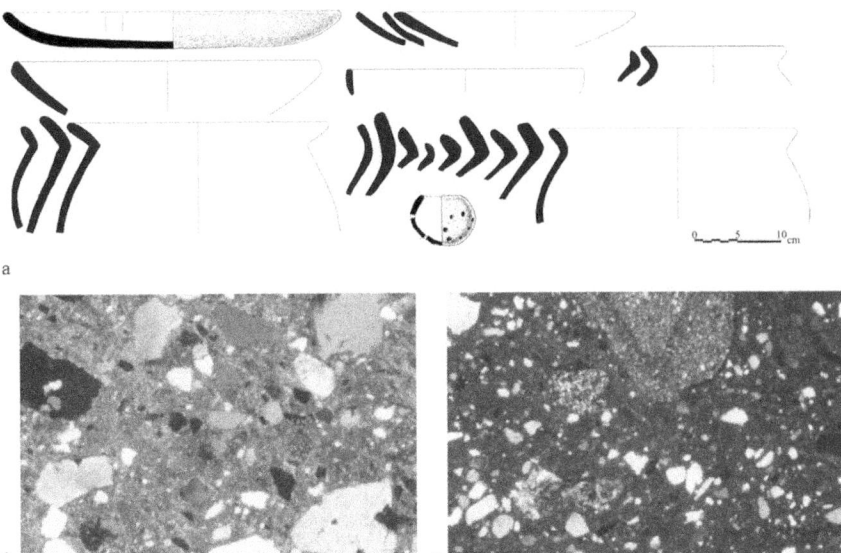

FIGURE 5.2. *Lamanai new sandy-paste manufacturing tradition: (a) vessel forms; (b) quartz-rich, sandy fabric (×25) identical to local clays; (c) sandy fabric (×25) containing large amounts of chert and chalcedony, mineralogically typical of pine-ridge savannah areas to the east, close to Altun Ha and Colha. Field of view = 3mm. (Pottery illustrations by Louise Belanger and Rebecca Curran; photomicrographs from Howie 2012, 155, figure 8.6a, b.)*

that, although paste preparation methods for fineware production changed significantly by the Early Postclassic period (e.g., the use of grog temper), potters continued to exploit the same local raw material resources as their predecessors. Recipes, although they changed, reflect complex knowledge of local component materials and their manufacturing and firing properties and behaviors. Certain surface-finishing techniques and firing methods also continued to be used in the manufacture of fineware alongside new techniques and a different approach to embellishment (Howie 2012, 208–211).

Why is this sort of knowledge essential in detecting immigration? At Lamanai, a new local tradition of coarseware manufacture appeared in the Terminal Classic and continued to at least the Late Postclassic (Howie 2012, 172; Wiewall and Howie 2010). Sandy, quartz-rich clays, common to areas of Pleistocene alluvium and sand that occur in northern Belize, distinguish raw-material resources that had not previously been exploited by Lamanai potters (figure 5.2). At Lamanai, the clays can be found in the area of "pine ridge" (savannah) that lies across the lagoon, forming its eastern shore. Large storage jars are the most common form of coarseware, but other forms were also produced. The jars are similar stylistically and petrographically to Late Classic jars at Altun Ha but with mineralogical and textural differences related to the use of local Lamanai resources. One hypothesis to explain the new tradition would be an influx of people into Lamanai from coastal areas to the east and/or northeast of the city. The putative immigrants seem to have integrated well with *Lamaneros*, but they retained aspects of their pottery-making traditions. They chose to use the quartz-rich sandy clays located across the lagoon instead of the limestone-derived raw materials in and around Lamanai because they had prior experience using them and understood well their properties and behaviors. The stimulus seems, however to have been a shift from the coast to inland areas, and we have to ask what sorts of conditions would explain this direction of movement when collapse is widely seen to have stimulated movement from Petén northward.

LAMANAI: STABLE ISOTOPE ANALYSES, CERAMIC PETROGRAPHY, AND INTRAREGIONAL MOBILITY

Stable isotope analysis geared specifically to explore movement of people at Lamanai was carried out by Donis (2013). A total of 63 individuals were included, with oxygen isotope values of a further 24 Lamanai individuals obtained by Howie and colleagues (Howie et al. 2010) as part of a study of the provenience characteristics of serving and drinking vessels placed in burials under residential building floors in the Terminal Classic through Early Postclassic periods. Donis's sample comprised Postclassic (36) and Historic or Spanish colonial (21) populations (Donis 2013, 52). Only the Postclassic results are discussed here. Methods comprised analyses of phosphate-oxygen isotopes of bone-tooth pairs, collagen carbon- and nitrogen-isotopes (diet); and examination of cranial and dental modification (Donis 2013, 117; Howie et al. 2010).

As reported by Donis (2013, 98, 121) and supported by Howie and colleagues (2010), the phosphate-oxygen isotope values of the Lamanai Postclassic dataset (and Terminal Classic to Early Postclassic dataset, in the case of the Howie study) are continuous, with no identifiable outliers. As a result, no individuals with geographic origins outside northern Belize could be specifically identified. However, the samples analyzed have a range of phosphate-oxygen isotope values more than 1.5 times larger than the expected Mesoamerican intrapopulational variability (Donis 2013, 121). When Donis compared the Postclassic and Historic results, she found that Postclassic-period bone and tooth enamel have a higher mean phosphate-oxygen value, and the mean difference is statistically significant (Donis 2013, 81). The Postclassic bone sample also has a larger range than the Historic-period sample, and the difference in variation between the two is statistically significant, with the Postclassic having a more than 1.5 times larger coefficient of variation (Donis 2013, 81–82, 99–100). According to Donis (2013, 100), the range of variation in phosphate-oxygen isotope values in the Postclassic, when compared to her Historic-period sample, suggests within-lifetime mobility, particularly intraregionally—that is, within the areas around Lamanai. Climate fluctuation cannot yet be ruled out as causal, however (Donis 2013, 99–100); more of the Lamanai skeletal sample needs to be analyzed before firm conclusions can be drawn. As regards sex-related patterns, Postclassic females from Lamanai exhibit larger differences between their enamel and bone phosphate-oxygen isotope values than males, which suggests greater within-lifetime mobility for females than males (Donis 2013, 123), a phenomenon that may reflect marriage practices.

Lamanai's material culture, such as the metal artifacts (Pendergast 1981; Simmons and Shugar 2013; Simmons et al. 2009), and dietary practices (White 1997; White and Schwarcz 1989) certainly indicate inter- and intraregional connections. A small sample of burials points to the kind of mobility that facilitates such connections. There is a burial of two individuals, N11-5/7 (the "Loving Couple") (Pendergast 1989; White et al. 2009), who were originally reported as having phosphate-oxygen isotope enamel values that were higher than bone by 1–2 percent, and it was suggested that they came to Lamanai separately at an early age—perhaps from West Mexico, based on the style of the bronze artifacts associated with the burial (White et al. 2009). Donis's analysis of the enamel of one of the molars indicates instead that the individuals spent the first few years of their lives at a site isotopically similar to Lamanai (Donis 2013, 89–90, 99). The cultural markers of West Mexico could mean that they were descendants of immigrants maintaining homeland traditions. If this was the case, it would suggest that Lamanai was a cosmopolitan community not so different from Teotihuacan, albeit on a smaller scale.

Other individuals display non-Lamanai traditions or cultural markers. The woman in Burial N10-4/9A exhibits lambdoidal cranial flattening not found in other burials at Lamanai during the Postclassic; where it occurs, the standard cranial modification at Lamanai is fronto-occipital (White 1996). The woman's dental modification is also inconsistent with dental modifications displayed by other individuals at the site (Howie et al. 2010; Williams and White 2006, 140). In her case, however, unlike the "Loving Couple," her oxygen isotope composition suggests that she was born elsewhere before moving to Lamanai at least 10–15 years before she died (Donis 2013, 115; Howie et al. 2016; White 1996).

Of the 34 vessels from Terminal Classic and Postclassic burials interred in residential building groups examined petrographically by Howie and colleagues (Howie et al. 2010), eight were identified as geologically inconsistent with local raw-material resources and hence were manufactured elsewhere. The petrographic characteristics of one vessel reflect a riverine inland source in northern Belize; six vessels derive from raw-material resources situated adjacent to the coast in east or northeast Belize, extending into southern Yucatán, with three petrographically distinct production localities represented; and one vessel,

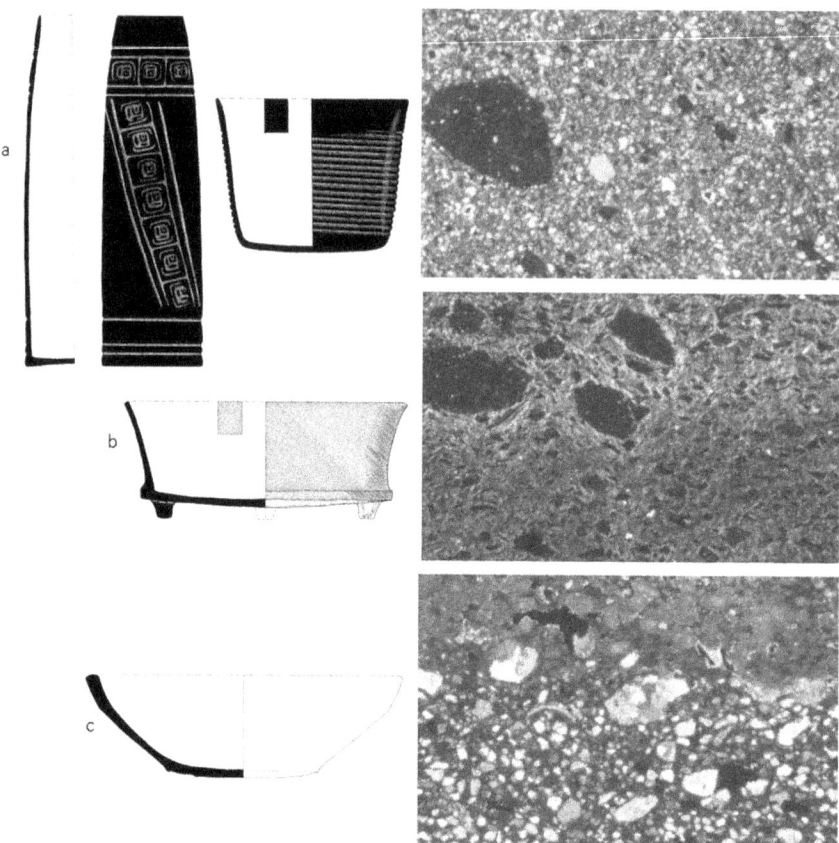

FIGURE 5.3. *Examples from Lamanai of nonlocal pottery included in burials within residential buildings. The vessels drawn on the left have pastes depicted in the photomicrographs on the right. (a) dolomitic marl-based fabric deriving from the coastal area of northeast northern Belize (×25); (b) fabric containing volcanoclastic temper (ash and crushed pumice) derived from source outside of northern Belize (×25); (c) crystalline calcite-tempered fabric containing snail shell and polycrystalline quartz derived from riverine clays in inland areas of northern Belize (×25). (Pottery illustrations by Louise Belanger; photomicrographs from Howie 2012, 146, figure 8.1g; 148, figure 8.3b; 157, figure 8.8c.)*

which contains volcanoclastic material (ash and crushed pumice), derives from a production locality outside the northern Belize region (figure 5.3). The individuals interred with nonlocal pottery are also distinctive in other respects. In one case the individual exhibits a style of dental modification not recorded elsewhere; in another, traces of red powder (cinnabar or red ochre) were found on the teeth. In both instances, the $\delta^{18}O$ values for enamel versus bone samples suggest relocation within the region since childhood, and dietary measures indicate atypical diets for Lamanai characterized by restricted consumption of marine

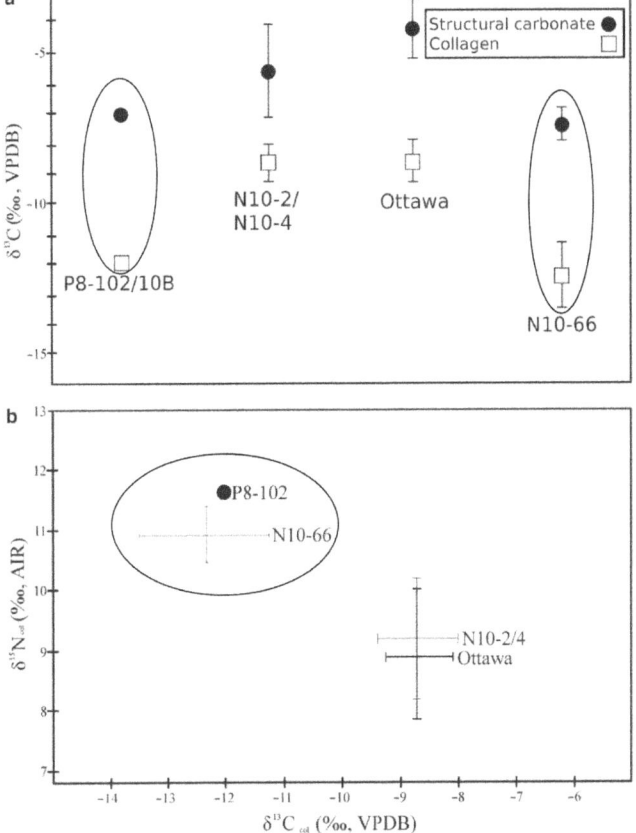

FIGURE 5.4. *Isotope values for enamel versus bone samples: means and standard deviations for (a) δ¹³C values of Lamanai collagen and bone bioapatite structural carbonate, and (b) δ¹⁵N versus δ¹³C values of Lamanai bone collagen. Residential groups with atypical diets for Lamanai are circled. (Howie et al. 2010, figure 3, 382.)*

resources (Howie et al. 2010) (figure 5.4). Other individuals interred within the same residential building groups were buried with locally produced stylistic imitations of the "foreign" pottery and had the same atypical diets. Taken together, the evidence strongly suggests the presence of immigrants within these residential units and an active attempt on the part of household members to maintain homeland traditions, as reflected in diet and grave goods. To date, therefore, evidence at Lamanai points to intraregional mobility of individuals in the Late / Terminal Classic and Early Postclassic, with movement of a group or population—those using sandy clays to make pots—initiated in the Terminal Classic but from that time becoming part of Lamanai cultural traditions.

The independence of the caye communities from the mainland is especially in evidence at the end of the Late Classic and throughout the Terminal Classic (end of the eighth through ninth centuries), when a new kind of burial dominated at Marco Gonzalez (Simmons and Graham 2017, 174). The excavations of Guderjan and colleagues (Guderjan and Garber 1995) on the north of Ambergris Caye (Chac Balam, San Juan, Ek Luum, Laguna de Cayo Francesa) recovered a greater chronological range of burials than is the case for Marco Gonzalez, but preservation of skeletal material in general was poor. Nonetheless, there is enough evidence to show that the burial positions of the Terminal Classic period in the north of the island seem to be more varied than those so far discovered at Marco Gonzalez.

In the interments at Marco Gonzalez, the individual was buried face down, with the lower legs flexed and bent backwards, and with the feet either over the buttocks or crossed between the thighs. This type of burial has been termed *VPLF* by Donis, for "ventrally placed, legs flexed" (Donis 2013, 112; Wrobel and Graham 2015, 87) (figure 5.5A). Out of 38 subfloor burials from Structures 14 and 12 at Marco Gonzalez, 30 were VPLF; four were supine with legs flexed in the manner of the VPLFs; and four were highly fragmented and incomplete (Simmons and Graham 2017; Wrobel and Graham 2013, 2015). In the excavations of Guderjan and colleagues in the north of the caye, there is only one certain VPLF—Burial 15 at Chac Balam—and two possible VPLFs from Chac Balam Burial 26 and Laguna de Cayo Francesa, Burial 1. None, however, had diagnostic artifacts (Glassman 1995).

The VPLF burial position does not appear on the mainland at Lamanai until the Early Postclassic Buk phase (late tenth to eleventh century) (Graham 2004; Pendergast 1982), where it is only one of a range of burial positions (Wrobel and Graham 2013, 2015) (figure 5.5b). VPLF burials at Lamanai generally occur along with Zakpah group ceramics. In fact, VPLF burials are either associated with Zakpah ceramics or have no ceramics at all, although there are sometimes other artifacts in these aceramic burials, such as shell objects (*Spondylus* or *Oliva* sp.), a jade pendant, or a chert blade. Of the total of 39 Buk-phase burials with VPLFs, five contained two individuals. One of the five had two VPLF interments; the other four each had a VPLF interment accompanied by an individual that was either extended and dorsally placed (2 instances); extended, ventrally placed (1 instance); or flexed on the right side (1 instance). Thus, the total of individuals laid out as VPLFs was 40.

Zakpah group ceramics are distinctive (see Pendergast 1982 or Buk-phase vessels in Graham 1987), with a distribution most commonly known from northern Belize inland and coastal sites, although examples are known from southern Belize (Howie 2012; Ting 2013; see Wrobel and Graham 2015, 86, figure 8.1).

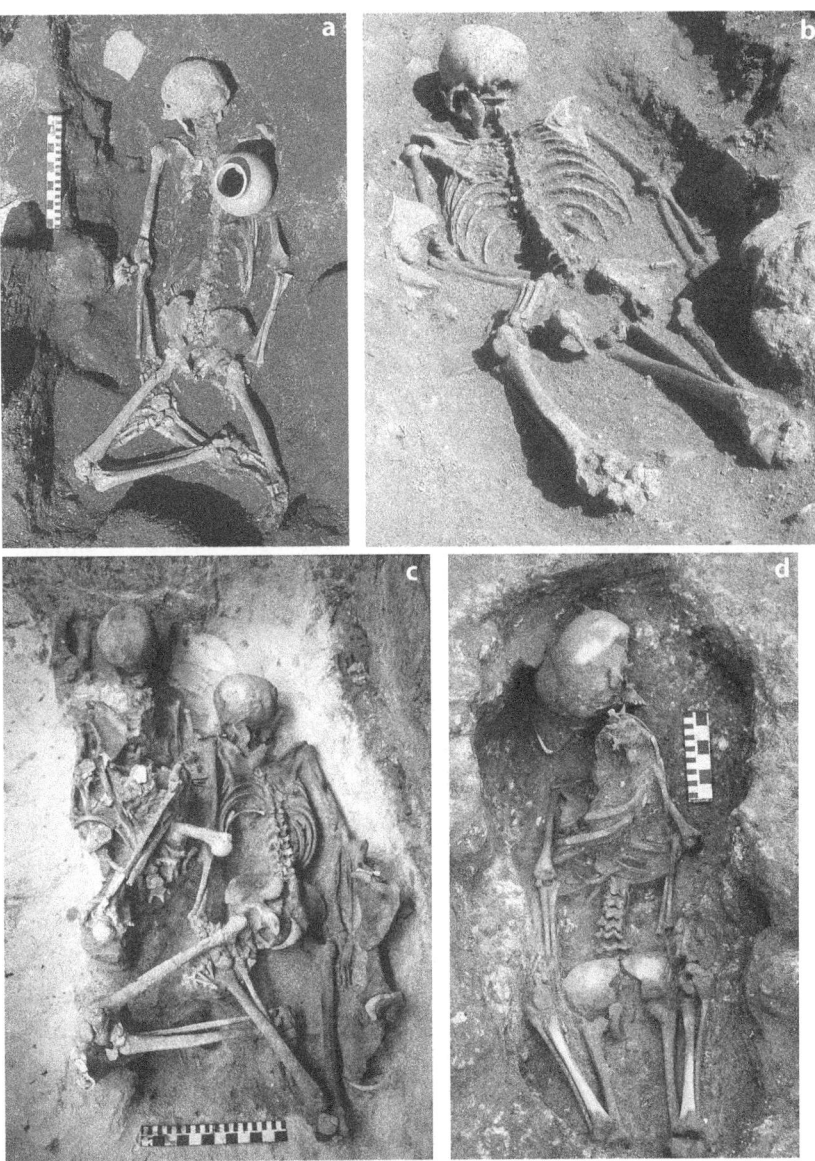

FIGURE 5.5. *Examples of VPLF burials from (a) Marco Gonzalez, Burial 14-27; (b) Lamanai, Burial N10-4/19; (c, d) San Pedro, from salvage excavations, Elvi's Restaurant. (Photos courtesy of Lamanai and Marco Gonzalez Projects.)*

Despite the changes in decorative techniques from Classic practices—incised or gouged as opposed to polychrome decoration, preference for a particular range of motifs (John 2008) and the use of grog temper—Zakpah-group ceramic production at Lamanai seems to have evolved locally, involving potters working within different technological traditions of manufacture; for example, different potters or groups of potters exploited traditional raw-material resources (Howie 2012, 139–178). As regards changes, a single approach to vessel manufacture replaced the multiple, internally consistent approaches of the Terminal Classic and Classic periods. By "single" we mean that Zakpah-group pottery exhibits a degree of stylistic and technological uniformity in that it shares stylistic, decorative, and petrographic characteristics, yet this "uniformity" is not standardized. Techniques instead are highly variable owing to differences in the technical procedures employed in production. Multiple tempers were employed in addition to the new use of grog, and raw-material ingredients were more rigorously processed to produce finer-textured fabrics than was the case in the Terminal Classic. In addition to incised and gouged decoration, the body geometry of vessels became more complex, with composite forms and hand-modeled elements (Howie 2012, 209–211).

Zakpah-group ceramics occur in abundance at Marco Gonzalez, although to date they have not been found in a primary context and hence not (yet?) with burials or caches. Petrographic analysis of Zakpah ceramics from Marco Gonzalez (Ting 2013) suggests, as does Howie's work at Lamanai (Howie 2012), that there is some sort of regional production specialization based at several communities in northern Belize. Lamanai burials with Zakpah ceramics have produced data from both ceramic and dietary analyses that suggest that the individuals interred were on the upper end of the social scale or at least had ample access to resources (see details in Howie et al. 2010; J. Metcalfe et al. 2009). The suggestion is based on the presence of copper/bronze artifacts (only two VPLF burials are associated with metal artifacts, however), dental modification traits, some distinctive cranial modification, and dietary variation. Only five VPLFs provide evidence through bone and enamel comparisons of having moved intraregionally, with one of these individuals (N10–4/9, Individual A), definitively born outside Lamanai, having come to the community after adolescence (Howie et al. 2010, 392–393). Of these five, only three—including N10–4/9, Individual A—are VPLFs. VPLFs along with Zakpah-group ceramics in burials are also found at Chau Hiix (Wrobel and Graham 2015, 87–88). Dietary isotopes suggest that all 10 individuals from the Chau Hiix burials except one (interred in an "urn"—probably one of the large Zakpah or Zalal pedestal-based, flanged jars) were distinct from those at Lamanai and were most likely from the coast (J. Metcalfe et al. 2009).

Both the dietary analyses of skeletal material and ceramic petrography carried out on Buk-phase samples at Lamanai provide evidence that the site's inhabitants had strong ties to communities on or near the coast (Howie et al. 2010; White 1997). We can therefore propose with some degree of support that there existed a coast-to-inland communication flow, with the attendant idea that people moved from the coast to inland communities and back fairly frequently. Can we also say that innovation in ideas about ritual and mortuary customs came to Lamanai via people traveling inland from the coast? Travel seems to have been the order of the day, and a well-developed degree of mobility—that is, regular movement of people across the land—characterized the Terminal Classic/Postclassic transition. A framework therefore existed that would have supported migration (at the level of the movement of families or groups) into Lamanai. What we know so far suggests largely intraregional mobility at the level of individuals, perhaps reflecting marriage patterns. There is also evidence to suggest migration in the Terminal Classic of people with a tradition of making pottery with sandy clays. In almost all cases, the movement is from east to west, or from coastal areas inland.

On the caye, we know from the burials salvaged from construction work in San Pedro that the VPLFs continued into Late Postclassic times (Pendergast and Graham 1991) (figure 5.5 c, d), whereas the burial practices at Lamanai in the later Postclassic would continue to be varied. This suggests that the island communities were integrated culturally in a way that was not characteristic of the mainland. With regard to the first appearance of the VPLF practice at Marco Gonzalez at ca. AD 800, the situation remains intriguing. Is it possible that enough people (foreign to the caye?) settled on the southern end of the island at the end of the Late Classic period to be termed a new population? (The presence of polychromes in two burials suggests that the town was built when polychromes were still being made and circulated.) At this point it is impossible to say. Although we have one burial from an Early Classic level with a supine interment (which has not been analyzed isotopically), we have no burials from the Late Classic with which to compare the later prone burials. Excavations by Guderjan and colleagues, however, show no VPLF individuals in burials dated to the Late Classic period (Glassman 1995).

The dramatic change from intensive salt processing on the island in the Late Classic period (ca. AD 600–750/800) to the building of a town (by ca. AD 800) reflects a renewed focus, at the time of the southern lowland Classic collapse, on circumpeninsular trade in items other than salt (Graham et al. 2017; Simmons and Graham 2017). A parallel to the appearance of the VPLFs in Maya history can perhaps be found in the sociopolitical and religious upheaval and warfare that characterized the Spanish Conquest, when a similarly dramatic change in burial practice occurred, accompanied by economic, social, and political change (Graham et al. 2013). If the VPLFs do not represent a new population on the caye, they could be the daughters and sons of an island generation that underwent conflict and lost, or that was accommodating to a new generation of merchant groups controlling trade, or that had adopted new cultural beliefs that entailed new mortuary practices—or any and all of these factors. Future extensive excavation as well as further dietary studies of the skeletal material (Williams et al. 2009) should go some way toward resolving this issue. We should also consider, however, that if conquest and/or conversion took place, and if the sixteenth century is any guide, then such phenomena can trigger movements of people on a relatively large scale. These movements need not have been of large scale in terms of the sizes of the groups moving, but may have been large in terms of the frequency and nature of the moves, thus deeply affecting the peninsula's historical trajectory and cultural continuity.

Who Moved, and in What Direction?

The question of who moved cannot be answered, but the evidence presented so far allows us to propose hypotheses that can be tested in future investigations at both Lamanai and Marco Gonzalez. The new tradition of coarseware manufacture at Lamanai in the Terminal Classic period (Howie 2012, 139–178) can perhaps best be explained by the east–west movement of small groups of people who once lived in communities on the plain, such as Altun Ha or Colha. Why people moved is another question, but evidence is beginning to emerge of a shift of some groups from the coastal plain to inland locations. The people practicing the new tradition of coarseware manufacture seem to have integrated without difficulty into the Lamanai community as witnessed by the facts that (1) the new tradition added to but did not replace other traditions and (2) the new tradition became part of local cultural practice and continued into at least the Late Postclassic. The toppling of Stela 9, with its early seventh-century dates, in the late eighth or early ninth century (Pendergast 1988), suggests some sort of turnover of the ruling stratum at ca. AD 800. There were implications for material culture: pottery slips lost their gloss, polychromes became sketchier, forms evolved, and civic buildings began to be constructed of wood. At the same time, there was continuity in caching and burial practices (Lentz et al. 2016). Given the combination of continuity of some cultural traditions with the loss of cultural value placed on glossy slips or masonry architecture, the "new" ruling elites may well have been local—or, from the region around Lamanai who settled locally—but not royal. The decreased emphasis on monumental masonry architecture could reflect an inability to call on the necessary labor, or it could simply show that priorities lay elsewhere. We hazard that population movements took place in the Terminal Classic, but were manifested in local shifts of small numbers of people, perhaps families, who moved as an effort to adjust to new conditions.

The VPLF burials seem to reflect a new mortuary ritual—and possibly a new belief related to death and dying—at both Marco Gonzalez and at Lamanai. Studies geared specifically to explore the movement of people have not yet been carried out at Marco Gonzalez. Initial stable isotope analyses were carried out by Donis at Lamanai (Donis 2013, 112–120), and a study of genetic relatedness among Early Postclassic groups in northern Belize was carried out by Wrobel, who compared the Lamanai and Chau Hiix material using dental morphology (Wrobel and Graham 2013, 2015). Results of both studies show that the VPLF burial position crosscuts other criteria, even those of status. The Lamanai burials represent different demographic groups; nonlocals or immigrants might be present but they are in the minority (Donis 2013, 119). On the caye at Marco Gonzalez, VPLFs represent a more sweeping change, but at this stage we have not compared the sample isotopically with burials from earlier periods. The fact that the VPLF mortuary practice is earlier on the caye than at Lamanai, is, however, highly significant. We do not yet know its origin, but the pattern of occurrence so far implies incremental dynamics rather than large-scale migration.

If the new mortuary practice was brought to Marco Gonzalez in the Terminal Classic period (beginning in the late eighth and continuing through the ninth and early tenth centuries) and then to Lamanai in the Early Postclassic (beginning in the late tenth century) by nonlocal individuals yet to be detected, they were a new kind of "nonelite" elite, and the practices were maintained (at Lamanai among other burial practices) by a broad population base. What is interesting is that the burials at Marco Gonzalez in the Terminal Classic period fit Classic-period practices in all but the VPLF position. At Lamanai, the Early Postclassic interments contained individuals, among them the VPLFs, all of whom could be said to have replaced the Classic-period elites and to have eschewed the symbols of Classic-period elite status.

WHERE TO GO FROM HERE?

Perhaps all we can propose at this stage is that the mortuary practices associated with VPLFs are part of a larger dynamic of change that characterized the Terminal Classic in parts of the eastern Maya lowlands. The overall direction of cultural change, at least in the eastern lowlands—as suggested by the new sandy-clay coarseware tradition at Lamanai and the earlier appearance of the VPLFs on the caye—was east to west, from the coast to inland locations. Migration is manifested in the movements of individuals and perhaps families or small groups, but such movements were facilitated, and adjusted to, owing to a resilience afforded by a long history of mobility. By and large, such movements were also intraregional.

In the Early Postclassic, the Zakpah group pottery at Marco Gonzalez seems to reflect the presence of a new kind of power base at Lamanai, and hence suggests the existence of a mainland-to-coast trajectory to complement the coast-to-mainland dynamic reflected in the arrival of the VPLF burial tradition at Lamanai. Zakpah-group pottery was produced at Lamanai and at other locations in northern Belize, possibly including Marco Gonzalez. As pointed out by Howie (Howie 2012), there was adherence to local traditions and practices at the same time that design elements, forms, and decorative technology were new. The new elements were a response to new demands that did not conform to Classic-period aesthetics. In addition, the widespread presence at Lamanai of Zakpah-group pottery in burials and caches in both ceremonial and residential contexts suggests the cessation of the Classic-period dynastic appropriation of luxury goods, and the decline of Classic-period values. The new demands and tastes, in the circumstances described, could have been generated by nonlocals, or perhaps by locals who had adopted, by one means or another, nonlocal values. If this hypothesis can be supported—and at present it is highly speculative—then migration of power-seekers with non–Classic Maya values must have taken place by the late tenth or early eleventh century. That these "power-seekers" came to dominate suggests that generating conflict against traditional elites, and overcoming them, was the mechanism of change. Given Mesoamerican rules of engagement (Aoyama and Graham 2015), such conflict did not necessitate large armies but instead could have been instigated by aggressive nouveau-elite factions. If conflict and competition were more or less confined to the non-commoner level, this would help to explain the population stability evidenced in the persistence of local manufacturing traditions.

The foregoing discussion is highly preliminary and by no means proven. It is intriguing to hypothesize, however, that the dynamic population movements in northern Belize and the cayes in the transition to the Postclassic period were a response to movements of power seekers or nouveau elites who either generated instability through conflict or took advantage of it. Although it is often said that we need to expand our studies of commoners, it is the individuals seeking wealth and power (and not royal status) in the late eighth through ninth centuries who were the harbingers of change. With their demands, values, and expectations, and very possibly with new rules of engagement in warfare and aggression, they seem to have had the potential to disrupt and undermine longstanding traditions of rulership and governance. At the same time, they encouraged, and took advantage of, stable community practices, particularly the practices of communities such as Lamanai and Marco Gonzalez, whose members were long successful in building flexible commercial and social networks tied to trade and exchange.

6

Maya on the Move

Mobility and Migration in the Classic Maya Kingdom of Copan, Honduras

NANCY GONLIN AND KRISTIN V. LANDAU

Archaeology is the story of migrations and how humans have left their mark across the world as they traversed it for a variety of reasons. From the smallest to the largest, archaeological sites contain a wealth of information that can answer questions about how, when, where, and why people in the past were on the move. Here, we hope to elucidate the ways in which the mobility of the inhabitants of the Classic Maya kingdom of Copan, Honduras, are decipherable from the archaeological record (figure 0.1, Introduction). The The mobility of our millennia-old species is manifested in various ways that are recoverable through different types of inquiry. Linguistic, archaeological, and bioarchaeological data have all been successfully used to tease apart the timing of movements of people (e.g., Cabana and Clark 2011a; Cucina 2015a; Leblanc 2015). For example, Jane Hill (2015, 362) concludes that "the geographic distribution of Mesoamerican linguistic diversity suggests that migration, both short- and long-range was an important social process in all periods of Mesoamerican prehistory." We also borrow findings from others who have conducted isotopic research on the inhabitants of Copan. As previous research has shown (Beekman and Christensen 2003,

DOI: 10.5876/9781646420735.c006

115), the integration of multiple datasets is most effective, if not requisite, for the anthropological study of migration. Models provided by David Anthony (1990) and Charles Tilly (1978) help to structure arguments that use archaeological data.

In this chapter, we amalgamate Nancy Gonlin's study of remains of ancient rural households throughout the Copan Valley with Kristin Landau's research in the urban neighborhood of San Lucas to argue that studies of population mobility need to incorporate multiple scales—geographic coverage that encompasses various communities, rural and urban domains, and recognition of contemporaneity issues. We hope to generalize from the particular examples provided here to contribute to the understanding of mobility within ancient cities and their hinterlands, and de-urbanizing processes that mirror the rise and fall of societies. Anthony (1990, 905) has astutely observed that "migration is a process, not an event, and as the process unfolds it generates its own dynamics." Archaeological signatures of this process manifest themselves in identifiable ways. Some material indicators for population mobility at Copan relevant to the present study are evidenced through construction episodes, settlement patterns, bioarchaeological data, burials, and artifactual signatures that are potentially indicative of ethnicity.

This volume focuses on population dynamics of ancient cities from macro- and microdemographic perspectives to assess mobility either across an entire region or in a particular area. Although, in their introduction to this volume, the editors consider mobility as a broad range of physical movements, and migration as a disruptive, unusual event, a global long-term perspective suggests to us that migration was quite common. Therefore, we understand *mobility* to refer to the *potential* or capacity for movement within a particular area (e.g., Graham and Howie, chapter 5, this volume; Inomata 2004; Ortega Muñoz 2015; Richards-Rissetto and Landau 2014), and *migration* as an umbrella category with several types.

Here, we promote Tilly's (1978; see also M. E. Smith 2014) discussion of types of migration (table 6.1) for its structuring of archaeological data. Tilly classified migration based on distance (over space and time) and social cleavage from community of origin (low to high). Moving short distances without a social break is "local migration"; moving a circuitous route over months or years and returning to the origin with minimal social break is "circular migration." "Chain migration" involves permanent movement to a new place with the encouragement and aid of those currently living there. For example, chain migration is the predominant type now experienced in the United States and European countries, with migrants requesting asylum to live with loved ones already abroad. "Career migration" involves a move to a new place, predominantly for work with like-minded colleagues, with a maximum break from previous social groups. In terms of this volume's characterization of migration, we would include chain

TABLE 6.1. Tilly's (1978) migration types

Distance	Social Cleavage	
	Low	High
Short	Local migration	Circular migration
Long	Chain migration	Career migration

and career migration as macrodemographic perspectives, and local and circular migration as microdemographic perspectives. Are these models realized with archaeological data, and are they useful in understanding ancient migration? Below, we first review processes of urbanization and de-urbanization at the ancient city of Copan, and then review categories of archaeological data by type (isotopes, artifacts, features, and architecture). Finally, we discuss what each data type might imply about Tilly's forms of migration, from local to career.

COPAN URBANIZATION

Situated at the western edge of Honduras, Copan is unique among the Classic (AD 250–900) lowland Maya centers for its frontier location at the Maya/Lenca linguistic boundary (figure 6.1). Ethnic heterogeneity may have prevailed before, during, and after the existence of the Maya dynasty that ruled the area for almost 400 years (Andrews and Fash 2005, 407–8; Bell and Canuto 2008; Canuto and Bell 2013; Demarest 1996; Fash 2001b; Gonlin 1993, 696–700; Landau 2010; Longyear 1952; Maca 2009; Schortman 1986; Viel 1993, 1999). Copan grew both in size and density from Middle (AD 400–600) to Late Classic (AD 600–900) times, as evidenced by increased numbers of contemporaneous houses in the city center and outlying valleys, and population crowding onto the best lands, resulting in the extraordinary population expansion during this time. David Webster (2018, 104) remarks that "this pattern, which seems to hold for much of the southern Lowlands, is one of the biggest demographic puzzles of Maya population history." Social, economic, and political processes within this ancient city waxed and waned as such demographic shifts occurred.

Evidence for early farmers in the Copan region dates as far back as the Preclassic period of Mesoamerica, to about 1400 BC, based on ceramics, but as long ago as 2400 BC as indicated by sediment cores (McNeil et al. 2010; Webster et al. 2013; Webster et al. 2005). Radiocarbon dates from beneath Copan's Acropolis place the establishment of the city to the Terminal Preclassic/Early Classic transition, around AD 100–420 (Sharer et al. 2005, 142). Rural occupation occurred at Los Achiotes (about 22 km east of Copan) and the local quarry of Cerro Chino (at the terminus of the western sacbe), where the remnants of offerings and a possible ritual building existed (Canuto 2004; Maca 2002). The areas immediately adjacent to the future Principal Group, El Bosque and Sepulturas, were

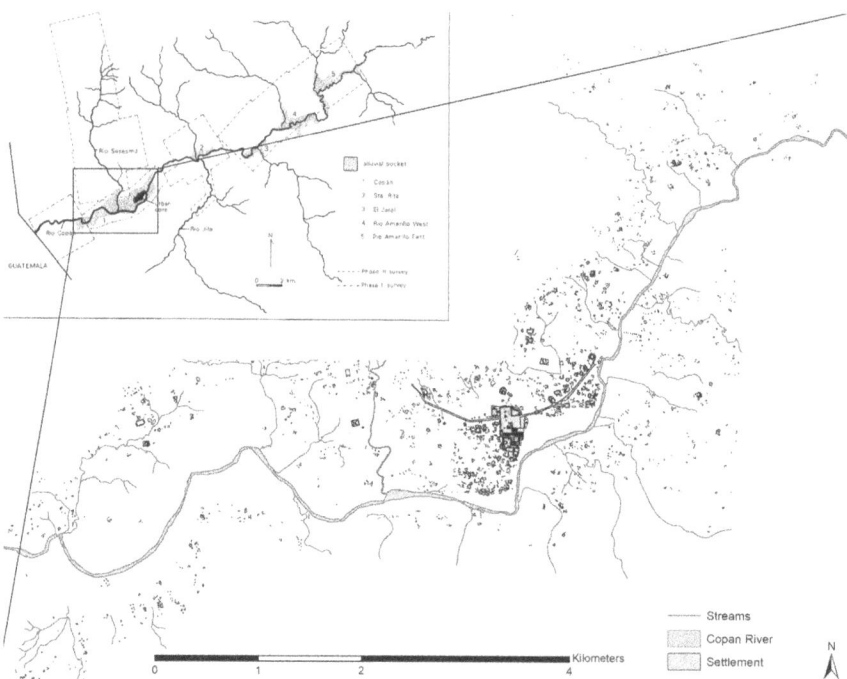

FIGURE 6.1. *Alluvial pockets (inset) along the Copan River in western Honduras, with enlargement of the settlement across the Copan Pocket, the largest area of fertile alluvium along the river's course. (Figure by Kristin V. Landau, based on data digitized by Richards-Rissetto [2010] from Fash and Long [1983].)*

also inhabited in the Preclassic. A few groups of people settled at higher elevations on the south side of the valley (Landau 2016; Ramos 2010). After *K'inich Yax K'uk' Mo'*, the first dynastic leader, arrived at Copan in AD 426, cut-stone architecture and monuments with hieroglyphic writing appeared at the center of the ancient city as we know it today. Refugees escaping the violent destruction of the Ilopango eruption, now dated to August/September of AD 539 (Payson Sheets, personal communication, April 21, 2019), might have sought shelter in nearby Copan at this time (Dull et al. 2001). Copan's apogee is thought to have occurred during the height of population expansion, during the twelfth and thirteenth rulers' reigns from AD 628 to 738 (Fash 2001b), as residents expanded their families and migrants reached the valley (Fash 2001b, chapter 2). However, peak population occurred by about AD 820 (Freter and Abrams 2016, 98), after which time residents abandoned the kingdom.

For our purposes, we define the urban core of Classic-period Copan as the 1.5 km² area that encompasses the major administrative and elite residences,

FIGURE 6.2. *Map of the urban core of Classic Copan, located in the Copan Pocket, which includes the Principal Group of monumental architecture (center) and its two urban neighborhoods of Las Sepulturas (east) and El Bosque (west). (Figure by Kristin V. Landau, based on data digitized by Richards-Rissetto [2010] from Fash and Long [1983].)*

including the Principal Group, El Bosque, and Sepulturas (figure 6.2). About half of the population at Copan's peak lived in the core (Webster et al. 2000, 177). The larger Copan Pocket includes the 24 km² surveyed urban and rural areas of the most fertile sections of the valley. Within the pocket, surveyors (Leventhal 1979; Willey and Leventhal 1979) identified subcommunities, or urban neighborhoods, and defined them as areas of higher density settlement between small streams. Results from excavations at two of these urban neighborhoods (Ostuman and San Lucas) are discussed below, along with the remains of households uncovered across the wider Copan Valley (Gonlin 1993; Webster and Gonlin 1988).

In the seventh century, the twelfth ruler erected stelae throughout the valley, possibly serving as territorial markers of the expanding kingdom (Fash 2001b; Marcus 1976; Spinden 1913). After the defeat and beheading of the thirteenth king by Quirigua in AD 738, residents of Copan did not see another strong leader until the last and sixteenth ruler took power 25 years later. The last dated—and unfinished—monument bears a Long Count inscription of AD 822. The characteristics and timing of abandonment after *Yax Pahsaj Chan Yopat*'s death are contentious issues at Copan, with some arguing for a slow decline over time (Freter 1988, 1993; Paine and Freter 1996; Paine et al. 1996; Webster and Freter 1990; Webster et al. 2000; Webster et al. 1993; Webster et al. 2004) and others for rapid abandonment and population replacement (Anovitz et al. 1999; Bill 1997; Braswell 1992; Braswell et al. 2000; Fash et al. 2004; Maca 2002; Manahan 2003, 2004; McNeil et al. 2010). Regardless of one's stance on this particular issue, major demographic shifts occurred throughout the region during the Classic and Postclassic periods, which have left their indelible mark in the archaeological record. It is to these markers of population mobility that we turn below.

DEMOGRAPHY BACKGROUND

Explanations for demographic shifts and their consequences ultimately depend on population estimates, which have been based on a variety of methods. The seminal volume by T. Patrick Culbert and Don S. Rice published in 1990 provided Mayanists with an overview of the then-state-of-the-art methods and interpretations of *Precolumbian Population History in the Maya Lowlands*. Counts of mounds, rooms, platforms, patios, burials, and sherds were and still are among the most popular ways by which archaeologists deduce the size of past populations. Other methods include chultun counts and their volumes (McAnany 1990), roofed surfaces of dwellings (Becquelin and Michelet 1994; Kolb 1985), insights from palynology (Rue 1986), agricultural modeling (Wingard 1992, 2016), and estimates of construction costs (Abrams 1984; Carrelli 2004). All methods ultimately depend upon the ability to recover one's preferred artifact/feature/site in quantities that accurately reflect past habitation and the ability to accurately control for contemporaneity.

Anthony (1990, 899–905) regards the study of migration as patterned human behavior, contrasting migrations of short distances with those of long distances to understand the structure of migrations and how different conditions favor different types. He refers to these conditions as "push-pull factors." Although we recognize that migrants did not necessarily have a choice in leaving or arriving, or if they did, that choice may have been coerced or severely constrained (Cameron 2013), we find the push-pull dichotomy a useful way of thinking from migrants' perspectives. The attractiveness of the Copan Valley to an agrarian population would have been high and serve to pull away people from their homelands. The rich alluvium in the Copan Pocket and other smaller pockets in the valley would have made for productive agriculture, a condition that is still true today. Abundant rainfall would have ensured harvests. Settlement near the river would have provided sources of protein, a mode of transportation and trade, (dry-season) drinking water, and areas for washing. The slightly higher elevation (600 masl) of Copan in comparison to other lowland Maya centers supported a lush tropical vegetation with numerous tree species, supplying the raw material for building, tools, and firewood (Lentz 1991). The forests supported populations of deer, peccary, monkeys, birds, jaguars, and many other species. Outcrops of rhyolite at Petapilla could have been quarried for ground-stone implements. Volcanic tuff was in great supply, as was limestone, and other building materials. Several clay sources are known throughout the valley that are ideal for pottery manufacture (Baudez 1983). Soil studies (Wingard 1992, 2016) and an analysis of the longevity of groups in various locales (Inomata 2004; Paine and Freter 1996; Paine, et al. 1996) generally support Anthony's modeling of migration in terms of the factors that impact a group's or an individual's decision to stay or leave.

Other than economic resources, additional pull factors might have included defense (safety in numbers within a valley surrounded by mountains), labor pooling or organic solidarity, religion and ideology, social promotion, and political control (see Cowgill 2003). For example, the massive defensive features at the Petexbatun site of Punta de Chimino likely attracted a large population during periods of endemic warfare in the Terminal Classic (Demarest, et al. 1997). Christopher Beekman (2015, 84; see also Inomata et al. 2015) suggests that new centers during the Early Classic engaged in a new migration strategy, "in which competing centers wooed newly mobile populations with novel interpretations of Mesoamerican ideology." Distinctive artistic styles used in sculpture, architecture, murals, and artifacts would have communicated new and exciting renditions of Mesoamerican cosmologies to "advertise" and maintain migrants at the incipient center. Houston and colleagues (2003) refer to this phenomenon in relation to Piedras Negras as a "moral community" convened by the holy lord. All in all, as the largest Maya frontier site with monumental architecture in the southeastern area, the Copan Valley would have much to offer agriculturalists and social climbers living in the region. What were the push factors that impelled settlers to leave their homelands to venture to the Copan Valley? While an understudied topic, we hypothesize that push factors might include unavailability of fertile land, overcrowding in the Late Classic, possible disease or lack of nutrients, resistance to hegemonic power, warfare (as in the case of Aguateca), or environmental change, among others. As other case studies have shown, perhaps ancient residents could also "vote with their feet" and it was the job of Copan leaders to maintain demographic stability (Beekman 2015, 82–83).

EVIDENCE OF MIGRATION IN THE COPAN VALLEY

While part of Copan's population growth over time into further outlying areas in the pocket can be attributed to reproductive rates, migration played an underappreciated role. For example, with a sample of 97 burials from Tikal, Guatemala, Andrew Scherer and Lori Wright (2015) determined through strontium isotope analysis that 11 individuals (11.3%) were of nonlocal origin at this major Classic

Maya center, a "remarkably high" number in comparison to other ancient cities around the world. Additionally, recent strontium isotope analysis on a sample of Copan's skeletal collection ($n = 141$) demonstrates that the migrant population may have been between 10 and 40 percent, depending on neighborhood affiliation (Miller 2015). This type of migration may fall into any three of Tilly's migration types. If residents moved from periphery to core or vice versa, local migration occurred. If new migrants joined previous ones, then chain migration operated; if individuals were moving to a new location altogether, then career migration would characterize this pattern. However, it is difficult to discern exactly which type or combination occurred; the categories and quality of archaeological data at this stage do not necessarily allow clear distinctions. Nevertheless, in some areas of Late Classic Copan, nearly half of the residents came from elsewhere, making it a veritable "city of immigrants." For modern comparison, based on the 2010 census, about 41 percent of Chicago residents were born outside of the city of Chicago; anthropological research has shown time and again that ancient and modern cities are not categorically different (e.g., M. E. Smith 2008b, 2010a; M. L. Smith 2003).

A prime example of career migration exists in the establishment of the Copan dynasty, for the city was founded by a migrant as detected through bioarchaeological studies (Buikstra et al. 2008; Buikstra, et al. 2004). According to chemical analyses by Price and colleagues (2010), *K'inich Yax K'uk' Mo'* appears to have been born and to have spent his early years in the southern and central Maya lowlands. Another tomb, west of Copan center, might hold the remains of an Early Classic king (one of the first six rulers), who migrated to Copan from the southern Maya lowlands (Price et al. 2014, figure 9). Copan's eighth ruler probably moved to the city from nearby Quirigua when he was between four and nine years old (Price et al. 2010). As one of the more straightforward "careers" in Maya society to analyze, it seems that migration from the Maya region to Copan was not uncommon for kings.

In a subsequent article, Price et al. (2014) determined strontium and oxygen values of 32 individuals selected from a rescue operation due west of the Acropolis, some of whom were commoners while others were elites, as evidenced by grave type, grave goods, and other metrics (Price et al. 2014, table 1). Since the sample size is small, conclusions drawn from these data are necessarily tentative. However, significantly, the researchers (Price et al. 2014, 43) note that "both sexes are equally represented not only among locals (4:4), but also among foreigners (5:5)." The similar male-to-female ratio among foreigners, along with the almost complete absence of younger individuals (i.e., subadults), provides demographic evidence for Tilly's (1978) chain migration, or possibly local migration—difficult to distinguish due to the resolution and variability in isotopic values. The absence of younger individuals along with a lack of material evidence that might distinguish local people from migrants in burial contexts suggest that nuclear families with few or no children settled in this area of Copan, likely as part of and with the help of already-present family units (Price et al. 2014, 43). Larger sample sizes and isotopic testing inclusive of central Honduran strontium and oxygen isotope values further suggest that migrants to Copan originated from non-Maya centers in Honduras, and that "migration was the norm rather than the exception throughout prehistory" (Miller Wolf and Freiwald 2018, 805; also Tsuda 2011).

MAYA ON THE MOVE WITHIN URBAN NEIGHBORHOODS

The majority of the Copan hinterlands are thought to have been settled during the mid-seventh century, during the long reign of the twelfth ruler (Fash 2001b). However, due to major post-abandonment soil deposition, earlier settlement may be buried under as many as 2 m of dirt in the valley and foothill zones (Fash and Sharer 1991; Hendon 2012). Therefore, targeted excavations that pay careful attention to chronology in specific areas or zones may best reveal the history of polity-wide settlement. Here we briefly discuss a few cases of mobility in the urban neighborhoods of San Lucas (1 km southeast of the center) and Ostuman (3.5 km west of the center) in the wider Copan Pocket (figure 6.3).

Recent work to the south of the urban core indicates that small families with cultural ties to central/eastern Honduras might have settled in San Lucas as early as the Preclassic. A rescue project unearthed the mammiform supports of a ceramic vessel (ca. AD 100) associated with a grave in a small architectural group (Ramos 2010). In another neighboring group, excavations revealed the burial of a poorly preserved woman in her mid-40s, who survived long-term nutritional deficiency and suffered complete antemortem tooth loss (Miller report in Landau 2014). She was buried in a simple grave with a large proportion of broken utilitarian serving wares dating to the Terminal Preclassic (cal. AD 196 ± 65 years, two-sigma). The eastern structure of this group was settled around the time that *K'inich Yax K'uk' Mo'* arrived at Copan; however, the high quantity of Acbi-phase *candeleros* recovered represents the continued shared tradition with regions in central Honduras and eastward (Douglass 2007). An artifact unique to southeast Mesoamerica, candeleros "reflect both a common cultural heritage as well as a continuing community interaction" with people outside of the Copan polity (Bill 2014, 90). Preclassic settlement and material culture in San Lucas hint that the first settlers may have been migrants from the east (Manahan and Canuto 2009), though determining migration from material culture can be highly problematic (Beekman and Christensen 2011; Tsuda 2011, 329).

The unique carved-rock outcrop in San Lucas, known locally as "Los Sapos" and associated with Group 12M-1, was likely a special ritual and possibly transformative place for royalty (figure 6.4). The bedrock jutting out of the surface of the

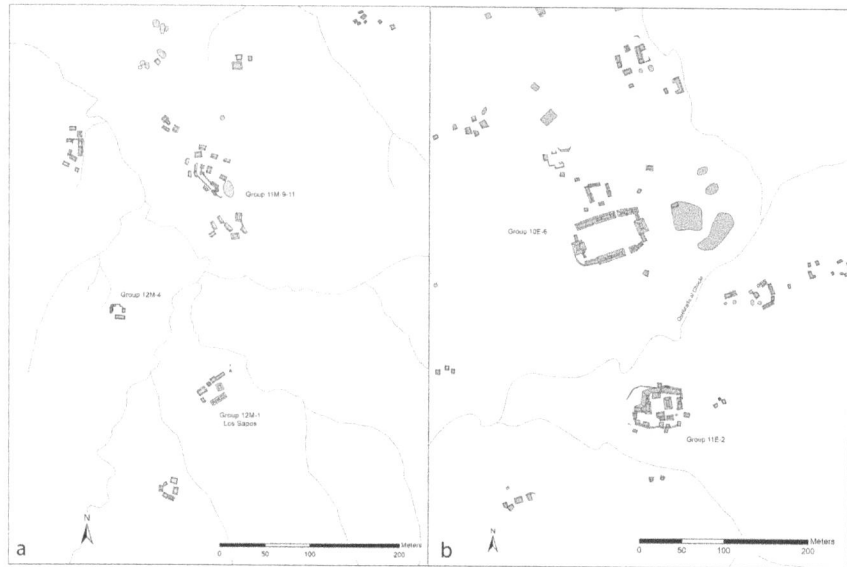

FIGURE 6.3. *Map of (a) San Lucas and (b) Ostuman architecture discussed in text. (Figure by Kristin V. Landau, based on data digitized by Richards-Rissetto [2010] from Fash and Long [1983].)*

earth was carved into aquatic animal figures (a toad and crocodile), architectural elements (raised and flat conical altars, three series of steps), and a male figure with headdress performing an act of autosacrifice. The toad depicts "el Rey Sapo" and possibly represents a species of toad that secretes a hallucinogenic substance through its conspicuous parotid glands (Bodamer 2002; Davis and Weil 1992; Dobkin de Rios 1974; Guernsey Kappelman 2000). Los Sapos occupies a sloped area between an architectural group behind it to the southwest and higher in elevation (Group 12M-1), and a deep depression to its northeast. Landau's (2016) excavations at the architectural group isolated a water canal that would have carried rainwater from the group's plaza, around a temple, and down and over Los Sapos. The aquatic symbolism and landscape features together suggest that the area was conceived as a sacred place for agricultural fertility and rain; an earlier field school (Fash 2001a) found a high proportion of artifacts relating to food preparation, and perhaps the celebration also involved feasting and food offerings to the gods. Small batrachian sculptures are known also from commoner habitation sites (11D-11-2 and 7D-3-1) in other locales of the Valley (Gonlin 2007, 101–103). Claude Baudez (2008) believed that Los Sapos represents the remains of what he called a local "popular religion" (vs. the aristocratic religion of the Maya elites) (L. Brown 2000; McAnany 2012). He hypothesized that the villagers who remained

FIGURE 6.4. *"El Rey Sapo" (a toad), one of the several aquatic figures carved into a natural outcrop of bedrock at Los Sapos, Group 12M-1. (Photograph by Kristin V. Landau.)*

after the fall of the city practiced this popular religion at Los Sapos. While ceramic dating here does not support Baudez's ideas, the existence of religious pluralism (Leventhal 1983) at Copan, perhaps attested to by Los Sapos, suggests the cosmopolitan nature of urban neighborhoods and generations of migrations.

Attention to dating and the life history of particular architectural groups in the San Lucas neighborhood also reveal local (likely within Copan) migrations of elite people. A large swath of land was engineered (i.e., flattened) for building and an architectural group was built and settled about 150 m due north of Los Sapos after AD 700. Originally classified as a commoner (Type 2) settlement, recent excavations show that Group 11M-9–11's specialized architectural style and sculpture supported several families. The largest building of this group is an anomaly for the area: with cut volcanic tuff stones, a vaulted arch, inset niche, windows, and sculpture, it is easily the most elite and unanticipated feature of San Lucas (figure 6.5). The sculpture pieces identified represent stylized maize foliation, and were likely once part of a *witz*, or mountain mask (personal communications, Karl Taube 2013 and Jorge Ramos 2014). This kind of iconography was also found in association with Temple 22 in Copan's center, the thirteenth ruler's elaborate throne room, showing an affiliation between these residents and royal symbols. According to ceramic chronology, the San Lucas building was constructed after AD 700 but was no longer occupied after the dynasty collapsed.

FIGURE 6.5. *Architectural features of the largest building of Group 11M-9–11 include cut volcanic tuff stones, vaulted arch, inset niche, windows, and sculpture. (Photograph by Kristin V. Landau.)*

Before the building was constructed and likely before the construction of the entire architectural complex, a large labor force undertook a massive leveling program whereby they brought fill material to San Lucas from the urban core, as much as a kilometer away and across the river. This fill likely originates from the urban core due to the high-status garbage found within it, including broken jade objects and misshapen Pachuca obsidian projectiles. The sudden establishment and settlement of Group 11M-9–11 by people with some connection to or support from Copan elites or royals at the urban core suggest that San Lucas hosted new migrants at a (short) geographic distance, but symbolic proximity to Copan's center.

Another area of the Copan Pocket, the intermontane valley of Ostuman, seems to have been settled by Maya individuals of high status by AD 650 (Whittington 1991). There are two larger architectural groups in the area located adjacent to one another: Groups 10E-6 (north) and 11E-2 (south) (see figure 6.3b). The largest building of the northern group was adorned with a sculptured stone mosaic, the farthest west from the urban core that any sculpture yet has been discovered at Copan. It also appears, according to further excavations in the southern group, that people lived in Ostuman after the AD 822 "collapse" of dynastic rule. A male individual was buried with a Pabellón Modeled-Carved vase, a type of Fine Orange vessel produced in Petén only after AD 830. Other vessels of this type were found in Copan's Salamar area (Ashmore 1991) and in the East Court of Copan's urban core. Although instrumental trace-element analysis on these vessels has yet to be performed (e.g., Domínguez Carrasco and Folan Higgins 2015), whether they are exotic in origin or locally made copies still points to travel (a kind of long-distance mobility) and knowledge of foreign ceramic form and decoration.

MAYA ON THE MOVE IN THE HINTERLANDS

There are various ways of detecting migratory behaviors in the Copan Valley. While isotopic analyses of human skeletons have focused on royalty or those buried in the urban core, other categories of evidence provide clues for under-standing the origins of the majority of the population. As Andrea Cucina (2015b, 78) notes, "although they do not leave behind 'interesting' traces of their existence, and therefore do not catch the attention of archaeologists, it is the movement of commoners that eventually modifies the structure of a popula-tion." In this section, we look at evidence from a few of the eight small sites (Type 1 in Copan's site hierarchy) in Copan's hinterland that were explored by David Webster's Rural Sites Project (Gonlin 1993; Webster and Gonlin 1988). Of interest is the lack of burials recovered from excavations of the remains of low-status households throughout the Copan Valley, a pattern that was first observed by AnnCorinne Freter (1988) in her extensive test-pitting program and later con-firmed with in-depth excavations of selected rural sites (Gonlin 1993, 1994, 2007; Webster and Freter 1990). Landau (2016) also found an unexpectedly low number of burials at San Lucas (only one, with an additional two left unexcavated from the nearby rescue operation). Gonlin (1993; 2007, 94–95) has previously written about the lack of burials in the rural area and potential explanations for the behaviors reflected in this pattern. The differences may lie in ethnic origins, lineage ties for Copan groups, economics, or as yet-undiscovered burial prac-tices among the kingdom's rural population. Notable for our studies here is the observation that when families abandon their homes to migrate to new areas, they may take burial remains with them (Barrientos et al. 2015).

Site 34A-12-2 is located 5.8 km from the urban core in the steep foothills of the Quebrada Sesesmil. This rural Copan homestead is atypical in that residents bur-ied their dead here. Uncovered were the remains of a rural household manifested in two small structures, which contain abundant evidence for the flourishing of inhabitants farming this region during the Middle/Late Classic transition, dur-ing a few generations of occupation. Chronology of this site is firmly established through two radiocarbon dates (cal. AD 415–540 ± 60 years and cal. AD 642–689 ± 50 years; Webster et al. 2000, 111), numerous obsidian hydration dates (cal. AD 614–723 ± 70 years) (Freter 1988, 260, 319), and ceramic seriation (Gonlin 1993, 369,

373). The farmers who migrated here brought with them, or acquired during their tenure, valuable objects that were placed with deceased members of the household. For example, a Middle Classic (Acbi) Arturo-Incised narrow-necked jar lay at the feet of a primary adult extended burial, just outside of the retaining walls of the northern structure. This individual was one of nine people (Gonlin 2007, 94) who were buried here over a period of a hundred years or so. Burials of men, women, children, and an infant, all marked in some manner, confirmed that the inhabitants had a vested interest in the land (McAnany 1995). An adult and juvenile were buried inside Structure 1, both of whom were found with missing bones. The clearly associated obsidian blade was hydration-dated to cal. AD 664 ± 70 years. These burials may represent the end of the occupation of this group, an interpretation that Barrientos and colleagues (2015) have posited for Naachtun, Guatemala. The missing bones may represent reentry of this burial, just prior to abandonment. The steeply sloped terrain may have served as a deterrent to continued agricultural productivity, and it is likely the family migrated to more fertile grounds, a pattern that was common to many groups located in such environments (Paine et al. 1996; Paine and Freter 1996). The statistical analysis of Paine and Freter (1996) demonstrated for various types of sites throughout the Copan Valley that those groups located on more fertile soils and more gently sloping land occupied their farmsteads longer than groups who had settled on agriculturally less-desirable lands.

Evidence for seasonal or circular migration was uncovered at Site 34A-12-1, just 65 m downhill from the residential site 34A-12-2. The ephemeral square structure (outlined by a single row of cobbles) was perched atop a knoll. Only two of its low-lying walls remained and the paucity of artifacts (0.93 kg of ceramics; nine broken obsidian blades; one obsidian chunk and one other obsidian artifact; no grinding stones; one stone celt; snail fragment; lump of burned clay) indicated an occupation less than year-round (Freter 1988; Gonlin 1993). If indeed this small structure functioned as a field hut, it represents an example of circular migration, following Tilly (1978), in that it was an interim residence for farmers.

One of the most elaborate caches recovered in the rural area comes from Site 7D-3-1 in the Río Amarillo pocket, 21 km from the urban core (Gonlin 2007). Inhabitants built three low-lying stone foundations upon which perishable superstructures were erected. Inside Structure 1 was a distinct area where cobble paving had been removed. Exploration into the remains of this residence produced sterile fill, except for where a stone cist was uncovered in the exact area of the missing pavement on top of the mound. A small obsidian eccentric in the form of a fishhook was recovered on the unpaved surface. The cist (80 cm × 120 cm) was built of two parallel walls of 7–10 courses of unworked stone about 70 cm high. Offerings had been placed at the bottom of the cist: a small (1 cm) flat piece of a highly polished greenstone, a plate of the Caterpillar type, a polychrome Copador cylinder, and a 10-cm-long chert spear point. It is evident that the cist was built during the initial stages of building construction and then reopened prior to the abandonment of the site. No burial was found inside and it is unknown what materials may have been removed. This feature may provide evidence of both house dedication and termination rituals, the latter indicating a probable definitive movement out of the locale, following Barrientos et al. (2015), and similar to the situation at Site 34A-12-2.

DISCUSSION AND CONCLUSIONS

Tilly (1978) presents a model of migration that one can test with archaeological data. As discussed at the beginning of the chapter, various types of migration are helpful in framing the abundant data at Copan. Evidence for circular migration in the form of a field hut (Site 34A-12-1) is one example of this type, which likely occurred more frequently than is visible archaeologically. The recovery of field huts is notoriously difficult, given their ephemeral nature and the fact that they are not typically the object. Career migration certainly occurred for the dynastic founder and other royals who are known to have come from afar. Whether this type also occurred in urban neighborhoods that attracted elites and their families can be hypothesized. However, the category of career migration should not be confined to only the royal and elite sectors of society, since farmers coming from afar to take up residence in rural areas were migrating for their careers as well. If in each of these instances, family members were encouraged to join their kin, the movement could be classified as chain migration. Bioarchaeological data are most productive in this arena of inquiry, though the chronology of determining the initial migrants may introduce contemporaneity issues. Local migrations seem to have occurred at both ends of the socioeconomic spectrum: agriculturalists farmed the landscape and then moved on to (literally) greener lands.

The numerous lines of evidence that we have presented paint a complex picture of Copan's migration history that illustrate demographic processes at multiple scales. Clearly, the urban core with its fertile lands and cultural life-style drew in settlers from near and far. Prior to AD 400, populations were low in number until the arrival of the first dynast, after which time the urban core became one of the most densely populated areas in the Classic Maya world. While not definitively informative of cultural or ethnic origins, strontium and oxygen isotopic analyses reveal that a very large percentage of Copan's Late Classic population did not grow up locally (Miller 2015). Additional research on the exact location and timeline of migrant settlement across the valley might allow us to model macroscale chain or career migration. Like the ethnic barrios identified at Teotihuacan (Manzanilla 2017), perhaps long-distance kinship networks persuaded faraway relatives to settle in a frontier city with plentiful resources (chain migration). Or Copan leaders provided attractive incentives for specialized craftspeople to migrate and work within emerging industries (career migration). Sudden construction episodes when more elaborate buildings were erected on previously unoccupied lands also provide evidence for the possibility of career migration. In the rural area, burials consisting of partial human remains may suggest the termination of residency, what Arnauld et al. (p. xx, this volume) refer to as "the extraction of buried ancestral remains." These types of markers may indicate local migration. One can imagine the draw of the city, its urban neighborhoods, and all it had to offer its occupants. Here, too, whether commoners or elites, residents marked their beginnings and endings in auspicious ways with material goods. This lifestyle continued on for quite some time until things went awry.

Others in the Copan kingdom chose to settle farther afield, as rural areas were occupied from the founding of the dynasty to beyond its collapse. Various factors attracted immigrants to the region as the polity grew into the tens of thousands during the Late Classic, with half its population outside the core area. Prime agricultural lands were occupied first and sustained the longest, though many other environs witnessed habitation. The hinterland areas were utilized by those of varying statuses, all of whom were able to partake in the benefits of belonging to a Classic Maya kingdom while simultaneously enjoying a degree of freedom outside the city core. Insights from Richards-Rissetto and Landau's (2014, 372) analysis on mobility as reflecting social interactions within the urban core suggest that "lower status residents were channeled to or past type 4 [elite] complexes to establish and reinforce social groups on an economic and/or political basis." Social inequality within the urban core was therefore a consistent aspect of daily life, but less prominent for residents living farther out. Low-status urban residents lived side-by-side with high status inhabitants and may have served them in some capacity, resulting in high-status dependence on low-status labor. This factor could have been a "push" for local migration from city center to periphery.

After the collapse of the ruling dynasty around AD 822, the urban core emptied out as de-urbanizing processes occurred and the region was largely abandoned. AnnCorinne Freter and Elliot Abrams (2016) have found in their research of particular groups in Copan's urban core (10L-2; 9J-5; 9N-8; 8N-11; 9M-22a; 11L structures) that typically the dominant structure in a group was abandoned first. This order of abandonment could indicate that either the administrator who lived there was not replaced or the leaders of the group were the first to leave (Freter and Abrams 2016, 112). In abandonment situations, not all are affected equally or all at the same time.

Recently, archaeologists working in tropical regions have called for a deemphasis on the terminology of "collapse," and instead a new focus on "urban diaspora" (Lucero et al. 2015). They argue that urban diaspora was not a postcollapse state of being, but a series of behavioral adjustments that best accommodated life during times and places of climate instability. Likewise, the argument is made for abandoning the terms "'looters' and 'squatters' living among the ruins of a decaying society" (Freter and Abrams 2016, 110). These terms have often been employed for inhabitants who remained and adjusted to changing circumstances. In the introduction to this volume, the editors point out how long-term climate change was one of the reasons for migration. In the case of the Classic Maya, this factor has been considered anew (e.g., Iannone 2014) and is being incorporated into numerous cultural evolutionary processes. Residents in the hinterlands of state-level societies often persisted, and families and individuals carried on their ways of living well beyond the fortunes of any dynasty. We agree with Inomata (2004), however, that the Classic Maya were on the move, as well illustrated in our multiscale urban and rural case studies from Copan.

ACKNOWLEDGMENTS

Thanks are due to the Honduran Institute of Anthropology and History for permitting our excavations, and for allowing us to present our work at the 2013 Annual Meeting of the Society for American Archaeology and in this publication. We are very pleased to have been invited by M. Charlotte Arnauld to participate in the symposium on mobility and migration and its subsequent publication by Charlotte, Grégory Pereira, and Christopher Beekman. Their editing on this chapter has been most helpful. Several granting agencies (National Science Foundation; Northwestern University) contributed to the collection of data presented here. Thanks are due to Christopher Hernandez, David M. Reed, Heather Richards-Rissetto, Cynthia Robin, K. Viswanathan, and David Webster for reading earlier drafts of this work. Bellevue College (for Nancy Gonlin) and Northwestern University and Alma College (for Kristin Landau) generously supported travel to present the initial work upon which this chapter is based, as well as provided institutional support.

7

Water, Land, and Ancient Maya Population Dynamics in the Puuc Hills, Mexico

NICHOLAS P. DUNNING, MICHAEL P. SMYTH,
ERIC WEAVER, AND DAVID ORTEGÓN ZAPATA

The Elevated Interior Region (EIR) of the Maya lowlands presented the ancient Maya with a significant environmental challenge: a five-month-long dry season and an acute lack of natural perennial water sources (Dunning et al. 2012). The hilly Puuc region of Yucatán and Campeche lies at the northern end of the EIR (figure 7.1), where water sources are particularly scarce and the dry season is pronounced. Capturing and storing large quantities of rainwater to survive the dry season offered the only means by which the ancient Maya could occupy the region in large numbers. On the other hand, the Puuc contains some of the best agricultural soils in the northern lowlands. Archaeological settlement patterns reflect a desire on the part of the Maya to access and control these soils, as well as the need to devise strategies to survive the dry season (Dunning 1992). These dual, basic, resource-oriented needs had a great impact on the nature of population movement in the region over many centuries, affecting both mobility and migration.

The Puuc is justly famous for the elaborate concrete veneer architecture that came to characterize the settlements in the region in the Late and Terminal Classic periods (table 7.1). For many years, it was assumed that the settlement

DOI: 10.5876/9781646420735.c007

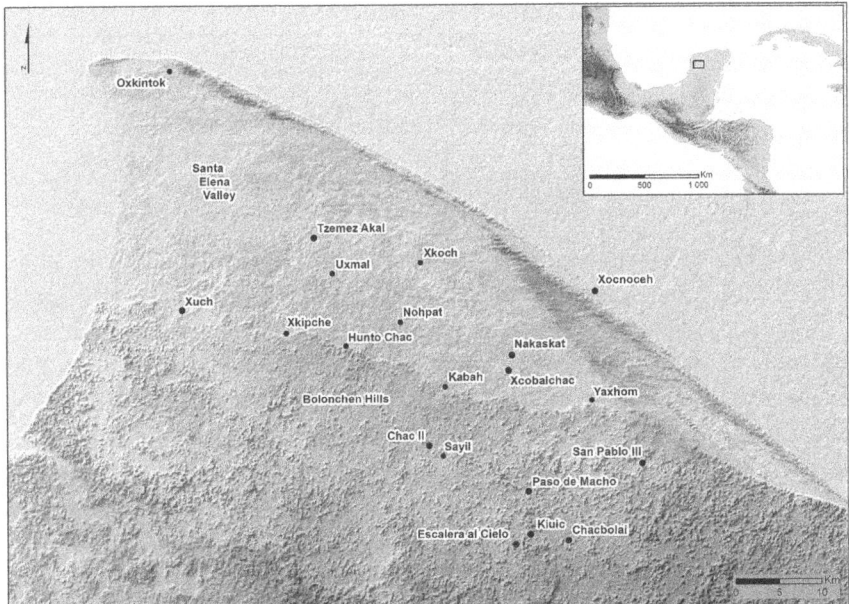

FIGURE 7.1. *Map of the Puuc region, showing sites mentioned in the text. (Map created by Nicholas Dunning. Base map is a hillshade derived from a Digital Elevation Model [DEM] produced by Jet Propulsion Laboratory–Airborne Synthetic Aperture Radar [AIRSAR], freely downloaded from http://airsar.jpl.nasa.gov/, accessed August 12, 2014. Courtesy NASA/JPL-Caltech.)*

history of the region was largely limited to an explosive surge in population during these same periods. Recent and ongoing research indicates that while the region did indeed experience an impressive Late/Terminal Classic florescence, regional settlement history is deeper and more complex, including at least some sizable pockets with Preclassic communities (Gallareta Negrón and Ringle 2004; Ringle 2011; Smyth and Ortegón Zapata 2008) and Early Classic components (Rivera Dorado 1996; Smyth 1998). Although the nature of ancient Maya settlement in the Puuc is far from being completely understood, especially during earlier time periods, certain patterns are emerging, including variation in mobility. Spatial mobility can be defined simply as the ability for a population to move (Inomata 2004; Kelly 1992). More specifically, as defined in the introduction to this volume by editors Arnauld, Beekman, and Pereira, mobility refers to regular physical movement facilitating social practices, whereas *migration* is movement based on unusual circumstances. In the Puuc, population movement was manifest at multiple scales ranging from seasonal mobility linked to productive resources to permanent migration between communities and regions.

TABLE 7.1. Chronological table of the Puuc region

	Middle/Late Preclassic	Early Classic	Late Classic	Terminal Classic
Chronology	800 BC–AD 250	AD 250–550	AD 550–750	AD 750–950
Ceramics	Mamom-Tihosuco	Cochuah	Motul	Cehpech
Architecture	Megalithic	Proto-Puuc	Early Puuc	Classic Puuc

In early colonial Yucatán, Maya society was self-organized into two basic classes: *almehenob* (nobility) and *mazehualob* (commoners). However, this superficial division obscures a more complex reality in which there were numerous subclasses of both nobility and commoners and the boundaries between the classes were somewhat fluid (Restall 1997, 88–92), a situation that was also likely true in earlier times (Arnauld et al. 2017b). Nobility and commoners were typically farmers, but their access to and control over farmland—and to water—was unequal. Archaeological evidence suggests that this situation has parallels in prehispanic times (Dunning 2004).

In addition to class, early colonial Yukatek Maya identity (and by inference, in earlier time periods as well) was closely tied to two other associations: *cah* (community of birth), and *chibal* (patronym group or lineage). This duality provided the Maya with a certain amount of structural mobility. On the one hand, people were tied to particular places and whatever resources they had come to control in that location. On the other hand, their lineage identity was significantly more portable and potentially facilitated their migration in times of need. While joining their lineage brethren in another *cah* may have meant forsaking their land and status, dire circumstances such as famine or war in their place of origin may have made such sacrifices seem necessary. It is important to note that the Maya *chibal* was anything but an egalitarian extended family. McAnany (1995, 111) has aptly described Maya lineages as "crucibles of inequality." A typical Yukatek *chibal* in the Late Postclassic/Early Postconquest included many lineage fragments and their dependents (Okoshi Harada 2011, 2012; Quezada 2014). Newly arrived members would likely have been appended at the bottom of the local hierarchy. The sociopolitical organization of even modestly sized towns was quite complex with numerous *chibal* barrios, a pattern that was also evident in Late/Terminal Classic Puuc towns (Prem and Dunning 2004). An examination of settlement systems in the Puuc region suggests that patterns of mobility and resource control changed over time.

THE PUUC PRECLASSIC AND EARLY CLASSIC

In the Puuc region, earlier settlement patterns are obscured by the large volume of later construction. Nevertheless, in a few places earlier patterns shine through. Megalithic architecture appears at a number of Puuc region sites, though often partially covered by later construction (Dunning 1992). Megalithic architecture is fairly widely distributed across the northern Maya lowlands and is highly distinctive: very large, well-dressed blocks with rounded edges overlie rubble cores on platforms that often have rounded corners (Mathews and Maldonado Cárdenas 2006). Although it was evident that megalithic architecture dated to an earlier phase of occupation, only more recently have excavations revealed that this phase encompassed the Mamon and Tihosuco ceramic complexes of the Middle/Late Preclassic periods (ca. 800 BC–AD 250) (Gallareta Negron and Ringle 2004; Smyth and Ortegón Zapata 2008) as well as extending perhaps a century into the Early Classic (Ringle 2011) (table 7.1). The majority of megalithic architecture currently known in the Puuc occurs at a number of large sites in the Santa Elena Valley, including Yaxhom, Nakaskat, Nohpat, and Xcoch (Dunning 1992). These sites are situated adjacent to basins with extensive tracts of high-quality agricultural soils. These sites also include large *aguadas* (depressions modified into reservoirs).

In addition to several aguadas, the large Preclassic site of Xcoch is also the location of a rare Puuc region cave penetrating to the deep permanent water table (Smyth and Ortegón Zapata 2008; Smyth et al. 2017; Weaver et al. 2015). The cave was clearly in use for millennia as an important center of ritual activity as attested to by countless ritually killed artifacts, extending from the Middle Preclassic into Postconquest times, and found throughout the labyrinthine cavern, especially in the deepest areas nearest the water pool. A *sacbe* (stone causeway) was constructed in the Late Preclassic, connecting the cave entrance with the city's largest reservoir, Aguada La Gondola, some 100 m to the west (figure 7.2). Notably, rare specialized polychrome water jars were found only within the cave and in excavations in the reservoir, indicating a ritual connection between these two places (Dunning et al. 2014a). In Maya cosmology caves are believed to be the dwelling places of rain gods and other water-related deities. The water found in sacred caves has long been used by Maya shamans in rainmaking and other rituals. At Xcoch it is easy to imagine a shaman making the arduous trek (including crawls and climbs) from the small water pool deep beneath the Earth, emerging from the cave mouth, and processing along the *sacbe* to the lip of the reservoir, then pouring forth the water offering and invoking the rain gods to follow with life-sustaining rains.

Excavations in another central reservoir (East Aguada) and one on the southern periphery of Xcoch (South Aguada 1) indicate that these were also constructed in the Preclassic. Smaller surface tanks were also constructed in the Preclassic to collect and store runoff from residential groups in the urban zone (Brewer et al. 2017; Weiss-Krejci and Sabbas 2002). Clearly, water-collection strategies were a significant part of urbanization in the Preclassic Puuc (see Ringle 2011 for the Preclassic origin of Aguada Xpotoit at Yaxhom). Excavations have

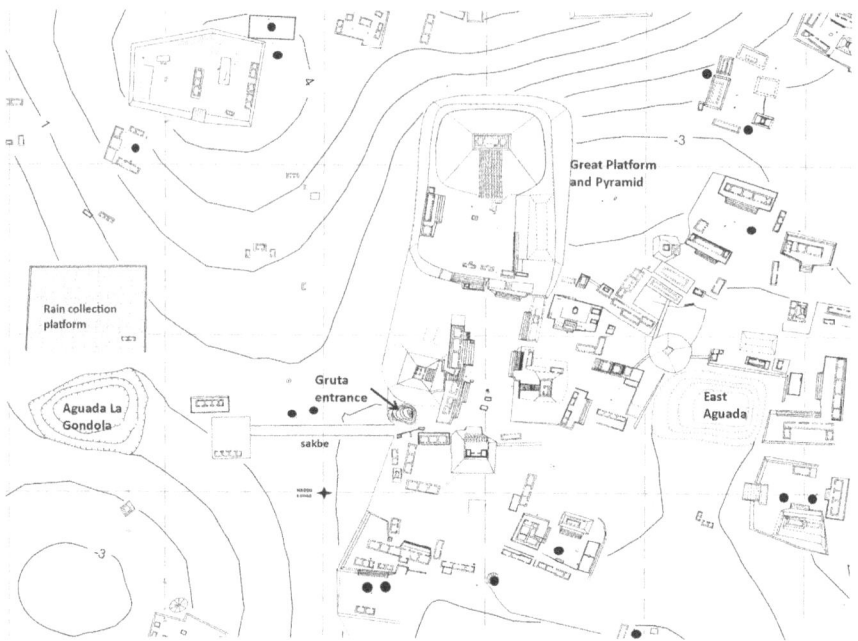

FIGURE 7.2. *Map of central Xcoch, including reservoirs and chultuns (black dots). (After Dunning et al. 2014a.)*

thus far uncovered evidence suggesting the construction of one chultun (a plastered, watertight subterranean household cistern) in the Preclassic (Smyth et al. 2014). However, the majority of Preclassic residential groups feature open-surface tanks, whereas chultuns are ubiquitously associated with later Classic residential architecture (figure 7.3).

Evidence from Xcoch indicates that this Preclassic community developed around its deep cave and symbolically related system of reservoirs that allowed for the concentration of an urban population (Dunning et al. 2014a; Smyth et al. 2014, 2017). The dependence of this population on a relatively centralized form of water capture and storage would have given the city's rulers great sway over its inhabitants. In addition to the larger reservoirs in the site center, smaller but sizable reservoirs are known for the southern and western peripheries of the site and may have been used both for residential populations as well as possible irrigation of nearby fields (Dunning et al. 2014a). These water sources would have provided a further extension of year-round settlement and political dominion into the hinterland around Xcoch.

Rural settlement in the Puuc during the Preclassic is poorly understood. The discovery of a solely Preclassic village site, Paso de Macho, deep within

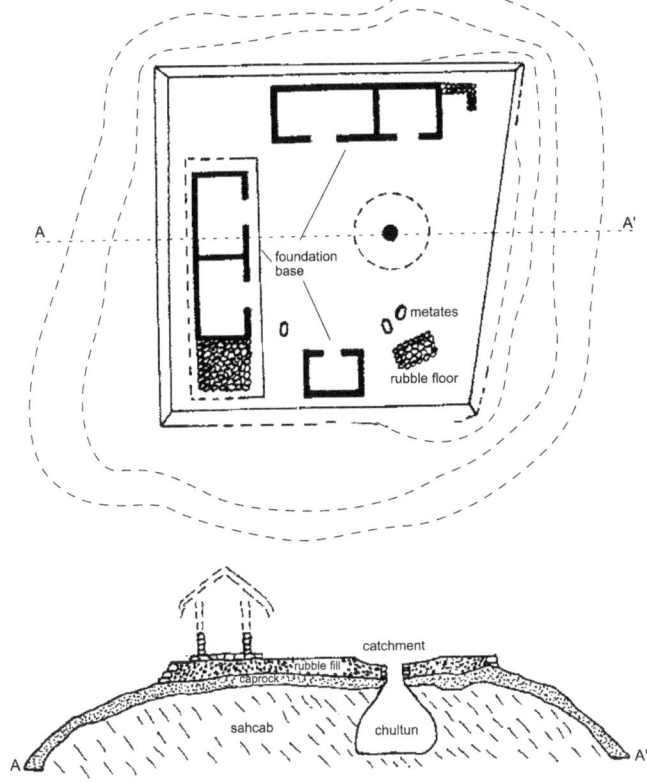

FIGURE 7.3. *Plan (top) and section A–A' (bottom) of a typical Puuc residential patio group including a chultun (water-catchment cistern). (After Dunning 1992.)*

the Bolonchen Hills indicates that at least some degree of more diffuse settlement took place at this time (Gallareta Negrón and Ringle 2004). This small site includes a diminutive ballcourt like many Preclassic sites in northwest Yucatán, modest monumental architecture and a few residential structures. There is a striking absence of chultuns and it is not understood how the residents of Paso de Macho obtained water in the dry season (Gallareta Negrón and Carrillo Sánchez 2005; Parker et al. 2017).

By the Early Classic period, chultuns were a standard component of residential architecture at Puuc sites such as Oxkintok (Rivera Dorado 1996) and Chac II (Smyth 1998), but precisely how and when this technology evolved is poorly understood. The extent of Early Classic Maya occupation in the Puuc is also poorly known: if early styles of Puuc architecture can be correlated with this time period, then settlement may have become fairly widespread, although most sites were likely comparatively small in size (Dunning 1992; Smyth 1998). At Xcoch there is evidence for a period of site abandonment or reduction between the Late Preclassic and Early Classic (Smyth et al. 2014; 2017), though how widespread this phenomenon may have been in the Puuc region is unknown. Paleoclimatic data from northern Yucatán and elsewhere in the Maya lowlands strongly suggest that recurring droughts may have dramatically affected the distribution of Maya settlement during the Preclassic/Classic transition (Brenner et al. 2000; Dunning et al. 2014b; Medina-Elizade et al. 2010, 2015; Smyth et al. 2017; Torrescano-Valle and Islebe 2015). It is distinctly possible that the advent and spread of chultun technology to capture and more effectively store rainwater was spurred by increasing aridity at the close of the Late Preclassic. Although evidence is currently minimal, the development of chultuns may have also facilitated out-migration from large centers such as Xcoch and the establishment of smaller, more widely dispersed settlements, because these residential scale features required much less labor to construct than civic reservoirs. Additionally, the ability to cap the narrow mouths of chultuns would have greatly reduced water lost to evaporation compared with open-air tanks and reservoirs, and reduced potential contamination and eutrophication.

THE PUUC LATE AND TERMINAL CLASSIC

In 1992, Dunning published a regional settlement-pattern study of the Puuc Hills, proposing a seven-tiered hierarchy of sites: three classes of major sites, three classes of minor sites, and a seventh class of likely seasonally occupied hamlets (Dunning 1992). Subsequent research has shown that this model was overly simplistic and "forced"—sometimes lumping diverse sites into single categories (Prem 2003). With the exception of the tiny class 7 sites, the model treated minor centers as essentially smaller versions of major centers, though lacking certain trappings of political authority (e.g., stelae and ballcourts). This simplification glossed over the considerable diversity that exists among Puuc minor centers.

    For this study, the definition of major centers remains the same: urban population concentrations with sizeable civic-ceremonial infrastructure including temple pyramids and large plazas, and the trappings of Classic Maya political authority such as large elite residential complexes ("palaces," dynastic stelae or other inscriptions, and ballcourts). Major centers can be interpreted as *batabil*, the seat of a ruler (*batab*), but with power typically shared with a council of lineage heads (*ah kuch cab*). Within the urban zone lineage/*chibal* barrios (*kuuchteel*) are often discernable (Carmean and Sabloff 1996; Hanks 2003; Prem and Dunning 2004). Major centers include those assigned settlement ranks of 1 through 3, though the region's rank 1 center, Uxmal, likely emerged as a higher-order political entity, *kuuchkabal*, that was the dominant center within a system of affiliated or subjugated *batabil*.

TABLE 7.2. General traits of Puuc-region minor centers and rural settlements

Trait	Minor Center	Suburb	Village	Manor	Seasonal Hamlet
Small temple pyramid	X				
Large vaulted residence	X			X	
Small vaulted residence	X	X	X	X	
Unvaulted residence	X	X	X	X	X
Small reservoir	X*	X*	X*	X*	
Chultuns	X	X	X	X	

* Found in most but not all examples.

The definition of minor-center sites, ranks 4 through 6 (Dunning 1992), needs to be refined. A closer examination reveals that minor sites were a diverse set of communities that included some true "minor centers" (simply smaller versions of major centers), but also what we are here calling "suburbs," "villages," and "manors." The definition of diminutive rank 7 sites remains the same: small, rural hamlets that were likely occupied only seasonally (table 7.2).

Some minor centers (rank 4 sites) do indeed appear to be scaled down versions of major centers complete with very modest monumental (nonresidential) architecture such as small pyramids, as well as large to modest elite dwellings (e.g., Xcobalchac; figure 7.4). Structurally, these sites appear to be smaller, more simplified iterations of larger centers. The scale of monumental architecture is much smaller and residential areas are less extensive and less complex. There are fewer outlying nodes indicative of lineage barrios. Though the mix of vaulted and unvaulted residential architecture is similar to that of larger centers, there may be a tendency for a smaller percentage of vaulted residences (e.g., the smaller percentage of vaulted edifices noted for Chunhuhub versus Xculoc; Michelet and Becquelin 2000). These minor centers likely represent the expansion of population in the Late Classic and migration in the form of "in-filling" between major centers in order to exploit remaining pockets of less intensively used land as well as to secure the territorial frontiers of established major centers (Dunning 1992), perhaps headed by the progeny of the rulers of major centers. Sites assigned ranks 5 and 6 in the 1992 classification are a more complex mix of settlement types, but include at least three distinct types: suburbs, villages, and manors. Suburbs and villages are essentially the same with regard to feature content but differ in geographical position with suburbs lying adjacent to larger centers and villages occupying rural positions.

Simms and others (2012) report on Escalera al Cielo, a minor settlement lying on hilltops some 1.4 km southwest of the major center of Kiuic. The site consists

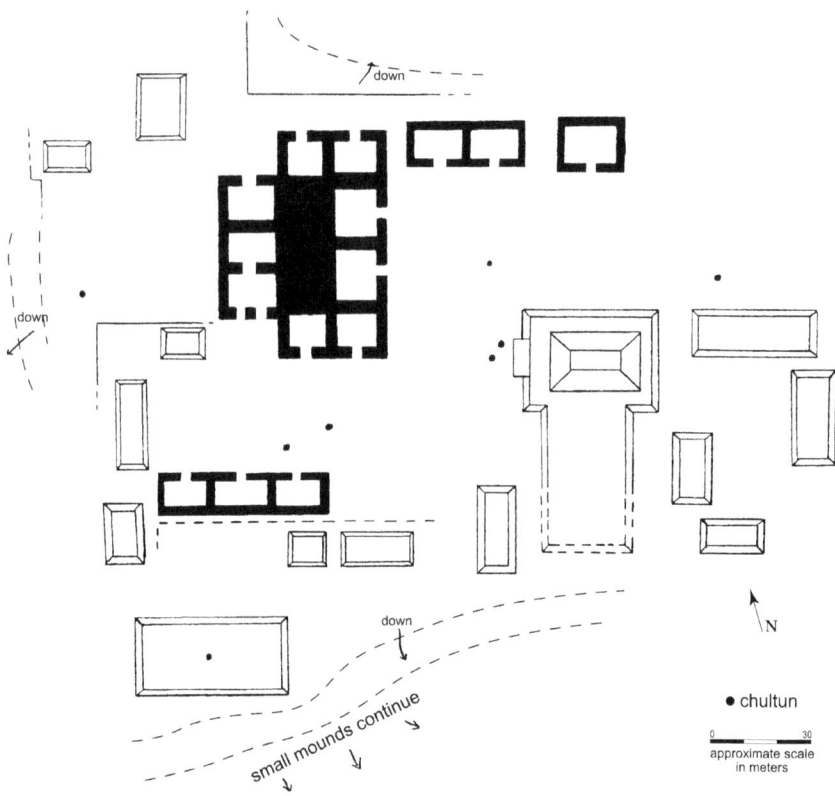

FIGURE 7.4. *Sketch map of Xcobalchac, Yucatán, a minor center. (After Dunning 1992.)*

of five or six residential patio groups clustered on conjoined hilltops. This hastily abandoned site contained intact artifact assemblages, indicating that its occupants were full-time agriculturalists. Escalera al Cielo is interpreted as a "suburban" out-post of Kiuic, controlling agricultural production on nearby lower terrain. *Suburb*, or *suburban estate*, is an apt description of some small sites in the near hinterland of major centers. Many Puuc urban centers contain apparent inner and outer residential zones (Dunning 1992, 2003). Within the inner zone, large areas of prime agricultural soils were left open and research suggests that these were typically under intensive cultivation (Dunning 1992, 2003; Smyth et al. 1995). There is also a clear spatial pattern situating elite households within or near the largest tracts of high-quality land (Dunning 1992; Isendahl 2002; Smyth et al. 1995) suggesting that land-based wealth was established by primacy within the community—the so-called "first founders" principle (Carmean 1991; McAnany 1995). The presence of boundary markers such as the "rubble pyramids" first identified at Sayil (Tourtellot 1988) and at some larger Puuc sites indicates that the inner residential zone was viewed as restricted space (Dunning 2003). As settlement pushed outward into an outer residential zone, land wealth was secured by outlying suburbs or estates such a Escalera al Cielo—a pattern noted for other urban centers of the Puuc as well (e.g., Groups A and B southwest of Sayil and XPRESS Groups E-2 and E-3 outside of Xkipche; Dunning 1992, 2003). Such suburbs have been interpreted as the possible domain of an "intermediate elite" or class of wealthy landed farmers still in close contact with a major center (Simms et al. 2012).

Trail and transect surveys extending beyond and between major and minor centers in the Puuc region demonstate detectable declines in settlement density along the margins of major centers as well as a general decrease in the percentage of vaulted stone residences and an increase in unvaulted buildings (Dunning 1992, 2003; Gallareta Negrón et al. 2010; Michelet 2000b; Michelet and Becquelin 2000). As noted above, some major centers include suburbs separated by relatively short distances from the main urban zone. Beyond this hinterland fringe between major and larger minor centers, three other types of settlement are often encountered: villages, manors, and hamlets.

Settlement clusters, or *villages*, that include middle-class architecture similar to that of suburban residential groups occur at greater distances from urban centers, expanding out into less-densely settled rural areas. Such villages are widely distributed in the Puuc (e.g., San Pablo III; figure 7.5). These communities exhibit a mixture of vaulted stone and unvaulted residential architecture, typically arranged in patio or platform groups, sometimes with one or more prominent groups.

In contrast to villages, *manors* are another distinct kind of small settlement, in this case dominated by a moderately large, vaulted, stone residential structure as well as more modest dwellings and outbuildings (e.g., Chacbolai; figure 7.6). The use of the term *manor* is not meant to necessarily imply a feudal model of land control such as has been suggested elsewhere (e.g., Adams and Smith 1981). Rather, it describes the presence of a clearly elite residence in a rural context (Nondédéo et al. 2013s; Taschek and Ball 2003). The origin of manor sites is unclear and may represent simply an extension of elite land-holdings away from major centers via a system of essentially "country estates," but could also represent several forms of migration. These include out-migration of some elites from major centers, either due to a failure to consolidate elite power, or as a form of power sharing (Arnauld et al. 2013b). Migrants from outside the Puuc may also have established rival minor centers and manors in underutilized parts of the landscape (Nondédéo 2013a). At present, the lack of complete settlement maps or excavation data for most sites makes answering these questions impossible.

In the Puuc region, Late and Terminal Classic year-round residences are indicated by the presence of rainwater and storage cisterns or chultuns (Dunning 1992; Prem 2003). The minor centers, suburbs, villages, and manors described above have abundant chultuns clearly indicative of permanent residence. Some

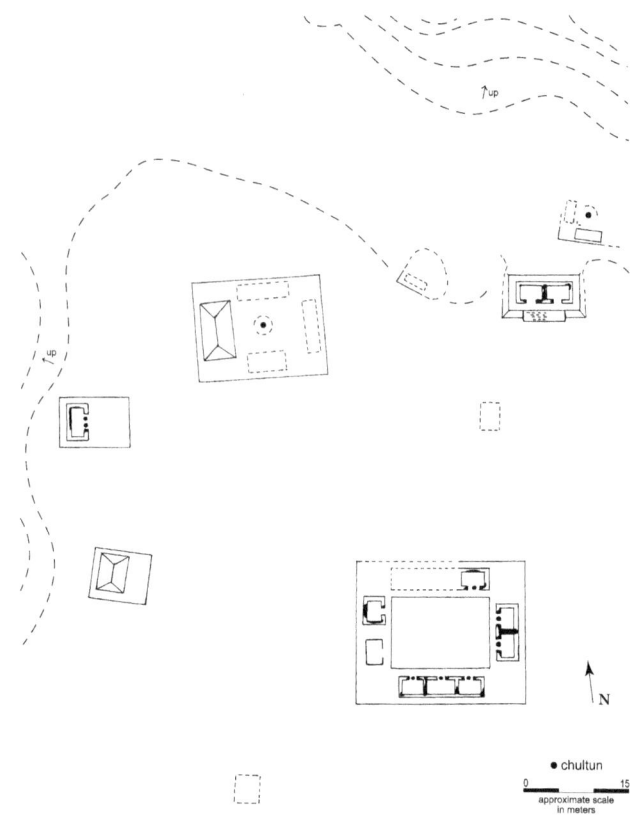

FIGURE 7.5. *Sketch map of San Pablo III, Yucatán, a rural village. (After Dunning 1992.)*

also have small reservoirs. It is unknown whether the elite residents of such centers also maintained residence within urban centers, though information from the sixteenth century suggest that many did (Quezada 2014; Williams-Beck 1998). These minor center elite and middle-class residences indicate the projection of elite land control into the countryside, a process likely facilitated by concentrating water management within site boundaries, however small the site.

The lowest tier of settlement within the Puuc is represented by small clusters of more archaeologically ephemeral features (Dunning 1992, 2003, 2004; Graff 1990). These clusters never include vaulted architecture, and rather feature some combination of poorer quality foundation braces (low support walls), small, low platforms, and "chich mounds" (amorphous rubble mounds), which exhibit little if any cut stone (figure 7.7a, b). Most important, these rural clusters almost never include chultuns. The lack of chultuns indicates that these settlements

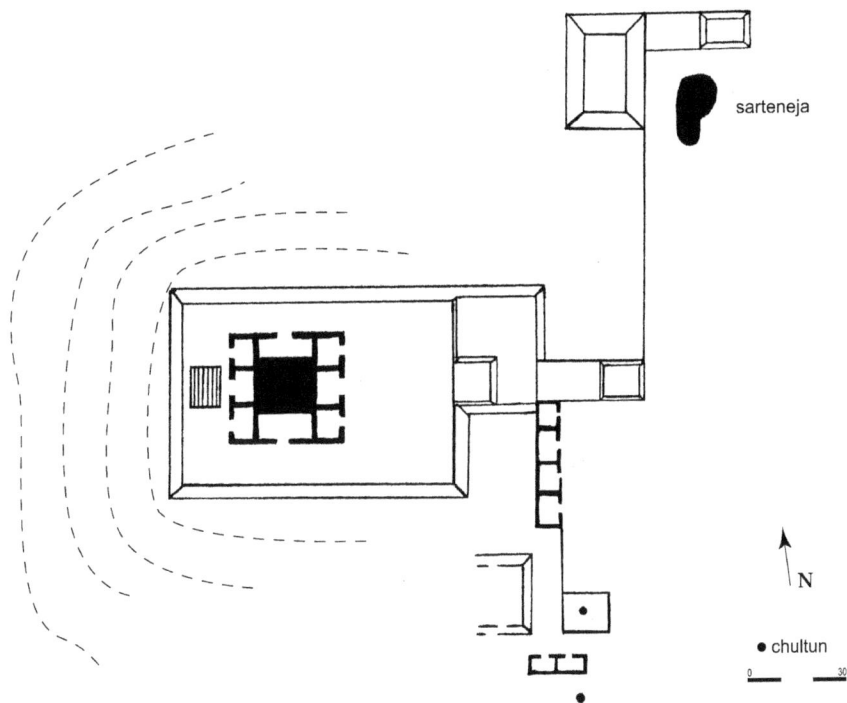

FIGURE 7.6. *Sketch map of Chacbolai, Yucatán, a rural manor. (After Dunning 1992.)*

did not possess the ability to capture and store and were either not occupied in the dry season or their inhabitants were dependent on larger communities to obtain water; two very distinct types of mobility. As farmsteads or field houses, occupied only during the rainy or growing season, these clusters could represent a further, though seasonal, expansion of population to work outlying lands each wet season, and who retreated to year-round settlements in the dry season. On the other hand, as dependent hamlets, these clusters could represent a possible indentured rural peasant population who relied on the back-breaking transportation of water from larger settlements during the dry season.

DISCUSSION

The ancient Maya were an agrarian society: their settlements were clearly tied to agriculturally significant variations within the natural landscape. The distribution of ancient settlement within the Puuc was especially conditioned by the availability of high-quality agricultural soils. This relationship is evident at several scales. Larger sites and earlier settled sites are typically situated favorably with respect to good land (Dunning 1992). Within sites the best areas of open garden or infield lands are spatially associated with elite residences (Smyth et al.

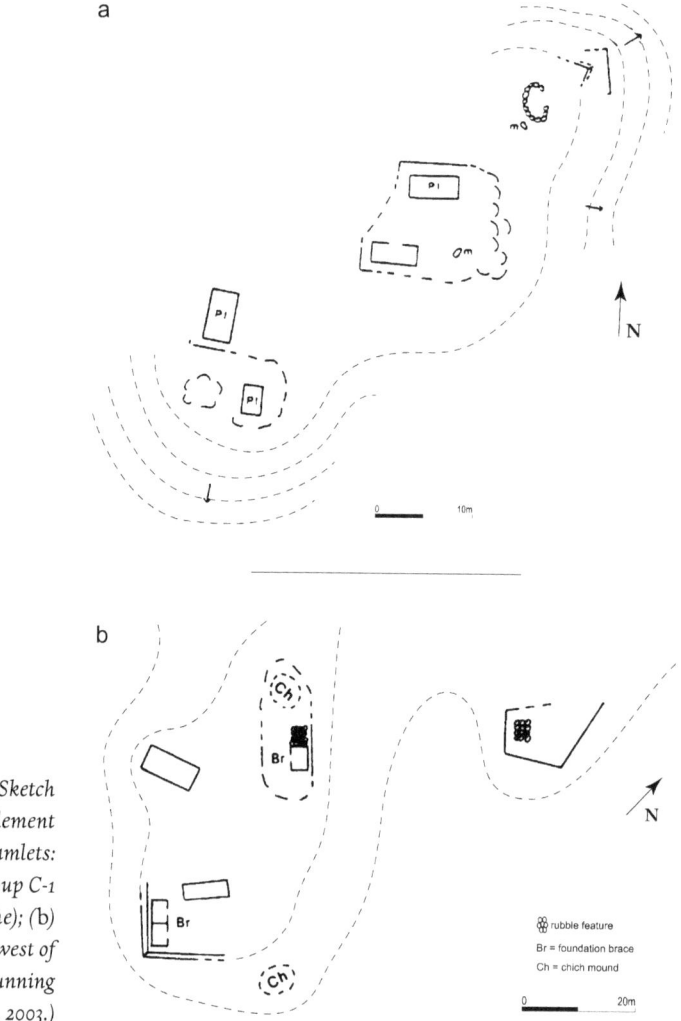

a

b

FIGURE 7.7. *Sketch maps of rural settlement clusters or hamlets: (a) XPRESS Group C-1 (west of Xkipche); (b) Site 7-12 (northwest of Xkokoh). (After Dunning 1992, 2003.)*

rubble feature
Br = foundation brace
Ch = chich mound

1995). Between large sites, suburban satellites, minor centers, villages, manors, and finally rural hamlets were positioned to take advantage of remaining available land (Dunning 2003; Gallareta Negrón et al. 2005, 2010). Clearly, in the Puuc, the control of land was closely linked to wealth and power (Isendahl et al. 2014). However, in this seasonally arid region, the control of water was also essential to the survival and success of any community.

The Preclassic center of Xcoch appears to be a good example of a *cah*: a community with a strong place-based identity centered on the cave underlying the heart of the city. This identity was further reinforced by the development of a system of urban reservoirs that tied the community to this life-giving infrastructure. As the system of reservoirs expanded outward, the number of social groups or the size of social groups could be expanded. The possible failure of this system at the end of the Preclassic in the face of intensifying drought pressure would have likely necessitated the abandonment or at least reduction of the site (Smyth et al. 2017).

Xcoch also illustrates the Maya concept of *ch'e'n*. Classic Maya texts typically refer to the *ch'e'n*—the home of gods and ancestors—at the heart of communities (Tokovinine 2013, 125). *Ch'e'n* are typically watery places such as caves, cenotes, or springs. In some cases, rulers and affiliate communities resided at these places of origin throughout the lengths of their dynasties. In other communities, the *ch'e'n* is referenced as a place distant in space and time and group identity includes a migration narrative, sometimes with multiple places. Nevertheless, even as dynasties multiplied and spread, they continued to associate themselves with a place of origin (Tokovinine 2013).

Ethnohistoric data from early colonial Yucatán indicate that the political economic organization of Maya society was closely tied to lineage or *chibal* structure, with group-based domination of communities, territories, and their interrelationships (Okoshi Harada 2011; Quezada 2014). This organization was reflected in the structure of communities, manifest in neighborhoods and compounds associated with lineage groups (Prem and Dunning 2004; Williams-Beck 1998), though some form of bureaucratic or special-interest-group participation is also possible (Ringle 2012).

In the Preclassic period, the creation of civic reservoirs in conjunction with monumental architecture may have facilitated urbanization by creating an important benefit for urban residents (Dunning et al. in press). As urban residence became commonplace through the Classic period, the increasing investment made by lineages and families in urban residential architecture itself likely made migration less attractive (Arnauld et al., chapter 8, this volume). Another social force that may have increased the attraction of urban places was the growth of networked urban markets in the Classic Period—as attested by both the proliferation of marketplaces and the spread of imported trade goods widely with urban populations (King and Shaw 2015; Ruhl et al. 2018).

The creation and spread of chultuns in the Classic period may be linked to the strengthening of *chibal*-based organization in the Puuc. Chultuns would have initially weakened the centripetal force of the ancient urban reservoirs by allowing settlement to spread over greater distances with only household-level investment. However, in dry years chultuns may not fill completely, making dependent populations vulnerable. At Xcoch the largest Preclassic central reservoir, La Gondola, was twice refurbished in the Classic period (Dunning et al. 2014a). There is a higher frequency of chultuns closer to the reservoir than farther away, suggesting that the water from the central tank may have been used to refill drying chultuns (a similar relationship exists between chultuns and cenotes, elite-controlled natural water sources, at Chichen Itza; R. Cobos, personal communication, 2011).

Despite the spatial freedom that chultun technology may have allowed in the settlement of the Puuc region, population mobility does not appear to have been unlimited. Dunning (2004) has characterized the Classic chultun-based settlement of the Puuc region as one of "nucleated dispersion." On the one hand, good land was intentionally left open for cultivation and settlement expanded to exploit the distribution of these lands. On the other hand, year-round settlement was spatially confined, with only seasonally occupied farmsteads and dispersed small villages and manors breaking out into more remote areas. In short, seasonal mobility within the Puuc region appears to have been highly structured.

Over time, disparities in land wealth grew both between and within lineages. Lineage leaders may have consolidated their wealth and power by limiting the dispersion of their members and clustering them within and around minor centers, villages, and manors where chultuns were allowed, but only occupying outlying lands during the rainy/growing season. In and around urban centers with multiple lineages and more complex sociopolitical organization, mobility would have been an intricately negotiated, tactical phenomenon. The growth of suburban settlements—as well as the founding and spread of minor centers, manors, and villages across the landscape likely resulted from the jockeying between lineages and their leaders for the control of land and other resources. However, in-migration of people from outside of the Puuc could also have factored in the filling of vacant land.

In stark contrast to the Puuc, Late/Terminal Classic settlement in the Río Bec region to its south was characterized by a remarkable degree of disaggregation (Lemonnier and Vannière 2013; Nondédéo et al. 2013a). There, urban centers were largely absent and the rural landscape was essentially "full." Small rural hamlets, manors, and farmsteads were strewn across the landscape with extensive networks of field walls, often linked to agricultural terracing, indicating an intensively managed and permanently occupied landscape.

Varying degrees of nonelite sedentism and mobility occurred across many parts of the Maya lowlands into the Late Preclassic (Inomata 2004; Inomata et al. 2015). Perhaps seasonal occupation of rural areas in the Puuc reflects a more widespread pattern that persisted into the Classic period elsewhere in the Maya lowlands (see Arnauld et al., chapter 8, this volume). In terms of spatial structure, the more aggregated settlement patterns of the Puuc are more akin to those found more widely across the EIR, including the northeastern Petén district of Guatemala. The absence of chultuns within rural settlement clusters in the Puuc may indicate a wider pattern of seasonal occupation of rural areas in other parts of the EIR where chultuns were not part of the usual adaptive technology making seasonality of occupation more difficult to discern.

Prolonged drought or increased drought frequency would have played havoc within Puuc communities that were utterly dependent on rainfall. Without adequate rainfall, the region was essentially uninhabitable. Soil exhaustion may also have contributed to environmental stress in the Terminal Classic (Andrews 2004; Dunning 1992). By the latter ninth century AD, the energy return on further expansion or intensification of agriculture in the Puuc was declining, making economic and population growth unsustainable, even without the added stress of drought (Isendahl et al. 2014). Thus, the attraction of the Puuc region for agrarian people would have been waning. By the late ninth century AD regional populations were shrinking and most sites were spiraling towards abandonment (Carmean et al. 2004).

Termination rituals, including stairway removal, are evident on monumental architecture at many major Puuc centers (Toscano Hernández and Huchim Herrera 2017), suggesting the end of elite control within the urban zone. This change coincided with the appearance of a new form of residential architecture, the "bench" or "C-shaped" structure, marking the establishment of small enclaves of residents often within former public spaces (e.g., Bey et al. 1997; Shaw and Johnstone 2006). These enclaves often persisted into the Postclassic and seem to represent a continuity of occupation by reduced numbers of people, rather than late outside intrusion (Paap 2017). On the other hand, the out-migration of population from the Puuc in the late ninth and tenth centuries AD is suggested by the severe reduction in sites of all scales. Unlike the apparent earlier short-distance migrations into intersite areas within the Puuc, the tenth century saw an overall exodus of population from the region. At the small suburban community of Escalera al Cielo, the residents appear to have packed some of their belongings while stashing others in anticipation of return; they never came back (Simms et al. 2012).

In contrast to other major Puuc centers in the late ninth century, Uxmal apparently experienced explosive population growth and a boom in the construction of monumental architecture (Carmean et al. 2004; Dunning et al. 2014a). Uxmal also boasted a set of at least thirteen reservoirs, an investment that may have allowed this center to thrive at least for a time when surrounding communities were abandoned. Whether the late concentration of population at Uxmal was achieved by force or by luring water-starved neighbors is unknown. However, Uxmal, too, eventually succumbed. As noted, a few Puuc sites show evidence of relatively ephemeral Postclassic occupation, but the region was never effectively reoccupied in prehispanic times. At Xcoch, while the city was abandoned in the Terminal Classic, the sacred cave, home to the rain gods, persisted as a pilgrimage site through the Postclassic and into colonial times—a final tribute to the lasting importance of this place.

8

Maya Residential Architecture, Mobility, and the Terminal Classic Abandonment of Lowland Urban Settlements

M. CHARLOTTE ARNAULD, EVA LEMONNIER,
DOMINIQUE MICHELET, AND MÉLANIE FORNÉ

Residential mobility was a great leveler.
KOHLER (1992, 631)

Mesoamerican societies underwent a long Classic/Postclassic transition through an Epiclassic stage (AD 600–900) that encompassed different types of mobility and migrations among other determinant processes (Beekman and Christensen 2003; Cowgill 2013). In the Maya area, "mythistoric migrations" narrated in chronicles represent founding events for the Postclassic highland societies—K'iche', Q'eqchi', and Poqomchi' in particular (Arnauld and Michelet 1991; Breton 2007; Fox 1987). Some centuries before, many lowland cities had been abandoned in a general desertion most often cited as a symptom of the Terminal Classic "collapse," or crisis, from AD 780 to 950 (Aimers 2007; Demarest et al. 2004; Iannone 2014; Lucero 2002). Along with other processes, this crisis involved a series of population movements with a broad displacement of settlements from the south-central lowlands to the northern lowlands (Turner and Sabloff 2012) and to the southern highlands. After centuries of apparent stability during the Classic

DOI: 10.5876/9781646420735.c008

period (AD 250–800), with the notable development of domestic stone architecture in urban contexts, Maya groups shifted residence in a series of movements. It will be some time before Mayanists can elucidate the causes and time-space coordinates for even a few of those movements. We suggest that what is needed first is a knowledge of the diverse types of mobility and migration that typically shaped urban settlements during the Early and Late Classic periods, as these movements eventually determined Terminal Classic urban dynamics, including the final dissolution of cities.

The present study concentrates on mobility in the Maya area on the spatial scale of a Classic city with its hinterlands, while also taking into account wider transfers of people and goods like those involved in trade mobility and the late migrations. Our spatial scale is a measure of the swidden (*milpa*) agriculture practiced in the Maya semitropical lowlands, possibly a distance of two-days' walk as the radius for the hinterland of any settlement (Atran 1993). Time is also a function of this crop system on which it is useful to take a *longue durée* perspective. Recent advances indicate that full agricultural production of food staples was achieved later than previously assumed, with enduring "mixed subsistence" of "hunters-fishers-gardeners" (Killion 2013). Also, farmers reached full sedentism with pottery use only by 1000 BC at the onset of the Middle Formative (Inomata et al. 2015). And the Neolithic demographic transition was still under way during the Late Formative (400 BC–AD 250), which would be due to the low productivity of early maize (Lesure et al. 2014). These assessments may still need further research, yet they show that the Maya urban centers that emerged during the Late Formative like El Mirador and Nakbe represented a remarkable stabilization of populations achieved in a few centuries. Those cities nevertheless disintegrated during the Terminal Preclassic crisis by AD 150, causing plausible movements (Dunning et al. 2014b). Some cities persisted whereas new ones formed in new places during the Early Classic (AD 250–600), and many later experienced a still unexplained demographic "surge" by AD 500–600 (e.g., Copan, Tikal, Caracol; Webster 2014; Webster et al. 2000). By Late Classic times (AD 600–800) domestic stone architecture with associated intensive agriculture constrained Maya farmers in new housing systems. What proportion of total lowland populations integrated those cities and systems is unknown, but at least for these people mobility related to subsistence may have changed. This second lowland urbanization process did not produce more sustainable cities since, during the Terminal Classic period (AD 780/800–950/1000), as mentioned, many cities were depopulated. The new Postclassic cities stimulated new forms of residential architecture that never reached the elaborateness of Classic houses.

Under what sociopolitical and economic conditions did those successive urbanization processes develop in an environment—the lowlands—well known to support only low-density demography and resource use? As part of an answer to that broad question, our inquiry in mobility-migration types aims to identify the archaeological correlates for diverse population movements that participated in urbanization and de-urbanization. Mobility and migration are topics particularly challenging for the archaeologist studying Mesoamerican lowland societies (see Cucina 2015a; Freiwald 2011a; Inomata 2004; Price et al. 2010, 2014; Ruz et al. 2009; and Wright 2012, among others; see also Sellet et al. 2006 for the Amazonian lowlands). In those regions as well as others, one available approach is residence construction (e.g., Burmeister 2000; M. E. Smith 2014), including variation in materials, building techniques, location, and shapes, along with associated aspects of garden intensification (Lemonnier and Vannière 2013) and formation process (Inomata et al. 2015). Analyzed in conjunction, those proxies reveal signatures of population movement types including initial settlement, growth or nongrowth, residence shift, and abandonment. This chapter presents an array of excavation results from several Maya lowland sites where we have worked during the past 30 years (figure 8.1), with the aim of defining archaeological patterns that correlate with mobility-migration types.

After introducing Maya lowland subsistence mobility and some of its archaeological correlates, the chapter deals with the Classic process of urban congregation with incipient masonry construction of dwellings in urban centers. It then concentrates on subsequent social dynamics at the settlement and neighborhood scales, leading to a discussion of de-urbanization as it possibly unfolded at the end of the Classic period.

MOBILITY TYPES RELATED TO SUBSISTENCE

Dispersion of resources in tropical lowlands requires that people diversify their strategies, combining localized intensive agriculture, extensive agriculture, hunting, fishing, collecting, and other associated activities (Dunning et al. 2012; Killion 1992, 2013; Scarborough and Burnside 2010). Milpa, or swidden agriculture, allowed Maya farmers to restore soil fertility by way of long periods of fallowing (3–15 years) after no more than two to three crops (generally one per year). Frequent shifting of cultivated fields requires periodic residence relocation (e.g., Atran 1993; see models in Wilk 1991, chapter 6). Also contributing to the semisedentary way of life, perishable material houses have to be rebuilt every 15 years (Inomata et al. 2015, 5; Wilk 1991, 210–211). Following the land-use and house cycles, farmers either rebuilt their house at the same place or shifted residence locations when they had exhausted accessible land. Ephemeral houses left little archaeological trace, at best anthropicized paleosoils and postholes in sterile bedrock, while in the early period the dead were not yet buried below houses or patios (Inomata et al 2015; see also Johnston 2004). In Middle Preclassic times, some farmers began dwelling near the residences of leaders or the collective

FIGURE 8.1. *Map of the Maya region with location of mentioned sites; case-studied sites in bold. (Map by Jean-François Cuenot, ArchAm Lab, Centre National de la Recherche Scientifique.)*

buildings in emerging central places. Probably in early existence with varying temporal and spatial patterns, an infield-outfield system developed: that is, farmers who had settled in villages or centers tended crops in both infield plots and outfield milpas located at a distance from their residence (Killion 1992; Netting 1977). The need to carry the crop load from fields to villages constrained the system (Atran 1993, 677). Transport may have rendered it more profitable to dwell seasonally on the field so as to consume the produce where it had been cropped, or at least during periods of intensive work on milpas. Dual residence resulted, with one urban house and a "field house," inasmuch as the subsistence system was not fully based on agriculture but also included use of secondary plants growing on milpas and fallowed fields, and, most important, the game attracted by cultivated maize (D. Brown 2002; Zetina Gutierrez and Faust 2011). Sometimes mentioned by archaeologists, field houses are rarely detected in lowland environments (see Garrison and Dunning 2009, 532; Lucero 2002, 815; Webster 2005, 61; Webster et al. 2000, 83, 109; Nancy Gonlin, personal communication, 2014; see also Gonlin and Landau, chapter 6, this volume). In those cases, mobility is mainly seasonal.

Shifting residences every five to 15 years corresponds to milpa temporary mobility. Moving from village or city residences to field houses for tending crops, hunting, and staple consumption and/or transport corresponds to milpa seasonal mobility. Both are part of complex subsistence movements, and their archaeological signatures are difficult to detect.

Longevity and Nongrowth of Small Household Units

Milpa temporary or seasonal mobility may only occasionally be detected, in high-resolution conditions of soil accumulation in dwelling units. Nevertheless, archaeologists can indirectly assess dual residence and associated infield-outfield systems through the careful study of the smallest dwelling units in sites. The Maya lived, and still live, in compounds of several houses where the members of an extended family dwell together, forming one household (Wilk and Ashmore 1988). The smallest household units visible in surface have one or two mounds (less than 0.5 m high) representing one or two nuclear kin families. They are the most abundant type of household units in Classic lowland cities, other types having more than two mounded structures. Except for Ceibal, where the proportion is only 36 percent, it is 80 percent at Dzibilchaltun and Mayapan (Tourtellot 1988, 106), 52.8 percent at Río Bec (Nondédéo et al. 2013a, table 7), and 55.6 percent at La Joyanca (Lemonnier 2009, 182). According to Haviland's domestic developmental cycle (Haviland 1988, based on Goody's 1958 model), they have a shorter lifespan than units having more structures. As we will see, this is not entirely validated, since small units rather show longevity with discontinuity, meaning primarily that they did not grow in size (Henderson 2003, 2012; Tourtellot 1988, figure 5.3). The nongrowth pattern implies that, even in normal conditions, at each generation the group lost some members who moved out to locate their house in another place, and that only one married member ensured continuity on the initial spot, himself having perhaps moved out temporarily before relocating at his parents' house (Wilk 1991, 95, 217; see Wilk and Ashmore 1988, 140, about bride service). This is what can be called "mobility embedded in continuity" (Takeshi Inomata, personal communication 2013), given that mobility is not hampered by permanent urban residence.

FIGURE 8.2. *Site map of La Joyanca, Guatemala, with location of test pits (S1 to S63) exca-vated in small household units. (Map by Eva Lemonnier, Projet La Joyanca–Tuspan B.)*

Mobility Embedded in Continuity: Group Gavilan at La Joyanca

In the test-pit program applied to La Joyanca neighborhoods in 2012 (Arnauld et al. 2017b), we sampled 30–60 percent of all modest units in each selected neighborhood (six among 11 neighborhoods; figure 8.2), complementing earlier excavations carried out in the large elite compounds of the site (Arnauld et al. 2004). On the site scale, the overall sample of excavated household units is 35 per-cent (65 units of a total of 185, all sizes considered). Among the 52 tested small units, 23 were one- or two-house units. One of those units, Group Gavilan, had previously (2000–2003) received full-coverage excavations (figure 8.3; Lemonnier 2009), and soil accumulation had been carefully analyzed in the process (Carozza et al. 2002, 2007). The types-modes of the ceramics recovered in large quantities

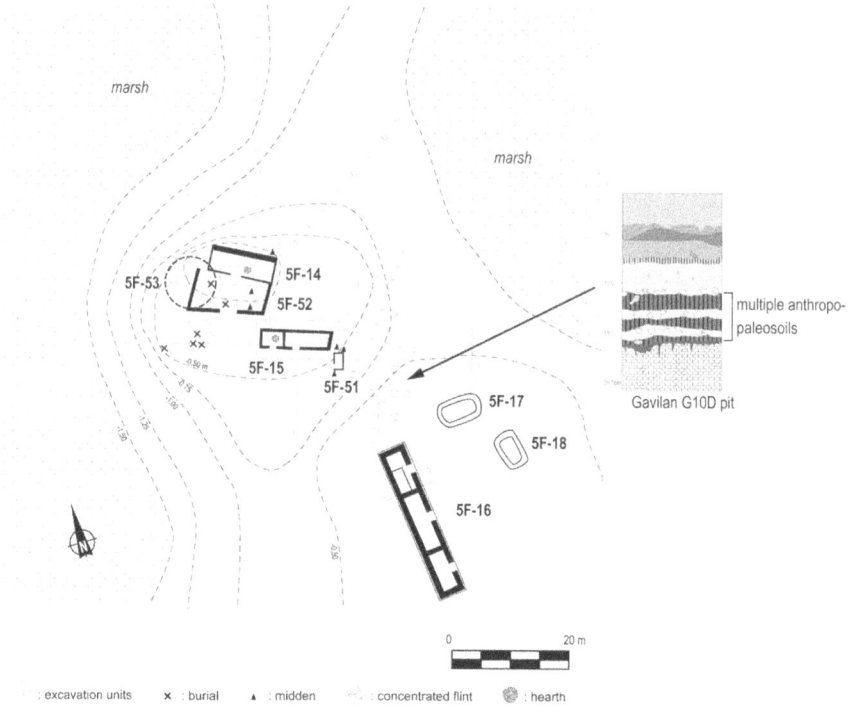

FIGURE 8.3. *Group Gavilan, or Unit 5F15, at La Joyanca, Guatemala, showing excavations carried out in 2000–2002 by Eva Lemonnier. (Modified from Lemonnier 2009, figure 5.1, Projet Petén Nord-Ouest-La Joyanca.)*

indicate that this unit was occupied continuously through 350 years, during Late Classic subphases 1–2 (AD 600–750, 750–850) and Terminal Classic subphase 1 (AD 850–950; Forné 2006). The four construction stages are summarized in table 8.1 (see Harris Matrix in Lemonnier 2009, figure 5.1).

In brief, three points are of interest for the mobility issue in the Gavilan sequence. First, it shows that during its 350-year lifespan the unit underwent growth from initially one to two residences, then three residences, if the neighboring vaulted structure is considered part of the same social group, which is stratigraphically plausible on the basis of Stages III–IV exterior-floor stratigraphy. With a total of six associated burials found, this is a moderate growth. Second, the presence of one burial early in the preplatform Stage I suggests that the initial settlers meant to stay there. And third, both house-platforms were entirely rebuilt at least once on newly spread fill and floor layers, but the more frequent rebuilding of each thatch-and-pole superstructure left no trace. In other words, even such a multicomponent sequence compacts the real story of both

TABLE 8.1. Summary of the life history of Group Gavilan (Unit 5F15), La Joyanca, Guatemala*

Construction Stages	Houses	Other Structures	Middens	Burials
Stage IV AD 850–950	5F14, 5F15 rebuilt on new fill and floor layers, with inner partition walls. Nearby vaulted 5F16 with inner benches	Added: 5F52 (house?) in 5F14 patio (not shared with 5F15)	Same middens accumulating	None preserved
Stage III AD 750–850	5F14, 5F15 each on a low stone-walled platform (40 cm high)	5F51, ancillary, storage	Several associated	One intrusive into filled-in 5F53
Stage II AD 675–750	Fill layer with stuccoed floor covering Stage I paleosoil, two short stone wall fragments	5F53, circular, ritual	None preserved	Four burials transitional from Stage II to Stage III
Stage I AD 600–675	Anthropicized paleosoil (Beta 155685, 1460 ± 50 BP cal AD 530–670, 2 sigma) over 35 m × 25 m area; two roughly dressed stones in line	None preserved	None preserved	One burial

* Spanning the Abril 1 (AD 600–750), Abril 2 (AD 750–850), and Tuspan 1 (AD 850–950) phases, on the basis of full coverage excavations by Eva Lemonnier (2009, 136–161). See also figure 8.3.

houses (see M. E. Smith 1992, 30–31, for a similar issue). What remains undetected is the sequence of repeated hiatuses resulting in soil accumulation deleted by later reconstruction, except possibly for multiple exterior anthropo-paleosoils (Carozza et al. 2002, 239) that may point to repeated natural soil accumulation during hiatuses (see figure 8.3 inset). The resulting pattern—longevity, low growth with few houses and burials, and compacted stratigraphic story—makes sense only if continuity and mobility are considered together. Continuity is reflected by the burial sequence in association with one ritual structure and the final construction of the vaulted structure, that is, an entirely masoned house or "durable house" (Beck 2007a). Mobility is indirectly assessed through low growth, low numbers of burials (compared to group mortality rates), and exterior floor stratigraphy, which indicates frequent hiatuses.

Mobility Embedded in Continuity: La Joyanca Neighborhoods

In 2012 we sampled units to be tested on the neighborhood scale, size being a secondary criterion of sampling (Arnauld et al. 2017b). As said, 23 small units (one or two visible mounds) in total, and 29 larger units were tested (with not all structures tested in any given unit). Five small units and two large ones were discarded due to poor dating. Instead of trying to count occupational components in each of the tested units, we evaluate their longevity and occupational continuity by counting the number of 50-year intervals (two generations) in their stratigraphic-ceramic history. The count is approximate in the three Late Preclassic/Early Classic phases, but more robust for the four Late/Terminal Classic phases.

Among the 27 large units, plus six elite compounds excavated previously, some 15 to 16 were founded before AD 600, most of them during the Late Preclassic subphases (400 BC–AD 200). Three of those early units and one late unit were still occupied from 950 to 1050. Hiatuses were detected in the ceramics and stratigraphy of 10 large units, indicating a degree of mobility. As for the 18 small units, half of them were founded well before AD 600, most during the Late Preclassic. Those units have an apparent longevity of 25 spans (until AD 850), and they nevertheless did not increase (i.e., no addition of structures on the platform). But, as the Gavilan case suggests, their compressed stratigraphy makes detecting hiatuses in occupation difficult (only two units). Seven were still occupied by 800–850, yet the Terminal Classic period (AD 850–1050) is rather characterized by late-founded large units (all counts based on Arnauld et al. 2017b, figures 6 and 9).

Plausible biases include low ceramic resolution (inflating longevity) and low stratigraphic resolution (reducing the detection of discrete hiatuses and construction episodes). Also, few burials were formally excavated. But even reducing lifespans and supposing many undetected hiatuses, nongrowing units still show that many generations of people discontinued and reconstructed ephemeral dwellings on the same, lightly renovated platforms. We suggest that this pattern corresponds to mobility embedded in continuity with limited growth.

This may well have been a generalized pattern that deserves more research in urban residential zones concerning, not only the stability of urban landscapes permitting such localized longevity, but also the hinterland/city relation (see M. L. Smith 2014). Beyond occasional high-mortality spurts, it indirectly reflects milpa mobility, or more generally, the long practice of households living in an urban context while still complying with mobility required by multiple subsistence strategies (see Wilk 1991, chapter 10, for modern Q'eqchi). Building houses on platforms, a technical answer to wet soil surface in rainy seasons, also satisfied the need to literally spot the urban place "owned" by the social group, rooted and legitimized by burials placed in those platforms (see Vapnarsky and Le Guen 2011 for modern Maya perception; Inomata et al. 2015). Even though mobility resulted in the absence of the group during one or two generations, memory of the place was kept through visits to the burial place. Hence, longevity, nongrowth, occupation hiatuses, and selective burials are explained not only by the mobility of some of the group members, but also by periodic group in-migration and out-migration.

Mobility Related to Masonry Architecture in Classic Urbanization

Just as the Gavilan people eventually built their durable house after three centuries of probably discontinuous presence at the same spot in the La Joyanca city, the ancient Maya who had settled in cities presumably sought to achieve social continuity and growth. These were basic preconditions for acquiring prestige and power locally. But clearly the mobility-continuity pattern suggests that lowland cities could not rapidly reach their maximal population size. Yet, large, collective ritual buildings were present even in early settlements, although associated residential zones were apparently reduced (see Inomata et al. 2015 for Ceibal, and Houston 2000, 177, for Piedras Negras). Maya peasants must have been enticed to sedentarize in cities so as to provide local elites with the labor force needed to create monumental architecture. Whether attracted by the prospect of stable life in better housing, or forced to settle in urban clusters (D. Chase et al. 1990, 500; de Montmollin 1989), Maya commoners probably migrated to cities where urbanization is archaeologically reflected in the sequences of residential zones that show not only an increase in dwelling units, but also a change from small thatch-and-pole houses to partially masoned, then large, vaulted residences. By AD 750 many compounds went through their second, third or fourth construction stage. At Río Bec the largest residences were built even later, from 700 to 900. In the Puuc zone, the proportion of household units having at least one vaulted dwelling can be high during Cehpech times (Becquelin and Michelet in press). An enormous body of datasets is available for analysis. More attention should be paid to correlating change in domestic masonry architecture with variation in occupancy rates (see Abrams 1994, 1998; Carmean 1991; Webster and Kirker 1995, for public architecture only).

The test-pit program applied in 2012 to the La Joyanca residential zone allowed us to calculate a shift in occupancy rate from 38.8 percent to 60.5 percent at the onset of the Late Classic phase 1 (by AD 600, early Abril 1). The percentages refer to the number of residential units, both large elite compounds and small commoner groups, with evidence of occupation during the La Joyanca ceramic phases subdivided into spans of 50 years (table 8.2; Arnauld et al. 2017b, figure 12). The rapidity of the shift may have been less than 100 years (AD 550–650), or more due to the low resolution of the Early Classic ceramic phase (La Flor, AD 200–600) compared to the higher resolution of the later phases (Abril 1–2 and Tuspan 1–2, 100 to 150 years each). In any case it is still a significant "surge" in population increase.

La Joyanca may have reached a maximal population of 1,291 to 1,639 inhabitants by AD 800–850 (late Abril 2), yet this had been calculated with an 80 percent occupancy rate (Lemonnier 2009, 201–204), which now appears too high compared to the results of our recent analyses (see table 8.2). However, it compensates for the change in domestic architecture that considerably enlarged the

TABLE 8.2. Distribution of 58 elite and smaller household units, La Joyanca, Guatemala*

Time transects (La Joyanca sequence)	Neighborhood													
	Armaldillo		Loro Real		Venado		Tepescuintle		Guacamaya		Zaraguate		Total	
	N	%	N	%	N	%	N	%	N	%	N	%	N	%
AD 200–250	0.0	0.0	2	3.4	7	12.1	6.0	10.3	6.5	11.2	1.0	1.8	22.5	38.8
AD 500–550	0.0	0.0	2	3.4	7	12.1	6.0	10.3	6.5	11.2	1.0	1.8	22.5	38.8
AD 600–650	3.0	5.2	4	6.9	7	12.1	7.5	13.0	11.5	19.9	2.0	3.4	35.0	60.5
AD 800–850	3.5	6.1	4	6.9	6	10.3	10.0	17.2	9.5	16.4	4.5	7.8	37.5	64.7
AD 950–1000	1.5	2.6	2	3.4	6	10.3	5.5	9.5	9.0	15.5	5.0	8.6	29.0	49.9

* Units occupied in 50-year time blocks or time transects (lines), in six La Joyanca neighborhoods (columns, sampled among eleven neighborhoods). All units were excavated and dated; seven units were discarded as poorly dated. The time transects were selected on the basis of graphs showing the distribution of occupied units so as to avoid as many error margins as possible. Raw counts and percentages are based on the total of 58 units (based on Arnauld et al. 2017b, figure 12).

elite compounds, increasing their housing capacities in comparison to commoner units. This change started earlier at La Joyanca, where the beginnings of monumental construction programs have been dated circa AD 600 (early Abril 1) in the public plaza and residential zone of the emerging city, particularly with vaulted structures (Arnauld 2002; Arnauld et al. 2004). Our interpretation is that the population surge is roughly coeval with the change in domestic architecture, not only in the elite compounds with vaulted residences, but even in small units where construction episodes with low stone walls and stuccoed floors on earth platforms considerably increased (Arnauld et al. 2017b, figure 8). Even if temporal details of the change remain to be studied, the AD 600 urbanization appears to involve a double process of long-term changes in housing patterns and population increase, the latter probably achieved in good part through in-migration, as in most preindustrial cities (Cowgill 1975; M. E. Smith 2014, 528; Tilly 1978).

Local paleoenvironmental evidence provided by two cores taken from Lake Tuspan (5 km west of La Joyanca) had initially suggested that the migration scenario would correlate with the end of the most intense erosional event recorded in the lake surroundings, which is dated AD 406–661 (Fleury et al. 2014), supposedly corresponding to maximal land use in the south hinterland. The Lake Tuspan sequence shows no later erosional episode (Carozza et al. 2007). By AD 661 local farmers either left the lake surroundings to dwell in La Joyanca, or shifted their land use and mobility patterns. Similar Early Classic population movements from small outlying sites into Piedras Negras and Yaxchilan have been proposed (Kingsley et al. 2012, 113; for other examples see Garrison and Dunning 2009; D. Rice and Rice 1990, 134–135; D. Rice et al. 1998). Farmers would have been attracted or—as envisioned by Tourtellot (1993, 225)—"captured" to support monumental construction (Inomata 2004, 186). But simultaneously they developed masonry architecture for their own needs. If established regionally, the time sequence of stone-masoned vault introduction in epicenters, elite compounds, and commoner residential zones would probably reflect that not only labor needs but also the perspective of achieving stability with growth had attracted hinterland families into urbanizing settlements. Urban attraction may have been the most intense and generalized movement through the Classic period all over the Maya lowlands.

MOBILITY TYPES RELATED TO CHANGES IN HOUSING SYSTEMS WITHIN CITIES

With many colleagues since 1986, we have been investigating seven Maya sites in the lowlands: Xcochkax, Xculoc, and Xcalumkin in the Puuc zone area (Michelet et al. 2000), Balamku and Río Bec in central Campeche (Arnauld et al. 1998; Michelet et al. 1998; Nondédéo et al. 2013a), La Joyanca in northwest Petén (Arnauld et al. 2004, 2014; Arnauld et al. 2013a), and Naachtun in northeast

Petén (Hiquet 2020; Nondédéo et al. 2013b; Sion 2016) (see figure 8.1). In all cases residential zones were surveyed, mapped, sampled, and excavated on both the household and neighborhood unit scales, that is, with systematic excavations of any one unit and its adjacent units. The diverse programs shared objectives in reconstructing social dynamics through the relative dating of building stages, occupation spans, and abandonment. Two simultaneous processes were identified, progressive autoconstruction and contraction of neighboring units into larger units, both having determined changes in mobility patterns.

Autoconstruction: Continuity with Growth

In one of the studied Puuc sites, Xcochkax, two adjacent units, 35 m distant, were horizontally excavated (Arnauld 1999; Michelet et al. 2000, 403–431). The sequence is only 200 years long (AD 800–1000). The dwelling system is distinct from the La Joyanca Gavilan example as Puuc units have one or more chultuns (water tanks) dug into the bedrock of small, natural karstic platforms. The case study bears on two such distinct platforms. Table 8.3 summarizes the sequence of alternate occupations on the western (largest) and eastern platforms, followed by the development on the former of a unit with possibly more than 18 rooms by successive additions of structures and chultuns. Furthermore, the architectural types of structures change through the six stages, in particular with the introduction of vaulted houses and a shrine. The increase in dwelling space (in square meters) has been shown to correlate with the increase in chultun volume, suggesting that the inhabitants carefully anticipated the growth of their group and their needs in water. Yet, in the sixth stage, the largest vaulted residence was left unfinished when the unit was abandoned.

The contrast with the La Joyanca Gavilan sequence is patent. Here the pattern combines short occupation with substantial growth—almost one reconstruction or expansion stage per generation—rapid improvement of domestic architecture, minimal stratigraphic accumulation, and no burial (except perhaps in the shrine, unexcavated). Hiatus in occupation seems questionable (see Haviland 1969, 429, for similar cases and analysis at Tikal). All or most members of the group maintained residence on the same western platform, a stability that the chultun technology warrants in the environmental conditions of the northern peninsula (see Dunning et al., chapter 7, this volume; also, the system is technically difficult to master, discouraging group fission, Arnauld 1999, 210). Stable coresidence in turn allowed the Xcochkax inhabitants to rapidly gain access to the vault technology that they applied to their shrine and last residence. The Gavilan inhabitants were also able to build a similar, although smaller, residence, but only after 300 years of discontinuous presence with limited growth. Both examples suggest that many Maya farmers built their own "durable houses" (Beck 2007b) by themselves, starting from simple houses. Continuity with

TABLE 8.3. Summary of the life histories of three adjacent units, Xcochkax, Puuc, Mexico*

Stage	Construction Modeled timespan (AD)	Houses	Other Structures	Chultun	Rooms (N)
Stage VI	950–980	Unfinished expansion of vaulted house (E4–10)	No data	Ch.2 still functioning	18+
Stage V	920–950	West Platform: 2 houses added (T2) & possibly main Stage III house partly rebuilt (T2)	Added: vaulted shrine with column Kitchens: 1 rebuilt and 1 added (T3)	Chultuns 2, 4, and 6 still functioning	16+
Stage IV	890–920	West Platform north tip: 1 added vaulted house (Type 1, E4–10)	No data	Chultun 6	7 + 2
Stage III	860–890	West Platform: 2 houses (T2–3) East Platform: abandoned	Kitchen (T3) with midden	Chultun 4	7
Stage II	830–860	West Platform: hiatus East Platform:1 house (T2-T3?) 2 substages: renovated floor	Kitchen (T3)	Chultun 5	3 to 4?
Stage I	800–830	West Platform: wall fragment East Platform: no occupation	None preserved	Chultun 3 filled: midden dated Stage I	No data

* Units are coded C-14, C-15, and C-16, and span the local Cehpech phase (AD 800–1000), based on full coverage excavations by M. Charlotte Arnauld (in Michelet et al. 2000, 177–196) with Fabienne de Pierrebourg. West and East Platforms are natural with subterranean water tank (chultun) dug out in bedrock. Structure Type 1 (T1), specialized cut stone, vaulted; Type 2 (T2), mixed stone, including cut lintels and jambs, high stone walls, unvaulted; Type 3 (T3), low stone walls, unvaulted.

frequent mobility (La Joyanca) slowed the process that, instead, was accelerated by stability of the group members and family growth (Xcochkax). Durable house architecture functioned as a sort of trap, catching populations. This specific process seems to have also functioned on wider spatial-social scales.

Contraction: Internal Mobility on the Neighborhood Scale

The Río Bec project built up on our previous experiences in household archaeology at Xcochkax, Balamku, and La Joyanca (also at Toniná; Arnauld 1999) focusing on the neighborhood scale as commended by Wilk (1988, 146). Broader areal excavations applied to series of adjacent units allowed us to document not only progressive autoconstruction but also simultaneous social contraction (Arnauld et al. 2012; Nondédéo et al. 2013a). The Río Bec environment locally favored intensive agriculture on terraced or enclosed fields surrounding the farmer dwellings (Lemonnier and Vannière 2013). The term sprawl (M. E. Smith 2010a) approximately qualifies the semirural, semiurban occupation of the whole Río Bec region south of Becan, where few sectors were left unoccupied and accessible to settlers or temporary *milperos*. Everywhere limited labor was locally required to tend crops in carefully bounded infields, and to build Río Bec–style vaulted houses (Arnauld et al. 2014). Thus, in this region mobility was hampered by several demographic and socioeconomic factors probably even more than in the Puuc region, a conclusion confirmed by the paucity of external trade relationships during the Late Classic period (Andrieu 2013; Arnauld et al. 2014). Yet, microscale dynamics may reflect intrasettlement mobility.

As defined by drainage channels, each Río Bec neighborhood encompasses one or two monumental, multiroom, decorated residences, some with appended towers, each with adjacent smaller house(s) and kitchen(s). These are the famous "Groups," labeled A, B, C, and so forth, among which smaller units with vaulted and unvaulted houses are dispersed (figure 8.4). Excavations of Groups A, B, and D entirely exposed 23 structures, mostly residences (with four kitchens), and every adjacent unit was test-pitted. Relatively high-resolution chronological assignments are based on a fine-grained ceramic typology built by Sara Dzul, as well as radiocarbon dating, and one Maya calendar date painted on a bench—in Structure 6N2, the residence paired with Edifice B (Taladoire et al. 2013). Complex construction stories assessed for the largest structures in Groups A, B, and D showed that the main construction stages may have lasted a hundred years each (Arnauld 2011; Michelet et al. 2013). This indicates that time length compensated for the limited availability of labor.

Moreover, from AD 550 to 850 the three sequences suggest that adjacent smaller units were abandoned during the lengthy construction stages. Figure 8.5 presents the stories of Group B compared to those of the La Joyanca Guacamaya neighborhood. Small units succeeded in building their own small masonry houses only to abandon them not much later. After AD 875 only the largest units were still occupied (along with neighboring Unit 6N4 in the case of Group B, figure 8.5a), resulting in three large "estates" that included terraced land of 3–4.5 ha each (Lemonnier and Vannière 2013, table 2). The need for labor makes it unlikely that many people were expelled in the process. Rather than eviction, integration into the social group of the most powerful houses provided the dominant families with labor, which meant a shift of residence from small to large units. In contrast with the Gavilan and Xcochkax cases presented above, in which farmers built their own vaulted houses, many Río Bec farmers integrated dominant residential compounds.

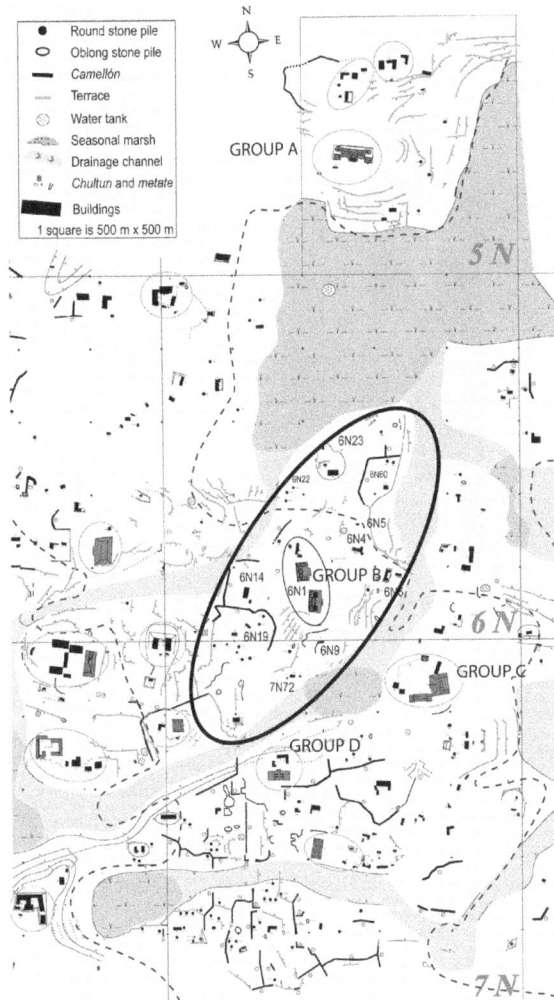

FIGURE 8.4. *Central sector of Río Bec, Mexico, in the nuclear zone (1.59 km²), with monumental Groups A (north), B (center), and D (south). (Modified from Lemonnier and Vannière 2013, figure 3, Projet Río Bec.)*

The Río Bec case study points to a contraction process referring to both a decreasing number of household units and a restriction of residential space for each nuclear family in a new modular housing system: the Río Bec–style residence (Nondédéo et al. 2013a, 379, 381, 382; Taladoire et al. 2013, 361–364). The process is reminiscent of analogues studied in the American Southwest where agrarian societies also adopted stone architecture in highly modular settlements (Flannery 2002; Kent 1992; Kohler 1992), although the latter appear more nucleated than Río Bec due to distinct infield systems. The comparison calls for more attention to be paid to granary and storage facilities in Maya housing systems—in vaulted rooms, presumably the space on wooden beams under the vault.

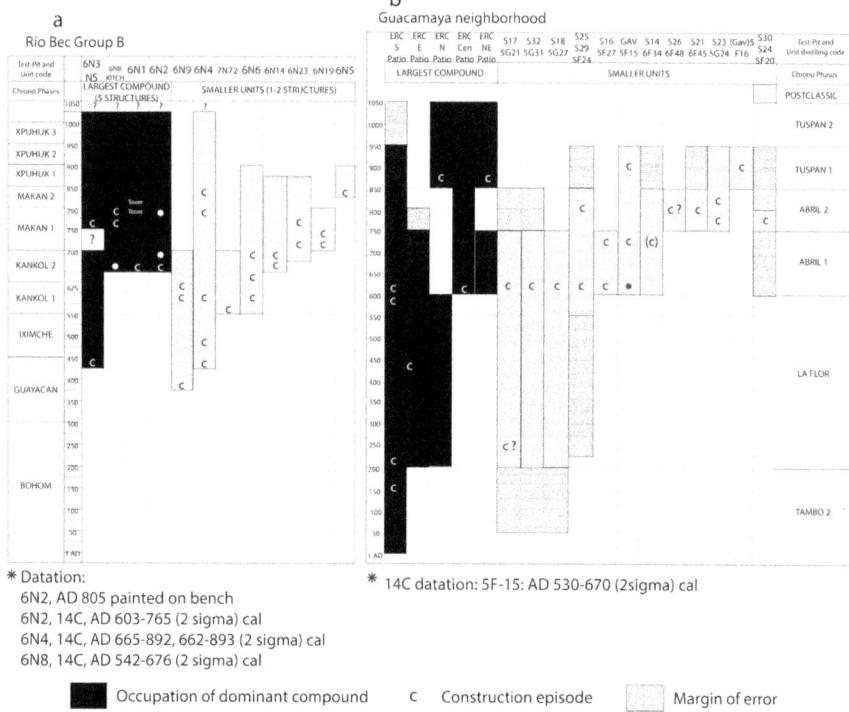

a
Río Bec Group B

b
Guacamaya neighborhood

* Datation:
6N2, AD 805 painted on bench
6N2, 14C, AD 603-765 (2 sigma) cal
6N4, 14C, AD 665-892, 662-893 (2 sigma) cal
6N8, 14C, AD 542-676 (2 sigma) cal

* 14C datation: 5F-15: AD 530-670 (2sigma) cal

■ Occupation of dominant compound   c Construction episode   ▨ Margin of error

FIGURE 8.5. *Comparing patterns of construction-occupation in two neighborhoods (AD 400–1100): (a) Group B, Río Bec, Mexico, seriated life histories of excavated dwelling units (9 units of a total of 12), elite compound on left side (the well-known "Group B," one log per structure), and smaller units on right side (one log per unit); (b) Guacamaya neighborhood, La Joyanca, Guatemala, 16 seriated units (of a total of 29), elite compound patios on left side, smaller units on right side. (Graph by Eva Lemonnier.)*

At La Joyanca the life stories of all tested smaller units have also been analyzed in relation with the construction stories of the larger compounds on the neighborhood scale (see figure 8.5; Arnauld et al. 2017b, figure 9). It appears that just after the construction of large vaulted multiroom residences a number of small units were abandoned as early as the Late Classic Abril 2 subphase (AD 750–850). Again, eviction or out-migration from the city is a possibility, but the Río Bec example rather suggests a process of settlement contraction, which seems plausible given the large dwelling capacity of vaulted multiroom residences in the elite compounds. At Naachtun, pending new evidence, after AD 800 people concentrated within Complex B-South, a large multipatio compound located in epicentral Group B, where the latest construction stages show clearly expanded, modular dwelling spaces (Nondédéo et al. 2013b, figure 5; Hiquet 2020; Sion

2016), whereas in the residential zone only one-third of the Late Classic units were still occupied (Hiquet and Sion 2018).

Generalized to many Late/Terminal Classic settlements with urban neighborhoods, the contraction process would have created powerful social groups clustered in a few residential compounds forming "social houses" (Arnauld et al. 2013b; Gillespie 2000; for possibly similar cases see LeCount and Yaeger 2010a, 75–76; Marken 2011; Zralka 2008, 129, 131). Such a tight affiliation of commoners with high-rank households would have been conditioned by access to good land adequate for intrasettlement, intensive agriculture, and would have entailed a loss of freedom in mobility for milpa agriculture, hunting, and trading activities (McAnany 1993, 77–83; Osborne 1991; Webster 2005). Generally, as intrasettlement agriculture required labor investment in infields (to build terraces, mark boundaries, plant fruit trees, etc.), farmers may have obtained the rights to inherit their improved land (McAnany 1993, 1995, 69–99; Roys 1943, 28; Wilk 1991, 120, 205, concerning cacao and copal trees, and some wetlands). Not only the affiliation to powerful houses must have transformed the traditional conditions of subsistence mobility, but land rights may have also favored stability of populations.

TERMINAL CLASSIC TRADE MOBILITY AND INTERSITE MIGRATIONS

By the end of the Classic period, continuous residence and stability in large social groups would have allowed a number of Maya families to afford growth with a sedentary life in prestigious dwellings. By the Terminal Classic period (AD 780–950) multipatio compounds with vaulted houses may have gathered a relatively high proportion of the whole settlement populations: 22–40 percent at La Joyanca (Lemonnier 2009, 203). While milpa mobility was inhibited, trade mobility appears to have increased rapidly as reflected by a generalized distribution of nonlocal items in quantity and diversity, particularly fine-paste carved ceramics, obsidian from Maya and Mexican Highlands, and volcanic and metamorphic stone metates (e.g., Braswell and Glascock 2003; Forné et al. 2013; Hruby 2006; Tokovinine and Beliaev 2013). Although to the detriment of architectural quality and monumentality (Sion 2016), social houses had presumably enough human resources to send members on trading trips, creating networks, alliances, and new opportunities in coastal settlements better connected to Mesoamerican dynamics (Turner and Sabloff 2012). By then, migrations had started out of Petexbatun, where warfare had been endemic by AD 750–810 (Demarest 2004, 117–121). Thus, new types of population movements began during the Terminal Classic period, in particular trade mobility and group migration. The former tended to be systemic, the latter was more related to circumstances and local crises.

Among the earliest archaeological evidence of Terminal Classic migrations has been the identification of "C-shaped houses" (D. Rice 1986) disseminated in elite compounds in various sites of the lowlands. It represents a type of non-vaulted, low-stone-walled, versatile dwelling, each having a long masoned bench and being easily partitioned for daily life and reception. Possibly intrusive at Ceibal, it helps trace movements of elite families up to Sayil and Uxmal. Quite distinct is the evidence of an unexpected, late (post–AD 870) trend to nucleation in peripheral sectors of the Río Bec region recently recovered by Philippe Nondédéo in Group I, Group V, El Porvenir, and Omelita, where huge "Río Bec Terminal style" residences were built at the core of large clusters of contemporaneous, similar, almost modular, lesser houses, suggestive of some late in-migration of people (Nondédéo et al. 2013a, 382, 392, figure 3). Another even more unexpected evidence of clustering was extensively excavated in 2003 at Balamku west of Río Bec, the p10A compound (figure 8.6). Postdating a Late Classic typical Río Bec–style unit with three separate vaulted houses, p10A encompasses 15 agglutinated rooms, nine with benches, opening on five small enclosed patios. Of unusual morphology in the Classic lowlands, p10A may represent the late settlement of some intrusive social group bringing an innovative, modular domestic architecture, although of poor quality. Analogous modular examples exist at Terminal Classic Calakmul on Structure II (Braswell et al. 2004). The modular system that agglutinated families appears at a moment (by AD 850–900) when some urban populations were migrating (Arnauld et al. 2017a; Demarest et al. 2004). It remains to be seen whether such late, poor-quality modular housing may have rendered the social groups more cohesive, prepared their out-migration, and facilitated their integration in host communities.

DISCUSSION: HOW TO MODEL CITY ABANDONMENT AS DE-URBANIZATION

A multiplicity of new housing systems created in urban contexts can be identified in the Maya lowlands roughly from AD 600 to 900. They reflect a variety of stability and mobility modes, allowing the archaeologist to model social dynamics in conjunction with paleoenvironmental datasets. Initially, Maya farmers may have been attracted to urban environments by the perspective of sedentary life and family growth. Once settled in emerging cities, they gradually improved their dwellings, either achieving the best-quality vaulted houses by themselves, or integrating elite compounds. An unknown proportion of commoners did not enter this alternative and never settled in urban settlements, or abandoned cities after discontinuous attempts. Specific correlations between urbanization, domestic architecture, and mobility are revealed by the case studies drawn from our research in the lowlands. De-urbanization must also be understood through the same kind of correlation.

FIGURE 8.6. *Compound p10A, Balamku, Mexico, located on the southern rim of the site's South Group; excavated in 2003. Benches are represented in gray. (Drawn by Laure Déodat, Balamku Projet, modified from Becquelin et al. 2005, 324, figure 14.)*

"Even though at first glance it may seem that there was massive population loss during and after the collapse, increasing evidence from hinterland studies suggests that what might have happened, instead, was both migration out of these areas and a reversion to non-platform houses constructed of thatch or wattle and daub, resulting in 'invisible' mounds in the archaeological record" (Lucero 2002, 821). We apply Lucero's remark primarily to the Maya who did not integrate large social groups, or split off at some moment. These people who reverted to the mobile, ephemeral dwelling system were presumably constrained by climatic conditions that were worsening from AD 830 to 1100. In contrast, the large groups who had engaged into trade activities and ceased to value high-quality architecture were more prepared to adopt drastic strategies of relatively massive out-migration following their already established alliances and networks.

Both such dispersion of commoners in hinterlands and more organized group migration of social houses must have been the most determinant processes that unfolded during the Terminal Classic and Early Postclassic over the Maya lowlands during the climatic transition to the Medieval Optimum (ca. AD 800–1100). As noted by Lucero, the former process is difficult to trace in forested environments. The latter, group migration, left silent residences that gradually went to ruin, but nevertheless frequently contained archaeological evidence of the circumstantial end of occupation. Abandonment, closure, termination, and postabandonment deposits have been discovered and are now analyzed in many Terminal Classic residential compounds (e.g., Lamoureux-St-Hilaire et al. 2015; Mock 1998). Some *de facto* deposits indicate violence suffered by inhabitants, closure deposits point to the migrant desire to cache properties and their intention to return, others reflect the rituals of definitive abandonment, and postabandonment deposits suggest that people still visited the abandoned houses.

The diversity per se is significant of the numerous, complex processes in which people were involved during what must have been a lengthy de-urbanization history on the regional scale. Even before complete abandonment of entire cities, contradictory expansion and reduction of residential zones point to diverse population movements, some of them correlated with still unfolding monumental, public or private construction (Forné 2006; Lamoureux-St-Hilaire et al. 2015; Zralka 2008; see Arnauld et al. 2017a; and Demarest 2004). Chronological refinement in studies of the Terminal Classic and Early Postclassic (AD 800–1200) lowland sites makes the difference between the perplexing vision of massive urban desertion and the more plausible implication of simultaneous, contradictory processes.

Through a series of dynamics that this chapter has attempted to reconstruct, by AD 800–900 the traditional balance between infield-outfield subsistence mobility, variable domestic architecture, and urbanization of politically central places had been radically transformed. From an elite perspective, trading mobility was perhaps as important as continuing diverse land-use strategies, stone architecture appeared disadvantageous due to maintenance and modification costs, and many epicentral royal courts lay abandoned, leaving central places devoid of their politicoreligious axis. New types of mobility by trading parties and their cohesive social groups may have logically prepared migrations from the southern to the northern lowlands, also to the Guatemalan and Chiapas highlands. From the other perspective, that of commoners, either migration was the mandatory option following the social groups they were attached to, or dispersion out of urban neighborhoods into hinterlands appeared attractive when the benefits of sedentary life in nucleated settlements were outgrown by the drawbacks of sparse neighbors, reduction of market places, and locally precarious water resources. Their stone houses then were of no avail, and they returned to thatch-and-pole houses, possibly field houses built close to milpas and lakes or marshes.

CONCLUSION

This chapter intended to define and describe specific mobility types to be archaeologically identified in order to better understand the Terminal Classic transformations. The specific Maya lowland subsistence system combined with the making of politically central places, and both together determined particular urbanization movements. Then gradually, Maya social structures—kinship, marriage rules, coresidence, ancestor veneration—along with urbanism and changing domestic architecture in turn determined new mobility types on the region, city, and neighborhood scales. Construction of new housing systems materialized different living ways and trajectories of life for individuals, households, and coresident groups. Those processes affected the traditional balance between subsistence mobility and housing, resulting in sedentism, stability, and even perhaps "capture" of those commoners who affiliated to high-rank social houses. In a number of lowland regions analogous to Río Bec, mobility became close to unsustainable, given social, demographic and agrarian conditions of settlements sprawling over wide regions. Again, new types of mobility appeared in relation with the emergence of large cohesive groups in Maya cities, and the Terminal Classic insertion of Maya societies into Mesoamerica, with the development of long-distance exchanges, changed trading routes, and royal dynastic displacements or termination. Groups began migrating, some cities expanded through population in-migration, others declined due to out-migration. Late practices of population capture in warfare may have also impacted cities or neighborhoods, a factor that would deserve a special treatment beyond settlement patterns and domestic architecture that are given priority in the present study.

Archaeological signatures have been presented for several broad categories of mobility, milpa temporary mobility, seasonal mobility, urban attraction, mobility embedded in continuity, settlement contraction, trade mobility, and group migration. To some point they appear to have operated sequentially during the Classic urbanization and de-urbanization processes. The latter never repeated in the same way, even though new cities again formed during the Postclassic periods (see Alexander 2012). Our past and present research efforts hopefully indicate that it is possible to identify and date systemic mobility (e.g., subsistence, milpa, and trade mobility) as well as to contrast these movements with more conjuncture-related, historical movements (e.g., group migration). Still other population movements inherently existed in urban phenomena (e.g., urban attraction, mobility embedded in continuity, and settlement contraction). For all of them, the main archaeological proxies consist of the diachronic changes in stone domestic architecture and intensive agriculture situated in the broad history of Maya lowland urbanization and de-urbanization that unfolded during the first millennium AD and further beyond.

The study of Postclassic Maya societies and settlements points to what the Maya preserved from their Classic urban civilization and what they actually gave up. No doubt that urban life reappeared at Chichen Itza and Mayapan, but with less-intensive infield agriculture, and without vaulted houses and most monumental public buildings that had been the hallmarks of the Classic civilization.

ACKNOWLEDGMENTS

We thank Pierre Becquelin (Tonina, Xculoc, and Xcalumkin projects); Philippe Nondédéo, Julien Sion, and Julien Hiquet (Naachtun project); and Véronique Breuil-Martínez, Erick Ponciano, Ernesto Arredondo, Salvador López, Didier Galop, and Jean-Michel Carrozza (La Joyanca projects) for sharing data with us.

We want to express our gratitude to INAH in Mexico and IDAEH in Guatemala for authorizing all projects, as well as to those who supported the La Joyanca projects, including Mrs. Gilberte Beaux (Basic Holdings Ltd), Licenciado Rodolfo Sosa (Basic Resources International, Bahamas, Ltd Sucursal Guatemala), Perenco, the French Ministry of Foreign Affairs, the Centre National de la Recherche Scientifique, and Université de Paris 1 Panthéon-Sorbonne (EXODES program).

PART III

Late Mesoamerican Migrations

9

Coalescence at Chicoloapan, Mexico

Migration and the Making of a Post-Collapse Community

SARAH C. CLAYTON

The Epiclassic period, from about AD 550 to 850, was a time of extraordinary social change in central Mexico. The powerful centralized state of Teotihuacan had broken down, its governing institutions dissolved, and the population of its monumental capital diminished to a fraction of its former size. The release of Teotihuacan's grip transformed a formerly consolidated subject territory into a fractious sociopolitical landscape coping with instability and violent conflict (see Morehart et al. 2012). These circumstances stimulated and may have at times necessitated—through displacement or forced relocation, for example—the significant movement of people. The reconfiguration of settlement across the Basin of Mexico (Charlton and Nichols 1997; Sanders et al. 1979) that resulted from these migrations is among the most archaeologically conspicuous changes related to the state's decline. As several previously established communities were abandoned, new settlements appeared in defensible locations, such as hill-tops. Some existing settlements experienced rapid and extensive growth, which required solving new sets of problems related to basic provisioning, security, the use of land and resources, and achieving a peaceable coexistence among

DOI: 10.5876/9781646420735.c009

increasing numbers of people. Alongside changes to regional settlement, new kinds of material culture and practices developed that departed substantially from earlier material traditions (Cowgill 2013).

Although shifting settlement patterns in the Basin of Mexico at this time are understood to have resulted from people's moving, *migration*—as a lived experience and active social process that impacted internal community dynamics—has rarely been closely examined in this context. These movements, which occurred under varying circumstances, amounted to more than just demographic rearrangements; they entailed leaving behind familiar people, places, and belongings, assuming the risks of travel, and negotiating new relationships. Migrations alter the courses of individuals' lives, affect social interactions within communities (Cameron 2013), and ultimately influence broader sociopolitical developments. Here, I consider the processes of migration and community building at Chicoloapan, a settlement in the southern Basin (figure 9.1) that grew significantly in the years surrounding Teotihuacan's decline. Drawing from settlement data and analyses of material culture, I examine how social practices and the built environment were configured to accommodate a growing and diverse population at a time of regional sociopolitical instability.

I find the concepts of *transformative relocation* (Nelson et al. 2014) and *coalescence* (Birch 2013; Kowalewski 2007) to be useful for relating Chicoloapan's growth to region-wide sociopolitical shifts, and for examining internal processes of community formation, respectively. Evidence from Chicoloapan, as an example of rapid settlement aggregation, sheds light on the strategies that people employ, under such conditions, to minimize social friction, promote cooperation, and establish consensual rules relating to space and resource access. The concept of coalescence offers a framework for investigating changes that occur when people come together under pressure, including the development of new practices, institutions, and material culture. For the Epiclassic Basin of Mexico, these concepts provide a way to see beyond changes in regional settlement patterns, toward understanding in fuller measure the social dynamics of community building.

MIGRATION AS TRANSFORMATIVE
RELOCATION IN CENTRAL MEXICO

Building upon recent advances in the study of migration (e.g., Cabana and Clark 2011a; Tsuda et al. 2015), Arnauld and colleagues (introduction, this volume) define *migration* as relocation that occurs under unusual circumstances. In contrast to *mobility*, which is systemic and habitual—such as periodic movement between rural and urban settlements (M. E. Smith 2014)—migration entails movement that is out of the ordinary, or disruptive with respect to routine practices. Although migration may be broadly considered to be a patterned human

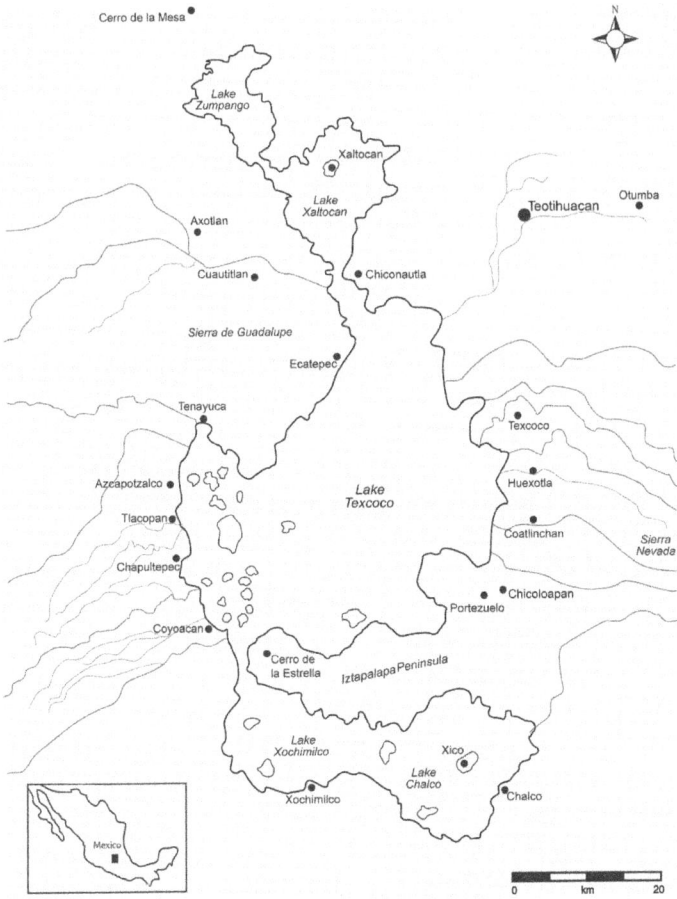

FIGURE 9.1. *Prehispanic settlements in the Basin of Mexico. (Map modified by author after https://commons.wikimedia.org/wiki/File: Lago_de_Texcoco-posclásico.png [Public Domain].)*

behavior (Anthony 1990), migrations are not routine, but involve crossing political, environmental, or social boundaries (Cameron 2013).

In some cases, migration relates closely to processes of sociopolitical decline and regeneration, including the depopulation of centers, the discontinuation of entrenched practices and the formation of new ones, and the profound reordering of social constructs. Nelson and colleagues (2014) offer the concept of *transformative relocation* to aid in understanding resettlement as part of systemic social reorganization (also see Arnauld et al., introduction, this volume). Transformative relocation involves moving and adopting new ways of life when existing socioecological structures lack the necessary flexibility to adapt to changing circumstances, or become *path dependent* (Hegmon 2017; Nelson et al. 2014). Path dependence is characterized by rigid resistance to change, even when revising established practices becomes imperative for solving critical problems. Path-dependent structures (e.g., political and economic institutions) eventually break down, and the movement of people to new locations facilitates this process of disaggregation and reformation. In an effort to identify variables that are cross-culturally relevant in this process, Nelson and coauthors compare transformative relocation among prehispanic societies in Mesoamerica and the southwestern United States. The framework they offer is helpful for examining the systemic vulnerabilities and responses that contributed to the dissolution of Teotihuacan and set in motion the resettlement of the Basin and the reformulation of social groups and constructs.

Inflexibility has long been viewed as a challenge for the long-term sustainability of states and the multiple, overlapping, and intersecting institutions that they comprise (Yoffee 1988). Cowgill (1988) stressed that states are not self-regulating systems; rather, they are beset with problems stemming from bureaucratic rigidity, conflicting interests, corruption, and inefficiency. Robert McC. Adams (1978), in discussing the trajectories of Mesopotamian polities, argued that an inverse relationship exists between political stabilization and the capacity to effectively adapt to unforeseen challenges. That is, complex societies suffer a "loss of resilience" (Adams 1978, 332) when they cling to strategies that contribute to short-term success but are antithetical to long-term stability. Path dependence is a similar concept, but specifically describes adherence to previously established practices, policies, infrastructures, or technologies beyond the exhaustion of their utility or past the point of reversibility (Hegmon 2017; Nelson et al. 2014).

For Teotihuacan, multiple path dependencies in political and economic spheres may have produced problems that could not be solved. Strategies that had initially propelled the state to regional dominance, including approaches to governance, settlement, and infrastructure, may have increasingly constrained innovation and limited the state's capacity to meet future needs. Millon (1988) argued, for example, that an early pattern of nucleation, in which the population concentrated in the capital and a few secondary centers, initially served the economic interests of the state but was problematic in the long term. Drawing from Adams's work on the loss of resilience, Millon suggested that an unforeseen consequence of this settlement strategy and the particular infrastructural investments it involved was the underutilization, inefficient management, and diminished access to goods, materials, and human resources from the hinterland. Although this trajectory may have weakened the centralized state, it is likely to have concurrently increased the resilience of many regional communities by enhancing their autonomy and self-sufficiency.

The concept of transformative relocation provides an avenue for relating processes of migration and resettlement to systemic sociopolitical shifts, such as political fragmentation, at larger scales, and for considering the reasons why profound social change becomes necessary. It does not, however, provide a framework for explaining or predicting the changes that occur after relocation, or the ways in which people reorganize communities once they have moved. Strategies of community formation engage with a variety of factors, including the size of relocating groups, the presence of established residents, local resource availability, and histories of interaction or conflict with other communities. For cases involving the aggregation of diverse groups (e.g., migrants from different places) during conditions of instability, the concept of *coalescence* aids in examining these strategies. I draw from Kowalewski's (2007) discussion of coalescence and from the subsequent application and elaboration of the model to diverse case studies (e.g., Arkush 2017; chapters in Birch 2013).

By examining this process at Chicoloapan, I hope to elucidate further the ways in which people manipulate and revise material culture—not simply because practices are transported to new places, but as a means of revolutionizing ways of living and constituting new social worlds. Before discussing Chicoloapan's trajectory, I put these developments into context by briefly reviewing the collapse of Teotihuacan, as it is understood archaeologically, and the changes that mark the transition from the centralized Classic to the fractious Epiclassic period.

THE COLLAPSE OF TEOTIHUACAN, AND EVOLVING VIEWS OF MIGRATION

Sometime around AD 550 (Beramendi-Orosco et al. 2008; Cowgill 2015b; Wolfman 1990), more than 100 buildings concentrated in the administrative core of Teotihuacan were burned in a manner that Millon (1988, 149) described as deliberate, selective, and violent. Sculptures were smashed and the remains of multiple individuals whose bodies had been dismembered were left in the rubble (Jarquín and Martínez 1982; Millon 1988). The temples were never rebuilt, and the state never recovered. These acts appear to have signified not just the decommissioning of temples as settings of ritual action, but also the end of a government that had been undergirded by religious concepts that the structures symbolized. The fiery destruction of monuments may be a clear indication of Teotihuacan's political demise; however, relating these events to the broader processes from which they culminated is not straightforward. Protracted and complex factors precipitated drastic changes in material culture as well as mass emigration from the city, decreasing its population from about 100,000 to perhaps 40,000 (Cowgill 2000).

Changes marking the transition to the Epiclassic period (table 9.1) include the appearance across the region of new ceramic forms and wares. These include a style of pottery called Coyotlatelco (Gaxiola González 2006), which is characterized by serving vessels decorated with designs in red paint on a natural or cream-slipped background (figure 9.2). Coyotlatelco pottery resembles ceramics present in the Bajío region of Guanajuato and Querétaro (Brambila Paz and Crespo 2005; Braniff Cornejo 2005; Cobean 1990, 180; Healan 2012; Mastache et al. 2002, 60; Rattray 1966). This has prompted much discussion about whether changes in the Basin resulted from the migration of groups from the northwest, and whether this interaction and movement played a role in the fragmentation of the state and subsequent developments. At times, this issue has been framed as an *either/or* question hinging on identifying the geographic origins of Coyotlatelco. That is, Coyotlatelco was *either* brought into the Basin by migrants who replaced local populations in a scenario of ethnic succession (e.g., Acosta 1972; Rattray 1989), *or* it originated within the Basin, in which case migrations either did not occur or had no appreciable impact (e.g., Sanders 2006). It is clear at this point that this is a false binary, loaded with the historical baggage of treating migration as a catchall explanation for culture change, rather than as a complex and dynamic social process (see Anthony 1990). Evidence from across the central highlands indicates that migrants from a variety of places were part of the region's multiethnic population for many generations (López Perez et al. 2006; Moragas Segura 2013). Parsons and colleagues (1996) argued, based on evidence from Chalco, that Coyotlatelco was present in the southern Basin of Mexico while the distinctive material culture of Metepec-phase Teotihuacan was still in use at the capital. Mastache and colleagues (2002, 60) present a similar scenario of temporal overlap but sociospatial separation between communities using Teotihuacan and Coyotlatelco material culture, respectively, in the Tula area. Beekman and Christensen (2003), who trace the origins of Coyotlatelco to the Bajío region, suggest that immigrants and their descendants coexisted with Teotihuacanos for up to two centuries. Similarly, Moragas Segura (2013, 186) suggests that migrants from the Bajío, whom she collectively identifies as Coyotlatelcos, arrived in the basin and were part of Teotihuacan's sociopolitical landscape from AD 450/500 onward.

Evidence for interaction among diverse groups in central Mexico through time, along with improved theoretical approaches to the study of migration, oblige us to discard simplistic models of culture change and to examine how these processes of movement, interaction, and innovation played out. The adoption of Coyotlatelco pottery was a widespread phenomenon, involving the exchange of materials and ideas and, ultimately, local production[1] and daily use within communities. A more productive question than "where did it originate?" is "why did people adopt it?" What needs and desires did it serve, and what part did it play as people negotiated social relationships and created new kinds of communities and ways of living at a time of substantial change?

Determining whether sizable groups of people relocated to the Basin from the Bajío and whether these migrations generally occurred before the state came

TABLE 9.1. General Mesoamerican chronology and corresponding Teotihuacan phases

Chronological Periods	Teotihuacan Phases	Approximate Years
Early Postclassic (AD 850–1150)	Atlatongo	AD 1000–1150
	Mazapan	AD 850–1000
Epiclassic (AD 550–850)	Coyotlatelco	AD 550–850
Early Classic (AD 200–600)	Metepec	AD 550–600
	Xolalpan	AD 450–550
	Tlamimilolpa	AD 200–350
Terminal Formative (150 BC–AD 200)	Miccaotli	AD 125–200
	Tzacualli	AD 1–125
	Patlachique	150–1 BC

FIGURE 9.2. *Sherds of Coyotlatelco bowls from domestic contexts at Chicoloapan. (Photograph by author.)*

apart or in its aftermath, while important, will not neatly explain the emergence of new cultural practices. In addition to considering the complex social reasons that people adopt, create, and abandon material culture, it is important to recognize that the migrations that occurred were not exclusively interregional. There was also substantial movement within the Basin, as residents of the capital and other affected settlements were displaced. Communities were in flux as opportunities and pressures changed; some broke apart, whereas others absorbed new members. Scholarship focused on migration between regions, while important, has overshadowed the significance of shorter-distance relocation within the Basin. These movements are often collectively glossed as "settlement reorganization," but were at least as transformative as long-distance migrations (Abell 2014; M. E. Smith 2014). Empirical research that closely examines the internal dynamics of multiple individual settlements is needed if we are to understand the ways in which both long- and short-distance migrations affected the broader cultural trajectory of the central Mexican highlands.

COALESCENT COMMUNITIES AND THE CASE OF CHICOLOAPAN

The concept of a *coalescent society* was first applied to polities in the southeastern United States that formed during the seventeenth and eighteenth centuries through the convergence, in the context of great social volatility, of diverse groups of refugees and remnant populations (Ethridge and Hudson 2002). These groups aggregated in new places and developed new integrative institutions, more inclusive modes of leadership such as councils and confederacies, and revised ritual practices, including mythmaking in the service of new organizing principles. The concept has been further developed, particularly by Kowalewski (2007, 2013), as a device for examining how societies have formed in various times and places through the aggregation of groups coping with crisis. Societies or communities (Arkush 2017; Birch 2013) that develop through coalescence do not represent a type, but vary in scale, in ecological setting, and in their particular histories, technologies, cultural practices, institutions, and responses to problems. Coalescence describes broadly similar strategies that people implement to solve the practical problems that arise under such circumstances as the collapse of a polity. These strategies exhibit a range of "parallelisms" (Kowalewski 2007) in diverse cultural settings.

Patterns characteristic of coalescence include the convergence of ethnically or socially distinct groups into large towns or villages, often in new locations that provide the potential for increased security and sufficient resources; changes in technology and the social means of production, including forms of agricultural intensification; the innovation of new social and governing institutions based on corporate leadership or collective decision-making, which resist personalized leadership and centralized authority; modification of the built environment to promote shared concepts of community and to condition social interaction; and the development of egalitarian or collective ideologies and identities, including migration stories that emphasize the incorporation and ordering of groups. As Kowalewski (2013) argues, these changes were active and deliberate, resulting from purposeful efforts by political actors to build communities. In an illustrative discussion of community formation in the Late Intermediate Period Andes (AD 1100–1450), Arkush (2017, 2) describes coalescent communities as *social experiments* conducted under pressure. Below, I draw from multiple lines of data relating to demographic growth, social organization, daily practices, and material culture to consider how such an experiment may have played out at Chicoloapan.

The history of settlement at Chicoloapan began in the Formative period, before the emergence of Teotihuacan, and continued for many centuries after its collapse, making this a strategic site for investigating long-term change. The settlement reached its largest extent during the Epiclassic period, having grown from a hamlet of perhaps a few dozen scattered farmsteads to a sprawling urban town of perhaps 6,000 or more people (Parsons 1971). At this time, it was part of a cluster of settlements that stretched 6–8 km across the southeastern edge of the Basin and featured houses of varying size, temples, plazas, and farms. The research discussed here is part of an active, multiyear field project focused on an area located in the modern municipality of Chicoloapan, which today's residents refer to as "Chicoloapan Viejo." The broad objective of this project is to understand how community life was reconfigured in the generations surrounding state collapse, including changes to economic practices, ritual, and forms of leadership. This research involves the excavation of domestic structures and activity areas; analyses of architecture, artifacts, and ecofacts; and the mapping of buried archaeological features via geophysical methods in order to reconstruct the spatial organization of the settlement and demographic change through time. Geophysical research at Chicoloapan is just beginning. Data from pedestrian survey, excavation, and the dating of early construction levels, however, indicate that the local population grew significantly in the generations surrounding Teotihuacan's decline (Clayton 2012; Parsons 1971). This growth resulted primarily from migration into the area during a relatively short time, rather than through internal demographic processes alone (Clayton 2016).

The origins of people who moved to Chicoloapan are not known, and although it is possible that they came from adjacent regions, it is highly likely that many relocated from elsewhere within the Basin of Mexico, as discussed above. This was not a new settlement; indeed, the longevity of habitation in the southern Basin may have contributed to the relative resilience of local populations who lived through politically volatile times. The dramatic enlargement of the local population, however, necessitated major changes in the use of space, resources, and modes of social interaction. Latecomers would have interacted in varying ways with longer-term residents. For many, the decision to settle in Chicoloapan may have been motivated by previous relationships, such as familial ties with established households in the area. It must be stressed that even relatively rapid aggregation is an intergenerational process of social change, producing populations that cannot be realistically characterized in binary terms as comprising "locals" and "migrants," no matter the results of isotopic analysis. *Migrant* is a culturally specific, shifting construct that might not accurately describe, in an *emic* sense, persons who relocate or their descendants, who might or might not be regarded as "local."

Some stylistic continuity in ceramic forms at Chicoloapan from the Classic to the Epiclassic period, discussed further below, suggests that although novel ideas and practices were adopted at this time, there was also a degree of syncretism, or blending of old and new traditions. Although it is likely that the population was multiethnic, it would be premature to discuss specific ethnic identities, given the complex relationship between identity and material culture. Stylistic and technological variation in domestic architecture across the settlement, however, suggests that its population comprised diverse households, possibly with varied origins. I focus the remainder of this discussion on the built environment and material culture at Chicoloapan and consider how these reflect the work of making community.

URBANIZATION AND THE BUILT ENVIRONMENT AT CHICOLOAPAN

Manipulation of the built environment is among the most effective, lasting, and archaeologically accessible material manifestations of community formation. Anthropologists have long viewed architecture, in its physical, visual, symbolic, spatial, and functional dimensions, as instrumental in conditioning social interactions. Architecture is prominently emphasized in research concerning coalescence (e.g., Birch 2013), because it materializes the constructs that undergird community relations, such as hierarchy, belonging and exclusion (Arkush 2017), and governance. In coalescent communities, architecture promotes integration, to varying degrees, and suppresses personal aggrandizement and tendencies toward the consolidation of authority. It does this by providing spatial contexts that facilitate and/or symbolize integrative activities (e.g., ballcourts, marketplaces, parks, and plazas), but also by delineating the spaces in which politicoreligious power may be enacted (e.g., temples) or by embedding such spaces within communities.

Comparative research grounded in collective-action theory (Fargher et al. 2011) has elucidated a range of architectural patterns that tend to associate with differing political structures, in which power is either shared or concentrated. Centralized leadership may be reflected in secular elite architecture (e.g., noble estates), extreme differences in house size, burials grouped by class, and configurations that emphasize a central civic precinct. This sort of layout formed the basic urban template of Postclassic central Mexican *altepetl*, which were arranged around central temples (M. E. Smith 2008a). Shared power, on the other hand, may be manifested in dispersed arrangements of civic architecture, such as public plazas, and minimal differences in house size. Fargher and colleagues (2011) describe Postclassic *tlahtocayotl* of eastern Puebla, which were not arranged around central temples, as examples of polities that are more collective. Collective leadership has been inferred based on the architectural patterns of post-collapse communities in other regions as well. A lack of palaces among Middle Bronze Age communities in Syria is argued (Cooper 2006), for example, to reflect deliberate efforts to hinder the concentration of power, and thereby to avoid the collapses to which earlier polities were prone.

As people moved to Chicoloapan during the early Epiclassic period, the population increased and the character of the settlement changed. What had long been a sparsely settled agrarian village effectively became a small city, featuring multiple temples, plazas, enclosures, and residential compounds. Although it was many orders of magnitude smaller than the great cities of Teotihuacan and Postclassic Tenochtitlan, it is important to recognize that these were anomalous with respect to Mesoamerican urban traditions. Chicoloapan was comparable in scale to the altepetl centers of the Postclassic Basin and Morelos, which had an estimated median of 4,750 inhabitants (M. E. Smith 2008a; Fargher et al. 2011, 309).

Results of pedestrian survey, surface collection, excavation, and limited geophysical prospection to date have yielded valuable information about Chicoloapan's built environment and, in turn, the social and political strategies of its residents. The most striking pattern to note is that the arrangement of civic-ceremonial architecture across the settlement represents a radical departure from the spatial logic of Teotihuacan. The settlement is not arranged around a central civic precinct. Temples and other forms of monumental architecture were conspicuous features of the landscape during the early Epiclassic period, but these structures were not spatially concentrated (figure 9.3). Ten sizable mounds are dispersed across the project area of 3.5 km², with others extending into the Chimalhuacan municipality to the west, associated with the site of Cerro Portezuelo (Hicks 2013) and into Ixtapaluca, to the east. Test excavations conducted in public plazas attached to Mounds 1 and 5 and in a large enclosed plaza 100 m east of Mound 5 reveal that these structures all contained early Epiclassic-period pottery in their early construction levels.

No mound at Chicoloapan has been directly excavated, as field research to date has concentrated on understanding the general spatial characteristics of the settlement and on more ephemeral domestic contexts, which face a greater threat of destruction by modern development. Several useful observations may be made, however. These are pyramidal platforms—likely temples—that ranged from 4 to 9 m in height and in most cases supported adobe structures, the collapsed walls of which are visible from the surface. They are relatively evenly spaced and correspond to clusters of archaeological features evident on the surface, the majority of which are the remains of residential structures, based on excavations conducted so far. Although the mounds are not massive in scale—especially compared to Teotihuacan, for example—all are visibly

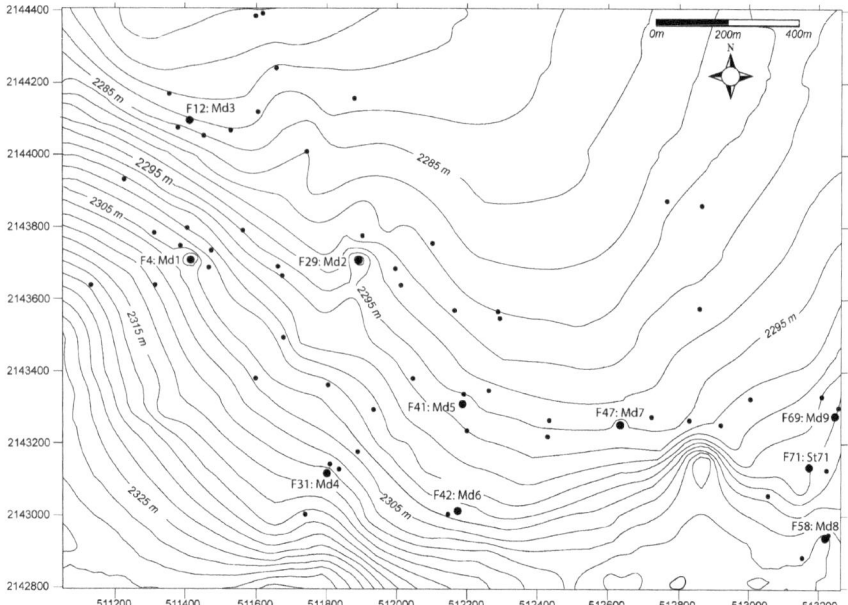

FIGURE 9.3. *Contour map of Chicoloapan, showing the distribution of pyramidal mounds (labeled) and other architectural features visible on the surface (indicated by smaller dots). (Map by author.)*

prominent and may be collectively viewed from the terraced hills that frame the southern edge of the settlement. Each mound is also visible from the nearest surrounding mounds, creating a pattern in which residential groups were spatially demarcated and defined in part by their access to a particular temple, but easily within view of other groups. Such placement is an artifact of deliberate urban planning. The structures were embedded within residential areas and probably served surrounding households. Their visual connectedness across space, however, likely promoted a sense of community for inhabitants of the settlement as a whole, even as they simultaneously facilitated a degree of autonomy and distinction among residential groups.

In addition to promoting a sense of community membership through a collectively understood pattern of civic architecture, the distribution of temples across the landscape may have facilitated forms of power sharing. That civic-ceremonial buildings were dispersed and set amongst houses suggests that leadership at Chicoloapan was more collective than centralized. Given the circumstances of the settlement's growth amid political upheaval, this strategy is likely to have been purposefully aimed at avoiding or rejecting the institutions associated with Teotihuacan.

DOMESTIC ARCHITECTURE

Excavations conducted in several domestic structures have contributed fundamental data concerning the organization and activities of Epiclassic households
in the Basin, including their subsistence and ritual practices, material culture,
and heterogeneity. The most horizontally extensive of these have concentrated
on three well-preserved residences—Structures 3, 7, and 9 (Op3, Op7/8, and Op9
in figure 9.4)—which were initially built and inhabited during Teotihuacan's
Metepec phase, or the early Epiclassic period. These represent the first detailed,
extensive excavations of household contexts from this period in the southern
Basin of Mexico.[2]

Domestic structures at Chicoloapan differed from those of Teotihuacan in
the materials and techniques used in their construction, their outward appearance, and their internal features. Residential construction involved the heavy use
of *either* adobe blocks or tamped, poured mud, sometimes in combination with
worked or unworked *tezontle* (a volcanic stone abundant in the area), although
the latter was often restricted to exterior walls. Architecture at Chicoloapan
has been heavily damaged by the plow and by water action, as the site sits on
an alluvial fan and much of the construction is earthen. This limits our ability to accurately determine the full size of individual structures. Geophysical
research during the next few years, including magnetic and electrical survey, will
enhance our understanding of intrasettlement variation in structure size, and
to determine whether there were extreme differences. It is clear, however, that
multiroomed structures were present, containing rooms of varying function,
including sunken patios with central hearths. Their configurations changed as
rooms were remodeled or added, and it was common to observe differences
in construction techniques through time within the same structure. However,
adobe blocks and *tapia* construction (see Hirth 2000, 101)—which entailed creating large slabs of hardened earth by pouring a mud mixture into construction
forms in place—have not been observed to co-occur.

Structures 3 and 7 are illustrative of stylistic variation observed among contemporaneous dwellings at Chicoloapan. Structure 3 (figure 9.5) is located in
the northwestern area of the site; Structure 7 (figure 9.6) is located nearer to
foothills along the southern margin of the settlement. The hills feature terraces
that likely date to the Epiclassic period, based on ceramics collected from the
surface, and may have facilitated agricultural intensification—a pattern among
coalescent communities. These structures were well preserved in some areas
and severely damaged by the plow in others. Both were determined to be residential based on the presence of hearths, food-preparation equipment (pottery,
grinding stones, and obsidian tools), and domestic trash, including faunal and
botanical remains. Ceramics and lithics included characteristically Epiclassic

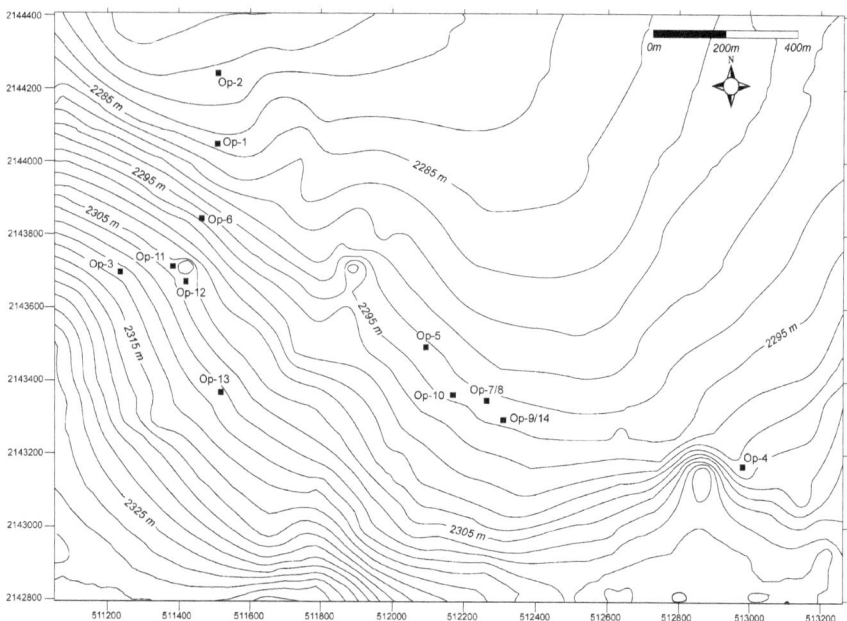

FIGURE 9.4. *Contour map of Chicoloapan, showing the locations of areas excavated (Operations 1–14). (Map by author.)*

materials such as Coyotlatelco pottery and primarily gray, rather than green, obsidian (see Parry and Glascock 2013; Spence 1981). Both structures featured plastered floors, but the construction techniques for walls differed markedly. The walls in Structure 3 were built using a combination of adobe bricks and unmodified *tezontle* cobbles of varying size; in contrast, the *tapia* technique was used to build most of the walls in Structure 7.

Both structures show evidence of extensive remodeling over multiple generations, and dated wood charcoal from secure contexts indicates that there was temporal overlap in the use of the structures (table 9.2). This suggests that the differences in their construction techniques represent synchronic, intracommunity variation in architectural style rather than changing practices through time. Dates from the earliest sampled context in Structure 3 suggest that it was built by AD 575–650; it is likely to have been abandoned circa AD 669–770. Structure 7 is likely to have been built earlier in the AD 500s. A plaster layer associated with a remodeling episode that occurred after its initial construction represents the earliest date obtained. The latest dated context of activity in Structure 7 was a hearth showing evidence of use between AD 624 and 675.[3]

Although socioeconomic inequality was a factor, persistent variation in the techniques and materials used to build houses is also likely to have expressed

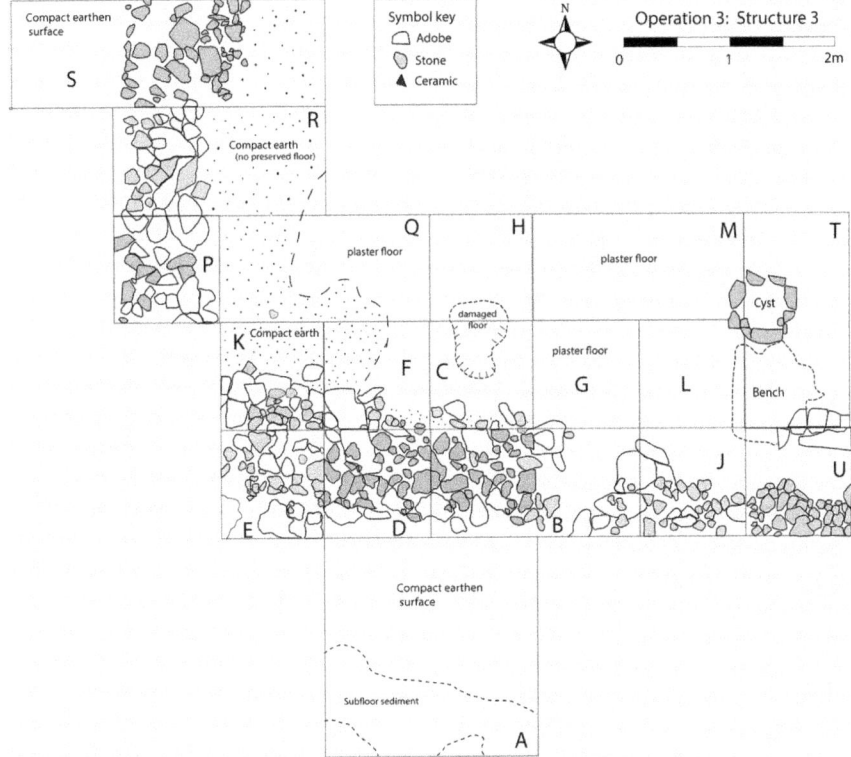

FIGURE 9.5. *Plan of the excavated portion of Structure 3, an Epiclassic house at Chicoloapan. (Drawing by author.)*

differences among residents at Chicoloapan that were not strictly status related. The process of building a house, like other forms of craft production, involves decisions about materials, techniques, and visual and functional outcomes, which are influenced by the social contexts in which a craft is learned. Variation in architectural style may relate to the participation of residents, perhaps from different places, in distinct contexts of learning or "communities of practice" (Abell 2014; Wenger 1998). Dissimilarities observed among houses at Chicoloapan suggest that groups may have distinguished themselves from one another in part through the aesthetic choices and building materials that they incorporated into their residential architecture.

POTTERY AND OTHER ARTIFACTS AT CHICOLOAPAN

Sweeping changes in artifact assemblages characterize the Classic/Epiclassic transition in the Basin of Mexico. In addition to the widespread adoption of

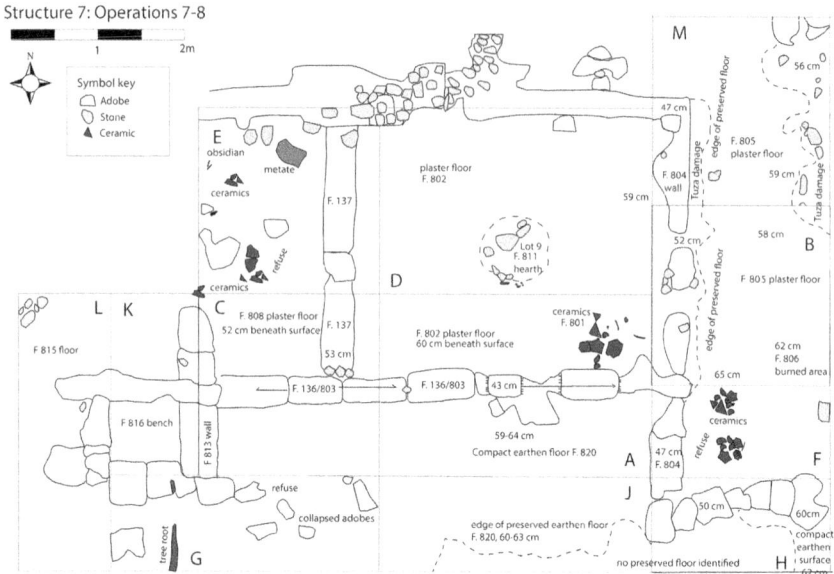

FIGURE 9.6. *Plan of the excavated portion of Structure 7. (Drawing by author.)*

TABLE 9.2. AMS radiocarbon dates from excavated contexts in Structures 3 and 7, Chicoloapan*

Structure	Sample No.	Uncal BP	Error	One-sigma	Two-sigma	Context
3	17	1284 BP	±22	AD 680–766	AD 669–770	floor
3	26	1321 BP	±22	AD 659–760	AD 655–766	subfloor
3	33	1443 BP	±23	AD 603–641	AD 575–650	ritual deposit
7	52	1375 BP	±22	AD 645–665	AD 624–675	hearth ash
7	53	1482 BP	±23	AD 561–608	AD 545–634	hearth ash
7	60	1506 BP	±33	AD 479–608	AD 430–636	plaster layer

* Calibrated based on Intcal13; analysis performed by the University of Arizona Accelerator Mass Spectrometry Laboratory.

Coyotlatelco decorated pottery, basic kitchen equipment was revised to accommodate shifting culinary practices. For example, there was a proliferation of *comales* and large scoops, neither of which were prominent in Classic-period assemblages. The paraphernalia of household ritual changed too. For example, the *candeleros* and composite censers that appear to have been ubiquitous among Teotihuacan's households (Rattray 2001) fell out of use—or perhaps were vehemently discarded. Long-handled "ladle censers" (e.g., Hicks 2013, 81; Morehart et al. 2012, 433) became common. As regional exchange networks were reformulated, proportions of obsidian artifacts made from different sources also changed. The use of green obsidian from the Pachuca source, which had dominated Teotihuacan assemblages, decreased, while obsidian artifacts from the Otumba and Ucareo sources became more frequent (Parry and Glascock 2013).

These changes are exhibited in the domestic assemblages of Chicoloapan, where Coyotlatelco pottery, large scoops, ladle censers, and obsidian tools from a variety of sources are present in strata associated with the early Epiclassic expansion of the settlement. Analyses of ceramics from diverse domestic contexts, including ritual features, refuse deposits, and construction fill, lead to the following observations. Early Epiclassic-period households used pottery that exhibits some continuity from earlier forms and wares in the area, as well as new materials that differed markedly from earlier material culture. Ceramic types characteristic of the early Epiclassic period in the southern Basin include Portezuelo Grey, Punctate Incised, Tezonchichilco, and Zone Incised (see Crider 2013). Some of these slightly resemble earlier local pottery; for example, Portezuelo Grey bowls often feature a "composite silhouette" shape that occurs in Classic-period pottery in the southern Basin (Clayton 2013). Coyotlatelco red-on-natural and red-on-cream vessels represent a new style, in that they do not appear to have local antecedents (Cowgill 2013). However, they occur abundantly and in direct association with Portezuelo Grey and other early Epiclassic types. What Coyotlatelco clearly does not represent is a wholly successive cultural complex, consistent with a model in which immigrant groups, bearing distinct materials and ideas, completely replaced a local population (e.g., Rattray 1989).

Although migration accounts in large part for demographic growth at Chicoloapan, no simple and direct link may be drawn between the presence of Coyotlatelco pottery and the arrival of groups from beyond the Basin. This does not preclude the possibility that individuals from the Bajío were among the many people who settled in this area. The use and production of Coyotlatelco pottery at Chicoloapan is more likely, however, to reflect intraregional movement and shifting interactions among communities.

CONCLUDING REMARKS

Seeing changes in material culture as part of the work of community making, rather than as transmissions of cultural content between groups (e.g., from "migrants" to "locals"), pushes us to consider the purposes that these changes served, rather than to focus on their geographic origins. The adoption of new material culture, practices, and institutions is critical to the success of communities that develop amid sociopolitical collapse. Kowalewski (2013) emphasizes the considerable effort and extraordinary creativity involved in these transformations.

The recognition of this fact—that lasting, functioning communities do not just come about but reflect effort and cooperation—obliges us to challenge tendencies to frame periods of decentralization, such as the Epiclassic, as dark ages characterized only by things coming apart. On the contrary, these were times of remarkable ingenuity. By revolutionizing the material culture of everyday life, from foodways to ritual, residents of Chicoloapan established new ways of relating to one another and put shared concepts of community into practice.

On a broader scale, the use of Coyotlatelco pottery—among other things—served to situate the community within a macroregional world that was awash in the exchange of ideas and materials during a time of heightened movement, interaction, and competition. In the absence of an overarching or unifying political structure, relationships among groups were in flux. Communities that came together in this context were actively positioning themselves with respect to their regional contemporaries. Participating in the exchange of similarly valued and commonly understood material goods, as a kind of cultural currency, may have fostered mutually beneficial relationships at a time when political instability called for such a strategy.

ACKNOWLEDGMENTS

This chapter is a revised version of a paper originally presented in a symposium organized for the Annual Meetings of the Society for American Archaeology, and I thank Charlotte Arnauld, Christopher Beekman, and Grégory Pereira for inviting me to participate. Funding for this project is provided by grants from the National Science Foundation (Awards 1219505 and 1724462), administered by the University of Wisconsin–Madison. Mexico's Consejo de Arqueología granted permission to conduct fieldwork at Chicoloapan. This research would not have been possible without the support of the local communities of San Vicente Chicoloapan and Coatepec, Ixtapaluca, who extended a warm welcome and offered their assistance in many ways. I am grateful to the Ejido de San Vicente Chicoloapan and to the ejidatarios who generously granted permission to excavate on their parcels. This project has benefited immensely from collaboration with Ricardo Cruz Jiménez, Guillermo García Román, Luis Barba Pingarron, Michelle Elliott, and Angela Huster. I also thank Don Roberto Perez Santana, Don Humberto Isla Perez, Enrique Perez Santana, Benito Martínez Cruz, Gaby Rodríguez, Reyna Gutierrez, Antonia Hernandez, Rosario Hernandez, and Berenice Villalpando for their assistance and friendship. Finally, I thank the students who have contributed to this research, including Kimberly Bauer, Hebe García, Christopher Schwartz, Kaedan O'Brien, Emily Eichstedt-Anderson, and Lily Houtman.

NOTES

1. Based on compositional analysis, Crider and colleagues (2007) demonstrate that most Epiclassic pottery was locally produced rather than traded, despite the widespread commonalities observed in decorative style. This pattern suggests that the Epiclassic economy was decentralized and that exchange among communities was limited; however, pottery is only one product among many that was exchanged. Obsidian tools, lime plaster, and other goods made from unevenly distributed raw materials circulated widely, indicating that regionally scaled economic interaction was frequent.

2. Excavations during the 1950s at nearby Cerro Portezuelo were restricted to test pits and the partial exposure of ceremonial structures (Clayton 2013; Hicks 2013).

3. A high-resolution, Bayesian chronological model of settlement growth and habitation, including additional AMS radiocarbon dates from other excavated features at Chicoloapan, is presented elsewhere (Clayton 2020).

10

Ephemeral Cities?

The Longevity of the Postclassic Tarascan Urban Sites of the Zacapu Malpaís, Mexico, and Its Consequences for the Migration Process

GRÉGORY PEREIRA, MARION FOREST,
ELSA JADOT, AND VÉRONIQUE DARRAS

The city is clearly defined by an organized area, a population, and a way of life, but also by temporality. It is conceived as a spatiotemporal object that is part of a long-term process and that stands out by a "temporal inertia that is much greater than that of the social phenomena and processes that are its origin" (Monnet 2003, 21). However, not all cities are part of a long-term process. As underlined by the geographer Alain Musset (2002), the history of the urban phenomenon also includes ephemeral cities that only existed for a few generations. His study focused on the cities of the Spanish Empire in America and recorded no fewer than 160 cities of this type. All of these amount to failures due to diverse factors (poor choice of location, natural catastrophes, vulnerability to attacks, etc.) and have often been swiftly forgotten.

These scattered examples of the first Spanish cities in the New World occur in a very specific context of colonization, but undoubtedly also illustrate a more general phenomenon that could be transposed to other chronocultural contexts—that of migrations where an exogenous population attempts to settle in an ecological and social environment over which it has little control. In this

DOI: 10.5876/9781646420735.c010

chapter, we want to explore this type of migratory pattern different from those discussed elsewhere in this book. Our objective here is to discuss archaeological indicators related to this type of urban migration.

Actually, it seems that these ephemeral cities also characterized certain phases of Mesoamerican history. According to ethnohistorical sources, the Postclassic period was marked by major political and demographic instability, which was partly linked to the arrival of new populations in already heavily populated lands. The wanderings of these new arrivals are a well-known theme in accounts of the origins of a number of societies from this period (Arnauld and Michelet 1991; Beekman and Christensen 2003; Navarrete 2010; see also Bullock, chapter 4, in this volume). The *Relación de Michoacán* (RM hereafter) provides a good example of this type of phenomenon—the consolidation, then the expansion of the Tarascan state from the 1420s to the 1440s (Espejel 2008, tomo I, 142–143) were preceded by diverse episodes of migration of a Chichimec group that founded the royal lineage—the Uacusecha. The written account in the second part of the manuscript enables us to explain the context of these migrations. These displacements were frequent—there were no fewer than eight successive displacements in less than three centuries for the direct ancestors of the *cazonci* or ruler—and they generally occur over short distances, such as within the same catchment area, or between two catchment areas or contiguous valleys. We also observe that these movements were focused around two rather short episodes (they occur over one or two generations) which appear to correspond to periods of crises marked by intercommunity conflicts and events described as supernatural.

From an archaeological viewpoint, the Middle Postclassic period[1] is characterized by the proliferation on *malpaís* zones (Holocene lava flows) of urban settlements of unprecedented dimensions and organization for the history of the region (Fisher and Leisz 2013; Michelet 1988, 1998; Michelet et al. 2005; Pollard 2008). Given their characterization in the RM, it is logical to address the ephemeral character of some of these establishments. This question is raised in particular in the case of the sites of the Malpaís de Zacapu, for which a link to the episode narrated at the beginning of the second part of the RM was suggested (Michelet 1988, 1998; Michelet et al. 2005). However, interpretations face a number of problems inherent to each of the two available sources.

As ethnohistorical data stem from ideologically driven discourse, they present a truncated and somewhat manipulated or idealized version of reality (Espejel 2008; Haskell 2008; Martínez González 2010; Michelet 1989). In addition, the narrator remains extremely vague in regards to certain important points: the leader and his "people" are often referred to, but no details are included as to the size and nature of the group in question (familial group? *calpulli*? more?). Moreover, it is seldom specified whether the new arrivals settle on new sites or whether they merge with preexisting communities. Lastly, the chronology of events is often unclear (Espejel 2008, tomo I, 110–113; Michelet et al. 1989, 106–108).

The contribution of archaeology is thus crucial for enhancing our understanding of these Postclassic migrations. These can be broached using different archaeological and bioarchaeological markers but the chronological resolution of the material indicators remains a major limitation. The correct interpretation of the latter requires a sufficient grasp of the question of site-occupation duration. To better understand the mobility of Postclassic populations, it is essential to characterize in detail the rhythms of site formation and abandonment. Yet—and this is one of the current research problems in our field of study—if we only reason on the basis of established chronoceramic phases, which have an estimated duration of over 200 years, there is a risk of clustering non-contemporaneous events together. In this chapter, we focus on the question of chronological resolution, an essential prerequisite for a satisfactory study of mobility on a pertinent timescale. This question is assessed using the data obtained from the sites of the Malpaís de Zacapu. With regard to the dating elements and the formation processes of the archaeological contexts, we attempt to estimate the occupation duration of two of these settlements. We then discuss their implications for the population movements to which they are linked.

THE POSTCLASSIC CITIES OF THE MALPAÍS DE ZACAPU

The Malpaís de Zacapu designates a complex of Holocene volcanic flows located to the northwest of the modern city of Zacapu (figure 10.1). This sector includes four main locales associated with diverse outliers occupied during the Postclassic period. Assuming a simultaneous occupation, the Malpaís de Zacapu would have grouped 10,000 to 12,000 habitants (Michelet 1998, 52) during the Milpillas phase (AD 1200–1450). Significant evidence of earlier occupation (Palacio phase: AD 900–1200) was identified at the site of El Palacio—the former Çacapo Tacanendan, occupied until the Conquest period and the only long-term site. On the other hand, such indications are tenuous at the other three locations (Las Milpillas, Malpaís Prieto, and El Infiernillo) where occupations are clearly associated with the Milpillas phase. This phase therefore marks a significant rupture with earlier periods and is characterized by the apparently rapid colonization of formerly unoccupied areas. The surface of the site of El Palacio doubled while several thousand structures were spread over a surface of nearly 250 ha across the three other sites (Forest 2014). Logically, the demographic expansion of the Milpillas phase is attributable to a massive population influx following the abandonment of regions further to the north (Arnauld and Faugère-Kalfon 1998; Michelet 1988, 1998; Michelet et al. 2005; Migeon 1990; Pereira et al. 2013). This occupation did not outlast the temporal limits of the Milpillas phase since, apart from the site of El Palacio, the other locales were deserted when the first

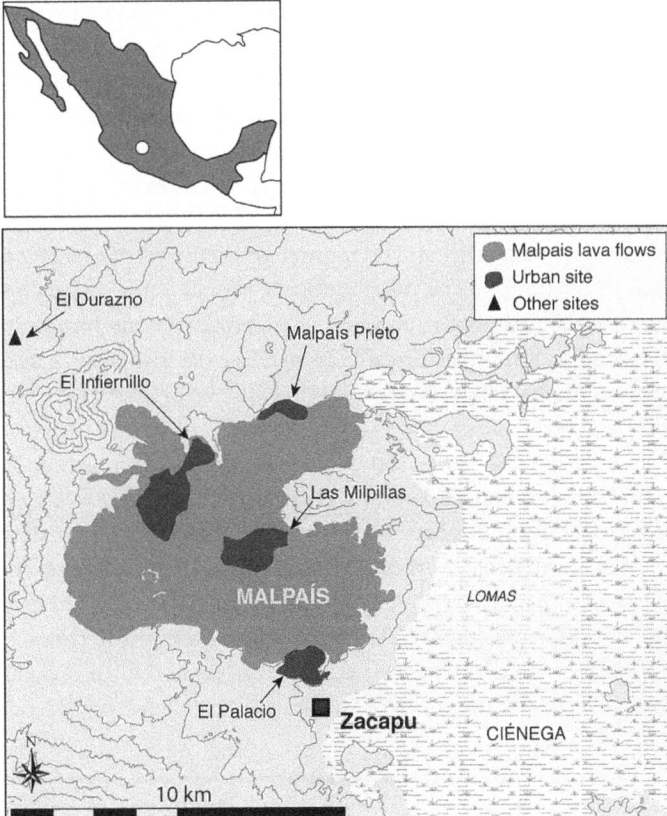

FIGURE 10.1. *Location of the sites of the Malpaís de Zacapu mentioned in the text. (Map by Grégory Pereira.)*

Spaniards arrived in the region. This is demonstrated by the absence of chronoceramic markers from the high period of the Tarascan kingdom (Tariacuri phase, AD 1450–1523), by the observation of systematic termination rituals involving the partial destruction of domestic hearths, and by the fact that these locations were not mentioned in the censuses drawn up by the Spaniards at the beginning of the sixteenth century (Michelet et al. 2005, 142; Migeon 1990, 30–45).

This reconstruction was developed in the 1980s after the first systematic research was carried out as part of the Michoacán project and has been reinforced by subsequent research conducted as part of the Uacusecha project (2010–2014). One of the aims of the new research has been to describe in more detail the types of occupation in this area. In order to do so, it is necessary to identify the markers likely to reveal the microevolution of the Malpaís sites. The duration of the Milpillas phase, estimated at 250 years (or 10–12 generations), is too long to satisfactorily assess site formation and abandonment procedures and, consequently, the mechanisms of Postclassic population movements. Preliminary data developed from a more systematic chronometric dating program provide some clarification. The first results concern the sites of Malpaís Prieto and Las Milpillas.

For Malpaís Prieto, the 11 AMS dates obtained come from four habitations and the main ceremonial zone.[2] The results (figure 10.2) point towards a maximum occupation span of 182 years between 1261 and 1443. However, as underscored by Bayliss and associates (2007), the total interval supplied by a series of dates is a poor indicator of the duration of a phenomenon, as the error margins considerably increase this duration. The distribution of probabilities is also compatible with a shorter period of about 100 years.[3] Unfortunately, the bimodal distribution of the results derived from the calibration curve does not enable us to clarify this short chronological range. It could just as easily be between 1260 and 1360 as between 1340 and 1440.

As for Las Milpillas, the seven dates obtained come from Group B, a complex of about 30 habitations linked to a ceremonial area excavated in 1984 and 1985 (Michelet et al. 1988; Migeon 1990). Three of these dates were obtained as part of the Michoacán project (Michelet 1992, 44), whereas the other four were analyzed as part of the Uacusecha project. Apart from sample INAH 721, which comes from an unreliable context, all the other dates are spread over a maximal period of 175 years, ranging between 1222 and 1397. As in the the preceding case, we can envisage a shorter duration (of 100 years or even less) that we can situate between 1250 and 1330.

These dates suggest two central hypotheses:

- If we take into consideration the widest interval provided by the dates from these two sites, we can propose a broadly contemporaneous occupation over a period of about 200 years (or about 8 generations), with the Las Milpillas occupation perhaps beginning before that of Malpaís Prieto.
- If, on the other hand, we favor the hypothesis of a shorter period for each complex (80–90 years, or 3–4 generations), and based on the chronological periods chosen for Malpaís Prieto, we can either envisage contemporaneity (based on the older interval), or succession throughout time (based on the recent interval for Malpaís Prieto).

These results are still preliminary. Pending new dates and the improvement of the typochronology, we propose approaching the question of occupation duration by examining four markers relative to site-formation processes:

1. Urban *Fabrique*: the topostratigraphic sequences relative to the architecture and spatial organization of the sites.
2. Waste Discard: the accumulation processes of domestic waste through the use of functional pottery.

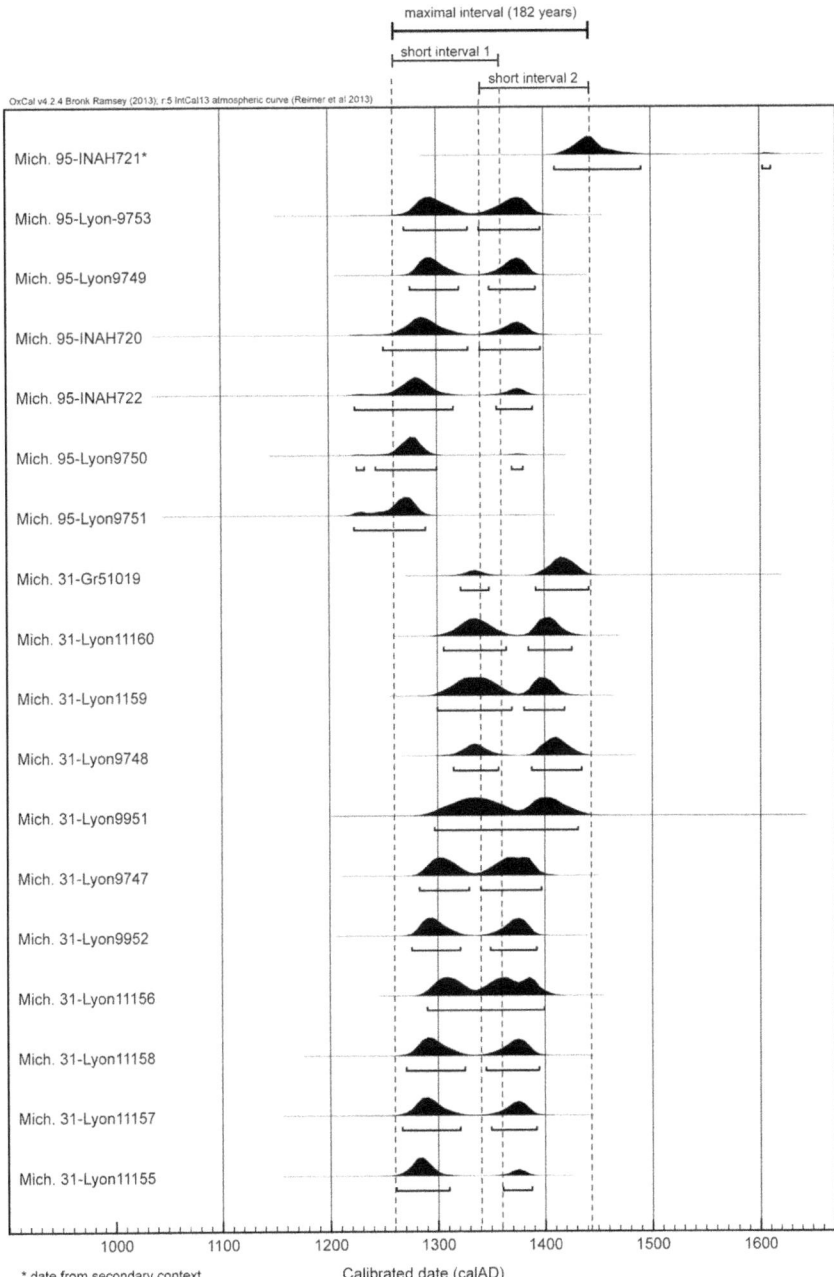

FIGURE 10.2. *Radiocarbon dates obtained from charcoal and bone samples from Las Milpillas and Malpaís Prieto sites. (Analysis performed by INAH Subdirección de Laboratorios y Apoyos Académicos, Centre de Datation par le Radiocarbone of Lyon and Centre for Isotope Research of the University of Groningen; graph by Grégory Pereira.)*

3. Obsidian Waste: the volume of waste linked to the production of prismatic blade cores.

4. Burials: the number of people buried on the sites compared to the theoretical predictions from demographic models.

For indicators 1, 2, and 4, we take the sites of Malpaís Prieto and Las Milpillas, which each of which has been subject to extensive excavations—as part of the Uacusecha (for the first) and Michoacán (for the second) projects. For indicator 3, we focus on the site of El Durazno, a workshop producing obsidian cores closely linked to both sites. We consider the four aforementioned indicators separately, and then we compare the results obtained and consider their implications for our understanding of the social phenomena studied here.

1. THE URBAN FABRIQUE AND THE STUDY OF THE MORPHOLOGICAL INTERVALS

The agglomerations of Malpaís de Zacapu make up vast urbanized grids, with multiple built and spatial components. It is essential to examine the nature and the function of these urban features in space and in time, as the urban fabrique process is our first marker for understanding the history of these sites and the societies that occupied them (Galinié 2000, 80; Garmy 2012, 30; Noizet 2007, 16).

How can we detect the detailed chronology of an urban event such as the cities of Malpaís when their occupation does not exceed 200 years? A city can be profoundly transformed in 200 years for political, social, or economic reasons, or because of all three factors. In Mesopotamia, during the fourth millennium BC, sociopolitical transformations and massive demographic transitions took place in less than 150 years—the arrival and rapid integration of new populations in the Uruk period at the city of Habuba Kebira resulted in the quadrupling of the urban area in less than two centuries (Huot 2004, 89; Vallet 1996, 53).

These transformations affect (or are caused by) the population (in composition and numbers), the dimensions of the city (its area and volume), the aspect of the city through its architectural facies (morphology and esthetics), and the function of the city (circulation, diverse networks, resource requirements) through its urban developments and density, which catalyze human interactions and lead to major societal transformations. The *fabrique* of an agglomeration is a question of time. For the archaeologist, this means a change in content, form (by appearance, disappearance, movement, growth) and transformations of its objects (by dispersal or clustering). As Galinié put it (2000, 52), "many things, even if we are of ignorant of how many, have been suppressed or replaced by others. Three principles are at work—accumulation, substitution, suppression."

In the present chapter, we evoke the case of Malpaís Prieto, which has undergone recent systematic and detailed investigation (Forest 2014). While

Malpaís Prieto also shows specificities that can be partly explained by different environmental conditions, the urban structure of the sites of Las Milpillas and El Infiernillo is very similar to that of Malpaís Prieto. The excavation and mapping work carried out (Forest 2014; Pereira and Forest 2011; Pereira et al. 2012, 2013) at Malpaís Prieto point to the construction of space in *morphological intervals* (Chouquer 2000, 124). We seek to identify continuities, transformations, or mutations that provide evidence of a complex urban history or, conversely, of a unique and homogenous occupation. Morphological intervals can be observed vertically (stratigraphy) or horizontally (extensions/reduction).

Horizontal Morphology: Study of the Urban Structure

The architectural facies of the Malpaís Prieto site (civic-ceremonial and domestic) present a very strong conceptual and morphological homogeneity, which, in the current state of our record of 1,500 site structures, gives no substantial information on the evolution of construction. Only the systems of equipment and façades could provide diachronic markers, as part of a specific enquiry, through the observation of the variation of the size and quality of the cut construction stones. For example, the temple-pyramids present distinctive facings. They are faced with fine slabs in the center and the west of the site and with rough facing in the eastern part. This morphological information could represent evidence of change in construction methods in time.

Two mechanisms must be considered in the detection of processes of urban growth at Malpaís Prieto, if we envisage that the agglomeration experienced demographic growth over several generations. The first mechanism would have consisted in the development of the core of the ancient site, which would gradually have spread out to the currently recorded 37 ha. This mechanism of urban *fabrique* is attested at Malpaís Prieto by the presence, at the edge of the site, of terraced plots necessary for the installation of new habitation areas, frozen in the process of development (figure 10.3). The site was seemingly in the process of expanding towards the exterior, characterized by the progressive displacement of its boundaries. However, the duration of this process could have been extremely varied (and therefore difficult to appreciate), depending on whether we consider it as a case of endogenous growth (based on the natural expansion of the initially installed groups) or a significant exogenous contribution (rapid immigration).

The second mechanism to consider, although we do not have stratigraphic or morphological proof, is the internal densification of preexisting areas. As a family expands, it builds a second house near the first. The very high urban density of Malpaís Prieto motivates us to consider this process, which would explain the very high density of the central areas of the site, and the often-complex layout of habitations and their connections (figure 10.3). This mechanism of urban growth occurs over two generations and is a process of endogenous expansion.

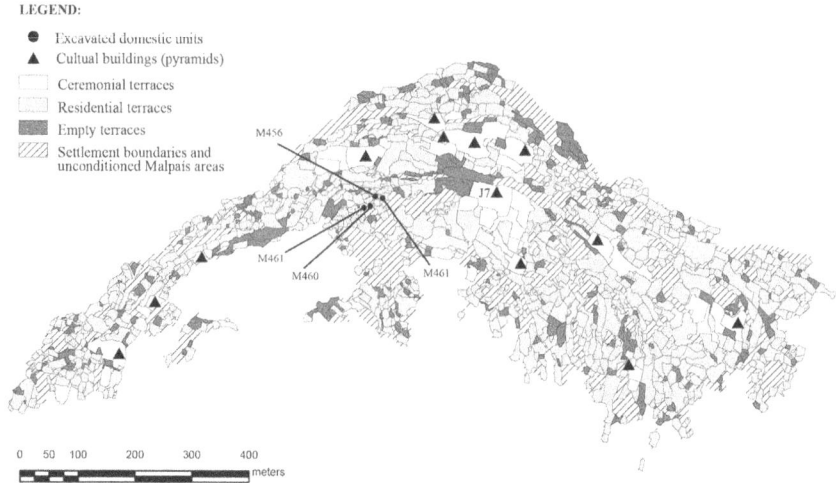

FIGURE 10.3. *Map of the Malpaís Prieto archaeological site and built terraces. (Map by Marion Forest.)*

The identification of these aspects would require more reliable records but we currently consider that both of these growth processes characterized Malpaís Prieto, explaining the internal density and the processes of ongoing external extension at the time of abandonment. On the basis of our observations, the primary cores of this agglomeration are located in the central and eastern parts of the site. The clearest extensions would thus be the western part and the habitation areas close to the site boundaries.

Vertical Morphology: Study of Stratigraphy and Architectural Transformations

With regard to the vertical transformations of built elements, the excavation data prevail and provide evidence of stratigraphic accumulation and morphofunctional transformations of the Malpaís Prieto edifices. We have modeled the degrees of importance in order to characterize these vertical transformations. It is difficult to associate these degrees with an accurate temporal duration (years, decades, centuries), but each of them corresponds to a distinct and very significant temporal and energy investment:

- Degree 1 corresponds to processes of repair and internal or external redevelopments linked to the upkeep or the maintenance of an edifice (reconstructing the floor of a domestic structure, for example). Production time is short and labor is minimal, probably limited to the familial sphere.

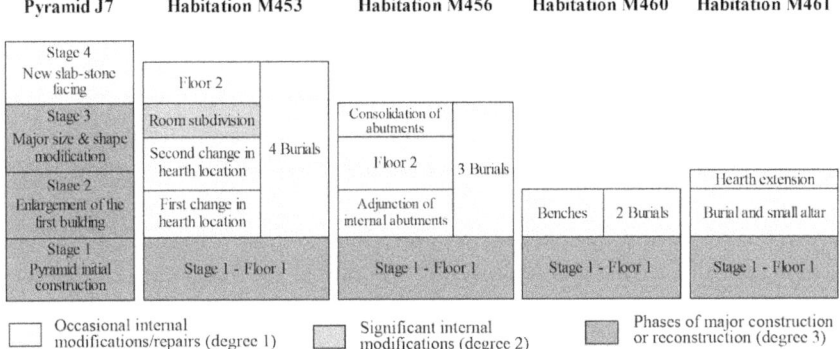

FIGURE 10.4. *Cumulative matrixes summarizing the morphofunctional history of five structures from the site of Malpaís Prieto. (Graph by Marion Forest.)*

- Degree 2 corresponds to redevelopments involving a change in the internal spatial organization of the structure, with no modification of the overall structure of the building. This degree of transformation involves more substantial resources and labor, but probably remained confined to the familial scale (nuclear or extended family). The time required for this type of transformation is still quite short.
- Degree 3 corresponds to major transformations of the structure involving overall modification (reconstruction with or without modification of the initial plan), a more elaborate project and the implementation of more considerable means. The production time required for this change is longer, for both the change in needs to occur, and the technical application of the project to take place.

A single structure can experience one or several transformations belonging to one of these three categories of intervention. Figure 10.4 presents a series of matrixes denoting the "cumulative" (and not strictly stratigraphic) history of four domestic structures and of the temple-pyramid J7 (main ceremonial center) of Malpaís Prieto. These edifices (four of which are beside each other) present distinct "morphological histories" as regards their type and complexity. Degree 1 and 2 events, which are the most frequent, can intervene over short, intragenerational temporalities: over several years or several decades the domestic area is installed, maintained, repaired, and modified, depending on the needs of the household. But the complete renovation of the floor of a house can occur over a generation. The repetition of these events in units M456 and especially M453 implies that these two houses were occupied for longer than the other two. However, it is difficult to consider the observed transformations as being symptomatic of long temporalities, spanning one or even two generations.

On the other hand, the matrixes comprising degree 3 events show a more complex history. The J7 pyramid underwent significant transformations that globally modified an edifice of monumental dimensions. These changes may occur rapidly, but they logically appear to correspond to longer rhythms, requiring more important decisions and more consequential resources. The existence of these edifices appears to demonstrate the development of intergenerational processes involving a higher number of participants than those connected to the family sphere. However, no source of information enables us to extend this spatial and architectural production schema further than several generations.

2. ACCUMULATION PROCESSES OF CERAMIC WASTE DISCARD IN A DOMESTIC CONTEXT

The accumulation processes of ceramic discard linked to domestic occupation are another way of estimating occupation span. Based on data from the excavation of four dwellings located on two habitation terraces from the site of Malpaís Prieto (M453 and M456 on UT1, M460 and M461 on UT2; see figure 10.3), we attempted to estimate the occupation span of these two residential areas by using the parameters proposed by accumulations studies. These show that the accumulation rates of discard from cooking pots are relatively constant and that these data can be used to estimate site-occupation span (David 1972; Schiffer 1975, 1987; Varien and Mills 1997). For this, we based our analysis on three functional classes of cooking vessels with an allegedly short use-life (Bronitsky 1986; Rice 1987; Skibo 1992).

In the ceramic assemblage of Malpaís Prieto, we considered that only three main forms of ceramics sustained regular thermal shocks (figure 10.5):

- cooking *ollas*, or jars
- cooking *cazuelas*, or deep dishes
- open braziers

In this last case, these are not cooking pots strictly speaking, but recipients that contained embers. They were thus exposed to strong thermal shocks and are likely to have a similar or even shorter use-life compared to cooking pots, as no water was added during use (Hildebrand and Hagstrum 1999).

We took into consideration ethnoarchaeological parameters such as the average use-life and number of cooking pots used on a daily basis in a household based on observations in Michoacán (Foster 1960), the storage and use of pots in protected or non-protected places, the presence of domestic animals or not, and so on (Varien and Potter 1997). In order to establish an average, we decided to keep the established duration of two years as the life expectancy of a cooking pot used every day ($L \approx 2$ years for the *ollas* and *cazuelas*) and one year for the

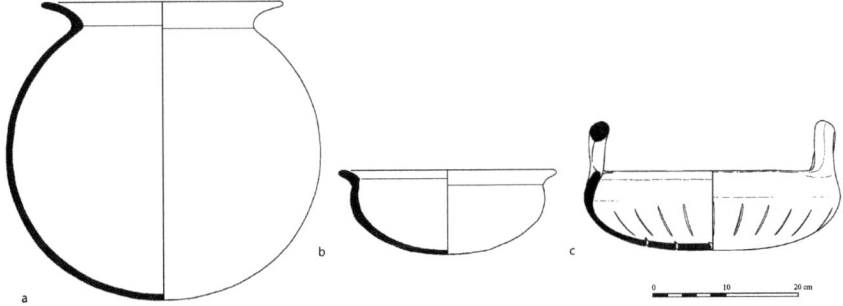

FIGURE 10.5. *Cooking vessels from residential areas at Malpaís Prieto: (a) olla, (b) cazuela, (c) brazier. (Drawing by Elsa Jadot.)*

braziers ($L \approx 1$ year). On the other hand, we lowered the systemic number to a total of 20 pots per house, including four cooking *ollas* ($S_{olla} = 4$), two cooking *cazuelas* ($S_{cazuela} = 2$), and one brazier ($S_{brazier} = 1$), in keeping with ethnological observations of the different classes of cooking pots made in a similar context (Hildebrand and Hagstrum 1999). We chose to use the minimum number of individuals (MNI) for the counts, rather than the mass, in order to calculate the accumulation span of ceramic discard, and thus the occupation duration of the associated structures. To estimate MNI, we adapted the discard equation proposed by Schiffer (1975, 1987), which suggests that the total ceramic discard (T_d) is equal to the time (t) corresponding to the duration after which the pots were discarded, multiplied by the number of pots present in a house at any given moment (also called systemic number S) and divided by the use-life of these pots (L). We established the following equations:

$$t = \text{MNI ollas} \times 24$$
$$t = \text{MNI cazuelas} \times 22$$
$$t = \text{MNI braziers} \times 11$$

The two studied habitation terraces each comprise two houses (M453 and M456 on UT1, M460 and M461 on UT2), for which we identified a dump, always located outside on a lateral access to the structure (figure 10.6). Here, we do not take into account the sherds found on the floors of the houses as they represent more episodic occupation remains (the "use assemblages" defined by Varien and Potter 1997), corresponding to shorter lapses of time and not to the total occupation span of the house. However, this sometimes denotes a phenomenon of reuse of ceramic discard, as is the case for Structure M456: discard sherds were reused in the system of construction of the house to level and raise the internal floor (UE24) between two occupation episodes. As this situation is

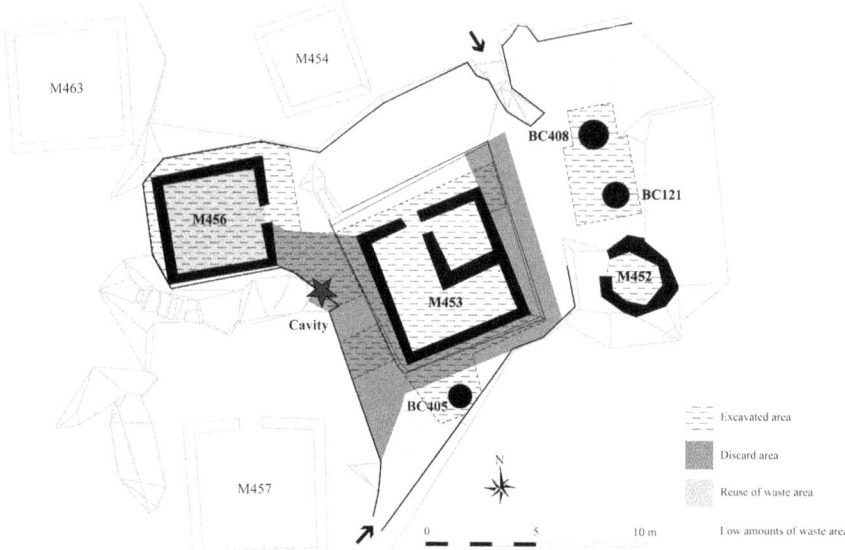

FIGURE 10.6. *Map of the UT1 residential terrace indicating the excavated areas, existing buildings, and discard areas. (Map by Elsa Jadot after Pereira et al. 2012, 6.)*

clearly understood, we can take these sherds into account for calculating the discard assemblage.

It appears that the houses of each terrace shared discard zones. In order to calculate this, we thus chose to regroup all the material from neighboring habitations (M453 and M456 on one side, M460 and M461 on the other), then divide the total sums by the number of structures (i.e., by two) to obtain estimations of the discard rate per household. As the contemporaneity of UT1 and UT2 has not been established, we considered this material separately. Then, there is the problem of the representativeness of the discovered material. The zones around the domestic structures were not extensively excavated and we thus only have part of the total waste. But as we know the exact surface excavated for each of these zones, we could estimate the percentage that they represent in relation to the whole area available for discard. We distinguished more or less dense discard areas on the non-built-up terrace zones: zones with a very high density of waste interpreted as dumps (exterior zones just beside houses), and areas where sherds were less systematically discarded (terrace zones further away from the structures). We performed these calculations by differentiating these two types of discard and used the percentage of excavated surface for each of them. In this way, we obtained estimations of the MNI for the three types of morphofunctional classes retained for this study (table 10.1).[4]

TABLE 10.1. Real and estimated MNI for the three types of morphofunctional classes issued from the habitation terraces UT1 and UT2

Residential terraces	Observed NMI			Estimated NMI		
	Ollas	Cazuelas	Braziers	Ollas	Cazuelas	Braziers
UT1	23	25	25	96	116	127
UT2	21	13	12	68	50	48

TABLE 10.2. Average duration of use (years) estimated for each habitation terrace based on types of cooking pots

Residential terrace	Ollas	Cazuelas	Braziers	Time span
UT1	24	58	64	24–64
UT2	17	25	24	17–25

We divided this sum by two to obtain estimates of the rate of discard per household (M453 and M456, as the other structures have different functions), giving an average of 48 *ollas* for each of them. When we used these MNI estimations per habitation in Schiffer's equation, we obtained estimates for the number of years of waste accumulation leading to the formation of the discard assemblage (table 10.2). With our example of an average of 48 *ollas* per UT1 house:

$$t = 48 \times 2 / 4 = 24$$

These results suggest a rather short occupation span for each of the studied terraces: about 17–25 years for M460/M461 (UT2), and 24–64 years for M453/M456 (UT1). They also indicate that the occupation duration for UT1 was longer than UT2, which is in keeping with the stratigraphic differences observed between the two terraces (see figure 10.4 above). We can thus suppose that the real occupation duration was limited in time, which is compatible with the hypothesis of a short occupation, spanning 1–3 generations.

3. ACCUMULATION PROCESSES OF OBSIDIAN WASTE IN AN ARTISANAL CONTEXT

In the same way as ceramic waste linked to domestic occupation, the volumes of obsidian waste produced in an artisanal context can also represent an interesting marker for evaluating the occupation duration of the Malpaís cities. The excavations carried out on these sites did not yield the remains of prismatic core manufacture. As shown by the site of El Durazno, located about 10 km northwest of Malpaís, this activity was not carried out in urban settings. This workshop is situated in a hamlet that appears to have been settled by a single social group with family links (Darras 2009). The occupation dates to the Milpillas phase and the technomorphological correspondences established between the obsidian artifacts from the Malpaís Prieto site and those produced in the Durazno workshops point to contemporaneity and economic interdependence between the two establishments. Thus evaluating the duration expressed by bulk material present at the Durazno workshop site is considered a valid proxy for the duration of occupation at the Malpaís Prieto site.

Work carried out at this site (Darras 2009, 2010, 2012) revealed the presence of two workshops producing polyhedral cores after the removal of first- and second-series blades, which were then exported and reduced at consumer sites by itinerant blade makers in the city of Malpaís Prieto. The available data suggest that the production units were responsible for the whole productive cycle, and studies also attempted to estimate the degree of involvement in the specialized activity by taking into account the three dimensions of production: raw material procurement, time spent making blades, and time spent supplying goods.

The quantities of raw material brought to the site were evaluated to provide an overall idea of the scale of production (Darras 2010). The results showed that Durazno Workshop 2 could have contained a total of 1,291.5 kg of obsidian waste. The calculation of the effective production volume, that is, the number and weight of prismatic cores made on site and supplied to consumer sites, showed that the workshop could have produced 1,212 cores from blocks weighing 1.5 kg each (Darras 2010), totaling 1,867 kgs. The volume of raw materials was then related to the time invested in its acquisition, transformation and supply. The results show that the 1,867 kg of raw material from Workshop 2 could correspond to a total of 1,698 work days (covering all the production cycle), and could have been transformed in 1,212 days. This led to the deduction that the fabrication of prismatic blades was an auxiliary activity that took up little craftsman time. This must be weighted using two parameters: the overall duration of the craft activity and the number of people involved in production, including raw material acquisition, manufacture, and core supply. As for the overall duration, it might have corresponded to the site-occupation period, or also have lasted for a shorter period. The speed of waste accumulation is contingent on productivity, depending on the number of individuals and their efficiency (partly measurable in terms of their technical competencies). Only one craftsman at a time per workshop is plausible, but raises the question of the transmission of knowledge and apprenticeship procedures. Moreover, there is another workshop at the site of Durazno and even if we think that their activity was synchronous, we cannot rule out the fact that each accumulation of waste could have been deferred in time.

In order to correlate the speed of accumulation of obsidian waste with a duration of activity, it was thus necessary to adopt two postulates: synchronous activity of two workshops, activity duration equal to occupation duration. The

TABLE 10.3. Parameters used to simulate the duration of production of the El Durazno obsidian workshops

Estimated duration of occupation or activity	Workshop 2 used as a reference		Both workshops	
	Direct Procurement*	Blade Production	Direct Procurement*	Blade Production
200 years	Trip of 1 day/5 years (black obsidian) Trip of 4/5 days/25 years (green obsidian)	6.1 cores/ year	Trip of 2 days/2.4 years (black obsidian) Trip of 4/5 days/ 25 years (green obsidian)	12.2 cores/ year
100 years	Trip of 1 day/ 2.5 years (black obsidian) Trip of 4/5 days/12.5 years (green obsidian)	12.2 cores/ year	Trip of 1 day/ 1.2 years (black obsidian) Trip of 4/5 days/6.2 years (green obsidian)	24.2 cores/ year
50 years	Trip of 1 day/1.2 years (black obsidian) Trip of 4/5 days /6.2 years (green obsidian)	24.2 cores/ year	1.6 trip of 1 day/year (black obsidian) Trip of 4/5 days/3.1 years (green obsidian)	48.5 cores/ year

* Individual trip with a load of 32 kg.

"number" and "efficiency" variables remain poorly defined. Three scenarios are considered with varying activity durations: two centuries, one century, and 50 years. The data obtained for Workshop 2 are extrapolated to the other workshop (by applying the same morphological criteria) (table 10.3).

What is the most plausible factor that helps us to discard some scenarios and choose the correct one? To correlate the output in numbers of produced blades (out of x cores) with the needs of the Malpaís Prieto population is attractive but would be too speculative because the total number of Durazno-type workshops servicing the Malpaís Prieto city is unknown. In addition, several Malpaís cities may have been supplied by the Durazno workshops. A more effective way is to evaluate the relevance of these scenarios through the intergenerational transmission mechanisms in the highly specialized craft of obsidian-working.

A scenario in which this activity spanned two centuries would suggest a very discontinuous production rhythm. According to two prehistorians with extensive experimental experience in pressure blade-making (Jacques Pelegrin and François Briois, personal communications, 2010), it is perfectly acceptable to practice artisanal production requiring complex *savoir faire* or competence on an occasional basis if the craftsman is experienced. In this perspective, our Tarascan artisans could have practiced blade-making from time to time without losing their *savoir faire*. However, occasional practice is incompatible with the notion of apprenticeship, as the apprenticeship of blade technology requires frequent and intensive practice. As it is inconceivable that such an activity could have been carried out over such a long period without the transmission of knowledge between generations, it is then necessary to imagine a different organization with, for example, apprentices based in other workshops.

By lowering the craft activity to 100, then to 50 years, doubles and then quadruples the number of cores made each year and makes it a regular activity throughout time, permitting an apprenticeship scenario. This model is rendered plausible at Durazno workshops by the presence of poorly made polyhedral cores, which appear to attest to the work of apprentices.

In this way, the accumulation of waste, combined with the "apprenticeship" mode of transmission, enables us to assess a rather short occupation duration for the Durazno-Malpaís sites of less than or equal to 100 years.

4. NUMBER OF BURIED PEOPLE

A potential marker of the occupation duration of a site is the number of dead "produced" by the population living there. It is logical to suppose that the number of deceased will be higher for longer durations of site occupation. However, this indicator raises many problems. First, it implies accepting the hypothesis that all the dead (or most of them) were buried at the site and the discovered graves are thus representative of the deceased population. We know that in many societies, this is not the general rule (Sellier 2011), as funerary practices entail differentiated treatments and places of burial. The data from the Malpaís sites illustrate a form of differentiated treatment based on age criteria involving two distinct areas (ceremonial areas and habitations) but they also suggest that taking these two areas into account may be representative of the deceased population. The excavations carried out in the ceremonial areas revealed cemeteries where age classes and sex are relatively well represented, apart from children who died under the age of five. The excavation conducted by Olivier Puaux (1989) in Group B of Las Milpillas illustrates this aspect well (Gervais 1987). Conversely, excavations carried out in habitations mainly yielded graves belonging to young children (Pereira 2020). When excavations of houses are exhaustive and extend to the levels underlying the floor, they show the regular presence of burial jars. The excavations in the four habitations of Malpaís Prieto described above (M453, M456, M460, M461) yielded the remains of 11 individuals, including two adults, an adolescent of 15–19 years, five children deceased between one and four years, two between one month and one year, and one perinatal. Even if the 0–1-year class seems slightly underrepresented, there is thus a certain complementarity between these two burial areas. Taken together, they comprise a distribution by age class compatible with the theoretical mortality schemas of archaic populations (Masset 1973; Séguy and Buchet 2011).

Based on this hypothesis of a good representativeness of graves from both contexts, we carried out a simulation consisting of comparing the estimated number of buried dead (table 10.4) with the expected number for a given occupation duration. The aim is to verify the compatibility of the results by varying the parameters of time. For this, we take the Group B neighborhood from Las Milpillas, studied in the 1980s as part of the Michoacán project (Michelet et al. 1988; Migeon 1990, 2015; Puaux 1989), as it is relatively well circumscribed spatially (a civic-ceremonial area associated with 32 habitations), and has yielded the remains of an exten-

TABLE 10.4. Presumed total of the Group B buried population from Las Milpillas, distributed by age class

Ages	Group B Cemetery*	Households[†]	Total
0	3	32	35
1–4	1	26	27
5–9	5	6	11
10–14	3	0	3
15–19	1	6	7
Adults	54	13	67
Total	67	83	150

* Data from Puaux (1989) and Gervais (1987).
[†] Figures extrapolated from the average numbers from households M453, 456, 460, and 461 from Malpaís Prieto, multiplied by 32, that is, the number of habitations associated with Group B cemetery.

sively excavated cemetery (67 individuals). The excavation of the habitations only just reached the levels underlying the floor and the data from these contexts are thus incomplete from a funerary perspective. Some graves discovered (Structure B14[5]) nonetheless indicate a comparable pattern to that observed during the more systematic excavations at Malpaís Prieto. We thus extrapolate the values obtained at the exhaustive house-floor excavations, considering that they must be similar to all the houses from Group B of Las Milpillas.

We are still left with the estimation of the theoretical number of deaths that could occur during the site occupation, which depends on the living population, the mortality rate, and the occupation duration. Here, we consider the following parameters:

- An occupation duration of a minimum of 80 years and a maximum of 175 years inferred from radiocarbon dates;
- A number of inhabitants per house estimated to 5 individuals, following the lower range proposed by Kolb (1985);
- An occupancy rate of 66 to 100% that allows us to estimate a range of living population between 105 and 160 people;
- A mortality rate of 2% to 4% that is an acceptable rate in populations without access to modern medical attention; and
- A population growth rate equal to 0 (a stationary population).

If we apply the parameter variation proposed above to the Group B habitations from Milpillas, we obtain the results in table (10.5).

TABLE 10.5. Estimation of the theoretical number of the Group B deceased population, Las Milpillas*

Parameters	80 years		175 years	
	5 inhabitants × 21 houses =	5 inhabitants × 32 houses =	5 inhabitants × 21 houses =	5 inhabitants × 32 houses =
Estimated living population, considering an occupancy rate of 66% or 100%	105	160	105	160
Expected number of remains (mortality rate: 2%)	168	256	368	560
Expected number of remains (mortality rate: 4%)	336	512	735	1,120

* Considering a mortality rate of 2% and 4% and a living population calculated as 5 inhabitants per house.

The results shown in table 10.5 indicate that the total number of buried remains from Group B (estimated at 150) only fits with the estimated number of dead people on the following conditions: a living population related with an occupancy rate of 33% (21 houses × 5 persons = 105) and a occupation limited to a short duration. This allows us to estimate a population of 168 people with a death rate of 2%. This once again supports the hypothesis of a short occupation.

DISCUSSION AND CONCLUSION

The results presented above must be treated with caution on account of the problem of the representativeness of the studied complexes. First of all, at the scale of the excavated zones, we cannot rule out that a considerable proportion of the archaeological assemblages may have escaped us, leading to an underestimation of occupation durations. On a larger scale, that of the site, there is no guarantee that the estimated durations for the excavated sectors can be extrapolated to the entire settlement.

In spite of these limitations, the hypothesis of a short occupation of the studied complexes, Las Milpillas and Malpaís Prieto, appears to be the most plausible. It is quite remarkable that the results provided by independent approaches, and obtained from different datasets, converge on a short chronological span of less than a century. On the scale of the domestic groups, the data from the four extensively excavated households at Malpaís Prieto (UT1 and UT2) reveal limited accumulation processes. This is also the case for the habitations excavated at Las Milpillas (Migeon 1990, 2015), where the studied structures display limited stratigraphic development. We can clearly propose that the UT1 habitations were occupied for longer than those of UT2. However, the accumulation of domestic waste suggests that the occupation duration did not span more than two or three generations. Also, on the scale of the residential group, we based our study on the funerary data from Group B from Las Milpillas. The comparison of the buried figures with the theoretical number of dead issued from the living population suggests that the duration required for the formation of the funerary complexes could not have been much longer than, again, two or three generations.

An independent signal leads to a similar conclusion: that of the knapping waste found at the El Durazno workshops, which supplied the Malpaís cities in obsidian prismatic blades. Here, the volumes of waste and the intergenerational transmission of *savoir faire* point to a maximal duration of a century. Ultimately, urban morphology data provide another scale of analysis. Even the main pyramid of Malpaís Prieto with its four main stages of successive extensions do not necessarily represent a long period. It suffices to recall the history of the construction of the Templo Mayor from Tenochtitlan to observe that this type of monument can present particularly complex stratigraphy that nonetheless extends over rather short durations.[6] Although it is logical that sites such as Malpaís Prieto or Las Milpillas required a certain period of time to develop and operate, one strong argument in favor of a short chronology is the remarkable homogeneity of the urban forms and structures (Forest 2014).

This relative brevity of the occupations perceptible on different scales has important consequences for the mobility of the groups considered and the underlying sociopolitical reasoning. If, like other authors, we accept that migratory systems are profoundly variable in terms of spatial, temporal, demographic, and structural scales (Anthony 1990; Cameron 2013; M. E. Smith 2014), the observed archaeological and ethnohistorical parameters enable us to sketch the outlines of the processes that might have operated in the region of Zacapu.

As emphasized in the introduction, the official Tarascan history conveyed by the RM describes considerable mobility of groups before the kingdom consolidated during the fifteenth century. The successive settlements of the ancestors of the *cazonci* were occupied for one to four generations, sometimes less. During their stay in the Zacapu Basin, they successively settled in two sites for a period of about one generation. Do the establishments of Malpaís de Zacapu provide direct archaeological evidence that can be correlated to these ethnohistorical events? If we consider that the Zacapu episode occurred during the thirteenth century[7] (Espejel 2008, tomo I, 117), the oldest radiocarbon dates indicate a temporal concurrence between the arrival of the Uacusecha and the beginning of the urbanization of Malpaís.[8]

However, it is clear that the text only mentions part of the reality and that the Malpaís cities have a longer and more complex history. Among other things, the dates show that the occupation continues during the major part of the fourteenth century, a period during which the ancestors of the *cazonci* would already have settled in the Pátzcuaro Basin. Above all, the RM recounts the history of a clan. However, certain passages also show that this group was not the only one involved in population movements. As an example of the latter, after the supernatural episode in which snakes caused the departure from Uayameo, four other Chichimeca groups cohabited with the Uacusecha and they also migrated towards new sites after being separated. Other sources (see Roskamp 2010) indicate that Nahua groups also migrated to Michoacán during the Postclassic period and that, in some cases, the migration histories of these groups may have been interwoven with those of Purhepecha speakers. The processes of fusion/fission of well-known groups in other regions (Cameron 2013, 222–223; see also Bullock, chapter 4, in this volume) must have been frequent, even though the RM largely overlooks the history of these populations that temporarily share the destiny of the Uacusecha.

The archaeological data might thus reveal another history that complements that of the ethnohistorical sources. They show that between the middle of the thirteenth century and the end of the fourteenth century, the volcanic flows of Malpaís were intensively occupied by a large population. The scale of the sites and the RM suggest that this episode corresponds to the aggregation of populations of possibly diverse origins. Although we are not in a position to accurately reconstruct the rhythm and the circumstances of this settlement formation—and we saw above that radiocarbon dates suggest two different scenarios—we can at least outline some essential characteristics:

1. The duration of the urban process (foundation/occupation/abandonment) probably did not exceed a century.
2. The limited prior occupation in the three main sites in the north of Malpaís (Malpaís Prieto, Las Milpillas, and El Infiernillo) rules out an endogenous phenomenon. This observation is less applicable to El Palacio, where there was a substantial Early Postclassic occupation.
3. In the light of the low growth rates of archaic populations, we can estimate that two-thirds of the total population of these three sites stemmed from immigration.[9]
4. It is difficult to envisage that numerically limited groups could have been responsible for the development of the sites of Malpaís Prieto and El Infiernillo, which were heavily constrained by the local environment. The Holocene lava flows on which these sites were founded present particularly uneven terrain, which would have required considerable artificial leveling before site occupation. We can thus suppose that these sites availed of massive and rapid population influxes from the beginning.
5. The groups installed in the Malpaís were highly organized. The settlements indicate spatial planning and the inhabitants shared (or adopted?) a

remarkably consistent sociopolitical organization schema, manifest from the politicoreligious sphere to domestic life (Forest 2014; Michelet 2000a).

Does this model attest to a shared, firmly grounded cultural tradition among the incoming groups, or to sufficiently persuasive (or coercive) powers to implement new forms of life in society? Whatever the case, it is clear that the arrival of populations in the Malpaís cannot be ascribed to the arrival of refugees or to the heteroclite regrouping of migrants of diverse origins. These were large, socially and politically structured groups.

We cannot, however, rule out the possibility that the Malpaís cities resulted from varied processes operating simultaneously or sequentially. It is probable that a large number of first immigrants were there from the outset and that they were responsible for the organization of the sites. But we can also envisage that the later arrival of other groups (isolated families or larger social groups) contributed to the rapid growth of the sites. The origins of these populations have yet to be archaeologically determined. Recent research in the nearby perimeter of the sites (Dorison 2019) shows that the process of urbanization described here cannot be the result of the nucleation of preexisting rural groups, as the latter were insufficient in number. Although we must therefore exclude a strictly local phenomenon (within a radius of 5 km), it is probable that the inhabitants of Malpaís did not come from very distant regions. Some of them could come from neighboring sectors located further north (Arnauld and Faugère-Kalfon 1998; Michelet and Arnauld 1991). Research carried out in the Lerma Valley (Pereira et al. 2005) and in the southern catchment area of the river (Faugère-Kalfon 1996) shows that the sedentary populations of these regions progressively abandoned them between the tenth and twelfth centuries and that they could have contributed to the formation of the Malpaís sites.

A final point to be considered is that part of the population movement probably also pertains to "local migrations," as defined by Tilly (1978; see also M. E. Smith 2014), which occurred during the occupation span of the sites. Certain bioanthropological markers, such as artificial cephalic modification (Natahi 2014; Pereira 1999, 2018), suggests the presence of people in the urban population who originated in the Zacapu Basin communities, starting before the arrival of the ethnohistorical Chichimecs. Their presence can be explained by a marriage alliance system such as alluded to by the RM. The future use of other bioanthropological markers should clarify the hypotheses presented above.

In conclusion, the data presented here enable us to better assess the forms of Chichimec migrations preceding the formation of the states of the Late Postclassic period. Archaeology shows that these groups were composed of large, highly organized populations capable of inventing new forms of urban life in hostile environments, which is very different from the stereotyped image of small groups of nomadic hunters conveyed by official history. These characteristics undoubtedly enabled these groups to establish a favorable balance of power with populations in the host regions, in order to develop alliances. But they would also have represented a threat to local groups and this probably led to the outbreak of conflicts and a profound remodeling of the regional sociopolitical landscape. Finally, these ephemeral cities of Malpaís de Zacapu must be considered as links in a longer sequence, patterned by episodes of fusion and fission, trial and error. It is in this sequence of new social experiences that we must seek out the origins of the melting pot of Tarascan society present at the beginning of the sixteenth century.

ACKNOWLEDGMENTS

The research presented in this article was funded by diverse institutions: the field and laboratory work conducted as part of the Uacusecha Project were funded by the French Ministère de l'Europe et des Affaires Etrangères, the UMR 8096 "Archéologie des Amériques" of the Centre National de la Recherche Scientifique (CNRS), and the Agence Nationale de la Recherche (ANR, Mésomobile program). The new radiocarbon dates were conducted as part of the EXODES program, funded by the University Paris 1, Panthéon-Sorbonne. We are also grateful to the Consejo de Arqueología of the Instituto Nacional de Antopología e Historia (INAH), who authorized field research, and also would like to thank M. Charlotte Arnauld, Dominique Michelet, and Isabelle Séguy for their useful comments on the manuscript of this chapter. The text was originally written in French and was translated by Louise Byrne.

NOTES

1. By *Middle Postclassic* we mean the period from AD 1200 to the beginning of the fifteenth century—that is, before the effective consolidation of the Tarascan state.

2. In all cases, the samples come from contexts strictly selected for their reliability (funerary contexts, primary detrital contexts).

3. On account of the still limited number of dates coming from stratigraphically controlled contexts, it is not yet possible to conduct satisfactory Bayesian analysis.

4. In this way, for UT1, 13 m² of dumping ground was excavated out of a total estimated surface of 81 m² (or 16%), and 38 m² of a zone with a low density of discard estimated at 143 m² (26.5%). To this we must add the discard reused in Structure M456. For example, for the *ollas* of UT1, we have: MNI = 7 in dumping areas (estimation of the total MNI total: 7 x 100 / 16 = 44), MNI = 13 in areas with a low density of discard (estimation of the total MNI: 13 x 100 / 26.5 = 49), and MNI = 3 for the reuse of M456. The total estimation of the MNI of the *ollas* for UT1 is thus equal to 96.

5. In this habitation, the remains of two children who died at the ages of 6 months and 9 months were discovered in a jar (Migeon 2015, 136).

6. After stage 2 of this monument, the countless reconstructions and repairs carried out occurred between 1427 and 1521, over a little less than a century (Matos Moctezuma 1981).

7. Due to the absence of dates in the text, we cannot provide any further details.

8. However, it is impossible to affirm which site corresponds to the Uiringuara Pexo of the *Relación de Michoacán*. Following Eduard Seler (2000, 173), it was the volcano known as La Alberca de los Espinos, whereas Claudia Espejel (2008, tomo II, 278–279) located the site on the flanks of the Cerro Tecolote, that is to the southwest of the present-day town of Zacapu.

9. This can be considered as a minimal estimation, as it was established on the basis of a supposed maximal growth rate of 0.2% (which is a high rate for preindustrial populations) (Cowgill 1975) and an occupation of these three sites throughout the whole duration of the Milpillas phase (which is not very likely, given the data exposed above). If we retain a rate of 0.1 %, the proportion of natural growth falls from 33% to 20%.

11

Itza Maya Migration and Mobility

A Tale of Two (or More) Cities

PRUDENCE M. RICE

Flight, temporary or permanent, has been the characteristic Maya response to crises throughout their recorded history.

FARRISS (1984, 75)

According to legend, the Itzas migrated southward from Chich'en Itza in Yucatán to Petén in 1420. At the spring equinox of that year, there was to be in Yucatán a marriage between princess Sacnicté, daughter of the Itza ruler Chac-Xib-Chac, and prince Ulmil Itzahal [Ulil Itzmal], son of the ruler of Mayapan, Hum-Aceel (Hunac Ceel). But on the final evening of the lengthy wedding festivities, a young man named Canek Ta-Itza, who had developed a passion for Sacnicté, conspired to kidnap her. In the middle of the night, after all the celebrants had collapsed in a drunken stupor, Canek Ta-Itza and forty collaborators seized Sacnicté and whisked her off toward Ticul (in the Puuc hills) and then into Petén. Arriving on the north shore of Lake Petén Itzá, the party was met by canoes and transported to the island where they established a new kingdom known as Taizá. Sacnicté was profoundly depressed by her circumstances: she refused to marry Canek Ta-Itza and, on the pretext of bathing in the lake, drowned herself. Ta-Itza blamed Ulmil Itzahal for her death and had

DOI: 10.5876/9781646420735.c011

him kidnapped. He was taken to another, distant lake and set free, whereupon he jumped
into the water and drowned. That lake is now known as Izabal (Itzahal).

PARAPHRASED FROM SOZA (1970, 403–415, AFTER
VILLAGUTIERRE SOTO-MAYOR 1983, 23–24)

Migration is a significant component of Epiclassic-to-Postclassic master narratives and origin myths throughout Mesoamerica. Because of this pervasiveness, it is difficult to know if the movements were factual or fictional: actual population displacements occurring for various reasons over the centuries, or mythic tropes embellished to serve the goals of political elites. In the Maya lowlands, indigenous histories tell us that peoples known as "Itza" reportedly participated in multiple short or internal movements—Cowgill's (1975, 509) "internal rearrangement in population density patterns"—as well as longer distance migrations.

In this essay, I investigate lowland Maya migrations and mobility pertaining to the history of the Itzas of central Petén, Guatemala. The definition of *migration* used here considers it to be movement across a physical or conceptual boundary into a new or different social and physical context, leading to new permanent (or semipermanent) residence (see also Cabana and Clark 2011b, 5–6). Two periods and two cities are of particular interest: the Epiclassic period (ca. AD 800–1000) and Chich'en Itza in Yucatán, and the Late Postclassic/Colonial period (ca. 1400–1697) Itza island capital of Tayza—variously known as Ta-itza, Tayasal, *noj peten* ("big island")—now Ciudad Flores in Petén. Sources of information include indigenous texts, Spanish colonial writings, and artifacts and architecture.

The primary indigenous sources, the Books of Chilam Balam, are replete with tales of migrations of "Itzas" between the southern and northern peninsula. They are maddeningly opaque, however, in terms of both revealing the identities of the Itzas (and other mobile groups) and providing an intelligible chronological framework. Because of this vagueness—a consequence of both unintentional and likely intentional obfuscation by the authors—it is nearly impossible to determine the historicity of the migrations from these books alone (see below). Thus a fundamental question concerns their veracity: are they true histories or garbled accounts? J. Eric Thompson (1945) considered them garbled, but M. Wells Jakeman (1946, 127n2) cautions that "before attributing such extensive ignorance of their own history to these native Maya historians, we should be certain that their record as it actually stands is definitely contradicted by the archaeological evidence."[1] It is possible, for example, that some data were retrodicted by copyists to conform to Postclassic or later ethnocalendric *k'atun*-cycling expectations. Herein lies the importance of archaeological data.

THE EPICLASSIC: WHO WERE THE MIGRANTS
AND WHY DID THEY MOVE?

The indigenous literature and archaeological evidence suggest that both the northern and southern Maya lowlands (figure 11.1) were plagued by internal migrations, incursions, and putative invasions or conquests by outsiders in the Epiclassic period. An understanding of migrations necessitates understanding migrants' goals and motivations, the "push-pull" factors behind their decisions (Lee 1966, 50–51): circumstances at home that push people to leave and circumstances in the destination that pull them in. What conditions might have triggered the Terminal Classic (or Epiclassic) lowland Maya migration streams discussed in the Chilam Balam books? As reviewed below, these books are vague on this early period, but archaeological and related data give some clues.

Migration Triggers: South-to-North Movements

Some movements are proposed to be northward migrations from central Petén, where epigraphic evidence suggests a Classic-period Itza homeland in the western basin of Lake Petén Itzá. The text on Late Classic Stela 2 at Motul de San José, on the northwest shore of the lake, identifies a ruler as a "holy Itsa' lord" with an Itza Emblem Glyph (Tokovinine and Zender 2012, 31, 43n1; see also Boot 2005, 38–39). Even earlier, glyphs incised on the supports of an unprovenienced late Early Classic (ca. AD 400–600) Petén-style black cylinder tripod claim that it belongs to the *yune Itza Ajaw* or "child of the Itza lord" (Boot 2005, 36; Voss 2001, figure 11). In each example, the term *"itza"* seems to refer to both a place (a toponym) and a people (an ethnonym).

Other likely southern migrant groups include Eastern Ch'olan speakers from Petén/Belize or Western Ch'olan speakers from the upper Usumacinta basin and Gulf coastal region of Acalan. The latter are variously referred to in the ethnohistorical literature as "Toltecs," "Mexicans," "Mexicanized Maya," Chontal Maya, and "Putun" (Gillespie 2011; Morley 1913; Thompson 1970).

Push factors leading to migration from the southern lowlands likely include Late Classic interpolity warfare and raiding in southwestern Petén, especially between cities allied with Tikal versus those with Calakmul (Boot 2005, 30–33; Demarest 2004; Webster 2002). Others reside in the many proposed causes of the southern Classic "collapse": drought, overpopulation, inadequate food supply, deforestation, soil exhaustion, disease or insect pests, or natural disasters (see, e.g., Adams 1973; Culbert 1977; Hamblin and Pitcher 1980; Lucero 2002; Sabloff 1973; Sharer 1977). Another push might have been the opportunity, after the demise of the Classic *k'ujul ajaws* ("holy lords"), for aspiring leaders to claim legitimacy through fictive origins or supernatural sanction in a distant place (see, e.g., Helms 1988, 1992). Affiliation with foreign polities and places, and even invocations of memories of them, can be critical to elite legitimacy and asserted

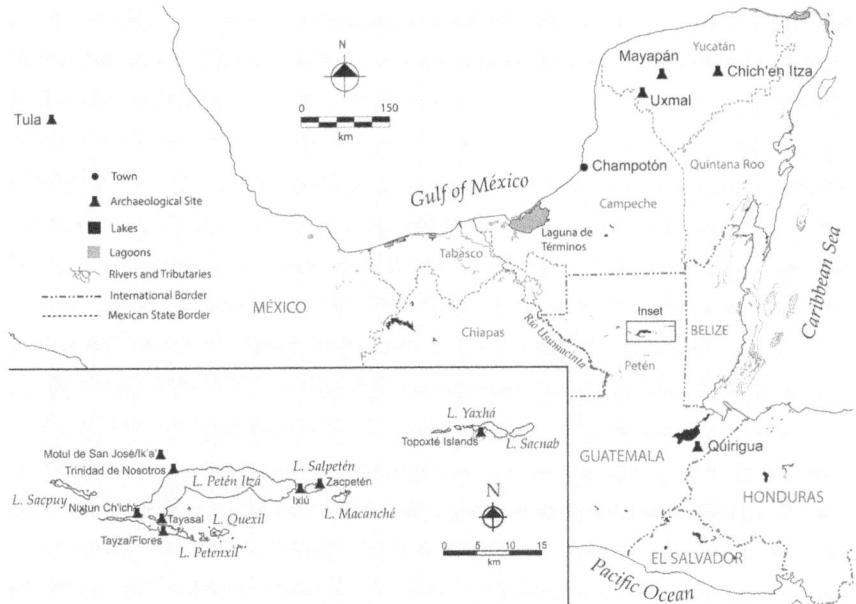

FIGURE 11.1. *The Maya lowlands and adjacent regions of Mesoamerica, showing modern political boundaries, sites mentioned in the text, and (as insert) the Petén Lakes region.*

either by claims of foreign origin and identity (e.g., stranger-kings), including display of legitimizing icons, or through symbolically more authoritative support mechanisms such as intermarriage.

Pull factors luring southern emigrants northward are not easy to identify. For farmers, the north has generally poorer, thinner soils and less rainfall. The latter is of particular concern, given the proposed role of drought in the Classic collapse (e.g., Douglas et al. 2015; Gill 2000; Haug et al. 2003; Iannone 2014). Nonetheless, Chich'en Itza reached its apogee during the drought conditions. In addition, the north has little surface water other than cenotes, either in lakes or rivers, and thus fewer aquatic resources (fish, turtles, water birds, etc.). Exploitable mineral resources (except for salt) are also scanty and forest resources differ little from those of the south.

One possible pull factor is ideological: the postulated Quetzalcoatl/feathered serpent cult (see below; López Austin and López Luján 2000; Ringle et al. 1998). Trade is another commonly invoked factor to explain Terminal Classic migrations, for example movements of eastern "Ytza" to appropriate distribution routes for Ixtepeque obsidian (Ball and Taschek 1989, 188–190). Participation in burgeoning circumpeninsular trade may have prompted internal migrations to the coast as well as reorganization of overland trade.

Migration Triggers: North-to-South Movements

Some northern lowlanders may have moved to the southern lowlands in the Epiclassic. In northern Belize, for example, a Terminal Classic patio-quad structure typical of Chich'en Itza was found at Nohmul (D. Chase and Chase 1982) and at Río Azul encroachments from the Puuc region of northwest Yucatán were evidenced by a small radial structure with balustraded serpent stairways and slatewares (Adams 1999, 147, 179). Puuc traits, including mosaic masks and "flowery noses," also appeared in the Mopan region of southeastern Petén (Laporte 2004, 229). Farther to the south, an intrusive group moved into Quirigua in the Terminal Classic period, introducing a "small stone *chacmool*" figure and Plumbate pottery (Sharer 1985, 249–252), and perhaps establishing a colony to control cacao production and trade along the Motagua River.

In central and southwestern Petén, too, nonlocal "influences," some Puuc-style, are seen on carved monuments and include multiple registers, pointed stela tops, decorated borders (P. Rice 2004, 223–226), and squared day-glyph cartouches associated with a highland Mexican Venus calendar (Lacadena 2010). Sites in the western basin of Lake Petén Itzá, including Tayasal, Flores, Trinidad de Nosotros, and Nixtun-Ch'ich', may have participated in different trade routes and/or experienced gradual in-migration as evidenced by new pottery types: Yucatecan slatewares (and a possible local imitation) and the occasional presence of Plumbate, which is largely absent elsewhere in the lakes district (A. Chase 1983, 1214–1217; 1990, 157; Moriarty 2012, 222; Rice 2009). In addition, new black-and-gray types, sometimes with incised monkeys, suggest trade or in-migration from the west or northwest (P. Rice 2020). The possible contemporaneity of two distinct ceramic complexes in the Tayasal Peninsula area suggested the possible "co-existence of two ethnic groups" (A. Chase 1983, 1215–1216), one representing immigrants from the north. At the large city of Nixtun-Ch'ich', green obsidian was recovered in relatively greater amounts (though still in small absolute quantities) as compared to other lakes-district sites. This site has a large ballcourt complex, not yet dated, with a footprint resembling that of the Great Ballcourt at Chich'en Itza and second in size only to that northern court.

Characteristics such as patio-quads, serpent stairways, stelae with multiple registers, slatewares, and Plumbate, are foreign to the southern lowlands and the lakes region. They suggest migration of northern people into the south—that is, "movement into a new or different context, leading to new permanent (or semipermanent) residence"—perhaps from the Puuc area and perhaps in groups. Identifying push factors in the north—particularly in the Puuc area—for these migrations is not easy, nor is identifying pull factors in the turbulent south.

The Epiclassic Founding and Decline of Chich'en Itza

The Itzas of Petén have long been associated with the city of Chich'en Itza in northern Yucatán, as indicated in the epigraph. Information on these relations comes from two sources: textual and archaeological.

TEXTUAL EVIDENCE

The primary textual sources for Chich'en Itza are the few surviving "prophetic histories," the Books of Chilam Balam, which many researchers have used to reconstruct Itza histories and plot their peregrinations (see, e.g., Andrews and Robles 1985; Ball and Taschek 1989; Barrera Vásquez and Morley 1949; Boot 1995, 1997, 2005; Jones 1998; Kowalski 1989; Kremer 1994; Peniche Rivero 1990; P. Rice 2018b, 2018c; Robles and Andrews 1986; Schele and Mathews 1998, 201–204; Thompson 1945, 1970; Tozzer 1957). These "books" are late compilations of quasihistorical chronicles, medical and astronomical lore, and prophecies of the speaker or spokesman (*chi'lam*) of the jaguar priest (*b'alam*), delivered every 20 years and updated into post-Colonial times. Concerning Itza history, the most useful of these texts are the *Chilam Balam of Tizimin* (Edmonson 1982) and the *Chilam Balam of Chumayel* (Edmonson 1986; Roys 1967), named for the Yucatán towns where they were recovered. The *Tizimin* is considered to reflect the viewpoint of the Postclassic/Colonial-period alliance of patrilines or patronym groups (*ch'ib'alob*) led by the Itzas in the eastern part of the northern Yucatán Peninsula, while the *Chumayel* concerns the Xiw-led alliances in the west.

In the Chilam Balams, events are related in 20-year calendrical intervals called *k'atuns* (*k'atunob*), named in retrograde order by their last day, always a day Ajaw, which repeats in cycles of ~256 Gregorian years. The most historical information comes from the *Chumayel*, which follows the calendar cycling of the Xiw-allied lineages (and also the Classic calendar): cycles begin in a K'atun 6 Ajaw and terminate in a K'atun 8 Ajaw, typically portrayed as a time of abandonment or symbolic destruction of a city followed by emigration.

The founding of the Itza capital of Chich'en Itza ("mouth [*chi'*] of the well or cenote [*ch'en*] of the Itza") is mentioned in several eighth-century *k'atuns* in the *Chumayel* but is barely registered in the *Tizimin*. Events begin in a K'atun 6 Ajaw (AD 692–711) with the "appearance of the Chichen Itza" (Edmonson 1986, lines 3, 13–14). This phrase suggests a gloss of either "the appearance of the *Itza people* [living at] the cenote" or "the discovery of Chichen Itza" (that is, the place; Roys 1967, 135). It has also been read as a "founding" of the city or its key alliance at the site now known as Dz'ibilchaltun (or perhaps Tihoo/T'ho, underlying modern Mérida) in a K'atun 11 Ajaw (Schele and Mathews 1998, 363–364n30, 364–368n31; also Boot 2005, 91).

The following K'atun 4 Ajaw (AD 711–731) refers to the birth of "the Giants" (*pawahtuns*? Roys 1967, 139–140) and "the touring of the lords." The founding lords (ancestors considered "giants"?) represented the four cardinal directions and include a *"Can Hek Witz"* ("Kan Ek' mountain") from the south. This is where lowland Maya migration stories distinguish the great and little "descents," a metaphor for arrival of ancestral immigrant groups, the leaders of which were to rule or govern for 13 *k'atuns* (the ~256-year cycle) over 13 communities. According to Franciscan friar Bernardo de Lizana (1995; orig. 1633), the priests "know that the inhabitants [of the peninsula] came in part from the west, in part from the east . . . And it is a fact that they say that from the east there came to this land but few people and from the west a good many" (in Tozzer 1941, 16n94).

The "great descent," or migration into Yucatán from the west, was said to have included both Itzas and Xiws from their homelands in the Gulf coast of today's Tabasco and Campeche. Eastern Petén and northern Belize were the proposed source of the "little descent" of migrations into the northern lowlands. The text on a Late Classic vase from Buenavista (western Belize) includes the nominal "Kokom" (Houston et al. 1992, 507n3; Tokovinine 2008, 248), the leading lineage of the Late Postclassic Itza alliance at Mayapan.

One translation of the *Chumayel* refers to the "remainder of the Itzas" departing Cozumel, arriving on the mainland, and taking the women as their wives (Roys 1967, 70); another, however, considers this passage to record the Xiws' entry from the east (Edmonson 1986, 269). This equivocation prompts the question whether, at some point, (some of) the Xiws were conflated with the *yala Itzas*, the "remainder" of the Itzas and apparently later arrivals. In any case, linguistic evidence supports the existence of geographic distinctions: dialectal differences between the *Tizimin* (Itza, east) and *Chumayel* (Xiw, west) are thought to have begun in the Epiclassic period (Hofling 2009).

In K'atun 13 Ajaw (AD 751–771) "the mat 'of the katun' was counted in order" (Roys 1967, 135); the Itzas "ordered the mat" (Edmonson 1986, lines 17–18). This "mat of the *k'atun*" is a metaphor for the seat (traditionally a woven mat) of political authority and its "ordering" refers to the simultaneous ending of the Itza cycle in a K'atun 13 Ajaw and founding of a new political seat at Chich'en Itza. Texts at some northern sites record the "arrival" in 770 of an individual with the name or title Kan/Chan Ek', best known from later Spanish sources in Petén (Edmonson 1986, 5n20). The "arrival" verb (*hul, huli* "to arrive [here]") usually means an arrival of great political import, as in "coming into power," making a significant change in the course of events, or even takeover and conquest (e.g., Stuart 2000, 477–478).[2]

The "founding" of a place does not necessarily mean its first or earliest occupation, but rather the formal initiation of its political ascendancy. Did a group known as "Itza" (either self-identified or identified by others) actually live near the cenote at this Late Classic date, or is the date a later contrivance to "fit" the cycles of Maya prophetic history? Archaeological evidence has revealed Preclassic and Early Classic pottery and dispersed settlement in the area of Chich'en Itza prior to this legendary foundation and migrations (see Kurjack et al. 1991; Ringle et al. 1998, table 1; Schmidt 2010; Volta and Braswell 2014, 386–391; Voss 2001, 161–162). It is impossible to know if these residents could be considered "ethnic" Itzas, however.

The 256-year cycle of 13 *k'atun* seatings ended in the K'atun 8 Ajaw of AD 928–948, at which time the holy city of Chich'en Itza was ritually terminated and the Itzas (or their ruling elites) went to a place called Chak'an Putun (generally thought to be Champotón). There, the *Chumayel* reports, they resided "under the trees, under the bushes, under the vines" (Edmonson 1986, lines 27–32, 59–61) and ruled for all or part of the next ~256-year cycle. After 40 years, in K'atun 4 Ajaw (968–987), it is claimed, some of the Itzas from Chak'an Putun returned and (re)conquered the land of Chich'en Itza (Edmonson 1986, lines 34–36, 48, also 175–176).

ARCHAEOLOGICAL EVIDENCE

The Chilam Balam books do not mention the data that have most influenced archaeologists' interpretations of Chich'en Itza: its architectural resemblances to the highland city of Tula, north of modern Mexico City. For decades, the standard—and highly debated—reconstruction of the history of Chich'en Itza involved the entry of "Toltecs" (warriors or merchants) from highland central Mexico into Yucatán. According to a more recent comprehensive interpretation by William Ringle and colleagues (1998), these resemblances came not from Toltec conquest but rather were associated with a cult centered on Quetzalcoatl (Nahuatl; Yucatecan *K'uk'ulcan* "bird serpent" or feathered serpent), a Mexican creator god with a wind avatar, Ehecatl. This cult and associated shrines spread along the Gulf coast through alliances, mercenaries, and pilgrims, and eventually reached the northern Maya lowlands.

Sometime after 900, new constructions in the northern part of the city, possibly built under the direction of a ruler named or titled K'uk'ulkan (Cobos 2011), created the Main Plaza of "Toltec" Chich'en Itza (see Kowalski and Kristan-Graham 2011). Major buildings included an enlarged *"castillo"* as a north-facing, nine-tiered radial structure, and several nearby temples with colonnades. Chich'en's Sotuta ceramic complex includes a Tula-like ritual subassemblage and new food-preparation forms known by Nahuatl terms: *molcajetes* (*mulcazitl?*) and *comales* (*comalli*). At Tula, *comales* appear in the Corral phase (AD 750–850) with *molcajetes* in the succeeding Tollan phase (Bey and Ringle 2011, 305).[3] Cuisine—including foods, utensils for preparation, and contexts of consumption—is a strong identity indicator (Dietler 2007; Tsuda 2011, 328; Twiss 2007). Thus, the new utensils with Nahuatl names reveal "a major culinary shift" associated with the Sotuta assemblage (Bey and Ringle 2011, 309; Ringle et al. 1998, 215) and suggest a different social composition of people using it. If traditional female roles of food-preparation can be assumed, Sotuta likely represents the presence of culturally "Mexican" emigrant families in the city—not solely elite male warriors or merchants as once proposed—who introduced certain dietary (and ritual) customs and tools.

Possible immigrants in Chich'en Itza include not only central Mexicans but also others, as the complex titles or patronyms of the city's ruling elites in inscriptions suggest they were foreigners (Grube and Krochock 2011). Mention of "Itzas" occurs in texts only at the Caracol structure, which was possibly a temple for issuing prophecies (Voss 2001, 158, 161).[4] Some artifacts and architecture suggest contacts with the western lowlands, perhaps pilgrims to this important city if not permanent settlers. For example, Chich'en's texts often appear on lintels in private rather than public settings, as is common in the Usumacinta valley; like western cities, Chich'en did not celebrate *k'atun* endings by erecting stelae. Among jades recovered from the Sacred Cenote, one bore the name and dates of a late seventh/early eighth–century ruler of Piedras Negras and another referred to a contemporaneous Palenque king (Ringle and Bey 2009, 330–332).

Decline

The decline of Chich'en Itza is as heavily debated as its founding and events are unclear in the Books of Chilam Balam. In particular, the bridal capture involving Hunac Ceel, Canek Ta-Itza, and Sacnicté leading to the flight of some Itzas to Petén, as mentioned in the epigraph, is temporally unanchored.[5] Political control of the city was probably largely weakened between 1050 and 1150, but Chich'en continued to be occupied as a key pilgrimage center into Colonial times. It is doubtful that the events described could be from the K'atun 8 Ajaw of 1185–1204 because archaeological evidence suggests that Mayapan was not yet a powerful city by that time (Masson and Peraza 2014a; also, Roys 1962, 69–70). By default, then, the attested date of 1420 seems reasonable and difficult to falsify.

Apart from dating, a revealing element in the last series of events gleaned from the Chilam Balams is the existence of branches or factions of Itzas: one faction, presumably the ruling elites, was overthrown and fled to Chak'an Putun; some who had gone to Chak'an Putun returned to Chich'en Itza to reclaim the land; and others, the "remainder," went to Tan Xuluk Mul, believed to be in Petén.

POSTCLASSIC AND LATER MIGRATIONS: THE ITZAS OF TAYZA

The presence of textually self-identified Late Classic and Terminal Classic Itzas in the Petén lakes area is difficult to substantiate archaeologically and, by the Early Postclassic, impossible epigraphically. Archaeological research in the northern lowlands has loosely traced the genesis of the opposed Late Postclassic alliances of Itzas versus Xiws to Chich'en Itza and Uxmal, respectively, but with little further detail. The southern lowlands lack an indigenous literature such as the Chilam Balam books, ambiguous though they may be.[6] Textual data on the lakes area's later inhabitants come from Spanish sources, primarily dating to the seventeenth century, but those writings have passed through at least two filters: what the Mayas chose to tell the Spaniards or to let them see, and what the Spaniards chose to present of that information (for example, writings by Franciscan missionaries vs. military men).

Itzas and Kowojs in Petén

In Late Postclassic and Contact-period Petén (ca. 1400–1700), the lakes district was occupied by two rival groups claiming ancestry in Yucatán: the Itzas in the Lake Petén Itzá basin in the west and the Kowojs in the east. When did these groups arrive in the lakes region, or were they (that is, were their ancestors) there from much earlier times? Spanish sources give some idea of the chronologies. The legend quoted in the epigraph reports that some Itzas fled to Petén from the north in 1420 and in 1618 friar Bartolomé de Fuensalida was given a similar date, being told that the Itzas of Tayza had migrated about a century before the first Europeans came to Yucatán (López de Cogolludo 1971, 2 [9], 256–257). Later in the seventeenth century, the Itza ruler Ajaw Kan Ek' claimed family relations at Chich'en Itza. Similarly, the Kowojs, whom we believe to be among the northern Xiw-allied *ch'ib'als*, told the Spaniards that they were from Mayapan and had come to Petén later, at the time of the early Spanish Conquest around 1520–1545 (Jones 1998, 11, 16, 430n24). These dates refer to the most recent migrations of these groups to Petén and we believe, from the volume of construction and refuse at the lacustrine sites, that Itzas' and Kowojs' (or Xiw-allied) ancestors lived there since around 1200, if not before.

We have identified archaeological signatures of Kowoj occupations at the Topoxte Islands in Lake Yaxha and at the Zacpeten peninsula in Lake Salpeten (Pugh 2001; P. Rice and Rice 2009). These include versions of temple assemblage architecture (related to that at Mayapan) and red-painted, cream-paste pottery. We have only begun to characterize the Itzas materially beyond their typical snail-inclusion paste (SIP) ware pottery, but architecturally they appear to be associated with "basic ceremonial groups" (Pugh and Shiratori 2018, 247–248; P. Rice and Rice 2016, 65–72), smaller hall structures (Pugh and Shiratori 2018, 239–242), and certain kinds of pottery decoration, particularly at their capital (P. Rice 2017, 2018d). Both Kowojs and Itzas conspicuously reused Classic-period monuments in the façades of their architecture (Cecil and Pugh 2018). This could be simply a matter of expedience, or an effort to prop up their legitimacy, given their immigrant status (C. Beekman, personal communication, 2015), or an appropriation and rememorialization of ancestral places.

Unfortunately, however, a simple Itza-versus-Kowoj dichotomy does not fully characterize the sociopolitical situation in seventeenth-century Petén, as each group was riven by factionalism. Archival research (Jones 1998) revealed at least two factions of Itzas: the ruling group at Tayza and the Chak'an bloc in the west. Similarly, ethnohistorical sources reveal at least two factions of Kowojs, the rivalry perhaps culminating in abandonment of their center at the Topoxte Islands in Lake Yaxha around AD 1450 (Wurster and Hermes 2000, 249). One faction, led by a shadowy figure known as Lascobox ("Lax Kowoj"), was located "one day's distance from 'the same lake'" [Yaxha?] (Jones 1998, 280). The other, an expansionist wing led by "Captain" Kowoj and his son Kulut Kowoj, was moving westward from Topoxte to Macanche Island and the Zacpeten peninsula, where they built their characteristic temple assemblages. These Kowojs allied with the Chak'an Itzas against the Tayza bloc led by Ajaw Kan Ek', an alliance materialized in pottery: Macanche Red-on-paste vessels are made of the Itzas' SIP ware but decorated with the distinctive swirly red-on-paste decoration of the Kowojs. Ultimately, by the late seventeenth century, the Kowojs reached the eastern end of Lake Petén Itzá, their goal being to usurp control of the Itzas' port of Saklamacal on the eastern shore of Lake Petén. There, at the site of Ixlu, the port's probable administrative center, the Kowojs solidified their claim by building a temple assemblage (P. Rice and Rice 2016, 61–64) and Macanche Red-on-paste pottery was noted at the Kowoj port city of Ketz on the northeast shore of Lake Petén Itzá (P. Rice and Cecil 2018, 226n7).

Unfortunately, from the limited evidence available, we cannot deduce how or when the factional conflicts began. Nonetheless, it is clear that Spanish proselytization and demands for submission provoked profound resistance, especially by the Chak'an–Kowoj coalition, and the region was plunged into warfare.

Tayza

In early 1697 a small army of Spaniards and others from Campeche marched south along the new *camino real* to encamp on the western shore of Lake Petén Itzá, where they built a ship to attack the Itzas' island capital (Jones 1998). On March 13, 1697, the attack was launched and Tayza became the last Maya political center to fall to European conquest. The Itzas who were not killed or drowned fled into the *monte* (forest), and their city was destroyed by the victorious Spaniards. A presidio was built upon the ruins and the island was named Nuestra Señora de los Remedios y San Pablo. Later, after the Spaniards had essentially abandoned the area, Remedios became a penal colony. In the nineteenth century it was renamed Flores and became the capital of the Department of El Petén. Subsequent heavy residential, administrative, and commercial construction has effectively precluded any large, controlled excavations into what might remain of the Itzas' capital. Unlike Chich'en Itza and Mayapan, where urban civic-ceremonial and domestic architecture stand exposed, evidence of Tayza's physical organization and residential composition is destroyed, buried, and invisible except for what we can extract from Spanish writings. Nonetheless, pottery and other evidence recovered from recent public works projects on the island have suggested that the southeastern quadrant of the site was probably the location of the residence of Kan Ek and other elite structures (P. Rice 2017, 2018a).

Spanish descriptions of the main temple or *castillo* ("castle") on the highest point in the center of the island suggest strong comparisons with the northern lowlands, as nothing like this structure has been found in Kowoj territory or at any other known Postclassic site in the south. The Tayza *castillo* was "square shaped, with a beautiful parapet and nine levels, all of fine stone, and each façade was about twenty yards [*varas*] wide, and very tall" (Villagutierre 1983, 313). If this description is accurate, the structure was clearly modeled on the larger *castillos* at Chich'en Itza and Mayapan, both dedicated to K'uk'ulcan/Quetzalcoatl (Jones 1998, 69). Those structures were radial pyramids (figure 11.2a, b): square in plan with nine tiers, four stairways, one on each face, and a masonry superstructure. The Chich'en *castillo*, 30 m high, faces ~21° east of north; its stairways comprise 364 steps (91 per side), commemorating the solar year; and its northern (front) stairway, with balustrades terminated by sculptured stone serpent heads, displays the famed "undulating serpent" pattern of shadow on the equinoxes. At Mayapan the *castillo* is 15 m high, has 260 steps (65 on a side) with serpent heads on the north stairway, faces ~5° east of north, and displays the same serpentine pattern around sunset on the winter solstice (Aveni 2010, 123; Peraza Lope and Masson 2014, 76, 78).

Additional descriptive detail about the Tayza *castillo* is lacking, but at about 16.5 m on a side it appears to have been half the size of the Mayapan temple (figure 11.2c). It was apparently topped by a masonry building with a *chacmool*-like "idol" sculpture on the top step (Villagutierre 1983, 313). If it shared further similarities with the northern *castillos*, this structure probably sat at the southern edge of what is now Flores's elevated central plaza, facing approximately north. It is not known if the temple had a calendrically significant number of steps, although 52 (a Calendar Round) on a side is a possibility. Sculptured stone serpent heads have not been noted in limited excavations in this central area of the island, but one was found downhill to the southeast. The Tayza *castillo* was reportedly presided over by the chief priest AjK'in Kan Ek', a cousin of the Ajaw Kan Ek', suggesting that he officiated in a Quetzalcoatl/ K'uk'ulcan-related cult centered on the island capital.

The similarities of the Tayza main temple to Quetzalcoatl/K'uk'ulcan *castillos* at Chich'en Itza and Mayapan, plus the fact that the Ajaw's sister lived at Chich'en Itza, lend support to the Itza legend of having migrated to Petén from Chich'en. It is likely, however, that Tayza's ruling dynasty, including priests of the feathered serpent cult, had long occupied the Lake Petén basin and the 1420 event was simply the latest of several groups or factions of Itzas to emigrate.

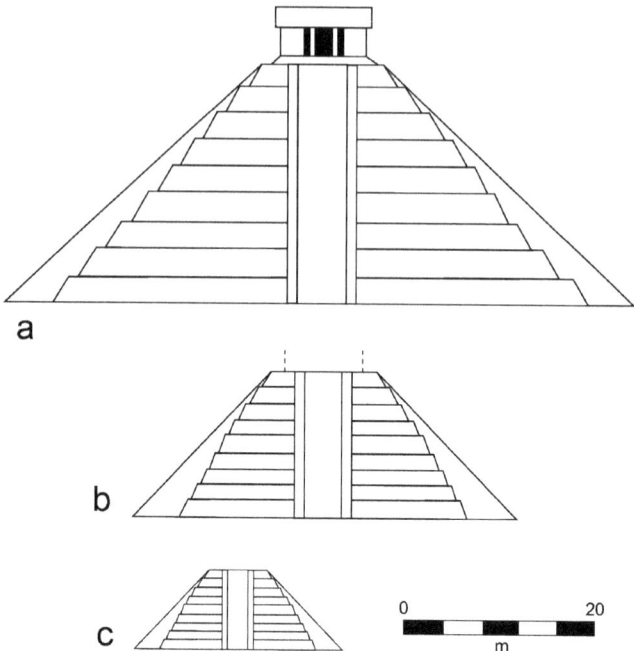

FIGURE 11.2. *Three lowland Maya K'uk'ulcan temples, drawn to the same scale: (a) Chich'en Itza; (b) Mayapan; (c) reconstruction of Tayza temple as radial.*

The stories of the others, such as the *yala Itza*, were recounted in the Books of Chilam Balam.

Spanish reports indicate that settlement organization at Tayza may have been quadripartite (P. Rice and Rice 2018, 29–34). An indigenous informant noted that the island had four named *barrios* called Kan Ek', Kal Jol, Makocheb', and Nojpeten (Jones 1998, 84). Versions of these names continued into the twentieth century. Unfortunately, their spatial locations and possible cardinal orientations are unknown, although modern street arrangements suggest quartering (P. Rice 2017, 2018a). Kan Ek' was likely the residential area of the Ajaw Kan Ek' and his retinue in the southeast, and Nojpeten may have been the name of the elevated civic-ceremonial center.

Archaeological investigation of quadripartition at Tayza is nigh impossible, given the destruction of Postclassic architecture and the island's dense modern settlement. In general, quadripartite organization of Postclassic lowland Maya cities has been largely unverifiable, although such arrangements are present in the highlands and commonly shown (perhaps idealized) on Mexican codices and early colonial maps (see, e.g., Paxton 2004). But quadripartitioning could not be satisfactorily identified at Mayapan, although placement of the site's causeways and gates suggest informal quarters (see C. Brown 1999; Hare et al. 2014, 155, 179; Peraza Lope and Masson 2014, 57–58). Colonial towns in Yucatán also provide little evidence of the idealized quadripartite plan with "four entrances, which were four gates to the four roads that divided the cah [town] into four parts" (Restall 1997, 20). At Tayza, the island's canoe-docking places may have been an equivalent to the formal entrances constructed as gates at land-locked cities.

IDENTIFYING LATE (CA. 1350/1400–1700) MIGRATION AND MOBILITY IN PETÉN

Varied conditions—social, political, and environmental—in the Late Postclassic and Contact/Colonial periods precipitated a massive and long-lived exodus of northern lowland Mayas southward into unpacified territory, including northern Petén and adjacent Belize (see Farriss 1984; Jones 1989; Quezada 2014).

Migration

Late Postclassic "push" factors triggering emigration include droughts, famines, a hurricane, epidemic disease, and the fifteenth-century collapse of the Mayapan confederacy and subsequent violence (e.g., an Itza massacre of Xiw rain priests around 1537) (see Jones 1989, 1998; Masson and Peraza Lope 2014b, 523–527). Later triggers were the intolerable conditions of colonialism: forced resettlements or *congregaciones*, harsh encomienda labor and tribute demands, introduced diseases (e.g., smallpox), and severe reprisals following occasional rebellions (Jones 1989, 1998; Masson and Peraza Lope 2014b, 523–527). Additional pushes include coastal slavers and piracy, and more famines, droughts, and hurricanes. Estimating that "considerably more than a third" of the indigenous Yucatán population lived permanently away from their home towns, Nancy Farriss identified three types of Colonial-period Maya mobility: flight (from colonial rule into unpacified territory), drift ("aimless" movements within colonial zones), and dispersal (flight from *congregación* resettlements, leading to new satellite settlements in the *monte*) (Farriss 1984, 73–76, 199, 200, 207).

The major Late Postclassic/Contact–period Kowoj and Itza settlements in the Petén lakes region (Topoxte, Zacpeten, Ixlu, Tayasal) are now well investigated archaeologically. However, the late sixteenth- and seventeenth-century Maya immigrants escaping from the north, as known through ethnohistorical research, have been largely invisible archaeologically in central Petén, unlike other areas of Mesoamerica, where they seem to be recognizable in barrios or neighborhoods.[7]

This invisibility is archaeologically problematic but may have multiple, potentially overlapping explanations:

- Assimilation: Migrants may have been quickly assimilated (perhaps by the second generation, as in modern times; Tsuda 2011, 328). Some elite migrant individuals or families were assimilated, perhaps among local kin, and assumed leadership roles (e.g., the Kan Ek's of Tayza). Migration streams were intermittent over two centuries or more, beginning in the late fourteenth century, allowing small groups to become gradually absorbed.
- Settlement location: Except for the site of Tayasal on the Tayasal Peninsula, the Contact-period population centers in the Petén lakes region were small, highly circumscribed, and relatively densely settled islands and peninsulas (sometimes fortified). Immigrants may have settled in the relatively less occupied mainland fringes or *monte* around major Postclassic settlements, perhaps in perishable housing (see Alexander and Andrade 2007).
- Material culture: The immigrants may have been mostly small groups of refugee families, who did not bring significant "ethnic"-identifying material goods with them (same is true in modern migration; see Tsuda 2011, 327–329). Northern immigrants' domestic architecture and material culture likely differed little from that in the south, and much may have been perishable (wood, fibers, gourds) in their new locations. Variability in material culture cannot be clearly attributed to the presence of small groups of northern interlopers as opposed to being introduced through trade (e.g., pottery) or through internal migrations or factions within the southern lowlands.
- Conflict zone: Existing internal conflicts among groups in the lakes area may have discouraged or limited in-migration, along with the Itzas' reputation as fierce warriors. A report on a 1604 expedition southeast of the Laguna de Términos noted that a group of Mayas fled toward Tayza to avoid forced conversion to Christianity, but the Itzas attacked them (Scholes and Roys 1968, 257, 507). Thus, comparatively few migrants may have ventured as far south as the central lakes district, instead stopping in the largely vacant intermediate area of what is now interior southern Campeche and Quintana Roo, and northern Petén.

On the one hand, we can suppose that, in the Petén lakes area, an influx of fifteenth-through-seventeenth-century migrants from the north would have been disruptive in terms of social order and governance, but neither Spanish texts nor available archaeological data speak directly to this issue. It is easy to imagine that the newcomers, whether few or many fleeing the disordered circumstances of the Mayapan collapse and Spanish Conquest, would have exacerbated existing social and political tensions between Itzas and Kowojs and fueled factionalism within each group. The only archaeological data that might be considered evidence of this turmoil is a late increase in decorative variability of slipped and painted pottery recovered at Flores (P. Rice 2017). It is not presently clear, however, if this decorative complexity might best be interpreted in terms of overt displays of social status or ethnopolitical identities and alliances (as in the hybrid Chak'an-Kowoj pottery), or something else.

On the other hand, if, following colonial historians (Quezada 2014; Restall 1997), the northern Mayas enjoyed wide-ranging *ch'ib'al* ties with the southern Itzas and Kowojs, this "pull" factor might explain ready assimilation and the lack of visibility. Or perhaps, as suggested in the last bullet point above, the northern refugees chose not to relocate to heavily settled and conflict-ridden areas like the lakes district, but rather fled to regions that were relatively unpopulated, such as eastern Chiapas. There, the modern Southern Lacandons are descendants of Yucatán refugees, whereas the Northern Lacandons appear to have descended at least in part from the Petén Mayas who fled the lakes region after conquest (Jones 1998; Palka 2005, 73–75; Pugh 2009; Schwartz 1990, 34–35).

Mobility and Material Remains

The local duplication of nonlocal material culture in the Itza region may be considered to provide supplementary evidence of human mobility. For example, the manufacture and use of "Mayapan-style" effigy censers in the Petén lakes region—identifiable as locally made by style and paste characteristics—and throughout the lowlands bespeak wide-ranging contacts. In particular, the Itzas' SIP ware was used in copying many northern or other ceramics, including "diving god" effigy censers, slateware, red-painted Kowoj decoration, Fine Orange pyriform shapes, a slipped ware resembling Plumbate, and, at Flores, a "Mixtec-style" long-handled openwork censer (A. Chase 1983, 1221, figure 4–13).

A focus on Postclassic and later mobility and in-migration into the Petén lakes district forces some reconsideration of ethnopolitically anomalous findings at two sites, Zacpeten and Ixlu. Zacpeten, in Lake Salpeten, became a Kowoj center at some time in the Postclassic period and its architecture features two of their signature temple assemblages, each built and then reconstructed once (Pugh 2001).[8] These assemblages are essentially mirror images of each other (i.e., they exhibit bilateral symmetry) and were characterized by only minor differences in construction and artifacts. They were interpreted as possibly representing a moiety-like social structure, but in light of both factionalism and in-migration, perhaps one of the assemblages was constructed by a Kowoj faction that absorbed some immigrant kin.

The northern temple assemblage, Group A, featured an unusual mass grave (Operation 1000) at its northwestern corner. Mass graves with disarticulated remains were also found on Topoxte Island (near the northwestern corner of the temple assemblage) and in several areas of Mayapan. Bioarchaeologist William Duncan (2009, 366) argued that the individuals in the graves at Topoxte and Zacpeten were exhumed from earlier interments, and represented ritual violation of the sites' ancestors. A radiocarbon assay from charcoal in a deposit just below the human remains at Zacpeten Op. 1000 yielded 2-sigma calibrated dates of AD 1321–1352 and 1389–1437 (Pugh 2001, 284), dating an arrival of Kowojs—possibly the expansionist faction moving west from Topoxte.

As mentioned, this expansionist faction eventually advanced from Zacpeten to the eastern edge of Lake Petén Itzá, contesting control of the Itza port at Ixlu. They established 12 new villages on the northern shore—perhaps with the aid of attested Kowoj immigrants from Mayapan in the early sixteenth century—and built a small temple assemblage in the northwest corner of Ixlu's Acropolis. In the western basic ceremonial group in the Main Plaza, the construction of shrine Structure 2023 was dedicated by the careful arrangement of 21 human skulls and four postcranial remains, all late-adolescent to young-adult males (Duncan 2005; P. Rice and Rice 2016, 69–76). Six skulls were positioned exterior to this small structure, establishing its east–west centerline, and 15 were placed in the center of its foundations in two north–south rows. Absent isotopic data, it is impossible to determine the sacrificial victims' origins, but various indicators, especially the red-painted decoration on the exterior of the structure, suggest that Structure 2023 might have been built by the Chak'an Itzas allied with the Kowojs against Tayza and the Ajaw Kan Ek' (P. Rice and Rice 2016, 85–88).

CONCLUDING THOUGHTS

To summarize, a group self-identifying as Itza, with a leader (or important elite personage or lineage) holding the title Ajaw Kan Ek', played important roles in two periods characterized by extremely fluid social landscapes in central Petén. The Itzas were present in the Late and Terminal Classic periods and possibly even the Early Classic. They—along with some of their allies—were among the four important lords who "appeared" at, "discovered," and/or founded the important city of Chich'en Itza in Yucatán in the early eighth century, according to the Books of Chilam Balam. Unfortunately, these early southern Itzas are still poorly known archaeologically. Textual sources report two Epiclassic or Early Postclassic migration streams or "descents" into the north, one from the east and the other from the west, although their relative timing is unknown. These streams seem to have had a lasting linguistic imprint in Yucatán, with east–west dialectal differences maintained into Colonial if not modern times (Hofling 2009, 77).

In the Postclassic and Contact periods, indigenous textual sources, Spanish reports, and archaeological evidence (from architecture and artifacts) testify to widespread population movements and interactions over short and long distances. The triggers for these migrations are better understood than those prompting the Epiclassic migrations, but some are the same: social and political unrest, factionalism, drought, and other natural disasters.

To conclude, I return to the original question underlying this essay: Were the lowland Maya migrations mentioned in the Chilam Balam books factually true, or were they garbled accounts, or simply mandatory tropes invoked to legitimize mythic histories and heroic origins? Jakeman (1946), in responding to Thompson's (1945) dismissal, suggested that contradictory archaeological evidence would help resolve the issue in Thompson's favor. The archaeological (and other) evidence I have reviewed here does not contradict the indigenous histories, and instead supports the factuality of at least some of the migrations. Some of the legendary Epiclassic mobility was factually, historically real, as supported by archaeological and linguistic-epigraphic data. Some of the Postclassic migrations and mobility were also real. Other stories were likely invented or embellished to serve political ends through the Postclassic and Contact or early Colonial periods. The situation may be similar to that of central Mexico, where the Mexicas' southward migrations to Lake Texcoco are portrayed in pictorial manuscripts as "ritual performances," transformative rites of passage in which the migration itself is the liminal stage (Boone 1991, 143–148). With respect to the Itzas, the key is to disentangle fact from fiction in those fluid and enshrouded circumstances.

ACKNOWLEDGMENTS

This essay reports some of the work of numerous colleagues and friends over the years, especially (in alphabetical order) Leslie Cecil, Bill Duncan, Grant Jones, Tim Pugh, Don Rice, and Miriam Salas. I thank Chris Beekman and Charlotte Arnauld for helpful suggestions on earlier versions of this contribution.

NOTES

1. More recent critiques of the chronicles have been more along the lines of literary criticism.

2. Other arrival verbs in the text are more neutral: "appeared" or "reached."

3. In the southern lowlands, grater bowls were common in Terminal Classic assemblages, but comales were rare until the Late Postclassic.

4. This calls to mind the meaning of the *its'* morpheme, which "is related to ideas of wisdom, magic, [and] occult power"; the Classic-period title *its'at* is usually translated as "sage, artist, scribe" with the general sense of "wisdom, knowledge, astuteness" (Barrera Vásquez 1991, 272, 273).

5. Harrison-Buck (2014, 695, 698) argues that the Hunac Ceel episode dates to AD 948 on the basis of the dating of Chich'en Itza's preeminence. This is not entirely implausible, as northern slatewares occasionally appear in the Terminal Classic in the western Petén lakes area.

6. At one time it was proposed that the Madrid Codex had been composed at Tayza (but see Paxton 2004).

7. Immigrants at Tipu, in west-central Belize, were attested by both Spanish sources (Jones 1989) and the incised decoration on archaeologically recovered pottery resembling that on the east coast of Quintana Roo to the north (personal observation).

8. The fact that these assemblages had two phases of construction parallels that of the *castillos* at Chich'en Itza and Mayapan, both of which saw major rebuilding of the original structure, perhaps on some calendrically significant anniversary.

12

Cohesive Social Groups and the Formation of Enclaves in West-Central Mexico

CHRISTOPHER S. BEEKMAN

Society is mobile. Individually and collectively, humans move in the course of their daily lives, in the execution of socioeconomic or religious activities, in reaction to or in anticipation of changing circumstances, and through forced relocation. To demote mobility and migration to a rare event is to treat human activity as a closed system and hold constant the shifting membership of institutions and communities simply for convenience of analysis. This predisposition to treat residential stability as a default distorts our understanding of human society and undermines attempts to understand how migration takes place. Many forms of mobility unfortunately leave limited traces. In this chapter, I address a form of migration in which a cohesive social group made a one-way relocation to a different environment (see Cabana and Clark 2011b, 5) that contributed to their greater archaeological or historical visibility. I refer to diaspora and the establishment of enclaves in west-central Mexico, particularly during the Postclassic period. As I mean to demonstrate, enclaves are more visible and amenable to study than some outcomes of migration and are an opportunity to ask questions about the process of migration and its aftermath. How common

DOI: 10.5876/9781646420735.c012

is migration and how do enclaves form? Are they as rare and historically contingent in structure as critics often suggest? What are the factors that contribute to their longevity or ephemerality? Research in the American Southwest has increasingly turned to the conditions under which migrant enclaves might have expressed or hidden aspects of their identity (Bernardini 2005; Stone 2003, 2015; Stone and Lipe 2011), but that region lacks the complex political institutions that define Mesoamerica. How do the choices available to actors change within the complex Mesoamerican social environment? In this chapter I consider several historically and/or archaeologically attested examples of enclaves along the border between the Late Postclassic Aztec and Tarascan empires for their origins, their involvement in specific activities, and their reproduction over time. This in turn suggests a framework for the interpretation of other communities as enclaves from prehistoric contexts. I conclude with a model for these enclaves and with observations on their frequency in the chosen study area.

COHESIVE SOCIAL GROUPS, ENCLAVES, AND DIASPORA

First, some definitions are in order. By *cohesive social groups* I refer to multiple migrants that retain a variety of contexts for traditional forms of interaction (a household, a network of interacting families forming a lineage or neighborhood) so that they can survive as a social and not solely a demographic unit. Individuals certainly migrated in the past as they do today, but may find it difficult or undesirable or unnecessary to maintain prior cultural attitudes when they lack the reinforcement of other members of that community (Fennell 2007, 43–44), or when they successfully integrate into a society (Bullock, chapter 4, this volume). Portes and Manning for instance (1986) find that individuals today migrate most frequently into better positions in the primary economic sector, equivalent in our terms to craft or ritual specialists who may be welcomed by the host community for their knowledge (see examples in Courlander 1971). On the negative side, several authors studying the African diaspora argue that abducted Africans were inhibited from passing on their traditions after arriving in the Americas due to the absence of open social interaction with others of similar cultural origin (Mintz and Price 1976; see Fennell 2007, 43). Put more abstractly, the individual actors in these cases became isolated from their prior social environment and reestablished a *habitus* appropriate to their new surroundings, which did not include others with similar cultural backgrounds. A cohesive social group on the other hand, with cultural requirements that must be satisfied internally (rituals, marital customs, distinct food or clothing, etc.), possesses numerous opportunities for cross-cutting interaction among members, what Portes and Manning (1986) call "institutional completeness" (see also Goldstein 2000). These features help to reproduce the community that migrants shared prior to migration (Beekman 2019; Shami 1993).

By *enclave*, I refer to a cohesive social group in a situation of contrast or opposition with other surrounding groups, such that members express or amplify their identity in response (drawing upon work such as Stone 2003). This may refer to a neighborhood within a larger town, or an entire settlement isolated within a broader landscape inhabited by other groups. In either case, I refer to the intrusive group as an *enclave*, and to the surrounding area as the *host community*. The term *diaspora* is often used loosely in conjunction with enclaves, such as a diaspora of enclaves. That term has been commonly used by historians in reference to the African diaspora, the Jewish diaspora, and so on, and highlight what Fennell (2007, 1) calls "dispersions of people to new locations due to abduction or to hostile circumstances in the lands from which they fled." This kind of diaspora does not always result in enclaves, as the migrants may be forcibly settled in conditions where they are isolated from others of similar origin.

Archaeologists have been biased towards alternative definitions of diaspora or enclaves that emphasize economic factors. Spence (2005; Spence et al. 2005) followed previous anthropologists referring to a diaspora as a string of enclaves involved in specific economic activities independent of political authorities (from A. Cohen 1969, 1971; Curtin 1984; Stein 1998). But the enclaves to which Santley (1989) referred were characterized as instruments of the Teotihuacan state, carrying political power and economic interests deep into its periphery. Still other uses of diaspora in the archaeological literature (L. Abrams 2012, 19–20) rely on R. Cohen's (2008) definition, which is noncommittal on the political ties of diaspora while emphasizing other factors such as an idealization of the origin place, horizontal ties between enclaves, and an uneasy relationship with the host community. I avoid here other terms used by these and other authors as synonyms for much the same ideas, including *barrio*, *network*, and *archipelago*. In order to proceed with a more flexible framework, I use the term *diaspora* in a more general sense as indicating a series of enclaves with a shared geographic or historical origin.

ENCLAVES AND DIASPORA IN POSTCLASSIC WEST-CENTRAL MEXICO

The setting is the eastern part of the modern state of Michoacán, and the states of Querétaro, Hidalgo, and México to the east. Towards the end of the Late Postclassic (ca. AD 1450–1520), the region formed the boundary between the Tarascan Empire to the west, and the Aztec Empire to the east (figure 12.1). The origin story of the Tarascan royal lineage, detailed in the *Relación de Michoacán* (Alcalá 2009), describes them as nomadic Chichimecs, who over several generations established an empire based in the Pátzcuaro Basin in central highland Michoacán (Pollard 1993, 2008). The Tarascan state is sometimes described as being more politically centralized than its enemies, and the Purhepecha language followed its expansion and replaced largely unknown predecessors (Pollard 1994, 81).

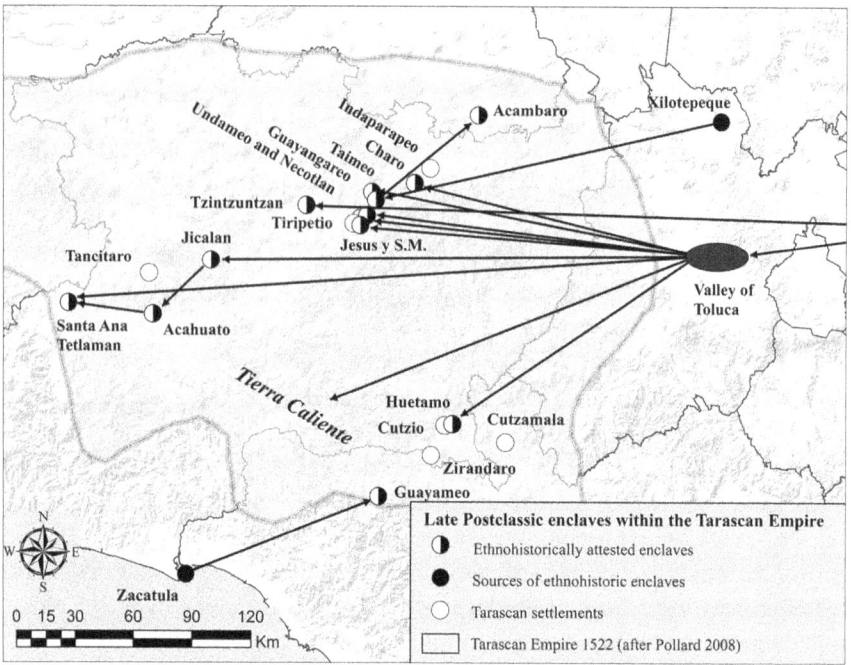

FIGURE 12.1. *Map of the Tarascan-Aztec border region, with enclaves and other communities mentioned in the text. (Map made in ArcGIS by the author.)*

Distinctive ceramics associated with the central lake basins of the Tarascan state had a widespread but mosaic-like distribution out to the peripheries of the empire (Lefebvre 2011, 86; Lister 1947, 73; Ramírez Urrea 1996), though such artifacts likely represented participation in the Tarascan State more than a Purhepecha ethnic identity (Albiez-Wieck 2011, 92–96). The rival Aztec polities of central Mexico also claimed descent from nomadic Chichimec ancestors from the north. However, their linguistic landscape was more diverse, including Nahuatl (a single language with ties to others far to the northwest) and various languages pertaining to the more established Otomanguean family. One analysis (Beekman and Christensen 2003, 2011) concluded that Nahuatl was introduced into central Mexico in the sixth century AD, spreading out from migrant communities only with its rise as a *lingua franca* under successive Postclassic empires. The final Aztec empire was lightly represented by material culture (M. E. Smith 1990; M. E. Smith and Berdan 1992; Umberger and Klein 1993), attributable to the way in which its institutions were laid down on top of, instead of replacing, those of conquered rivals. Both Tarascan and Aztec empires established or appropriated border sites that faced off against one another (Gorenstein et al. 1985; Lefebvre 2011; Silverstein 2001).

Several cohesive social groups crossed this hostile boundary and settled enclaves within the Tarascan Empire through negotiation with and approval by the ruler, or *Irecha*. The 1580 *Relación Geográfica* for Celaya relates how four couples brought 60 Otomi families from Hueychiapan in Xilotepeque, in the valley of Toluca just east of the border, and requested lands from the *Irecha* in exchange for services (Acuña 1987, 60–61). They were initially assigned lands in Guayangareo, and later Acambaro when they did not like their original settlement. They were self-governing and paid no goods as tribute. They did however provide military service to protect the Tarascan-Aztec frontier, as did Chichimeca who were similarly settled here by the *Irecha* (Acuña 1987, 61, 63). At some point the *Irecha* sent four Tarascan families (or lineages [Lefebvre 2017, 212]) to Acambaro. Tarascan (i.e., Purhepecha) was described as the general language throughout the region (Acuña 1987, 63–64); these four families were therefore not another enclave of distinct language, but political emissaries who nonetheless stood out through their use of ceramics from the Pátzcuaro Basin. They resided on the valley floor, while Chichimec and Otomi inhabitants used a development of the older Lerma ceramic complex and resided on the hill known today as Cerro el Chivo (Gorenstein et al. 1985, 98–100). In 1580, Tarascan remained the primary language, and Chichimeca, Otomi, and Mazahua continued in use (Acuña 1987, 60). The *Irecha* mentioned in this document is Tariacuri, rather than the later ruler cited in the remainder of our examples below, but this is likely an error as Tariacuri was dead before the Tarascans extended their imperial reach to the area of Celaya and Acambaro (Alcalá 2009, location 2024).

The Acambaro enclave more likely dates to the late fifteenth century, when similar migrations out of the valley of Toluca were resettled within the empire. The *Relaciones Geográficas* for Taimeo and Necotlan report that an entire town of Otomi left the Toluca area to escape persecution. An Otomi noble with the nonetheless Nahuatl-sounding name of Ucelo Apanze (Ocelhuapantzin; Acuña 1987, 186) met with the *Irecha* Tzitzispandaquare to request permission to settle. In return for tribute, the *Irecha* told them they could populate the towns of Taimeo, Necotlan, and Matalcingo/Charo in the eastern highlands, and other unnamed towns in the Tierra Caliente 100 km to the south. By 1579, these Otomi were said to dress and speak like the Tarascans (Acuña 1987, 187). The *Relación Geográfica* for Taimeo differs in stating that the leader of the migrants was named Timax and that the migrants served as warriors and suppliers for the Tarascan forts (Acuña 1987, 276–277). These Otomi were described as bilingual in 1579.

Clearly related to these enclaves are those described by Diego Basalenque (1886, 304–305). The same *Irecha* Tzitzispandaquare (here known by his nickname of Characu), recruited Matlatzinca from Toluca for a war further to the west, and upon its successful resolution they requested lands within the Tarascan Empire. The *Irecha* agreed and let them choose from the region between Indaparapeo and Tiripetio to settle. The noblest families settled by the rivers at Charo, the same town mentioned above for the Otomi migrants. The lesser nobles settled in Santiago Undameo, near Necotlan. The common families settled in the high areas around Jesús y Santa María, also near Necotlan (see Acuña 1987, 185). All these migrants were renamed *Pirinda*, which referred in some way to their new position in the middle of the empire. Matlatzinca was still spoken when Basalenque wrote in the late 1600s (Basalenque 1886, 303–314), without specifying the situation in each town.

The Tierra Caliente of southern Michoacán was home to additional enclave communities, which were probably part of the same diaspora as those already described. The 1580 *Relación Geográfica* for the Tarascan communities of Sirandaro (modern Zirandaro) and Cuseo (modern Cutzio) (Acuña 1987, 262–263, 268–269) describes how each town had a foreign enclave—Apaneca lived in Sirandaro's subject town of Guayameo, while Matlatzinca occupied the Huetamo neighborhood adjoining Cutzio. The Apaneca were resettled captives from the coastal polity of Zacatula, while the Matlatzinca originated in Toluca and left the region voluntarily to avoid persecution by the local lords. Their noble leader petitioned the *Irecha* Tzitzispandaquare for land, and the Matlatzinca were settled in Huetamo. This enclave is likely related to those discussed for central Michoacán, as an Arroyo Pirinda runs through Huetamo today. Sirandaro and its enclave at Guayameo were tasked with supporting the Tarascan fort at Cutzamala (Acuña 1987, 266). By 1552, two locally made pictographic codices in central Mexican style detailed the tribute paid by the Tarascans of Cutzio and Otomi of Huetamo to a Spanish encomendero (Roskamp 2003). Roskamp (2003, 63–64) suggests that the migrants at Huetamo were also linked to copper mining. It is not clear why the 1552 record identifies Otomi rather than Matlatzinca at Huetamo, but the languages are related and the term *Otomi* may have been used (as it certainly was elsewhere) as a generic term for non-Nahuas (Roskamp 2003, 71). Whatever may have initially been the case, by 1580 none of the migrants spoke anything but Purhepecha and were said to differ in no wise from other community members (Acuña 1987, 263, 269).

Other enclaves in the Tierra Caliente claimed more distant origins. The *Lienzo de Jicalán* (previously known as the *Lienzo de Jucutacato*) and the *Probanza de Santa Ana Tetlaman* (previously known as the *Relación de Tancítaro*) date to 1565 and 1577, respectively (Carrasco 1969; Jiménez Moreno 1948; Mendizábal 1926; Roskamp 1998, 2010). The first is a pictorial record of the migration of Nahuatl speakers from the Gulf Coast locale of Chalchicueyehcan, through central Mexico and the valley of Toluca, through various places in Michoacán, until finally settling in Jicalan on the edge of the Tierra Caliente. The *Probanza* is a textual document that closely follows the story of the *Lienzo* but ends in Santa Ana Tetlaman further to the west. The two sources differ in their claims to the land and mines (see also Roskamp and Retiz 2013). The first claims to have settled before the Tarascan imperial expansion, and the second states that they requested lands from the *Irecha* Tzitzispandaquare, receiving both land and the task of guarding the frontier. Whether granted by the *Irecha* or not, the migrants obtained rights to copper mines and sources of coloring for the decoration of gourds, and securing a renewal of access to these materials was likely the reason for these documents (Roskamp 1998). Roskamp (1998, 2003, 2010) has studied these pictorial and textual documents in detail, concluding that the central Mexican pictorial style followed in the *Lienzo* and in the above-mentioned *Codices of Huetamo* and *Cutzio* was likely brought by the migrants. By 1580, the *Relación Geográfica* that covers these communities and the rest of the corregimiento of Tancitaro still referred to the pueblos of Santiago Acahuato and Santa Ana Tetlaman as occupied by Nahuatl speakers (Acuña 1987, 296, 297). Kelly cites several later sources that attest to Nahuatl in the area into the eighteenth century (Kelly 1947, 22–23). The population of Huetamo had abandoned their native languages, but they preserved a distinctive art style and maintained the use of their own church separately from that of the inhabitants of Cutzio despite their close proximity, a point considered worth noting by the author of the *Relación Geográfica*.

One recently recognized enclave at the heart of the Tarascan Empire held significant political power. Monzón et al. (2009) published a document by Melchor Caltzin, documenting the rights and privileges of a Nahuatl enclave in the capital city of Tzintzuntzan. According to the document, the *Irecha* Tzitzispandaquare enlisted the help of 20 Nahuatl-speaking merchants in the successful conquest of Tzintzuntzan from a rival Tarascan lineage. The members of this enclave became directly involved in Tarascan power politics, and received a series of privileges that were the subject of decades of disputes into the sixteenth century (Monzón et al. 2009; Roskamp 2010).

The cases discussed here present a number of commonalities. Migrants cited political persecution for their decision to change location, which necessarily meant changing their political allegiance. The migrants initially were cohesive social groups with a common identity, whether as a lineage or other customary affiliation. Several were led by nobles, who might be ethnolinguistically distinct from the migrants themselves. Empty territory could be settled without asking permission, although eventually all of the groups voluntarily petitioned the *Irecha* for land in return for tribute or service. This is not unlike the way native peoples petitioned the Spanish authorities with supporting documentation to renew resource rights. Name changes, such as from Matlatzinca to Pirinda, accompanied a shift in identity. The migrants' identity often came to be redefined around their new role within the empire, whether as metalworkers, soldiers, or merchants. The Otomi who populated Necotlan and Charo had not taken on any particular role beyond that as tribute payers, and in the absence of a distinct occupational identity, they ceased to stand out from their Tarascan host community a century later. The Matlatzinca/Otomi at Huetamo and the Apaneca of Guayameo both served to protect the Tarascan border, and neither continued to stand out through expressive means such as language use. The Matlatzinca however maintained separation from the Tarascans by using their own church while the Apaneca may not have maintained a distinct identity because they were war captives unable to rebuild a wider range of institutions from their prior communities. A further contributing factor may be that the Apaneca enclave at Guayameo was 35 km from the Tarascan community of Zirandaro, but the Huetamo enclave was adjacent to Tarascan Cutzio and constantly in view. The latter were constantly reminded of their outsider status, and reacted by maintaining it. Holding political power gave the Nahua enclave in Tzintzuntzan further reason to maintain their identity and language as part of a strategy of privilege maintenance. Most of the enclaves discussed were part of a larger diaspora out of the Toluca valley during the reign of a single Tarascan ruler, but beyond shared origins and similar destinations there is little indication that they maintained contact with one another after settling into their new homes.

PARALLELS IN THE MIGRATION ANNALS

The common characteristics noted here are not unusual and can be found throughout the ethnohistoric accounts of the earlier Postclassic migrations into central Mexico. To keep this discussion condensed, I cite here only a few examples. First, persecution is often cited as a reason for migration, such as in the account of how Nahuatl-speaking Pipil came to be in Central America.

> Being in such great affliction, and in such terrible servitude, those that had been lords of this land and who had held it peacefully, demanded council of their wise men that they might tell them what to do, since they could no longer suffer such tyrannical tribute, so much work and death . . . At the end of the eight days they advised that everyone should gather together, in a single day, as secretly as possible, all their women, children, and belongings and move on and quit that land. (Torquemada 1723, volume I, 332)[1]

Yet there may be a fine line between chafing under the demands of ruling elites and hoping to establish one's self in a similar position. There are examples of secondary elites who chose to migrate with their followers in search of political opportunities, as in the following excerpt from the migration story of Xolotl in the *Anónimo Mexicano* of the late sixteenth century. "The lord died, leaving his two sons, one called Achcauhtzin, [the other] Xolotl. The first became the lord of the rulership; the second was restless at heart because he had not been made the ruler" (Crapo and Glass-Coffin 2005, 11). Such lesser nobles may be the ones described in the examples above as leading and representing their supporters in negotiations for land with the local ruler.

Migrant groups often underwent a name change that signified their new status and affiliation with a different political power, the Culhua Mexica being the best-known example. In the following quote, a group of Chichimeca adopted the name of the place where they settled, while the Mexica appended Tepaneca to their name because of the group to whom they had pledged fealty. "Since the Texcalticpac Chichimeca might attack them, he had sent ambassadors there near to the Tepaneca Mexica, who indeed was named Huitzilihuitzin" (Crapo and Glass-Coffin 2005, 32).

Migrants were expected to request permission to settle from the local lord. The deal was typically sealed with a marriage, with the local ruler being the wife-giver:

> In the forty and seventh year after the noble Xolotl arrived, another three rulers came, bringing many well-adorned warriors. He who led them was called Acolhua, so that they took the name of his lineage . . . And . . . happily lord Xolotl and his son Nopaltzin received them, and he gave them in marriage the two girls whom he guarded. He gave Cuetlaxochitl to Acolhua as wife, and he gave him the nobility of Azcaputzalco. And to Chiconquauhtli he gave Cihuaxochitl as wife, and he gave him the nobility of Xaltocan (Crapo and Glass-Coffin 2005, 16)

There is no mention of a marital alliance between the *Irecha* and the Otomi or Matlatzinca. This suggests differences in how the Tarascan empire incorporated such groups, through transactions more than through kinship relations.

Some migrants aimed to take land by force, and there may have been pressure upon a local ruler to accept a request to settle in his/her lands: "At this time there already was a ruler of Huexotzinco. Their leader was called Xiuhtlehui. Already the Tlaxcalteca watched him. They already surrounded and enclosed him. Because of this, he was greatly disturbed. Then many people came into his territory from other regions" (Crapo and Glass-Coffin 2005, 32–33).

ARCHAEOLOGICAL EXAMPLES

With this preliminary characterization of migrations, enclaves, and diaspora in west-central Mexico, we can review several intrusive communities that have been identified archaeologically within the same general region (figure 12.2). The Middle/Late Formative (650–100 BC) Chupicuaro culture of southern Guanajuato and neighboring Querétaro and Michoacán has long been associated with cemeteries and fine ceramics desirable on the art market. Recent work has corrected this mortuary bias with the identification of sites with circular architecture transitioning in the Terminal Formative to enclosed patios (Darras and Faugère 2005). Intrusive Chupicuaro ceramics have been identified

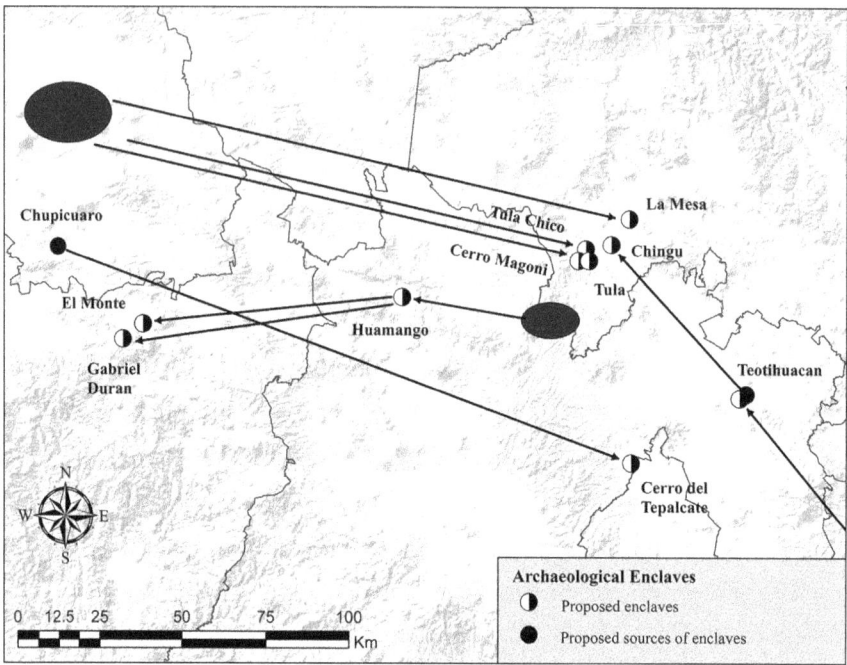

FIGURE 12.2. *Map of the central Mexican region, with the proposed enclaves discussed in the text. (Map made in ArcGIS by the author.)*

throughout central Mexico at numerous sites, but a recent critical analysis by Darras (2006) has whittled away many as misidentifications, very small sample sizes, or too poorly documented to evaluate. However, the Ticoman III (350–250 BC) occupation at Cerro del Tepalcate on the western shore of Lake Texcoco remains of great interest for the large number of actual Chupicuaro ceramics recovered there since the 1940s (Pareyón Moreno 2013, 182–186; Porter 1956, 550, 571). The site shows no indication of economic specialization and was of brief occupation, covering just 3.6 ha and consisting of a single mounded structure. Darras (2006, 85, 91, 93) suggests that Cerro del Tepalcate may have been founded as the lead edge of broader west–east population movements over the course of the Formative.

The best-known prehistoric enclave is undoubtedly Tlailotlacan, the Zapotec enclave of Teotihuacan. Although discussed in a number of sources, it is Spence (1996, 2005; Spence et al. 2005) who has placed Tlailotlacan within a wider theoretical consideration of enclaves and diaspora. The Zapotec enclave is composed of multiple apartment compounds and other structures occupied during the Early Tlamimilolpa through Metepec phases (AD 100–650)—a surprisingly long and robust occupation. Spence estimates a population of 800 people, predominantly of commoner status (Spence 2005, 179–180). The occupants lived in Teotihuacan-style apartment compounds, and the Zapotec presence has been inferred from Oaxacan-style family tombs, architectural façades, and ceramics making up about 5 percent of the total assemblage. One or two Zapotec-style tombs indicate the retention of prior forms of worship (Croissier 2007). Initial interpretations of these archaeological data as indicative of a foreign enclave have been supported by stable isotopic analyses of skeletal remains (Price et al. 2000; White, Spence, Longstaffe, and Law 2004), though not without complications. The isotopic data support ongoing immigration into the enclave and interaction with central Oaxaca, as well as complex mobility patterns in which enclave members spent time at other locations, potentially other Zapotec enclaves in central Mexico (White, Spence, Longstaffe, and Law 2004; see also M. E. Smith and Lind 2005). Spence (2005, 198) posits that the Zapotec were involved in specialized economic activities such as importing Thin Orange or lime for construction into Teotihuacan. This is primarily supported through inferences of interaction with other Zapotec enclaves than based upon evidence at Teotihuacan itself. Tlailotlacan may have been an enclave of migrant workers and their families. Its remarkable duration of occupation suggests other factors in its maintenance however. The presence of other foreign residents has been noted at Teotihuacan, based on archaeological data (Spence et al. 2005), isotopic results (Price et al. 2000; White, Storey, Longstaffe, and Spence 2004), or epigraphy/visual culture (Taube 2003). But most had less archaeological visibility because they met their daily needs through the Teotihuacan markets, itself an indication that these foreigners were not self-sufficient and cohesive social groups.

Another case from Classic-period central Mexico tests the outer limits of what should be considered in an enclave model. The 254-ha settlement of Chingu lies in the Mezquital valley of Hidalgo, 60 km northwest of Teotihuacan (Díaz Oyarzábal 1980). Survey and mapping operations there in the 1970s recognized three-temple architecture and small apartment compounds like those at Teotihuacan, as well as construction methods, site orientation, burials, and a ceramic complex most characteristic of the Tlamimilolpa phase (ca. AD 100–350), with limited evidence for earlier and later occupations. Other ceramics recovered from the site and region appear to be local in nature, and Chingu takes on the appearance of a wholesale intrusion or conquest by Teotihuacan into the Mezquital valley, complete with religious and political institutions. A concentration of Oaxacan ceramics found within an area of the site with obsidian and ceramic workshops (Díaz Oyarzábal 1980, 64–65) intriguingly suggests the potential role of Zapotecs in craft production. Díaz Oyarzábal's proposal that Chingu managed the exploitation of sources of lime for construction on behalf of Teotihuacan has since been confirmed (Barba et al. 2009). Chingu corresponds to Santley's use of the term *enclave* as a direct instrument of the

Teotihuacan state, and it stood in isolation compared to the local material culture of the Mezquital valley. Yet its size, complexity, and complete replication of Teotihuacan culture differs notably from those populations accepted and resettled by the Tarascan state. These characteristics suggest that it might be better characterized as a colony than an enclave, established through different mechanisms but retaining the isolated character of our other examples.

Finally, two settlements have been identified in the Ucareo valley of northeast Michoacán, and dated to the Middle Postclassic (Hernandez and Healan 2008). Both include habitation areas and mounded architecture but are the only sites identified for the Middle Postclassic period in the study area. Rather than enclaves (as I have been using the term), El Monte and the Gabriel Duran site are really the only two settlements for the entire period, covering 26 and 8 ha, respectively. Yet analysis found the ceramics to be distinct from those in earlier and later periods in the local sequence, and "indistinguishable" from those recovered from Huamango, 85 km away in the northern Toluca valley (Piña Chan 1981). Interestingly, the ceramics at Huamango are similarly distinct from those of its neighbors (Hernandez and Healan 2008, 275), and therefore all three sites suggest a settlement diaspora of unknown origin. Hernandez and Healan (2008, 277–279) interpret the Ucareo valley sites as potentially an attempt to take over the collapsing obsidian trade networks after the fall of Tula, either on their own behalf or that of a central Mexican state. The shallow occupations described for all three sites suggest that it was a short-lived effort.

The archaeological cases expand upon those described in the historic texts, and provide material details otherwise unavailable, as few of the sites identified in the documents have been subject to archaeological research. Specialized economic roles are interpreted for the Classic and Postclassic archaeological examples, and at least one of them was arguably the result of conquest by a larger political entity. The politically sponsored enclaves occurred over notably shorter distances from their parent community, just 60–85 km on a straight line. The distances between parent and enclave for the less politically directed examples described in the documents are 135–210 km, and even greater if the detailed wanderings of the *Lienzo de Jicalán* are taken at face value. This may reflect limits on the capacity of polities to support populations beyond too great a distance, and on the ability of a colony to consistently transport resources back to the parent polity.

DISCUSSION AND CONCLUSIONS

In Cabana's (2011) discussion of the history of research into migration, she describes how processual archaeologists characterized migration as a form of mobility not subject to theoretical analysis because it was nonsystemic and therefore seen as random. Migration has only been rehabilitated as a subject for analysis with the gradual loosening or abandonment of processualism's more arbitrary underpinnings—structural-level analysis, systemic behaviors, ecologically inspired models, and the priority of economic and adaptive explanations (compare Ammerman and Cavalli-Sforza 1979, 1984; Anthony 1990; Stone 2003). Migration as described in wave-of-advance models such as that classically set forth by Ammerman and Cavalli-Sforza (1984) do not occur in the real world because, as expressed by Bernardini (2005, 15), they describe the movement of people, not a people. They privilege demography and genetics over social interaction. They recognize no role for social identity, for social ties between migrants, and they collapse the potential range of interactions with established populations to replacement or conversion to an adaptively superior way of life (Bellwood 2001; Renfrew 2002). Social groups are important in defining the units of migration and in the maintenance of cultural heritage after migration has taken place, and play an important role in the migrations of both middle-range and complex societies. The cohesive social groups discussed here could correspond to the families or lineages described by Bernardini (2005) for the Hopi migrations, but there is greater emphasis upon leadership in the Mesoamerican accounts. Similarly, political entities that can abduct people for their own purposes, exploit disaffected subjects to the point of migration, or direct the formation of colonies, are increasingly important in more complex societies.

The findings expressed here and elsewhere put a different face on the many methodological improvements that have taken place in our ability to recognize migration. While metric/nonmetric skeletal analyses, ancient DNA, and isotopic studies are now making many prior interpretations testable, it is only by a better theoretical understanding of how migrants move, congregate spatially, and mark themselves visually that we will know how to isolate and sample populations for these analyses. If we are looking for migrants, we will not necessarily recognize them by their use of distinctive material culture—that occurs only in particular cases of postmigration behavior. As Spence (2005, 181) has stressed, no enclave will perfectly replicate its premigration communities due to obvious differences in the surrounding social environment, the characteristics of the initial migrants, the challenges and resources presented by the natural environment, and so on. While in-migrants may be identifiable, that does not mean that they will look like their origin communities, and over time the differences from the host community may recede as their interests become increasingly aligned. Researchers seeking to understand these dynamics will need to adopt sampling techniques that test for community heterogeneity rather than assuming the remains from a site to represent a homogeneous sample population.

As noted previously, individuals, couples, or other small groups of migrants are far less likely to retain expressive cultural differences from their host community for multiple reasons. From the individual's perspective, they may be at a disadvantage for social interaction if they set themselves off from other members of the community by continuing to use their native language, dress in native clothing, and so on. Individuals are likely to obtain their clothes, food, pottery, and such from the same sources as their neighbors in the absence of a migrant community, and the reproduction of their traditional community is in any case impossible in the absence of social institutions. From the perspective of host community members, individual migrants are not considered a threat in isolation, and so are more easily accepted. The same difficulties for community replication hold for groups of migrant workers who may be demographically biased towards one gender, of a single economic class, or who otherwise poorly replicate the range of social categories and institutions of their origin community. Continuing enclaves of this sort do occur, but through the emergence of new social institutions to form a community (e.g., Voss 2008, 42, 44), which may necessarily alter the archaeological appearance of the group.

Cohesive social groups lie at the opposite end of these continua. When religious specialists, community leaders, and producers of goods and services specific to the group are included in the formation of an enclave, they allow traditional forms of marriage, ritual, authority, dietary practices, and economy to continue in a manner closer to that of their prior community. Furthermore, Portes and Manning (1986) proposed that migrant groups that monopolized an economic niche not in competition with the host society could thrive without necessarily assimilating (see also Curtin 1984). Those authors thought in terms of economic roles specific to the capitalist economy. However, any group responsibility or task that engaged its members differentially further set them apart from the host community through the enactment of distinct daily practices. Groups assigned to monitor the frontier, or who engaged in mining and metalworking as a group, held a more layered and durable identity than those who paid tribute like any other subject of the Tarascan Empire. As noted by Portes and Manning (1986, table 3), this separate identity could make the enclave unpopular with the host community but lead to acceptance by community leaders with wider economic or political interests. One exciting area for future research will be how often these enclaves formed contiguous neighborhoods that might be recognized through settlement archaeology (Arnauld et al. 2012).

A further variable is the degree to which the enclave receives external support. Spence et al. (2005, 166–168) review the ways in which ongoing communication with other enclaves continued to reinforce the identity of the Oaxaca barrio at Teotihuacan. The Otomi and Matlatzinca migrant communities resettled within the Tarascan Empire may have kept ties with their fellows from the same diaspora, but the circumstances of the migration suggest that they had limited contacts with communities back in the Toluca valley where they originated. Their eventual absorption into the empire would have been hastened on this count. The colony at Chingu is of an entirely different order, as it was proposed to have been founded by Teotihuacan for political and economic purposes. Presumably, this kind of enclave could have continued until support from its parent community was withdrawn, as it apparently was by the end of the Tlamimilolpa phase. Hernandez and Healan (2008) proposed that the enclaves associated with Huamango and stretching into the Ucareo area of Michoacán were founded to control the obsidian mining industry in the Middle Postclassic, but their ephemerality may indicate that the support of their political sponsor was very short lived.

Enclaves are predominantly seen as being in a precarious position, surrounded by foreign groups and continually in danger of assimilation into the dominant culture. However, sufficiently large cohesive social groups were in a position to expand their importance over time. Several archaeologists have argued that migrants out of northwestern Mexico moved into the Mezquital valley of Hidalgo in the sixth century AD and initially occupied hilltop sites different from the indigenous communities occupying the farmland on the valley floor (e.g., Mastache and Cobean 1989; Mastache, et al. 2002; see Spence et al. 2011 for supporting isotopic evidence). The hilltop sites of La Mesa, Cerro Magoni, and others displayed ceramic differences from one another, and some had multiple neighborhoods or foci for public architecture (Anderson 2015). Following the proposals made here, these were cohesive groups maintaining social distance from both indigenous inhabitants of the valley, other communities of migrants, and even other migrant groups within the same settlement. Communities of diverse origin are evidenced in the following Corral phase (AD 700–850) by isotopic data (Spence et al. n.d.) and separate civic loci (Mastache and Cobean 1989), even though the new Coyotlatelco ceramic complex was shared across the valley population (Cobean 1990). A far more detailed analysis can be found elsewhere (Beekman and Christensen 2011), but the initial mosaic landscape of enclaves at La Mesa, Cerro Magoni, and later Tula Chico gave way to the multiethnic city of Tula by the ninth century AD. Nahuatl is described in native documents as the language of the dominant group at Tula during the Early Postclassic, and of succeeding empires at Azcapotzalco, and of course Tenochtitlan. The political and economic success of Nahuatl speakers over the next several centuries allowed the language to be adopted horizontally across central Mexico, creating a continuous distribution out of what began as separate enclaves in a broader diaspora.

Finally, the number of enclaves in west-central Mexico would appear to be unusually high. This may be due simply to the intensive research in this corner of Mesoamerica. But the region selected for discussion corresponds to what is today a triple linguistic frontier between Otomanguean, southern Uto-Aztecan, and Purhepecha language families. Since enclaves by definition remain distinct from the host society, those discussed here may stand out because they had crossed a linguistic boundary into a region where communication barriers hindered the establishment of common interests and where ethnolinguistic identity was communicated more sharply through expressive culture (language and certain aspects of material culture). Indeed, language family-scale boundaries were crossed for every case where we have linguistic evidence. I have previously considered the linguistic differences in this area to have been important variables in the failure of styles and concepts to cross from east to west during the Early and Middle Formative periods (Beekman n.d.). Language also played an important and complex role in sustaining cultural and political boundaries in Querétaro and Hidalgo from the Epiclassic through Early Colonial periods (Beekman and Christensen 2011). Language is the most intangible of all forms of expressive culture, but it nonetheless plays a role in the definition of cohesive social groups whose coordinated study may present various opportunities for the study of ancient migration.

NOTE

1. "Viéndose en tanta aflicción, y en tan grave servidumbre, los que antes estaban Señores de aquella Tierra, y la poseían pacíficamente, demandaron Consejo a sus Alfaquíes, que les dixesen, que debían hacer, que ya no podían sufrir tan Tiranos Tributos, y tantos Trabajos, y Muertes . . . Al termino de los ocho días dixeron: Que se apercibiesen para que todos en un día, los más secreto, que pudiesen, levantasen sus Mugeres, y Niños, y sus Haciendas, y se fuesen adelante, y dexasen aquella Tierra."

PART IV

Discussion

13

Migration and Its Close Linkages

DOMINIQUE MICHELET

A . . . reason for the renewal of archaeological interest in migration is simply the
recognition of its importance. Studies in modern migration have established the existence
of close linkage between migration as a phenomenon and a host of other processes or
behavioral patterns as urbanization, industrialization, agricultural strategies, family
structure, gender and ideology.

D. W. Anthony (1990, 897)

The historiography of the archaeology of migrations has been presented elsewhere,[1] and is also repeatedly discussed in the present volume, in particular in
the introduction to this volume by Charlotte Arnauld and colleagues, and in
chapter 12 by Christopher Beekman. Therefore, it is not necessary to treat this
theme in detail here, apart from to reaffirming that population movements at
different spatiotemporal scales have always been, and remain, the norm rather
than the exception in human history. In light of this, it is thus not only logical
but also essential for archaeology and related sciences dealing with the study of
material remains, to take migrations into consideration. On the list of major

DOI: 10.5876/9781646420735.c013

challenges in archaeology today, established by Kintigh et al. (2014) and based on nearly 200 replies to a large-scale survey among mainly American and European archaeologists, one of the five leading topics concerns "movement, mobility, and migration."

In the Mesoamerican area and at its margins,[2] the existence of migrations, especially large scale and/or with a strong politicocultural impact, has been highlighted for a long time. This has been done for several reasons: to account for the more or less drastic variations in settlement patterns in specific places or regions, to elucidate the presence of certain elements of the material culture where they were not expected, or due to the influence of ethnohistorical texts citing migrations. But these evident population movements do not represent the totality of the movements of individuals or groups that might have existed and that partly shaped the history of Mesoamerica. Even low-visibility movements may have existed that had determinant, structural effects on dynamics.

The editors of this book and the instigators of the preceding symposia clearly wish to exhort the scientific community working on precolumbian Mesoamerica to widen research perspectives related to migrations, a concern shared in particular with Cameron's call (2013) to "broaden the view." They thus convened the participants to discuss a particular theme: the relation of population movements to types of settlement designated as "urban," or "cities." Each participant was invited to question the role of population mobility in relatively abrupt urbanization or, inversely, de-urbanization processes, and to assess their effect in periods of greater apparent stability, which could be considered the "ordinary" state of urban units.

After a close reading of the different contributions of this volume as well as part of the extensive literature on archaeological migrations (in Mesoamerica or elsewhere), we decided to highlight several broad and, hopefully, useful considerations. These focus on the variability and the complexity of population movements and on some of the methodological problems raised by the approaches used to detect, evaluate, and understand them. However, we would first like to make some preliminary comments concerning the frame of reference initially outlined for this work but that is not followed by all the chapters of the book—although this does not diminish the interest of the contributions.

To begin with, it is important to acknowledge that the use of the term *urban* and the concept of cities is still not exempt from difficulties today. Controversies divide the community of Mesoamerican archaeologists as to what could or could not be construed as "urban."[3] Perhaps it would have been preferable to use more neutral terms such as "centers" or "agglomerations,"[4] since one of the main objectives of this volume was to encourage reflection on the population exchanges that may have occurred between diverse types of settlements and their hinterlands, between cores and peripheries, and between what modern terminology opposes as *rural* and *urban*, a dichotomy not necessarily pertinent for early Mesoamerican societies. Indeed, we cannot contest that even in the most "urban" centers of Mesoamerica, a non-negligible proportion of the inhabitants were engaged in agricultural activities; this is clearly true for Maya lowland sites, which are today readily labeled "green cities" (Arnauld and Michelet 2004; A. Chase and Chase 2016), but also for settlements with high residential density in the highlands. Moreover, we observe that the first case study discussed in this volume (Freiwald, chapter 1) concerns the site of Barton Ramie, which is recognized as "rural" by the author, although this does not prevent her from questioning the native or immigrant status of the individuals buried there, and from proposing stimulating results. Even within this type of site we observe the presence of people from elsewhere. It is thus necessary to broaden the field of research originally proposed, which was centered on the movements of populations strictly related to phenomena of attraction (or of dispersal) engendered by centers. However, we ought not to forget this specific question—how did such and such population movement shape such and such a center, by contributing to its demography, but also to its settlement structure? Undoubtedly, this is an important perspective for the study of the various centers that developed in Mesoamerica.

In their appropriate attempt to encourage the research community to extend the analysis of population movements beyond major migratory episodes, which at times changed the course of history of certain parts of Mesoamerica, the editors advance a terminological clarification and propose a distinction between migration and mobility. Although their definition of the concept of mobility is not different from the use of the term by other authors (see for example, van Dommelen 2014, 480), not all of the contributors to this volume adhere to it. For Gonlin and Landau (chapter 6) as well as for Graham and Howie (chapter 5) and others, the word *mobility* should be used only to designate the capacity of a given population to move, whereas any effective movement is related to a form of migration. Similarly, we can observe that the authors of the collective and multidisciplinary volume coordinated by Cabana and Clark did not succeed in agreeing on a definition of *migration*, leading the editors of the volume to propose a "minimal" definition of migration as "a one-way relocation to a different environment by at least one individual" (Cabana and Clark 2011a, 5). Each contributor was called upon to refine and enrich this definition according to his or her own approach. Note, however, that in a holistic perspective on the word *migration*, this minimal definition does not include what several authors have called *circular migrations*, that is, movements of people who subsequently return to their point of origin.

In the present case, the word *migration* alone may have been sufficient insofar as we admit, from the outset, that it could encompass very diverse types of movement. Most, if not all of these can be divided into two classes: large- and small-scale migrations in the very broad sense of the word, including spatial, temporal, and social scales (the last depending on the nature and the size of the migrant population). Incidentally, we must acknowledge that a quantitatively small and spatially short, but relatively long-term "routine" migration may have serious consequences for the receiving as well as the originating locations. Such an example may be confounded with the material results, in principle more easily accessible to archaeology, of another process—the fast and massive migration of people between the same points. The distinction between these two processes can be made principally based on the control of the temporal parameter. This last point is methodologically crucial, and is emphasized with good reason by the authors of the introduction to this volume. It is therefore essential to acknowledge that the identification of one or other form of migration does not depend on the appraisal of only a first, a second, or a third type of parameter, but on the combined evaluation of the different parameters at work.

We now continue the discussion by approaching the question of the forms of population movements before focusing on how to assess them, using archaeological data.

VARIABILITY IN MIGRATION: FROM TYPOLOGIES TO VARIABLE OPERATIVE MODES

In the 1960s and the 1970s, archaeology, especially in the United States, turned away from the problem of ancient migrations for several reasons. Among these are undoubtedly the true or falsely suspected links between what were pejoratively called "migrationism" and diffusionism. However, other archaeologies (for example those related to Late Antiquity and to the beginning of the Middle Ages in northwestern Europe that dealt with the "invasions") and also other disciplines like history, did not abandon the theme. According to the references cited by the contributors of this book, the analysis by Charles Tilly of migrations in modern Europe (Tilly 1978) played a particularly important, even seminal, role. Indeed, the study by this historian is not a mere examination of concrete cases, but he develops a theorization and classification of the forms of migration. This work may have attracted, and indeed continues to attract, archaeologists primarily because it proposes a typology of population movements differentiating four or five "standard" forms of movements, and archaeology is commonly involved in typological practice. Tilly differentiates *local migration* (in which the distance traveled and the cultural gap experienced by the migrants between the point of departure and the point of arrival are limited), *circular migration* (in which the migrant social entity returns to its point of origin after one or several episodes of expatriation), *chain migration* (in which migrants are "received" where they arrive, particularly by predecessors), and *career migration* (in which the generally

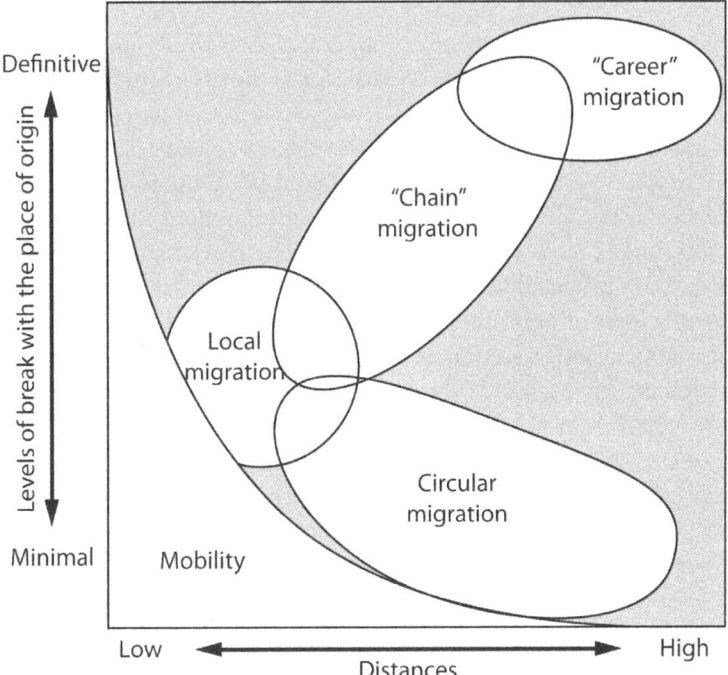

FIGURE 13.1. *The different forms of migrations and mobility as schematized by Tilly (1978). (Redrawn by Sylvie Eliès; UMR 8096, ArchAm.)*

permanent migrants move to become part of new systems and new structures). We can then observe that in situations where distances are too short and divergences between the two poles of displacement are too few, we would see simple *inframigratory mobility*, in which the dividing line between mobility and migration is floating, and in any case arbitrary. Tilly's famous schema (figure 13.1; see also Gonlin and Landau's table 6.1 in this volume) is of particular interest here for the two parameters that, according to Tilly, make up the different forms of population displacement: the physical distances between the departure and arrival zones on one hand, and the degree of sociocultural rupture experienced by the actors on the other.

We must also notice the care taken by the author to represent in his diagram the existence of possible overlaps between the different forms of migration. But the two parameters used in Tilly's figure are clearly not the only ones. Other approaches could emphasize the importance of the temporalities involved in these phenomena, with long-term processes, at one end, and relatively occasional events, at the other. And there are some supplementary parameters that model the structure of mobility and migrations: for example, the size of the populations involved, ranging from several isolated individuals to whole sets of populations, with intermediary groups, and with family groups in particular. This last parameter is specifically relevant in the case of movements to (or from) relatively nucleated settlements, as suggested in chapter 4 (this volume) by Bullock and chapter 8 (this volume) by Arnauld and colleagues.

In his famous article published in 1990, David W. Anthony postulates that if we want to make progress in the archaeology of migrations, we must first focus on the structure of each migratory phenomenon. This is, at least implicitly, an invitation to conduct analyses leading to a categorization—or a typology—of the forms or processes of population movements (Anthony 1990, figure 1). Anthony then lists the factors that, according to him, are the most decisive in the structure of any mobility or migration: the social organization in which the agents are involved, their economic situations (although these are by no means the only important circumstances, as Anthony himself acknowledges), and the technical conditions of the movements. Although he denounces the focus of archaeologists on the causes of population movements, which explains the failure of several works on the subject, the theorization he advances of what he prefers to call the "conditions" of this kind of phenomenon can be just as counterproductive if we treat them as engraved in stone. This is precisely what Cameron (2013) rightly criticizes, emphasizing in particular the fact that not all movements of people correspond to more or less calculated decisions. We will simply recall here that, according to Anthony, these "conditions" revolve around three main variables: attractive elements (the pull side of things), expulsive elements (the push aspect), and the existence, or absence, of different types of obstacles on the paths of travel. As Cameron argues, there is not always a pull factor behind migration, and some movements are not the result of well-thought-out choices. This is particularly the case with what she calls "random demographic processes"—a point that illustrates the pertinence and the importance of what we called above "small-scale movements," and what others label as "population circulation" events. To come back to Anthony's proposals, it is important to mention that he advocates separating short-distance migrations from long-distance ones. Among the latter, he points out five conditions that he does not present as distinct types, although at least one of them could be considered as such by many researchers: "leapfrogging," "migration stream" (in which movement occurs in one direction along a given road, as opposed to "migration waves," which are extensively spread out), and "return migration" (which appears to be equivalent to Tilly's "circular migration"). To this list he adds the two specific dimensions of "migration frequency" (how many migrations do people undertake?) and "migration demography" (which fractions of a population migrate?).

Ultimately, whether or not we use typological categories to cover the whole possible spectrum of population movements (which is Tilly's concern) or whether we limit ourselves to a more or less systematic examination of the parameters at work so as to define the structure or the form of mobility or a migration (Anthony's perspective), the most important aspect to retain from this brief overview is the very extensive variety of elements to take into account concomitantly, in order to describe and understand an observed or supposed population movement. But first, we need to detect those movements.

ARCHAEOLOGICAL SIGNATURES OF POPULATION MOVEMENTS: A FEW COMMENTS ON THEIR USE, IN PARTICULAR IN PRECOLUMBIAN MESOAMERICA

Today, there is a consensus among specialists of past societies, in particular Mesoamerica, that three main categories of evidence can be examined to detect, confirm, or infer the reality of past population movements: material culture and practices representative of each society, settlement patterns, and biological remains of individuals and groups in question. A fourth category of testimony can be added to this set of information sources, particularly for migrations thought to have occurred in times close to the Conquest, namely ethnohistorical texts—real narratives, often detailed, or simple allusions—referring to movements with sufficiently profound consequences to have been recalled in oral traditions and written down long after the events.[5] At that point, based on examples from the chapters of this volume as well as other comparable cases, the issue is to discuss certain problems linked to the use of these different kinds of sources and to outline how to improve and solidify them. Our aim at present is thus not to draw up a complete panorama of all the cited domains, but to formulate a series of comments, liable to clarify and optimize our approaches to mobility and migrations.

Material Culture and More

We no longer automatically associate elements from material cultures with cultures or ethnicities directly, or consider that changes in this domain can (or must) indicate possible population transfers and migrations. Behind this approach to migrations through the observation of replacements or simple transformations of assemblages of objects—which affect styles in the broad sense, or technologies that allowed their manufacture—lies the question of cultural identity.[6] It is incontestable that types of objects can be archaeologically associated with one or another population, and, in this respect, the case of sites located in sectors considered cultural border zones, at least during certain periods, can be particularly enlightening. In this way, Copan and its surroundings could provide a major example, even though chapter 6, by Gonlin and Landau, is not addressed to this subject. Nonetheless, if we construct the identities of populations too closely on the basis of material remains, we run the risk of reifying and fossilizing them and, conversely, of minimizing or even obliterating the dynamics that could have developed within each group with no exterior input. As for the more or less rapid modifications observed throughout time in the material culture of a particular place, they do not necessarily involve durable and definitive displacements of individuals or entire populations. In their analysis of the occupations of the Belize valley, particularly at Baking Pot, between the Classic and Postclassic periods, Hoggarth and colleagues (chapter 2, this volume) note important changes in the inventories of artifacts (ceramics, lithics, metal), which is hardly surprising, as these episodes are separated in time by nearly four centuries. Nonetheless, the authors find the real indicator of the arrival of new groups after AD 1280 elsewhere: in the biochemical characteristics of the skeletons of the people buried there.

An exemplary case of the occurrence of archaeological objects possibly linked to demographic transformation including migration is that of Coyotlatelco pottery—the significance of its presence may have been overestimated, although it is still undoubtedly underexploited, in spite of the abundant works concerning this material (see, among others, López Perez et al. 2006; Solar Valverde 2006). The introduction of this pottery to central Mexico, and Teotihuacan in particular, has been taken as an argument supporting the model of an invasion having played a key role in the fall of the metropolis, as this pottery was associated for a long time with a tradition from the western-northwestern portion of Mesoamerica. However, the data reported by Clayton (chapter 9, this volume), based on her work at the site of Chicoloapan to the southeast of the Basin of Mexico, imply that the development of this pottery, which remains possibly connected to new arrivals, was much more complex than initially thought. In particular, the duration of the phenomenon is an issue, since the appearance of this ware in the Basin of Mexico may have preceded political disruption at Teotihuacan.

Alongside material culture, several practices registered in material remains can also be examined for signs of population movements. The first of these, which appears throughout the pages of this book, is clearly that of funerary practices. The main observation regarding the latter is that they are far from clear cut. On the one hand, Graham and Howie (chapter 5, this volume) presume that new populations arrived in the maritime community of Marco Gonzalez at the end of the Late Classic and the beginning of the Terminal Classic on the basis of a new burial position (a position that will also be seen at Lamanai, at a much later date). But conversely, at Barton Ramie, in a group of 28 analyzed individuals, three were identified as nonlocals according to strontium isotope ratio comparisons from bones and teeth, but they did not display any specific funerary treatment (Freiwald, chapter 1, this volume). The same is true of Cholula—out of 20 individuals recognized as nonnatives of the city (according to the analyses of Price and Burton as discussed by Bullock, chapter 4, this volume), not one of them presents signs of any particular mortuary behavior, nor any specific osteological indicators. The adoption of the funerary practices of a place has often rightfully been interpreted as the expression of migrants' efforts to assimilate. As for the fact that an individual does not present a local isotopic signature, it does not necessarily mean that he belongs to a cultural, ethnic, or linguistic group distinct from the local individuals.

We will thus provisionally conclude here that the measurement of population movements based on elements from the material culture—either artifacts or practices—especially when these are taken in isolation, is far from clear or simply not possible. In contrast, these elements, combined with other markers, are not redundant and are often very useful as they potentially corroborate one another, and can also reveal specific conditions related to migrations—for example, the degree of assimilation of newcomers in a previously established population. This type of secondary (or lateral) interpretation can be of great interest, particularly for the analysis of forms of affiliation (for example, neighborhoods) in diverse settlements. This is precisely the heart of the contribution that Beekman (chapter 12, this volume) devotes to this byproduct of certain migrations—the formation of foreign enclaves in particular places or spaces. At the boundary between the Aztec Empire and the Tarascan kingdom, and specifically inside the latter, there were Nahuatl, Otomi, and Matlatzinca enclaves, better known today through historic records than through archaeological remains.[7] But conversely, the Zapotec enclave and the sector where people from the Gulf Coast lived at Teotihuacan, were initially identified on the basis of material culture elements—the shape of the graves, on one hand, and the plan of residential structures on the other. The important point here is to recognize, as Beekman does, the link between enclaves and the cohesive social groups underlying them.

Settlement Patterns

Settlement patterns—not to be confused with building morphology, which is part of the aforementioned category of remains—are part of the material culture of past societies. However, we discuss them separately here because these remains have often been directly hypothesized to correlate with migrations, as these events involve the establishment and abandonment of sites. The *a priori* rather rapid development of the urban settlements in the Malpaís of Zacapu, which is the focus of the contribution by Pereira and others (chapter 10, this volume), could certainly have been interpreted as part of a population displacement, even without reading the first lines of the *Relación de Michoacán*. In the same way, although Dunning and colleagues (chapter 7, this volume) supply new data showing the existence of Preclassic settlements in the Puuc region, in particular at Xcoch, it is reasonable to consider that the population increase in this Maya region during the eighth century of our era could never have occurred without the influx of migrants. Conversely, several major episodes of site abandonment are known in Mesoamerican history, such as in the central Maya lowlands between the end of the eighth and tenth centuries. As Graham and Howie (chapter 5, this volume) and Arnauld and colleagues (Arnauld et al. 2017a) present elsewhere, discussions of the abandonment of the central Maya lowlands at the end of the Classic period bear mainly on the abandonment of masonry-built dwellings in both large and small sites. It is reasonable to ask whether part of the retreating population may have lived, at least for some time, without necessarily going very far away, in residences made of perishable materials that are only slightly visible, if at all, to the type of archaeology conducted up until now in this zone. Also, worth mentioning is the hypothesis whereby the disappearance of all villages, some of them very extensive, along the northeastern frontier of Mesoamerica towards the year 1000 would not necessarily have been accompanied by the retreat of all the inhabitants towards more southern regions. Some of them could have chosen to stay locally or in some vicinity by adapting to new lifestyles and inventing new cultures, on the model of the semisedentary Pames discovered by the first missionaries, particularly in the Sierra Gorda. Large-scale population movements can sometimes be correlated with deep changes at the place of departure in subsistence systems, dwelling morphology, and settlement patterns.

All ancient migrations, regardless of their type or size, are an integral part of paleodemography. This element is not taken sufficiently into consideration in the contributions of this volume, except in those by Cucina and colleagues (chapter 3) and Pereira and colleagues (chapter 10). The dynamics of a given population depends on its birth rate, its death rate, and what demographers call the "migratory balance." In the case of pre-Jenerian populations (those that precede smallpox vaccination), models of natural development (or, more precisely, models intrinsic to populations) can be established. Variations between the development curves supplied by these models and real population developments[8] cannot be attributed to factors other than migration, especially when they are significant, since population fertility and life expectancy are not likely to change in the short term, except in exceptional cases, such as for example during epidemics. Thus, the analysis of ancient migrations in Mesoamerica and elsewhere has much to gain from increased collaboration with paleodemographers. Of course, when fluctuations in settlement networks seem to point to relatively important immigration or emigration and, better still, when this can be confirmed by a paleodemographic study, there are still a number of outstanding issues that need to be addressed—the origin of the migrants in the case of the sudden appearance of large settlements (see the following section), or their destination in the case of an exodus. The approach to population movements through the evolution of settlements can also be developed in another way, as shown for example by Arnauld and others (chapter 8, this volume). This focuses on growth, or nongrowth, of individual residential complexes or whole establishments in the long term. Growth or at least stability should *a priori* be the norm and, where there is nongrowth, its absence must be explained—for example, by generational expulsion events or, more generally, what Cameron (2013, 225) called "fission." For her part, Rice (chapter 11, this volume) stresses the importance, in certain cases, of factionalism. Ultimately, there is a whole spectrum of possible identification of population movements based on the analysis of settlement patterns at several distinct scales but, most important, it is necessary to take these diverse scales into consideration—households, neighborhoods, whole centers—no matter how big or small they are.

BioArchaeology

With the development of bioarchaeological sciences, already outlined by Anthony (1990) more than 30 years ago, and which will no doubt continue to give rise to new types of analyses in the future, the identification of migratory flows has made tremendous progress. Multiple methods are used and, although the study of strontium isotopes on human remains is currently thriving, as shown by several chapters in this book, here again it is important to combine different approaches. In this way, analyzing the dental morphology of Classic Maya population at the Yucatecan port of Xcambo provides critical information (for example, by showing that there are few biological links between the individuals from the coast and those from inland zones), while the study of the structure of Early to Late Classic populations provides other types of information, and biogeochemistry also brings new promising datasets. Concerning this extremely productive field of research, some comments are in order. In the cases presented in this volume, in particular those concerning strontium ratio analyses, several figures are surprising. For example, the only two adults dating from the Postclassic period at Baking Pot are identified as being of foreign origin, whereas the third individual from the same period, a child, is unsurprisingly considered to be local (Hoggarth et al., chapter 2, this volume). Does it not seem vital here to try to broaden the sample? Actually the authors of the study are aware of this as they write, "drawing conclusions from a small sample of only three individuals poses more questions than answers." In fact, when we are dealing with migrations considered to be of low intensity, whether on a regional or a larger scale, it is not unthinkable to rely on a small sample, but on the condition of not translating those small figures into percentages.

Concerning the events considered to have involved massive (im)migrations or with drastic consequences, it is undoubtedly imprudent to rely on the study of only few individuals. Returning to Teotihuacan and the question of the arrival of Coyotlatelco populations (who could have been foreigners and who may have played a determinant role in the crisis that the city and its system of government suffered around the middle of the sixth century or even a little afterwards), the analyses of buried individuals were undertaken in the very early stages of the development of strontium ratio measurements (Manzanilla 2005b; Price et al. 2000). The studied burials were situated in cave-tunnels discovered and excavated to the east of the Pyramid of the Sun. In the second article cited above, dental ratios are not given for the 13 individuals from Cueva del Pirul, whereas, of the four individuals from Cueva de las Varillas where bone and dental ratios are published, at least three of them are of nonlocal origin and may have come from diverse places. However, the burials from this latter cave appear to be from the postcollapse phase (Mazapan) rather than from the Metepec phase. In the first referenced work, it appears that eight individuals were analyzed from the Cueva del Pirul and probably date to the Metepec phase (Manzanilla 2005b, 266). Two of them are clearly nonnatives, two seem to be local, and four of them yield measurements that are difficult to interpret. In any case, these results show that an extensive biogeochemical program is required to shed more light on this major topic concerning the determination of the foreign or native character of the bearers of Coyotlatelco ceramics.[9]

Regarding the biogeochemical proxies and their limitations, some of the conclusions reached by Freiwald in chapter 1 of this volume should be highlighted. Her assessment that these approaches "only work for the first-generation migrants" and that "each sample will only identify a single move and miss the multiples moves an individual might have made," seems to be particularly pertinent. In short, demonstrating that the place of death is not the place of birth or childhood does not illustrate the exact moves an individual made throughout life. Do the results of the analysis indicate a single migration to the place of death, or did the individual in question die during a simple occasional move, or again did the individual share his/her time between several places of residence? Again, sampling is a central issue. If a relatively extensive sample can be obtained at the settlement scale, it could show variations in different parameters for that particular settlement, which once related to their specific contexts, could help us to detect movement patterns. Lastly, in the future we must be attentive to data that paleogenetic analyses are fortunately able to provide.

Narratives and Archaeology

Again, this is a vast subject and we comment on only a few aspects. In Mesoamerica, the ethnohistorical texts mentioning or, at times, detailing migrations, principally refer, and with good reason, to later precolumbian societies. It has been observed for a long time that recording a migration at the foundation of an important political entity (Mexican, Tarascan, K'iche'[10]) seems to have been a veritable literary commonplace at the time of the Conquest, sometimes with some historical basis but also with revealing ideological content. The available texts deliberately present colorful versions of realities to imbue them with symbolic value, particularly in order to legitimate the ruling powers, but these cannot be reduced to pure fabrications. Even though it is likely that the authors or inspirers of these texts were more concerned with producing canonical and exemplary narrations than with precisely reporting facts, a refusal to recognize that these documents have some historical basis is challenged by the existence of material data that validate parts of them. It is thus legitimate to systematically and critically compare the different texts and material data—see, for example, Michelet (2010) concerning the initial part of the Tarascan case or, strictly speaking, the Uacusecha saga. Another important reference is the article by Beekman and Christensen (2003) on the Nahua migrations, which widens the strict case of the Mexica and illustrates the potential of archaeology to contribute a theoretical perspective to ancient migrations. Before this comparative exercise, which can result in the rejection or modification of certain assertions in these accounts, but also conversely in the confirmation of others, the main advantage of these historic-legendary writings is to point to the possible existence of population movements that we would otherwise know nothing of, and to encourage archaeology to search for evidence of their material traces. The chapter on the Itza in this volume, carefully analyzed by P. Rice (chapter 11), is emblematic of this. Without the elements concerning them, transmitted by the Chilam Balam, archaeology alone could probably not have detected the major double migration undertaken by at least part of the group: first towards the north of Yucatán, perhaps during the Late Classic period onwards, then again towards the region of the Petén lakes, late in the Postclassic period. The different mentions of the Itza in the Chilam Balam, and their multiple and complex movements are difficult to understand and interpret, and some of these moves may have been mythical. However, when these texts are taken seriously, they can serve as a basis for other research, specifically archaeological, and can thus, at least partially, advance our knowledge of the moves of the Itza or even open new perspectives on the migrations of other populations.

Last, but Not Least . . .

As said with regard to the relevance of correlating written sources on migrations with archaeology, it is important to reiterate here that the analysis of population movements in past societies, of whatever form or size, necessitates the combined use of several types of evidence. This is more or less explicitly illustrated in practically all the chapters of this volume. Nonetheless, another last point deserves emphasis: the importance of the control of time, as precisely as possible (Cowgill 2015b), in the analysis of the studied phenomena. Here we wish to briefly present one last example, namely the (migratory) arrival of the

Uacusechas in the Zacapu Basin (northern Michoacán) as a precursor to the development of the Tarascan state, an issue to which we have devoted research. When archaeology began to develop in this zone during the 1980s, we immediately identified large urban sites in the Malpaís of Zacapu, and later traced their development from the middle of the thirteenth century until their general abandonment (except for one) in a very organized manner towards the middle of the fifteenth century. Then the first pages of the second part of the *Relación de Michoacán* suddenly became clear. Let us recall that the latter referred to the arrival to this exact place of a group of migrants, the Uacusechas, with a leader and a tutelary deity, as well as to the (seemingly rapid) continued migration onwards of this group to form the ruling elite of the future Tarascan kingdom. At the time of our initial research, as a result of a poor understanding of event chronology and of the thin stratigraphic sequences obtained in the first test pits we excavated, we believed the whole settlement process and the occupation to be more or less synchronous within a phase of 200 years—the Milpillas phase (AD 1250–1450). In this context, we thought that what had occurred was a rapid and numerically important immigration, followed by moderate onsite growth of the populations involved. As shown in chapter 10 (this volume) by Pereira and colleagues, new work conducted in the same sector from 2009 onwards has provided rich additional information. The urban sites in question underwent much more substantial *in situ* development than previously thought. For example, four successive stages of construction were detected in the main pyramid at the site of Malpaís Prieto. Furthermore, the local histories of the several sites do not appear to have covered the whole phase and could not have been strictly synchronous, at least in the case of the two sites with more rigorous ^{14}C dating results. Henceforth, a very different image of migration emerges—one of less brutal, more progressive, more continuous migration, maybe proceeding from site to site following a kind of leapfrog movement, as Anthony (1990) would have labelled it. The Uacusecha case is not yet totally settled, but we can see that the migrations indicated by the archaeological data from the 1980s and those suggested by new information are not the same.

As highlighted in one comment by Bullock (chapter 4, this volume), beyond the identification of migrants, which will be in principle guaranteed in the near future by the biogeochemistry of human remains, the real challenge for tomorrow (and still today) with regards to the study of past migrations is to reconstruct the real processes of mobility and migrations.

CONCLUSIONS

Having long struggled with archaeological and ethnohistorical issues bearing on population movements in western Mexico as well as with the question of the retraction of the northeastern Mesoamerican frontier, we welcome the contributions of this volume for the potential they offer in discussing the diversity of archaeological signatures, markers, and proxies, and in bringing forth many ways of combining disciplinary approaches. The focus on Mesoamerica is well chosen, considering the relevance in this culture area of urban developments during the Classic and Postclassic eras, even though we prefer that the variable dimensions of settlement shapes, sizes, composition, and patterns be carefully assessed before rural/urban concepts are applied that, in many cases, force ancient realities and complex data sets into modern preconceptions. Indeed, the frequency of Mesoamerican large settlements, a number of them certainly quite "urban," and their marked variation from Preclassic to Classic and Postclassic in size and nature do raise the issue of their demography, the latter necessarily including migration processes. It is all the more pertinent that, generally as a cultural area, Mesoamerica is notable for the relatively limited longevity of its main cities or political capitals, and their relatively frequent relocation in space, the paradigmatic example being central Mexico with its series of large metropolises formed and abandoned in succession. Even in those settlements that possessed undeniable longevity, strong fluctuations point to population movements.

Even if still to be clarified and reworked, this framework (the relation of "large" with "small" neighbor settlements) now seems adequate to refine the theoretical and methodological approaches to the old issue of migration. Indeed, it can be advanced, although with caution, that Mesoamerican archaeology has reached a point at which most regions have been reasonably covered by local and supralocal settlement pattern studies, defining at least hypothetical time-space processes over rather large distances. This is not to say that surveys and excavations have been exhaustive and that all resulting interpretative models are well grounded. But some degree of knowledge has been attained for many regions that include multitiered settlement networks, allowing us to devise plausible scenarios of population movements when considering the now more-controlled evidence bearing on time constraints, environmental variation, material culture diversity, and, in some cases, written traditions. This is where the working definition of *mobility* as a less disruptive process than *migration* must find a path and open perspectives, as this volume proposes using a relatively large array of case studies along with a diversity of combined approaches. Our comments have highlighted problems of time resolution and precision of sampling size, and of the still-limited role of certain bioarchaeological methods. But the goal remains to optimize our conceptual tools in order to approach the unusual complexity of the migratory phenomenon. Most ancient population movements (in groups, not as individuals) should be demographically visible, but paleodemography is unfortunately underdeveloped in Mesoamerican studies. Large, rapid population movements may appear to be archaeologically visible, although their varied modes may not be immediately recognized, as shown by our Michoacán

Malpaís case study. But many low-visibility small-scale movements also occurred and were as determinant as the large ones in structuring societies, their settlements, and their dynamics.

NOTES

1. For a short summary from an interesting perspective, which is not that of an archaeologist working in America, we can refer to van Dommelen (2014).

2. With regard to these, see for example Hers (1989), Michelet (2001), and Stresser-Péan (2000) for the northern frontier, or chapter 6 by Gonlin and Landau in the preceding pages concerning a sector of the southeast limits.

3. See the paradigmatic positions of Sanders and Webster (1988), on one hand, and D. Chase et al. (1990), on the other. The latter was recently updated, particularly in A. Chase and Chase (2016). For an overall perspective and details of the Mesoamerican case, it is best to refer to Sanders et al. (2003), and Mastache et al. (2009), as well as Cowgill (2004) or M. E. Smith (2007), among others.

4. On the origins of the Greek city, see Mazarakis-Ainian (2017) and, on the concept of agglomeration, Chantraine (2009, supplement on the etymology of κώμη).

5. But their importance also stems from the fact that these narrations are related to a desire to write the history of groups in mythical schemas, which often value foreign origins.

6. A. Gallay (Gallay et al. 2012), among others, through his work in the Niger valley, showed that, if form could give rise to imitations or adoptions without population movements, techniques are not easily transmitted and have more chance of revealing specific know-how, or sometimes even a particular ethnicity.

7. At Tzintzuntzan, we refer to the presence of a Nahua community (Roskamp 2010). But was this a true enclave in the spatial sense of the term?

8. Theoretically retrievable in mortuary remains, or even in the quantitative study of settlements, or other seemingly cruder indicators, such as the quantities of ceramics per period.

9. Manzanilla's (2017) edited volume on migration at Teotihuacan does not address the issue of the role of newcomers at the end of the metropolis's political apogee. However, as it widely documents the complex multiethnic Teopancazco neighborhood through time, it is well in phase with the present volume's perspective.

10. For an analysis of the parallels between the histories of these three groups, one can refer in particular to Martínez González (2010, table).

References

Abell, Natalie. 2014. "Migration, Mobility and Crafts People in the Aegean Bronze Age: A Case Study from Ayia Irini on the Island of Kea." *World Archaeology* 46: 551–568.

Abrams, Elliot M. 1984. "Systems of Labor Organization in Late Classic Copán, Honduras: The Energetics of Construction." PhD diss., Pennsylvania State University, State College, PA.

Abrams, Elliot M. 1994. *How the Maya Built Their World: Energetics and Ancient Architecture.* Austin: University of Texas Press.

Abrams, Elliot M. 1998. "Structures as Sites: The Construction Process and Maya Architecture." In *Function and Meaning in Classic Maya Architecture*, ed. Stephen D. Houston, 123–140. Washington, DC: Dumbarton Oaks.

Abrams, Lesley. 2012. "Diaspora and Identity in the Viking Age." *Early Medieval Europe* 20: 17–38.

Acosta, Jorge R. 1972. "El epílogo de Teotihuacan." In *Teotihuacan XI Mesa Redonda*, I: 149–156. México, DF: Sociedad Mexicana de Antropología, Instituto Nacional de Antropología e História.

DOI: 10.5876/9781646420735.c014

Acuña, René. 1987. *Relaciones Geográficas del Siglo XVI: Michoacán*. México, DF: Universidad Nacional Autónoma de México.

Adams, Richard E. W. 1973. "The Collapse of Maya Civilization: A Review of Previous Theories." In *The Classic Maya Collapse*, ed. T. P. Culbert, 21–34. Albuquerque: School of American Research and University of New Mexico Press.

Adams, Richard E. W. 1999. *Rio Azul: An Ancient Maya City*. Norman: University of Oklahoma Press.

Adams, Richard E. W., and William D. Smith. 1981. "Feudal Models for Classic Maya Civilization." In *Lowland Maya Settlement Patterns*, ed. W. Ashmore, 335–350. Albuquerque: School of American Research and University of New Mexico Press.

Adams, Robert McC. 1978. "Strategies of Maximization, Stability, and Resilience in Mesopotamian Society, Settlement, and Agriculture." *Proceedings of the American Philosophical Society* 122(5): 329–335.

Aimers, James J. 2004. *Cultural Change on a Temporal and Spatial Frontier: Ceramics of the Terminal Classic to Postclassic Transition in the Upper Belize River Valley*. British Archaeological Reports, International Series. Oxford, UK: Archaeopress.

Aimers, James J. 2007. "What Maya Collapse? Terminal Classic Variation in the Maya Lowlands." *Journal of Archaeological Research* 15: 329–377.

Aimers, James J., Terry G. Powis, and Jaime J. Awe. 2000. "Preclassic Round Structures of the Upper Belize River Valley." *Latin American Antiquity* 11(1): 71–86.

Albiez-Wieck, Sarah. 2011. "Contactos exteriores del estado tarasco: Influencias desde dentro y fuera de Mesoamérica." PhD diss., Rheinischen Friedrich-Wilhelms-Universität Bonn.

Alcalá, Jerónimo de. 2009. *Relación de Michoacán*. Electronic publication. Barcelona: Red-ediciones.com S. L.

Alexander, Rani T. 2012. "Maya Collapse or Resilience? Lessons from the Spanish Conquest and Yucatan's Caste War." In *The Ancient Maya of Mexico: Reinterpreting the Past of the Northern Maya Lowlands*, ed. Geoffrey Braswell, 325–346. London: Equinox.

Alexander, Rani T., and S. Andrade. 2007. "Frontier Migration and the Built Environment in Southwestern Campeche." *Estudios de Cultura Maya* 30: 175–196.

Alexiades, Miguel N., ed. 2009. *Mobility and Migration in Indigenous Amazonia: Contemporary Ethnoecological Perspectives*. Oxford: Berghahn Books.

Ammerman, Albert J., and Luigi Luca Cavalli-Sforza. 1979. "The Wave of Advance Model for the Spread of Agriculture in Europe." In *Transformations: Mathematical Approaches to Culture Change*, ed. Colin Renfrew and Kenneth L. Cooke, 275–293. New York: Academic Press.

Ammerman, Albert J., and Luigi Luca Cavalli-Sforza. 1984. *The Neolithic Transition and the Genetics of Population*. Princeton, NJ: Princeton University Press.

Anderson, J. Heath. 2015. Cerro Magoni: A Link between Epiclassic Tula and the Bajío? Paper presented at the 80th Annual Meeting of the Society for American Archaeology, San Francisco, California. tDAR ID: 396128.

Andrews, Anthony P., E. Wyllys Andrews, and Fernando Robles C. 2003. "The Northern Maya Collapse and Its Aftermath." *Ancient Mesoamerica* 14(1): 151–156.

Andrews, Anthony P., and Shirley B. Mock. 2002. "New Perspectives on the Prehispanic Maya Salt Trade." In *Ancient Maya Political Economies*, ed. Marilyn A. Masson and David A. Freidel, 307–334. Walnut Creek, CA: Altamira Press.

Andrews, Anthony P., and Fernando Robles C. 1985. "Chichen Itza and Coba: An Itza-Maya Standoff in Early Postclassic Yucatan." In *The Lowland Maya Postclassic*, ed. Arlen F. Chase and Prudence M. Rice, 62–72. Austin: University of Texas Press.

Andrews, Bradley W. 2004. "Sayil Revisited: Inferring Terminal Classic Population Size and Dynamics in the West-Central Yucatan Peninsula." *Human Ecology* 32: 593–613.

Andrews, E. Wyllys, and William L. Fash. 2005. "Issues in Copán Archaeology." In *Copán: The History of an Ancient Maya Kingdom*, ed. E. W. Andrews and W. L. Fash, 395–425. Santa Fe, NM: School of American Research Press.

Andrieu, Chloé. 2013. "Late Classic Maya Lithic Production and Exchange at Río Bec and Calakmul, Mexico." *Journal of Field Archaeology* 38(1): 21–37.

Anovitz, Lawrence M., J. Michael Elam, Lee R. Riciputi, and David R. Cole. 1999. "The Failure of Obsidian Hydration Dating: Sources, Implications, and New Directions." *Journal of Archaeological Science* 26(7): 735–752.

Anthony, David W. 1990. "Migration in Archeology: The Baby and the Bathwater." *American Anthropologist* 92(4): 895–914.

Aoyama, Kazuo, and Elizabeth Graham. 2015. "Ancient Maya Warfare: Exploring the Significance of Lithic Variation in Maya Weaponry." *Lithics: Journal of the Lithic Studies Society* 36: 5–17.

Arango, Joaquín. 2000. "Explaining Migration: A Critical View." *International Social Science Journal* 52(165): 283–296.

Arkush, Elizabeth. 2017. "Coalescence and Defensive Communities: Insights from an Andean Hillfort Town." *Cambridge Archaeological Journal* 28(1): 1–22.

Arnauld, M. Charlotte. 1999. "Croissance et différenciation interne de groupes d'habitation dans deux sites mayas des basses terres (Mexique)." In *Habitat et société, Actes des XIXe Rencontres Internationales d'Archéologie et d'Histoire d'Antibes*, ed. F. Braemer, S. Cleuziou, and A. Coudart, 201–222. Antibes, France: Editions Association pour la promotion et la diffusion des connaissances archéologiques.

Arnauld, M. Charlotte. 2002. "Arquitectura política y residencial en La Joyanca, noroccidente del Petén (Guatemala)." *Mexicon* XXIV(3): 55–62.

Arnauld, M. Charlotte. 2011. Fase y generación en la arquitectura residencial de Río Bec (Campeche). Paper presented at the VII Mesa Redonda de Palenque, Los mayas y las concepciones del tiempo, Palenque, Mexico, November 28.

Arnauld, M. Charlotte. 2014. "El proyecto Maya de vida y sociedad." In *Nah, Otoch. Concepción, factura y atributos de la Morada Maya*, ed. Fabienne de Pierrebourg and Mario Humberto Ruz, 37–64. Izamal: Secretaría de Educación del Estado de Yucatán, Universidad Nacional Autónoma de México.

Arnauld, M. Charlotte, Chloé Andrieu, and Mélanie Forné. 2017a. "'In the Days of My Life.' Elite Activity and Interactions in the Maya Lowlands from Classic to Early Postclassic Times (The Long Ninth Century, AD 760–920)." *Journal de la Société des Américanistes*, special issue "Maya Times. Measures and Textures of Time among the Maya: The Said, the Written and the Lived," 41–96. http://journals.openedition.org/jsa/15362; DOI:10.4000/jsa.15362. July 14, 2018.

Arnauld, M. Charlotte, Véronique Breuil-Martinez, and Erick Ponciano A. 2004. *La Joyanca (La Libertad, Guatemala), antigua ciudad maya del noroeste del Petén.* México, DF, and Ciudad de Guatemala: Centre Français d'Études Mexicaines et Centraméricaines, Centro de investigaciones regionales de Mesoamérica, Asociación Tikal.

Arnauld, M. Charlotte, and Brigitte Faugère-Kalfon. 1998. "Evolución de la ocupación humana en el centro-norte de Michoacán (Proyecto Michoacán, CEMCA) y la emergencia del Estado tarasco." In *Génesis, culturas y espacios en Michoacán*, ed. Véronique Darras, 13–34. México, DF: Centre Français d'Études Mexicaines et Centraméricaines.

Arnauld, M. Charlotte, Marie France Fauvet-Berthelot, Dominique Michelet, and Pierre Becquelin. 1998. "Balamkú: historia del Grupo Sur (Campeche, México)." In *XI Simposio de Investigaciones Arqueológicas en Guatemala*, ed. J. P. Laporte and H. L. Escobedo, 135–150. Ciudad de Guatemala: Museo Nacional de Arqueología y Etnología de Guatemala, Asociación Tikal.

Arnauld, M. Charlotte, Eva Lemonnier, Mélanie Forné, Didier Galop, and Jean-Paul Métailié. 2013a. "The Rise and Fall of a Secondary Polity: La Joyanca (Guatemala)." In *Millenary Maya Societies: Past Crises and Resilience. Sociedades mayas milenarias: crisis del pasado y resiliencia*, ed. M. Charlotte Arnauld and Alain Breton, 148–168. http://www.mesoweb.com.

Arnauld, M. Charlotte, Eva Lemonnier, Mélanie Forné, Julien Sion, and Erick Ponciano Alvarado. 2017b. "Early to Late Classic Population Mobility in the Maya site of La Joyanca and Hinterlands, Northwestern Petén, Guatemala." *Journal of Anthropological Archaeology* 45: 15–37.

Arnauld, M. Charlotte, Linda R. Manzanilla, and Michael E. Smith, ed. 2012. *The Neighborhood as a Social and Spatial Unit in Mesoamerican Cities.* Tucson: University of Arizona Press.

Arnauld, M. Charlotte, and Dominique Michelet. 1991. "Les migrations postclassiques au Michoacan et au Guatemala: problèmes et Perspectives." In *Vingt études sur le Mexique et le Guatemala réunies à la mémoire de Nicole Percheron*, ed. A. Breton, J.-P. Berthe, and S. Lecoin, 67–92. Toulouse and México, DF: Collection Hespérides, Presses Universitaires du Mirail and Centre Français d'Études Mexicaines et Centraméricaines.

Arnauld, M. Charlotte, and Dominique Michelet. 2004. "Le développement des cités mayas." *Annales, Histoire, Sciences Sociales* 59(1): 78–103.

Arnauld, M. Charlotte, Dominique Michelet, Chloé Andrieu, Alfonso Lacadena, Eva Lemonnier, Boris Vannière, Philippe Nondédéo, and Julie Patrois. 2014. "Río Bec.

Des grandes maisons et des Récoltes." *Journal de la Société des Américanistes* 100(2): 107–144.

Arnauld, M. Charlotte, Dominique Michelet, and Philippe Nondédéo. 2013b. "Living Together in Río Bec Houses: Co-Residence, Rank and Alliance." *Ancient Mesoamerica* 24(2): 469–493.

Arnauld, M. Charlotte, Dominique Michelet, Boris Vannière, Philippe Nondédéo, and Eva Lemonnier. 2012. "Houses, Emulation and Cooperation among the Rio Bec Groups." In *The Neighborhood as a Social and Spatial Unit in Mesoamerican Cities*, ed. M. Charlotte Arnauld, Linda R. Manzanilla, and Michael E. Smith, 202–228. Tucson: University of Arizona Press.

Ashmore, Wendy. 1991. "Site-Planning Principles and Concepts of Directionality among the Ancient Maya." *Latin American Antiquity* 2(3): 199–226.

Atran, Scott. 1993. "Itza Maya Tropical Agro-Forestry." *Current Anthropology* 34(5): 633–700.

Aubry, B. Scott. 2009. "Population Structure and Interregional Interaction in Pre-Hispanic Mesoamerica: A Biodistance Study." PhD diss., Ohio State University, Columbus, OH.

Audet, Carolyn M. 2002. "Excavations of Structure 198, Baking Pot, Belize." In *The Belize Valley Archaeological Reconnaissance Project: A Report of the 2001 Field Season*, ed. C. S. Griffith and Jaime J. Awe, 91–110. Belmopan: Belize Department of Archaeology.

Audet, Carolyn M. 2006. "Political Organization in the Belize Valley: Excavations at Baking Pot, Cahal Pech and Xunantunich." Ph. diss., Vanderbilt University, Nashville, TN.

Audet, Carolyn M., and Jaime J. Awe. 2004. "What's Cooking at Baking Pot: A Report of the 2001 to 2003 Seasons." *Research Reports in Belizean Archaeology* 1: 49–59.

Audet, Carolyn M., and Jaime J. Awe. 2005. "The Political Organization of the Belize River Valley: Evidence from Baking Pot, Belize." *Reports in Belizean Archaeology* 2: 357–364.

Aveni, A. F. 2010. "Cosmology and Cultural Landscape: The Late Postclassic Maya of North Yucatán." In *Astronomers, Scribes, and Priests: Intellectual Interchange between the Northern Maya Lowlands and Highland Mexico in the Late Postclassic Period*, ed. G. Vail and C. Hernández, 115–132. Washington, DC: Dumbarton Oaks.

Awe, Jaime J. 2015. The Mexican Intrusion: Yucatec Influences in Terminal Classic Western Belize. Paper presented at the Belize Archaeology and Anthropology Symposium. San Ignacio, Belize, June 30.

Awe, Jaime J., Claire E. Ebert, Carolyn Freiwald, and Kirsten Green. 2017. "The Dead Do Tell Tales: Unravelling the Case of the Cahal Pech's Jane or John Doe." *Research Reports in Belize Archaeology* 14: 213–225.

Baden, William W. 1987. "A Dynamic Model of Stability and Change in Mississippian Agricultural Systems." PhD diss., University of Tennessee, Knoxville, TN.

Baden, William W. 2005. "Modelling Prehistoric Maize Agriculture as a Dissipative Process." In *Continuing the Revolution: Nonlinear Political and Economic Models for Archaeology*, ed. Christopher S. Beekman and William W. Baden, 95–122. London: Ashgate Press.

Baker, Brenda J., and Takeyuki Tsuda, eds. 2015. *Migration and Disruptions: Toward a Unifying Theory of Ancient and Contemporary Migrations*. Gainesville: University Press of Florida.

Balasse, Marie, Stanley H. Ambrose, Andrew B. Smith, and T. Douglas Price. 2002. "Seasonal Mobility Model for Prehistoric Herders in the South-Western Cape of South Africa Assessed by Isotopic Analysis of Sheep Tooth Enamel." *Journal of Archaeological Science* 29(9): 917–932.

Ball, J. W., and J. T. Taschek. 1989. "Teotihuacan's Fall and the Rise of the Itza: Realignments and Role Changes in the Terminal Classic Maya Lowlands." In *Mesoamerica after the Decline of Teotihuacan, AD 700–900*, ed. Richard A. Diehl and Janet C. Berlo, 187–200. Washington, DC: Dumbarton Oaks.

Barba, L., J. Blancas, L. R. Manzanilla, A. Ortiz, D. Barca, G. M. Crisci, D. Miriello, and A. Pecci. 2009. "Provenance of the Limestone used in Teotihuacan (Mexico): A Methodological Approach." *Archaeometry* 51: 525–545.

Barnard, Hans, and Willemina Wendrich, eds. 2008. *The Archaeology of Mobility: Old World and New World Nomadism*. Los Angeles: Cotsen Institute of Archaeology, University of California, Los Angeles.

Barrera Vásquez, A. 1991. *Diccionario Maya. Maya-Español; Español Maya*. México, DF: Editorial Porrúa.

Barrera Vásquez, A., and S. G. Morley. 1949. *The Maya Chronicles*. Carnegie Institution of Washington Contributions to American Anthropology and History, 10(48): 1–86. Washington, DC: Carnegie Institute.

Barrientos, Isaac, Julien Sion, Chloé Andrieu, Daniel Salazar, and Julio Cotom. 2015. "Evidencias de reingreso a los espacios sepulcrales en grupos habitacionales del Clásico Tardío-Terminal en Naachtun, Petén, Guatemala." In *XXVIII Simposio de Investigaciones Arqueológicas de Guatemala*, ed. B. Arroyo, L. Méndez Salinas, and L. Paiz, 465–479. Ciudad de Guatemala: Museo Nacional de Arqueología y Etnología. http://www .asociaciontikal.com/simposio-28-ano-2014-2/03. Consulted February 8, 2018.

Basalenque, Diego. 1886 [1673]. *Historia de la Provincia de San Nicolás de Tolentino de Michoacán, del Orden de N. P. S. Agustín*. México, DF: Tip. Barbedillo y Comp.

Baudez, Claude F. 1983. *Introducción a la Arqueología de Copán, Honduras*. Tegucigalpa, Distrito Central, Honduras: Secretaría de Estado en el Despacho de Cultura y Turismo.

Baudez, Claude F. 2008. Religion Aristocratique et Religion Populaire à Copán. Unpublished manuscript in possession of the chapter author.

Bayliss, Alex, Christopher Bronk Ramsey, Johannes van der Plicht, and Alasdair Whittle. 2007. "Bradshaw and Bayes: Towards a Timetable for the Neolithic." *Cambridge Archaeological Journal* 19(S1): 1–28.

Beck, Robin A., Jr., ed. 2007a. *The Durable House: House Society Models in Archaeology.* Center for Archaeological Investigations, Occasional Paper No. 35. Carbondale: Southern Illinois University.

Beck, Robin A., Jr. 2007b. "The Durable House: Material, Metaphor and Structure." In *The Durable House: House Society Models in Archaeology*, ed. Robin A. Beck, 3–24. Center for Archaeological Investigations, Occasional Paper No. 35. Carbondale: Southern Illinois University.

Becquelin, Pierre, and Dominique Michelet. 1994. "Demografía en la zona Puuc: El recurso del Método." *Latin American Antiquity* 5(4): 289–311.

Becquelin, Pierre, and Dominique Michelet. In press. *Xcalumkín, historia de un centro maya-puuc*, Volumen 1: *El asentamiento*. México, DF: Centre d'Etudes Mexicaines et Centraméricaines.

Becquelin, Pierre, Dominique Michelet, M. Charlotte Arnauld, Gregory Pereira, Fabienne de Pierrebourg, Eric Taladoire, Philippe Nondédéo, Marie-France Fauvet-Berthelot, Juan Reveles, and Antonio Benavides Castillo. 2005. "Balamku: la historia del sitio vista desde el Grupo Sur y su Periferia." *Investigadores de la Cultura Maya* 13(2): 317–332.

Beekman, Christopher S. 2015. "Causes and Consequences of Migration in Epiclassic Northern Mesoamerica." In *Migration and Disruptions: Toward a Unifying Theory of Ancient and Contemporary Migrations*, ed. Brenda J. Baker and Takeyuki Tsuda, 73–96. Gainesville: University Press of Florida.

Beekman, Christopher S. 2019. "The El Grillo Complex of Central Jalisco and the Reestablishment of Community and Identity." In *Migrations in Late Mesoamerica*, ed. Christopher S. Beekman, 109–147. Gainesville: University Press of Florida.

Beekman, Christopher S. n.d. "Regional and Corporate Identities in Formative Western Mexico." In *Rearranging Identities and Society in Formative Period Mesoamerica*, ed. Catharina Eleonora Santasilia, Guy David Hepp, and Richard Diehl. Manuscript in possession of the author.

Beekman, Christopher S., and William W. Baden. 2011. "El cultivo del maíz y su impacto regional: Agotamiento de los suelos en el Corredor de La Venta, Jalisco." In *Patrones de Asentamiento y Actividades de Subsistencia en el Occidente de México. Reconocimiento a la Doctora Helen P. Pollard*, ed. Eduardo Williams and Phil C. Weigand, 351–382. Zamora, México: Colegio de Michoacán.

Beekman, Christopher S., and Alexander F. Christensen. 2003. "Controlling for Doubt and Uncertainty through Multiple Lines of Evidence: A New Look at the Mesoamerican Nahua Migrations." *Journal of Archaeological Method and Theory* 10(2): 111–164.

Beekman, Christopher S., and Alexander F. Christensen. 2011. "Power, Agency, and Identity: Migration and Aftermath in the Mezquital Area of North-Central Mexico." In *Rethinking Anthropological Perspectives on Migration*, ed. Graciela S. Cabana and Jeffery J. Clark, 147–171. Gainesville: University Press of Florida.

Bell, Ellen E., and Marcello A. Canuto. 2008. "The Ties that Bind: Administrative Strategies in the El Paraíso Valley, Department of Copán, Honduras." *Mexicon* 30: 10–20.

Bellwood, Peter. 2001. "Early Agriculturalist Population Diasporas? Farming, Languages, and Genes." *Annual Review of Anthropology* 30: 181–207.

Ben-Sira, Z. 1997. *Immigration, Stress, and Readjustment*. Westport, CT: Praeger Publishers.

Bentley, R. Alexander. 2006. "Strontium Isotopes from the Earth to the Archaeological Skeleton: A Review." *Journal of Archaeological Method and Theory* 13(3): 135–187.

Bentley, R. Alexander, R. Krause, T. Douglas Price, and B. Kaufmann. 2003. "Human Mobility at the Early Neolithic Settlement of Vaihingen, Germany: Evidence from Strontium Isotope Analysis." *Archaeometry* 45(3): 471–486.

Beramendi-Orosco, Laura E., Galia González-Hernández, Jaime Urrutia-Fucugauchi, Linda R. Manzanilla, Ana M. Soler-Arechalde, Avto Goguitchaishvili, and Nick Jarboe. 2008. "High-Resolution Chronology for the Mesoamerican Urban Center of Teotihuacan Derived from Bayesian Statistics of Radiocarbon and Archaeological Data." *Quaternary Research* 71(2): 99–107.

Berlin, H., and S. Rendon, eds. 1947. *La Historia Tolteca-Chichimeca: Anales de Quauhtinchan*. México, DF: Antigua Librería Robredo.

Bernardini, Wesley. 2005. *Hopi Oral Tradition and the Archaeology of Identity*. Tucson: University of Arizona Press.

Bernardini, Wesley R. 2011. "Migration in Fluid Social Landscapes." In *Rethinking Anthropological Perspectives on Migration*, ed. Graciela S. Cabana and Jeffery J. Clark, 31–44. Gainesville: University Press of Florida.

Bey, George J., III, Craig Hanson, and William Ringle. 1997. "Classic to Postclassic at Ek Balam, Yucatan: Architectural and Ceramic Evidence for Defining the Transition." *Latin American Antiquity* 8: 237–254.

Bey George J., III, and W. M. Ringle. 2011. "From the Bottom Up: The Timing and Nature of the Tula–Chichén Itzá Exchange." In *Twin Tollans: Chichén Itzá, Tula, and the Epiclassic to Early Postclassic Mesoamerican World*, ed. J. K. Kowalski and C. Kristan-Graham, 299–234. Washington, DC: Dumbarton Oaks.

Bill, Cassandra R. 1997. "Patterns of Variation and Change in Dynastic Period Ceramics at Copan, Honduras." PhD diss., Tulane University, New Orleans, LA.

Bill, Cassandra R. 2014. "Shifting Fortunes and Affiliations on the Edge of Ruin: A Ceramic Perspective on the Classic Maya Collapse and Its Aftermath at Copan." In *The Maya and Their Central American Neighbors: Settlement Patterns, Architecture, Hieroglyphic Texts, and Ceramics*, ed. G. E. Braswell, 83–111. New York: Routledge.

Binford, Lewis R. 1980. "Willow Smoke and Dogs' Tails: Hunter-Gatherer Settlement Systems and Archaeological Site Formation." *American Antiquity* 45(1): 4–20.

Binford, Lewis R. 1982. "The Archaeology of Place." *Journal of Anthropological Archaeology* 1: 5–31.

Birch, Jennifer, ed. 2013. *From Prehistoric Villages to Cities: Settlement Aggregation and Community Transformation*. New York: Routledge.

Black, Richard, Stephen R. G. Bennett, Sandy M. Thomas, and John R. Beddington. 2011. "Migration as Adaptation." *Nature* 478: 447–449.

Blanton, Richard E. 1978. *Monte Alban: Settlement Patterns at the Ancient Zapotec Capital*. New York: Academic Press.

Blanton, Richard E., Laura Finsten, Stephen A. Kowalewski, and Gary Feinman. 1996. "Migration and Population Change in the Prehispanic Valley of Oaxaca, Mexico." In *Arqueología Mesoamericana. Homenaje a William T. Sanders*, Volumen 2, ed. Guadalupe Mastache, Jeffrey P. Parsons, Robert S. Santley, and Mari Carmen Serra Puche, 11–36. México, DF: Instituto Nacional de Antropología e Historia.

Bodamer, Benton B. 2002. "Toad Trip: Shamanic Transformation, Rain Divination, and the Role of Toads in Precolumbian and Modern Mesoamerican Ritual." Unpublished BA Thesis, Department of Anthropology, Harvard University, Cambridge, MA.

Boldsen, J., G. Milner, L. Konigsberg and J. Wood. 2002. "Transition Analysis: A New Method for Estimating Age from Skeletons." In *Paleodemography: Age Distributions from Skeletal Samples*, ed. R. Hoppa and J. Vaupel, 73–106. Cambridge, UK: Cambridge University Press.

Boone, Elizabeth Hill. 1991. "Migration Histories as Ritual Performances." In *To Change Place: Aztec Ceremonial Landscapes*, ed. Davíd Carrasco, 121–151. Boulder: University Press of Colorado.

Boot, E. 1995. "'Kan Ek' at Chich'en Itsa. A Quest into a Possible Itsa Heartland in the Central Peten, Guatemala." *Yumtzilob* 7(4): 333–339.

Boot, E. 1997. "'No Place Like Home': Maya Exodus, Itsa Maya Migrations between ca. AD 650 and AD 1450." *Veertig Jaren Onderweg*, ed. Henri J. M. Claessen and H. F. Vermeulen, 165–187. Leiden, Netherlands: DSWO Press, Rijksuniversiteit Leiden.

Boot, E. 2005. *Continuity and Change in Text and Image at Chichén Itzá, Yucatán, Mexico*. Leiden, Netherlands: CNWS Publications.

Brambila Paz, Rosa, and Ana María Crespo. 2005. "Desplazamientos de poblaciones y creación de territorios en el Bajío." In *Reacomodos demográficos del Clásico al Posclásico en el centro de México*, ed. Linda Manzanilla, 155–174. México, DF: Instituto de Investigaciones Antropológicas, Universidad Universidad Nacional Autónoma de México.

Braniff Cornejo, Beatriz. 2005. "Los chichimecas a la caída de Teotihuacan y durante la conformación de la Tula de Hidalgo." In *Reacomodos demográficos del Clásico al Posclásico en el centro de México*, ed. Linda Manzanilla, 45–56. México, DF: Instituto de Investigaciones Antropológicas, Universidad Nacional Autónoma de México.

Braswell, Geoffrey E. 1992. "Obsidian-Hydration Dating, the Coner Phase, and Revisionist Chronology at Copan, Honduras." *Latin American Antiquity* 3(2): 130–147.

Braswell, Geoffrey E., John E. Clark, Kazuo Aoyama, Heather I. McKillop, and Michael D. Glascock. 2000. "Determining the Geological Provenance of Obsidian Artifacts from the Maya Region: A Test of the Efficacy of Visual Sourcing." *Latin American Antiquity* 11(3): 269–282.

Braswell, Geoffrey E., and Michael D. Glascock. 2003. "The Emergence of Market Economies in the Ancient Maya Worlds: Obsidian Exchange for Terminal Classic

Yucatan, Mexico." In *Geochemical Evidence for Long Distance Exchange*, ed. Michael D. Glascock, 33–52. Westport, CT: Bergin and Garvey.

Braswell, Geoffrey E., Joel D. Gunn, Maria del Rosario Dominguez, William L. Folan, Laraine A. Fletcher, Abel Morales Lopez, and Michael D. Glascock. 2004. "Defining the Terminal Classic at Calakmul, Campeche." In *The Terminal Classic in the Maya Lowlands: Collapse, Transition, and Transformation*, ed. Arthur A. Demarest, Prudence M. Rice, and Don. S. Rice, 162–194. Boulder: University Press of Colorado.

Brenner, Mark, Barbara W. Leyden, Jason H. Curtis, Bruce H. Dahlin, and Rosario Medina Gonzalez. 2000. "Un registro do 8,000 años del paleoclima del noroeste de Yucatán." *Revista de la Univeridad Autónoma de Yucatán* 15: 52–65.

Breton, Alain. 2007. *Rabinal Achi. A Fifteenth-Century Maya Dynastic Drama*, trans. Teresa Lavender Fagan and Robert Schneider. Boulder: University Press of Colorado.

Brewer, Jeffrey L., Christopher Carr, Nicholas P. Dunning, Debra Walker, Armando Anaya Hernández, Megan Peuramaki-Brown, and Kathryn Reese-Taylor. 2017. "Employing Airborne Lidar and Archaeological Testing to Determine the Role of Small Depressions in Water Management at the Ancient Maya site of Yaxnohcah, Campeche, Mexico." *Journal of Archaeological Science Reports* 13: 291–302.

Bronitsky, Gordon. 1986. "The Use of Materials Science Techniques in the Study of Pottery Construction and Use." In *Advances in Archaeological Method and Theory*, Volume 9, ed. Michael Brian Schiffer, 209–276. Orlando, FL: Academic Press.

Brown, C. T. 1999. "Mayapán Society and Ancient Maya Social Organization." PhD diss., Tulane University, New Orleans, LA.

Brown, Denise F. 2002. "La organización social y espacial de ciudades mayas; aportaciones de la antropología social." In *Tercer Congreso Internacional de Mayistas. Memoria*, Volumen 1, 280–290. México, DF: Universidad Nacional Autónoma de México.

Brown, Linda A. 2000. "From Discard to Divination: Demarcating the Sacred through the Collection and Curation of Discarded Objects." *Latin American Antiquity* 11(4): 319–333.

Brumfiel, Elizabeth M., and John M. Fox, eds. 1994. *Factional Competition and Political Development in the New World*. Cambridge, UK: Cambridge University Press.

Buikstra, Jane E., James H. Burton, Paul D. Fullagar, T. Douglas Price, Vera Tiesler, and Lori E. Wright. 2008. "Strontium Isotopes and the Study of Human Mobility in Ancient Mesoamerica." *Latin American Antiquity* 19(2): 167–180.

Buikstra, Jane E., T. Douglas Price, Lori E. Wright, and James A. Burton. 2004. "Tombs from the Copán Acropolis: A Life History Approach." In *Understanding Early Classic Copán*, ed. E. E. Bell, M. A. Canuto, and R. J. Sharer, 191–212. Philadelphia: University of Pennsylvania Museum of Archaeology and Anthropology.

Buikstra, J., and D. Ubelaker, eds. 1994. *Standards for Data Collection from Human Skeletal Remains*. Proceedings of a Seminar at the Field Museum of Natural History Organized by Jonathan Haas. Arkansas Archaeological Survey Research Series 44. Fayetteville: Arkansas Archaeological Survey.

Bullock, M. 2013. "Pathological Skeletal Lesions and Selective Mortality in the Post-classic Population of Cholula." In *Estudios de Antropología Biológica*, Vol. XVI, ed. L. Escorcia, M. Herrera, and B. Robles, 67–94. México, DF: Escuela Nacional de Antropología e Historia and Asociación Mexicana de Antropología Biológica, Universidad Nacional Autónoma de México.

Bullock, M., L. Marquez, P. Hernandez, and F. Ruiz. 2013. "The Paleodemographic Age-at-Death Distributions of Two Mexican Skeletal Collections: A Comparison of Transition Analysis and Traditional Aging Methods." *American Journal of Physical Anthropology* 152(1): 67–78.

Bullock, M., T. D. Price, J. Burton, K. Hirth, and J. C. Jimenez. In prep. Immigration to the Postclassic Urban Center of Cholula: A Strontium and Oxygen Isotope Study.

Bullock Kreger, M. 2010. "Urban Population Dynamics in a Preindustrial New World City: Morbidity, Mortality, and Immigration in Postclassic Cholula." PhD diss., Pennsylvania State University, State College, PA.

Burmeister, Stefan. 2000. "Archaeology and Migration: Approaches to an Archaeological Proof of Migration." *Current Anthropology* 41: 539–567.

Buzon, Michael R., Antonio Simonetti, and Robert A. Creaser. 2007. "Migration in the Nile Valley during the New Kingdom Period: A Preliminary Strontium Isotope Study." *Journal of Archaeological Science* 34: 1391–1401.

Cabana, Graciela S. 2011. "The Problematic Relationship between Migration and Culture Change." In *Rethinking Anthropological Perspectives on Migration*, ed. Graciela S. Cabana and Jeffery J. Clark, 16–28. Gainesville: University Press of Florida.

Cabana, Graciela S., and Jeffery J. Clark, eds. 2011a. *Rethinking Anthropological Perspectives on Migration*. Gainesville: University Press of Florida.

Cabana, Graciela S., and Jeffery J. Clark. 2011b. "Introduction: Migration in Anthropology: Where We Stand." In *Rethinking Anthropological Perspectives on Migration*, ed. Graciela S. Cabana and Jeffery J. Clark, 3–15. Gainesville: University Press of Florida.

Cadwallader, Martin T. 1992. *Migration and Residential Mobility: Macro and Micro Approaches*. Madison: University of Wisconsin Press.

Calnek, E. 1976. "The Internal Structure of Tenochtitlan." In *The Valley of Mexico: Studies in Pre-Hispanic Ecology and Society*, ed. Eric Wolf, 287–302. Albuquerque: University of New Mexico Press.

Cameron, Catherine M. 1995. "Migration and the Movement of Southwestern Peoples." *Journal of Anthropological Archaeology* 14: 104–124.

Cameron, Catherine M. 2011. "Captives and Culture Change: Implications for Archaeologists." *Current Anthropology* 52(2): 169–209.

Cameron, Catherine M. 2013. "How People Moved Among Ancient Societies: Broadening the View." *American Anthropologist* 115(2): 218–231.

Campbell, Benjamin C., and Michael H. Crawford. 2012. "Perspective on Human Migration: Introduction." In *Causes and Consequences of Human Migration*, ed. Michael H.

Crawford and Benjamin C. Campbell, 1–8. Cambridge, UK: Cambridge University Press.

Campbell, Bruce M. S., and Mark Overton. 1991. *Land, Labour and Livestock: Historical Studies in European Agricultural Productivity*. Manchester, UK: Manchester University Press.

Canuto, Marcello A. 2004. "The Rural Settlement of Copán: Changes through the Early Classic." In *Understanding Early Classic Copán*, ed. E. E. Bell, M. A. Canuto, and R. J. Sharer, 29–50. Philadelphia: University of Pennsylvania Museum of Archaeology and Anthropology.

Canuto, Marcello A., and Ellen E. Bell. 2013. "Archaeological Investigations in the El Paraíso Valley: The Role of Secondary Centers in the Multiethnic Landscape of Classic Period Copan." *Ancient Mesoamerica* 24(1): 1–24.

Carmean, Kelli. 1991. "Architectural Labor Investment and Social Stratification at Sayil, Yucatan, Mexico." *Latin American Antiquity* 2: 151–165.

Carmean, Kelli, Nicholas P. Dunning, and Jeff K. Kowalski. 2004. "High Times in the Hill Country: A Perspective from the Terminal Classic Puuc Region." In *The Terminal Classic in the Maya Lowlands: Collapse, Transition, and Transformation*, ed. A. A. Demarest, P. M. Rice, and D. S. Rice, 424–449. Boulder: University Press of Colorado.

Carmean, Kelli, and Jeremy Sabloff. 1996. "Political Decentralization in the Puuc Region, Yucatan, Mexico." *Journal of Anthropological Research* 52: 317–330.

Carot, Patricia. 2001. *Le site de Loma Alta, Lac de Zacapu, Michoacan, Mexique*. Monographs in American Archaeology 9, British Archaeological Reports International Series 920. Oxford, UK: Archaeopress.

Carozza, Jean-Michel, Didier Galop, and Jean-Paul Métailié. 2002. "Estudios palinológico y geomorfológico en el sitio La Joyanca y su cercanía." In *Proyecto Petén Noroccidente: La Joyanca, Informe N°4, cuarta temporada de campo, 2002*, ed. Véronique Breuil-Martinez, E. Salvador Lopez, and Tristan Saint-Dizier, 230–244. Ciudad de Guatemala: Centre Français d'Études Mexicaines et Centraméricaines.

Carozza, J. M., D. Galop, J.-P. Métailié, B. Vanniere, G. Bossuet, F. Monna, J. A. Lopez-Saez, M. C. Arnauld, V. Breuil, M. Forné, and E. Lemonnier. 2007. "Landuse and Soil Degradation in the Southern Maya Lowlands from Pre-Classic to Postclassic Times: The Case of La Joyanca (Petén, Guatemala)." *Geodynamica Acta* 20(4): 195–207.

Carrasco, Pedro. 1969. "Nuevos datos sobre los Nonoalca de Habla Mexicana en el Reino Tarasco." *Estudios de Cultura Nahuatl* 8: 215–221.

Carrasco, Pedro. 1971. "Social Organization of Ancient Mexico." In *Archaeology of North Mesoamerica*, Part 1, *Handbook of Middle American Indians*, Vol. 10, ed. G. Ekholm and I. Bernal, 349–375. Austin: University of Texas Press.

Carrelli, Christine. 2004. "Measures of Power: The Energetics of Royal Construction at Early Classic Copán." In *Understanding Early Classic Copan*, ed. E. E. Bell, M. A. Canuto, and R. J. Sharer, 113–127. Philadelphia: University of Pennsylvania Museum.

Castro, L. J., and A. Rogers, 1983. "Patterns of Family Migration: Two Methodological Approaches." *Environment and Planning A* 15(2): 237–254.

Castro, Luis J., and Andrei Rogers. 1984. "What the Age Composition of Migrants Can Tell Us." Reprinted from *Population Bulletin of the United Nations* 15 (1983): 63–79. *Research Reports. International Institute for Applied Systems Analysis* RR-84-3. Vienna, Austria: Novographic.

Ceballos, Teresa. 2003. "La cronología cerámica del puerto maya de Xcambó, Costa Norte de Yucatán: complejo Xtambú." Licenciatura Thesis, Facultad de Ciencias Antropológicas, Universidad Autónoma de Yucatán, Mérida, Mexico.

Cecil, Leslie G., and Timothy W. Pugh. 2018. "Souls of the Ancestors: Postclassic Maya Incensarios, Architecture, and Mana." *Ancient Mesoamerica* 29: 157–170.

Champion, Tony, and Graeme Hugo. 2004. "Introduction: Moving Beyond the Urban-Rural Dichotomy." In *New Forms of Urbanization: Beyond the Urban-Rural Dichotomy*, ed. Tony Champion and Graeme Hugo, 3–24. Aldershot, UK: Ashgate.

Chantraine, Pierre. 2009. *Dictionnaire étymologique de la langue grecque*, original edition and supplement. Paris: Librairie Klincksieck.

Charlton, Thomas H., and Deborah L. Nichols. 1997. "Diachronic Studies of City-States: Permutations on a Theme—Central Mexico from 1700 BC to AD 1600." In *The Archaeology of City-States: Cross Cultural Approaches*, ed. Deborah L. Nichols and Thomas H. Charlton, 169–208. Washington, DC: Smithsonian Institution Press.

Chase, Arlen F. 1983. "A Contextual Consideration of the Tayasal-Paxcaman Zone, El Peten, Guatemala." PhD diss., University of Pennsylvania, Philadelphia, PA.

Chase Arlen F., and Diane Z. Chase. 2016. "The Ancient Maya City: Anthropogenic Landscapes, Settlement Archaeology, and Caracol, Belize." *Research Reports in Belizean Archaeology* 13(1): 3–14.

Chase, Diane Z. 1982. "Spatial and Temporal Variability in Postclassic Northern Belize." PhD diss., University of Pennsylvania, Philadelphia, PA.

Chase, Diane Z. 1997. "Southern Lowland Maya Archaeology and Human Skeletal Remains: Interpretations from Caracol (Belize), Santa Rita Corozal (Belize), and Tayasal (Guatemala)." In *Bones of the Maya: Studies of Ancient Skeletons*, ed. Stephen L. Whittington and David M. Reed, 15–27. Washington, DC: Smithsonian Institution Press.

Chase, Diane Z., and Arlen F. Chase 1982. "Yucatec Influence in Terminal Classic Northern Belize." *American Antiquity* 47(3): 596–614.

Chase, Diane Z., and Arlen F. Chase. 1988. *A Postclassic Perspective: Excavations at the Maya Site of Santa Rita Corozal, Belize*. Monograph 4. San Francisco: Pre-Columbian Art Research Institute.

Chase, Diane Z., Arlen F. Chase, and William A. Haviland. 1990. "The Classic Maya City: Reconsidering the 'Mesoamerican Urban Tradition.'" *American Anthropologist* 92(2): 499–506.

Chinchilla Mazariegos, Oswaldo, Vera Tiesler, Oswaldo Gomez, and T. Douglas Price. 2015. "Myth, Ritual and Human Sacrifice in Early Classic Mesoamerica: Interpreting a Cremated Double Burial from Tikal, Guatemala." *Cambridge Archaeological Journal* 25(1): 187–210.

Chouquer, Gérard. 2000. *L'étude des paysages: Essais sur leurs formes et leur histoire.* Paris: Errance.

Clark, Jeffery J. 2001. *Tracking Prehistoric Migrations: Pueblo Settlers among the Tonto Basin Hohokam.* Anthropological Papers No. 65. Tucson: University of Arizona Press.

Clark, P., and D. Souden. 1988. "Introduction." In *Migration and Society in Early Modern England*, ed. P. Clark and D. Souden, 11–48. Totowa, NJ: Barnes and Noble.

Clayton, Sarah C. 2012. Investigaciones de campo en las cercanías de Cerro Portezuelo. Report submitted to the Consejo de Arqueología, México, DF.

Clayton, Sarah C. 2013. "Measuring the Long Arm of the State: Teotihuacan's Relations in the Basin of Mexico." *Ancient Mesoamerica* 24(1): 87–105.

Clayton, Sarah C. 2016. "After Teotihuacan: A View of Collapse and Reorganization from the Southern Basin of Mexico." *American Anthropologist* 118(1): 104–120.

Clayton, Sarah C. 2020. "The Collapse of Teotihuacan and the Regeneration of Epiclassic Societies: A Bayesian Approach." *Journal of Anthropological Archaeology* 59: article number 101203.

Clayton, Sarah C., and Ricardo Cruz Jiménez. 2017. El colapso de Teotihuacan y el crecimiento de ciudades epiclásicas: investigaciones recientes en Chicoloapan Viejo. Paper presented at the Sixth Mesa Redonda Teotihuacan, México, DF.

Cobean, Robert H. 1990. *La Cerámica de Tula, Hidalgo.* Latin American Archaeology Publications. Pittsburgh, PA: University of Pittsburgh.

Cobos Palma, Rafael. 2011. "Multepal or Centralized Kingship? New Evidence on Governmental Organization at Chichén Itzá." In *Twin Tollans: Chichén Itzá, Tula, and the Epiclassic to Early Postclassic Mesoamerican World*, rev. ed., ed. Jeff Karl Kowalski and Cynthia Kristan-Graham, 249–271. Washington, DC: Dumbarton Oaks Research Library and Collection, Trustees for Harvard University.

Coe, William R. 1990. *Excavations in the Great Plaza, North Terrace and North Acropolis of Tikal.* Tikal Report No. 14, Vol. III. Philadelphia: The University Museum, University of Pennsylvania.

Cohen, Abner. 1969. *Customs and Politics in Urban Africa: A Study of Hausa Migrants in Yoruba Towns.* Berkeley: University of California Press.

Cohen, Abner. 1971. "Cultural Strategies in the Organization of Trading Diasporas." In *The Development of Indigenous Trade and Markets in West Africa*, ed. Claude Meillassoux, 266–281. Oxford, UK: Oxford University Press.

Cohen, Mark Nathan. 2008. "Implications of the NDT for World Wide Health and Mortality in Prehistory." In *The Neolithic Demographic Transition and Its Consequences*, ed. Jean-Pierre Bocquet-Appel and Ofer Bar-Yosef, 481–500. New York: Springer.

Cohen, Robin. 2008. *Global Diasporas: An Introduction.* 2nd edition. Oxon: Routledge.

Cohen, S., D. Tyrrell, and A. Smith. 1991. "Psychological Stress and Susceptibility to the Common Cold." *New England Journal of Medicine* 325: 606–612.

Cohen, S., and G. Williamson. 1991. "Stress and Infectious Disease in Humans." *Psychological Bulletin* 109: 5–24.

Cook, Sherburne F., and Woodrow W. Borah. 1974. *Essays in Population History: Mexico and the Caribbean*, Vol. 2. Berkeley: University of California Press.

Cooper, Lisa. 2006. "The Demise and Regeneration of Bronze Age Urban Centers in the Euphrates Valley of Syria." In *After Collapse: The Regeneration of Complex Societies*, ed. Glenn M. Schwartz and John J. Nichols, 18–37. Tucson: University of Arizona Press.

Copeland, Sandi R., Matt Sponheimer, Darryl J. de Ruiter, Julia A. Lee-Thorp, Daryl Codron, Petrus J. le Roux, Vaughan Grimes, and Michael P. Richards. 2011. "Strontium Isotope Evidence for Landscape Use by Early Hominins." *Nature* 474(7349): 76–78.

Cortés, H. 1985. *Cartas de Relación*, ed. Marío Hernández Sánchez-Barba. Madrid: Dastin, S. L.

Courlander, Harold. 1971. *The Fourth World of the Hopis*. Albuquerque: University of New Mexico Press.

Cowgill, George L. 1975. "On Causes and Consequences of Ancient and Modern Population Changes." *American Anthropologist* 77(3): 505–525.

Cowgill, George L. 1988. "Onward and Upward with Collapse." In *The Collapse of Ancient States and Civilizations*, ed. Norman Yoffee and George L. Cowgill, 244–276. Tucson: University of Arizona Press.

Cowgill, George L. 2000. "The Central Mexican Highlands from the Rise of Teotihuacan to the Decline of Tula." In *The Cambridge History of the Native Peoples of the Americas*, Volume II: *Mesoamerica, Part I*, ed. R. E. W. Adams and M. J. Macleod, 250–317. Cambridge, UK: Cambridge University Press.

Cowgill, George L. 2003. "Teotihuacan: Cosmic Glories, Mundane Needs." In *The Social Construction of Ancient Cities*, ed. M. L. Smith, 37–55. Washington, DC: Smithsonian Institution.

Cowgill George L. 2004. "Origins and Development of Urbanism: Archaeological Perspectives." *Annual Review of Anthropology* 33: 525–549.

Cowgill, George L. 2013. "Possible Migrations and Shifting Identities in the Central Mexican Epiclassic." *Ancient Mesoamerica* 24(1): 131–149.

Cowgill, George L. 2015a. *Ancient Teotihuacan: Early Urbanism in Central Mexico*. New York: Cambridge University Press.

Cowgill, George L. 2015b. "We Need Better Chronologies: Progress in Getting Them." *Latin American Antiquity* 26(1): 26–29.

Crapo, Richley, and Bonnie Glass-Coffin. 2005. *Anónimo Mexicano*. Logan: Utah State University Press.

Crider, Destiny L. 2013. "Shifting Alliances: Epiclassic and Early Postclassic Interactions at Cerro Portezuelo." *Ancient Mesoamerica* 24: 107–130.

Crider, Destiny L., Deborah L. Nichols, Hector Neff, and Michael D. Glascock. 2007. "In the Aftermath of Teotihuacan: Epiclassic Pottery Production and Distribution in the Teotihuacan Valley, Mexico." *Latin American Antiquity* 18(2): 123–143.

Croissier, Michelle M. 2007. "The Zapotec Presence at Teotihuacan, Mexico: Political Ethnicity and Domestic Identity." PhD diss., University of Illinois at Urbana-Champaign.

Cucina, Andrea, ed. 2015a. *Archaeology and Bioarchaeology of Population Movement among the Prehispanic Maya*. New York: Springer.

Cucina, Andrea. 2015b. "Population Dynamics during the Classic and Postclassic Period Maya in the Northern Maya Lowlands: The Analysis of Dental Morphological Traits." In *Archaeology and Bioarchaeology of Population Movement among the Prehispanic Maya*, ed. Andrea Cucina, 71–84. New York: Springer.

Cucina, Andrea, and Allan Ortega Muñoz. 2014. "Afinidades biológicas de la población de Oxtankah en el ámbito regional del sur de Quintana Roo, periodo Clásico." *Estudios de Cultura Maya* 44: 59–84.

Cucina, Andrea, Allan Ortega-Muñoz, and Sandra Elizalde-Rodarte. 2018. "Biological Affinities and Mortuary Archaeology in Coastal Northern Populations of Yucatan at the End of the Postclassic Period: Demic Considerations." In *Bioarchaeology of Pre-European Mesoamerica: An Interdisciplinary Approach*, ed. Cathy Willermet and Andrea Cucina A., 99–132. Gainesville: University Press of Florida.

Cucina, Andrea, T. Douglas Price, Evelia Magaña, and Thelma Sierra. 2015. "Crossing the Peninsula: The Role of Noh Bec, Yucatán, in Ancient Maya Classic Period Population Dynamics from the Analysis of Dental Morphology and Sr Isotopes." *American Journal of Human Biology* 27(6): 767–778.

Cucina, Andrea, Vera Tiesler, Thelma Sierra Sosa, and Hector Neff. 2011. "Trace-Element Evidence for Foreigners at a Maya Port in Northern Yucatan." *Journal of Archaeological Science* 38(8): 1878–1885.

Culbert, T. Patrick. 1977. "Maya Development and Collapse: An Economic Perspective." In *Social Process in Maya Prehistory: Studies in Honour of Sir Eric Thompson*, ed. N. Hammond, 510–530. London: Academic Press.

Culbert, T. Patrick, and Don Stephen Rice, eds. 1990. *Precolumbian Population History in the Maya Lowlands*. Albuquerque: University of New Mexico Press.

Curtin, Philip D. 1984. *Cross-Cultural Trade in World History*. Cambridge, UK: Cambridge University Press.

Dahlin, Bruce H., and Traci Ardren. 2002. "Modes of Exchange and Regional Patterns: Chunchucmil, Yucatán." In *Ancient Maya Political Economies*, ed. Marilyn A. Masson and David Freidel, 249–284. Walnut Creek, CA: Altamira Press.

Daneels, Annick, and Gerardo Gutiérrez Mendoza, eds. 2012. *El poder compartido: Ensayos sobre la arqueología de organizaciones políticas segmentarias y oligárquicas*. México, DF: Publicaciones de la Casa Chata, Centro de Investigaciones y Estudios Superiores en Antropología Social.

Darling, J. Andrew, John C. Ravesloot, and Michael R. Waters. 2004. "Village Drift and Riverine Settlement: Modeling Akimel O'odham Land Use." *American Anthropologist* 106(2): 282–295.

Darras, Véronique. 2006. "Las Relaciones entre Chupícuaro y el Centro de México durante el Preclásico Reciente. Una Crítica de las Interpretaciones Arqueológicas." *Journal de la Société de Americanistes* 92: 69–110.

Darras, Véronique. 2009. "Peasant Artisans: Household Prismatic Blade Production in the Zacapu Region, Michoacan (Milpillas phase 1200–1450 AD)." *Archaeological Papers of the American Anthropological Association* 19(1): 92–114.

Darras, Véronique. 2010. *Paysans artisans de l'ouest mésoaméricain. Approche tech-noéconomique et sociale: des Tarasques aux Chupicuaro*. 2 vols. Habilitation à diriger des recherches, Université Paris 1 Panthéon-Sorbonne, Paris.

Darras, Véronique. 2012. "Development of Pressure Blade Knapping in North-Central and West Mexico." In *The Emergence of Pressure Knapping: From Origin to Modern Experimentation*, ed. P. Desrosiers, 417–462. New York: Springer.

Darras, Véronique, and Brigitte Faugère. 2005. "Cronología de la cultura Chupícuaro: estudio del sitio La Tronera, Puruaguita, Guanajuato." In *El antiguo occidente de México: Nuevas perspectivas sobre el pasado prehispánico*, ed. Eduardo Williams, Phil C. Weigand, Lorenza López Mestas, and David C. Grove, 255–282. Zamora, México: Colegio de Michoacán.

das Neves, Virginia A. 2012. "Childhood Origin and Diet of the Ancient Maya: A Pilot Study of Strontium, Oxygen and Carbon Isotope Analyses on Human Tooth Enamel from the Northwestern Belize Site of Nojol Nah, Located in Blue Creek, Orange Walk District." Master's Thesis, Australia National University, Canberra.

David, Nicholas. 1972. "On the Life Span of Pottery, Type Frequencies, and Archaeological Inference." *American Antiquity* 37(1): 141–142.

Davies, Diane. 2012. "Past Identities, Present Legitimization: The Re-Use of a Late Preclassic Residential Group at the Maya Site of San Bartolo, Guatemala." PhD diss., Tulane University, New Orleans, LA.

Davis, Kingsley. 1973. *Cities and Mortality: International Population and Urban Research*. Institute of International Studies, reprint 433. Berkeley: University of California.

Davis, Wade, and Andrew T. Weil. 1992. "Identity of a New World Psychoactive Toad." *Ancient Mesoamerica* 3: 51–59.

Demarest, Arthur A. 1996. "Closing Comment." *Current Anthropology* 37(5): 821–830.

Demarest, Arthur A. 2004. "After the Maelstrom: Collapse of the Classic Maya Kingdoms and the Terminal Classic in Western Petén." In *The Terminal Classic in the Maya Lowlands: Collapse, Transition, and Transformation*, ed. Arthur A. Demarest, Prudence M. Rice, and Don S. Rice, 102–124. Boulder: University Press of Colorado.

Demarest, Arthur A., Matt O'Mansky, Claudia Wolley, Dirk Van Tuerenhout, Takeshi Inomata, Joel Palka, and Héctor L. Escobedo. 1997. "Classic Maya Defensive Systems and Warfare in the Petexbatun Region: Archaeological Evidence and Interpretations." *Ancient Mesoamerica* 8(2): 229–253.

Demarest, Arthur A., Prudence M. Rice, and Don S. Rice, eds. 2004. *The Terminal Classic in the Maya Lowlands: Collapse, Transition and Transformation.* Boulder: University Press of Colorado.

De Montmollin, Olivier. 1989. "Land Tenure and Politics in the Late/Terminal Classic Rosario Valley, Chiapas, Mexico." *Journal of Anthropological Research* 45: 293–314.

Díaz Oyarzábal, Clara Luz. 1980. *Un sitio clásico del área de Tula, Hidalgo.* Serie Arqueología. México, DF: Instituto Nacional de Antropología e Historia.

Dietler, M. 2007. "Culinary Encounters: Food, Identity, and Colonialism." In *The Archaeology of Food and Identity,* ed. K. C. Twiss, 218–242. Center for Archaeological Investigations. Carbondale: Southern Illinois University.

Dobkin de Rios, Marlene. 1974. "The Influence of Psychotropic Flora and Fauna on Maya Religion." *Current Anthropology* 15(2): 147–164.

Domínguez Carrasco, María del Rosario, and William J. Folan Higgens. 2015. "Ceramic Traditions in the Calakmul Region: An Indicator of the Movement of Ideas or Populations?" In *Archaeology and Bioarchaeology of Population Movement among the Prehispanic Maya,* ed. Andreas Cucina, 13–24. New York: Springer.

Donis, A. E. 2013. "Exploring the Movement of People in Postclassic and Historic Period Lamanai Using Stable Isotopes." MA thesis, University of Western Ontario, London.

Dorison, Antoine. 2019. *Archéologie des systèmes agraires préhispaniques de la région de Zacapu, Michoacán, Mexique, VIIe-XVe siècle apr. J.-C.* Phd diss., Université Paris 1-Panthéon-Sorbonne, Paris.

Douglas, Peter M. J., Mark Pagani, Marcelo A. Canuto, Mark Brenner, David A. Hodell, T. I. Eglinton, and Jason H. Curtis. 2015. "Drought, Agricultural Adaptation, and Sociopolitical Collapse in the Maya Lowlands." *Proceedings of the National Academy of Sciences USA* 112: 5607–5612.

Douglass, John G. 2007. "Smoke, Soot, and Censers: A Perspective on Ancient Commoner Household Ritual Behavior from Naco Valley, Honduras." In *Commoner Ritual and Ideology in Ancient Mesoamerica,* ed. N. Gonlin and J. C. Lohse, 123–142. Boulder: University Press of Colorado.

Driver, David W., and James F. Garber. 2004. "Minor Centers between Seats of Power." In *The Ancient Maya of the Belize Valley,* ed. J. F. Garber, 287–304. Gainesville: University Press of Florida.

Dufour, D. L., and B. A. Piperata. 2004. "Rural-to-Urban Migration in Latin America: An Update and Thoughts on the Model." *American Journal of Human Biology* 16: 395–404.

Dull, Robert A., John Southon, and Payson D. Sheets. 2001. "Volcanism, Ecology, and Culture: A Reassessment of the Volcán Ilopango TBJ Eruption in the Southern Maya Realm." *Latin American Antiquity* 12(1): 25–44.

Duncan, W. N. 2005. *The Bioarchaeology of Ritual Violence in Postclassic El Petén, Guatemala (AD 950–1524).* Carbondale: Southern Illinois University.

Duncan, W. N. 2009. "The Bioarchaeology of Ritual Violence at Zacpetén." In *The Kowoj: Identity, Migration, and Geopolitics in Late Postclassic Petén, Guatemala*, ed. P. M. Rice and D. S. Rice, 340–367. Boulder: University Press of Colorado.

Dunn, Richard K., and S. J. Mazzullo. 1993. "Holocene Paleocoastal Reconstruction and Its Relationship to Marco Gonzalez, Ambergris Caye, Belize." *Journal of Field Archaeology* 20(2): 121–131.

Dunning, Nicholas P. 1992. *Lords of the Hills: Ancient Maya Settlement in the Puuc Region, Yucatan, Mexico*. Monographs in World Prehistory No. 15. Madison, WI: Prehistory Press.

Dunning, Nicholas P. 2003. "Along the Serpent's Maw: Environment and Settlement in Xkipché, Yucatán." In *El asentamineto de Xkipché*, ed. H. J. Prem, 263–316. México, DF: Instituto Nacional de Antropología e Historia.

Dunning, Nicholas P. 2004. "Down on the Farm: Classic Maya Houselots as Farmsteads." In *Ancient Maya Commoners*, ed. J. Lohse and F. Valdez, 96–116. Austin: University of Texas Press.

Dunning, Nicholas P., and George F. Andrews. 1994. "Ancient Maya Architecture and Urbanism at Siho and the Western Puuc Region, Mexico." *Mexicon* 16: 53–61.

Dunning, Nicholas P., Timothy Beach, and Sheryl Luzzadder-Beach. 2012. "Kax and Kol: Collapse and Resilience in Lowland Maya Civilization." *Proceedings of the National Academy of Sciences* 109: 3652–3657.

Dunning, Nicholas P., J. Brewer, Christopher Carr, Armando Anaya Hernández, Timothy Beach, Jennifer Chmilar, Liwy Grazioso Sierra, Robert Griffin, David Lentz, Sheryl Luzzadder-Beach, Kathryn Reese-Taylor, William Saturno, Vernon Scarborough, Michael Smyth, and Fred Valdez. In press. "Harvesting *Ha*: Ancient Water Collection and Storage in the Elevated Interior Region of the Maya Lowlands." In *Sustainability and Water Management in the Maya World and Beyond*, ed. Jean Larmon, Lisa Lucero, and Fred Valdez. Boulder: University Press of Colorado.

Dunning, Nicholas, David Wahl, Timothy Beach, John Jones, Sheryl Luzzadder-Beach, and Carmen McCane. 2014b. "The End of the Beginning: Drought, Environmental Change, and the Preclassic to Classic Transition in the East-Central Maya Lowlands." In *The Great Maya Droughts*, ed. Gyles Iannone, 107–126. Boulder: University Press of Colorado.

Dunning, Nicholas, Eric Weaver, Michael Smyth, and David Ortegon Zapata. 2014a. "Xkoch: Home of Maya Rain Gods and Water Managers." In *The Archaeology of Yucatan: New Directions and Data*, ed. T. W. Stanton, 65–80. British Archaeological Reports, International Series. Oxford, UK: Archaeopress.

Durán, Diego. 1971. *Books of the Gods and Rites and The Ancient Calendar*, trans. F. Horcasitas and D. Heyden. Norman: University of Oklahoma Press.

Ebert, Claire E., Brendan J. Culleton, Jaime J. Awe, and Douglas J. Kennett. 2016. "AMS ^{14}C Dating of Preclassic to Classic Period Household Construction in the Ancient Maya Community of Cahal Pech, Belize." *Radiocarbon* 58(1): 69–87.

Edmonson, Munro S., trans. and ed. 1982. *The Ancient Future of the Itza: The Book of Chilam Balam of Tizimin*. Austin: University of Texas Press.

Edmonson, Munro S., trans. and ed. 1986. *Heaven Born Merida and Its Destiny: The Book of Chilam Balam of Chumayel*. Austin: University of Texas Press.

Ehret, Jennifer J., and James M. Conlon. 2000. "Results of the Surface Collection Program at Baking Pot: The Northeast Baking Pot and North Caracol Farm Settlement Clusters." In *The Western Belize Regional Cave Project: A Report of the 1999 Field Season*, ed. C.S. Griffith, R. Ishihara, and Jaime J. Awe, 55–72. Durham: University of New Hampshire, Durham.

El-Najjar, M., D. Ryan, C. G. Turner II, and B. Lozoff. 1976. "The Etiology of Porotic Hyperostosis among the Prehistoric and Historic Anasazi Indians of Southwestern United States." *American Journal of Physical Anthropology* 44: 477–487.

Emberling, G. 1997. "Ethnicity in Complex Societies: Archaeological Perspectives." *Journal of Archaeological Research* 5: 295–344.

Ericson, Jonathon E. 1985. "Strontium Isotope Characterization in the Study of Prehistoric Human Ecology." *Journal of Human Evolution* 14(5): 503–514.

Espejel C., Claudia. 2008. *La justicia y el fuego. Dos claves para leer la Relación de Michoacán*. Zamora, México: El Colegio de Michoacán.

Ethridge, Robbie, and Charles Hudson, eds. 2002. *The Transformation of the Southeastern Indians: 1540–1760*. Jackson: University Press of Mississippi.

Ezzo, Joseph A., Clark M. Johnson, and T. Douglas Price. 1997. "Analytical Perspectives on Prehistoric Migration: A Case Study from East-Central Arizona." *Journal of Archaeological Science* 24(5): 447–466.

Faist, Thomas. 2013. "The Mobility Turn: A New Paradigm for the Social Sciences?" *Ethnic and Racial Studies* 36(11): 1637–1646.

Fargher, Lane. F., Verenice Heredia Espinoza, and Richard E. Blanton. 2011. "Alternative Pathways to Power in Late Postclassic Highland Mesoamerica." *Journal of Anthropological Archaeology* 30(3): 306–326.

Farriss, Nancy M. 1984. *Maya Society under Colonial Rule*. Princeton, NJ: Princeton University Press.

Fash, William L. 2001a. Informe de Actividades: Enero a Agosto 2001. Archivos del Centro Regional de Investigaciones Arqueológicas, Copán ruinas, Honduras.

Fash, William L. 2001b. *Scribes, Warriors and Kings: The City of Copán and the Ancient Maya*. New York: Thames and Hudson.

Fash, William L., E. Wyllys Andrews, and T. Kam Manahan. 2004. "Political Decentralization, Dynastic Collapse, and the Early Postclassic in the Urban Center of Copán, Honduras." In *The Terminal Classic in the Maya Lowlands: Collapse, Transition, and Transformation*, ed. A. A. Demarest, P. M. Rice, and D. S. Rice, 327–363. Boulder: University Press of Colorado.

Fash, William L., and Kurt Long. 1983. "Mapa Arqueológico del Valle de Copán." In *Introducción a la Arqueología de Copán*, ed. C. F. Baudez, Tomo III. Tegucigalpa, Honduras: Instituto Hondureño de Antropología e Historia.

Fash, William L., and Leonardo López Luján, eds. 2009. *The Art of Urbanism: How Mesoamerican Kingdoms Represented Themselves in Architecture and Imagery*. Washington, DC: Dumbarton Oaks.

Fash, William L., and Robert J. Sharer. 1991. "Sociopolitical Developments and Methodological Issues at Copan, Honduras: A Conjunctive Perspective." *Latin American Antiquity* 2(2): 166–187.

Faugère-Kalfon, Brigitte. 1996. *Entre Zacapu y Río Lerma: culturas en una zona Fronteriza*. Cuaderno des Estudios Michoacanos 7. México, DF: Centre Français d'Études Mexicaines et Centraméricaines.

Fazekas, I., and F. Kosa. 1978. *Forensic Fetal Osteology*. Budapest, Hungary: Akademiai Kiado.

Fennell, Christopher C. 2007. *Crossroads and Cosmologies. Diasporas and Ethnogenesis in the New World*. Gainesville: University Press of Florida.

Fenner, Jack N., and Lori E. Wright. 2014. "Revisiting the Strontium Contribution of Sea Salt in the Human Diet." *Journal of Archaeological Science* 44: 99–103.

Finnegan, Gregory Allan. 1976. "Population Movement, Labor Migration, and Social Structure in a Mossi Village." PhD diss., Brandeis University, Waltham, MA.

Fisher, Christopher, and Stephen Leisz. 2013. "New Perspectives on Purépecha Urbanism Through the Use of Lidar at the Site of Angamuco, Mexico." In *Space Archaeology: Mapping Ancient Landscapes with Air and Spaceborne Imagery*, ed. D. Harrower and M. Harrower, 191–201. New York: Springer.

Flannery, Kent V. 2002. "The Origins of the Village Revisited: From Nuclear to Extended Households." *American Antiquity* 67(3): 417–433.

Fleury, Sophie, Bruno Malaizé, Jacques Giraudeau, Didier Galop, Viviane Bout-Roumazeilles, Philippe Martinez, Karine Charlier, Pierre Carbonel, and M. Charlotte Arnauld. 2014. "Impacts of Maya Land Use on the Laguna Tuspán Watershed (Petén, Guatemala) as Seen through Clay and Ostracod Analysis." *Journal of Archaeological Science* 49: 372–382.

Forest, Marion. 2014. "Approches spatio-archéologiques de la structure sociale des sites urbains du Malpaís de Zacapu." PhD diss., Université de Paris 1—Panthéon/Sorbonne.

Forest, Marion, and Dominique Michelet. 2012. "Organisation sociale, organisation spatiale: le cas des sites urbains du Malpaís de Zacapu, Michoacán, Mexique." In *Cahier des thèmes transversaux ArcScAn, Vol. X*, ed. Patrice Brun, 95–107. Maison de l'Archéologie et de l'Ethnologie. Nanterre: Centre National de la Recherche Scientifique, Université de Paris. https://hal.archives-ouvertes.fr/CAHIER_TH_ARSCAN/.

Forné, Mélanie. 2006. *La cronología cerámica de La Joyanca, Noroeste del Petén, Gua-temala.* British Archaeological Reports, International Series, No.17. Oxford, UK: Archaeopress.

Forné, Mélanie, Chloé Andrieu, Arthur A. Demarest, Paola Torres, Claudia Quintanilla, Ronald L. Bishop, and Olaf Jaime Riveron. 2013. *Crisis y cambios en el Clásico Tardío: los retos económicos de una ciudad entre Tierras Altas y Tierras Bajas Mayas.* www.mesoweb .com.

Foster, George M. 1960. "Life-Expectancy of Utilitarian Pottery in Tzintzuntzan, Micho-acan, Mexico." *American Antiquity* 25(4): 606–609.

Fowler, William R. 1989. *The Cultural Evolution of Ancient Nahua Civilizations: The Pipil-Nicarao of Central America.* Norman: University of Oklahoma Press.

Fowles, Severin M. 2011. "Movement and the Unsettling of the Pueblos." In *Rethinking Anthropological Perspectives on Migration*, ed. Graciela S. Cabana and Jeffery J. Clark, 45–67. Gainesville: University Press of Florida.

Fox, John W. 1987. *Maya Postclassic state formation.* New York: Cambridge University Press.

Fox, Robin. 1967. *The Keresan Bridge.* London School of Economics Monographs on Social Anthropology, No. 35. London: Athlone.

Frankenberg, Susan R., and Lyle W. Konigsberg. 2011. "Migration Muddles in Pre-history: The Distinction between Model-Bound and Model-Free Methods." In *Rethinking Anthropological Perspectives on Migration*, ed. Graciela S. Cabana and Jeffery J. Clark, 278–292. Gainesville: University Press of Florida.

Freiwald, Carolyn. 2011a. "Maya Migration Networks: Reconstructing Population Movement in the Belize Valley during the Late and Terminal Classic." PhD diss., University of Wisconsin, Madison.

Freiwald, Carolyn. 2011b. "Patterns of Population Movement at Xunantunich, Cahal Pech, and Baking Pot During the Late and Terminal Classic (AD 600–900)." *Research Reports in Belize Archaeology* 9: 89–100.

Freiwald, Carolyn. 2012. "Actuncan Burials: The 2011 Field Season." In *The Actuncan Archaeological Project: Report of the 2011 Field Season*, ed. Lisa LeCount and Angela Keller, 93–108. Belmopan: Belize Institute of Archaeology.

Freiwald, Carolyn. 2019. "Excavation and Curation Strategies for Complex Burials in Tropical Environments." *Advances in Archaeological Practice.* 7(1): 10–22.

Freiwald, Carolyn. 2020. "Migration and Mobility among the Ancient Maya." In *The Maya World*, ed. S Hutson and T Ardren, 203–222. Abingdon: Routledge.

Freiwald, Carolyn, and Nicholas J. Billstrand. 2014. "Burial 11 in Structure 41 at Actuncan, Belize." In *The Actuncan Archaeological Project: Report of the 2013 Field Season*, ed. Lisa J. LeCount, 49–74. Belmopan: Belize Institute of Archaeology.

Freiwald, Carolyn, and Destiny Micklin. 2013. "Burial Pratices in Group 1 Patio." In *The Actuncan Archaeological Project: Report of the 2012 Field Season*, ed. Lisa J. LeCount, 81–92. Belmopan: Belize Institute of Archaeology.

Freiwald, Carolyn, David W. Mixter, and Nicholas Billstrand. 2014a. "Burial Practices at Actuncan: A Seated Burial and Ongoing Analysis from the 2001–2013 Field Seasons." *Research Reports in Belize Archaeology* 11: 95–110.

Freiwald, Carolyn, and Timothy Pugh. 2018. "The Origins of Early Colonial Cows at San Bernabé, Guatemala: Strontium Isotope Values at an Early Spanish Mission in the Petén Lakes Region of Northern Guatemala." *Environmental Archaeology* 23(1): 80–96.

Freiwald, Carolyn, Jason Yaeger, Jaime J. Awe, and Jennifer Piehl. 2014b. "Isotopic Insights into Mortuary Treatment and Origin at Xunantunich, Belize." In *The Bioarchaeology of Space and Place: Ideology, Power and Meaning in Maya Mortuary Contexts*, ed. G. D. Wrobel, 107–141. New York: Springer Press.

Freter, AnnCorinne. "The Classic Maya Collapse at Copan, Honduras: A Regional Settlement Perspective." PhD diss., Department of Anthropology, Pennsylvania State University, 1988.

Freter, AnnCorinne. 1993. "Obsidian-Hydration Dating: Its Past, Present, and Future Application in Mesoamerica." *Ancient Mesoamerica* 4(2): 285–303.

Freter, AnnCorinne, and Elliot M. Abrams. 2016. "Chronology, Construction, and the Abandonment Process: A Case Study from the Classic Maya Kingdom of Copan, Honduras." In *Human Adaptation in Ancient Mesoamerica: Empirical Approaches to Mesoamerican Archaeology*, ed. Nancy Gonlin and Kirk D. French, 97–123. Boulder: University Press of Colorado.

Gage, Timothy G., Sharon N. DeWitte, and James W. Wood. 2012. "Demography Part I: Mortality and Migration." In *Human Biology: An Evolutionary and Biocultural Perspective*, ed. Sara Stinson, Barry Bogin, and Dennis O'Rourke, 694–755. Hoboken, NJ: Wiley Liss.

Galinié, Henri. 2000. *Ville, Espace Urbain et Archéologie*. Collection Sciences de La Ville 16. Maison des Sciences de la Ville, de l'Urbanisme et des Paysages. Tours: Université François-Rabelais.

Gallareta Negrón, Tomas, George Bey III, and William Ringle. 2010. Proyecto Arqueológico Regional de Bolonchén, Temporada de Campo 2000–2010. México, DF: Informe Técnico al Consejo de Arqueología del Instituto Nacional de Antropología e Historia.

Gallareta Negrón, Tomás, and Ramón Carrillo Sánchez. 2005. "The Labná-Kiuic Intersite Survey." In *The 2001 Season of the Labná-Kiuic Archaeological Project*, ed. William Ringle, 53–60. Foundation for the Advancement of Mesoamerican Studies, Inc. www.famsi.org/reports/00019/00019Ringle01.pdf. Accessed June 4, 2018.

Gallareta Negrón, Tomas, and William Ringle. 2004. The Earliest Occupation of the Puuc Region, Yucatan, Mexico: New Perspectives from Xocnaceh and Paso de Macho. Paper presented at the 103rd Annual Meeting of the American Anthropological Association, Atlanta, GA.

Gallay, Alain, Éric Huysecom, Anne Mayor, and Agnès Gelbert. 2012. *Potières du Sahel: à la découverte des traditions céramiques de la Boucle du Niger (Mali)*. Gollion: Infolio.

Galley, C. 1998. *The Demography of Early Modern Towns: York in the Sixteenth and Seventeenth Centuries.* Liverpool, UK: Liverpool University Press.

Garmy, Pierre. 2012. *Villes, Réseaux et Systèmes de Villes: Contribution de L'archéologie.* Paris: Editions Errance.

Garrison, T. G., and Nicholas P. Dunning. 2009. "Settlement, Environment, and Politics in the San Bartolo-Xultun Territory." *Latin American Antiquity* 20(4): 525–552.

Gaxiola González, Margarita. 2006. "Tradición y estilo en el estudio de la variabilidad cerámica del epiclásico en el centro de México." In *El fenómeno Coyotlatelco en el centro de México: Tiempo, Espacio y Significado,* ed. Laura Solar Valverde, 17–40. México, DF: Instituto Nacional de Antropología e Historia.

Gerry, John P. 1993. "Bone Isotope Ratios and Their Bearing on Elite Privilege among the Classic Maya." *Geoarchaeology* 12(1): 41–69.

Gerry, John P., and Harold W. Krueger. 1997. "Regional Diversity in Classic Maya Diets." In *Bones of the Maya: Studies of Ancient Skeletons,* ed. S. L. Whittington and D. M. Reed, 196–207. Washington, DC: Smithsonian Institution Press.

Gervais, Véronique. 1987. Edad de la muerte en Las Milpillas (Michoacán). México, DF: Centre Français d'Études Mexicaines et Centraméricaines. Manuscript in possession of the chapter author.

Gill, R. 2000. *The Great Maya Droughts.* Albuquerque: University of New Mexico Press.

Gillespie, Susan D. 2000. "Rethinking Ancient Maya Social Organization: Replacing 'Lineage' with 'House.'" *American Anthropologist* 102(3): 467–484.

Gillespie, Susan D. 2001. "Personhood, Agency, and Mortuary Ritual: A Case Study from the Ancient Maya." *Journal of Anthropological Archaeology* 20: 73–112.

Gillespie, Susan D. 2011. "Toltecs, Tula, and Chichén Itzá: The Development of an Archaeological Myth." In *Twin Tollans: Chichén Itzá, Tula, and the Epiclassic to Early Postclassic Mesoamerican World,* ed. Jeff Karl Kowalski and Cynthia Kristan-Graham, 61–92. Washington, DC: Dumbarton Oaks.

Gilli, Adrian, David A. Hodell, George D. Kamenov, and Mark Brenner. 2009. "Geological and Archaeological Implications of Strontium Isotope Analysis of Exposed Bedrock in the Chicxulub Crater Basin, Northwestern Yucatán, Mexico." *Geology* 37(8): 723–726.

Glassman, David M. 1995. "Skeletal Biology of the Prehistoric Maya of Northern Ambergris Caye." In *Maya Maritime Trade, Settlement, and Populations on Ambergris Caye, Belize,* eds, Thomas H. Guderjan and James F. Garber, 73–93. Lancaster, CA: Labyrinthos.

Goldstein, Paul. 2000. "Communities without Borders: The Vertical Archipelago and Diaspora Communities in the Southern Andes." In *The Archaeology of Communities: A New World Perspective,* ed. Marcello A. Canuto and Jason Yaeger, 182–209. London: Routledge.

Gómez Chávez, Sergio. 1998. "Nuevos Datos sobre la Relación entre Teotihuacan y el Occidente de México." In *Antropología e historia del Occidente de México, XXIV Mesa*

Redonda de la Sociedad Mexicana de Antropología, 1461–1493. México, DF: Sociedad Mexicana de Antropología, Universidad Nacional Autónoma de México.

Gonlin, Nancy. 1993. "Rural Household Archaeology at Copán, Honduras." PhD diss., Pennsylvania State University, State College, PA.

Gonlin, Nancy. 1994. "Rural Household Diversity in Late Classic Copan, Honduras." In *Archaeological Views from the Countryside: Village Communities in Early Complex Societies*, ed. G. M. Schwartz and S. E. Falconer, 177–197. Washington, DC: Smithsonian Institution Press.

Gonlin, Nancy. 2007. "Ritual and Ideology among Classic Maya Commoners at Copán, Honduras." In *Commoner Ritual and Ideology in Ancient Mesoamerica*, ed. N. Gonlin and J. C. Lohse, 83–121. Boulder: University Press of Colorado.

González de la Mata, Rocio, and Andrew P. Andrews. 1998. "Navegación y comercio en la costa oriental de la Península de Yucatán." In *Los Mayas*, ed. P. Schmidt, Mercedes de la Garza, and Enrique Nalda, 451–467. México, DF: CONACULTA, Instituto Nacional de Antropología e Historia.

González-Hermosillo A., F., and L. Reyes García. 2002. *El códice de Cholula: La exaltación testimonial de un linaje Indio*. México, DF: Instituto Nacional de Antropología e Historia, Gobierno del Estado de Puebla, Centro de Investigaciones y Estudios Superiores en Antropología Social, and Grupo Editorial Miguel Ángel Porrúa.

Goodman, A., and G. Armelagos. 1985. "Factors Affecting the Distribution of Enamel Hypoplasias within the Human Permanent Dentition." *American Journal of Physical Anthropology* 68: 579–493.

Goodman, A., D. Martin, G. Armelagos, and G. Clark. 1984. "Indications of Stress from Bone and Teeth." In *Paleopathology at the Origins of Agriculture*, ed. M. Cohen and G. Armelagos, 13–49. Orlando, FL: Academic Press.

Goodman, A., and J. Rose. 1990. "Assessment of Systematic Physiological Perturbations from Dental Enamel Hypoplasias and Associated Histological Structures." *American Journal of Physical Anthropology* 33 (Supplement 11): 59–110.

Goody, Jack, ed. 1958. *The Development Cycle in Domestic Groups*. Cambridge Papers in Social Anthropology, no. 1. New York: Cambridge University Press.

Gorenstein, Shirley, David Chodoff, John Hyslop, Helen Perlstein Pollard, Michael Snarskis, and Lee Anne Wilson. 1985. *Acámbaro: Frontier Settlement on the Tarascan-Aztec Border*. Vanderbilt University Publications in Anthropology 32. Nashville, TN: Vanderbilt University Press.

Graff, Donald H. 1990. "Investigación preliminaria de los asentamientos rurales en la zona Puuc, Yucatan, México." In *Boletín del Consejo de Arqueología*, 135–137. México, DF: Instituto Nacional de Antropología e Historia.

Graham, Elizabeth. 1985. "Facets of Terminal to Post-Classic Activity in the Stann Creek District, Belize." In *The Lowland Maya Postclassic*, ed. Arlen F. Chase and Prudence M. Rice, 215–229. Austin: University of Texas Press.

Graham, Elizabeth. 1986. "Barton Ramie Ceramic Types at Colson Point, North Stann Creek: A Focus on the Protoclassic." *Cerámica de Cultura Maya* 14: 32–38.

Graham, Elizabeth. 1987. "Terminal Classic to Historic-Period Vessel Forms from Belize." In *Maya Ceramics: Papers from the 1985 Maya Ceramic Conference*, ed. P. M. Rice and R. J. Sharer, 73–98. BAR International Series 345. Oxford, UK: BAR.

Graham, Elizabeth. 1989. "Brief Synthesis of Coastal Site Data from Colson Point, Placencia, and Marco Gonzalez, Belize." In *Coastal Maya Trade*, ed. Heather McKillop and Paul F. Healy, 135–154. Occasional Papers in Anthropology, No. 8. Peterborough, Ontario, Canada: Trent University.

Graham, Elizabeth. 1994. *The Highlands of the Lowlands: Environment and Archaeology in the Stann Creek District, Belize, Central America*. Monographs in World Archaeology No. 19. Madison, WI: Prehistory Press; Toronto, Canada: Royal Ontario Museum.

Graham, Elizabeth. 1998. *Report on the Investigations at Middle Caye, Glovers Reef Atoll, 1997 and 1998*. Submitted to Belize Institute of Archaeology, Belmopan.

Graham, Elizabeth. 2004. "Lamanai Reloaded: Alive and Well in the Early Postclassic." In *Research Reports in Belizean Archaeology* 1, ed. Jaime Awe, John Morris, and Sherilyne Jones, 223–242. Belmopan, Belize: Institute of Archaeology, National Institute of Culture and History.

Graham, Elizabeth. 2006a. "A Neotropical Framework for *Terra Preta*." In *Time and Complexity in Historical Ecology: Studies in the Neotropical lowlands*, ed. William Balée and Clark Erickson, 57–86. New York: Columbia University Press.

Graham, Elizabeth. 2006b. "An Ethnicity to Know." In *Maya Ethnicity: The Construction of Ethnic Identity from Preclassic to Modern Times*, ed. Frauke Sachse, 109–124. Acta MesoAmericana, Vol. 19. Markt Schwaben: Verlag Anton Saurwein.

Graham, Elizabeth. 2011. *Maya Christians and Their Churches in Sixteenth-Century Belize*. Gainesville: University Press of Florida.

Graham, Elizabeth, Richard Macphail, Simon Turner, John Crowther, Julia Stegemann, Manuel Arroyo-Kalin, Lindsay Duncan, Richard Whittet, Cristina Rosique, and Phillip Austin. 2017. "The Marco Gonzalez Maya Site, Ambergris Caye, Belize: Assessing the Impact of Human Activities by Examining Diachronic Processes at the Local Scale." *Quaternary International* 437: 115–142.

Graham, Elizabeth, and David M. Pendergast. 1989. "Excavations at the Marco Gonzalez Site, Ambergris Caye, Belize." *Journal of Field Archaeology* 16(1): 1–16.

Graham, Elizabeth, David M. Pendergast, and Grant D. Jones. 1989. "On the Fringes of Conquest: Maya-Spanish Contact in Colonial Belize." *Science* 246(4935): 1254–1259.

Graham, Elizabeth, Scott E. Simmons, and Christine D. White. 2013. "The Spanish Conquest and the Maya Collapse: How 'Religious' Is Change?" *World Archaeology* 45(1): 161–185.

Graulich, Michel. 1981. "The Metaphor of the Day in Ancient Mexican Myth and Ritual." *Current Anthropology* 22(1): 45–60.

Graulich, Michel. 1984. "Aspects mythiques des pérégrinations Mexicas." In *The Native Sources and the History of the Valley of Mexico*, ed. Jacqueline de Durand-Forest, 25–72. British Archaeological Reports, International Series 204. Oxford, UK: Archaeopress.

Green, Kirsten. 2016. "The Use of Stable Isotope Analysis on Burials at Cahal Pech, Belize in Order to Identify Trends in Mortuary Practices over Time and Space." PhD diss., University of Montana, Missoula.

Greene, Kevin. 1986. *The Archaeology of the Roman Empire*. Berkeley: University of California Press.

Grube, Nikolai, and Ruth J. Krochock. 2011. "Reading between the Lines: Hieroglyphic Texts from Chichén Itzá and Its Neighbors." In *Twin Tollans: Chichén Itzá, Tula, and the Epiclassic to Early Postclassic Mesoamerican World*, ed. J. K. Kowalski and C. Kristan-Graham, 487–526. Washington, DC: Dumbarton Oaks.

Grupe, Gisela, T. Douglas Price, Meter Schroter, Frank Sollner, Clark M. Johnson, and Brian L. Beard. 1997. "Mobility of Bell Beaker People Revealed by Strontium Isotope Ratios of Tooth and Bone: A Study of Southern Bavarian Skeletal Remains." *Applied Geochemistry* 12: 517–525.

Guderjan, T. H., and J. F. Garber, eds. 1995. *Maya Maritime Trade, Settlement, and Populations on Ambergris Caye, Belize*. Lancaster, CA: Labyrinthos.

Guernsey Kappelman, Julia. 2000. "Late Formative Toad Altars as Ritual Stages." *Mexicon* XXII: 80–84.

Guerra, Rafael, and Renee Collins. 2015. "Excavations at the Lower Dover Palace Complex: Results of the 2014 Field Season." In *The Belize Valley Archaeological Project: A Report of the 2014 Field Season*, ed. Julie A. Hoggarth and Jaime J. Awe, 224–239. Belmopan, Belize: Belize Institute of Archaeology, National Institute of Culture and History.

Hamblin, R. L., and B. L. Pitcher. 1980. "The Classic Maya Collapse: Testing Class Conflict Hypotheses." *American Antiquity* 45(2): 246–267.

Hanks, William. 1990. *Referential Practice: Language and Lived Space among the Maya*. Chicago, IL: University of Chicago Press.

Hanks, William F. 2003. "'Reducción' and the Remaking of the Social Landscape in Colonial Yucatan." In *Espacios Mayas: Usos, Representaciones, Creencias*, ed. Alain Breton, Aurore Monod Becquelin, and Mario Humberto Ruz, 161–180. México, DF: Universidad Nacional Aútonoma de México.

Hanna, Jonathan A., Elizabeth Graham, David M. Pendergast, Julie A. Hoggarth, David L. Lentz, and Douglas J. Kennett. 2016. "A New Radiocarbon Sequence from Lamanai, Belize: Two Bayesian Models from One of Mesoamerica's Most Enduring Sites." *Radiocarbon* 58(4): 771–794.

Hard, Robert J., and William L. Merrill. 1992. "Mobile Agriculturalists and the Emergence of Sedentism: Perspectives from Northern Mexico." *American Anthropologist* 94(3): 601–620.

Hare, Timothy S., Marilyn A. Masson, and Carlos Peraza Lope. 2014. "The Urban Cityscape." In *Kukulcan's Realm: Urban Life at Ancient Mayapán*, ed. M. A. Masson and C. Peraza Lope, 149–191. Boulder: University Press of Colorado.

Harrison-Buck, E. 2014. "Reevaluating Chronology and Historical Content in the Maya Books of Chilam Balam." *Ethnohistory* 6(4): 681–713.

Harrison-Buck, E., and P. A. McAnany. 2006. "Terminal Classic Circular Shrines and Ceramic Material in the Sibun Valley, Belize: Evidence of Northern Yucatec Influence in the Eastern Maya Lowlands." *Research Reports in Belizean Archaeology* 3: 287–299.

Haskell, David. 2008. "The Cultural Logic of Hierarchy in the Tarascan State: History as Ideology in the *Relación de Michoacán*." *Ancient Mesoamerica* 19, 231–241.

Haug, G. H., D. Gunther, L. C. Peterson, D. M. Sigmun, K. A. Hughen, and B. Aeschlimann. 2003. "Climate and the Collapse of Maya Civilization." *Science* 299(5613): 1731–1735.

Haviland, William A. 1969. "A New Population Estimate for Tikal, Guatemala." *American Antiquity* 34(4): 429–433.

Haviland, William A. 1988. "Musical Hammocks at Tikal: Problems with Reconstructing Household Composition." In *Household and Community in the Mesoamerican Past*, ed. Richard R. Wilk and Wendy Ashmore, 121–135. Albuquerque: University of New Mexico Press.

Healan, Dan M. 2012. "The Archaeology of Tula, Hidalgo, Mexico." *Journal of Archaeological Research* 20: 53–115.

Hegmon, Michelle. 2017. "Path Dependence." In *The Oxford Handbook of Southwest Archaeology*, ed. Barbara Mills and Severin Fowles, 155–168. Oxford, UK: Oxford University Press.

Hegmon, Michelle, Jacob Freeman, Keith W. Kintigh, Margaret C. Nelson, Sarah Oas, Matthew A. Peeples and Andrea Torvinen. 2016. "Marking and Making Differences: Representational Diversity in the U.S. Southwest." *American Antiquity* 81(2): 253–272.

Helmke, Christophe G. B. 2008. "Excavations of Structures B1 and B7 at Baking Pot, Belize." In *The Belize Valley Archaeological Reconnaissance Project: A Report of the 2007 Field Season*, ed. C. G. B. Helmke and Jaime J. Awe, 109–144. Belmopan: Belize Institute of Archaeology.

Helmke, Christophe G. B., and Jaime J. Awe. 2012. "Ancient Maya Territorial Organisation of Central Belize: Confluence of Archaeological and Epigraphic Data." *Contributions in New World Archaeology* 4: 57–88.

Helms, Mary W. 1988. *Ulysses' Sail: An Ethnographic Odyssey of Power, Knowledge, and Geographical Distance*. Princeton, NJ: Princeton University Press.

Helms, Mary W. 1992. "Long-Distance Contacts, Elite Aspirations, and the Age of Discovery in Cosmological Context." In *Resources, Power, and Interregional Interaction*, ed. Edward M. Schortman and Patricia A. Urban, 157–174. New York: Plenum.

Henderson, Hope. 2003. "The Organization of Staple Crop Production at Kaxob." *Latin American Antiquity* 14(4): 469–496.

312 | *References*

Henderson, Hope. 2012. "Understanding Households on Their Own Terms: Investigating on Household Sizes, Production and Longevity at Kaxob, Belize." In *Ancient Households of the Americas: Conceptualizing What Households Do*, ed. John G. Douglass and Nancy Gonlin, 269–298. Boulder: University Press of Colorado.

Hendon, Julia A. 2012. "Neighborhoods in Pre-Hispanic Honduras: Settlement Patterns and Social Groupings within Sites or Regions." In *The Neighborhood as a Social and Spatial Unit in Mesoamerican Cities*, ed. M. C. Arnauld, L. Manzanilla, and M. E. Smith, 159–180. Tucson: University of Arizona Press.

Hernández, Christine L., and Dan M. Healan. 2008. "The Role of Late Pre-Contact Colonial Enclaves in the Development of the Postclassic Ucareo Valley, Michoacán, Mexico." *Ancient Mesoamerica* 19: 265–282.

Hernández Reyes, C. 1970. "Restos arquitectónicos del horizonte postclásico en Cholula." In *Proyecto Cholula, Serie Investigaciones 19*, ed. I. Marquina, 89–92. México, DF: Instituto Nacional Antropología e Historia.

Hers, Marie-Areti. 1989. *Los toltecas en tierras Chichimecas*. Cuadernos de historia del arte 35, Instituto de Investigaciones Estéticas. México, DF: Universidad Nacional Autónoma de México.

Hicks, Frederic, 1982. "Tetzcoco in the Early Sixteenth Century: The State, the City, and the Calpolli." *American Ethnologist* 9: 230–249.

Hicks, Frederic. 1986. "Prehispanic Background of Colonial Political and Economic Organization in Central Mexico." In *Supplement to the Handbook of Middle American Indians*, Volume 4, *Ethnohistory*, ed. R. Spores, 35–54. Austin: University of Texas Press.

Hicks, Frederic. 1991. "Gift and Tribute: Relations of Dependency in Aztec Mexico." In *Early State Economics*, ed. H. Claessen and P. Van de Velde, 199–213. New Brunswick, NJ: Transaction Publishers.

Hicks, Frederic. 2013. "The Architectural Features of Cerro Portezuelo." *Ancient Mesoamerica* 24(1): 73–85.

Hildebrand, John A., and Melissa B. Hagstrum. 1999. "New Approaches to Ceramic Use and Discard: Cooking Pottery from the Peruvian Andes in Ethnoarchaeological Perspective." *Latin American Antiquity* 10(1): 25–46.

Hill, Jane H. 2015. "Mesoamerica and the Southwestern United States: Linguistic History." In *The Global Prehistory of Human Migration*, ed. Peter Bellwood, 362–368. West Sussex, UK: John Wiley and Sons Ltd.

Hillson, Simon. 2014. *Tooth Development in Human Evolution and Bioarchaeology*. Cambridge, UK: Cambridge University Press.

Hiquet, Julien. 2020. "Essor monumental et dynamiques des populations, le cas de la cité maya de Naachtun, Guatemala, au Classique Ancien 150–550 apr. J.-C." PhD diss., Université de Paris 1 Panthéon-Sorbonne, Paris.

Hiquet, Julien, and Julien Sion. 2018. Households, Growth, Contraction, and Mobility at the Classic Maya Center of Naachtun. Paper presented at the 83rd Society for American Archaeology, Washington, DC, April 12.

Hirth, Kenneth. 2000. *Ancient Urbanism at Xochicalco: The Evolution and Organization of a Pre-Hispanic Society*, Volume 1. Salt Lake City: University of Utah Press.

Hirth, Kenneth G. 2003. "The Altepetl and Urban Structure in Prehispanic Meso-america." In *El urbanismo en Mesoamerica (Urbanism in Mesoamerica)*, Volumen 1, ed. William T. Sanders, Alba Guadalupe Mastache, and Robert H. Cobean, 57–84. México, DF and University Park: Instituto Nacional de Antropología e Historia and Pennsylvania State University.

Hirth, Kenneth G., ed. 2009. *Housework: Craft Production and Domestic Economy in Ancient Mesoamerica*. Archeological Papers No. 19. Washington, DC: American Anthropological Association.

Hodell, David A., Rhonda L. Quinn, Mark Brenner, and George Kamenov. 2004. "Spatial Variation of Strontium Isotopes (87Sr/86Sr) in the Maya Region: A Tool for Tracking Ancient Human Migration." *Journal of Archaeological Science* 315: 585–601.

Hoerder, Dirk. 2004. "Migration as Balancing Process: Individual and Societal Connections of Mobility." In *Migration, Mobility, and Borders: Issues of Theory and Policy*, ed. Thomas Geisen, Anthony Andrew Hickey, and Allen Karcher, 15–34. Frankfurt: IKO, Verlag für Interculturelle Kommunikation.

Hofling, C. A. 2009. "The Linguistic Context of the Kowoj." In *The Kowoj: Identity, Migration, and Geopolitics in Late Postclassic Petén, Guatemala*, ed. P. M. Rice and D. S. Rice, 70–79. Boulder: University Press of Colorado.

Hoggarth, Julie A. 2012. "Household Adaptation and Social Reorganization in the Aftermath of Collapse at Baking Pot, Belize." PhD diss., University of Pittsburgh, PA.

Hoggarth, Julie A., Sebastian F. M. Breitenbach, Brendan J. Culleton, Claire E. Ebert, Marilyn A. Masson, and Douglas J. Kennett. 2016. "The Political Collapse of Chichen Itza in Climatic and Cultural Context." *Global and Planetary Change* 138: 25–42.

Hoggarth, Julie A., Brendan J. Culleton, Jaime J. Awe, and Douglas J. Kennett. 2014. "Questioning Postclassic Continuity at Baking Pot, Belize. Using Direct AMS ^{14}C Dating of Human Burials." *Radiocarbon* 56(3): 1057–1075.

Holland, T., and M. O'Brien. 1997. "Parasites, Porotic Hyperostosis, and the Implications of Changing Perspectives." *American Antiquity* 62: 183–193.

Hoppa, Robert D., and James W. Vaupel J., eds. 2002. *Paleodemography: Age Distribution from Skeletal Samples*. Cambridge, UK: Cambridge University Press.

Houston, Stephen D. 2000. "Into the Minds of Ancients: Advances in Maya Glyph Studies." *Journal of World Prehistory* 14(2): 121–201.

Houston, Stephen D., Hector Escobedo, Mark Child, Charles Golden, and René Muñoz. 2003. "The Moral Community: Maya Settlement Transformation at Piedras Negras, Guatemala." In *The Social Construction of Ancient Cities*, ed. Monica L. Smith, 212–253. Washington, DC: Smithsonian Institution Press.

Houston, Stephen D., D. Stuart, and K. A. Taube. 1992. "Image and Text on the 'Jauncy Vase.'" *The Maya Vase Book: A Corpus of Rollout Photographs of Maya Vases*, Volume 3, 499–512. New York: Kerr Associates.

Howie, Linda. 2012. *Ceramic Change and the Maya Collapse: A Study of Pottery Technology, Manufacture and Consumption at Lamanai, Belize.* British Archaeological Reports, International Series 2373. Oxford, UK: Archaeopress.

Howie, Linda, Terry Powis, and Elizabeth Graham. 2016. "Sitting on the Dock of the Bay: Ceramic Connections between Lamanai and the Chetumal Bay Area over More Than Two Millennia." In *Perspectives on the Ancient Maya of Chetumal Bay,* ed. Debra S. Walker, 162–185. Gainesville: University Press of Florida.

Howie, Linda, Christine D. White, and Fred J. Longstaffe. 2010. "Potographies and Biographies: The Role of Food in Ritual and Identity as Seen through Life Histories of Selected Maya Pots and People." In *Pre-Columbian Foodways: Interdisciplinary Approaches to Food, Culture, and Markets in Ancient Mesoamerica,* ed. John E. Staller and Michael D. Carrasco, 369–398. Dordrecht, Netherlands: Springer.

Hruby, Zachary X. 2006. "The Organization of Chipped Stone Economies at Piedras Negras, Guatemala." PhD diss., University of California, Riverside.

Huot, Jean-Louis. 2004. "L'urbanisation (3500–2700 Av. J.-C.)." In *Une archéologie des peuples du Proche-Orient, II: Des premiers villageois aux peuples des cités-États (X-IIIe millénaire av. J.-C.),* ed. J.-L. Huot, 73–104. Paris: Editions Errance.

Iannone, Gyles. 1996. "Problems in the Study of Ancient Maya Settlement and Social Organization: Insights from the 'Minor Centre' of Zubin, Cayo District, Belize." PhD diss., Institute of Archaeology, University of London.

Iannone, Gyles, ed. 2014. *The Great Maya Droughts in Cultural Context: Case Studies in Resilience and Vulnerability.* Boulder: University Press of Colorado.

Ibarra-Rivera, L., S. Mirabal, M. M. Regueiro, and R. J. Herrera. 2008. "Delineating Genetic Relationships among the Maya." *American Journal of Physical Anthropology* 135(3): 329–347.

Inomata, Takeshi. 2004. "The Spatial Mobility of Non-Elite Populations in Classic Maya Society and Its Political Implications." In *Ancient Maya Commoners,* ed. Jon C. Lohse and Fred Valdez, Jr., 175–196. Austin: University of Texas Press.

Inomata, Takeshi, Jessica MacLellan, Daniela Triadan, Jessica Munson, Melissa Burhama, Kazuo Aoyama, Hiroo Nasu, Flory Pinzóne, and Hitoshi Yonenobu. 2015. "Development of Sedentary Communities in the Maya Lowlands: Coexisting Mobile Groups and Public Ceremonies at Ceibal, Guatemala." *Proceedings of the National Academy of Science* 112(14): 4268–4273.

Isendahl, Christian. 2002. *Common Knowledge: Lowland Maya Urban Farming at Xuch.* Department of Archaeology and Ancient History, Studies in Global Archaeology No. 1. Uppsala, Sweden: Uppsala University.

Isendahl, Christian, Nicholas P. Dunning, and Jeremy Sabloff. 2014. "Growth Dependency and Decline in Classic Maya Puuc Political Economies." *AP3A: Archaeological Papers of the American Anthropological Association* 24: 43–55.

Jackson, Lawrence, and Heather McKillop. 1989. "Defining Coastal Maya Trading Ports and Transportation Routes." In *Coastal Maya Trade,* ed. Heather McKillop and Paul

F. Healy, 91–110. Occasional Papers in Anthropology No. 8. Peterborough, Canada: Trent University.

Jakeman, M. W. 1946. "The Identity of the Itzas." *American Antiquity* 12(2): 127–130.

Jarquín P., Ana M., and Enrique Martínez V. 1982. "Las Excavaciones en el Conjunto 1D." In *Memoria del Proyecto Arqueológico Teotihuacan 80–82*, ed. I. Rodríguez G., R. Cabrera C., and N. Morelos. G., 89–126. México, DF: Instituto Nacional de Antropología e Historia.

Jimenez, Socorro. 2002. "La cronología cerámica del puerto maya de Xcambó, costa norte de Yucatán: Complejo Cerámico Xcambó y Complejo Cerámico Cayalac." Licenciatura thesis, Universidad Autónoma de Yucatán, Mérida, México.

Jiménez Moreno, Wigberto. 1948. "Historia antigua de la zona Tarasca." In *El occidente de México, Cuarta Mesa Redonda*, 146–157. México, DF: Sociedad Mexicana de Antropología.

John, Jennifer R. 2008. "Postclassic Maya Ceramic Iconography at Lamanai, Belize, Central America." PhD diss., Institute of Archaeology, University College London.

Johnston, Kevin. 2004. "The 'Invisible Maya': Minimally Mounded Residential Settlement at Itzan, Peten, Guatemala." *Latin American Antiquity* 152: 145–175.

Jones, Grant D. 1989. *Maya Resistance to Spanish Rule: Time and History on a Colonial Frontier*. Albuquerque: University of New Mexico Press.

Jones, Grant D. 1998. *The Conquest of the Last Maya Kingdom*. Palo Alto, CA: Stanford University Press.

Joyce, Arthur A., and Marcus Winter. 1996. "Ideology, Power, and Urban Society in Pre-Hispanic Oaxaca." *Current Anthropology* 37(1): 33–47.

Kahn, Jennifer. 2013. "Anthropological Archaeology in 2012: Mobility, Economy, and Transformation." *American Anthropologist* 115(2): 248–261.

Katzenberg, Mary A., and H. Roy Krause. 1999. "Application of Stable Isotope Variation in Human Tissues to Problems in Identification." *Journal of the Canadian Society of Forensic Sciences* 22: 7–19.

Kelly, Isabel T. 1947. *Excavations at Apatzingán, Michoacán*. Viking Fund Publications in Anthropology No. 7. New York: Viking Fund.

Kelly, Robert L. 1992. "Mobility/Sedentism: Concepts, Archaeological Measures, and Effects." *Annual Review of Anthropology* 21: 43–66.

Kelly, Robert L. 1995. *The Foraging Spectrum: Diversity in Hunter-Gatherer Lifeways*. Washington, DC: Smithsonian Institution Press.

Kent, Susan. 1992. "Studying Variability in the Archaeological Record: An Ethnoarchaeological Model for Distinguishing Mobility Patterns." *American Antiquity* 57(4): 635–660.

Killgrove, Kristina, and Janet Montgomery. 2016. "All Roads Lead to Rome: Exploring Human Migration to the Eternal City through Biochemistry of Skeletons from Two Imperial-Era Cemeteries (1st–3rd c AD)." *PloS one* 11(2): e0147585.

Killion, Thomas W., ed. 1992. *Gardens of Prehistory: The Archaeology of Settlement Agriculture in Greater Mesoamerica*. Tuscaloosa: University of Alabama Press.

Killion, Thomas, W. 2013. "Nonagricultural Cultivation and Social Complexity: The Olmec, Their Ancestors, and Mexico's Southern Gulf Coast Lowlands." *Current Anthropology* 54(5): 569–606.

King, Eleanor M., and Leslie Shaw. 2015. "Research on Maya Markets." In *The Ancient Maya Marketplace: The Archaeology of Transient Space*, ed. Eleanor King, 1–32. Tucson: University of Arizona Press.

Kingsley, M., C. W. Golden, A. K. Scherer, and L. M. Marroquin de Franco. 2012. "Parallelism in Occupation: Tracking the Pre- and Post-Dynastic Evolution at Piedras Negras, Guatemala through Its Secondary Site, El Porvenir." *Mexicon* XXXIV: 109–117.

Kintigh, Keith W., Jeffrey H. Altschul, Mary C. Beaudry, Robert D. Drennan, Ann P. Kinzig, Timothy A. Kohler, W. Fredrick Limp, Herbert D. G. Maschner, William K. Michener, Timothy R. Pauketat, Peter Peregrine, Jeremy A. Sabloff, Tony J. Wilkinson, Henry T. Wright, and Melinda A. Zeder. 2014. "Grand Challenges for Archaeology." *American Antiquity* 79(1): 5–24.

Kirchhoff, P. 1947. Prologue: "La historia tolteca chichimeca: Un estudio Historico-sociologico." In *La Historia Tolteca Chichimeca: Anales de Quauhtinchan*, ed. H. Berlin and S. Rendon. México, DF: Antigua Librería Robredo.

Knudson, Kelly J. 2008. "Tiwanaku Influence in the South Central Andes: Strontium Isotope Analysis and Middle Horizon Migration." *Latin American Antiquity* 32(6): 3–23.

Kohler, Timothy A. 1992. "Archaeology, Field Houses, Villages, and the Tragedy of the Commons in the Early Northern Anasazi Southwest." *American Antiquity* 57(4): 617–635.

Kolb, Charles C. 1985. "Demographic Estimates in Archaeology: Contributions from Ethnoarchaeology on Mesoamerican Peasants." *Current Anthropology* 26(5): 581–599.

Kowalewski, Stephen A. 2007. "Coalescent Societies." In *Light on the Path: The Anthropology and History of the Southeastern Indians*, ed. T. J. Pluckhahn and R. Ethridge, 94–122. Tuscaloosa: University of Alabama Press.

Kowalewski, Stephen A. 2013. "The Work of Making Community." In *From Prehistoric Villages to Cities: Settlement Aggregation and Community Transformation*, ed. J. Birch, 201–218. New York: Routledge.

Kowalski, Jeff Karl. 1989. "Who Am I among the Itza? Links between Northern Yucatan and the Western Maya Lowlands and Highlands." In *Mesoamerica after the Decline of Teotihuacan, AD 700–900*, ed. Richard A. Diehl and Janet C. Berlo, 173–185. Washington, DC: Dumbarton Oaks.

Kowalski, Jeff Karl, and Cynthia Kristan-Graham, eds. 2011. *Twin Tollans: Chichén Itzá, Tula, and the Epiclassic to Early Postclassic Mesoamerican World*, rev. ed. Washington, DC: Dumbarton Oaks.

Kremer, J. 1994. "The Putun Hypothesis Reconsidered." In *Hidden among the Hills: Maya Archaeology of the Northwest Yucatan Peninsula*, ed. H. J. Prem, 289–307. Mockmuhl, Germany: Verlag Von Flemming.

Krueger, Harold. 1985. Sr Isotopes and Sr/Ca in Bone. Paper presented at the Biomineralization Conference, Warrenton, VA, April 14–17.

Kubler, George. 1984. "Pre-Columbian Pilgrimages in Mesoamerica." *Diogenes* 32(125): 11–23.

Kurjack, E. B., R. Maldonado, and M. Greene Robertson. 1991. "Ballcourts of the Northern Maya Lowlands." In *The Mesoamerican Ballgame*, ed. V. L. Scarborough and David Wilcox, 145–159. Tucson: University of Arizona Press.

Lacadena, Alfonso. 2010. "Highland Mexican and Maya Intellectual Exchange in the Late Postclassic: Some Thoughts on the Origin of Shared Elements and Methods of Interaction." In *Astronomers, Scribes, and Priests: Intellectual Interchange between the Northern Maya Lowlands and Highland Mexico in the Late Postclassic Period*, ed. Gabrielle Vail and Christine Hernandez, 383–406. Washington, DC: Dumbarton Oaks.

Lachniet, Matthew S., and William P. Patterson. 2009. "Oxygen Isotope Values of Precipitation and Surface Waters in Northern Central America (Belize and Guatemala) are Dominated by Temperature and Amount Effects." *Earth and Planetary Science Letters* 284: 435–446.

Laffoon, Jason E., Gareth R. Davies, Menno I. Hoogland, and Corinne I. Hofman. 2012. "Spatial Variation of Biologically Available Strontium Isotopes ($^{87}Sr/^{86}Sr$) in an Archipelagic Setting: A Case Study from the Caribbean." *Journal of Archaeological Science* 39(7): 2371–2384.

Lagunas, Z. 1994. "Las prácticas funerarias en Cholula Prehispánica." *Mirada Antropológica* 1: 82–94.

Lambert, J.D.H., and J. T. Arnason. 1982. "Ramon and Maya Ruins: An Ecological, not an Economic, Relation." *Science* 216(4543): 298–299.

Lamoureux-St-Hilaire, Maxime, Scott Macrae, Carmen A. McCane, Evan A. Parker, and Gyles Iannone. 2015. "The Last Groups Standing: Living Abandonment at the Ancient Maya Center of Minanha, Belize." *Latin American Antiquity* 26(4): 550–569.

Landau, Kristin. 2010. Appropriating Ancient Maya Political Strategy: Archaeology, Stela A and National Identity in Honduras. Paper presented at the Annual Meeting of the American Anthropological Association, New Orleans, LA.

Landau, Kristin. 2014. Proyecto Arqueológico de los Barrios de Copán, OP 70, Suboperaciones 1–24, Enero 2012–Octubre 2013. Report submitted to the Instituto Hondureño de Antropología e Historia, Tegucigalpa.

Landau, Kristin. 2016. "Maintaining the State: Centralized Power and Ancient Neighborhoods in Copán, Honduras." PhD diss., Northwestern University, Evanston, IL.

Landers, J. 1993. *Death and the metropolis: Studies in the Demographic History of London 1670–1830*. Cambridge: Cambridge University Press.

Laporte, Juan-Pedro. 2001. "Dispersión y estructura de las ciudades del sureste de Petén, Guatemala." In *Reconstruyendo la ciudad maya: El urbanismo en las sociedades antiguas*, ed. Andrés Ciudad, María Josefa Iglesias, and M. C. Martínez Martínez, 137–161. Madrid: Sociedad Española de Estudios Mayas.

Laporte, Juan-Pedro. 2004. "Terminal Classic Settlement and Polity in the Mopan Valley, Petén, Guatemala." In *The Terminal Classic in the Maya Lowlands: Collapse, Transition, and Transformation*, ed. A. A. Demarest, P. M. Rice, and D. S. Rice, 195–230. Boulder: University Press of Colorado.

LeBlanc, Steven A. 2015. "Mesoamerica and the Southwestern United States: Archaeology." In *The Global Prehistory of Human Migration*, ed. Peter Bellwood, 369–375. West Sussex, UK: John Wiley and Sons Ltd.

LeCount, Lisa J., and Jason Yaeger. 2010a. "A Brief Description of Xunantunich." In *Classic Maya Provincial politics: Xunantunich and Its Hinterlands*, ed. Lisa J. LeCount and Jason Yaeger, 67–78. Tucson: University of Arizona Press.

LeCount, Lisa J., and Jason Yeager. 2010b. "Provincial Politics and Current Models of the Maya State." In *Classic Maya Provincial Polities: Xunantunich and Its Hinterlands*, ed. L. J. LeCount and J. Yaeger, 20–45. Tucson: University of Arizona Press.

Lee, E. 1966. "A Theory of Migration." *Demography* 3(1): 47–57.

Lefebvre, Karine. 2011. "Acámbaro, en los confines del reino Tarasco: una aculturación discreta (1440–1521 d.C.)." *Trace* 59: 74–89.

Lefebvre, Karine. 2017. "La Toponimía frente a la Arqueología y a la Historia: Aportes sobre la Ocupación de la Región de Acámbaro en el Momento de la Conquista." In *La Memoria de los Nombres: La Toponimía en la Conformación Histórica del Territorio, de Mesoamérica a México*, ed. Karine Lefebvre and Carlos Paredes Martínez, 209–230. México, DF: Centro de Investigaciones en Geografía Ambiental, Universidad Nacional Autónoma de México.

Leloup, Fabienne. 1996. "Migration: A Complex Phenomenon." *International Journal of Anthropology* 11(2–4): 101–115.

Lemonnier, Eva. 2009. *La structure de l'habitat du site maya classique de La Joyanca dans son environnement local (Petén, Guatemala)*. Paris Monographs in American Archaeology 23, British Archaeological Reports, International Series 2016. Oxford, UK: Archaeopress.

Lemonnier, Eva, and Boris Vannière. 2013. "Agrarian Features, Farmsteads, and Homesteads in the Río Bec Nuclear Zone, Mexico." *Ancient Mesoamerica* 24(2): 397–413.

Lentz, David L. 1991. "Maya Diets of the Rich and Poor: Paleoethnobotanical Evidence from Copan." *Latin American Antiquity* 2(3): 269–287.

Lentz, David L., Elizabeth Graham, Xochitl Vinaja, Venicia Slotten, and Rupal Jain. 2016. "Agroforestry and Ritual at the Ancient Maya Center of Lamanai." *Journal of Archaeological Science Reports* 8: 284–294.

Leppard, Thomas P. 2014. "Mobility and Migration in the Early Neolithic of the Mediterranean: Questions of Motivation and Mechanism." *World Archaeology* 46(4): 484–501.

Lesure, Richard G., Lana S. Martin, Katelyn J. Bishop, Brittany Jackson, and C. Myles Chykerda. 2014. "The Neolithic Demographic Transition in Mesoamerica." *Current Anthropology* 55(5): 654–664.

Leventhal, Richard M. 1979. "Settlement Patterns at Copan, Honduras." PhD diss., Harvard University, Cambridge, MA.

Leventhal, Richard M. 1983. "Household Groups and Classic Maya Religion." In *Prehistoric Settlement Patterns: Essays in Honor of Gordon R. Willey*, ed. E. Z. Vogt and R. M. Leventhal, 55–76. Cambridge, MA: Peabody Museum of Archaeology and Ethnology.

Leventhal, Richard M. 2010. "Changing Places: The Castillo and the Structure of Power at Xunantunich." In *Classic Maya Provincial Polities: Xunantunich and Its Hinterlands*, ed. L. J. LeCount and J. Yaeger, 79–96. Tucson: University of Arizona Press.

Lévi-Strauss, Claude. 1979. *La voie des Masques*. Paris: Plon.

Liffman, Paul M. 2000. "Gourdvines, Fires, and Wixárika Territoriality." *Journal of the Southwest* 42(1): 129–165.

Lind, Michael D. 1994. "Cholula and Mixteca Polychromes: Two Mixteca-Puebla Regional Sub-styles." In *Mixteca-Puebla: Discoveries and Research in Mesoamerican Art and Archaeology*, ed. H. B. Nicholson and E. Quiñones Keber, 79–100. Culver City, CA: Labyrinthos.

Lister, Robert H. 1947. "Archaeology of the Middle Rio Balsas Basin, Mexico." *American Antiquity* 13: 67–78.

Lizana, Fray Bernardo de 1995. *Historia de Yucatan: Devocionario de Nuestra Señora de Izmal y conquista Espiritual*. México, DF: Universidad Nacional Autónoma de México.

Lockhart, J. 1992. *The Nahuas after the Conquest. A Social and Cultural History of the Indians of Central Mexico, Sixteenth through Eighteenth Centuries*. Palo Alto, CA: Stanford University Press.

Longyear, John M. 1952. *Copán Ceramics: A Study of Southeastern Maya Pottery*. Washington, DC: Carnegie Institute of Washington.

López, S., Z. Lagunas, and C. Serrano. 1976. *Enterramientos humanos de la zona arqueológica de Cholula, Puebla*. Colección Científica Antropología Física 44. México, DF: Instituto Nacional de Antropología e Historia.

López, S., Z. Lagunas, and C. Serrano. 2002. *Costumbres funerarias y sacrificio humano en Cholula Prehispánica*. México, DF: Instituto de Investigaciones Antropológicas, Universidad Nacional Autónoma de México.

López Austin, A., and L. López Lujan. 2000. "The Myth and Reality of Zuyuá. The Feathered Serpent and Mesoamerican Transformations from the Classic to the Postclassic," trans. Scott Sessions. In *Mesoamerica's Classic Heritage. From Teotihuacan to the Aztecs*, ed. D. Carrasco, L. Jones, and S. Sessions, 21–84. Boulder: University Press of Colorado.

López de Cogolludo, D. 1971. *Los tres siglos de la dominación española en Yucatan, o sea historia de esta Provincia*. Graz, Austria: Akademische Druck-u. Verlagsanstalt.

López Pérez, Claudia, Claudia Nicolás, and Linda Manzanilla. 2006. "Atributos morfológicos y estilísticos de la cerámica Coyotlatelco en el centro ceremonial de Teotihuacan." In *El fenómeno Coyotlatelco en el centro de México: Tiempo, espacio y significado*, ed. Laura Solar Valverde, 216–230. México, DF: Instituto Nacional de Antropología e Historia.

Lucero, Lisa J. 2002. "The Collapse of the Classic Maya: A Case for the Role of Water Control." *American Anthropologist* 104(3): 814–826.

Lucero, Lisa J. 2006. *Water and Ritual: The Rise and Fall of Classic Maya Rulers*. Austin: University of Texas Press.

Lucero, Lisa J., Roland Fletcher, and Robin Coningham. 2015. "From 'Collapse' to Urban Diaspora: The Transformation of Low-Density, Dispersed Agrarian Urbanism." *Antiquity* 89(347): 1139–1154.

Luu, L. B. 2005. *Immigrants and the Industries of London, 1500–1700*. Aldershot, UK: Ashgate Publishing.

Maca, Allan L. 2002. "Spatio-temporal Boundaries in Classic Maya Settlement Systems: Copan's Urban Foothills and the Excavations at Group 9J-5." PhD diss., Harvard University, Cambridge, MA.

Maca, Allan L. 2009. "Ethnographic Analogy and the Archaeological Construction of Maya Identity at Copan, Honduras." In *The Ch'orti' Maya Area: Past and Present*, ed. B. Metz, C. L. McNeil, and K. M. Hull, 90–107. Gainesville: University Press of Florida.

MacKie, E. 1963. "Some Maya Pottery from Grand Bogue Point, Turneffe Islands, British Honduras." Appendix in D. R. Stoddart, "Effects of Hurricane Hattie on the British Honduras Reefs and Cays, October 30–31, 1961." *Atoll Research Bulletin* 95: 131–135.

MacKinnon, J. Jefferson, and Susan M. Kepecs. 1989. "Prehispanic Saltmaking in Belize: New Evidence." *American Antiquity* 54(3): 522–533.

Maggiano, Isabel, Michael Schultz, Horst Kierdorf, Thelma Sierra, Corey Maggiano, and Vera Tiesler. 2008. "Cross-sectional Analysis of Long Bones, Occupational Activities and Long-distance Trade of the Classic Maya from Xcambo. Archaeological and Osteological Evidence." *American Journal of Physical Anthropology* 130: 470–477.

Manahan, T. Kam. 2003. "The Collapse of Complex Society and its Aftermath: A Case Study from the Classic Maya Site of Copán, Honduras." PhD diss., Vanderbilt University, Nashville, TN.

Manahan, T. Kam. 2004. "The Way Things Fall Apart: Social Organization and the Classic Maya Collapse of Copán." *Ancient Mesoamerica* 15(1): 107–125.

Manahan, T. Kam, and Marcello A. Canuto. 2009. "Bracketing the Copán Dynasty: Late Preclassic and Early Postclassic Settlements at Copan, Honduras." *Latin American Antiquity* 20(4): 553–580.

Mansell, Eugenia Brown, Robert H. Tykot, David A. Freidel, Bruce H. Dahlin, and Traci Ardren. 2006. "Early to Terminal Classic Maya Diet in the Northern Lowlands of the Yucatán (Mexico)." In *Histories of Maize: Multidisciplinary Approaches to the Prehistory, Linguistics, Biogeography, Domestication, and Evolution of Maize*, ed. John Staller, Robert Tykot, and Bruce Benz, 173–185. Burlington, MA: Academic Press.

Manzanilla, Linda. 2003. "The Abandonment of Teotihuacan." In *The Archaeology of Settlement Abandonment in Middle America*, ed. Takeshi Inomata and Ronald Webb, 91–102. Salt Lake City: University of Utah Press.

Manzanilla, Linda, ed. 2005a. *Reacomodos demográficos del Clásico al Posclásico en el centro de México*. México, DF: Instituto de Investigaciones Antropológicas, Universidad Nacional Autónoma de México.

Manzanilla, Linda. 2005b. "Migrantes epiclásicos en Teotihuacan. Propuesta metodológica para el análisis de migraciones del Clásico al Posclásico." In *Reacomodos demográficos del Clásico al Posclásico en el centro de México*, ed. Linda Manzanilla, 261–273. México, DF: Instituto de Investigaciones Antropológicas, Universidad Nacional Autónoma de México.

Manzanilla, Linda R. 2015. "Cooperation and Tensions in Multiethnic Corporate Societies Using Teotihuacan, Central Mexico, as a Case Study." *Proceedings of the National Academy of Sciences* 112(30): 9210–9215.

Manzanilla Linda R., ed. 2017. *Multiethnicity and Migration at Teopancazco: Investigations of a Teotihuacan Neighborhood Center*, Gainesville: University Press of Florida.

Manzanilla, Linda R., and Claude Chapdelaine, eds. 2009. *Domestic Life in Prehispanic Capitals: A Study in Specialization, Hierarchy, and Ethnicity*. Memoirs of the Museum of Anthropology, Number 46, Studies in Latin American Ethnohistory and Archaeology, Volume VII (General ed. Joyce Marcus). Ann Arbor: University of Michigan.

Manzanilla, Linda, and Claudia López Pérez. 1998. "Ocupación Coyotlatelco de túneles al este de la Pirámide del Sol en Teotihuacan." In *Antropología e historia del occidente de México: XXIV Mesa Redonda*, Volumen 3, 1611–1627. México, DF: Sociedad Mexicana de Antropología.

Marcus, Joyce. 1976. *Emblem and State in the Classic Maya Lowlands*. Washington, DC: Dumbarton Oaks.

Marfia, A. M., V. Krishnamurthya, E. A. Atekwana, and W. F. Panton. 2004. "Isotopic and Geochemical Evolution of Ground and Surface Waters in a Karst Dominated Geological Setting: A Case Study from Belize, Central America." *Applied Geochemistry* 19: 937–946.

Marken, Damien B. 2011. "City and State: Urbanization, Rural Settlement and Polity in the Classic Maya Lowlands." PhD diss., Southern Methodist University, Dallas, TX.

Márquez, Lourdes, Patricia Hernández, and Almudena Gómez. 2002. "La población urbana de Palenque en el Clásico Tardío." In *La organización social entre los mayas prehispánicos, coloniales y modernos. Memoria de la Tercera Mesa Redonda de Palenque*, Tomo II, ed. Vera Tiesler, Rafael Cobos, and Merle Greene, 13–33. México, DF: Instituto Nacional de Antropología e Historia, Universidad Autónoma de Yucatán.

Martínez González, Roberto. 2010. "La dimensión mítica de la peregrinación Tarasca." *Journal de la Société des Américanistes* 96(1): 39–73.

Masset, Claude. 1973. "La démographie des populations inhumées. Essai de Paléodémographie." *L'Homme* 13(4): 95–131.

Masson, Marilyn A. 1997. "Cultural Transformation at the Maya Postclassic Community of Laguna de On, Belize." *Latin American Antiquity* 8(4): 293–316.

Masson, Marilyn A. 2000. *In the Realm of Naachan Kan*. Boulder: University Press of Colorado.

Masson, Marilyn A. 2002a. "Introduction." In *Ancient Maya Political Economies*, ed. Marilyn A. Masson and David A. Freidel, 1–30. Walnut Creek, CA: Altamira Press.

Masson, Marilyn A. 2002b. "Community Economy and the Mercantile Transformation in Postclassic Northeastern Belize." In *Ancient Maya Political Economies*, ed. Marilyn A. Masson and David A. Freidel, 335–364. Walnut Creek, CA: Altamira Press.

Masson, Marilyn A., and David A. Freidel, eds. 2002. *Ancient Maya Political Economies*. Walnut Creek, CA: Altamira Press.

Masson, Marilyn A., and Carlos Peraza Lope, eds. 2014a. *Kukulcan's Realm: Urban Life at Ancient Mayapán*. Boulder: University Press of Colorado.

Masson, Marilyn A., and Carlos Peraza Lope 2014b. "Militarism, Misery, and Collapse." In *Kukulcan's Realm: Urban Life at Ancient Mayapán*, M. A. Masson and C. Peraza Lope, 521–539. Boulder: University Press of Colorado.

Masson, Marilyn A., and Robert M. Rosenswig. 2005. "Production Characteristics of Postclassic Maya Pottery from Caye Coco, Northern Belize." *Latin American Antiquity* 16(4): 355–384.

Mastache, Alba Guadalupe, and Robert H. Cobean. 1989. "The Coyotlatelco Culture and the Origins of the Toltec State." In *Mesoamerica after the Decline of Teotihuacan, AD 700–900*, ed. Richard Diehl and Janet Berlo, 49–67. Washington, DC: Dumbarton Oaks.

Mastache Alba Guadalupe, Robert H. Cobean, Ángel García Cook, and Kenneth G. Hirth, eds. 2009. *El urbanismo en Mesoamérica / Urbanism in Mesoamerica*, Vol. 2. México, DF: Instituto nacional de antropología e historia; State College, PA: Pennsylvania State University.

Mastache, Alba Guadalupe, Robert H. Cobean, and Dan Healan. 2002. *Ancient Tollan: Tula and the Toltec Heartland*. Boulder: University Press of Colorado.

Mathews, Jennifer P., and Ruben Maldonado Cárdenas. 2006. "Late Formative and Early Classic Interaction Spheres Reflected in the Megalithic Style." In *Lifeways in the Northern Maya Lowlands: New Approaches to Archaeology in the Yucatan Peninsula*, ed. Jennifer Mathews and Bethany Morrison, 95–118. Tucson: University of Arizona Press.

Matos Moctezuma, Eduardo. 1981. *Una visita al Templo Mayor de Tenochtitlan*. México, DF: Instituto Nacional de Antropología e Historia.

Mazakaris-Ainian, Alexandes. 2017. "Κώμη et πόλισ, réflexion sur la formation de la cité dans la Grèce Ancienne." In *Comptes rendus des séances de l'Académie des inscriptions et Belles-lettres*, 21–50. Paris: Académie des inscriptions et belles-lettres.

McAnany, Patricia A. 1990. "Water Storage in the Puuc Region of the Northern Maya Lowlands: A Key to Population Estimates and Architectural Variability." In *Precolumbian Population History in the Maya Lowlands*, ed. T. P. Culbert and D. S. Rice, 263–284. Albuquerque: University of New Mexico Press.

McAnany, Patricia A. 1993. "The Economics of Social Power and Wealth among Eight-Century Maya Households." In *Lowland Maya Civilization in the Eighth Century* AD, ed. J. A. Sabloff and J. S. Henderson, 65–90, Washington, DC: Dumbarton Oaks.

McAnany, Patricia A. 1995. *Living with the Ancestors: Kinship and Kingship in Ancient Maya Society*. Austin: University of Texas Press.

McAnany, Patricia. 2010. *Ancestral Maya Economies in Archaeological Perspective*. Cambridge, UK: Cambridge University Press.

McAnany, Patricia. 2012. "Terminal Classic Maya Heterodoxy and Shrine Vernacularism in the Sibun Valley, Belize." *Cambridge Archaeological Journal* 22(1): 115–134.

McAnany, Patricia, Jeremy Sabloff, Lamoureux-St-Hilaire, and Gyles Iannone. 2016. "Leaving Classic Maya Cities: Agent-Based Modeling and the Dynamics of Diaspora." In *Social Theory in Archaeology and Ancient History*, ed. G. Emberling, 259–290. New York: Cambridge University Press.

McCafferty, Geoffrey. 1994. "The Mixteca-Puebla Stylistic Tradition at Early Postclassic Cholula." In *Mixteca-Puebla: Discoveries and Research in Mesoamerican Art and Archaeology*, ed. H. B. Nicholson and E. Quiñones Keber, 53–77. Culver City, CA: Labyrinthos.

McCafferty, Geoffrey. 1996. "The Ceramics and Chronology of Cholula, Mexico." *Ancient Mesoamerica* 7: 299–323.

McCafferty, Geoffrey. 2000. "Tollan Chollolan and the Legacy of Legitimacy during the Classic-Postclassic Transition." In *Mesoamerica's Classic Heritage: From Teotihuacan to the Aztecs*, ed. D. Carrasco, L. Jones, and S. Sessions, 341–367. Boulder: University Press of Colorado.

McCafferty, Geoffrey. 2001. *Ceramics of Postclassic Cholula, Mexico: Typology and Seriation of Pottery from the UA-1 Domestic Compound*. Monograph 43. Los Angeles: Cotsen Institute of Archaeology, University of California Los Angeles.

McCafferty, Geoffrey. 2007. "Altar Egos: Domestic Ritual and Social Identity in Postclassic Cholula, Mexico." In *Commoner Ritual and Ideology in Ancient Mesoamerica*, ed. N. Gonlin and J. Lohse, 213–250. Boulder: University Press of Colorado.

McIlvaine, Britney Kyle. 2015. "Implications of Reappraising the Iron-Deficiency Anemia Hypothesis." *International Journal of Osteoarchaeology* 25: 997–1000.

McKillop, Heather. 1996. "Ancient Maya Trading Ports and the Integration of Long-Distance and Regional Economies: Wild Cane Cay in South-Coastal Belize." *Ancient Mesoamerica* 7(1): 49–62.

McKillop, Heather. 2002. *Salt: White Gold of the Ancient Maya*. Gainesville: University Press of Florida.

McKillop, Heather. 2009. "The Geopolitics of the Coastal Maya Economy in Southern Belize: Relations between the Coastal and Inland Maya." In *Research Reports in Belizean Archaeology* 6, ed. John Morris, Sherilyne Jones, Jaime Awe, George Thompson, and Christophe Helmke, 55–61. Belmopan, Belize: Institute of Archaeology, National Institute of Culture and History.

McKillop, Heather. 2016. "Coastal Economies: Comparing Northern and Southern Belize." In *Perspectives on the Ancient Maya of Chetumal Bay*, ed. Debra S. Walker, 279–291. Gainesville: University Press of Florida.

McKillop, Heather, and Kazuo Aoyama. 2018. "Salt and Marine Products in the Classic Maya Economy from Use-Wear Study of Stone Tools." *Proceedings of the National Academy of Sciences* 115(43): 10948–10952.

McNeil, Cameron L., David A. Burney, and Lida Pigott Burney. 2010. "Evidence Disputing Deforestation as the Cause for the Collapse of the Ancient Maya Polity of Copan, Honduras." *Proceedings of the National Academy of Sciences* 107(3): 1017–1022.

Medina-Elizade, Martin, Stephen Burns, David W. Lea, Yemane Asmerom, Lucien von Gunten, Victor Polyak, Mathias Vuille, and Ambarish Karmalkar. 2010. "High Resolution Stalagmite Climate Record from the Yucatan Peninsula Spanning the Maya Terminal Classic Period." *Earth and Planetary Science Letters* 10538. (doi: 10.1016 /j.epsl.2010.08.016).

Medina-Elizade, Martin, Stephen Burns, X. Jiang, C. C. Shen, F. Lases-Hernandez, and J. M. Polonco-Martinez. 2015. "High-resolution Stalagmite Record from the Yucatan Peninsula Spanning the Preclassic Period." *Global and Planetary Change* 138: 96–102.

Medrano, Lucy. 2005. "Tratamientos póstumos del cuerpo humano en la tradición funeraria de Xcambó, Yucatán." Licenciatura Thesis, Universidad Autónoma de Yucatán, Mérida, 2005.

Meissner, Nathan J. 2014. "Technological Systems of Small Point Weaponry of the Postclassic Lowland Maya (AD 1400–1697)." PhD diss., Southern Illinois University, Carbondale.

Mendizábal, Miguel O. de. 1926. *El Lienzo de Jucutácato. Su Verdadera Significación*. México, DF: Talleres Gráficos del Museo Nacional de Arqueología, Historia y Etnografía.

Mensforth, R., C. Lovejoy, J. Lallo, and G. Armelagos. 1978. "Part Two: The Role of Constitutional Factors, Diet and Infectious Disease in the Etiology of Porotic Hyperostosis and Periosteal Reactions in Prehistoric Infants and Children." *Medical Anthropology* 2: 1–59.

Messmacher, M. 1967. "Los patrones de asentamiento y la arquitectura en Cholula." In *Cholula: Reporte Preliminar*, ed. M. Messmacher, 6–17. México, DF: Editorial Nueva Antropología.

Metcalfe, Jessica Z., Christine D. White, Fred J. Longstaffe, Gabriel Wrobel, Della Collins Cook, and K. Anne Pyburn. 2009. "Isotopic Evidence for Diet at Chau Hiix, Belize: Testing Regional Models of Hierarchy and Heterarchy." *Latin American Antiquity* 20 (1): 15–36.

Metcalfe, Sarah, Ann Breen, Malcolm Murray, Peter Furley, A. Fallick, A. McKenzie. 2009. "Environmental Change in Northern Belize since the Latest Pleistocene." *Journal of Quaternary Science* 24(6): 627–641.

Michelet, Dominique. 1988. "Apuntes para el análisis de las migraciones en el México Prehispánico." In *Movimientos de población en el Occidente de México*, ed. T. Calvo and G. López Castro, 13–23. México, DF: Centre Français d'Études Mexicaines et Centraméricaines-El Colegio de Michoacán.

Michelet, Dominique. 1989. "Histoire, mythe et apologue: Note de lecture sur la seconde partie de la Relación [. . .] de Michoacán." In *Enquêtes sur l'Amérique moyenne: Mélanges offerts à Guy Stresser-Péan*, ed. Dominique Michelet, 105–112. Etudes Mésoaméricaines. México, DF: Instituto Nacional de Antropología e Historia, Consejo Nacional para la Cultura y las Artes et Centre d'Etudes Mexicaines et Centraméricaines.

Michelet, Dominique. 1992. "El Centro-Norte de Michoacán: características generales de su estudio Regional." In *El Proyecto Michoacán 1983–1987. Medio ambiente e introducción a los trabajos arqueológicos*, ed. D. Michelet, 9–52, México, DF: Centre Français d'Études Mexicaines et Centraméricaines.

Michelet, Dominique. 1998. "Topografía y prospección sistemática de los grandes asentamientos del Malpaís de Zacapu: claves para un acercamiento a las realidades Sociopolíticas." In *Génesis, culturas y espacios en Michoacán*, ed. Véronique Darras, 47–59. México, DF: Centre Français d'Études Mexicaines et Centraméricaines.

Michelet, Dominique. 2000a. "'Yácatas' y otras estructuras ceremoniales tarascas en el Malpaís de Zacapu, Michoacán" In *Arqueología, historia y antropología. In memoriam José Luis Lorenzo Bautista*, ed. J. Litvak and L. Mirambell, 117–137. Colección científica 415, México, DF: Instituto Nacional de Antropología e Historia.

Michelet, Dominique. 2000b. "Tipología de los edificios inventariados en el área de estudio y intentos de Interpretación." In *Mayas del Puuc: Arqueología de la Región de Xculoc, Campeche*, ed. Dominique Michelet, Pierre Becquelin, and Marie-Charlotte Arnauld, 459–480. México, DF: Centre Français d'Études Mexicaines et Centraméricaines.

Michelet, Dominique. 2001. "Northeastern Mexico." In *The Oxford Encyclopedia of Mesoamerican Cultures*, Volume 2, ed. Davíd Carrasco, 375–378. New York: Oxford University Press.

Michelet, Dominique. 2010. "De palabras y piedras: reflexiones en torno a las relaciones entre arqueología e historia en el Michoacán protohistórico, sector de Zacapu." *Istor, Revista de historia Internacional* 40: 27–43. www.istor.cide.edu/istor.html, July 14, 2018.

Michelet, Dominique, and Marie Charlotte Arnauld. 1991. "Les migrations postclassiques au Michoacán et au Guatemala: Problèmes et perspectives." In *Vingt études sur le Mexique et le Guatemala réunies à la mémoire de Nicole Percheron*, ed. A. Breton, J.-P. Berthe, and S. Lecoin, 67–92. Toulouse: Presses Universitaires du Mirail.

Michelet, Dominique, M. Charlotte Arnauld, and Marie-France Fauvet-Berthelot. 1989. "El proyecto del CEMCA en Michoacán. Etapa I: un Balance." *TRACE* 16: 70–87.

Michelet, Dominique, M. Charlotte Arnauld, Philippe Nondédéo, Gregory Pereira, Fabienne de Pierrebourg, and Eric Taladoire. 1998. "La saison de fouilles de 1998 à Balamkú (Campeche, Mexique): des avancées Substantielles." *Journal de la Société des Américanistes* 84(1): 183–199.

Michelet, Dominique, and Pierre Becquelin. 2000. "Hábitat y unidades 'organizativas.'" In *Mayas del Puuc: Arqueología de la Región de Xculoc, Campeche*, ed. Dominique

Michelet, Pierre Becquelin, and Marie-Charlotte Arnauld, 480–497. México, DF: Centre Français d'Études Mexicaines et Centraméricaines.

Michelet, Dominique, Pierre Becquelin and M. Charlotte Arnauld. 2000. *Mayas del Puuc. Arqueología de la región de Xculoc, Campeche*. México, DF: Gobierno del Estado de Campeche, Centre Français d'Etudes Mexicaines et Centraméricaines.

Michelet, Dominique, Alain Ichon, and Gérald Migeon. 1988. "Residencias, barrios y sitios posclásicos en el Malpais de Zacapu." In *Primera reunión sobre les sociedades prehispánicas en el Centro-Occidente de México*, 177–191. Cuaderno de Trabajo 1. Querétaro, México: Instituto Nacional de Antropología e Historia.

Michelet, Dominique, Philippe Nondédéo, Julie Patrois, Céline Gillot, and Emyly González. 2013. "Structure 5N2 (Groupe A): A Río Bec Paradigmatic Palace?" *Ancient Mesoamerica* 24(2): 415–431.

Michelet, Dominique, Grégory Pereira and Gérald Migeon. 2005. "La llegada de los uacusechas a la región de Zacapu, Michoacán: datos arqueológicos y Discusión" In *Reacomodos demográficos del Clásico al Posclásico en el centro de México*, ed. L. Manzanilla, 137–153, México, DF: Universidad Nacional Autónoma de México.

Micklin, Destiny. 2015. "Using Isotope Analysis to Understand the Interaction between Migration and Burial at the Eastern Structure of Group 1 at Actuncan, a Maya Archaeological Site in Belize." Master's Thesis, University of Texas at Arlington.

Migeon, Gérald. 1990. "Archéologie en pays tarasque. Structure de l'habitat et ethnopréhistoire des habitations tarasques de la région de Zacapu (Michoacán, Mexique) au Postclassique Récent." Thèse de doctorat, Université de Paris 1 Panthéon-Sorbonne, Paris.

Migeon, Gérald. 2015. *Residencias y Estructuras Civico-Ceremoniales Posclásicas Tarascas de la Región de Zacapu (Michoacán, México)*. BAR International Series 2729. Oxford, UK: Archaeopress.

Miller, Katherine A. 2015. "Family, 'Foreigners,' and Fictive Kinship: A Bioarchaeological Approach to Social Organization at Late Classic Copan." PhD diss., Arizona State University, Tempe AZ.

Miller Wolf, Katherine A., and Carolyn Freiwald. 2018. "Re-Interpreting Ancient Maya Mobility: A Strontium Isotope Baseline for Western Honduras." *Journal of Archaeological Science* 20: 799–807.

Millon, René. 1988. "The Last Years of Teotihuacan Dominance." In *The Collapse of Ancient States and Civilizations*, ed. Norman Yoffee and George L. Cowgill, 102–164. Tucson: University of Arizona Press.

Mintz, Sidney W., and Richard Price. 1976. *An Anthropological Approach to the Afro-American Past: A Caribbean Perspective*. Occasional Papers in Social Change, Volume 2. Philadelphia, PA: Institute for the Study of Human Issues.

Mitchell, Patricia T. 2006. "The Royal Burials of Buenavista del Cayo and Cahal Pech: Same Lineage, Different Palaces?" MA thesis, San Diego State University, CA.

Mock, Shirley B. 1997. "Monkey Business at the Northern River Lagoon: A Coastal-Inland Interaction Sphere in Northern Belize." *Ancient Mesoamerica* 8(2): 165–183.

Mock, Shirley Boteler, ed. 1998. *The Sowing and the Dawning: Termination, Dedication, and Transformation in the Archaeological and Ethnographic Record of Mesoamerica*. Albuquerque: University of New Mexico Press.

Molloy, J., and W. Rathje. 1974. "Sexploitation among the Late Classic Maya." In *Mesoamerican Archaeology: New Approaches*, ed. N. Hammond, 431–444. Austin: University of Texas Press.

Monnet, Jérôme. 2003. "From Urbanism to Urbanity: A Dialog between Geography and Archaeology about the City." In *El urbanismo en Mesoamérica. Urbanism in Mesoamerica*, Volume 1, ed. W. T. Sanders, A. G. Mastache, and R. H. Cobean, 21–42. México, DF: Instituto Nacional de Antropologia e Historia, and Pennsylvania State University.

Monod Becquelin, Aurore. 2012. "Introduction: La frontière Épaisse." *Ateliers d'Anthropologie* 37. http://ateliers.revues.org/9169. Consulted April 22, 2016.

Montgomery, Janet. 2010. "Passports from the Past. Investigating Human Dispersals Using Strontium Isotope Analysis of Tooth Enamel." *Annual Review of Human Biology* 37: 325–346.

Monzón, Cristina, Hans Roskamp, and J. Benedict Warren. 2009. "La Memoria de Don Melchor Caltzin (1543): Historia y legitimación en Tzintzuntzan, Michoacán." *Estudios de Historia Novohispana* 40: 21–55.

Moragas Segura, Natália. 2013. "Sociedades en colapso: La transición del Clásico al Epiclásico en Teotihuacan." *Diálogo Andino* 41: 185–197.

Morehart, Christopher T., Abigail Meza Peñaloza, Carlos Serrano Sánchez, Emily McClung de Tapia, and Emilio Ibarra Morales. 2012. "Human Sacrifice during the Epiclassic Period in the Northern Basin of Mexico." *Latin American Antiquity* 23(4): 426–448.

Moriarty, M. D. 2012. "History, Politics, and Ceramics: The Ceramic Sequence of Trinidad de Nosotros, El Petén, Guatemala." In *Motul de San José: Politics, History, and Economy in a Classic Maya Polity*, ed. A. Foias and K. F. Emery, 194–228. Gainesville: University Press of Florida.

Morley, S. G. 1913. "Archaeological Research at the Ruins of Chichen Itza, Yucatan." In *Reports upon the Present Condition and Future Needs of the Science of Anthropology*, ed. W. H. R. Rivers, A. E. Jenks, and S. G. Morley, 61–91. Washington, DC: Carnegie Institution of Washington.

Morrissey, James. 2015. "Rethinking 'Causation' and 'Disruption': The Environment-Migration Nexus in Northern Ethiopia." In *Migration and Disruptions: Toward a Unifying Theory of Ancient and Contemporary Migrations*, ed. Brenda J. Baker and Takeyuki Tsuda, 196–222. Gainesville: University Press of Florida.

Motolinía, Fray Toribio de Benavente. 1971. *Memoriales o Libro de las Cosas de la Nueva España y de los naturales de Ella*, ed. Edmundo O' Gorman. México, DF: Universidad Nacional Autónoma de México.

Müller, F. 1970. "La Cerámica de Cholula." In *Proyecto Cholula*, ed. I. Marquina, 129–142. Serie Investigaciones 19. México, DF: Instituto Nacional de Antropología e Historia.

Müller, F. 1973. "La extensión arqueológica de Cholula a través del Tiempo." *Comunicaciones, Proyecto Puebla-Tlaxcala* 8: 19–21.

Müller, F. 1978. *La alfarería de Cholula*. México, DF: Instituto Nacional de Antropología e Historia.

Murata, Satoru. 2011. "Maya Salters, Maya Potters: The Archaeology of Multi-Crafting on Non-Residential Mounds at Wits Cah Ak'al, Belize." PhD diss., Boston University, MA.

Musset, Alain. 2002. *Villes nomades du Nouveau Monde*. Paris: Editions de l'Ecole des Hautes Etudes en Sciences Sociales.

Natahi, Selim. 2014. "Étude des crânes tarasques d'El Palacio, Michoacan, Mexique. Pratique de la déformation crânienne intentionnelle et homogénéité biologique du Groupe." Mémoire de Master 2, PACEA, Université de Bordeaux 1, France.

Navarrete, Federico. 2010. *Los orígenes de los pueblos indígenas del valle de México. Los altépetl y sus Historias*. México, DF: Universidad Nacional Autónoma de México.

Nelson, Ben A., and Steven LeBlanc. 1986. *Short-Term Sedentism in the American Southwest: The Mimbres Valley Salado*. Albuquerque: University of New Mexico Press.

Nelson, Ben A., Adrian S. Z. Chase, and Michelle Hegmon. 2014. "Transformative Relocation in the U.S. Southwest and Mesoamerica." In *The Resilience and Vulnerability of Ancient Landscapes: Transforming Maya Archaeology through IHOPE*, ed. Arlen F. Chase and Vernon L. Scarborough, 171–182. Archaeological Papers of the American Anthropological Association, no. 24. Hoboken, NJ: Wiley.

Nelson, Ben A., and Destiny Crider. 2005. "Posibles Pasajes Migratorios en el Norte de México y el Suroeste de Los Estados Unidos Durante el Epiclásico y el Postclásico." In *Reacomodos demográficos del Clásico al Posclásico en el centro de México*, ed. Linda Manzanilla, 75–102. México, DF: Instituto de Investigaciones Antropológicas, Universidad Nacional Autónoma de México.

Nelson, Margaret Cecile, and Colleen A. Strawhacker, eds. 2011. *Movement, Connectivity, and Landscape Change in the Ancient Southwest*. Boulder: University Press of Colorado.

Netting, R. McC. 1977. "Maya Subsistence: Mythologies, Analogies, Possibilities." In *The Origins of Maya Civilization*, ed. R. E. W. Adams, 299–334. Albuquerque: School of American Research, University of New Mexico Press.

Noguera, E. 1954. *La cerámica arqueológica de Cholula*. México, DF: Editorial Guarania.

Noizet, Hélène. 2007. *La Fabrique de La Ville. Espaces et Sociétés à Tours (IXe–XIIIe Siècle)*. Paris: Histoire Ancienne et Médiévale, Publications de la Sorbonne.

Nondédéo, Philippe, M. Charlotte Arnauld, and Dominique Michelet. 2013a. "Río Bec Settlement Patterns and Local Socio-Political Organization." *Ancient Mesoamerica* 24(2): 373–396.

Nondédéo, Philippe, Alejandro Patiño, Julien Sion, Dominique Michelet, and Carlos Morales-Aguilar. 2013b. "Crisis multiples en Naachtun: aprovechadas, superadas e

Irreversibles." In *Millenary Maya Societies: Past Crises and Resilience/Sociedades mayas milenarias: crisis del pasado y Resiliencia*, ed. M. Charlotte Arnauld and Alain Breton, 122–147. www.mesoweb.com/publications/MMS.

Novotny, Anna. 2015. "Creating Community: Ancient Maya Mortuary Practice at Mid-Level Sites in the Belize River Valley, Belize." PhD diss, Arizona State University, Tempe.

Novotny, Anna C., Jaime J. Awe, Catharina E. Santasilia, and Kelly J. Knudson. 2018. "Ritual Emulation of Ancient Maya Elite Mortuary Traditions during the Classic Period (AD 250–900) at Cahal Pech, Belize." *Latin American Antiquity* 29(4): 1–19.

Noyola, A. 1992. "Unidades habitacionales prehispánicas excavadas en el estado de Puebla." *Notas Mesoamericanas* 14: 19–36.

Okoshi Harada, Tsubasa. 2011. *Codice de Calkini*. México, DF: Universidad Autónoma de México.

Okoshi Harada, Tsubasa. 2012. "Post-Classic Maya 'Barrios' in Yucatan: A Historical Approach." In *The Neighborhood as a Social and Spatial Unit in Mesoamerican Cities*, ed. M. Charlotte Arnauld, Linda R. Manzanilla, and Michael E. Smith, 331–351. Tucson: University of Arizona Press.

Oland, Maxine H., and Marilyn A. Masson. 2005. "Late Postclassic–Colonial Period Maya Settlement on the West Shore of Progresso Lagoon." *Research Reports in Belizean Archaeology* 2: 223–230.

Olivera, M. 1978. *Pillis y macehuales: Las formaciones sociales y los modos de producción de Tecali del siglo XII al XVI*. México, DF: Centro de Investigaciones Superiores del Instituto Nacional de Antropología e Historia, Ediciones de la Casa Chata.

O'Rourke, Dennis, and Jane Enk. 2012. "Genetics, Geography and Human Variation." In *Human Biology: An Evolutionary and Biocultural Perspective*, ed. Sara Stinson, Barry Bogin, and Dennis O'Rourke, 99–142. Hoboken, NJ: Wiley Liss.

Ortega-Muñoz, Allan. 2015. "The Use of Theoretical and Methodological Bases in Population Movements Studies: Paleo- and Archaeo-Demographic Approaches." In *Archaeology and Bioarchaeology of Population Movement among the Prehispanic Maya*, ed. Andrea Cucina, 59–70. New York: Springer.

Ortega-Muñoz, Allan, Andrea Cucina, Vera Tiesler, and Thelma Sierra-Sosa. 2018. "Population and Demographic Shift Along the Coast of Yucatan from the Early to Late Classic: A View from Xcambo, Mexico." *Latin American Antiquity* 29(3): 591–609.

Ortman, Scott G., and Catherine M. Cameron. 2011. "A Framework for Controlled Comparisons of Ancient Southwestern Movement." In *Movement, Connectivity and Landscape Change in the Ancient Southwest*, ed. Margaret Nelson and Colleen Strawhacker, 233–252. Boulder: University Press of Colorado.

Ortner, Donald. 2003. *Identification of Pathological Conditions in Human Skeletal Remains*. Second Edition. San Diego, CA: Academic Press.

Ortner, Donald, Erin Kimmerle, and Melanie Diez. 1999. "Probable Evidence of Scurvy in Subadults from Archaeological Sites in Peru." *American Journal of Physical Anthropology* 108: 321–331.

Ortner, Donald, and Walter G. J. Putschar. 1981. *Identification of Pathological Conditions in Human Skeletal Remains*. Smithsonian Contributions to Anthropology 28. Washington, DC: Smithsonian Institution Press.

Osborne, Robin. 1991. "The Potential Mobility of Human Populations." *Oxford Journal of Archaeology* 10(2): 231–252.

Oxenham, Marc Fredrick, and Ivor Cavill. 2010. "Porotic Hyperostosis and Cribra Orbitalia: The Erythropoietic Response to Iron-Deficiency Anaemia." *Anthropological Science* 118: 199–200.

Paap, Iken. 2017. "Archaeological Fieldwork in the Transitional Zone Between Puuc and Chenes (Campeche, Mexico)." In *Recent Investigations in the Puuc Region of Yucatán*, ed. Meghan Rubenstein, 87–98. Pre-Columbian Archaeology 8. London: Archaeopress.

Paine, Richard R., and AnnCorinne Freter. 1996. "Environmental Degradation and the Classic Maya Collapse at Copan, Honduras (AD 600–1250): Evidence from Studies of Household Survival." *Ancient Mesoamerica* 7(1): 37–47.

Paine, Richard R., AnnCorinne Freter, and David L. Webster. 1996. "A Mathematical Projection of Population Growth in the Copán Valley, Honduras, AD 400–800." *Latin American Antiquity* 7(1): 51–60.

Palka, Joel W. 2005. *Unconquered Lacandon Maya*. Gainesville: University Press of Florida.

Palka, Joel W. 2014. *Maya Pilgrimage to Ritual Landscapes: Insights from Archaeology, History, and Ethnography*. Albuquerque: University of New Mexico Press.

Palkovich, A. 1987. "Endemic Disease Patterns in Paleopathology: Porotic Hyperostosis." *American Journal of Physical Anthropology* 74: 527–537.

Papademetriou, Demetrios G., and Philip L. Martin. 1991. *The Unsettled Relationship: Labor Migration and Economic Development*. New York: Greenwood Press.

Pareyón Moreno, Eduardo. 2013. *El Cerro del Tepalcate*. Compilación de Roberto García Moll. México, DF: Instituto Nacional de Antropología e Historia.

Paris, Elizabeth H. 2008. "Metallurgy, Mayapan, and the Postclassic Mesoamerican World System." *Ancient Mesoamerica* 19(1): 43–66.

Parker, Evan, George J. Bey III, Tomás Gallareta Negrón, Betsy Kohut. 2017. Excavation of a Rural Middle Preclassic Maya Village: Investigations at Paso del Macho, Yucatán, México. Paper presented at the 82nd Annual Meeting of the Society for American Archaeology, Vancouver, British Columbia, April 1.

Parry, William J., and Michael D. Glascock. 2013. "Obsidian Blades from Cerro Portezuelo: Sourcing Artifacts from a Long-Duration Site." *Ancient Mesoamerica* 24: 177–184.

Parsons, Jeffrey R. 1971. *Prehistoric Settlement Patterns in the Texcoco Region, Mexico*. Memoirs of the Museum of Anthropology No. 3. Ann Arbor: University of Michigan.

Parsons, Jeffrey R., Elizabeth Brumfiel, and Mary Hodge. 1996. "Developmental Implications of Earlier Dates for Early Aztec in the Basin of Mexico." *Ancient Mesoamerica* 7(2): 217–230.

Patterson, Erin, and Carolyn Freiwald. 2016. "Migraciones regionales en las Tierras Bajas Centrales: Nuevos valores de isótopos de estroncio en La Corona y El

Perú-Waka'." In *XXVI Simposio de investigaciones arqueológicas en Guatemala*, ed. B. Arroyo, L. Méndez Salinas, and G. Ajú Álvarez, 797–807. Guatemala City: Instituto de Antropología e Historia Asociación Tikal.

Paulsen, Allison. 1976. "Environment and Empire: Climatic Factors in Prehistoric Andean Culture Change." *World Archaeology* 8(2): 121–132.

Paxton, M. 2004. "Tayasal Origin of the Madrid Codex: Further Consideration of the Theory." In *The Madrid Codex: New Approaches to Understanding an Ancient Maya Manuscript*, ed. G. Vail and A. F. Aveni, 89–127. Boulder: University Press of Colorado.

Pendergast, David M. 1981. "Lamanai, Belize: Summary of Excavation Results, 1974–1980." *Journal of Field Archaeology* 8(1): 29–53.

Pendergast, David M. 1982. "Lamanai, Belice, durante el Posclásico." *Estudios de Cultura Maya* XIV: 19–58.

Pendergast, David M. 1986. "Stability through Change: Lamanai, Belize, from the Ninth to the Seventeenth Century." In *Late Lowland Maya Civilization: Classic to Postclassic*, ed. Jeremy A. Sabloff and E. Wyllys Andrews V, 223–249. Albuquerque: University of New Mexico Press/School of American Research.

Pendergast, David M. 1988. *Lamanai Stela 9: The Archaeological Context*. Research Reports on Ancient Maya Writing 20. Washington, DC: Center for Maya Research.

Pendergast, David M. 1989. "The Loving Couple: A Mystery from the Maya Past." *ROM Archaeological Newsletter*, Series II, No. 35.

Pendergast, David M., and Elizabeth Graham. 1991. "The Town beneath the Town: 1991 Excavations at San Pedro, Ambergris Caye, Belize." *Royal Ontario Museum Archaeological Newsletter*, Series II, No. 45: 1–4.

Peniche Rivero, P. 1990. *Sacerdotes y comerciantes: el poder de los mayas e itzaes de Yucatán en los siglos VII a XVI*. México, DF: Fondo de Cultura Económico.

Peraza Lope, Carlos, and Marilyn A. Masson. 2014. "Politics and Monumental Legacies." In *Kukulcan's Realm: Urban Life at Ancient Mayapán*, ed. Marilyn A. Masson and Carlos Peraza Lope, 39–104. Boulder: University Press of Colorado.

Peregrine, Peter N., Ilia Peiros, and Marcus Feldman. 2009. *Ancient Human Migrations: A Multidisciplinary Approach*. Salt Lake City: University of Utah Press.

Pereira, Grégory. 1999. *Potrero de Guadalupe: anthropologie funéraire d'une communauté prétarasque du nord du Michoacán, Mexique*. British Archaeological Reports, International Series 816. Oxford, UK: Archaeopress.

Pereira, Grégory. 2018. "Dinámicas poblacionales y modificación cefálica artificial en el Michoacán Prehispánico." In *Modificaciones cefálicas culturales en Mesoamérica. Una perspectiva Continental*, ed. V. Tiesler and C. Serrano S., 653–683. México, DF: Universidad Nacional Autónoma de México.

Pereira, Grégory. 2020. "Un acercamiento al tratamiento funerario de los niños en el Michoacán Prehispánico." In *Ritos y prácticas funerarias, discursos y representaciones de la muerte. Un acercamiento multidisciplinario e intercultural*, ed. N. Béligand, 95–115. México, DF: Centre Français d'Études Mexicaines et Centraméricaines.

Pereira, Grégory and Marion Forest. 2011. *Informe sobre los trabajos de campo realizados en el sitio El Malpaís Prieto, Michoacán, México: temporada 3 (Febrero-Mayo del 2010)*. Report submitted to the Consejo de Arqueología, México, DF.

Pereira, Grégory, Marion Forest, Dominique Michelet, and Elsa Jadot. 2012. *Proyecto Uacúsecha. Informe sobre los trabajos de campo realizados en el sitio El Malpaís Prieto y otros asentamientos de la región de Zacapu, Michoacán: Temporada 4 (2011–2012)*. Report submitted to the Consejo de Arqueología, México, DF.

Pereira, Grégory, Dominique Michelet, Elsa Jadot, Aurélie Manin, Michelle Elliott, Antoine Dorison, and Marion Forest. 2013. *Informe sobre los trabajos de campo realizados en el sitio El Malpaís Prieto y otros asentamientos de la región de Zacapu, Michoacán: Temporada 5 (2012)*. Report submitted to the Consejo de Arqueología, México, DF.

Pereira, Grégory, Dominique Michelet, and Gérald Migeon. 2013. "La migración de los purépecha hacia el norte y su regreso a los Lagos." *Arqueología Mexicana* XXI(123): 55–60.

Pereira, Grégory, Gérald Migeon, and Dominique Michelet. 2005. "Transformaciones demográficas y culturales en el Centro-Norte de México en vísperas del Posclásico: los sitios del Cerro Barajas (suroeste de Guanajuato)." In *Reacomodos demográficos del Clásico al Posclásico en el centro de México*, ed. Linda Manzanilla, 123–136. México, DF: Universidad Nacional Autónoma de México.

Peterson, P., C. Chao, T. Molitor, M. Murtaugh, F. Strgar, and B. Sharp. 1991. "Stress and Pathogenesis of Infectious Disease." *Reviews of Infectious Disease* 13: 710–720.

Piedrasanta, Ruth, Raúl Monterroso, Ramón Rivas, Oscar Batres, Mario Ardón, Ricardo Zavala, and Luis Pedro Taracena. 2010. *Arquitectura de Remesas*. Ciudad de Guatemala: Centro Cultural de España en Guatemala / Ministerio de Asuntos Exteriores y Cooperación / Agencia Española de Cooperación Internacional para el Desarrollo. http://www.cervantesvirtual.com/obra/arquitectura-de-remesas-2/. Consulted April 22, 2016.

Piehl, Jennifer C. "Performing Identity in an Ancient Maya City: The Archaeology of Houses, Health and Social Differentiation at the Site of Baking Pot, Belize." PhD diss., Tulane University, 2006.

Piña Chan, Román, ed. 1981. *Investigaciones sobre Huamango y Región Vecina*. México, DF: Gobierno del Estado de México.

Plunket, Patricia, and Gabriela Uruñuela. 2005. "Recent Research in Puebla Prehistory." *Journal of Archaeological Research* 13: 89–127.

Plunket, Patricia, and Gabriela Uruñuela. 2006. "Social and Cultural Consequences of a Late Holocene Eruption of Popocatépetl in Central Mexico." *Quaternary International* 15: 19–28.

Plunket, Patricia, and Gabriela Uruñuela. 2008. "Mountain of Sustenance, Mountain of Destruction: The Prehispanic Experience with Popocatépetl Volcano." *Journal of Volcanology and Geothermal Research* 170: 111–120.

Pohl, Mary E. D., and John M. D. Pohl. 1994. "Cycles of Conflict: Political Factionalism in the Maya Lowlands." In *Factional Competition and Political Development in the New*

World, ed. Elizabeth M. Brumfiel and John W. Fox, 138–157. Cambridge: Cambridge University Press.

Pollard, Helen Perlstein. 1993. *Taríacuri's Legacy. The Prehispanic Tarascan State.* Norman: University of Oklahoma Press.

Pollard, Helen Perlstein. 1994. "Ethnicity and Political Control in a Complex Society: The Tarascan State of Prehispanic Mexico." In *Factional Competition and Political Development in the New World*, ed. Elizabeth M. Brumfiel and John W. Fox, 79–88. Cambridge: Cambridge University Press.

Pollard, Helen Perlstein. 2008. "A Model of the Emergence of the Tarascan State." *Ancient Mesoamerica* 19: 217–230.

Porter, Muriel Noé. 1956. "Excavations at Chupícuaro, Guanajuato, Mexico." *Transactions of the American Philosophical Society* 46: 515–637.

Portes, Alejandro, and Robert D. Manning. 1986. "The Immigrant Enclave: Theory and Empirical Examples." In *Competitive Ethnic Relations*, ed. Susan Olzak and Joane Nagel, 47–68. Orlando: Academic Press.

Prem, Hanns J. 2003. "Aspectos de los patrones de asentamiento en la región Puuc central." In *Escondido en la selva: arqueología en el norte de Yucatán*, ed. H. J. Prem, 273–308. México, DF: Instituto Nacional de Antropología e Historia.

Prem, Hanns J., and Nicholas P. Dunning. 2004. "Investigations at Hunto Chac, Yucatan." *Mexicon* 26: 26–36.

Price, T. Douglas, James H. Burton, and R. Alexander Bentley. 2002. "Characterization of Biologically Available Strontium Isotope Ratios for the Study of Prehistoric Migration." *Archaeometry* 44(1): 117–135.

Price, T. Douglas, James H. Burton, Paul Fullagar, Lori E. Wright, Jane E. Buikstra, and Vera Tiesler. 2008. "Strontium Isotopes and the Study of Human Mobility in Ancient Mesoamerica." *Latin American Antiquity* 19(2): 167–180.

Price, T. Douglas., James H. Burton, Paul D. Fullagar, Lori E. Wright, Jane E. Buikstra, and Vera Tiesler. 2015. "Strontium Isotopes and the Study of Human Mobility among the Ancient Maya." In *Archaeology and Bioarchaeology of Population Movement among the Prehispanic Maya*, ed. Andrea Cucina, 119–132. Heidelberg, New York, Dordrecht, London: Springer Briefs in Archaeology, Springer Cham.

Price, T. Douglas, James H. Burton, Robert J. Sharer, Jane E. Buikstra, Lori E. Wright, Loa P. Traxler, and Katherine A. Miller. 2010. "Kings and Commoners at Copán: Isotopic Evidence for Origins and Movement in the Classic Maya Period." *Journal of Anthropological Archaeology* 29(1): 15–32.

Price, T. Douglas, and Hildur Gestsdóttir. 2006. "The First Settlers of Iceland: An Isotopic Approach to Colonization." *Antiquity* 80(307): 130–144.

Price, T. Douglas, Corina Knipper, Gisela Grupe, and Václav Smrcka. 2004. "Strontium Isotopes and Prehistoric Human Migration: The Bell Beaker Period in Central Europe." *European Journal of Archaeology* 7(1): 9–40.

Price, T. Douglas, Linda Manzanilla, and William Middleton. 2000. "Immigration and the Ancient City of Teotihuacan in Mexico: A Study Using Strontium Isotope Ratios in Human Bone and Teeth." *Journal of Archaeological Science* 27(10): 903–913.

Price, T. Douglas, Seiichi Nakamura, Shintaro Suzuki, James H. Burton, and Vera Tiesler. 2014. "New Isotope Data on Maya Mobility and Enclaves at Classic Copan, Honduras." *Journal of Anthropological Archaeology* 36: 32–47.

Price, T. Douglas, Vera Tiesler, William J. Folan, and Robert H. Tykot. 2018. "Calakmul as a Central Place: Isotopic Insights on Urban Maya Mobility and Diet during the First Millennium A.D." *Latin American Antiquity* 29(3): 439–454.

Prowse, Tracy L., Henry P. Schwarcz, Peter Garnsey, Martin Knyf, Roberto Macchiarelli, and Luca Bondioli. 2007. "Isotopic Evidence for Age-Related Immigration to Imperial Rome." *American Journal of Physical Anthropology* 132(4): 510–519.

Puaux, Olivier. 1989. "Les pratiques funéraires tarasques: approche archéologique et Ethnohistorique." PhD diss., Université de Paris 1-Panthéon-Sorbonne.

Pugh, Timothy W. 2001. "Architecture, Ritual, and Social Identity at Late Postclassic Zacpetén, Petén, Guatemala." PhD diss., Southern Illinois University, Carbondale.

Pugh, Timothy W. 2003. "The Exemplary Center of the Late Postclassic Kowoj Maya." *Latin American Antiquity* 14(4): 408–430.

Pugh, Timothy W. 2004. "Activity Areas, Form, and Social Inequality in Residences at Late Postclassic Zacpetén, Petén, Guatemala." *Journal of Field Archaeology* 29(3/4): 351–367.

Pugh, Timothy W. 2009. "The Kowoj and the Lacandon: Migrations and Identities." In *The Kowoj: Identity, Migration, and Geopolitics in Late Postclassic Petén, Guatemala*, ed. Prudence M. Rice and Don S. Rice, 368–384. Boulder: University Press of Colorado.

Pugh, Timothy W., Katherine Miller, Carolyn Freiwald, and Prudence Rice. 2016. "Technologies of Domination at Mission San Bernabé, Petén, Guatemala." *Ancient Mesoamerica* 27(1): 49–70.

Pugh, Timothy W., Jose Romulo Sanchez, and Yuko Shiratori. 2012. "Contact and Missionization at Tayasal, Petén, Guatemala." *Journal of Field Archaeology* 37(1): 3–19.

Pugh, Timothy W., and Yuko Shiratori. 2018. "Postclassic Architectural Traditions and the Petén Itzas." In *Historical and Archaeological Perspectives on the Itzas of Petén, Guatemala*, ed. Prudence M. Rice and Don S. Rice, 227–251. Boulder: University Press of Colorado.

Pumain, Denise. 2004. "An Evolutionary Approach to Settlement Systems." In *New Forms of Urbanization: Beyond the Urban-Rural Dichotomy*, ed. Tony Champion and Graeme Hugo, 231–247. Ashgate, UK: Aldershot.

Quesnel, André. 2009. "De la communauté territoriale à l'organisation familiale en archipel: la mobilité spatiale des familles rurales en Afrique de l'ouest et au Mexique." In *Les mondes de la Mobilité*, ed. Françoise Dureau and Marie-Antoinette Hily, 67–103. Rennes, France: Presses Universitaires de Rennes.

Quezada, Sergio. 2014. *Maya Lords and Lordship: The Formation of Colonial Society in Yucatan, 1350–1600*, trans. Terry Rugley. Norman: University of Oklahoma Press.

Quiñones Keber, E. 1995. *Codex Telleriano-Remensis: Ritual, Divination, and History in a Pictorial Aztec Manuscript.* Austin: University of Texas Press.

Quirk, Joel, and Darshan Vigneswaran. 2015. "Mobility Makes States." In *Mobility Makes States. Migration and Power in Africa*, ed. Darshan Vigneswaran and Joel Quirk, 1–34. Philadelphia: University of Pennsylvania Press.

Ramirez Urrea, Susana. 1996. "La cerámica de la fase Amacueca de la Cuenca de Sayula." *Estudios del Hombre* 3: 81–126.

Ramos, Jorge H. 2010. *Informe de Investigación Preventiva, Fase III, en Propiedad La Pintada.* Report on file at Centro Regional de Investigaciones Arqueológicas, Copán, Honduras.

Rand, Asta J., Paul F. Healy, and Jaime J. Awe. 2015. "Stable Isotopic Evidence of Ancient Maya Diet at Caledonia, Cayo District, Belize." *International Journal of Osteoarchaeology* 25(4): 401–413.

Rattray, Evelyn Childs. 1966. *An Archaeological and Stylistic Study of Coyotlatelco Pottery.* Monographs of the Department of Anthropology, Volume 7–8. México, DF: University of the Americas.

Rattray, Evelyn C. 1987. "Los barrios foráneos de Teotihuacan." In *Teotihuacan: Nuevos Datos, Nuevas Síntesis, Nuevos Problemas*, ed. Emily McClung de Tapia and Evelyn C. Rattray, 243–276. México, DF: Instituto de Investigaciones Antropológicas, Universidad Nacional Autónoma de México.

Rattray, Evelyn C. 1989. "Un taller de bifaciales de obsidiana del periodo Coyotlatelco en la Hacienda Metepec, en Teotihuacan." In *La obsidiana en Mesoamerica*, ed. Margarita Gaxiola González and John E. Clark, 243–252. México, DF: Instituto Nacional de Antropología e Historia.

Rattray, Evelyn C. 1990. "The Identification of Ethnic Affiliation in the Merchants' Barrio, Teotihuacan." In *Etnoarqueología: Primer Coloquio Bosch-Gimpera*, ed. Yoko Sugiura and Mari Carmen Serra, 113–138. México, DF: Universidad Nacional Autónoma de México.

Rattray, Evelyn C. 2001. *Teotihuacan: Ceramics, Chronology, and Cultural Trends.* México, DF: Instituto Nacional de Antropología e Historia and University of Pittsburgh.

Renfrew, Colin. 2002. "'The Emerging Synthesis'. The Archaeogenetics of Farming/Language Dispersals and Other Spread Zones." In *Examining the Farming/Language Dispersal Hypothesis*, ed. Peter Bellwood and Colin Renfrew, 3–16. McDonald Institute Monographs. Cambridge, UK: University of Cambridge.

Restall, Matthew. 1997. *The Maya World: Yucatec Culture and Society 1550–1850.* Palo Alto, CA: Stanford University Press.

Reyes García, Luis. 1988a. *Cuauhtinchan del Siglo XII al XVI: Formación y desarrollo histórico de un señorío Prehispánico.* Second edition. México, DF: Centro de Investigaciones y Estudios Superiores en Antropología Social.

Reyes García, Luis. 1988b. *Documentos sobre tierras y señoríos en Cuauhtinchan.* Second edition. México, DF: Centro de Investigaciones y Estudios Superiores en Antropología Social.

Rice, Don S. 1986. "The Peten Postclassic: A Settlement Perspective." In *Late Lowland Maya Civilization: Classic to Postclassic*, ed. J. A. Sabloff and E. W. Andrews V, 301–346. Albuquerque: University of New Mexico Press.

Rice, Don S., and Prudence M. Rice. 1990. "Population Size and Population Change in the Central Peten Lakes Region, Guatemala." In *Precolumbian Population History in the Maya Lowlands*, ed. T. P. Culbert and Don S. Rice, 123–148. Albuquerque: University of New Mexico Press.

Rice, Don S., Prudence M. Rice, and Timothy Pugh. 1998. "Settlement Continuity and Change in the Central Peten Lakes Region: The Case of Zacpeten." In *Anatomía de una civilización: Aproximaciones interdisciplinarias a la cultura Maya*, ed. A. Ciudad Ruiz, F. Marquinez, J.M. Garcia Campillo, M.J. Iglesias Ponce de León, A. Lacadena García-Gallo, and L.T. Sanz Castro, 207–252. Madrid: Sociedad Española de Estudios Mayas.

Rice, Prudence M. 1987. *Pottery Analysis: A Sourcebook*. Chicago, IL: University of Chicago Press.

Rice, Prudence M. 2004. *Maya Political Science: Time, Astronomy, and the Cosmos*. Austin: University of Texas Press.

Rice, Prudence M. 2009. "Mound ZZ1, Nixtun-Ch'ich', Petén, Guatemala: Rescue Operations at a Long-Lived Structure in the Maya Lowlands." *Journal of Field Archaeology* 34(4): 403–422.

Rice, Prudence M. 2017. "Visualizing Tayza, Capital of the Petén Itzas: Teasing 'Meanings' from Postclassic Pottery Styles." *Latin American Antiquity* 28(3): 177–95.

Rice, Prudence M. 2018a. "The Archaeology of Tayza." In *Historical and Archaeological Perspectives on the Itzas of Petén, Guatemala*, ed. Prudence M. Rice and Don S. Rice, 310–339. Boulder: University Press of Colorado.

Rice, Prudence M. 2018b. "Itza Origins: Texts, Myths, Legends." In *Historical and Archaeological Perspectives on the Itzas of Petén, Guatemala*, ed. Prudence M. Rice and Don S. Rice, 77–96. Boulder: University Press of Colorado.

Rice, Prudence M. 2018c. "Lowland Maya Epiclassic Migrations." In *Historical and Archaeological Perspectives on the Itzas of Petén, Guatemala*, ed. Prudence M. Rice and Don S. Rice, 97–113. Boulder: University Press of Colorado.

Rice, Prudence M. 2018d. "Styles and Motifs: Decorated Pottery of the Itzas at Tayza." *Historical and Archaeological Perspectives on the Itzas of Petén, Guatemala*, ed. Prudence M. Rice and Don S. Rice, 340–374. Boulder: University Press of Colorado.

Rice, Prudence M. 2020. "Terminal Classic Interactions between the Western Petén Lakes Chain and the Western Lowlands." In *The Nuts and Bolts of the Real "Business" of Ancient Maya Exchange*, ed. Marilyn A. Masson, David A. Freidel, and Arthur A. Demarest, 434–450. Gainesville: University Press of Florida.

Rice, Prudence M., and Leslie G. Cecil. 2018. "Postclassic Pottery and Identities." In *Historical and Archaeological Perspectives on the Itzas of Petén, Guatemala*, ed. Prudence M. Rice and Don S. Rice, 205–226. Boulder: University Press of Colorado.

Rice, Prudence M., and Don S. Rice, eds. 2009. *The Kowoj: Identity, Migration, and Geo-politics in Late Postclassic Petén, Guatemala*. Boulder: University Press of Colorado.

Rice, Prudence M., and Don S. Rice, eds. 2016. *Ixlú: A Contested Maya Entrepôt in Petén, Guatemala*. Latin American Archaeological Reports, Center for Comparative Archaeology. Pittsburgh, PA: University of Pittsburgh.

Rice, Prudence M., and Don S. Rice. 2018. "Classic-to-Contact-Period Continuities in Maya Governance in Central Petén, Guatemala." *Ethnohistory* 65(1):25–50.

Richards, Michael, Katerina Harvati, Vaughan Grimes, Colin Smith, Tanya Smith, Jean-Jacques Hublin, Panagiotis Karkanas, and Eleni Panagopoulou. 2008. "Strontium Isotope Evidence of Neanderthal Mobility at the Site of Lakonis, Greece Using Laser-Ablation PIMMS." *Journal of Archaeological Science* 35(5): 1251–1256.

Richards-Rissetto, Heather M. 2010. "Exploring Social Interaction at the Ancient Maya City of Copan, Honduras: A Multi-Scalar Geographic Information Systems (GIS) Analysis of Access and Visibility." PhD diss., University of New Mexico, Albuquerque.

Richards-Rissetto, Heather M., and Kristin Landau. 2014. "Movement as a Means of Social (Re)production: Using GIS to Measure Social Integration across Urban Landscapes." *Journal of Archaeological Science* 41: 365–375.

Rico-Gray, V. and J. G. García-Franco. 1991. "The Maya and the Vegetation of the Yucatan Peninsula." *Journal of Ethnobiology* 11(1): 135–142.

Ringle, William M. 2011. The Yaxhom Valley Survey: Pioneers of the Puuc Hills, Yucatan. Report to the National Geographic Society on Research Award 8913–11. Washington, DC: National Geographic Society.

Ringle, William M. 2012. "The Nunnery Quadrangle of Uxmal." In *The Ancient Maya of Mexico: Reinterpreting the Past of the Northern Maya Lowlands*, ed. G. Braswell, 191–227. Sheffield, UK: Equinox.

Ringle, William M., and George J. Bey III. 2009. "The Face of the Itzas." In *The Art of Urbanism: How Mesoamerican Kingdoms Represented Themselves in Architecture and Imagery*, ed. William L. Fash and Leonardo López Luján, 329–383. Washington, DC: Dumbarton Oaks Research Library and Collection, Trustees for Harvard University.

Ringle, William M., Tomas Gallareta Negron, and George J. Bey III. 1998. "The Return of Quetzalcoatl: Evidence for the Spread of a World Religion during the Epiclassic Period." *Ancient Mesoamerica* 9(2): 183–232.

Rivera Dorado, Miguel. 1996. *Los Mayas de Oxkintok*. Madrid: Ministerio de Educación y Cultura.

Rivera Villanueva, José Antonio and Claudia Serafina Berumen Félix. 2011. *Documentos de los Tlaxcaltecas en la Nueva Galicia, Siglos XVI-XVIII*. San Luís Potosí: Gobierno del Estado de Tlaxcala, Fideicomiso Colegio de Historia de Tlaxcala, El Colegio de San Luís.

Roberts, C., and K. Manchester. 1997. *The Archaeology of Disease*. New York: Cornell University Press.

Robinson, David J. 1981. "Indian Migration in Eighteenth Century Yucatan: The Open Nature of the Closed Corporate Community." In *Studies in Spanish American Population History*, ed. David J. Robinson, 149–173. Dellplain Latin American Studies No. 8. Boulder, CO: Westview Press.

Robles C., Fernando, and Anthony P. Andrews. 1986. "A Review and Synthesis of Recent Postclassic Archaeology in Northern Yucatan." In *Late Lowland Maya Civilization, Classic to Postclassic*, ed. J. A. Sabloff and E. W. Andrews V, 53–98. Santa Fe, NM: School of American Research, and Albuquerque: University of New Mexico Press.

Rogers, Andrei, and Luis J. Castro. 1981. "Age Patterns of Migration: Cause-Specific Profiles." *Research Reports, International Institute for Applied Systems Analysis* RR-81-6: 125–159.

Rogers, Andrei, and Luis J. Castro. 1984. "Model Migration Schedules." In *Migration, Urbanization, and Spatial Population Dynamics*, ed. A. Rogers, L. Castro, and N. Keyfitzet, 41–91. Boulder: Westview Press.

Rogers, Andrei, Luis J. Castro, and N. Keyfitzet, eds. 1984. *Migration, Urbanization, and Spatial Population Dynamics*. Boulder, CO: Westview Press.

Rogers, Andrei., R. Raquillet, and Luis J. Castro. 1978. "Model Migration Schedules and their Applications." *Environment and Planning A* 10(5): 475–502.

Rojas, Gabriel de. 1985. "Relación de Cholula." In *Relaciones Geográficas del Siglo XVI: Tlaxcala*, Vol. 2, ed. R. Acuña, 123–145. México, DF: Universidad Nacional Autónoma de México.

Romano, Arturo 1973. "Deformación cefálica intencional en la población prehispánica de Cholula, Pue." *Comunicaciones, Proyecto Puebla-Tlaxcala* 8:49–50.

Romano, Arturo 1974. "Deformación cefálica intencional." In *Antropología Física, Época prehispánica. México, panorama histórico y cultural III*, ed. Juan Comas, 197–227. México, DF: Instituto Nacional de Antropología e Historia.

Roskamp, Hans. 1998. *La Historiografía Indígena de Michoacán: El Lienzo de Jucutácato y los Títulos de Carapan*. School of Asian, African, and Amerindian Studies. Leiden, Netherlands: Research School Centre of Non-Western Studies.

Roskamp, Hans. 2003. *Los Códices de Cutzio y Huetamo. Encomienda y Tributo en la Tierra Caliente de Michoacán, Siglo XVI*. Zamora, México: Colegio de Michoacán, Colegio Mexiquense.

Roskamp, Hans. 2010. "Los Nahuas de Tzintzuntzan-Huitzitzilan, Michoacán. Historia, mito, y legitimación de un señorío Prehispánico." *Journal de la Société des Américanistes* 96(1): 75–106.

Roskamp, Hans, and Mario Rétiz. 2013 "An Interdisciplinary Survey of a Copper-Smelting Site in West Mexico: The Case of Jicalán el Viejo, Michoacán." In *Archaeometallurgy in Mesoamerica: Current Approaches and New Perspectives*, ed. A. N. Shugar and S. E. Simmons, 29–50. Boulder: University Press of Colorado.

Roys, Ralph L. 1943. *The Indian Background of Colonial Yucatan*. Carnegie Institution of Washington Publication 548. Washington, DC: Carnegie Institute of Washington.

Roys, Ralph L. 1962. "Literary Sources for the History of Mayapan." In *Mayapan, Yucatan, Mexico*, ed. H.E.D. Pollock, R. L. Roys, T. Proskouriakoff, and A. L. Smith, 25–96. Washington, DC: Carnegie Institute of Washington.

Roys, Ralph L. 1967. *The Book of Chilam Balam of Chumayel*. Norman: University of Oklahoma Press.

Rue, David. 1986. "A Palynological Analysis of Prehispanic Human Impact in the Copán Valley, Honduras." PhD diss., Pennsylvania State University, State College, PA.

Ruhl, Thomas, Nicholas P. Dunning, and Christopher Carr. 2018. "LiDAR Reveals Possible Network of Ancient Maya Marketplaces in Southern Campeche, Mexico." *Mexicon* 40: 83–91.

Rushton, Elizabeth A., Sarah E. Metcalfe, and Bronwen S. Whitney. 2013. "A Late-Holocene Vegetation History from the Maya Lowlands, Lamanai, Northern Belize." *The Holocene* 23: 485–493.

Ruz, Mario Humberto, J. Garcia Targa, and Andres Ciudad R., eds. 2009. *Diasporas, migraciones y exilios en el mundo Maya*. Madrid: Sociedad Española de Estudios Mayas, and Mérida: Universidad Nacional Autónoma de México.

Sabloff, J. A. 1973. "Major Themes in the Past Hypotheses of the Maya Collapse." In *The Classic Maya Collapse*, ed. T. P. Culbert, 35–40. Santa Fe, NM: School of American Research and University of New Mexico Press.

Sahagún, Fray Bernardino de. 1950–1969. *General History of the Things of New Spain: Florentine Codex*. Trans. A. Anderson and C. Dibble. Salt Lake City: University of Utah Press.

Sanders, William T. 2006. "Late Xolalpan-Metepec/Oxtotipac-Coyotlatelco; Ethnic Succession or Changing Patterns of Political Economy: A Reevaluation." In *El fenómeno Coyotlatelco en el centro de México: Tiempo, espacio y significado*, ed. Laura Solar Valverde, 183–200. México, DF: Instituto Nacional de Antropología e Historia.

Sanders, William T., Alba Guadalupe Mastache, and Robert H. Cobean, eds. 2003. *El urbanismo en Mesoamérica/Urbanism in Mesoamerica*, Volumen 1. University Park: Instituto Nacional de antropología e Historia, Pennsylvania State University.

Sanders, William T., Jeffrey R. Parsons, and Robert S. Santley. 1979. *The Basin of Mexico: Ecological Processes in the Evolution of a Civilization*. New York: Academic Press.

Sanders, William T., and David Webster. 1988. "The Mesoamerican Urban Tradition." *American Anthropologist* 90(3): 521–546.

Santley, Robert S. 1989. "Obsidian Working, Long-Distance Exchange, and the Teotihuacan Presence on the South Gulf Coast." In *Mesoamerica after the Decline of Teotihuacan, AD 700–900*, ed. Richard A. Diehl and Janet Catherine Berlo, 131–152. Washington, DC: Dumbarton Oaks.

Sapignoli, Maria. 2014. "Mobility, Land Use, and Leadership in Small-Scale and Middle-Range Societies." *Reviews in Anthropology* 43(1): 35–78.

Sattenspiel, Lisa, and Henry Harpending. 1983. "Stable Populations and Skeletal Age." *American Antiquity* 48: 489–498.

Saturno, William Andrew. 2000. "In the Shadow of the Acropolis: Rio Amarillo and its Role in the Copan Polity." PhD diss., Harvard University, Cambridge, MA.

Scarborough, Vernon L., and William R. Burnside. 2010. "Complexity and Sustainability: Perspectives from the Ancient Maya and the Modern Balinese." *American Antiquity* 75(2): 329–334.

Schachner, Gregory. 2012. *Population Circulation and the Transformation of Ancient Zuni Communities*. Tucson: University of Arizona Press.

Schele, Linda, and Peter Mathews. 1998. *The Code of Kings. The Language of Seven Sacred Maya Temples and Tombs*. New York: Scribner.

Scherer, Andrew K. 2004. "Dental Analysis of Classic Period Population Variability in the Maya Area." PhD diss., Texas A & M University, College Station, TX.

Scherer, Andrew K. 2007. "Population Structure of the Classic Period Maya." *American Journal of Physical Anthropology* 132: 367–380.

Scherer, Andrew K., Alyce de Carteret, and Sarah Newman. 2014. "Local Water Resource Variability and Oxygen Isotopic Reconstructions of Mobility: A Case Study from the Maya Area." *Journal of Archaeological Science* 2: 666–676.

Scherer, Andrew K., and Lori E. Wright. 2015. "Dental Morphometric and Strontium Isotope Evidence for Population History at Tikal, Guatemala." In *Archaeology and Bioarchaeology of Population Movement among the Prehispanic Maya*, ed. Andrea Cucina, 109–118. New York: Springer.

Schiffer, Michael Brian. 1975. "Archaeology as Behavioral Science." *American Anthropologist* 77: 836–848.

Schiffer, Michael Brian. 1987. *Formation Processes of the Archaeological Record*. Albuquerque: University of New Mexico Press.

Schmidt, Peter J. 2010. "Chichen antes de los Itza." In *XXIII Simposio de Investigaciones Arqueológicas en Guatemala, 2009*, ed. Bárbara Arroyo, A. Linares, and Lorena Paiz. Guatemala City: Museo Nacional de Arqueología e Etnología, Ministerio de Cultura y Deportes, and Instituto de Antropología e Historia.

Scholes, France V., and Ralph L. Roys. 1968. *The Maya Chontal Indians of Acalan-Tixchel*. Second edition. Norman: University of Oklahoma Press.

Schortman, Edward. 1986. "Interaction between Maya and non-Maya along the Late Classic Southeast Maya Periphery." In *The Southeast Maya Periphery*, ed. Patricia Urban and Edward Schortman, 114–137. Austin: University of Texas Press.

Schwake, Sonja A. 2008. "The Social Implications of Ritual Behavior in the Maya Lowlands: A Perspective from Minanha, Belize." PhD diss., University of California, San Diego.

Schwartz, N. 1990. *Forest Society: A Social History of Petén, Guatemala*. Philadelphia: University of Pennsylvania Press.

Schwarz, K. R. 2009. "Eckixil: Understanding the Classic to Postclassic Survival and Transformation of a Peten Maya Village." *Latin American Antiquity* 20(3):413–441.

Scott, Richard G., and Christy G. Turner. 1997. *The Anthropology of Modern Human Teeth: Dental Morphology and its Variation in Recent Human Populations*. Cambridge Studies in Biological Anthropology. Cambridge, UK: Cambridge University Press.

Séguy, Isabelle, and Luc Buchet. 2011. *Manuel de Paléodémographie*. Editions Institut National des Etudes Démographiques. Paris: Les Manuels.

Seler, Eduard. 2000 [1905]. "Los antiguos habitantes de Michoacán." In *Relación de Michoacán*, ed. M. Franco Mendoza, 147–233. Zamora, México: Colegio de Michoacán, Gobierno del Estado de Michoacán.

Sellet, Frederic, Russel Greaves, and Pei-Lin Yu. 2006. *Archaeology and Ethnoarchaeology of Mobility*. Gainesville: University Press of Florida.

Sellier, Pascal. 2011. "Tous les morts? Regroupement et sélection des inhumés: les deux pôles du 'recrutement Funéraire.'" In *Le regroupement des morts. Genèse et diversité Archéologique*, ed. D. Castex, P. Courtaud, H. Duday, F. Le Mort, and A.-M. Tillier, 83–94. Bordeaux, France: Maison des Sciences de l'Homme d'Aquitaine/Ausonius.

Serrano, Carlos, Marta Pimienta, and Alfonso Gallardo. 1993. "Mutilación dentaria y filiación étnica en los entierros del Templo de Quetzalcoatl, Teotihuacan." In *II Coloquio Bosch-Gimpera*, ed. María Teresa Cabrero, 263–276. México, DF: Universidad Nacional Autónoma de México.

Shami, Seteney. 1993. "The Social Implications of Population Displacement and Resettlement: An Overview with a Focus on the Arab Middle East." *International Migration Review* 27: 4–33.

Sharer, Robert J. 1977. "The Maya Collapse Revisited: Internal and External Perspectives." In *Social Process in Maya Prehistory. Studies in Honour of Sir Eric Thompson*, ed. N. Hammond, 531–552. London: Academic Press.

Sharer, Robert J. 1985. "Terminal Events in the Southeastern Lowlands: A View from Quirigua." In *The Lowland Maya Postclassic*, ed. Arlen F. Chase and Prudence M. Rice, 245–253. Austin: University of Texas Press.

Sharer, Robert J., David W. Sedat, Loa P. Traxler, Julia C. Miller, and Ellen E. Bell. 2005. "Early Classic Royal Power in Copán: The Origins and Development of the Acropolis (ca. AD 250–600)." In *Copán: The History of an Ancient Maya Kingdom*, ed. E. W. Andrews and W. L. Fash, 139–199. Santa Fe, NM: School of American Research Press.

Shaw, Justine M., and Dave Johnstone. 2006. "El papel de la arquitectura postmonumental en el norte de Yucatán." *Los Investigadores de la Cultura Maya* 14: 267–278.

Shiratori, Yuko. 2014. Constructing Social Identity through the Past: Migration Myths and Exchange Systems of the Contact Period Itza. Paper presented at the Chacmool Conference, Calgary, Alberta.

Sierra Sosa, Thelma. 1999a. "Xcambó: Codiciado enclave económico del Clásico Maya." *Arqueología Mexicana* 37: 40–47.

Sierra Sosa, Thelma. 1999b. "Xcambó: Codiciado puerto del clásico Maya." *I'Inaj Semilla de Maíz* 10: 19–27.

Sierra Sosa, Thelma. 2004. "La arqueología de Xcambó, Yucatán, centro administrativo salinero y puerto comercial de importancia regional durante el Clásico." PhD diss., Universidad Nacional Autónoma de México.

Sierra Sosa, Thelma, Andrea Cucina, T. Douglas Price, James Burton, and Vera Tiesler. 2014. "Maya Coastal Production, Exchange, and Population Mobility. A View from the Classic Period Port of Xcambó, Yucatán, México." *Ancient Mesoamerica* 25: 221–238.

Silverstein, Jay. 2001. "Aztec Imperialism at Oztuma, Guerrero. Aztec-Chontal Relations during the Late Postclassic and Early Colonial periods." *Ancient Mesoamerica* 12: 31–48.

Simmons, Scott E. 2005. "Investigations in the Church Zone. Maya Archaeometallurgy at Spanish Colonial Lamanai, Belize." In *Research Reports in Belizean Archaeology* 2, ed. Jaime Awe, John Morris, Sherilyne Jones, and Christophe Helmke, 231–239. Belmopan, Belize: Institute of Archaeology, National Institute of Culture and History.

Simmons, S. E., and E. Graham. 2017. "Maya Coastal Adaptations in Classic and Postclassic Times on Ambergris Caye, Belize." In *Trading Spaces: The Archaeology of Interaction, Migration and Exchange*, ed. M. Patton and J. Manion, 167–180. Proceedings of the 46th Annual Chacmool Conference, Chacmool Archaeology Association. Calgary, Canada: University of Calgary.

Simmons, Scott E., David M. Pendergast, and Elizabeth Graham. 2009. "The Context and Significance of Copper Artifacts in Postclassic and Early Historic Lamanai, Belize." *Journal of Field Archaeology* 34(1): 57–75.

Simmons, Scott E., and A. N. Shugar. 2013. "Maya Metallurgical Technology in Late Postclassic-Spanish Colonial Times: The View from Lamanai, Belize." *ArcheoSciences* 1: 105–123.

Simms, Stephanie R., Evan Parker, George Bey III, and Tomas Gallareta Negrón. 2012. "Evidence from Escalera al Cielo: Abandonment of a Terminal Classic Puuc Maya Hill Complex in Yucatan, Mexico." *Journal of Field Archaeology* 37: 270–288.

Sion, Julien. 2016. "La caractérisation socio-économique des élites mayas au Classique terminal (830–950 apr. J.C.): le Groupe B-Sud de Naachtun (Guatemala)." PhD diss., Université de Paris 1 Panthéon-Sorbonne.

Skibo, James M. 1992. *Pottery Function: A Use-Alteration Perspective.* New York: Plenum Press.

Skinner, M., and A. Goodman. 1992. "Anthropological Uses of Developmental Defects of Enamel." In *Skeletal Biology of Past Peoples: Advances in Research Methods*, ed. S. Saunders and M. Katzenberg, 153–174. New York: Wiley-Liss.

Slovak, Nicole M., and Adina Paytan. 2011. "Applications of Sr Isotopes in Archaeology." *Advances in Isotopic Geochemistry* 5: 743–768.

Smith, Carol A. 1982. "Modern and Premodern Urban Primacy." *Comparative Urban Research* 9: 79–96.

Smith, Michael E. 1984. "The Aztlan Migrations of the Nahuatl Chronicles: Myth or History?" *Ethnohistory* 31(3): 153–186.

Smith, Michael E. 1990. "Long-Distance Trade under the Aztec Empire." *Ancient Meso-america* 1: 153–169.

Smith, Michael E. 1992. "Braudel's Temporal Rhythms and Chronology Theory in Archaeology." In *Archaeology, Annales, and Ethnohistory*, ed. A. B. Knapp, 23–34. Cambridge, UK: Cambridge University Press.

Smith, Michael. E. 2004. "The Archaeology of Ancient State Economies." *Annual Review of Anthropology* 33: 73–102.

Smith, Michael E. 2007. "Form and Meaning in the Earliest Cities: A New Approach to Ancient Urban Planning." *Journal of Planning History* 6: 3–47.

Smith, Michael. E. 2008a. *Aztec City-State Capitals*. Gainesville: University Press of Florida.

Smith, Michael E. 2008b. Ancient Cities: Do They Hold Lessons for the Modern World? Paper presented at the 73rd Annual Meeting of the Society for American Archaeology, Vancouver, British Columbia, Canada, March 25–30.

Smith, Michael E. 2010a. "Sprawl, Squatters and Sustainable Cities: Can Archaeological Data Shed Light on Modern Urban Issues?" *Cambridge Archaeological Journal* 20(2): 229–253.

Smith, Michael E. 2010b. "The Archaeological Study of Neighborhoods and Districts in Ancient Cities." *Journal of Anthropological Archaeology* 29: 137–154.

Smith, Michael E. 2011. "Tula and Chichén Itzá: Are We Asking the Right Questions?" In *Twin Tollans: Chichén Itzá, Tula, and the Epiclassic to Early Postclassic Mesoamerican World*, rev. ed., ed. J. K. Kowalski and C. Kristan-Graham, 469–499. Washington, DC: Dumbarton Oaks.

Smith, Michael E. 2014. "Peasant Mobility, Local Migration and Premodern Urbanization." *World Archaeology* 46(4): 516–533.

Smith, Michael E., and Frances F. Berdan. 1992. "Archaeology and the Aztec Empire." *World Archaeology* 23: 353–367.

Smith, Michael E., and Frances F. Berdan. 2003. "Postclassic Mesoamerica." In *The Postclassic Mesoamerican World*, ed. Michael E. Smith and Frances F. Berdan, 3–13. Salt Lake City: University of Utah Press.

Smith, Michael E., and Michael D. Lind. 2005. "Xoo-Phase Ceramics from Oaxaca found at Calixtlahuaca in Central Mexico." *Ancient Mesoamerica* 16: 169–177.

Smith, Monica L., ed. 2003. *The Social Construction of Ancient Cities*. Washington, DC: Smithsonian Institution Press.

Smith, Monica L. 2014. "The Archaeology of Urban Landscapes." *Annual Review of Anthropology* 43: 307–323.

Smyth, Michael P. 1998. "Before the Florescence: Chronological Reconstructions at Chac II, Yucatan, Mexico." *Ancient Mesoamerica* 9: 137–150.

Smyth, Michael P., Christopher Dore, and Nicholas P. Dunning. 1995. "Interpreting Prehistoric Settlement Patterns: Lessons from the Maya Center of Sayil, Yucatan." *Journal of Field Archaeology* 22: 321–347.

Smyth, Michael, Nicholas P. Dunning, Eric Weaver, Philip van Beynen, and David Ortegón Zapata. 2017. "The Perfect Storm: Climate Change and Settlement Response in the Puuc Hills Region of Yucatan." *Antiquity* 91: 490–509.

Smyth, Michael P., and David Ortegón Zapata. 2008. "A Preclassic Center in the Puuc Region: A Report on Xcoch, Yucatan, Mexico." *Mexicon* 30: 63–68.

Smyth, Michael P., David Ortegón Zapata, Nicholas P. Dunning, and Eric Weaver. 2014. "Settlement Dynamics, Climate Change, and Human Response at Xcoch in the Puuc Region, Yucatan, Mexico." In *The Archaeology of Yucatan: New Directions and Data*, ed. T. W. Stanton, 45–64. British Archaeological Reports, International Series. Oxford, UK: Archaeopress.

Snead, James E., Clark L. Erickson, and J. Andrew Darling, eds. 2011. *Landscapes of Movement: Trails, Paths, and Roads in Anthropological Perspective*. Philadelphia, PA: Pennsylvania Museum Press and the University of Pennsylvania Press.

Solar Valverde, Laura, ed. 2006. *El Fenómeno Coyotlatelco en el Centro de México: Tiempo, Espacio y Significado*. México, DF: Coordinación Nacional de Arqueología, Instituto Nacional de Antropología e Historia.

Somerville, Andrew D., Mikael Fauvelle, and Andrew W. Froehle. 2013. "Applying New Approaches to Modeling Diet and Status: Isotopic Evidence for Commoner Resiliency and Elite Variability in the Classic Maya Lowlands." *Journal of Archaeological Science* 40(3): 1539–1553.

Somerville, Andrew D., Margaret J. Schoeninger, and Geoffrey E. Braswell. 2016. "Political Alliance, Residential Mobility, and Diet at the Ancient Maya City of Pusilha, Belize." *Journal of Anthropological Archaeology* 41: 147–158.

Soza, J. M. 1970. *Monografía del departamento de El Petén*, Vol. II. Second edition. Ciudad de Guatemala: Editorial José de Pineda Ibarra.

Spence, Michael W. 1981. "Obsidian Production and the State in Teotihuacan." *American Antiquity* 46(4): 769–788.

Spence, Michael W. 1992. "Tlailotlacan, a Zapotec Enclave in Teotihuacan." In *Art, Ideology, and the City of Teotihuacan*, ed. Janet Berlo, 59–88. Washington, DC: Dumbarton Oaks.

Spence, Michael W. 1996. "A Comparative Analysis of Ethnic Enclaves." In *Arqueología Mesoamericana, Homenaje a William T. Sanders*, Volúmen I, ed. Alba Guadalupe Mastache, Jeffrey R. Parsons, Robert S. Santley, and Mari Carmen Serra Puche, 333–354. México, DF: Instituto Nacional de Antropología e Historia.

Spence, Michael W. 2005. "A Zapotec Diaspora Network in Classic-Period Central Mexico." In *The Archaeology of Colonial Encounters: Comparative Perspectives*, ed. Gil J. Stein, 173–205. Santa Fe, NM: School of American Research Press.

Spence, Michael W., Christine D. White, Robert H. Cobean, Alba Guadalupe Mastache, and Fred J. Longstaffe. n. d. The Residential History of the La Mesa People: The Oxygen-Isotope Evidence. Manuscript in possession of the chapter author.

Spence, Michael W., Christine D. White, Patricia Fournier, Emily Webb, and Fred J. Longstaffe. 2011. The Chapantongo Site: Oxygen Isotope Analysis and Epiclassic

Population Mobility in the Valley of Mezquital. Paper presented at the 76th Annual meeting of the Society for American Archaeology, Sacramento, California, month and day.

Spence, Michael W., Christine D. White, Evelyn C. Rattray, and Fred J. Longstaffe. 2005. "Past Lives in Different Places: The Origins and Relationships of Teotihuacan's Foreign Residents." In *Settlement, Subsistence, and Social Complexity: Essays Honoring the Legacy of Jeffrey R. Parsons*, ed. Richard E. Blanton, 155–197. Los Angeles: Cotsen Institute, University of California Los Angeles.

Spinden, Herbert Joseph. 1913. *A Study of Maya Art, Its Subject Matter and Historical Development*. Cambridge, MA: The Museum.

Spotts, John. 2013. "Local Achievers or Immigrant Elites? Ancestral Relics or Warrior Trophies? Some Classic Period Cultural Historical Questions Addressed through Strontium Isotope Analysis of Burials from Buenavista, Belize." Master's thesis, San Diego State University, CA.

Stein, Gil J. 1998. "Rethinking World-Systems: Power, Distance, and Diasporas in the Dynamics of Interregional Interaction." In *World-Systems Theory in Practice: Leadership, Production, and Exchange*, ed. P. Nick Kardulias, 153–177. Lanham, MD: Rowman and Littlefield.

Stone, A., D. Reents, and R. Coffman. 1985. "Genealogical Documentation of the Middle Classic Dynasty, Caracol, El Cayo, Belize." In *Fourth Palenque Round Table, 1980*, Vol. VI, ed. E. Benson, 267–275. San Francisco, CA: Pre-Colombian Art Research Institute.

Stone, Tammy. 2003. "Social Identity and Ethnic Interaction in the Western Pueblos of the American Southwest." *Journal of Archaeological Method and Theory* 10: 31–67.

Stone, Tammy. 2005. "Factional Formation and Community Dynamics in Middle-Range Societies." In *Nonlinear Models for Archaeology and Anthropology: Continuing the Revolution*, ed. Christopher S. Beekman and William W. Baden, 79–94. London: Ashgate Press.

Stone, Tammy. 2015. *Migration and Ethnicity in Middle Range Societies: A View from the Southwest*. Salt Lake City: University of Utah Press.

Stone, Tammy, and William D. Lipe. 2011. "Standing Out versus Blending In: Pueblo Migrations and Ethnic Marking." In *Movement, Connectivity, and Landscape Change in the Ancient Southwest*, ed. Margaret Nelson and Colleen Strawhacker, 275–296. Boulder: University Press of Colorado.

Storey, Rebecca. 1992. *Life and Death in the Ancient City of Teotihuacan: A Modern Paleodemographic Synthesis*. Tuscaloosa: University of Alabama Press.

Stresser-Péan, Guy. 2000. *San Antonio Nogalar: la Sierra de Tamaulipas y la frontera noreste de Mesoamérica*. México, DF: Centro de Investigaciones y Estudios Superiores en Antropología Social, El Colegio de San Luís, Universidad de Tamaulipas, and Centre Français d'Études Mexicaines et Centraméricaines.

Stuart, David. 2000. "The Arrival of Strangers: Teotihuacan and Tollan in Classic Maya History." In *Mesoamerica's Classic Heritage: Teotihuacan to the Aztecs*, ed. Davíd

Carrasco, Lindsay Jones, and Scott Sessions, 465–513. Boulder: University Press of Colorado.

Stuart-Macadam, P. 1985. "Porotic Hyperostosis: Representative of a Childhood Condition." *American Journal of Physical Anthropology* 66: 391–398.

Stuart-Macadam, P. 1987. "Porotic Hyperostosis: New Evidence to Support the Anemia Theory." *American Journal of Physical Anthropology* 74: 521–526.

Stuart-Macadam, P. 1991. "Porotic Hyperostosis: Changing Interpretations." In *Human Paleopathology: Current Syntheses and Future Options*, ed. D. Ortner and A. Aufderheide, 36–39. Washington, DC: Smithsonian Institution Press.

Sutinen, Jessica. 2014. "Identifying Non-Local Individuals at the Ancient Maya Centre of Minanha, Belize through the Use of Strontium Isotope Analysis." Master's Thesis, Trent University, Peterborough, Ontario, Canada.

Taladoire, Eric, Sara Dzul, and Mélanie Forné. 2013. "Chronology of the Río Bec Settlement and Architecture." *Ancient Mesoamerica* 24(2): 353–372.

Taschek, Jennifer T., and Joseph W. Ball. 2003. "Nohoch Ek Revisited: The Minor Center as Manor." *Latin American Antiquity* 14: 371–388.

Taube, Karl A. 2003. "Tetitla and the Maya Presence at Teotihuacan." In *The Maya and Teotihuacan: Reinterpreting Early Classic Interaction*, ed. Geoffrey E. Braswell, 273–314. Austin: University of Texas Press.

Thomas, T. 1995. "Acculturative Stress in the Adjustment of Immigrant Families." *Journal of Social Distress and the Homeless* 4: 131–142.

Thompson, J.E.S. 1945. "A Survey of the Northern Maya Area." *American Antiquity* 11(1): 2–24.

Thompson, J.E.S. 1970. "Putun (Chontal Maya) Expansion in Yucatan and the Pasión Drainage." In *Maya History and Religion*, 3–47. Norman: University of Oklahoma Press.

Thornton, Erin Kennedy. 2011. "Reconstructing Ancient Maya Animal Trade through Strontium Isotope (^{87}Sr / ^{86}Sr) Analysis." *Journal of Archaeological Science* 38(1): 3254–3263.

Tiesler, Vera, ed. 2014. *The Bioarchaeology of Artificial Cranial Modifications: New Approaches to Head Shaping and Its Meanings in Pre-Columbian Mesoamerica and Beyond*. Interdisciplinary Contributions to Archaeology. New York: Springer.

Tiesler, Vera. 2015. "Shifts in Artificial Head Forms, Population Movements, and Ethnicity among the Postclassic Maya." In *Archaeology and Bioarchaeology of Population Movement among the Prehispanic Maya*, ed. Andreas Cucina, 143–154. New York, Springer.

Tiesler, Vera, and Andrea Cucina. 2012. "Filiación, relaciones inter-poblacionales y enlaces culturales en las Tierras Bajas mayas durante el Clásico." *Estudios de Cultura Maya* 40: 97–122.

Tiesler, Vera, Andrea Cucina, Thelma Sierra Sosa, Marlene Falla, and Richard Meindl. 2005. "Comercio, dinámicas biosociales y estructura poblacional del asentamiento costero de Xcambó, Yucatán." *Los Investigadores de la Cultura Maya* 13(2): 365–372.

Tiesler, Vera, Andrea Cucina, Travis W. Stanton, and David A. Freidel. 2017. *Before Kukulkán. Bioarchaeology of Maya Life, Death, and Identity at Classic Period Yaxuná*. Tucson: University of Arizona Press.

Tilly, Charles. 1978. "Migration in Modern European History." In *Human Migration: Patterns and Policies*, ed. William H. McNeil and Ruth S. Adams, 48–72. Bloomington: Indiana University Press.

Ting, K. Carmen. 2013. "Change, Continuity and the Maya Collapse: Reconstructing the Ceramic Economy in the Eastern Maya Lowlands during the Classic to Postclassic Transition." PhD diss., Institute of Archaeology, University College London, UK.

Tokovinine, A. 2008. "The Power of Place: Political Landscape and Identity in Classic Maya Inscriptions, Imagery, and Architecture." PhD diss., Harvard University, Cambridge, MA.

Tokovinine, Alexandre, and Dmitri Beliaev. 2013. "People of the Road: Traders and Travelers in Ancient Maya Words and Images." In *Merchants, Markets, and Exchange in the Pre-Columbian World*, ed. Kenneth G. Hirth and Joanne Pillsbury, 169–199. Washington, DC: Dumbarton Oaks.

Tokovinine, A., and M. Zender. 2012. "The Lords of Windy Water: The Royal Court of Motul de San José in Classic Maya Inscriptions." In *Motul de San José: Politics, History and Economy in a Classic Maya Polity*, ed. A. E. Foias and K. F. Emery, 30–66. Gainesville: University Press of Florida.

Torquemada, Juan de. 1783 [1615]. *Monarquía Indiana*. Madrid: Nicolás Rodriguez Franco.

Torrescano-Valle, Nuria, and Gerald Islebe. 2015. "Holocene Paleoecology, Climate History, and Human Influence in the Southwestern Yucatan Peninsula." *Review of Paleobotany and Palynology* 217: 1–8.

Toscano Hernández, Lourdes, and José Huchim Herrera. 2017. "Terminaciones Rituales en los Principales Edificios de la Región Puuc." In *Recent Investigations in the Puuc Region of Yucatán*, ed. Meghan Rubenstein, 81–86. Pre-Columbian Archaeology 8. London: Archaeopress.

Tourtellot, Gair. 1988. "Developmental Cycles of Households and Houses at Seibal." In *Household and Community in the Mesoamerican Past*, ed. Richard R. Wilk and Wendy Ashmore, 95–120. Albuquerque: University of New Mexico Press.

Tourtellot, Gair. 1993. "A View of Ancient Maya Settlements in the Eighth Century." In *Lowland Maya Civilization in the Eighth Century A.D*, ed. Jeremy A. Sabloff and J. S. Henderson, 219–241. Washington, DC: Dumbarton Oaks.

Tourtellot, Gair, and Jason J. González. 2004. "The Last Hurrah: Continuity and Transformation at Seibal." In *The Terminal Classic in the Maya Lowlands: Collapse, Transition, and Transformation*, ed. Arthur A. Demarest, Prudence M. Rice, and Don. S. Rice, 60–82. Boulder: University Press of Colorado.

Tozzer, Alfred M., trans. and ed. 1941. *Landa's Relación de las Cosas de Yucatan*. Cambridge, MA: Peabody Museum of Archaeology and Ethnology, Harvard University.

Tozzer, Alfred M. 1957. *Chichen Itza and Its Cenote of Sacrifice: A Comparative Study of Contemporaneous Maya and Toltec.* Cambridge, MA: Peabody Museum of Archaeology and Ethnology, Harvard University.

Trask, Willa. 2018. "Missionization and Shifting Mobility on the Southeastern Maya-Spanish Frontier: Identifying In-Migration to the Maya site of Tipu, Belize through the Use of Strontium and Oxygen Isotopes." PhD diss., Texas A&M University, College Station, TX.

Trask, Willa, Lori E. Wright, and Keith Prufer. 2012. "Isotopic Evidence for Mobility in the Southeastern Maya Periphery: Preliminary Evidence." *Research Reports in Belizean Archaeology* 9: 61–74.

Tsuda, Takeyuki G. 2011. "Modern Perspectives on Ancient Migrations." In *Rethinking Anthropological Perspectives on Migration*, ed. Graciela S. Cabana and Jeffrey J. Clark, 313–338. Gainesville: University Press of Florida.

Tsuda, Takeyuki G., Brenda J. Baker, James F. Eder, Kelly J. Knudson, Jonathan Maupin, Lisa Meierotto, and Rachel E. Scott. 2015. "Unifying Themes in Studies of Ancient and Contemporary Migrations." In *Migration and Disruptions. Toward a Unifying Theory of Ancient and Contemporary Migrations*, ed. Brenda J. Baker and Takeyuki Tsuda, 15–32. Gainesville: University Press of Florida.

Turner, Bethany L., George D. Kamenov, George D. Kingston, and George D. Armelagos. 2009. "Insights into Immigration and Social Class at Machu Picchu, Peru Based on Oxygen, Strontium, and Lead Isotopic Analysis." *Journal of Archaeological Science* 36(2): 317–332.

Turner, B. L., II, and Jeremy A. Sabloff. 2012. "Classic Period Collapse of the Central Maya Lowlands: Insights about Human-Environment Relationships for Sustainability." *Proceedings of the National Academy of Sciences* 109(35): 13908–13914.

Twiss, Katheryn. C. 2007. "We Are What We Eat." In *The Archaeology of Food and Identity*, ed. Katheryn C. Twiss, 1–15. Center for Archaeological Investigations. Carbondale: Southern Illinois University.

Tykot, Robert H. 2002. "Contribution of Stable Isotope Analysis to Understanding Dietary Variation among the Maya." *Archaeological Chemistry. Materials, Methods, and Meaning*, ed. Kathryn A. Jakes, 169–184. Symposium Series 831. Washington, DC: American Chemical Society.

Ubelaker, D. 1989. *Human Skeletal Remains: Excavation, Analysis, Interpretation.* Manuals on Archaeology 2. 2nd edition. Washington, DC: Taraxacum Press.

Umberger, Emily, and Cecilia F. Klein. 1993. "Aztec Art and Imperial Expansion." In *Latin American Horizons*, ed. Don Stephen Rice, 295–336. Washington, DC: Dumbarton Oaks.

Uruñuela, G., and P. Plunket, P. 2005. "La transición del Clásico al Posclásico: Reflexiones sobre el Valle de Puebla-Tlaxcala." In *Reacomodos demográficos del Clásico al Postclásico en el centro de México*, ed. Linda Manzanilla, 303–324. México, DF: Universidad Nacional Autónoma de México.

Valdés, Juan Antonio, and Federico Fahsen. 2004. "Disaster in Sight: The Terminal Classic at Tikal and Uaxactun." In *The Terminal Classic in the Maya Lowlands: Collapse, Transition, and Transformation*, ed. Arthur A. Demarest, Prudence M. Rice, and Don S. Rice, 140–161. Boulder: University Press of Colorado.

Vallet, Régis. 1996. "Habuba Kebira ou la naissance de l'urbanisme." *Paléorient* 22(2): 45–76.

Van Dommelen, Peter. 2014. "Moving On: Archaeological Perspectives on Mobility and Migration." *World Archaeology* 46(4): 477–483.

Vapnarsky, Valentina. 2009. "La migración en las voces mayas: historia hacia la cultura." In *Diasporas, migraciones y exilios en el mundo maya*, ed. Mario H. Ruz, Julio Garcia Targa, and Andrés Ciudad-Ruiz, 327–352. Mérida: Sociedad Española de Estudios Mayas, Universidad Nacional Autónoma de México.

Vapnarsky, Valentina, and Olivier Le Guen. 2011. "The Guardians of Space and History: Understanding Ecological and Historical Relationships of the Contemporary Yucatec Maya to their Landscape." In *Ecology, Power, and Religion in Maya Landscapes*, ed. Christian Isendahl and Bodil Liljefors Persson, 191–208. Acta Mesoamerica Vol. 23. Markt Schwaben: Verlag Anton Saurwein.

Varien, Mark D., and Barbara J. Mills. 1997. "Accumulations Research: Problems and Prospects for Estimating Site Occupation Span." *Journal of Archaeological Method and Theory* 4(2): 141–191.

Varien, Mark D., and James M. Potter. 1997. "Unpacking the Discard Equation: Simulating the Accumulation of Artifacts in the Archaeological Record." *American Antiquity* 62(2): 194–213.

Velásquez Morlet, Adriana, Edmundo López de la Rosa, Ma del Pilar Casado López, and Margarita Gaxiola. 1988. *Zonas arqueológicas Yucatán*. México, DF: Instituto Nacional de Antropología e Historia.

Viel, René H. 1993. *Evolución de la Cerámica de Copán, Honduras*. Tegucigalpa, Honduras: Instituto Hondureño de Antropología e Historia.

Viel, René H. 1999. "The Pectorals of Altar Q and Structure 11: An Interpretation of the Political Organization at Copan, Honduras." *Latin American Antiquity* 10(4): 377–399.

Villagutierre Soto-Mayor, Juan de. 1983. *History of the Conquest of the Province of the Itza*. Culver City, CA: Labyrinthos.

Volta, B., and G. E. Braswell. 2014. "Alternative Narratives and Missing Data: Refining the Chronology of Chichen Itza." In *The Maya and Their Central American Neighbors: Settlement Patterns, Architecture, Hieroglyphic Texts, and Ceramics*, ed. G. E. Braswell, 356–402. New York: Routledge.

Voss, A. W. 2001. "Los itzáes en Chichén Itzá: los datos Epigráficos." *Los Investigadores de la Cultura Maya* 9(1): 151–173.

Voss, Barbara. 2008. "Between the Household and the World System: Social Collectivity and Community Agency in Overseas Chinese Archaeology." *Historical Archaeology* 42: 37–52.

Walker, Debra S. 1990. "Cerros Revisited: Ceramic Indicators of Terminal Classic and Postclassic Settlement and Pilgrimage in Northern Belize." PhD diss., Southern Methodist University, Dallas, TX.

Walker, P., R. Bathurst, R. Richman, T. Gjerdrum, and V. Andrushko. 2009. "The Causes of Porotic Hyperostosis and Cribra Orbitalia: A Reappraisal of the Iron-Deficiency-Anemia Hypothesis." *American Journal of Physical Anthropology* 139: 109–125.

Wanner, Isabel, Thelma Sierra, Kurt Alt, and Vera Tiesler. 2007. "Lifestyle, Occupation, and Whole Bone Morphology from the Pre-hispanic Maya Coastal Population from Xcambó, Yucatán, México." *International Journal of Osteoarchaeology* 17: 253–268.

Weaver, Eric, Nicholas Dunning, and Michael Smyth. 2015. "Investigation of a Ritual Cave Site in the Puuc Region of Yucatan, Mexico: Actun Xcoch." *Journal of Cave and Karst Studies* 77: 120–128.

Webster, David L. 2002. *The Fall of the Ancient Maya: Solving the Mystery of the Maya Collapse*. London: Thames and Hudson.

Webster, David L. 2005. "Political Ecology, Political Economy, and the Culture History of Resource Management at Copan." In *Copán: The History of an Ancient Maya Kingdom*, ed. E. Wyllys Andrews and William L. Fash, 33–72. Santa Fe, NM, and Oxford, UK: School of American Research Press.

Webster, David. 2014. "Maya Drought and Niche Inheritance." In *The Great Maya Droughts in Cultural Context: Case Studies in Resilience and Vulnerability*, ed. Gyles Iannone, 333–349. Boulder: University Press of Colorado.

Webster, David. 2018. *The Population of Tikal: Implications for Maya Demography*. Paris Monographs in Archaeology 49. Oxford, UK: Archaeopress.

Webster, David, and AnnCorinne Freter. 1990. "Settlement History and the Classic Collapse at Copan: A Redefined Chronological Perspective." *Latin American Antiquity* 1(1): 66–85.

Webster, David L., AnnCorinne Freter, and Nancy Gonlin. 2000. *Copán: The Rise and Fall of an Ancient Maya Kingdom*. Belmont, CA: Wadsworth.

Webster, David, AnnCorinne Freter, and David Rue. 1993. "The Obsidian Hydration Dating Project at Copan: A Regional Approach and Why It Works." *Latin American Antiquity* 4(4): 303–324.

Webster, David L., AnnCorinne Freter, and Rebecca Storey. 2004. "Dating Copán Culture History: Implications for the Terminal Classic and the Collapse." In *The Terminal Classic in the Maya Lowlands: Collapse, Transition, and Transformation*, ed. Arthur A. Demarest, Prudence M. Rice, and Don S. Rice, 291–326. Boulder: University Press of Colorado.

Webster, David L., and Nancy Gonlin. 1988. "Household Remains of the Humblest Maya." *Journal of Field Archaeology* 15(2): 169–190.

Webster, David L., Kenneth Hirth, and Lee Newsome. 2013. *Final Report to NSF: Chronology of El Gigante Cave, Honduras*. Report to the National Science Foundation, Alexandria, VA.

Webster, David, and Jane Kirker. 1995. "Too Many Maya, Too Few Buildings: Investigating Construction Potential at Copan, Honduras." *Journal of Anthropological Research* 51: 363–387.

Webster, David L., David Rue, and Alfred Traverse. 2005. "Early *Zea* Cultivation in Honduras: Implications for the Iltis Hypothesis." *Economic Botany* 22(2): 166–173.

Webster, David, and William Sanders. 2001. "La Antigua ciudad mesoamericana: teoría y Concepto." In *Reconstruyendo la ciudad maya: El urbanismo en las sociedades antiguas*, ed. Andrés Ciudad, María Josefa Iglesias, and M. C. Martínez Martínez, 43–64. Madrid: Sociedad Española de Estudios Mayas.

Weiss, Kenneth M. 1973. "Demographic Models for Anthropology." *American Antiquity* 32: 1–186.

Weiss-Krejci, Estella. 2003. "The Maya Corpse: Body Processing from Preclassic to Postclassic Times in the Maya Highlands and Lowlands." In *Jaws of the Underworld: Life, Death and Rebirth among the Ancient Maya*, ed. Pierre R. Colas, Genevieve LeFort, and Bodil L. Pearson, 71–86. Mockmuhl: Verlag Anton Saurwein.

Weiss-Krejci, Estella, and Thomas Sabbas. 2002. "The Potential Role of Small Depressions as Water Storage Features in the Central Maya Lowlands." *Latin American Antiquity* 13: 343–357.

Wells, E. Christian, Karla L. Davis-Salazar, José E. Moreno-Cortés, Glenn S. L. Stuart, and Anna C. Novotny. 2014. "Analysis of the Context and Contents of an Ulua-Style Marble Vase from the Palmarejo Valley, Honduras." *Latin American Antiquity* 25(1): 82–100.

Wells, E. Christian, and Ben A. Nelson. 2007. "Pilgrimage and Material Transfers in Prehispanic Northwest Mexico." In *Mesoamerican Ritual Economy: Archaeological and Ethnological Perspectives*, ed. E. Christian Wells, 137–165. Boulder: University Press of Colorado.

Welsh, W.B.M. 1988. *An Analysis of Classic Lowland Maya Burials*. British Archaeological Reports, International Series 409. Oxford, UK: Archaeopress.

Wenger, Etienne. 1998. *Communities of Practice: Learning, Meaning, and Identity*. Cambridge, UK: Cambridge University Press.

White, Christine D. 1996. "Sutural Effects of Fronto-Occipital Cranial Modification." *American Journal of Physical Anthropology* 100(3): 397–410.

White, Christine D. 1997. "Ancient Diet at Lamanai and Pacbitun: Implications for the Ecological Model of Collapse." In *Bones of the Maya: Studies of Ancient Skeletons*, ed. S. L. Whittington and D. Reed, 171–180. Washington, DC: Smithsonian Institution.

White, Christine D., Paul E. Healy, and Henry R. Schwartz. 1993. "Intensive Agriculture, Social Status and Maya Diet at Pacbitun, Belize." *Journal of Anthropological Research* 49: 347–375.

White, Christine D., Fred J. Longstaffe, and Kimberley R. Law. 2001. "Revisiting the Teotihuacan Connection at Altun Ha." *Ancient Mesoamerica* 12(1): 65–72.

White, Christine D., Fred J. Longstaffe, David M. Pendergast, and Jay Maxwell. 2009. "Cultural Embodiment and the Enigmatic Identity of the Lovers from Lamanai." In

Bioarchaeology and Identity in the Americas, ed. Kelly J. Knudson and Christopher M. Stojanowski, 155–176. Gainesville: University Press of Florida.

White, Christine, Fred J. Longstaffe, Michael Spence, Evelyn Rattray, and Rebecca Storey. 2010. "The Teotihuacan Dream: An Isotopic Study of Economic Organization and Immigration." In *The 'Compleat Archaeologist': Papers in Honour of Michael W. Spence*, ed. Christopher J. Ellis, Neal Ferris, Peter A. Timmins, and Christine D. White, 279–297. *Ontario Archaeology* 85–88 (2008–2009) and London Chapter OAS Occasional Publication 9.

White, Christine D., T. Douglas Price, and Fred J. Longstaffe. 2007. "Residential Histories of the Human Sacrifices at the Moon Pyramid, Teotihuacan: Evidence from Strontium and Oxygen Isotopes." *Ancient Mesoamerica* 18: 159–172.

White, Christine D., and Henry P. Schwarcz. 1989. "Ancient Maya Diet: As Inferred from Isotopic and Elemental Analysis of Bone." *Journal of Archaeological Science* 16: 451–474.

White, Christine D., Michael W. Spence, Fred J. Longstaffe, and Kimberley R. Law. 2000. "Testing the Nature of Teotihuacan Imperialism at Kaminaljuyú using Phosphate Oxygen-Isotope Ratios." *Journal of Anthropological Research* 56(4): 535–558.

White, Christine D., Michael W. Spence, Fred J. Longstaffe, and Kimberley R. Law. 2004. "Demography and Ethnic Continuity in the Tlailotlacan Enclave of Teotihuacan: The Evidence from Stable Oxygen Isotopes." *Journal of Anthropological Archaeology* 23: 385–403.

White, Christine D., Michael W. Spence, Fred J. Longstaffe, Hilary Stuart-Williams, and Kimberley R. Law. 2002. "Geographic Identities of the Sacrificial Victims from the Feathered Serpent Pyramid, Teotihuacan: Implications for the Nature of State Power." *Latin American Antiquity* 13(2): 217–236.

White, Christine D., Michael W. Spence, Hilary Le Q. Stuart-Williams, Henry P. Schwarcz. 1998. "Oxygen Isotopes and the Identification of Geographical Origins: The Valley of Oaxaca versus the Valley of Mexico." *Journal of Archaeological Science* 25: 643–655.

White, Christine D., Rebecca Storey, Fred J. Longstaffe, and Michael W. Spence. 2004. "Immigration, Assimilation, and Status in the Ancient City of Teotihuacan: Isotopic Evidence from Tlajinga 33." *Latin American Antiquity* 15: 176–198.

Whittington, Stephen L. 1991. *The Ostuman Archaeological Project*. Final report submitted to the National Science Foundation and Instituto Hondureño de Antropología e Historia. Archivos del Central Regional de Investigaciones Arqueológicas, Copán Ruinas, Honduras.

Whittington, Stephen L., and David M. Reed. 1997. "Commoner Diet at Copán: Insights from Stable Isotopes and Porotic Hyperostosis." In *Bones of the Maya*, ed. S. L. Whittington and D. M. Reed, 157–170. Washington, DC: Smithsonian Institution Press.

Whyte, I. 2000. *Migration and Society in Britain: 1550–1830*. Houndmills, Basingstoke, Hampshire, UK: MacMillan Press.

Wiewall, Darcy, and Linda Howie. 2010. "More than Meets the Eye: Ceramic Production and Consumption at Lamanai, Belize, during the Postclassic to Spanish Colonial Periods." In *Research Reports in Belizean Archaeology 7*, ed. John Morris, Sherilyne Jones, Jaime Awe, George Thompson, and Melissa Badillo, 201–217. Belmopan, Belize: Institute of Archaeology, National Institute of Culture and History.

Wilk, Richard R. 1988. "Maya Household Organization: Evidence and Analogies." In *Household and Community in the Mesoamerican Past*, ed. Richard R. Wilk and Wendy Ashmore, 135–151. Albuquerque: University of New Mexico Press.

Wilk, Richard R. 1991. *Household Ecology. Economic Change and Domestic Life among the Kekchi Maya in Belize*. Tucson: University of Arizona Press.

Wilk, Richard R., and Wendy Ashmore. 1988. *Household and Community in the Mesoamerican Past*. Albuquerque: University of New Mexico Press.

Willermet, Cathy, Heather J. Edgar, Corey Ragsdale, and B. Scott Aubry. 2013. "Biodistances among Mexica, Maya, Toltec, and Totonac Groups of Central and Coastal Mexico." *Chungará, Revista de Antropología Chilena* 45(3): 447–460.

Willey, Gordon R., William R. Bullard Jr., John B. Glass, and J. C. Gifford. 1965. *Prehistoric Maya Settlements in the Belize Valley*. Cambridge, MA: Peabody Museum.

Willey, Gordon R., and Richard M. Leventhal. 1979. "Prehistoric Settlement at Copan." In *Maya Archaeology and Ethnohistory*, ed. N. Hammond and G. R. Willey, 75–102. Austin: University of Texas Press.

Williams, Jocelyn S., Shannen M. Stronge, Gyles Iannone, and Fred J. Longstaffe. 2017. "Examining Chronological Trends in Ancient Maya Diet at Minanha, Belize, using the Isotopes of Carbon and Nitrogen." *Latin American Antiquity* 28(2): 269–287.

Williams, Jocelyn S., and Christine D. White. 2006. "Dental Modification in the Postclassic Population from Lamanai, Belize." *Ancient Mesoamerica* 17(1): 139–151.

Williams, Jocelyn S., Christine D. White, and Fred J. Longstaffe. 2009. "Maya Marine Subsistence: Isotopic Evidence from Marco Gonzalez and San Pedro, Belize." *Latin American Antiquity* 20(1): 37–56.

Williams-Beck, Lorraine A. 1998. *El Dominio de los Batabob: El Área Puuc Occidental Campechana*. Campeche, México: Secretaría de Educación Pública, Universidad Autónoma de Campeche.

Wingard, John Davis. 1992. "The Role of Soils in the Development and Collapse of Classic Maya Civilization at Copán, Honduras." PhD diss. Pennsylvania State University, University Park, PA.

Wingard, John D. 2016. "Complementarity and Synergy: Stones, Bones, Soil, and Toil in the Copan Valley, Honduras." In *Human Adaptation in Ancient Mesoamerica: Empirical Approaches to Mesoamerican Archaeology*, ed. Nancy Gonlin and Kirk D. French, 73–93. Boulder: University Press of Colorado.

Wolfman, Daniel. 1990. "Mesoamerican Chronology and Archaeomagnetic Dating, AD 1–1200." In *Archaeomagnetic Dating*, ed. Jeffrey L. Eighmy and Robert S. Sternbeg, 261–308. Tucson: University of Arizona Press.

Wood, J., G. Milner, H. Harpending, and K. Weiss. 1992. "The Osteological Paradox: Problems of Inferring Prehistoric Health from Skeletal Samples." *Current Anthropology* 33: 343–370.

Wright, Lori E. 2005a. "Identifying Immigrants to Tikal, Guatemala: Defining Local Variability in Strontium Isotope Ratios of Human Tooth Enamel." *Journal of Archaeological Science* 32(4): 555–566.

Wright, Lori E. 2005b. "In Search of Yax Nuun Ayiin I: The Tikal Project's Burial 10." *Ancient Mesoamerica* 16: 89–100.

Wright, Lori E. 2006. *Diet, Health, and Status among the Pasión Maya: A Reappraisal of the Collapse*. Vol. 2. Nashville, TN: Vanderbilt University Press.

Wright, Lori E. 2007. *Ethnicity and Isotopes at Mayapán*. Report to the Foundation for Ancient Mesoamerican Studies, Inc. http://www.famsi.org/reports/05068/. Consulted August 15, 2015.

Wright, Lori E. 2012. "Immigration to Tikal, Guatemala: Evidence from Stable Strontium and Oxygen Isotopes." *Journal of Anthropological Archaeology* 31(3): 334–352.

Wright, Lori E., and Bruce Bachand. 2009. "Strontium Isotopic Identification of an Early Classic Migrant to Punta de Chimino, Guatemala." In *Maya Archaeology 1*, ed. Stephen Houston, Charles Golden, and Joel Skidmore, 28–35. San Francisco, CA: Mesoweb Press.

Wright, Lori E., and F. Chew. 1998. "Porotic Hyperostosis and Paleoepidemiology: A Forensic Perspective on Anemia among the Ancient Maya." *American Anthropologist* 100: 924–939.

Wright, Lori E., Juan Antonio Valdés, James H. Burton, T. Douglas Price, and Henry P. Schwarcz. 2010. "The Children of Kaminaljuyu: Isotopic Insight into Diet and Long Distance Interaction in Mesoamerica." *Journal of Anthropological Archaeology* 29(2): 155–178.

Wrobel, Gabriel D. G. 2004. "Metric and Nonmetric Dental Variation among the Ancient Maya of Northern Belize." PhD diss., Indiana University, Bloomington.

Wrobel, Gabriel D., Carolyn Freiwald, Amy Michael, Christophe Helmke, Jaime Awe, Douglas J. Kennett, Sherry Gibbs, Josalyn M. Ferguson, and Cameron Griffith. 2017. "Social Identity and Geographic Origin of Maya Burials at Actun Uayazba Kab, Roaring Creek Valley, Belize." *Journal of Anthropological Archaeology* 45: 98–114.

Wrobel, Gabriel, and Elizabeth Graham. 2013. "Los Entierros de la Fase Buk en Belice: Comprobando las relaciones genéticas entre grupos del Posclásico Temprano en Belice a través de la morfología Dental." In *Afinidades Biológicas y Dinámicas Poblacionales entre los Antiguos Mayas. Una vision multidisciplinaria*, ed. Andrea Cucina, 19–38. Mérida, México: Universidad Autónoma de Yucatán.

Wrobel, Gabriel, and Elizabeth Graham. 2015. "The Buk Phase Burials of Belize: Testing Genetic Relatedness among Early Postclassic Groups in Northern Belize Using Dental Morphology." In *Archaeology and Bioarchaeology of Population Movement among the Prehispanic Maya*, ed. Andrea Cucina, 85–95. New York: Springer.

Wrobel, Gabriel, D., Christophe G. B. Helmke, and Carolyn Freiwald. 2014. "A Case Study of Funerary Cave Use from Je'reftheel, Central Belize." In *The Bioarchaeology of Space and Place: Ideology, Power and Meaning in Maya Mortuary Contexts*, ed. Gabriel D. Wrobel, 77–106. New York: Springer.

Wurster, Wolfgang W., and Bernard Hermes. 2000. "Fechas de carbono 14." In *El sitio maya de Topoxté: investigaciones en una isla del lago Yaxhá, Petén, Guatemala*, ed. Wolfgang W. Wurster, 247–249. Mainz am Rhein, Germany: Verlag Philipp von Zabern,

Yaeger, Jason. 2003. "Small Settlements in the Upper Belize River Valley: Local Complexity, Household Strategies of Affiliation, and the Changing Organization." In *Perspectives on Ancient Maya Complexity*, ed. Gyles Iannone and Samuel V. Connell, 42–58. Monograph 49. Los Angeles, CA: Cotsen Institute of Archaeology, University of California Los Angeles.

Yaeger, Jason, and Carolyn Freiwald. 2009. "Complex Ecologies: Human and Animal Responses to Ancient Landscape Change in Central Belize." *Research Reports in Belizean Archaeology* 8: 83–92.

Yoffee, Norman. 1988. "Orienting Collapse." In *The Collapse of Ancient States and Civilizations*, ed. Norman Yoffee and George L. Cowgill, 1–19. Tucson: University of Arizona Press.

Zetina Gutierrez, M. de G., and B. Faust. 2011. "De la agroecología maya a la arqueología demográfica: ¿cuántas casas por familia?" *Estudios de Cultura Maya* 38: 97–120.

Zhu, Yu. 2004. "Changing Urbanization Process and in situ Rural-Urban Transformation: Reflections on China's Settlement Definition." In *New Forms of Urbanization. Beyond the Urban-Rural Dichotomy*, ed. Tony Champion and Graeme Hugo, 207–230. Aldershot, UK: Ashgate.

Zralka, Jaroslaw. 2008. *Terminal Classic Occupation in the Maya Sites Located in the Area of Triangulo Park, Peten, Guatemala*. Prace Archeologicze Monographs N°62. Krakow, Poland: Jagiellonian University Press.

Zweig, Christina L. 2011. "A Report of the 2010 Excavations at Structures M-100 and M-101, Baking Pot, Belize." In *The Belize Valley Archaeological Reconnaissance Project: A Report of the 2010 Field Season*, ed. Julie A. Hoggarth and Jaime J. Awe, 29–44. Belmopan: Belize Institute of Archaeology.

M. CHARLOTTE ARNAULD earned her doctoral degree at the Université Paris I Panthéon-Sorbonne and is currently emeritus research director at the Centre National de la Recherche Scientifique (CNRS). As a Mesoamerican archaeologist she has directed or codirected five long-term projects in Maya highland Verapaz, lowland La Joyanca in Guatemala, Balamku and Río Bec in southern Mexico, and Zacapu in western Mexico. She specializes in Maya urban studies, exploring neighborhood dynamics and related population mobility as part of her broader work in Maya social archaeology, including related aspects of the Classic collapse. Her publications include *Archéologie de l'habitat en Alta Verapaz (Guatemala)*, coedited volumes on the archaeology of La Joyanca and western Mexico, and on *The Neighborhood as a Social and Spatial Unit in Mesoamerican Cities* (with L. Manzanilla and M. E. Smith). She has published papers in *Journal de la Société des Américanistes*, *Ancient Mesoamerica*, and *Journal of Anthropological Archaeology*. Her coedited volume *Maya Kingship: Rupture and Transformation of from Classic to Postclassic Times* (with T. Okoshi, A. F. Chase, and P. Nondédéo) is forthcoming.

JAIME J. AWE is associate professor of anthropology at Northern Arizona University, director of the Belize Valley Archaeological Reconnaissance Project, and an emeritus member of the Belize Institute of Archaeology. He received degrees in Anthropology at

Trent University in Ontario, Canada, and his PhD from the Institute of Archaeology at University College London. As the first director of the Belize Institute of Archaeology (2003–2014), he was responsible for managing the archaeological heritage of the country. During his extensive career, Dr. Awe has conducted important research and conservation at most of the major archaeological sites in Belize. His research interests include topics that span the Preceramic period to the time of European contact. Presently, he continues an active program of research in Belize, conducting multidisciplinary investigations with his colleagues and graduate students at the major Maya cities of Cahal Pech, Baking Pot, Xunantunich, and Lower Dover.

CHRISTOPHER S. BEEKMAN earned his PhD from Vanderbilt University and is a professor of anthropology at the University of Colorado, Denver. His research focuses on sociopolitical practices in ancient western Mexico, and that region's interaction with its neighbors. He has directed excavation projects at Llano Grande and Navajas, and surveys in the La Primavera region and in the Magdalena Valley (with Verenice Heredia Espinoza) in Jalisco, Mexico. He is currently working with Verenice Heredia Espinoza on the unpublished collections from Los Guachimontones, Jalisco. Among his edited or coedited books are *Nonlinear Models for Archaeology and Anthropology* (2005, with William Baden), *Shaft Tombs and Figures in West Mexican Society* (2016, with Robert Pickering), *Migrations in Late Mesoamerica* (2019), and *Anthropomorphic Representations in Highland Mesoamerica: Gods, Ancestors, and Human Beings* (2020, with Brigitte Faugère). He is currently finalizing the volume *Waves of Influence* (coedited with Colin McEwan) to be published with Dumbarton Oaks.

MEGGAN BULLOCK is a bioarchaeologist specializing in ancient Mesoamerican populations. She earned her PhD from the Pennsylvania State University and is an adjunct professor of physical anthropology at the Escuela Nacional de Antropología e Historia in Mexico, where she offers courses on method and theory in bioarchaeology. Her previous research has focused on health and disease in urban environments and methodological issues in paleodemography and paleopathology. She has studied human skeletal remains from the prehispanic urban center of Cholula, attempting to address the issue of migration in studies of urban health and demography. Her more recent research has incorporated the concept of social identity and its use in bioarchaeology. She is also interested in the study of physical and structural violence in past populations through the study of pathological and traumatic lesions in human skeletal remains. Her publications are concerned with questions related to the paleodemography and paleopathology of skeletal remains from Mexico.

SARAH C. CLAYTON is an archaeologist and associate professor in the Department of Anthropology at the University of Wisconsin, Madison. Her research explores the ways in which the growth and decline of premodern cities transformed surrounding landscapes and ways of life. An active field researcher in central Mexico, her recent work examines the regional dynamics and cultural legacy of Teotihuacan, the largest city of its time in North America. She currently directs a multiyear project at Chicoloapan (on the outskirts of Mexico City). Her research has been published in *American Anthropologist, Ancient Mesoamerica, Cambridge Archaeological Journal*, and *Latin American Antiquity*, and she has contributed several chapters to volumes of *The Cambridge World History*.

ANDREA CUCINA received his PhD in paleopathology (Catholic University, School of Medicine 1998; *Laurea* honoris in Biological Sciences with major in physical anthropology, University of Rome "La Sapienza," 1991). Currently, he is a full research professor in the School of Anthropological Sciences, Universidad Autónoma de Yucatán (UAY), and a member of the Sistema Nacional de Investigadores (SNI Level II). His main interest is dental anthropology among archaeological and recent human populations. He has carried out field and lab research in Italy, the Dominican Republic, Pakistan, Florida, Mexico, and Guatemala. His main topics of investigation focus on paleodiet, paleopathology, development, archaeometry, population affinities, and migratory dynamics among the ancient Maya, as well as biological distance analyses in South America, the Caribbean, and Europe. He has authored and coauthored more than eighty scientific publications in peer-reviewed indexed journals and edited several scientific books from international and national (UADY, UNAM) editorial presses.

VÉRONIQUE DARRAS is a research director at the CNRS. She received her doctoral degree from the Université Paris 1 Panthéon–Sorbonne. Her research focuses on cultural developments in central-western Mesoamerica, from Preclassic to Postclassic, with an interest in Chupícuaro and pre-Tarascan cultures. She reconstructs social and economic systems based on spatial patterns, craft production, and exchange networks, with a special concern for obsidian and ceramic materials. Her research is based on field archaeology and technological studies using the analytical tool of *chaîne opératoire*. She has also published on the symbolism of materials by cross-referencing archaeological and ethnohistorical data. She has recently led several research programs in northern Michoacan and the Lerma Valley, Mexico, including one focused on the migratory phenomena that led to the emergence of major cultural entities in central-western Mesoamerica, such as the Tarascan state.

NICHOLAS P. DUNNING is professor and head in the Department of Geography and GIS at the University of Cincinnati. He became interested in the ancient Maya via serendipity by once checking out the wrong book from the public library in Honolulu. Dunning obtained his PhD from the University of Minnesota. He has worked on numerous archaeological projects in Guatemala, Belize, and Mexico—including repeatedly in the Puuc region. He has also recently worked in Chaco Canyon, New Mexico, and on various islands in the West Indies. Dunning has published several books, including most recently *Tikal: Paleoecology of an Ancient Maya City*, and some 150 refereed articles and book chapters. When not digging in the dirt at ancient sites, Dunning spends his time digging in the dirt in a large organic vegetable garden.

MARION FOREST is an archaeologist, currently a postdoctoral researcher and instructor in the Department of Anthropology at Brigham Young University. Her research questions include the social and spatial processes associated with the emergence, transformation, and decline of urban settlements in the highlands of Mexico. After she completed her PhD at the University Paris I, she was awarded a postdoctoral fellowship by the Fyssen Foundation to continue her project at Arizona State University, investigating early Tarascan urbanism (west Mexico) based on both remote sensing and ground-based work. Her most recent publication in *Advances in Archaeological Practice* addresses the use of LiDAR-derived data and crowd-sourced research in archaeology student training.

MÉLANIE FORNÉ received her doctoral degree from Université Paris 1. She has been engaged in fieldwork research for 15 years in Guatemala. Her research focused on ceramics, as a strong marker for microchronology, using traditional typology and combining it with a modal approach. She worked on several archaeological sites, including La Joyanca, Naachtun, Cancuen, and Uaxactun, among others. She directed Centro de Estudios Mexicanos y Centroamericanos (CEMCA) in Guatemala for three years. She wrote and drew a comic book "Ixtz'unun" (26 chapters published in the Guatemalan newspaper *Prensa Libre*), in which she pictured the daily life of Maya children during the Classic period. Since 2014, she has lived in France and specialized in illustration, graphics, and web design.

CAROLYN FREIWALD studies diet and migration in Mesoamerica, combining history, archaeology, chemistry, and biology to reconstruct human and animal mobility and landscape use. She earned her PhD from the University of Wisconsin, Madison, and worked at the UW-Madison Zoological Museum before accepting a position at the University of Mississippi. She has created isotope baseline maps in central and southern Mexico, northern Guatemala, Belize, western Honduras, and the Dominican Republic, and used those to identify migration into early Mesoamerican villages, Classic-period Maya cities, and Colonial-period missions. She has also addressed where the Maya hunted wild game, the origins of some of the earliest cows and pigs in northern Guatemala, and how nonlocal foods like salt might affect similar studies across the Maya region. She has published her research in the *Journal of Archaeological Science*, *Current Anthropology*, the *American Journal of Physical Anthropology*, and *Ancient Mesoamerica*, as well as in numerous book chapters. Her work also addresses curation and ethical concerns working with human remains and archaeological collections both in the United States and Latin America.

NANCY GONLIN received her PhD from Pennsylvania State University. She specializes in household archaeology, ritual, ecological perspectives, and the study of the daily and nightly lives of ancient Mesoamericans. She has created a new perspective called the archaeology of the night and presented a TEDx talk on this subject, among other media. She is Registered Professional Archaeologist 16354. Gonlin serves as the coeditor for the journal *Ancient Mesoamerica*. She has coauthored a textbook on *The Archaeology of Native North America* and a case study of Copan. Gonlin's coedited volumes include *Commoner Ritual and Ideology in Ancient Mesoamerica*, *Ancient Households of the Americas*, *Human Adaptation in Ancient Mesoamerica*, *Archaeology of the Night*, and *Night and Darkness in Ancient Mesoamerica*.

ELIZABETH GRAHAM received her PhD from Cambridge University. She is professor of Mesoamerican archaeology at the Institute of Archaeology, University College London. She has carried out archaeological investigations in Belize since 1973. Her recent field-work focuses on the site of Marco Gonzalez on Ambergris Caye in Belize. Her research interests include the role of commercial dynamics and warfare in the Maya collapse, the changing rules of engagement in warfare, the impact of Spanish colonial activities (*Maya Christians and Their Churches in Sixteenth-Century Belize*), and the role of the remains of human activities in soil genesis.

JULIE A. HOGGARTH received her PhD at the University of Pittsburgh and is currently an assistant professor in Anthropology at Baylor University. Her research centers on societal collapse, climate change, and building high-precision radiocarbon chronologies in the Belize River Valley of western Belize. She is the codirector of the Belize Valley Archaeological Reconnaissance (BVAR) project, which has operated a regional project at multiple sites in the upper Belize River Valley since 1988.

LINDA HOWIE is a professional researcher, educator, and entrepreneur who works at the crossroads of anthropology, materials engineering, and the earth sciences, using scientific methods to investigate the material biographies of ancient and historic artifacts and build-ing materials, and their wider cultural significance. Her research in archaeology focuses on determining the geographic origins of pottery and stone artifacts, reconstructing ancient and historic production technologies, and tracing patterns of resource extraction, fabrication processes, and exchange networks. She earned her PhD in archaeology and archaeological science at the University of Sheffield. She currently holds academic posi-tions at Fanshawe College and Western University. She is the owner of two London-based businesses: *HD Analytical Solutions* and *Material Legacy*. Partnerships range from private collectors to industry, and to academic and government research professionals working in geology, mineral and mining exploration and development, planetary science, cultural heritage resource management, materials engineering, ecology, and architecture.

ELSA JADOT received her Doctorate from the University of Paris 1. She is an associ-ate researcher at the CNRS. Her research focuses on ceramic technology in ancient Michoacán from the Epiclassic to early Colonial periods to link the ceramic production process with the emergence and transformations of Tarascan civilization. Her current work focuses on the consequences of Spanish colonization, with an emphasis on the technical and cultural evolution of local ceramic production. Her research has appeared in *Ancient Mesoamerica*, *Latin American Antiquity*, and in the edited volume *Archéologie de la frontière* (Lucas Aniceto et al., eds.).

KRISTIN V. LANDAU earned her PhD from Northwestern University and is an assis-tant professor of anthropology at Alma College, Michigan. She directs the Proyecto Arqueológico de los Barrios de Copán, which studies citywide political and economic dynamics from the perspective of outlying neighborhoods. Additionally, she specializes in collaborative archaeology, Geographic Information Systems, and ceramic and obsidian analysis. Her recent publications have appeared in *Journal of Computer Applications in Archaeology*, *Journal of Archaeology and Education*, and *Cambridge Archaeological Journal*.

EVA LEMONNIER received her PhD from Université Paris 1 and her dissertation was published in the BAR International Series. She is associate professor of archaeology at the Université Paris 1 and has worked at La Joyanca (2000–2003) and Naachtun (2010–2017) in Guatemala, as well as at Balamku (1999) and Río Bec (2006–2008) in Mexico. She now coordinates the Río Bec 2 Project (2019–2022), with a focus on sociopolitical change and land use patterns. Her research on population mobility, neighborhoods, agrarian systems, and urban/rural relationships has been published in *Journal of Anthropological Archaeology* and *Ancient Mesoamerica*, and as chapters in edited volumes. She is attempting to correlate agricultural production, demography, social dynamics, and economic prosperity to examine the specifics of the urbanization process among the Maya.

DOMINIQUE MICHELET is honorary director of research at CNRS and received his PhD from the University of Paris 1. He has worked on the northern frontier of Mesoamerica and in central-west Mexico (Michoacán), both regions where prehispanic population movements were important. In the Maya realm, he has also participated and/or led research programs in the Puuc region (Xculoc, Xcalumkin) as well as in the northern Southern lowlands (Balamku, Río Bec, Naachtun). Among his publications, he is the author of *Río Verde, San Luis Potosí*, has coedited *Mayas del Puuc, Arqueología de la región de Xculoc* (with Pierre Becquelin and M. Charlotte Arnauld), and contributed numerous articles and chapters to edited volumes, including *Reacomodos demográficos del Clásico al Posclásico en el centro de México* (edited by Linda Manzanilla).

DAVID EZEQUIEL ORTEGÓN ZAPATA earned his Licenciatura from the UAY. His research includes the ceramics, settlement patterns, and iconography of many northern lowland Maya sites, including Chaac II, Sayil, Xcoch, Acanceh, Yaxuná, Ek Balam, Kabah, and Uxmal. He contributed to mapping Chichen Itza, Uxmal, Ek Balam, Muluchtzekal, Sanacté, Sabacche, and Cansahcab, and to rescue work in several places in the Yucatán including Ake, Kantunil, Yaaxhom Valley, Sahe, Playa del Carmen, and the Chichen Itza periphery. He has also engaged in restoration work at Edzna, Chichen Itza, and Sabacche, and survey in the Chenes and Puuc sectors, Campeche.

GRÉGORY PEREIRA received his PhD from Université Paris 1 in 1997 and is currently a research director at the CNRS. Dr. Pereira's research focuses on mortuary patterns in ancient Mesoamerica and on sociopolitical transformations and migrations at the northern Mesoamerican frontier (the Michoacán and Bajío regions in western Mexico). He has directed excavation projects at Cerro Barajas, Guanajuato (in collaboration with Gérald Migeon and Dominique Michelet) and he is currently coordinating the Uacusecha Project at the Zacapu basin, Michoacán. He also collaborates with various projects in western (Michoacán Project) and central Mexico (Moon Pyramid Project, Templo Mayor Project), the Gulf Coast (Vista Hermosa Project), and the Maya area (Balamku and Río Bec Project). He has coedited several books, including *Tradiciones cerámicas del Epiclásico* *en el Bajío y regiones aledañas: cronología e interacción* (with Chloé Pomédio and Eugenia Fernández Villanueva), *La Ciudad Perdida: Raíces de los soberanos tarascos* (with Eliseo Padilla Gutiérrez), and *Vista Hermosa: Nobles, artesanos y mercaderes en los confines del mundo huasteco* (with Guy and Claude Stresser-Péan).

PRUDENCE M. RICE received her PhD from Pennsylvania State University. She is an archaeologist with a research specialization in pottery analysis and has taught at the University of Florida and Southern Illinois University, Carbondale. At the latter, she served as department chair and associate vice chancellor for research before retiring in 2011. She has led or co-led (with husband Don S. Rice) field projects in Peten, Guatemala, and Moquegua, Peru. Among her publications are *Pottery Analysis* (2d ed.), and *Space-Time Perspectives on Early Colonial Moquegua.*

THELMA NOEMÍ SIERRA SOSA is a research professor at the Instituto Nacional de Antropología e Historia (INAH), where she has been since 1982. She holds a PhD in Mesoamerican studies from the Universidad Nacional Autónoma de México (UNAM). She has carried out several research projects in the Yucatán peninsula, focusing on a wide array of topics, including Maya settlement patterns, architecture, and trade, and bioarchaeology. She has authored and coauthored many scientific papers and book chapters, including *Los Patrones de Asentamiento de San Gervasio: Isla de Cozumel*, which received the National Award for best research by the INAH. Since 2005 she has been a member of the Mexican National System of Investigators (SNI). She is currently lead investigator in several archaeological projects including the Proyecto Arqueológico Xcambo, and Proyecto Cono Sur, both in Yucatán.

MICHAEL P. SMYTH is president of the Foundation for Americas Research, Inc. (www.FARINCO.org). He received his PhD in anthropology from the University of New Mexico and has served as faculty at the Universities of New Mexico, Cincinnati, Kentucky, Central Florida, Stetson, and Buffalo, and at Rollins College. He has worked and researched for over 35 years in Mexico, including the Puuc region and the sites of Sayil, Chac II, and Xcoch, Yucatán. Smyth has also directed sponsored research into climate change, environmental systems, and the formation of Colombian Andean chiefdoms. He has published numerous articles on Maya storage and subsistence systems, ethnic interactions, hydraulic chiefdoms, human ecodynamics, and is currently researching the Preclassic regional hierarchy and early farmers around Xcoch in the Santa Elena Valley of the Puuc hills.

VERA TIESLER is research professor at the UAY, in Mérida, Mexico, where she heads the Laboratory of Bioarchaeology. She received her PhD in anthropology from UNAM, with five accredited years of medical school (Germany and Mexico). Her work focuses on the Maya burial record and includes active fieldwork at Palenque, Calakmul, Yaxuna, and Chichen Itza. By exploring skeletal information jointly with precolumbian art, artifacts, and ethnohistoric sources, Tiesler's research addresses ancient lifestyles and death practices, physical appearance and permanent body enhancement, violence, sacrifice, and body processing. Recent books include *New Perspectives in Human Sacrifice and Ritual Body Treatments among the Ancient Maya* (Tiesler and Cucina, eds.), *The Bioarchaeology of Artificial Cranial Modifications*, *Before Kukulkán: Maya Life, Death, and Identity at Classic Period Yaxuna, Yucatan, Mexico* (Tiesler, Cucina, Stanton, Freidel), *Social Skins of the Head: Body Beliefs and Ritual in Ancient Mesoamerica and the Andes* (Tiesler and Lozada, eds.), and *Smoke, Flames, and the Human Body in Mesoamerican Ritual Practice* (Tiesler and Scherer eds.).

ERIC WEAVER completed an MA in geography at the University of Cincinnati. His research has concentrated on anthropogenic usage of caves in Mexico, the American Southwest, and Kentucky. He has also worked on GIS modeling at several sites, including Tikal. He has authored or coauthored articles in *Journal of Cave and Karst Studies* and *Proceedings of the National Academy of Sciences*, and in chapters in several edited volumes. He is currently the natural resources branch chief at El Malpaís and El Morro National Monuments, New Mexico.

Index

Cook, Sherburne F., 71
Copador cylinder, 145
Copan, 17, 24, 46, 78, 131, 137, 139, 141, 145–46, 235, 275; abandonment of, 136; case studies from, 147; Classic, 134–35, *135*; farmers in, 133; hinterland of, 143–45; Group 11M-9-11: 141, 142, *142*; Las Sepulturas, 133, *135*; Late Classic, 138; migration at, 145; population of, 132, 135, 137; Preclassic, 133; urban core of, 134–35, *135*, 142, 143; urbanization of, 133–36
Copan Pocket, *134*, 135, 136, 139, 142
Copan River, alluvial pockets along, *134*
Copan Valley, 132, 135, 136, 137–39, 143, 144
copper items, 55, *55*, 56, 257
Corral phase, 239, 265
cosmology, 60, 137, 151
Cowgill, George, 5, 6, 192, 233
Coyotlatelco, 276, 279; pottery of, 193, 194, 202, 204, 205, 206, 280
Cozumel, 76, 110, 238
craft production, 7, 62, 89, 90, 94, 95, 203
cranial modifications, 97, 98 (table), 120, 121
Crawford, Michael H., 64
cribra orbitalia, 83, 84, 102 (table), 103
Cuauhtinchan, 86, 87, 89, 90
Cucina, Andrea, 16, 76, 143, 278
Cueva de las Varillas, 280
Cueva del Pirul, 280
Culbert, T. Patrick, 136
Culhua Mexica, 259
cultural practices, 6, 80, 81, 98, 109, 111, 196
cultural traditions, 80, 123, 128, 229
culture, 59, 81, 116, 252; Chupicuaro, 259; expressive, 266; material, 5, 12, 13, 14, 16, 17, 18, 49, 54–56, 57, 61, 128, 139, 190, 193, 195, 197, 198, 205, 206, 246, 254, 266, 270, 275–77, 283; Maya, 41; migration and, 194; Postclassic, 82; settlement, 44; Teotihuacan, 262
Cutzio, 256, 257, 258

Darras, Véronique, 18, 260
data: archaeological, 49, 62, 64, 79, 97, 131, 132, 133, 233, 261, 272, 282; bioarchaeological, 61, 62, 85, 91–92, 94–104, 132, 145; biogeochemical, 49, 56–57; dental morphological, 67; ethnohistorical, 161, 209; isotopic, 49, 85, 92, 248, 261, 265; paleoenvironmental, 182
de Fuensalida, Bartolomé, 241
de Lizana, Bernardo, 238
de-urbanization, 3, 6, 9, 60, 133, 166, 185, 270; abandonment as, 182–84

decoration, 18, 125, 241, 250n7
demographic solution curve, *72*
demography, 13, 14, 17, 18, 25, 26, 78, 80, 89, 178, 252, 263, 283; ancient population, 60; anthropological, 85, 94; background, 136–37; genetic, 64; low-density, 166; migration, 274; shift in, 133, 276; urban, 9
dental modifications, 13, 34, 72, 120, 121, 122
dental morphology, 60, 82, 129; diversity and, 66–68; scored, 67 (table)
depopulation, 44, 50, 54, 57, 165, 191
diaspora, 10, 19, 259, 265; cohesive, 252–53; enclaves and, 253–58; urban, 146
Díaz Oyarzábal, Clara Luz, 261
diet, 14, 25, 34, 46, 120, 121, 240, 264; analysis of, 26, 29, 39, 126, 128; atypical, 122, 123
diseases, 78, 83, 84, 85, 100, 102, 103, 104, 137, 234, 245, 278
displacement, 10, 164, 185, 189, 209, 215, 276; cycles of, 9; demographic, 11; population, 5, 233, 273, 277
diversity, 154, 283; biological, 60; dental morphology and, 66–68
Donis, A. E., 114, 120, 124, 129
drought, 160, 163, 234, 235, 245, 248
Duncan, William, 247
Dunning, Nicholas, 17, 154
Durazno workshops, 214, 221, 222, 223, 224, 227; duration/production of, 223 (table)
Dzul, Sara, 178

Early Classic, 8, 16, 48, 61, 65, 66, 67, 68, 69, 70, 71, 74, 75, 114, 115, 117, 127, 133, 137, 149, 150–54, 165, 171, 172, 173, 175
Early Postclassic, 18, 52, 54, 56, 112, 114, 116, 117, 118, 119, 120, 123, 124, 129, 183, 184, 228
economic activities, 3, 61, 88, 94–95, 96, 104, 109
economic issues, 9, 63, 76, 80, 86, 100, 104, 111, 165–66, 252, 253, 260
economy, 6, 60, 61, 264; archaeology and, 62; Epiclassic, 207n1; neoclassic, 63
Eichrom Industries, 33
El Bosque, 133, 135, *135*
El Infiernillo, 210, 215, 228
El Monte, 262
El Palacio, 210, 228
El Porvenir, 182
El Rey Sapo, 140, *141*
Elevated Interior Region (EIR), 148
elites, 140, 154, 258; Copan, 142; intermediate, 157; minor center, 158; political, 65, 233
Emberling, G., 99

enamel, 46, 83, 122; hypoplasias, 83, 100, 101 (table); isotope values for, *123*

enclaves, 259; cohesive, 252–53; diaspora and, 253–58; ethnic, 10, 92, 99; term, 253, 261–62

environmental challenges, 9, 19, 137, 148, 163, 176, 191, 283

Epiclassic, 10, 15, 19, 163, 190, 193, 197, 198, 199, 201–2, 205, 206, 233, 248, 266; migration during, 234–40; social change in, 189

Escalera al Cielo, 155–56, *157*, 163

Espejel, Claudia, 231n8

ethnicity, 75, 86, 89, 94, 95, 96, 98, 111, 143, 145, 194; element indicative of, 132; repressing, 99

ethnohistory, 12, 15, 71, 79, 85, 87, 88, 90, 91, 94, 104, 258, 270, 282

exchange, 4, 17, 57, 59, 75, 90, 91, 95, 116, 185, 194, 206, 255; population, 56, 270; regional, 62, 204; trade and, 112, 114, 117, 130

fabric, 119, 126; crystalline calcite-tempered, 122; dolomitic marl-based, *122*; sandy, *119*; volcanoclastic temper, *122*

factionalism, 242, 246, 247, 248, 279

family groups, 88, 168, 179, 181, 269, 274; movement of, 94–95

famine, 87, 88, 150, 245

Fargher, Lane F., 198

farmers, 133, 165, 166, 176

farms, 7, 159, 162, 197

Farriss, Nancy M., 232, 245

Fazekas, I., 82

feathered serpent, 235, 239

Fine Orange, 143, 247

fineware, 119

"first founders" principle, 156

Flores, 233, 236, 242, 243, 246, 247

food preparation, 14, 18, 140, 240

food supply, 9, 234

Forest, Marion, 18

Formative, 87, 165, 197, 260

Forné, Mélanie, 17

Freiwald, Carolyn, 16, 92, 280

Freter, AnnCorinne, 143, 144, 146

funerary complexes, formation of, 227

funerary practices, 18, 39, 41, 51, 91, 96, 97, 98, 276, 277. *See also* burials

Gabriel Duran site, 262

Gage, Timothy G., 77–78

Galinié, Henri, 214

genetics, 13, 80, 263

geology, 13, 24, 27, 29, 46

Gerry, John, 29, 39

Gonlin, Nancy, 17, 132, 143, 271, 273, 275

governance, 59, 130, 192, 198, 246

Graham, Elizabeth, 16, 60, 132, 271, 276, 278

Great Ballcourt, 236

Great Pyramid, 79, 82, 105n1

greenstone, 50, 144

Group 11M-9-11. *See* Copan

Group B (Río Bec), 157, 178, 180, 212, 224, 226; burials at, 225, 225 (table); construction-occupation of, *180*; deceased population of, *227*; funerary data from, 227

Group Gavilan. *See* La Joyanca

Group Guacamaya. *See* La Joyanca

Guanajuato, 194, 259

Guayameo, 256, 258

Guderjan, Thomas H., 124, 127

habitational zones, 82, 92, 95, 96, 98, 99

habitation terraces, 218, 219; duration of use for, 221 (table)

habitations, 146, 197, 207n3, 215, 224

habitus, 6, 9, 114, 252

Habuba Kebira, 214

Haviland, William A., 168

Healan, Dan A., 262, 265

hearths, 201, 202, 211

Hernández, Christine L., 262, 265

hiatuses, 54, 171, 172, 176

Hidalgo, 253, 261, 265, 266

Hill, Jane, 131

hinterlands, 7, 12, 15, 16, 17, 61, 92, 132, 139, 146, 147, 152, 156, 157, 165, 172, 175, 183, 184, 192, 270; movement in, 143–45; settlement in, 25, 41

Historia Tolteca-Chichimeca (Berlin and Rendon), 86, 87, 89

Hoggarth, Julie, 16, 53, 276

Hohokam, 15

home bases, 92, 95–96

Hopis, 263

households, 18, *169*; elite/smaller, 174 (table); Epiclassic, 201; excavated, 169; longevity/nongrowth of, 168

houses, 12, 13, 179; C-shaped, 182; Classic, 165; construction of, 184–85; durable, 8, 171, 173, 176; ephemeral, 166; Epiclassic, *203*; field, 159, 167, 168; mobility and, 175–81, 185; modular, 182; non-platform, 183; social, 181; urban, 167; vaulted, 178, 182

Houston, Stephen D., 137

Howie, Linda, 16, 60, 114, 120, 121, 130, 132, 271, 276, 278

Huamango, 262, 265

Huetamo, 256, 257, 258

Hugo, Graeme, 60, 75

Hunac Ceel, 232, 240, 249n5

hunters and gatherers, 4, 7

hyperostosis, 83, 84, 103, 102 (table), 110

hypoplasias, 83, 100, 101 (table), 102

Ibarra-Rivera, L., 43

iconography, 12, 81, 96, 141

identity, 13, 160, 215, 239; cultural, 275; egalitar-ian/collective, 196; ethnic, 10, 98, 99, 106n8, 198, 266; ethnopolitical, 247; linguistic, 18, 258, 266; material culture and, 198; migrant, 257; occupational, 258; place-based, 160; social, 263; Yukatek Maya, 150

ideology, 137, 269; egalitarian/collective, 196; Postclassic, 55

immigrants, 86, 87, 110, 138, 146, 229, 238; ethnic groups and, 89, 99; material culture and, 246; status of, 271; tracking, 13

immigration, 14, 118–20; massive, 279; mobil-ity and, 10; rapid, 215; settlement networks and, 278

in-migration, 5, 56, 78, 172, 175, 236, 246, 247

inequality, 68, 150; social, 146; socioeconomic, 202–3

Inomata, Takeshi, 6, 147

intermarriage, 88, 95, 235

Irecha, 255, 256, 257, 259

isotopes, 85, 133; age at-death distribution for, *84*

isotopic analyses, 13, 16, 17, 41, 46, 48–49, 80, 113, 197, 261

isotopic evidence, 17, 34, 37, 44, 46–49

isotopic signatures, 28, 92; local/nonlocal, 79, 106n5

isotopic studies, 25, 27–29, 40, 41, 72, 82, 90, 92, 97

isotopic values, 24, 25, 27, 39, 44, 47, 92, 97, 138

Itza Emblem Glyph, 234

Itzas, 53, 233, 237, 246, 248, 281; Classic-period, 234; Kowojs and, 241–45; material culture in, 247; migration of, 232, 238, 239; Tayza and, 240–45

Ixlu, 242, 245, 247, 248

Ixtepeque, 57, 235

jades, 124, 142, 240

Jadot, Elsa, 18

Jakeman, M. Wells, 233, 249

jars: Arturo-Incised narrow-necked, 144; cook-ing, 218; flanged, 126; Late Classic, 120; polychrome water, 151; Zalal, 126

Jesús y Santa María, 256

Kal Jol, 244

Kan/Chan Ek', 238

Kan Ek', 238, 243, 244, 246

k'atun, 233, 237, 238, 239, 240

K'atun 4 Ajaw, 239

K'atun 6 Ajaw, 237

K'atun 8 Ajaw, 237, 239, 240

K'atun 11 Ajaw, 237

K'atun 13 Ajaw, 238

K'iche', 164, 280

K'inich Yax K'uk Mo', 134, 138, 139

kinship, 145, 184, 259

Kintigh, Keith W., 270

Kiuic, 156

Kohler, Timothy A., 164

Kosa, F., 82

Kowalewski, Stephen A., 193, 195, 196, 205

Kowoj, 53, 246, 247, 248; Chak'an and, 242; Itzas and, 241–45

Krueger, Harold W., 26, 29, 33

K'uk'ulcan, 239, 243

K'uk'ulcan temples, 244

Laguna de Cayo Francesca, 124, 125

Laguna de On, 52

Laguna de Términos, 246

La Joyanca, 168, 169, 170, 180, 181; construction programs in, 175; dwelling system from, 176; elite/smaller household units in, 174 (table); Group Gavilan, 169, *170*, 171 (table), 172, 173, 176, 178; Group Guacamaya, 178, *180*; household archaeology at, 177; map of, *169*; population of, 173; Unit 5F15, *170*, 171 (table)

Lake Petén Itzá, 48, 56, 232, 234, 236, 241, 242, 243, 248. *See also* Petén Lakes

Lake Salpeten, 241, 247

Lake Texcoco, 249, 260

Lake Yaxha, 241, 242

Lamanai, 17, 38, 48, 52, 53, 112–13, 114, 117, 123, 124–28, 130, 276; analysis at, 129; bells at, 56; Buk phase at, 116; burials at, 124, 126, 128, 129; ceramic inventory at, 116; ceramic petrography at, 118–20; copper items at, 55, 56; location of, *115*; manufacturing traditions at, *119*; marine resources at, 122; material culture at, 121; nonlocal pottery from, *122*;

provisional chronology for, 113 (table); ritual/mortuary customs at, 127

Landau, Kristin, 17, 132, 140, 143, 146, 271, 273, 275

landscapes, 3, 15, 140, 145, 157, 199, 200, 253, 265; ethnic, 18; isotopic, 28; linguistic, 254; natural, 159; rural, 8, 162; social, 248; sociopolitical, 189, 194, 230; urban, 111, 172

Las Milpillas, 212, 214, 224, 226, 227, 228; burials at, 225, 225 (table); radiocarbon dates from, 213; urban structure of, 215

Las Sepulturas. *See* Copan

Late Classic, 25, 39, 44, 48, 52, 53, 54, 61, 65, 66, 67, 68, 69, 70, 71, 72, 73, 74, 75, 76, 78, 112, 114, 115, 116, 117, 120, 123, 124, 127, 133, 143, 145, 146, 148, 150; ceramics from, 118; life table of, 70 (table); overcrowding in, 137; population of, 149; sample/demographic solution curve for, 72

Late Formative, 8, 165, 259

Late Postclassic, 18, 54, 56, 117, 119, 128, 150, 229, 233, 238, 240, 241, 245; reoccupation during, 44

Late Preclassic, 151, 154, 162, 172

leadership, 195, 197, 200, 246, 263; centralized, 198; collective, 199; corporated, 196

Lemonnier, Eva, 17, 170

Lerma Valley, 229, 255

lesions, 84; pathological, 100–101, 102; proliferative, 101, 103 (table), 104; skeletal, 83, 85; sphenoid, 85, 104 (table)

Lienzo de Jicalán, 256, 257, 262

Lienzo de Jucutacato, 256

life expectancy, 69, 77, 78, 218, 278

life table, Late Classic, 70 (table)

limestone, 27, 46, 118, 120, 137

linguistics, 12, 15, 80, 131, 133, 238, 248, 249, 254, 265, 266, 267

lithics, 16, 95, 96; changes in, 276; Epiclassic, 201–2

locals: cranial modification of, 97; health of, 100; migrants and, 197; nonlocals and, 73; paleopathological analyses of, 104; term, 106n5

Long Count, 135

Los Achiotes, 133

Los Sapos, 139, 140, 141

Lucero, Lisa J., 182, 183

Macanche Island, 242

Madrid Codex, 249n6

Main Plaza, 239, 248

maize, 39, 141, 165, 168

Makocheb', 209, 244

Malpaís, 221, 223, 224, 227, 277, 284; groups in, 228; immigrants to, 229; microevolution of, 211; urban sites in, 282

Malpaís de Zacapu, 209, 227, 230; location of, 211; Postclassic sites of, 210–12, 214

Malpaís Prieto, 210, 212, 214–15, 216, 217, 218, 222, 223, 225, 226, 227, 228, 242, 282; architectural facies of, 215; cooking vessels from, 219; map of, 216; morphological history in, 217; radiocarbon dates from, 213; urban density of, 215; UT1 habitation terrace, 221 (table); UT1 residential terrace, 220; UT2 habitation terrace, 221 (table)

Manning, Robert D., 252, 264

manors, 155, 157, 160, 162; rural, 159

Manuscript of 1553 (Reyes García), 87

Marco Gonzalez, 17, 38, 112, 115, 117, 124–28, 130, 276; burials at, 52, 113, 128; ceramic inventory at, 116; Early Postclassic at, 118; location of, 115; mortuary practice at, 129; pottery at, 129; provisional chronology for, 113 (table); salt from, 114; Terminal Classic at, 116; VPLF at, 127

markers, 39, 47, 98, 135, 156, 211, 212, 214, 221, 224, 277, 283, 360; archaeological, 210; bioanthropological, 16, 229; bioarchaeological, 210; biological, 13; cultural, 13, 121; diachronic, 215; migration, 27, 146; mobility, 136

Márquez, L., 77

marriage, 90, 94, 96, 121; alliances, 95; exogamic, 8; integration and, 95; local, 88; rules, 184

Masson, Marilyn A., 52

Mastache, Alba Guadalupe, 194

material culture, 5, 12, 13, 14, 16, 17, 18, 49, 54–56, 57, 61, 99, 116, 121, 128, 139, 190, 193, 197, 205, 206, 246, 254, 266, 270, 275–77, 283; changes in, 44; Classic-period, 44; identity and, 198; nonlocal, 247; Postclassic, 55

materials, 80, 190, 269, 275; building, 53, 137, 203; mobility and, 247–48; new types of, 55; raw, 137; skeletal, 128

Matlatzinca, 256, 257, 258, 259, 264, 277

Maya, 17, 18, 38, 59, 69, 76, 114, 129, 133, 165, 168, 182, 185, 238, 241, 242; ancient, 173; archeological literature on, 43; Belize, 109; Chontal, 53, 234; Classic, 12, 15, 43, 64, 78, 131, 137–38, 145, 146, 147, 153, 161, 279; flight of, 232; luxury goods and, 60; Mexicanized, 234; migration of, 139–43, 233; mobility of, 6; movement of, 143–45; non-Classic, 130; Petén and, 247;

reservoirs, 17, 151, 154, 158, 161, 163

residences, 65–66, 199, 200; economic considerations and, 90; elite, 154, 157; postmarital, 89–90; Puuc, *153*; Río Bec Terminal style, 182; urban, 168; vaulted stone, 157

residential zones, 95, 96, 172, 173, 175, 176, 179, 184

resources, 118, 166; aquatic, 235; economic, 137; marine, 59, 122; mineral, 235; raw-material, 126

Rice, Don S., 136

Rice, Prudence, 18, 279, 281

Richards-Rissetto, Heather M., 134, 135, 140, 146

Ringle, William M., 239

Río Amarillo pocket, 144

Río Azul, 236

Río Bec, 162, 168, 173, 175, 177, 178–79, 180, 182, 185; central sector of, 179. *See also* Group B

rituals, 12, 17, 96, 127, 171, 173, 193, 252; dedication, 145; funerary, 18, 98; household, 204; termination, 145, 163, 211

RM. See *Relación de Michoacán*

Roskamp, Hans, 256, 257

rural settlement clusters, map of, *160*

Rural Sites Project, 143

sacbe, 133, 151

Sacnicté, 232, 240

Sacred Cenote, 240

San Cristóbal, 48

San Juan, 124

San Lucas, 132, 139, 141, 142, 235; map of, *140*

San Pablo III, map of, *158*

San Pedro, 52, 117, 125, 127

Sanders, William T., 61

Santa Ana Tetlaman, 256, 257

Santa Elena Valley, 151

Santa Rita Corozal, 52, 53

Santiago Acahuato, 257

Santiago Undameo, 256

Santley, Robert S., 253, 261–62

Saturday Creek, burials at, 39

Sayil, 156, 157, 182

Scherer, Andrew, 137–38

Schiffer, Michael Brian, 219, 221

Schwarz, K. R., 56

sculpture, 137, 140, 141, 142, *142*, 193, 243

sedentism, 4, 5, 181, 182, 185

Seler, Eduard, 231n8

settlement patterns, 12, 41, 44, 49, 53–54, 69, 132, 148, 185, 277–79

settlements, 18, 23, 25, 54, 77, 145, 152, 157, 162, 181, 192, 246, 264, 280, 282; commoner, 235; composition of, 14; decline of, 185; density of, 14, 135; evolution of, 228, 278–79; growth of, 189; longer-term, 95; nucleated, 184; Postclassic, 246; prehispanic, *191*; reconfiguration of, 189; regional, 190; rural, 155 (table), 190; size of, 12, 14; urban, 5, 12, 175, 190

shells, 96, 115, *122*, 124

Shiratori, Yuko, 52

Shugar, A. N., 56

Sibun Valley, 54

Sierra Sosa, Thelma N., 69, 74

Simmons, Scott E., 56

Site 7-12, map of, *160*

skeletons, 28, 60, 68, 82, 83, 96, 106n3; age-at-death distribution for, *84*; biochemical characteristics of, 276; cultural modifications of, 97

slatewares, 53, 236, 247, 249n5

Smith, Michael E., 89

Smyth, Michael P., 7, 17

social boundaries, 9, 24, 191

social change, 189, 193, 197

social contexts, 95, 99, 233

social dynamics, 5, 166, 182, 190

social groups, 7, 11, 15, 89, 95, 132, 146, 148, 161, 181, 182, 192, 229, 251, 261, 263, 265, 266, 277; cohesive, 252–53, 264

social interactions, 3, 5, 196, 197, 198, 252, 263, 264

social organization, 4, 25, 41, 77, 80, 197

social relationships, 7, 81, 94, 95, 98, 194

social structures, 6, 81, 184, 247

social unrest, 86, 195, 248

socioeconomic structures, 81, 88, 91, 105, 145, 178, 251

sociopolitical conditions, 61, 150, 162, 165–66, 189, 190, 191, 192, 205, 230

soils, 137, 144, 148, 168, 169, 171, 172, 235; agricultural, 151, 156, 159; deposition of, 139; exhaustion of, 7, 163, 234; formation of, 29, 46; restoration of, 166

Soto-Mayor, Villagutierre, 233

Sotuta, 239, 240

South Group. *See* Balamku

Southern Lacandons, 247

Soza, J. M., 233

Spanish Conquest, 86, 117, 127, 210, 241, 246, 275, 280

Spanish Lookout, 25, 52

Milton Keynes UK
Ingram Content Group UK Ltd.
UKHW010702160724
445389UK00014B/758